YOUR
INTEGRAL LIFE MATTERS

Create a Life and Legacy Management Mindset for Personal, Organizational, Community and Societal Success in the American Tradition*

Dr. Rudy Garrity

* A free introductory life and legacy management webinar is included for purchasers

* Self-Fulfillment   * High Performance   * Common Good
* Human Enlightenment   * Financial Security   * Mid-Life Transition
* Senior Legacy   * Write Your Life Story

(Contact: rgarrity@alforum.org)

Initial Text Copyright 2016 by Rudolph Blaine Garrity

All rights reserved.

Published by ALF Press
The American Learnership Forum
673 Potomac Station Drive, NE #602
Leesburg, VA 20176-1819
Email: rgarrity@alforum.org

Printed by Create Space, an Amazon.com Company

Permission is granted for individuals to use limited portions the author's original content in this publication for their own personal use so long as prominent acknowledgement of the author's name and book title is annotated therein. All content and graphics used must contain attribution in the form: © American Learnership™ by Dr. R. Garrity.

Permission must be requested and granted in writing for individuals or organizations to use the author's original content for any purpose including internal or external training, coaching and consulting (exception is granted when ALF gifts or promotes the book to selected individuals for business use.) Use of this book's original content will not be granted for commercial use by any person, or firm, other than those specifically considered current American Learnership Forum clients, affiliates or partners. Send requests to become ALF partners, or licensees to rgarrity@alforum.org.

Permission to use the perspectives and works of other authors' work referenced in this book must be solicited from their respective publishers. Additionally, purchase of others' works referenced, herein, for a "publisher's library" as done in this book is highly recommended.

PUBLISHER'S NOTE: Every effort has been made to ensure the accuracy of the information used or developed in the writing and production of this book. However, readers are advised to reflect on their own knowledge and experience when considering how the information contained, herein, may be effectively used in their own personal and professional development.

ISBN- 13: 998-0-9985617-1-4

2017 First Printing

To All Readers

Heads-Up for a Powerful Mindset and Results

Welcome to a human learning and performance initiative in which contemporary adult education materials and experience are integrated and demonstrated for Americans seeking successful lives and careers in today's fast-paced and conflicted societal environment. Discovering our purpose, objectives, skills, and available resources are essential for adaptation to the rapid change, information overload, and situational complexity we find in our everyday experience. However, longer – term life, family, and career mastery is almost always dependent on our willingness for continuous learning, leading, knowing, and adapting to the changing circumstances and ordinary life/career transitions we face over a lifetime from age 25 to 75. Also, that which is worth learning is also a family responsibility.

To use an analogy, it could be said that the human mind is an extension of the knowledge and materials on deposit in a well-stocked American university. In this handbook we refer to this phenomenon as the "University of the Mind" – a powerful holistic, cross-disciplinary concept if there ever was one to represent that all we could or should know to succeed up the ladder of life and career. Learning from experience takes a lifetime to accomplish and share.

A question that often lies just beyond our cognitive reach, given how much there is to know and accomplish within our daily lives is: How much information, knowledge and unknown unknowns are relevant, available and waiting to be discovered – but are outside our cognition and emotion capabilities? A basic topic of this American Learnership™ (lifelong learning and leadership) Handbook has been to research and document many best concepts and practices currently available across the American social system-of-systems landscape – and to integrate them cognitively for practical results. Over 10 years of work and a number of articles, books and courses has permitted a summary of that work to evolve so that a seminal effort might be presented regarding the cognitive vs emotional, static vs dynamic, and centrifugal and centripetal factors can be understood as influential factors in our daily activities.

This handbook, and its products and services at our companion American Learnership Forum (ALF) website (www.alforum.org) are tools for learning and performance. The Master Class and Read-Handbook tabs on the ALF site are used to conduct webinars, and includes curricula, videos, chapter PDFs, and exercises. At this point in this book, we heartily suggest you read the Preface and Introductory descriptions that follow.

To participate in both our free and discounted webinars, or to become an ALF partner or affiliate, send your: Name, Email, Phone and Address to rgarrity@alforum.org (ATTN: Master Class). At this time we suggest you scan the figures below to see if they speak to you in their own way. They are holistic, integral and return again as reminders.

ALF Social System-of-Systems Worldview

Personal Self-Fulfillment

A Mindful "Way-of-Being"

A Non-Profit Education, Coaching, Consulting and Fundraising Community

Organizational High Performance

The American Learnership™ Forum

"The Reinvigoration of America" -- "Head, Hands & Heart Community Support"

Community Common Good

A Business Alliance for Citizen Development and Enhancement of the American Culture

Dr. Rudy Garrity
Founder/CEO
www.alforum.org

Societal Enlightenment

ALF Adult Life Management with 2nd Life Encore Potential

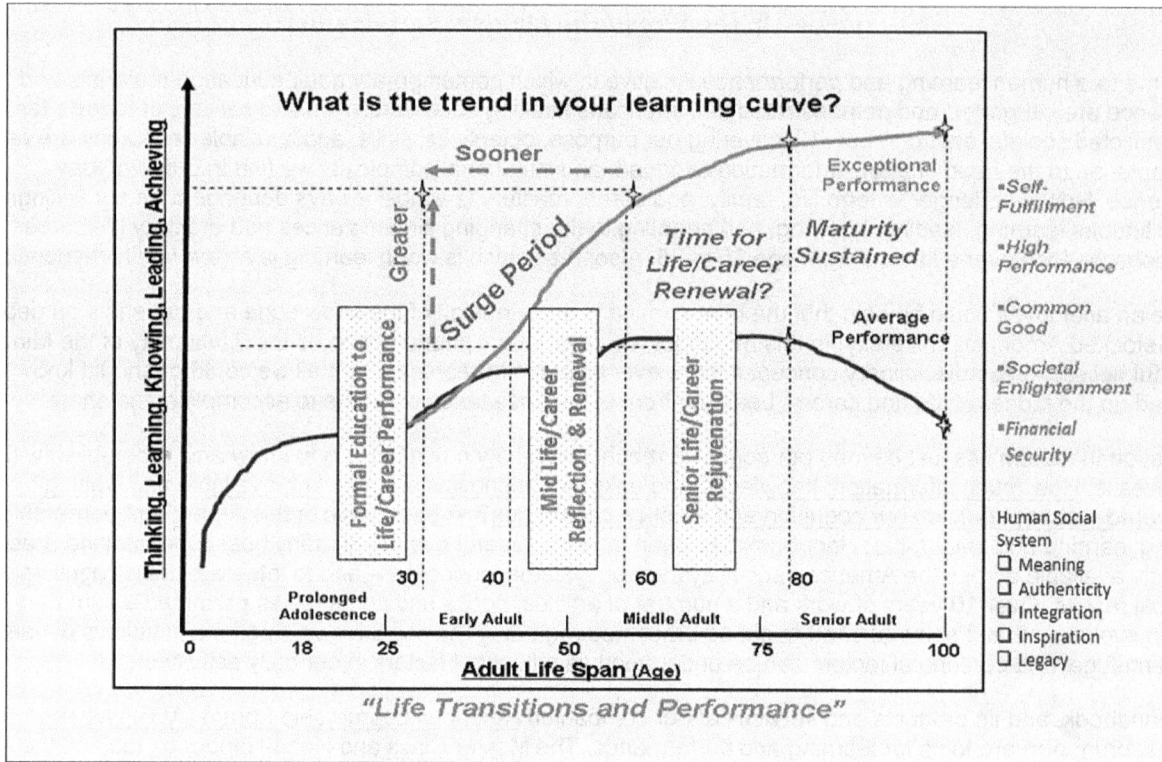

What is the trend in your learning curve?

"Life Transitions and Performance"

ALF Methodology for Integral Learning

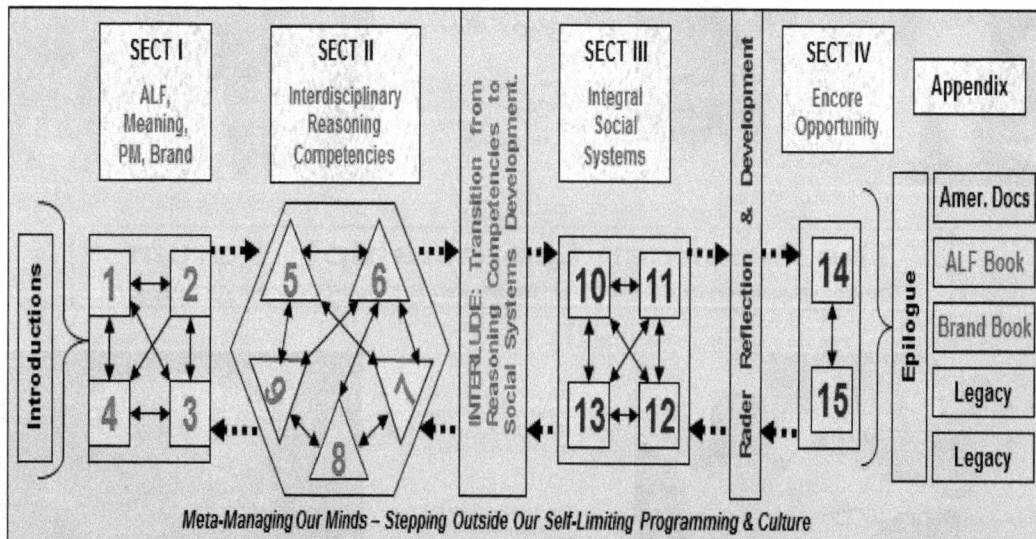

A Life Management Educational Asset

Your Integral Life Matters: Create a Life and legacy Management Mindset for Personal, Organization, Community and Societal Success

Meta-Managing Our Minds – Stepping Outside Our Self-Limiting Programming & Culture

Preface

Welcome to the American Learnership Forum (ALF) Inc.

The ALF advocates the application of a Life Management and Professional Performance Mindset and Brand for American citizens, businesses, communities and overall societal enlightenment. For that purpose the Handbook and its companion Educational Website (Curriculum, Graphics, Videos, Chapters and Exercises) promote: *YOUR INTEGRAL LIFE MATTERS: Create a Life and Legacy Management Mindset for Personal, Organizational, Community and Societal Success in the American Tradition*

We recommend that readers of this Handbook; and participants in our ALF Master Class and related courses, keep in mind that the ALF challenge is to construct and share an overarching meta-level concept for Integral Adult Life Management along with a compelling methodology for achieving real-life practical results. Additionally, we emphasize the importance of establishing one's professional brand and presence as a "lifelong learner" motivated toward achieving interdisciplinary reasoning, social systems development, a memorable living legacy, a distinguished way-of-being and a notable personhood in their lifetime.

The Life Management program is intended to be an exceptionally powerful supplement for American adults desiring continuous education and development that exceeds what is available elsewhere. Many formal, time-consuming and expensive courses have limited usefulness in integrating the breadth and scope of knowledge, skills and abilities one needs to know and apply when dealing with life's increasing pace, uncertainty and complexities. We often overlook the beneficial effect of a holistic mindset in living, working and relationships, and in building cross-disciplinary competence for interpersonal matters with thoughtful reasoning and balance. Being helpful, motivated, competent, inclusive, authentic and trustworthy are human factors worth pursuing in a well-managed life, culture and community.

Participation in this Integral Life Matters program is welcomed for adults aged 25 to 75 who at any stage of life/career transition where a desire for wide-ranging practical learning -- wherein open thinking, thoughtful conversation, and a shared learning opportunity (with minimum partisan, ethnic or sectarian conflict) -- can serve as "good time" spent with others. This program is offered as a well-researched cross-disciplinary methodology for self-management to achieve self-fulfillment, high performance, the common good and human enlightenment. Conversation that welcomes multiple points of view is trusted as a great way for everyone to discover their own unique goals, capabilities and journey toward happiness.

To participate as a class or course member, receive recognition for achievement, and even write your own e-book, contact author Dr. Rudy Garrity for detailed information at rgarrity@alforum.org or 703-587-0942 (subject line: "Master Class") Inquiries on becoming an ALF affiliate owner or partner are welcomed.

ALF Website: http://www.alforum.org/read-handbook.html (Website, Curriculum, Chapter PDFs, and Videos

Mastermind for Project Leaders: American Family Life Management and Professional Performance

The ALF Mastermind Project represents the most comprehensive and detailed investigation of the concepts, goals, models, methods and values that, in total, characterize the breadth and depth of human needs, wants and desires in human social organization. Over the early period of the adult lifespan, career-educated citizens establish families, grow children, achieve early adult tasks, and plan for lives with only moderate levels of advanced information. These capabilities are hard to anticipate.

As mid-life nears, many family and career objectives have been accomplished, new avenues of interest and occupation become known, and the urge for some degree of change becomes a regular factor in our mid-life minds. Our transition into adulthood begins to wane as mid-life transitions and opportunities become compelling. Nuclear families and associations are adjusted to the "new normal" as social changes forge relationships across other cultures and locations. New achievements and losses are experienced.

After 10-15 years even our mid-life phase begins to wane and a transition to a senior or elder life phase becomes a necessity. Our past is clearly longer while our future threatens to diminish as friends and families meet their mortality. Who were we? Why were we? What have we become? What do we yet have to do? Is time left? We alone, need to assess and draw conclusions on whom we were and have become.

The ALF Mastermind Project provides an overarching and most thorough methodology for discovering and integrating adult life thinking, learning, knowing, leading, sharing and achieving personal, organizational, community and societal tasks and objectives – i.e. integral life management – that this author has read or experienced during purposeful research. The totality of this work is offered – not as a dogmatic model for others to follow – but as a reference for review during others' study and learning.

This ALF educational program consists of other projects focused more explicitly on the issues and topics of interest for Americans (and others) at different times and places in their respective lifetimes. More information on these projects is at the ALF website: http://www.alforum.org/alf-master-class.html .

Ages 25-50 Projects:

1. My Integral Life, Work, Wealth, Health and Legacy Success ** (Personal Fulfillment)

2. My Authentic Personal and Professional Brand ** (Enterprise High Performance) Plus optional e-books.

Ages 50-75 Projects:

1. My Mid-Life/Career Transition and Personal Renewal ** (Encore Life Planning)

2. My Senior Lifelong Learning and Memorable Legacy ** Plus optional e-books and Family Letters)

CONTENTS   PAGE

Introduction

Your Integral Life Matters: Create a Life Management Mindset for Personal, Organizational, Community and Societal Success in the American Tradition

A. National and International Learning and Development

For the last twenty five years national and global political and economic forces have appeared to be undercutting America's accomplishments at building a democratic consensus home and abroad on what sustainable human development requires. Individuals, organizations and communities normally amenable to incremental change are experiencing a multi-factored explosion of disruptive attitudes, and challenges to elected authority that elevate human mindlessness and social chaos to a new and threatening art form.

American leaders and citizens are enveloped in an avalanche of terror threats to our national security, an explosion of technological innovations to be accommodated, a host of socio-economic disparities that breed hostility, and prominent ecological abuse that only the powerful and wealthy among us could rationalize as being good for national and global human development.

It appears that the American government, institutional leaders and cultural elites are at an apex of dysfunction; and that their inability to learn, analyze, prioritize, synthesize and achieve social consensus is ascendant in a culture at war with itself. An undercurrent of educationally limited, ill-informed, and emotionally driven citizens and noncitizens appear to be in a tsunami of acrimonious communication with those in positions of authority and power. Concurrently, significant evidence of duplicitous governance, pervasive inequality, socio-economic insensitivity and escalating ecological damage has been convincingly demonstrated. We can clearly see our adversary. It is us! We can do better!

The American Learnership vision for the future (this Life Management Mindset Handbook) is that (1) benefits from lifelong learning, reflection and renewal; (2) support mindful rather than mindless thinking and behavior; (3) inspire people at all income levels toward self-fulfillment, high performance, the common good, and human enlightenment; and (4) when shared, this powerful philosophy, improvement architecture and practical tools can be beneficial to all societies and nations. Additionally, this Mindset Handbook recognizes and elaborates on the recent development of the integral learning and knowledge management disciplines – especially their capability to integrate knowledge, skills and abilities across multiple disciplines and fields of study. And lastly, America is the leader – and will continue to be the leader of the free world's socio-economic relations and cultural development – as well as being the primary influencer of international finance and markets.

[**Author's Note:** An important factor in this mindset handbook is that a "theory to practice" commitment is maintained throughout. Overarching meta-concepts are derived from consolidation of lower level practical tools and experiences into a richer tapestry of contemporary research and principles with broader influence and scope. While many thought leaders and writers stress changing one's purpose and intentions as critical for human growth and development, the content of this Mindset Handbook additionally argues for *proactive lifelong learning and professional performance branding* wherein concepts and tools are continuously improved and used to achieve practical objectives that serve individual, business and community needs within a relevant timeframe. The principle here is that aspiration (vision and motivation) requires perspiration (skills and work) for a well lived life and a balanced social system-of-systems.

Expectations at Program Completion

The intent, herein, is to illustrate the potential *lifelong learning and knowledge building* that may be achieved when empowered adults become skilled and engaged in "interdisciplinary reasoning" for "integral social development." This capability, may be contrasted with the more commonly used methods of societal deliberation and decision-making where issue analysis is riddled with personal bias, limited relevant information, and overlooked contextual factors that (unfortunately) are directly pertinent to the personal, business, community or societal situation at hand.

The thesis of this Mindset Handbook is approached with *four overriding expectations* concerning how one should investigate, organize and draw conclusions given the scope and interdisciplinary nature of human issues and topics. What boundaries must be drawn, what dependencies must be clearly explained, what sequencing between cause and effect is fundamental, and how information can be prioritized and presented for different groups with a variety of interests.

1. The **first goal** or expectation is that the author has attempted to learn, improve, apply and share a snapshot of the best life management knowledge and experience he has discovered during his 45+ adult years. The content and

context of this handbook and mindset is rich with authoritative source material written by others to whom recognition is given. Significant analysis, written explanation and graphical content has been added by the author to enable the subsequent establishment of an interdisciplinary and integral educational curriculum for others' edification in concepts that are intellectually, emotionally and practically useful. A *whole brain* (writing and graphical) learning methodology is utilized throughout to communicate a high degree of life management **SUBSTANCE** to be shared with others' for their own knowledge and skill development. As always, each reader reserves the right to accept, reject or modify the recommendations they themselves receive from others. Think of a buffet table with many possible choices. Some items are must haves, certain ones might be sampled, and a few will definitely not be selected. People choose to meet their own needs and interests.

2. The **second goal** to achieve is directed towards those who make the inevitable comment upon seeing the breadth and depth of the subject matter offered: "Quickly tell me <u>what</u> this is and <u>why</u> I should care." The approach used is to help others to understand and apply a systematic life management **PROCESS** (method) for managing their own growth and development – even though they may not care to learn or fully use what the author has chosen to advocate at a particular point in the manuscript. Early on, a metaphor of a *University of the Mind* is introduced in which readers and participants are requested to conceptualize their own brains as being huge databases functionally similar to the intellectual content stored and taught in university libraries. All content is useful to human experience and development, but needs to be selectively accessed and used – in an integrated and meaningful manner – only when appropriate. This approach advises that one's brain can be thought of being organized in a system-of-systems taxonomy that favors one's real life social structure and practical experience – and, that recent research indicates the human brain has distributed data holding compartments analogous to a university. Everyone in life is charged to make responsible choices in their use of data and information when in pursuit of their objectives and unique interests. The attentive reader and communicator cannot avoid learning both substance and process when enmeshed within an interdependent learning experience.

3. The **third goal** selected is to introduce and evaluate a life management **META-SYSTEM MENTAL MODEL** way of reasoning, learning and action in which the total course material of a typical university, that is, all its educational subjects and strategies, are viewed as consisting of the purposeful differentiation of knowledge and skills by selected "experts." Some educators have commented that this differentiation process reduces individuals' range of perspective and holistic reasoning capabilities. Alternatively, it may be more useful for human learning and development to reconstruct the interdisciplinary linkages among stove-piped knowledge domains – and then focus on the more comprehensive and integral mental models necessary for enhanced reasoning and decision making. Today, we live in complex and fast-paced situations and the popular concept of *mindfulness* should focus less on stress reduction through behavior modification, and more on building a mindful capacity and resilience for proactive mind management. A contemporary term for this achievement is for a person to build enhanced *complexipacity*

4. The **fourth goal** of this learning project is to define a life management **LEARNING AND LEGACY BRANDING METHODOLOGY** that enables our life management Handbook readers and life planning coaches to record personal stories that reflect accurately and substantively on their life/career experiences and accomplishments. This, in fact, is what this author has achieved for himself and for others' consideration as they too, reflect and grow through their life experiences. The process used in this Mindset Handbook is for the author to conduct a *blended learning and interactive mentoring initiative wherein participants are assisted in learning, preparing and publishing their own e-books as illustrated in Appendices B and C*. This practical outcome illustrates how everyone can apply the life management knowledge, skills and abilities advocated. They receive greater life/career presence and self-fulfillment, business leadership and consulting skills, and local community recognition and inclusion in their services to others. (The author will assist interested readers in publishing their personal life learning and legacy planning e-books.)

In conclusion, the methods presented and knowledge advocated in this Mindset Handbook, should be thought of as creating a "working hypothesis" for evaluation by adult learners of the (a) quality of the SUBSTANCE shared, (b) for the effectiveness of the PROCESS utilized, (c) for the comprehensiveness and maturation of the META-SYSTEM MODEL employed, and (d) for the value received by LEGACY BRANDING oneself as having demonstrated notable achievement. Together, any well-organized person will benefit from taking the time to reflect and act on the *What, Why and How* their personal and professional time on earth has been spent.

The overarching ALF social system-of-systems meta-model used in this Life Management handbook and mindset illustrate the concept that Personal system development focused on SELF FULFILLMENT, coupled with Organization system development emphasizing HIGH PERFORMANCE and Community system development concerned with the

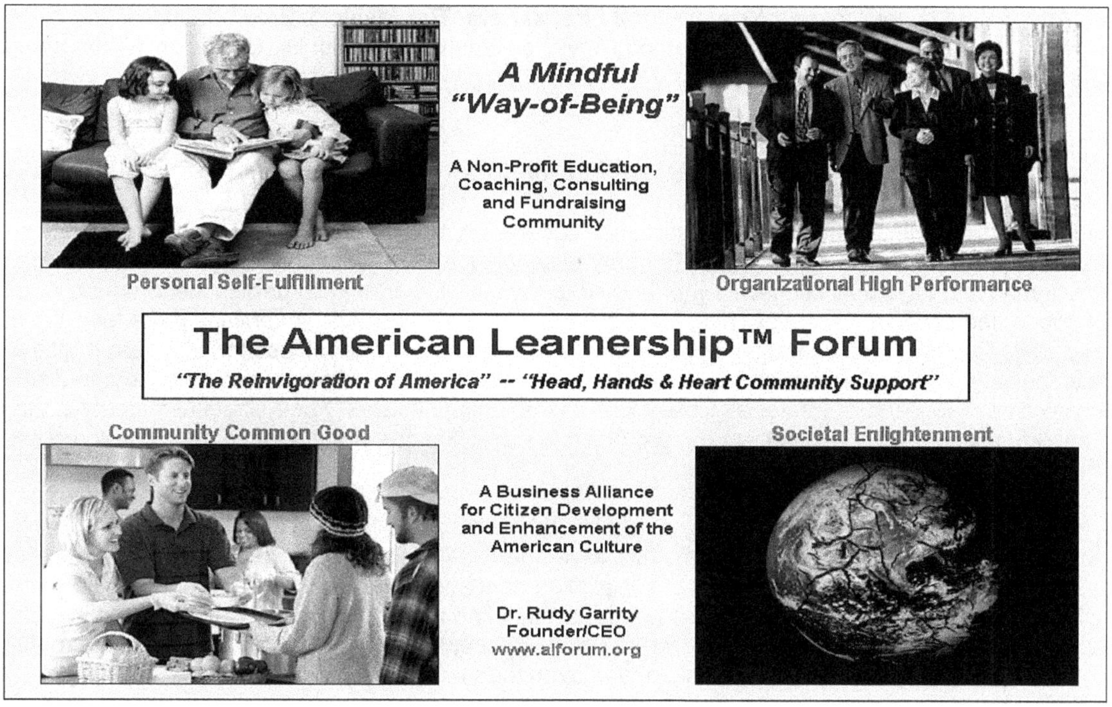

Figure 1

COMMON GOOD, can empower a nation's citizenry to achieve Societal HUMAN ENLIGHTENMENT and social progress. (Figure 1)

Mindset Handbook Structure and Use

This handbook and mindset are flexibly configured to support a variety of learning methodologies that educators and learning facilitators may use in assisting individuals and groups in attaining the practical knowledge, skills and abilities needed for their personal (family), organization (business) and community (societal) social lives – and, at any stage of their adult lives between ages 25 to 75. Textual descriptions and graphical depictions combine for whole-brain exercise, while differences in learning styles and personal preferences are noted and respected.

Our readers and course participants have choices on how to proceed (Reference chapters in the Table of Contents). Also, ALF will occasionally host FREE webinars to introduce this Mindset Handbook to purchasers and potential business partners. Contact Dr. Garrity www.alforum.org, for Life Management assistance. Choices:

1. Young adults ages 25-50. **Life/Career Transition and Growth**
   Study Appendix A; then read chapters1-13, the Epilogue and Appendices B and C.
   Options: Prepare draft of e-book: *My Integral Life, Work, Wealth, Health and Legacy Success; or*
   Prepare draft of e-book: *My Authentic Personal and Professional Brand*

2. Mid-life/career adults ages 50-65. **Mid-Life/Career Transition and Renewal**
   Study Appendix A; skip chapters 1-13, then read the Second Interlude and chapters 14-15.
   Next review chapters 1-13, the Epilogue and Appendices B and C for e-book preparation.
   Options: Prepare draft of e-book: *My Integral Life, Work, Wealth, Health and Legacy Success, or*
   Prepare draft of e-book: *My Authentic Personal and Professional Brand*

3. Senior adults ages 65-80. **Senior Rejuvenation, Authentic Living and Legacy Success**
   Study Appendix A; skip chapters 1-13, then read the Second Interlude and chapters 14-15.
   Next read chapters 1-13, the Epilogue, and Appendix B for e-book preparation.
   Options: Prepare draft of e-book: *My Integral Life, Work, Wealth, Health and Legacy Success, or*
   Prepare draft of *My Senior Life Learning and Memorable Legacy (Letter).*

4. <u>Attend the Master Class </u>for **Your Integral Life Matters.** This Mentor's Program applies the complete Life Management Mindset Handbook methodology. Participants work with Dr. Garrity on **All** the above subject matter and earn an ALF Certification. Reference: http://www.alforum.org

B. The American Experiment in Life, Liberty and the Pursuit of Happiness

The American experiment in democratic governance deserves a mixed review in terms of its efficiency and effectiveness. A majority of Americans benefit from the security, wealth, and technological capability offered to those who through education, social connectivity, or birthright have the opportunity to participate, produce, and consume valued goods and services. However, in terms of serving the interests of *ALL Americans* more fully, the nation is failing to live up to its Constitutional guarantee of life, liberty, and the pursuit of happiness for all. There is little doubt that American society, in terms of its social and financial responsibilities, should be able to produce and distribute its bounty more equitably and in greater alignment with its founding principles. For a sizeable minority in the population these opportunities may not exist; or are missed due to their lack of preparation; or social barriers are perceived to be too difficult for them to overcome.

While the increasing pace of life, complexity of issues, and unpredictability of events threaten to consume many in whirlpools of societal turbulence, the systems that have been designed for support often fail to respond adequately. Chaos and rigidity co-exist to the detriment of social alignment and cohesion. Using the Federal government as an example, pluralistic gridlock that even James Madison might find difficult to accept has slowed policy and budget deliberations to a crawl. Americans seem to be losing their ability to recognize and act on issues of mutual concern. Unless a crisis is imminent, little action is taken, and even then that which is done may be ill-advised.

A critique of the growth and development of modern American society in terms of the core civic and ethical values envisioned in the American founding would hardly be complementary. The extent of our impressive economic and technological accomplishments coupled with seemingly intractable political, social, ecological, and international predicaments could have been difficult to anticipate and prevent, but surely we might have done much better than we have. The question of whether American society can proactively learn to manage its future for positive results, or simply act as inept caretakers of a diminishing heritage, may be worth considering. It appears that we, as citizens, are not sufficiently engaged in the most important conversations required to fully understand, expertly negotiate and firmly secure enlightened national progress here at home.

On the international scene, we may ask ourselves: "Where are the future U.S. leaders with outstanding minds and ethical personal character who can influence and establish America's national vision, mission and policies that are constitutionally authentic and internationally welcomed? Concurrently, we could ask ourselves to reflect on our seemingly self-imposed commitment to be the leader of the "free world." Are we willing to "walk our talk" by confronting the ignorant traditions, rampant greed, and inhumane behavior of billions of people distributed throughout planet earth? To what degree is human progress on an international scale the responsibility of American? Is human progress limited to only a minority our nation's and the world's people? What share of the planet's human burden falls is the responsibility of the United States? Can we even articulate these multi-dimensional questions in an informed manner?

America's Founding, Purpose and International Influence

Appendix A contains selected documents that provide a foundation for America's purpose, principles, ideals and culture. Included are the U.S. Declaration of Independence and the Original Bill of Rights to our Constitution. It is important to notice that the content and citizenry preferences used throughout are guided by the societal laws, operating procedures and cultural priorities established over time – and now represent the American way of thinking and being.

[**Author's Note**: It is suggested that the readers allot time early in their schedule to scan these important guides and prepare to include their own knowledge and perspectives as a foundation for understanding and use of this Handbook's focus on human aspirations and objectives. The *Universal Ideals* identified in Chapter One later in the document are considered as contemporary American values and practices that contribute to both the content and context of American life. These factors established the socio-economic environment within which the research and writing of this manuscript was conducted. *Notwithstanding this approach, the vast majority of concepts and practices recommended, herein, are considered to be equally applicable to other nations and cultures.*]

A 21st Century Recap

A short sample of contemporary American societal issues and dilemmas is offered as a reminder that, notwithstanding the progress and standard of living enjoyed by many Americans, our potential is far from being achieved in a fair and equitable manner. As a nation we are hamstrung when any sizable segment of the population fails to exercise its rights and honor its responsibilities to itself and the larger community. Selected areas for immediate American concern include:

1. Addictions (lack of responsibility and self-control). The recognition of excessive drug and alcohol abuse, smoking and eating disorders, and sexual perversions and predators; At issue: Cost and effectiveness of the War on Drugs, selective medical use of marijuana, the doubling of heroin deaths in the last two years, etc.

2. Education (inadequate preparation for today's jobs). The lack of knowledge, skills, and motivation for performance in the competitive global workplace, over- and under-educated people; At issue: Educational standards and opportunity, curriculum content, knowledge of math and science, etc.

3. Social/Moral (crime, anti-social attitudes and behavior). Significant cynicism, intolerance, bias, lack of respect, self-centeredness, pastiche personalities, illegitimate births, and crimes against persons and property; At issue: abortion rights, gay rights, rights of community and obligations of citizens, etc

4. Economy (worker productivity, lack of economic opportunity, and inequitable distribution of goods and services). Welfare, poverty, and hunger; At issue: jobs, health care, global business and trade, generational under-employment, etc.

5. Politics (lack of responsible participation). Lack of respect for government and the political system, public scandals, cronyism; At issue: church/state relations, influence peddling, pluralistic gridlock, etc.

6. Ecology (overuse and destruction of environment). Overpopulation, pollution, resource depletion; At issue: destruction of rain forests, global warming, energy production etc.

7. Technology (tools and technologies). Unanticipated economic and social impacts; At issue: ethical issues of biotechnology, controls against computer pornography, cybercrime etc.

8. International (conflicts, wars, and human deprivation). Inequality of life and freedom; At issue: Middle East Wars, African genocide, starvation, and spreading of disease, etc.

Weighing heavily on the minds of those concerned with American citizen and human system development is how we approach these societal issues with respect for the freedoms we cherish, and with reinforcement of the obligations we owe each other within the complexity and diversity of our American societal experiment. Armed with a belief in the unbounded potential of American ingenuity and our extraordinary progress in science, medicine, government, and economics; we often explain to ourselves that, in time, all our nation's problems can be resolved, but we just have not achieved sufficient consensus and identified required resources.

From a broader perspective, how should we interpret America's relationship with the rest of the world? Have we yet determined just how much responsibility and interdependency we need to establish with other nations and continents? Even if we attempt to retreat economically, politically and/or militarily, will others let us do so? Must America always be the biggest humanitarian contributor and the last resort in repelling ignorant and savage behavior elsewhere? What can we reasonably do and afford? And, what should a citizen assume in terms of their personal opportunities and responsibilities?

Integral Life Management and Achievement

Our lives are experienced in a linear (horizontal) manner as we go through our individual aging processes (birth, adolescence, early adult, middle adult and senior adult). Most often we have little understanding of what we can expect at each stage, and are lucky to have others who can assist us in developing a vision for ourselves and the knowledge and skills required to succeed at every level we attain (Figure 2)

As we grow and develop our human capabilities (knowledge, emotions, physical) evolve in an interdisciplinary manner and at an uneven pace and rate of maturity within the complex environment we inhabit. The pace of development in our lives proceeds with similarly early in life, but as we acquire independence and exposure we become more responsible for our own trajectory once we enter early adulthood. As we get older we can find that we get locked into patterns of choices and behaviors that are increasingly restraining our options moving forward. For many, a crisis begins to develop wherein we become compelled to make life/career changes so that we may follow alternative paths towards newly discovered goals and objectives. Questions such as: What is our unique meaning and more satisfying direction? What practical steps might get us there? Which life achievement curve do we prefer? This *Integral Life Matters* handbook will assist you in choosing and pursuing an optimal life management strategy and memorable legacy. Earlier and faster are essential accomplishments in this model.

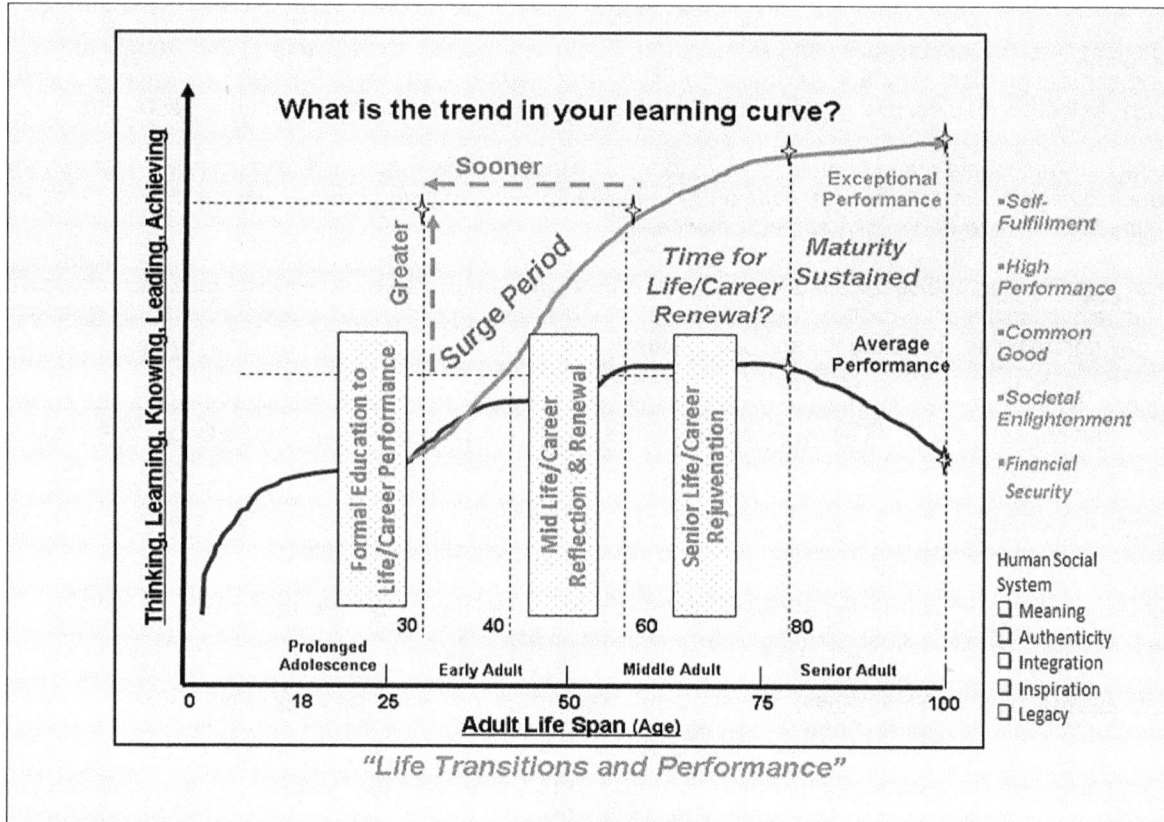

Figure 2

Summary of Contents

The comprehensive contents of this Mindset Handbook are presented for lifelong learning and conversation as:

Ambitions: This section on *Preliminary Insights and Ambitions* contains "think pieces" as a foundation for enriched consideration of the American Learnership and Integral Knowledge Management subjects that follow. These insights should enable readers and seminar participants to stretch any self-imposed boundaries on our thinking, learning and desired performance. The ability and willingness to proactively engage life management responsibilities is critical for everyone's lifelong learning and success.

Section I: This section on *American Learnership: Life Management and Professional Branding* introduces the proprietary "American Learnership" concept as a powerful and comprehensive methodology for achieving optimum benefit from initiatives designed to improve knowledge building for social systems development. Readers are invited to reflect on the meaningful ideals and inspirational goals that motivate and assist us in understanding the benefits of *lifelong learning*, the *meaning of life*, *life project management* and *personal branding*.

Section II: This section on *American Learnership: Interdisciplinary Reasoning Competencies* describes the interrelatedness of five knowledge building skills that systematically enable meaningful thinking, learning, knowing, leading and achieving. These skills are *Systems Thinking, Pattern Recognition, Situational Learning, Knowledge Management*, and *Adaptive Leadership*. These competencies form an interdisciplinary and powerful methodology for driving social systems development.

Section III: This section on *American Learnership: Integral Social Systems Development* provides a comprehensive explanation of how we citizens can function within four interdependent knowledge building social system domains to become exceptionally successful. These are *Personal Systems Development, Organization Systems Development,*

Community Systems Development, and *Societal Systems Development.* These competencies increase the speed and quality of knowledge building.

Section IV: This section on *American Learnership Encore: Mid-Life Opportunities and Experiences* provide senior adults the opportunity to review and improve on their accumulated learning, knowledge building and life accomplishments, and to bring closure to a successful life well-lived. Commitment to a 50+ Encore Initiatives for senior life management and legacy branding allows elders to remain productive and vigorous through life's end.

Epilogue: *Summarization and Review of Selected Major Topics:* A review at this stage solidifies reader comprehension:

A. Implications for Integral Learning and Knowledge Management
B. American Learnership Practitioner Characteristics (25)
C. Wealth Accumulation and Financial Security
D. Life Transitions and Architecture for Integrated Living and Development.

Appendix: *Supporting information; Participant products and services.*

A. American Founding Documents
B. Personal e-Book Publishing (option): *My Integral Life, Work, Wealth, Health and Legacy Success*
C. Personal e-Book Publishing (option): *My Authentic Personal and Professional Brand*
D. Encore Example: The Author's Encore Journey
E. Complete Your Unique Life Project (option): *My Senior Life Learning and Memorable Legacy (Letter)*
F. American Learnership Organization and Author

C. Ambitions: Preliminary Insights and Aspirations

*The improvement of understanding is for two ends: first our own increase of knowledge;
secondly, to enable us to deliver that knowledge to others. — John Locke*

Many of us go through our lives completing tasks and meeting responsibilities without thinking too much about where we are going and how we are going to get there. Only occasionally when a person or an event breaks our pattern of concentration do we take the time to reflect on what we have been doing and to determine whether it is meaningful to us, or to anyone else, that we continue along the same path. When we do find time to mull over our direction, extent of commitments, and rate of progress, the thoughts that often emerge are:

When will I discover my true calling, and begin to live a more integrated and meaningful life?

How can I become more knowledgeable and competent in a rapidly changing and stressful world?

How can I manage my way through these mid-life/career disappointments, and have a second chance to succeed?

How can I make my life a memorable event, and become an example for those who follow in the future?

These questions, and others with similar heart-felt overtones, are clues to lives that lack the cognitive and emotional development that people in advanced societies have come to expect. How can we make the appropriate personal changes? How can we even think about what has happened and what is needed to be done? These are daunting challenges. These concerns and challenges mark the cornerstone of this work.

The research for this Life Management Mindset Handbook has been an investigation into Americans' lives, careers, legacies and societal best practices; and a framework for integrating the resulting theories, perspectives, and practices so they may be understood, embraced, and applied for personal, organizational, and community improvement.

Other authors have conducted research, analyzed their findings, and presented their perspectives – and this handbook attempts to give many of them the credit they deserve within the context of its social architecture. The Handbook is a compilation of selected topics and authors whose perspectives have informed the author's own development over a lifetime of social development and career progression. A buffet table is set and we can all browse, select, and discuss that which is mentally nourishing in our own lives and careers. We can become more efficient, effective, innovative, and compassionate in managing our way through this one life we have to lead.

A few context setting factors that come to mind to begin this conversation are presented. These are meant to prod you, the reader, to reflect on your own efforts to make sense out of the sometimes incoherent patterns of human thinking and behavior we all experience – and to emerge determined to find your answers the above questions.

1. Conscious Pursuit of Personal Development (Mindset)

Personal development may be easier to understand and support as a concept than it is to define and implement in a systematic manner. Because individuals are distinct from one another (age, gender, and education) and experience different life circumstances (ethnicity, culture, and career) we might expect that everyone is significantly unique as they make choices in pursuit of a satisfying life. And yet, philosophers, researchers, academics and social scientists have compiled considerable data and information that suggest that at a fundamental level of human reasoning and behavior we have common needs, interests and attitudes that drive our perspectives and preferences.

Researcher and author Steve Pavlina (*Personal Development for Smart People: The Conscious Pursuit of Personal Growth*, 2008) has assembled an impressive body of knowledge and insight that suggest there are certain high-level concepts leading to practical actions that every one of us should be able to learn and apply in all areas of our lives and careers. For Pavlina, "smart people" are those that have acquired a working knowledge of seven principles, with "intelligence" being the foremost and the result of the interaction among the other six:

a. Intelligence – Human *intelligence* is derivative from the mutually reinforcing primary and secondary principles that follow. When these principles are learned and applied throughout our lives we are empowered to learn, grow, lead, achieve and contribute to human betterment.

b. Truth – The first primary principle of personal development. We primarily grow as human beings by discovering new truths about ourselves and our reality. We can accelerate our growth by consciously seeking *truth* and deliberately turning away from falsehood and denial.

c. Love – The second primary principle of personal development. *Love* is an emotion, but more than that it is the willingness to connect to another person, place or thing to create a meaningful relationship. Forming connections may be the essence of a purposeful life.

d. Power – The third primary principle of personal development. Our ability to consciously and deliberately assist and create the world around us is a function of our *power* to cultivate a life of our own choosing. We need not accept becoming a victim of our environment.

e. Oneness – The first secondary principle comes from combining *truth* and *love*. Whereas love is the ability to connect by choice, oneness recognizes the *truth* that everything is *already connected* – the natural state of being. *Oneness* creates an empathetic connection with everything else.

f. Authority – The second secondary principle is derived from *truth* and *power*. Truth without power accomplishes nothing. Power without truth generates wasted action. The principle of *authority* teaches us to blend knowledge and action to produce intelligent results. Living a self-directed life requires that others be influenced by our apparent *authority*.

g. Courage – The third secondary principle results from the combination of *love* and *power*. While it is clear that a sense of power often leads to bold action, it is equally true that when power is coupled with the love from our deepest connections we can act both bold and *courageously* in the face of risk and obstruction.

[**Author's Note**: Additional information on Steve Pavlina's perspectives and contributions are at www.StevePavlina.com]

2. Knowledge, Values, Culture and Societal Progress (Mindset)

In social, political and economic literature researchers are able to define the societal *knowledge* that promotes the emergence of strong cultures with the power to drive societal progress. The general effect is that the *values*, attitudes, beliefs, orientations and underlying assumptions prevalent among a group of people *(the culture)* can be shown to reliably influence that group's economic development, material well-being, social-economic equity, and political-competency *(societal progress)*. The assumption is that the group is able to define the values, assumptions and behaviors they agree should be the standard assessment criteria and the measures of acceptable performance. It has been suggested that cultures that value self-reliance, equal rights, democracy and productive work are better positioned to empower their citizenry to make intelligent choices toward greater human enlightenment and progress.

The question that arises is "Is the culture itself judged to be worthy of the task before it?" Has the culture developed and been accepted as intellectually and behaviorally mature for the group's continued development? The two factors for basic reflection by the group's leaders are (a) has the group learned the most relevant, scientific and logically established processes, methods, facts and truths essential to their historical time and experience (e.g. their Intelligence Quotient), and (b) has the group learned and accepted the personal and societal relationship responsibilities sought by their most respected and progressive leaders (e.g. their Emotional Quotient).

The well regarded American Senator, Daniel Patrick Moynihan once said: "The central conservative truth is that it is culture, not politics, which determines the success of a society." One response might be is that politics represents the arena in which policy battles are fought by selected warriors chosen by powerful and competing constituents. And, in America the general set of rules by which these battles are fought are guided by the U.S. Founding documents of which the Constitution and its Amendments are preeminent.

3. Transitioning from a Mindless to a Mindful Way-of-Being (Mindset)

Sigmund Freud once said: "We know that the first step toward the intellectual mastery of the world in which we live is the discovery of general principles, rules and laws which bring order out of chaos. By such mental operations we simplify the world of phenomena, but we cannot avoid falsifying it in doing so, especially when we are dealing with processes of development and change." Whenever we become lazy or trapped by our simplifications and convenience-based way of thinking, we are in danger of operating on the basis of *premature cognitive commitments* in which our frames of reference and preference dominate our mental processing and exclude new, more accurate, and more useful information – and we begin to operate *mindlessly*.

Mindlessness is perpetuated by (a) unconscious, motivated-not-knowing, (b) using restrictive categories for approved knowledge, (c) a sense of limited scope or resources, (d) a refusal to consider the influence of context, (e) the influence of pre-established values and perceptions, (f) a strong preference for linear, cause and effect thinking, (g) a lack of education, emotional development, and/or experience, and (h) excessive trust in "experts" with little real basis for their views. Upon reflection, it might be that most of humankind lives within social, ethnic, religious, cultural, political, and economic circumstances that perpetuate this mindlessness. Maybe the time has come the raise the bar of our expectations, and to declare that given the hundred thousand years or so of our *homo-sapiens* ancestors roaming around the earth we should have accomplished more. Maybe we can learn to become more mindful in our reasoning and behavior as we progress into our respective futures.

According to Ellen Langer in her book *Mindfulness* (1989), mindfulness can be distinguished by three key qualities: (a) creation of new categories, (b) openness to new information, and (c) awareness of more than one perspective. The willingness and ability to create new categories occurs when people pay attention to the information coming their way in terms of the situational context involved. A state of mindfulness also allows a person and/or group to welcome new, relevant information as a source of learning and improvement; it understands that change is continuous and as complexity grows new factors and relationships warrant consideration. And lastly, being astute to others' knowledge and experience requires that not only new information but others' perspectives are considered when trying to understand people and situations. Mindfulness is the result of open-minded, systems thinking and human pattern recognition. On the global scale, the world can be divided between the have and have-nots, the mindful and the mindless. We have a choice.

4. Whole-Brain Training and Learning (Mindset)

Our human brain is structured with a prefrontal lobe *executive capability* to organize and to push and pull data and information to/from multifarious brain data locations. This functionality enables thinking and reasoning (sense-making) amid many influencing factors, thereby enabling human response and behavior appropriate to the situation at hand. The sum total of all the brain activity required for daily assessments, decisions, actions and reflections has proven to be extraordinary as human learning and development has progressed over millennia.

A word that uniquely captures the synthesis of these mutually supportive brain functions is *integral*. When our learning elicits integral learning, knowledge and understanding of the situations in which we find ourselves, we are empowered to reason and take action in a rapidly changing and complex world. Brain training that enhances the integral learning and knowledge building capacity of the human brain can be considered as a useful metaphor for learning and leading an efficient and effective life and career, and for constructing a holistic personal legacy that becomes meaningful for posterity.

The author and readers of this Mindset Handbook are considered to be subjects in an experiment on *integral brain learning through cognitive and emotional immersion*. We are part of an experiment in which whole-brain stimulation occurring through an immersion into a plethora of interrelated subjects and perspectives alternately frustrates, and then illuminates, our mental processing and sense of order. The approach is to provide enough new information to stimulate interest and establish a learning opportunity, but not so much to dwell on the topic at the expense of the larger, whole life integration objective. Hundreds of perspectives, models, frameworks and other "think pieces" are included to assist you the reader in making a self-assessment of what you think, feel, and plan to do to craft and fulfill your personal and professional life of objectives.

The educational objective is to create *holistic brain learning* by stimulating cognitive association and emotional sensation. Everyone desiring to stay mentally sharp and relevant throughout their lifetime can benefit from participating in reasoning and stimulating dialogue. The expectation is this mindset-building experience is a bit more interesting than doing crossword puzzles or Sudoku.

5. Integral Learning and Knowledge Management (Mindset)

The field of Knowledge Management has been articulately defined by the George Washington University educational team of Michael Stankosky and Francesco Calabrese during 2000 to 2010. While the discipline of learning was included as a major pillar and supporting factor, more research shows that comprehensive learning (context as well as content) is more critical to knowledge building and management than previously thought. In fact, it is now fair to say that knowledge creation and sharing cannot be fully effective if situational learning has not been thoroughly accomplished.

As important as knowledge management has become in understanding personal and organizational effectiveness and development, we need to appreciate that we are first and foremost awash in a sea of data, information and various personalities relating to the situations within which we learn. Some situations are routine and need little attention while at the other end of a continuum – without the use of the right information at the right time for the right purpose by the right people – those situations might well be personally or professionally limiting.

Every situation we encounter requires a fair amount of information gathering and analysis followed by decision-making concerning (a) what to do with that knowledge and (b) if further action is appropriate. Every situation is an interdisciplinary learning opportunity and the learning we acquire contributes to our store of knowledge we deem to be trustworthy and useful. Situational learning may therefore be valued as a predicate for knowledge management – and without efficient management of both learning and knowledge; attempts to improve organizational leadership and human performance cannot be fully effective.

6. A University of the Mind (Mindset)

A major example of how life and work has been systematically divided and organized into units of knowledge and performance is illustrated in Figure 3. Shown is the approach used by a well-known university to depict the various schools, departments, and programs that have a logical connection to the University's Knowledge Management Program. The breadth of the university's educational program inspires this author to propose the concept *University of the Mind – to* be a "Mindset" that describes the "similarity between a university and the human mind" wherein their modular construct, breadth of knowledge, and responsibility to accommodate activities requiring both integration and differentiation. This perspective poses the challenge: How can we select, record, modify, apply, and share patterns of belief and information among individuals and social systems when and where they are needed?

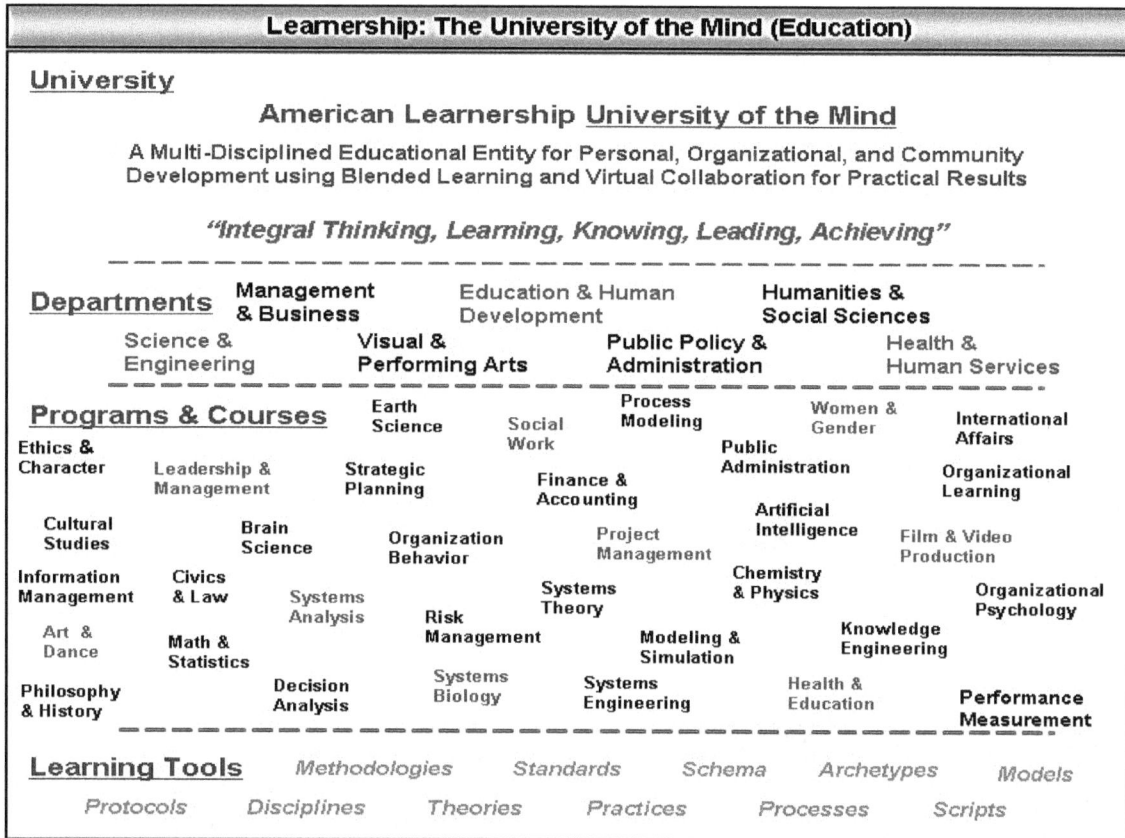

Learnership: The University of the Mind (Education)

University

American Learnership University of the Mind

A Multi-Disciplined Educational Entity for Personal, Organizational, and Community Development using Blended Learning and Virtual Collaboration for Practical Results

"Integral Thinking, Learning, Knowing, Leading, Achieving"

- -

Departments

| Management & Business | Education & Human Development | Humanities & Social Sciences |
| Science & Engineering | Visual & Performing Arts | Public Policy & Administration | Health & Human Services |

- -

Programs & Courses

Ethics & Character Leadership & Management Strategic Planning Earth Science Social Work Process Modeling Finance & Accounting Public Administration Women & Gender International Affairs Organizational Learning

Cultural Studies Brain Science Organization Behavior Project Management Artificial Intelligence Film & Video Production

Information Management Civics & Law Systems Analysis Risk Management Systems Theory Chemistry & Physics Organizational Psychology

Art & Dance Math & Statistics Modeling & Simulation Knowledge Engineering

Philosophy & History Decision Analysis Systems Biology Systems Engineering Health & Education Performance Measurement

- -

Learning Tools

Methodologies Standards Schema Archetypes Models

Protocols Disciplines Theories Practices Processes Scripts

Figure 3

7. Systems Integration for a Differentiated World (Mindset)

Societal development occurs within a complex tapestry of interrelated fields of knowledge, culture, and societal structure sometimes referred to as the human social system. While our lives are lived as integrated experiences, we are formally educated to think and work within narrowly differentiated scientific and sociological disciplines. This paradox, while somewhat understandable for teaching children and less experienced people, can restrict adult minds from expanding to their full cognitive and emotional maturity.

Even as we recognize that differentiation and fragmentation may often lead to greater productivity and efficiency in our activities, we cannot afford to sacrifice the greater human potential and effectiveness that result from lifelong learning in an integral, interdisciplinary, system-of-systems context. A complex environment where important interdependencies must be accommodated while decision-making and problem solving are in full sway calls for formal education and practical training that competently addresses real life and career challenges and opportunities.

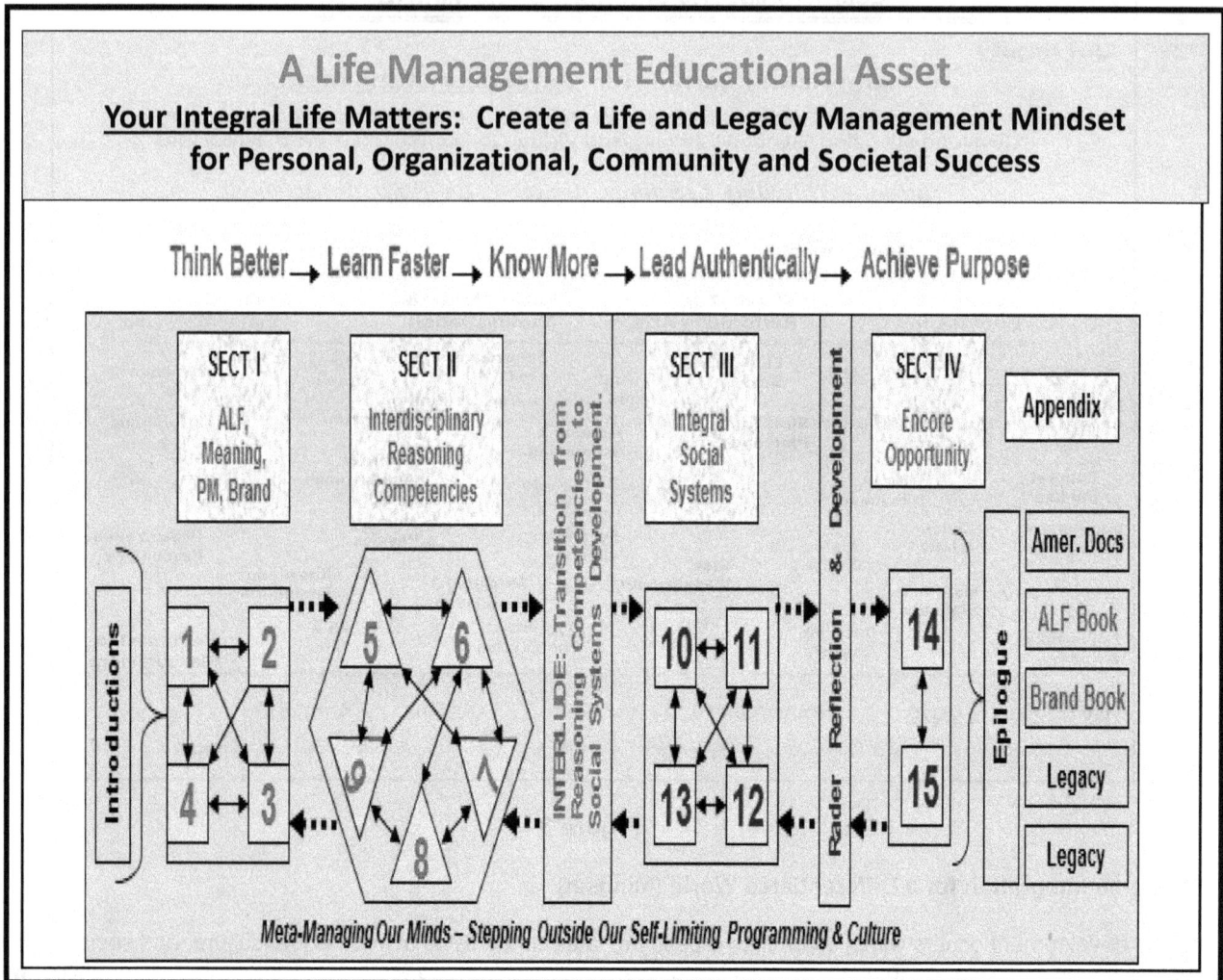

Figure 4

What is needed as we develop into adulthood is greater emphasis on interdisciplinary education and skill development that incorporates systems thinking, pattern recognition, situational assessment, broad-based knowledge sharing, and adaptive personal and organizational skills development. This Mindset Handbook is an example of one such learning opportunity, and many new perspectives and insights will unfold for the reader that will ultimately enhance your self-management, professional performance and continuous growth and achievement.

8. A Life Learning Educational Asset (LLEA) (Mindset)

The emphasis here on both the evolutionary content and context of interdisciplinary disciplines – across an adult lifetime of often overlapping and changing forces – requires a willingness to introduce concepts early-on that will only come to more meaningful fruition somewhat later as additional factors and actions are indicated. As an example in Figure 4 the integrated human social systems domains of personal, organizational, community and societal development (Chapters 10-12) can only be dynamically understood after foundational learning processes are introduced here in the Introduction, anchored in an architecture, purpose, process and desire for individual personhood (Chapters 1-4). When these cognitive and emotional topics are interlaced into motion – where systems thinking, pattern recognition, situational learning, knowledge management and adaptive leadership are sequentially synthesized (Chapters 5-9) – change and growth are energized in those same target social domains.

As lifelong adult learning is experienced, a person's mid-life and senior years are where a second chance at innovation and interpersonal compassion – followed by expressions of orderly self-fulfillment – are illuminated as evidence of an integral life well lived.

9. American Traditions (Mindset)

This body of research, documentation and graphics has been produced after a period of 30 years of adult experience and development, six years of doctoral study and dissertation preparation, and nine years of university teaching and business consulting. In that time your author has been an American citizen reared in the social and civic values of the growing and expanding American culture and development. Including some professional development and recreational travel outside the United States, his experience is heavily weighted on U.S. foundational documents, such as the Declaration of Independence, the Constitution, the Bill of Rights and Amendments and the United Nation's Declaration of Human Rights.

The knowledge and experience gleaned from life, work, debate and cultural conversation with others has enabled this author to assimilate the competence and confidence to selectively assert a best practices mindset for societal living, working, and collaboration that – while certainly not perfect in considering other relevant perspectives – can be advocated and recommend as contributing to the advancement of people in most cultures, races, religions, localities and political persuasions in this twenty-first century timeframe. This belief is supported by the accumulation of an immense number of references that suggest the breadth, depth and integration of concepts and practices worthy of emulation at appropriate opportunities. Appendix A contains selections from some of these founding documents for review and reference here and in subsequent curricula.

10. Capacity for Inquiry, Learning and Advocacy (Mindset)

The writing of this document was pursued in the spirit and understanding that all societal trends and issues are open to personal interpretation. It is recognized that events have meaning in terms of the values, attitudes, and beliefs of those who witness or participate in them; our perception is our reality. In terms of this project, a need for an awareness of differing perspectives and the resulting effects on individual and group thinking and action is appreciated. The search for core values, attitudes, and beliefs is pursued to discern those for which there is wide support and compelling evidence of usefulness as applied to societal development. As for how well American society has already progressed and the potential quality of its future, a continuum of human perspectives is recognizable:

a. The Optimist's View. Optimists, at one end of a continuum, tend to expect the best possible outcomes from current trends or situations. Optimists see the positive results of the American experience and can point to trends that portend an even better future ahead. From this perspective, America's achievements have been extraordinary and have enabled the majority of its citizens to enjoy unparalleled prosperity. Internationally, America dominated the twentieth century and is positioned for leadership in this century also. The optimists trust that the positive aspects of individual, organizational, and community life will emerge and succeed in making the future better than the past – at least for themselves and those they care about. Optimists believe that society will eventually improve education, reduce crime, defeat bias, streamline bureaucracy, overcome poverty, improve life expectancy, etc. Things will definitely get better; somehow.

b. The Pessimist's View. Pessimists, at the other end of the continuum, tend to expect the worst possible outcomes from current trends or events. Their views are the opposite from those of the optimists and they argue that evidence of their views is easy to find in everyday events. The pessimist's viewpoint has probably never been stated better than by Dorothy Sayers, a commentator on Dante (Dante's Inferno) and modern society, who stated, in part: "And since we are today fairly well convinced that society is in a bad way and not necessarily evolving in the direction of perfectibility, we find it easy enough to recognize the various stages by which the deep of corruption is reached" (Sayers, 1954). In terms of this perspective, America's problems with education, crime, poverty, disease, dishonesty, corruption, etc. will not be solved, because we lack the will, the ability, or both to take action.

c. The Hopeful Realist's View. Hopeful realists, somewhere along the continuum between the optimists and the pessimists are inclined toward rational consideration of facts and cause-and-effect relationships, and believe that resources may be summoned by informed and willing persons to achieve desired improvement. By avoiding what may be termed the optimist's wishful thinking and the pessimist's allegiance with hopelessness, the hopeful realist engages problems and opportunities with personal determination and commitment to the future. Allen Tough in *Crucial Questions About the Future* (1991) says "…if in doubt, adopt a cautiously optimistic attitude…Face fully the deep-seated problems of the world, but also retain plenty of hope, energy, and enthusiasm." (p.43)

This Mindset Handbook has been researched and written as a hopeful realist. Almost any text with social commentary or newspaper of the day is sufficient reference to see the obvious -- America is severely troubled. If stating that the nation and society are in decline is too much for some to bear, it is certainly true that the nation's potential is not being fully realized. The challenge is to find strength in our roots, locate our common ground, learn the lessons that are being taught, strive for our higher goals, and act in the interest of ourselves and others.

Conclusion

With these perspectives in mind, we can now move forward to Section I: American Learnership: Life Management and Professional Branding.

Chapter 1, <u>An Introduction to American Learnership</u> -- provides an overarching summary of the foundational concepts and insights that make "Learnership" a distinctive trademark. The principles, graphics and practices advocated are meant to stretch readers' thinking and suggest new approaches for becoming successful – all within a logical social system-of-systems framework. The foundational relationship between American Learnership and Integral Knowledge Management begins in this chapter.

Chapter 2, <u>Discovering the Meaning of Your Life</u>, offers a comprehensive method for reflection, learning and the identification of one's own life management objectives to create a sense of purpose and motivation. The learnership social system domains and guideline objectives used to organize this task were (a) Personal self-fulfillment, (b) Organization high performance, (c) Community common good, and (d) Societal human enlightenment. When pursued in an integrated manner, the learner is assured of achieving personal development and greater life satisfaction.

Chapter 3, <u>Being the Project Manager of Your Life</u>, provides an introduction to a well-regarded business management skill with a description of how that tool could be used equally well in managing one's learning and life trajectory. The project management methodology adds value due to its use of process management and systems thinking techniques that require employing discrete steps in working towards a desired objective. Periodic review of project challenges and updating of necessary project changes keeps the life management initiative moving forward toward meaningful objectives at a reasoned pace.

Chapter 4, <u>Creating Your Authentic Personal and Professional Brand</u>, describes how the reader may responsibly learn more about themselves and then use that learning to chart a course of action that enables their purpose and capabilities to be understood and valued by others in their network and field of business.

<u>Section 1</u>

American Learnership:
Life Management and Professional Branding

Section I: This section on *American Learnership: Life Management and Professional Branding* introduces the proprietary "American Learnership" concept as a powerful and comprehensive methodology for achieving optimum benefit from initiatives designed to improve knowledge building for social systems development. Readers are invited to reflect on the meaningful ideals and inspirational goals that motivate and assist us in understanding the benefits of *lifelong learning*, the *meaning of life, life project management* and *personal branding.*

The Value of Unification

"Whenever a large number of facts accumulate concerning any branch of knowledge, the human mind feels the need for some unifying concept with which to correlate them. Such integration is not only artistically satisfying, by bringing harmony into what appeared to be discord; it is also practically useful. It helps one see a large field from a single point of view. When surveyed from a great elevation, some details in the landscape become hazy, or even invisible; yet it is only from there that we can see the field as a whole, in order to ascertain where the more detailed exploration of the ground would be most helpful for its further development." — Hans Selye, M.D., *The Stress of Life*

Chapter One

Introduction to American Learnership

Major Chapter Topics

Introduction to American Learnership

Understanding Learning and American Learnership

Learning is a process that is the cornerstone of all human activity. Without learning, there is no human growth and development – personhood is not possible. And, at the microscopic level, the genes of the human genome – the foundational recipes for both our anatomy and behavior – cannot develop without exposure to and influence from their human (host) environment (Genome, 1999, by Ridley). It is a fact that life itself depends upon the ability of the human organism to learn from the interaction of its ingrained predispositions (nature) and its experience with its surroundings (nurture). The ability for our genes to evolve is based on their capacity for microscopic change and mutation. For complex human beings, our ability to learn and develop is tightly linked to our capacity and willingness to engage, understand, and accommodate our environment. Norman Vincent Peale said: *"The successful person is always a learner'*.

Learners are people with an ability to learn, which makes everyone to some degree a learner. Most of us fail to learn to excel at the pace, depth, breadth and length of time required to be categorized as first rate learners. To continually discover new, worthwhile and satisfaction-giving topics requires learners committed to open, inquisitive, proactive and action-oriented ways of learning. Their cognitive and emotionally based modes of sensing/thinking, interpreting/deciding, and realizing/acting need coherent interplay with their personal attributes. Good learners are able to learn effectively within the context of increasing time constraints, constant change, and the increasing complexity of modern life. Learning is essential for knowing.

Leading thinkers and influential writers throughout history have constructed theories on the what, why and how of learning in an effort to assist learners in their personal growth and development. This book acknowledges those insightful contributions and provides a meta-cognitive approach for integration and use of many of those interdependent and supportive perspectives. Juvenal said *"All wish to possess knowledge, but few comparatively speaking are willing to pay the price."*

Knowing is a capability that results from learning. Efficient and effective learners know more useful information about the people, things, and situations in life that matter. Learners and learning are focused on knowledge and knowing. In particular, having in our brains (or at our disposal) the information and knowledge required to understand, plan, execute, and reflect on our life activities incrementally advances growth and development. Knowing is essential for achieving. Gail Sheehy said: *'The secret of a leader lies in the tests he has faced over the whole of his life and the habit of action he develops in meeting those tests".*

Leading is a process that has to do with our ability to use our knowledge to influence others' thinking and behavior. Because learning creates change, leading is also essential if the new state of knowledge is to be shared and actualized. The process of leading change includes creating a future vision, building a case for change, involving important stakeholders, and implementing compelling improvements – all of which should demonstrate the viability of the new knowledge and encourage early adaptation by those affected. Without effective leading little is accomplished – much like racing the engine on a high performance car but never putting the vehicle in gear. Leading is essential for putting knowledge into action. John Quincy Adams, 6th President of the United States, once said: *"If your actions inspire others to dream more, learn more, do more, and become more, you are a leader".*

Leadership, the distinguishing characteristic of leaders is that they are able to get others to travel to an unfamiliar location, accomplish a desired objective, or change a personal perspective without fully knowing all the information that might be relevant. Leaders create a sense of direction, motivation and trust in others so that their personal thoughts, needs or plans are considered and action is taken. Some of the traits positively correlated with effective leadership include being competent, focused, fair, objective and friendly; having a positive attitude, and showing good initiative.

Peter Vaill (Learning as a Way of Being) suggests the concept of learning leadership or "leaderly learning" wherein leaders adopt a style of management that demonstrates that they are open to learning their way through issues and problems. Major focus is placed on effectively integrating the technical (content), purposeful (direction) and relational (meaningful) aspects of organizational matters through effective collaboration and joint decision making. This, unfortunately, is clearly not a dominant skill in today's competitive business environment. Leonardo da Vinci said:" *Learning is the only thing the mind never exhausts, never fears, and never regrets. It is the only thing that will never fail us".*

Learnership, learning is a complex process with the object of knowledge creation and use in virtually all human affairs. And, learners are people with an ability to learn – although the development of this ability and willingness to use it varies widely across the general population. It follows, then, that there should be a term to describe people who are exceptional and influential learners; their capabilities and their influence on others. Learnership is the suggested term, and it is derived from: (1) learner – one who seeks to learn or to gain knowledge through experience or study, and (2) – ship (suffix) – to show or possess a quality, state, or condition. Additionally, learnership captures the essence and skill of leadership in which people are skillful in influencing others.

Learnership is a *process in service of knowledge*: its creation and its application. Highly developed skill in learnership virtually assures highly developed and comprehensive use of knowledge across multiple interdisciplinary social systems. In today's terminology, it could be said that learnership makes the concept of "*Total Knowledge Management*" (TKM) a distinct possibility.

Learnership is about *learning*, and about being a learner. More importantly, it's about the journey or *process* that begins when we learn to become a skilled and purposeful learner and make a lifelong commitment to create and realize our individual potential. It's about the resilience that grows when learning yields achievement even when faced with obstacles and inequities. It's about the possibilities we discover through personal reflection and social interaction. It's a *life management methodology* whose pace quickens as we become more mindful of our experiences and relationships and begin to manage our co-evolution within the expanding universe.

Learnership is about *knowing,* and how lifelong learning leads to the acquisition and storage of information and "relevant" knowledge that may be employed in a multifaceted manner in order to become an *intelligent and competent person*. The more knowledge we can acquire, store, access, and apply in a timely and rational manner, the more efficient and effective we become in all aspects of our lives. Knowing is both a cognitive and emotional ability; and it is a physical capability in that the body can be trained to perform a wide range of skills. People are known to have multiple intelligences such as linguistic, mathematical, musical intelligence. Knowing more about a subject or situation is a positive indicator that appropriate action is likely to be taken.

Learnership is about *leading*, and about influencing action. Learning leads to knowledge but knowledge without action denies the learner and others the growth and development they may value. The ability of leaders to create a sense of urgency or opportunity focused on new levels of personal or organizational development is a significant attribute. Individual and societal aspirations can be realized when objectives are clearly identified, best practices are understood, collaborative teamwork is established, and persistent effort is applied. A commitment to higher performance and community service is only potent when learning is shared and applied through the efforts of learning leaders.

Learnership is a *whole person competence*. The objective of learnership is to be a significant catalyst in the pursuit of personal self-fulfillment, organizational high performance, the community common good and societal enlightenment. From an introspective and feeling perspective, learnership is the lifelong crafting of our potential "to become," to establish a presence that transcends our own existence, and to influence the development of future generations. From a performance-oriented and cognitive perspective, learnership is demonstrated by our steadfast pursuit of lifelong learning, knowledge management, and personal achievement in all areas of life's responsibility and opportunity. Learnership conveys "a way-of-being" in which lifelong learning and knowledge management are thoroughly integrated into one's goal-seeking behavior so as to invigorate our experience and performance.

Learnership is *not a new phenomenon*, but it is a new term and a more comprehensive articulation of the preferred attitudes, areas of knowledge, and constructive activities that give each of us the edge in planning and experiencing a more successful and satisfying life and career.

Learnership can be *practiced by just about anyone*. Many people throughout history have had the understanding and courage to become lifelong learners, doers, and contributors. They have charted their unique course, realized their own purpose, and enriched the lives of countless others as they pursued their particular journeys. Unfortunately, the world's history has been that the vast majority of people in all societies and cultures have missed what the "accomplished elite" have experienced. Maybe by adopting the learnership learning-to-learn strategy, many more of us can learn to manage our learning, our knowing, our leading, and our achievements.

The concept of *Your Integral Life Matters: A Life Management Handbook for American Learning, Leading and Legacy Success* is intended to inspire the same generative perspective towards personal development, higher performance and social contribution expressed in such seminal works as Carl Rodgers' A Way of Being and Peter

Vaill's *Learning as a Way of Being*. The attempt, herein, is to establish a gestalt-like description of how our own cognitive development and personal performance can not only serve our own purposes, but also be an inspiration to others' growth and achievement.

A life worth living is informed by skillful reasoning, reflective learning, and the application of knowledge to desired ends. Learnership is meant to convey an optimum lifestyle in which efficient learning and effective leading are the behavioral hallmarks of lifelong learners determining their unique and successful "ways-of-being." What also needs to be understood is that the connective link between learning and leading is knowing (our mind's knowledge repository) – and it is this storehouse of information and knowledge that provides the "content" that is created and put to work within the process of learning and leading.

At a summary level, learnership is an interpersonal capability distinguished by:

1. A synthesis of learning and leadership process skills in which the patterns of reasoning and behavior demonstrated by "learning-leaders" guide and motivate the performance of individuals in their pursuit of personal, organizational, community and societal accomplishment.

2. A focus on the what, why, and how of societal knowledge creation and application so individuals may (a) take responsibility for their own lifelong learning and knowledge creation, and (b) be motivated to achieve extraordinary results by discovering their unique purpose and crafting their journey so as to apply their increasing knowledge toward meaningful personal and social objectives.

3. A desire to participate and lead the development and implementation of a comprehensive strategy for lifelong societal learning, knowing, and leading that leads toward holistic and integrated human social systems development. Henry Miller said: "*The real leader has no need to lead – he is content to point the way*".

The Learnership Philosophy

Learnership is a component of one's life philosophy on what is worth knowing and doing and on how human needs can be accomplished. Viewed from a broad perspective, learnership practitioners maintain a distinctive worldview that frames their thinking, learning, knowing, leading, and behavior. Their inclination to determine the: who, what, when, where, why, how, and for whom on a wide range of societal issues and human activity signifies a sense of personal responsibility for contributing to the welfare of themselves, their organizations, and their communities. When seen in action, learnership practitioners impact others as learning-leaders. When they are in leadership roles, they display what Peter Vaill calls "leaderly learning" in that they learn within and through the situation in which they are involved.

For *learnership practitioners*, living and learning are inseparable and they enjoy the daily opportunity to grow, learn, and evolve as described by Peter Senge, et al, in their book entitled *Presence: An Exploration of Profound Change in People, Organizations, and Society* (2005). These lifelong learners hold deeply held core beliefs and exude personal confidence that through inquiry and dialogue they will *learn to grow and to transition to a higher level-of-being.*

From an educational viewpoint, learnership contributes to the individual learner's ability to construct their own knowledge of social reality and to succeed within that structure (Reference: *The Social Construction of Reality* by Berger and Luckmann, 1967). Meta-cognitive reflection provides the learner with opportunity to reframe personally held views and modify ingrained programs for thinking and behavior.

On the philosophical level, learnership may be understood and appreciated as enthusiasm to participate in life and contribute to human progress by engaging in a broad set of mutually supportive and symbiotic practices that enrich peoples' knowledge and understanding. *Learning to learn, and to use what is learned for the betterment of humankind is an essential characteristic of the learnership philosophy.* Emphasis is on:

1. Purpose and Meaning – A commitment to engage with others in answering life's basic questions:

    a. What do I stand for? (A sense of purpose)

    b. How do I fit in with what has come before? (A sense of history)

    c. How am I related to other people/events/objectives? (A sense of order)

    d. <u>What can I hope for as I take action</u>? (A sense of outcome)

2. <u>Societal Development</u> – A willingness to embark on humanity's journey toward an understanding of life's mysteries, definition of human purpose, and equalization of societal opportunities.

3. <u>Higher-Level-of-Being</u> – A desire to motivate oneself and others to pursue a unique purpose, confront personal challenges, develop enlightened perspective, and experience mindful accomplishment.

4. <u>Goal Achievement</u> – A synthesis of skills in lifelong learning and knowledge management that lead toward the accomplishment of the universal human goals of self-fulfillment, high performance, the common good, and human enlightenment.

5. <u>Responsibility and Motivation</u> – A focus on the what, why, and how of lifelong learning and knowledge management so individuals may (a) take responsibility for their own learning and development, and (b) be motivated to achieve extraordinary results by first discovering their unique skills and purpose.

6. <u>Role Performance</u> – A capacity to improve human performance by applying the skills of kinship, fellowship, leadership, followership, stewardship, citizenship, statesmanship, and philanthropy.

7. <u>Use of Dialogue</u> – An appreciation for interpersonal dialogue anchored in open inquiry, rapid learning, interpersonal understanding, reasoned decision-making, and constructive action that achieves consensual results.

8. <u>Knowledge Management</u> – A willingness to participate in knowledge development focused on issues and challenges in the political, economic, social, technological, ecological, and geological spheres of societal knowledge and endeavor.

9. <u>Adult Life Cycle</u> – A developmental perspective on one's own lifetime that recognizes that individuals, organizations, and communities pass through phases of development, each with its own objectives, responsibilities, and rewards.

10. <u>Self-Renewal</u> – An understanding of life's uncertainty, complexity, and   temporality – and the value of transformative learning for occasional reinvigoration of one's life and career.

11. <u>Learning-to-Learn</u> – A willingness to learn and apply contemporary skills and methods designed to increase the quality and speed of one's learning.

12. <u>Secular Reasoning</u> – A commitment to participate in the public sphere using fact-based objectivity and authentic subjectivity in order that "common ground" among community participants is obtained. Political and sectarian debate is kept to a minimum due to their tendency to reduce collaboration and slow necessary consensus.

13. <u>Future Orientation</u> – A desire to explore and discover new knowledge and innovations that can enhance the lives and careers of current and future individuals and societies.

The Learnership Architecture

Ralph Waldo Emerson once said that "Life is a succession of lessons which must be lived to be understood." Of course, the problem here is that by the time we live long enough to understand what is worth knowing, it is often too late to chart an informed course of action meaningful for the life we are now living.

How then is it possible to capture the wisdom of exemplars – borne of time, experience and reflection – and make knowledge both discoverable and usable in our expanding, fast-paced world? Is there an agile but systematic process for thinking, learning and knowing that can empower more of us to discover our unique purpose and to accomplish our respective goals, needs and contributions?

The thesis of my book is that we can learn to manage ourselves – and to even lead others in their own development – towards the intellectual and emotional maturity that makes significant personal accomplishment probable. And, this may be done regardless of our personal histories or social status. The theoretical construct through which this occurs has three major propositions:

1. That systems thinking, pattern recognition, situational learning, knowledge management and adaptive leadership are foundational mental activities that serve as building blocks for managing what is worth thinking, learning, knowing, leading, and pursuing to select and achieve a holistic set of life goals.

2. That to understand and accomplish these life goals, an architecture consisting of the five competencies and four interdependent social systems requires our thoughtful reflection. These social systems consist of our personal social system, our organizational social system, our community social system, and our perspective on societal social systems among nations and geopolitical networks.

3. That the concurrent use and integration of the five reasoning competencies and four social systems allows those so inclined to achieve a mindful way-of-being. That is, they become skilled in their ability to dynamically process information and confident that knowledge acquired is relevant to their needs.

Figure 1-1 illustrates the relationship among these major reasoning competencies, system-of-systems, and human aspiration to "get our minds around matters essential in our lives. Ideally, these interdependent systems are developed and applied in a balanced manner with due consideration for personal, organizational, and community needs and responsibilities.

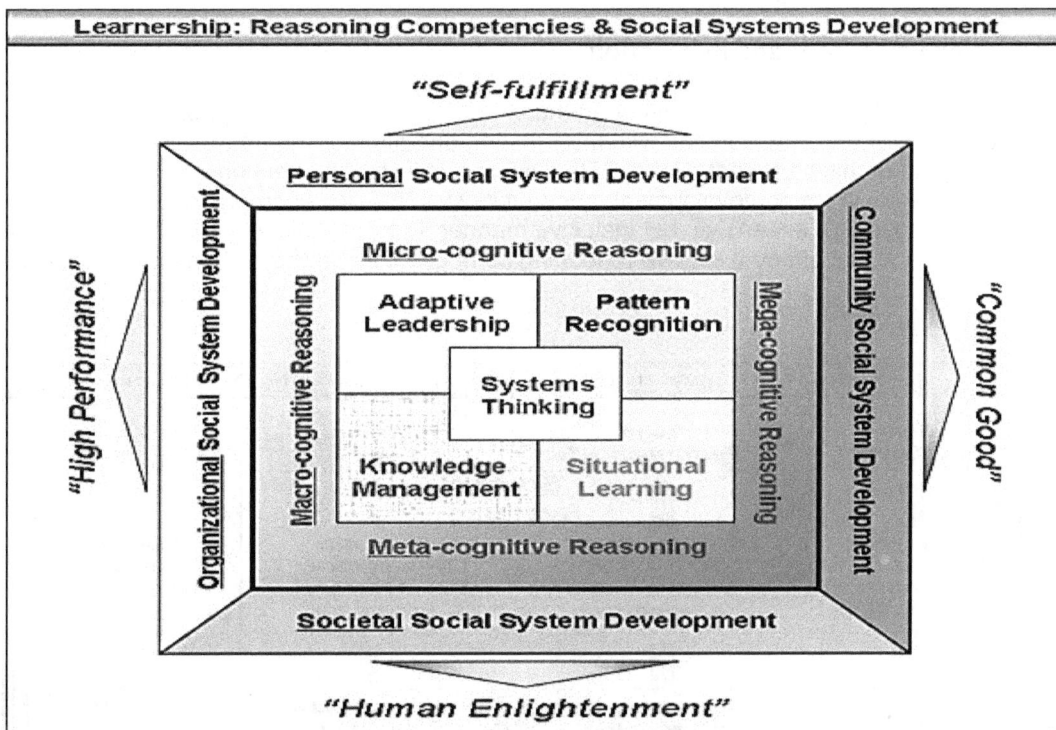

Figure 1-1

Building Reasoning Competency

The practice of learnership emphasizes five critical competencies that enable us to reason more efficiently and effectively, and to become more emotionally and psychologically balanced. Specifically, they enable us to better manage our thinking, learning, knowing, leading and goal-seeking activities. These competencies serve as catalysts in our efforts to manage and improve our performance in the four major social systems we inhabit – the personal, organization, community and societal social systems of life. The competencies are defined below, and are then succeeded by descriptions of the four interdependent social systems they enable.

1. System Thinking (ST). A system perspective on social matters that illustrates the interdependency and mutual support among the personal, organizational, and community subsystems within which we learn, develop, and strive for success. The system thinking competency helps us develop a broader, more integrated outlook, and to expand the contextual environment of our thoughts and decisions.

2. Pattern Recognition (PR). By definition, a pattern can be an archetype, a model, an ideal worthy of imitation, a representative sample of something, or a composite of traits or features characteristic of individuals. All biological life forms maintain and exhibit patterns of activity; and, the social development of humankind is inextricably anchored to our thought processes as revealed in our behavior.

3. Situational Learning (SL). A major life activity is dealing with the wide variety of situations we encounter on a daily basis. Some situations are routine and need little attention while at the other end of the continuum they may be significantly life and/or career threatening. What is important to understand is that every situation we encounter requires some amount of information gathering and analysis followed by decision making and action.

4. Knowledge Management (KM). Human development can only proceed as far as our combined knowledge will allow. Whether we view ourselves as individuals, organizations or communities, we are both empowered and constrained by our current knowledge, and our willingness and ability to acquire additional knowledge. Contemporary studies and writings indicate that knowledge may be systematically created, managed and used to enhance human development and to produce the products and services we need and desire.

5. Adaptive Leadership (AL). No amount of knowledge has practical value until it is applied to human needs or concerns. Someone needs to articulate what is known, show relevancy to the situation or challenge at hand, and propose a course of action that can create a meaningful result. It is the work of leaders to craft visions and futures that inspire others to accept change and become participants in the journey forward.

Social Systems Development and Integration

A fundamental purpose of learnership is to direct attention to the challenges and opportunities we in society must recognize as we reflect on the past, contend with the present, and plan for the future. The subject is structured in terms of a meta-system architecture that allows us to systematically focus attention on personal systems development, organization systems development, community systems development, and societal system development in an increasingly expansive, but inclusive manner. Figure 1-2 is a dynamic flow model of the potential, cumulative, societal effect of the five reasoning competencies on the meta-system social development framework.

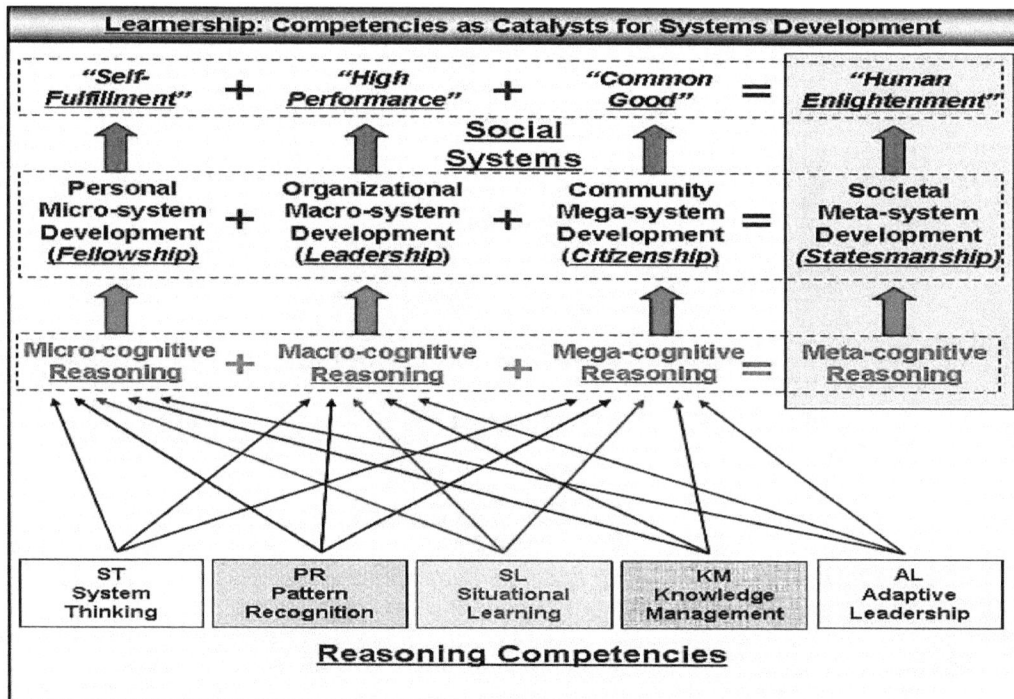

Figure 1-2

1. Personal Systems Development (PSD). PSD is social synthesis at the micro-cognitive level, and is the starting point for managing the quality of our individual lives. Priority at this level is focused on continuous improvement of our health, character and ability. The universal goal selected for individuals is *self-fulfillment*, and the key role to be played is that of *fellowship*. Learning, knowing, and leading inform and activate PSD.

2. Organizational Systems Development (OSD). OSD is social synthesis at the macro-cognitive level, and uses recognized benchmarks for achieving highly efficient and effective organizational performance. The organ-

izational elements selected for intense management focus are the organization's direction, operations and performance. The universal goal selected for organizations is *high performance*, and the key role to be played is *leadership*. Learning, knowing, and leading inform and activate OSD.

3. <u>Community Systems Development (CSD)</u>. CSD, is social synthesis at the mega-cognitive level, and is conceived as the pathway for experiencing a rewarding community life. The community elements under development at this level are the institutions of government, education and business. The universal goal selected for communities is the *common good*, and the key role to be played is *citizenship*. Learning, knowing, and leading inform and activate CSD.

4. <u>Societal Systems Development (SSD)</u>. SSD is social synthesis at the meta-cognitive level, and consists of fully integrated reasoning and development across all four levels of social synthesis. SSD strives to capture the spirit of John Sullivan's *To Come to Life More Fully* (1990), and suggests milestones for our timeless journey towards holistic personhood. The universal goal selected for the societal level is *human enlightenment*, and the key role to be played is *statesmanship*. Learning, knowing, and leading inform and activate SSD. (Reference Figure 1.2)

Creating Human Capital

1. <u>Human Capital (Personal)</u>. Having come this far, we as individuals might already think to ask the age-old: "What's in It for Me (WIIFM)?" The answer could well be that learnership offers us an opportunity to enhance our own self-worth, to advance our quality of life, to increase our productive value, and to build our quotient of human capital." *Personal human capital* may be defined as the investment that we ourselves and others have made in becoming potentially valuable participants in our personal, organizational, and community lives. The more we learn and know, and the better we contribute, the greater is our acceptance and respect by others.

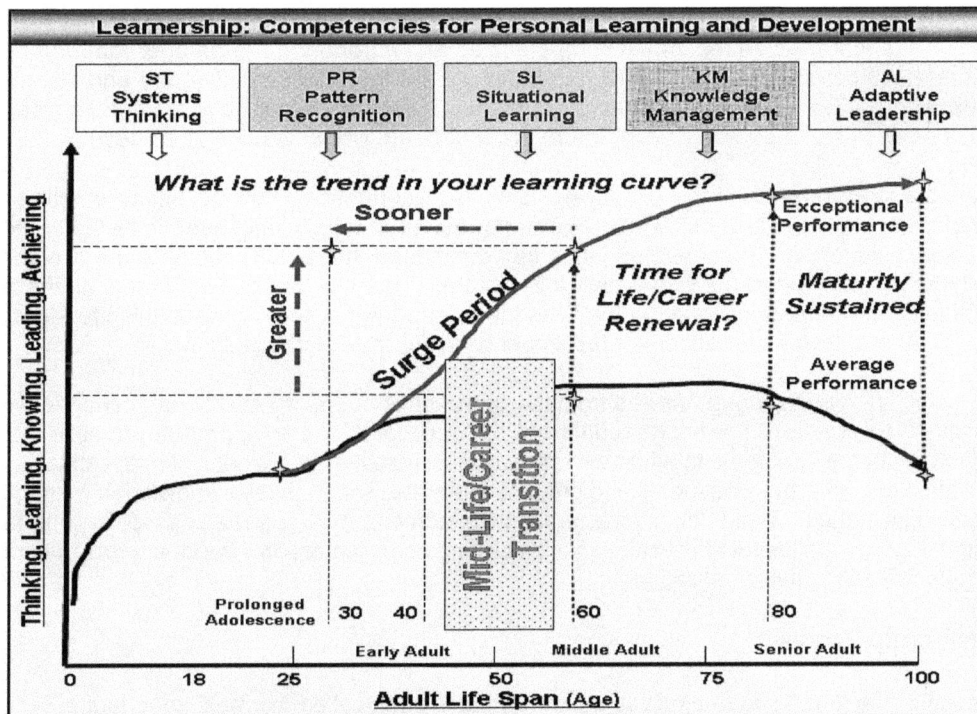

Figure 1-3

Figure 1-3 is a graphical illustration of the importance of getting an early start on building personal human capital. The horizontal axis defines a typical adult life span, and the vertical axis depicts the increasing ability of individuals to acquire the essential reasoning skills (thinking, learning, knowing, leading, and achieving). These skills are valuable for each of us in crafting a full and rewarding life, however, few of us ever really "get our act together and take in on the road" as effectively as we should.

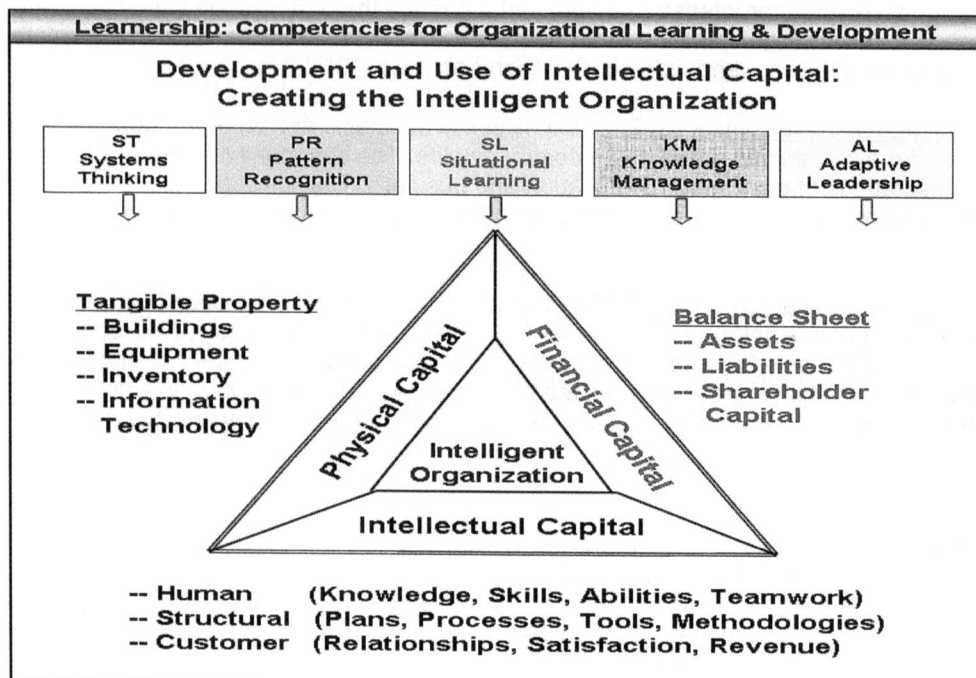

Figure 1-4

The good news is that the five reasoning competencies just introduced are an aggregation of hundreds of best practices that have consistently been shown to be important factors in effective life and work management – and, they can be learned. Some important questions we might ask are: "What have we accomplished in the past? How are we positioned to succeed now? What future state of being would we like to achieve?"

Any reasonable interpretation of the U.S. or world social, economic or political situation tells us that many fellow citizens experience a lifetime of below average performance in which limitations in heredity, education, health, location, social position, or personal motivation has consigned them to the lower of the two lines on the graph. Additionally, those who are in the proverbial "mid-life crisis" may be wondering "Is this all there is?" and "Maybe I should re-think what I am doing with my life?" "Is there time for me, too, to make this life journey memorable and meaningful?" "Can I, too, experience self-fulfillment and high performance?"

2. Human Capital (Organizational). Viewed from the perspective of the organizational manager, we might be tempted to ask "What's in this for us?" The answer could well be "Learnership is an opportunity to build the skills, knowledge, and contributions of the workforce to a firm's mission or business results. Organizational capital is the term applied to the organization's long-term investments and productive assets; and in today's knowledge management vernacular intellectual capital in the form of human, structural and customer capital is a major asset for long-term high performance. Figure 1-4 illustrates the relationships among an organization's various forms of capital with special attention to its need for intellectual capital.

The Learnership Process

Human capital is the term used to direct attention to what is often called the most important asset of an organization – its workforce. Typically, human capital development activities focus on improving the operation of the personnel office, e.g. recruitment, training, performance measurement, and termination. In more advanced organizations, additional effort is spent on career development which attempts to link employee training to the evolving needs of the organization. Unfortunately, there is little evidence that this level of intervention has much effect on the long-term stability and performance of the workforce in a world churning uncertainty, complexity, downsizing and new found employee independence.

The learnership principles and practices synthesized in this text have distinct advantages in establishing the systematic reasoning, collaborative dialogue, and learning leadership necessary for quantum improvement in employee motivation and workforce competence and performance.

[**Author's Note**: Figures 1-5 and 1-6 are high level illustrations of the learnership practitioner development program supported by the perspectives and models presented and advocated in this book. The perspectives, knowledge and skills implicit in the learnership philosophy and the learnership architecture are available to everyone who wishes to significantly optimize his or her life and career performance across a wide range of topics and issues. The use of a system/process model is particularly germane to the purpose of this concept and presentation.]

Learnership Universal Ideals and Knowledge Spheres

Learnership builds upon the social system-of-systems framework within which all human growth and development depends. Since the dawning of the human species people have had to communicate, coordinate, and collaborate with one another in order to secure their own survival and that of their families. Human history indicates that more interdependent arrangements and increasingly complex relationships were created as the evolutionary process of human development proceeded through the centuries.

Along the way leaders from many cultures, religions and states suggested various ideals, principles, values, and practices that were deemed to be superior for human society adherence. In the American tradition those "*ideals*" given almost "*universal support*" included: *truth-honesty, beauty-goodness, freedom-democracy, justice-equality, love-happiness,* and *responsibility-trust.* These ideals set the moral context for social relations and political and economic progress (Figure 1-5).

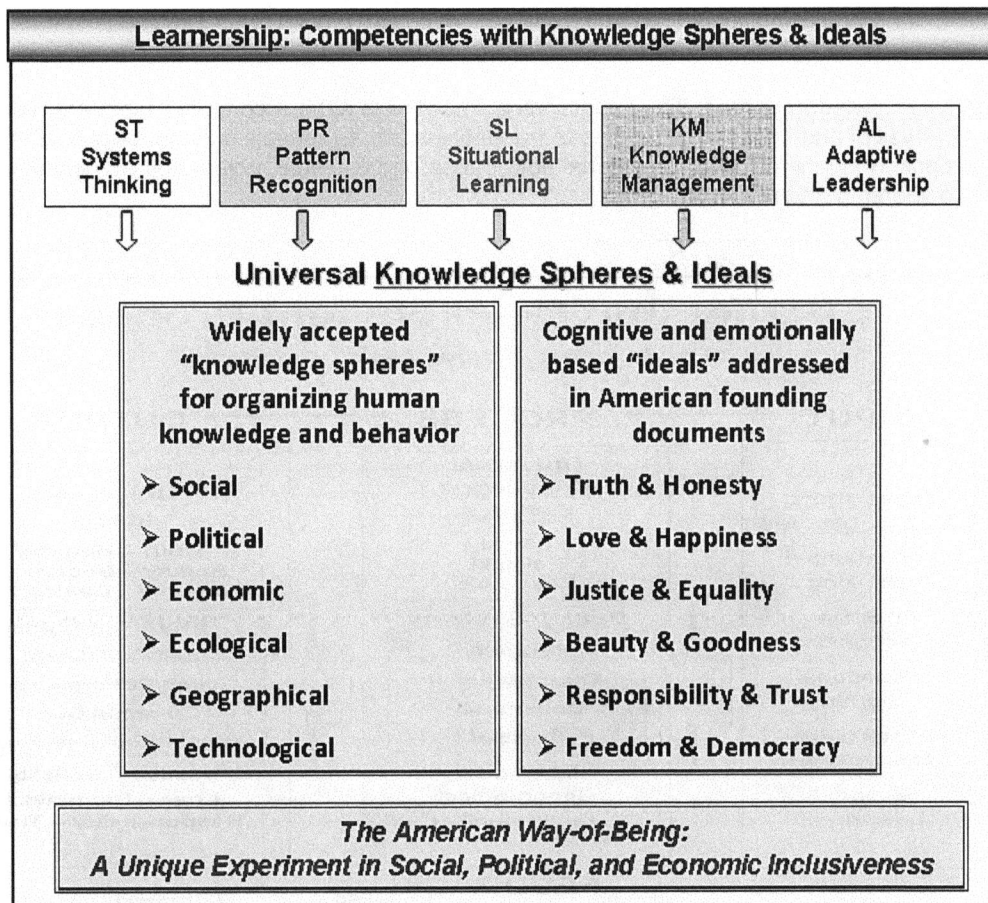

Figure 1-5

Additionally in the figure, a typology of six "*universal knowledge spheres*" is shown that often occurs in futures research to illustrate distinct categories of societal knowledge and behavior. The combination of these ideals and knowledge spheres are defined in learnership as "context setting" elements that continuously influence the other factors in the learnership model. These international knowledge domains are described as follows:

1. Social Knowledge Sphere. The social knowledge sphere addresses the associations and living arrangements among individuals and groups in society. Focus is on the dynamics of social activity among individuals,

organizations and institutions. Major emphasis is on education, learning, culture, human relations, interpersonal communication and media activities across international nation-states and countries.

2. Political Knowledge Sphere. The political knowledge sphere deals with the study, structure, or affairs of government, politics, or the state. Focus is on citizenship, governance, foreign policy, political and cultural choices, and national defense activities across international nation-states and countries.

3. Economic Knowledge Sphere. The economic knowledge sphere concerns the production, development and management of income and wealth. Focus is on the production and distribution of goods and services. Primary emphasis is on business management, financial management, and social systems economic development activities across international nation-states and countries.

4. Technological Knowledge Sphere. The technological knowledge sphere concerns the application of scientific methods and tools to societal activities. Emphasis here is on the study, development, and application of scientific methods and materials to achieve societal objectives. Major focus is on biotechnology, information technology, and materials technology activities across international nation-states and countries.

5. Ecological Knowledge Sphere. The ecological knowledge sphere concerns the relationships between organisms, their environments and the goal of sustainable habitats. Emphasis is on the life processes and characteristic phenomena of living organisms. Focus is on bio-system management, energy production, population and demographics, and the availability of food and health services activities across international nation-states and countries.

6. Geographical Knowledge Sphere. The geographical knowledge sphere concerns the preservation of geographical, physical and continental regions of the entire earth. Emphasis is on international issues and relationships concerning nation-states' territorial boundaries and conflicts, population and immigration challenges, and property ownership and resource rights.

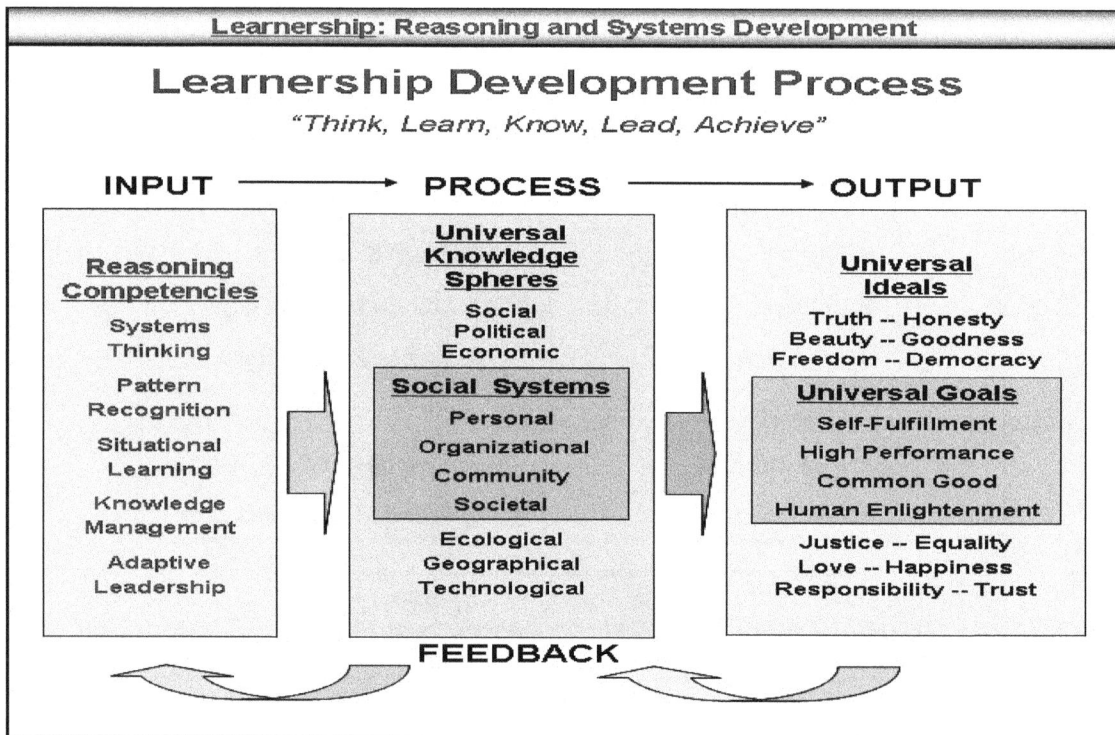

Figure 1-6

Learnership Practitioner Social Systems and Universal Goals

The core of the practitioner development process focuses on the four *Social System of Systems* within which everyone resides and the *Universal Goals* most of us seek to achieve:

1. <u>Personal Social System</u>. At the smallest (micro) level we each seek our own sense of *self-fulfillment.*

2. <u>Organizational Social System</u>. At the next higher (macro) level we desire to become *high performance* employees in our employment.

3. <u>Community Social System</u>. At the second highest (mega) level we hope to live in neighborhoods and cities that are able to construct and enjoy the *common good.*

4. <u>Societal Social System</u>. At the highest (meta) level we aspire to occasionally contribute to what may be termed *human enlightenment.*

"*Learnership practitioner*" is the term used in this Handbook to give distinction to a special class of artful learners – those who immerse themselves in a lifelong quest for relevant learning, meaningful knowledge, and personal achievement. These are people who, over time, continuously learn and develop the capability to understand and integrate the myriad of influences and experiences to which life exposes them. They display a personal "presence" which others often interpret as being rational, balanced and competent. Additional attributes often characteristic of learnership practitioners are below and in this Handbook's Epilogue:

1. Are people who systematically increase their understanding of life's opportunities and challenges; develop their skills through *questioning and learning*; and produce products and services of value to themselves and others.

2. Have historically been contributors to societal development due to their *innovation and problem-solving proclivities*. They are people who have eclectic learning interests and acquire the skills and technologies that enable their achievements.

3. Are also *knowledge managers* in their own right in that they continually identify, acquire, organize, use and share new found knowledge within their respective social systems. They learn and lead within their personal social system, develop and apply knowledge practices and tools in their organizational roles, and contribute as informed problem solvers within their local communities.

4. Understand and appreciate the fundamental theories in their fields of interest and education. However, they are *primarily committed to the practical application* of what they need to learn and know in order to pursue their goals and achieve their priorities. In particular, these highly interdependent personalities appear to have a high degree of resilience and resourcefulness in acquiring new knowledge and in their ability to learn from practical experience. These people have good cognitive and reflective skills, but unlike their more academic counterparts, those skills are valued to the degree they align with their need to turn "knowledge into action" in a timely manner.

5. Have *learned-to-learn*, they get psychological rewards from the process of learning, and they do it all their lives. They may be distinguished from the majority of others who are bound by the excessive differentiation and lack of integration of the traditional educational curricula that fail to connect theory to practice, and have little motivational impact when taught in formal classroom settings.

6. Operate as *free agent learners* and may be distinguished from many others in that they are not bound by the limitations of the traditional educational curricula taught in formal school and classroom settings. Instead, they are, and have been imbued with the "adult learning," "learn-as-needed," "just-in-time-training," and "virtual knowledge worker" practices encouraged by the rapidly changing social, economic, and technological work practices of the last two decades.

7. Pursue *cycles of rapid learning* across formal and informal boundaries and social and electronic networks. Instant messaging, internet scanning, and blog participation are viewed as sources of potentially useful information, while smart phones and laptops are essential tools for communications, learning, and knowledge-building.

8. Possess a *curiosity concerning the world around them* that enables history, learnership practitioners have been "people with distinguished lives and careers." They are here today working among us in large numbers, and will be valued for their unique contributions by generations yet to come.

9. Relish the opportunity *to fully absorb their experiences and to learn from them.* They also become influential through their ability to put their knowledge into action.

10. A willingness to embark on *humanity's journey toward mindful growth* and an understanding of life's mysteries and human purpose.

11. A *desire to motivate oneself and others* to discover life's opportunities, pursue a unique purpose, confront personal challenges, develop enlightened perspective, and attain a higher level-of-being.

12. An *appreciation for interpersonal dialogue* based on open inquiry, rapid learning, interpersonal understanding, and reasoned decision making.

13. A capacity to *improve human relations* by exemplifying the principles of leadership, followership, stewardship, citizenship, fellowship, and statesmanship.

14. A willingness to *participate in issue resolution* in the political, economic, social, technological, territorial, and ecological domains of societal knowledge and endeavour.

15. A *developmental perspective* on how individuals, organizations and communities progress through their respective phases of development – each with its own objectives, challenges and rewards.

16. A *systems perspective* on societal learning and development that balances the human need for both stability and change to achieve higher levels of societal development and performance.

17. A focus on *personal learning and knowledge management* as key capabilities in the development of social systems: personal, organizational, community, and societal.

18. A desire to *replace differentiation with integration* as a lifelong perspective – and the ultimate foundation for a mindful journey through life.

19. A commitment to *use knowledge, science, and practical experience* to overcome excessive reliance on mysticism, superstition, and supernatural intervention when operating in the public spheres where everyone needs to feel comfortable and secure.

20. An advocate of the *means between the extremes* – weighing personal rights with social responsibilities in order to negotiate adequate, inclusive outcomes.

21. An appreciation for *balancing inquiry and advocacy* in all one attempts to accomplish. No one knows all that could be known to reduce potential risk and to guarantee success.

22. A capacity to *perform multiple roles* such as consultant, coach, facilitator, student, mentor, thought leader, and project manager as situations require.

23. A willingness to apply the *Learnership Integrated Systems Architecture* (LISA) model at all levels of personal and social systems development.

Thomas Friedman, in his recent book *The World is Flat* (2005) suggested a few new thoughts that integrate well into the above *learnership practitioner* description. When explaining what will be required for those individuals worldwide to remain vital and competitive during the rapid changes in the immediate future, Friedman emphasizes: (a) learning-to-learn, (b) pattern recognition and problem solving, (c) striving to become untouchable, and (d) becoming a "*versalist.*"

Learning-to-learn is a fundamental anchor in learnership philosophy and practice. It is the capacity to recognize individual, organizational and societal patterns of thinking and action. Problem solving and decision-making are essentially learnership reasoning practices. Striving to become an "untouchable" in the new world economy requires that we keep ourselves well educated and skilled in order to remain marketable in the international marketplace.

Lastly, the manner in which many more careerists will stay competitive will be to strike a balance between being a specialist and a generalist – both of which have their place in the economy. We who become "*versalists,*" however, will progress through our careers by continually adding new specialties to our respective repertoires thereby allowing us multiple opportunities for gainful employment. Two additional learnership practitioner capabilities should be added to the above list:

24. A personal *commitment to learning reasoning competencies* that improve systems thinking, pattern recognition, situational learning, knowledge management, and adaptive leadership.

25. An expectation that *personal development depends primarily on being responsible and responsive* to the ever-changing political, economic, and social forces occurring locally or on a global scale.

If there is a new social contract implicit between employers and employees today it should be this: You give me your labor and I will guarantee that as long as you work here, I will give you every opportunity – through either career advancement or training to become more employable and more versatile. — Thomas Friedman

Achieving a Mindful Way-of-Being

Learnership practitioners are people who systematically increase their understanding of life's opportunities and challenges; develop their skills through questioning and learning; and produce products and services of value to themselves and others. They are knowledge managers in that they continually identify, acquire, organize, use and share new found knowledge within their respective social systems. They learn and lead within their personal domains, they develop and apply knowledge practices and tools in their organizational roles, and they contribute as informed problem-solvers within their local communities.

Using learnership, they seek to optimize the integration of their personal self-fulfillment, organizational high performance, community common good and societal human enlightenment. They may even experience what Csikszentmihalyi (*Flow*, 1990), Senge et al (*Presence*, 2007), and Langer (*Mindfulness*, (1989) have eloquently described in their well-regarded writings. This is the learnership practitioner's vibrant and rewarding mindful way-of-being.

[**Author's Note**: It is important to address at this point that a divergence of perspectives on the definition of mindfulness has become evident over the last decade or more. Currently much press and social media coverage have advocated what may be termed "mindfulness meditation" which is based on teachings of Theravada Buddhism. This involves paying attention to one's thoughts, sensations and feelings. In practice, this requires focusing on a single object or concentrating on a narrowly defined term or topic so as to eliminate disruptive sensations. The objective is to relax and quiet down in order to remove accumulated personal stress.

Another definition, perhaps more productive from a learning perspective, is what may be termed "attentive mindfulness" in which a person purposely sheds their cognitive and emotional mental constraints so as to accept input regarding behavior and information from a wide range of meaningful sources that may not have formerly been recognized but containing relevant value. The latter perspective which conforms to the dictionary definition and learning research is advocated by Langer. That said, both *mindfulness meditation* and *attentive mindfulness* have a role in self-reflection and personal development situations. The latter approach is used in this handbook.]

American Societal Intelligence

Much has now been said in this introductory chapter about learnership, the learnership philosophy, the learnership process model, the potential of learnership theory and practice in developing intellectual (specifically human) capital, and the development of learnership practitioners. In preparing to move forward, a final commentary is provided to illustrate specific speed bumps in achieving the five competencies and benefiting personally and professionally within each of the four learnership social systems (domains).

Decades of study and experience have been reviewed in an attempt to understand why the suggestions of so many experts in a wide variety of fields have so little practical effect on the quality of our personal, organizational, and community lives. As individuals, workers, and citizens it seems that too many of us are slow learners and even slower implementers of what is known to be superior practices in thinking, learning, knowing, leading, and achieving. Learnership practitioners are those who have forever demonstrated their knowledge and skills consistent with the factors addressed herein, and the rest of us who are now ready to seize the opportunities before us to proactively manage our own development in response to the personal and social performance weaknesses summarized below.

Reasoning Competencies – Internal Resistance to be Overcome:

1. Systems Thinking – A *limited interest and skill* in open thinking and dialogue – thereby failing to understand the contextual forces that must be accommodated in order to properly scope problems and issues for effective decision-making.

2. Pattern Recognition – An *inability to discern* the differences among peoples' preferences, temperaments, and intentions as well as being inadequately skilled in organizational and community procedures, processes, and methods through which work is efficiently accomplished.

3. Situational Learning – An *inability to apply critical analysis* to life and work experiences and to reflect on those experiences in a systematic manner to acquire timely cognitive and emotional learning.

4. Knowledge Management – An *unwillingness to perceive knowledge as a manageable* commodity, and to learn the tools and practices currently available for improved performance.

5. Adaptive Leadership – A *shortage of knowledge and skill* in understanding pervasive drivers for change, and an inability to plan and facilitate group learning strategies that can assure organizational relevancy and competitiveness.

Social System Development – External Factors to be Confronted:

6. Personal Social System – The *unwillingness to review one's own accomplishments and weaknesses* in the areas of health, ability and character to determine what immediate changes are required to craft a life worthy of respect and recognition. A lack of a respectful relationship among family, friends, and associates is also an indicator of weakness.

7. Organizational Social System – An *unwillingness to assess organizational direction, operations and performance* against best industry practices; determine opportunities for improvement; and steadfastly participate in the implementation of corrective measures. A lack of educated and skilful leadership of teams and functions contribute to this dysfunction.

8. Community Social System – *Being indifferent to the benefits of trustworthy, responsible and collaborative dialogue* among the education, government and business sectors and institutions that can lead to thoughtful community relationships. Similarly, the lack of an informed and active citizenry willing to provide for the common good is a deficiency.

9. Societal Social System – *Being insensitive to the deteriorating effects of social, political, and economic inequity and excess* that threaten humanity's health, freedom, and overall well-being. The lack of statesmanship among states and cultures that could prevent the occurrence of misunderstanding and hostility were it to be available.

Cultural/Societal Intelligence

At the Metacognitive level of social analysis we can see significant human progress and potential in the American 230 years of socio-economic experimentation. And yet, given what we could have learned from our experiences, the results of our imperfect thinking, questionable decision-making and perpetual inability to resolve issues concerning basic human health and safety – are we an intelligent culture? – are we an intelligent society?

A learnership objective is to help Americans plan and manage our lives to achieve optimum performance and happiness within the limits of our unique circumstances. Learnership provides a synthesis of expert opinion and best practices. Learnership practitioners are people – many like us, who are willing to develop ourselves and engage in constructive social activity. Learnership practitioners live, work and participate in their respective communities and are the citizens of our American society. Can we do better?

While it is obvious that not everyone has the same level of inherited capabilities or environmental support, everyone has the ability to make better choices and pursue worthwhile objectives. Everyone should be enabled to experience personal progress, self-esteem, and significant accomplishment. The time is now for us to learn, lead and act – with purpose, foresight and compassion.

Implications for Integral Learning and Knowledge Management

The comprehensive American Learnership Process Model and the Learnership Integrated Systems Architecture (LISA) in this chapter provide an all-inclusive framework suitable for both the book's primary subject of Integral Learning and Knowledge Management (ILKM). Both topics are based on the premise that "*total learning, total knowing, and total leading*" are a natural triad of activities in a lifetime of human development and achievement. More specifically,

Situational Learning and Knowledge Management will be shown to be interdependent competencies supporting Adaptive Leadership in achieving Social System-of-Systems Progress.

The ILKM concept is anchored here in chapter one and is further developed in subsequent chapters through adaptive leadership (chapter nine). After that, it is applied in the four social system domains of personal, organization, community and societal development (chapters ten to thirteen). Along the way, the field of Knowledge Management will be observed to be evermore *interdisciplinary* in educational scope and *integral* for social systems enrichment.

Personal Reflection

This topic appears at the send of each chapter and is meant to serve two purposes: (a) be a reader's guide to main points and "takeaways," and (b) to encourage everyone to take a moment to engage their mental cognition and intuition on what the chapter means to them – especially at this time in their lives. Questions for chapter reflection follow immediately below; and for those readers inclined to maintain a self-assessment, your thoughts may be recorded in your *American Learnership for Life, Work, Wealth, Health and Legacy Success which is located at* Appendix B.

Insights, Commitments and Skills

If you plan to participate in the *American Learnership for Life, Work, Wealth, Health and Legacy Success* self-development program, it is suggested you record your insights, commitments and skills to be developed here in this chapter, and then again in Appendix B:

My learning in terms of new insights, changing priorities, new commitments or skills I want to acquire:

1. Insights (Example): Remind myself that …

2. Commitments (Example): Continue to ask myself …

3. Skills (Example): Apply my knowledge and skills to …

[**Author's Note**: This chapter begins the reader's data collection for recordation in Appendix B. The information collected in Appendix B can, therefore, be used for the "optional" practical exercise entitled: *My Integral Life, Work, Wealth, Health and Legacy Success*.]

Conclusion

This introductory summary is intended as a foundation for conducting a chapter by chapter discussion and reflection on the print book entitled*: Your Integral Life Matters: A Life Management Handbook for American Learning, Leading and Legacy Success*. The purpose of these conversations, webinars and written projects is to provide adult learners a body of knowledge that crosses real-life interdisciplinary boundaries that are difficult to adequately understand and explain by people with only rudimentary knowledge and experience in one or two educational and career disciplines. Breadth and depth really do matter in human learning, development, performance and accomplishment.

Chapter Two

Discovering the Meaning of Your Life

Major Chapter Topics

Discovering the Meaning of Your Life

Purpose: The <u>WHAT</u> and <u>WHY</u> of Your Life

> *I guess the essence of life for me is finding something you really enjoy doing that gives meaning to life, and then being in a situation where you can do it. -- Isaac Asimov.*

The Meaning of "Meaning"

How strongly is Figure 2-1 a concern for you at this stage of your life? Was it more of a concern when you were younger, or is becoming more present as you grow older?

In the pursuit of discovering what we term our "*meaning*" it is essential that we understand that while "meaning" is often thought to be something dynamic we objectively demonstrate outside ourselves, in fact, "meaning" always begins inside ourselves as our worldview of appropriate beliefs, values, motives and preferred actions before we reveal them to others. Our own pre-programmed and ingrained belief system established in our brain tells us what and who we are – and whether the time has come to share and declare ourselves to others. And, because we all have different brain stores of data, images, beliefs and values it is certain that variations of "meaning" exist even among those who say they are committed to the same "meaning."

Figure 2-1

In his book *Re-Create Your Life* (1997), author Morty Lefkoe says that our consciousness creates our own realities, and he encourages us to occasionally set aside our beliefs long enough to consider a different way for viewing our lives. In doing so we should apply five well accepted principles:

1. Existence is a function of consciousness.

2. Language is the primary tool we use to make distinctions.

3. There is no inherent meaning (or "the truth") in the world.

4. When you create a belief, you create your reality.

5. When you eliminate a belief, you change your reality and create new possibilities.

The importance of this cognitive activity is that when we search for, and think about, meanings that are central to our existence; and prioritize them for use of our intellect and resources we should do so in an informed manner. Accuracy, efficiency and effectiveness all matter in accomplishing this fundamentally personal responsibility.

There is a learning process and decision-making activity required for each of us to say with conviction that "this is what I believe; this is my meaning in life; this is how I make my decisions; this is what motivates me; and this is how I manage myself, contribute to others and impact the world." Engaging this topic from a variety of viewing points allows us to clarify our personal meanings and make better choices that influence our unique sense of self, vision, mission and personhood.

Maslow's Hierarchy of Needs and Motivation

Abraham Maslow presented his hierarchy of human needs ranging from *Physiological Needs* at the bottom to *Self-Actualization* needs at the top – with the other three needs *Safety*, *Love and Belonging*, and *Esteem*. It is not known whether he ever actually presented that information in a pyramid as illustrated in Figure 1. What is notable is that he referred to the lowest needs as *deficiency needs* with the belief that a lack of physical capabilities and sufficient safety, love and belonging, and esteem – if not corrected over time – would limit one's ability to achieve self-actualization. A short definition of each need follows: (Figure 2-2)

1. Physiological Needs – These are the physical requirements for human survival. This has to be minimally satisfied for any progress to a higher level.

2. Safety Needs – These needs are also very basic and include personal security, financial security and health and well-being.

3. Love and Belonging – These needs are interpersonal and involves feelings of belongingness. They become more important as the lower two needs are adequately met.

4. Esteem – This need emerges as the three lower needs are met and a person becomes more independent due their lower three needs being met to a reasonable degree.

5. Self-Actualization – This need or desire becomes a greater force as a person overcomes major deficiencies the four lower levels of the hierarchy, and even masters them so at level 5 one can focus on becoming "all that he or she desires to become."

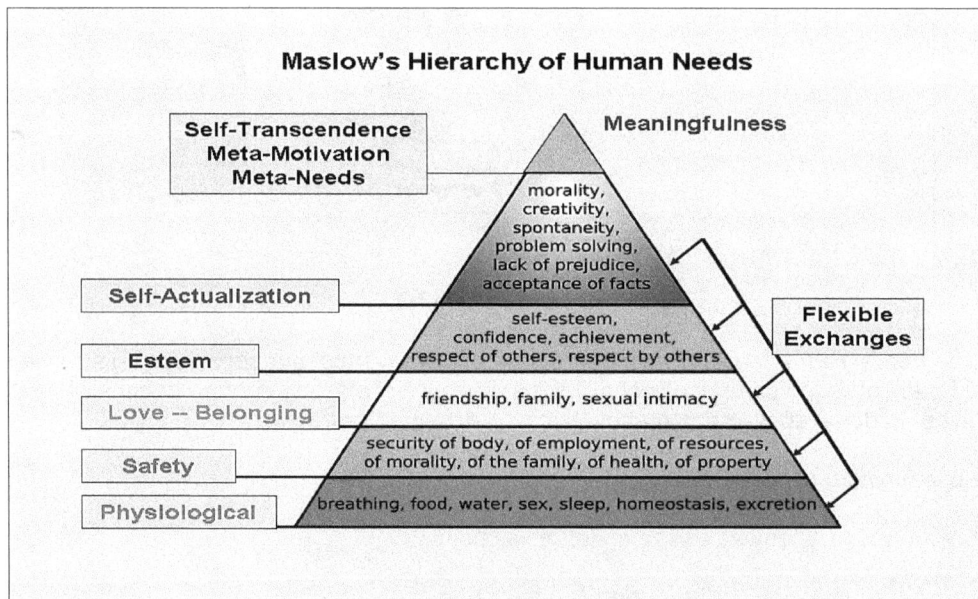

Maslow's Hierarchy of Human Needs

Self-Transcendence Meta-Motivation Meta-Needs

Meaningfulness

morality, creativity, spontaneity, problem solving, lack of prejudice, acceptance of facts

Self-Actualization

self-esteem, confidence, achievement, respect of others, respect by others

Flexible Exchanges

Esteem

Love -- Belonging

friendship, family, sexual intimacy

Safety

security of body, of employment, of resources, of morality, of the family, of health, of property

Physiological

breathing, food, water, sex, sleep, homeostasis, excretion

Figure 2-2

Due to his seminal work, Maslow is still highly regarded even though many respected researchers and psychologists have updated or modified his work as they expanded the range of psychology and sociology knowledge using more modern methods and tools. One area of interest concerns obvious differences between people raised in individualistic (self) cultures and those raised in collectivist (others) cultures.

To appreciate Maslow's theory completely, Figure 2-2 in this text places emphasis on two additional aspects of his theory. The first is the addition to the model of "flexible exchanges" which is meant to emphasize individuals may be significantly different as to their psychological preferences, cultural upbringing or stage of development in which they currently reside. It may be that we can temporarily subsume certain lower level need in order to emphasize a higher level need. We can make changes as the circumstances we are in take a dramatic turn. The model depicts a theory for most normal situations, but is not predictive for everyone.

A second added feature of the model is particularly important for use in this book. This is shown as a capstone added here on top of Maslow's hierarchy. As Maslow's work matured he recognized that only a minority of exceptional people in any society or nation could achieve a high degree of self-actualization. So what, then, could they expect and experience going forward?

His view was that *meta-needs* would develop, leading to *meta-motivation*, and culminating in *self-transcendence*. He said that once a person had navigated his hierarchy of needs, and substantively accommodated them, they were now willing to travel a new path of their own making to achieve self-directed growth. They would aspire to meta-needs which seem to be generally related to a concept used later in this book entitled: "Universal Ideals." Maslow's meta-needs are shown in general alignment with those selected universal ideals in Table 1:

Universal Ideals	Maslow's Meta-needs
Truth – Honesty	Truth (reality)
	Simplicity (essence)
Beauty – Goodness	Beauty (rightness of form)
	Goodness (benevolence)
	Perfection (harmony)
	Wholeness (unity)
	Richness (complexity)
Freedom – Democracy	Autonomy (self-sufficiency)
	Liveliness (spontaneity)
Justice – Equality	Justice (fairness)
	Uniqueness (individuality)
Love – Happiness	Playfulness (ease)
Responsibility – Trust	Completion (ending)
	Meaningfulness (values)

Table 2-1

The one Maslow meta-need that jumps into the foreground in the design of this book is *meaningfulness* a term easily seen as having interdependency with *mindfulness*. Something is meaningful when it is valued and relevant, and to be viewed in that manner it would also need to be understood within its specific context. Not doing so would be *mindless* which defeats the concept of meaningfulness as a practical objective. Questions for potential study interest might be: (a) How can we enlighten and empower people to proactively strive towards *human growth and development*? (b) When in life should we expect to experience a level of self-actualization that allows us to witness on the horizon our own opportunity *for self-transcendence*?

What Questions do People Often Ask?

Most of us try innumerable times through our lives to answer the following basic questions about ourselves and how we fit in with what our acquired knowledge and experience has given us to work. For many of us we discover that the answers are heavily influenced by situational factors at the time we ask. Chances are that throughout our lives we are on a journey of discovery, and while the questions don't change, the answers may change significantly.

Contrary to the view that some people espouse, our purpose and meaning is not pre-programmed into us before birth. While DNA and genes inherited through *nature* certainly set the stage for what and who we become, we do know that *nurture* has an immense effect during the whole time of our lives. Beginning in early childhood there are choices to be made even with the smallest amount of knowledge and experience. And certainly before we attain adulthood, the rights and responsibilities that result from both our own decision-making, and that contributed by others, encourages us to define ourselves and to draw maps for our life and career journeys – even if they prove to be only temporary and in need of periodic updating.

At the most fundamental level, research indicates that we humans report the need to discover the *Purpose* and the *Meaning* of our lives. We engage with others in answering a few fundamental life management questions:

1. **What do I stand for?** (*A sense of purpose*)

2. **How do I fit in with what has come before?** (*A sense of history*)

3. **How am I related to other people/events/forces?** (*A sense of order*)

4. **What can I hope for as I take action?** (*A sense of outcome*)

The difficulty some people experience with this list of questions is that they may be too broad a concept for us to understand at a more practical level. Also, even if we have a high level sense of our purpose or meaning, we have little of value because without a sense of history, order and outcome no action is intended – and knowledge without action is socially meaningless.

Initially it may be easier to identify specific day to day concerns for which finding answers will have a timely outcome – and a "to-do" aspect. Some examples in the "finding meaning" through understanding our personal needs or contemplating our occasional aspirations include:

1. **"When will I** discover *my true calling*, and begin to live a more integrated and meaningful life?"

2. **"How can I** become *more knowledgeable and competent* in a rapidly changing and stressful world?"

3. **"How can I** manage my way through these *mid-life/career disappointments*, and have a second chance to succeed?"

4. **"How can I** make my *life a memorable* event, and become an example for those in the future?"

And, from a more introspective point of view, we could focus on exploring the *motivation* and *energy* needed to more fully understand human development. Exploration into these topics may be helpful:

1. **Our interest** in developing an *interdisciplinary perspective* on human relationships and events

2. **Our need** to achieve a sense of personal *integration* and *wholeness* in a *differentiated* world

3. **Our aspiration** for a life well-lived on a seemingly *mindful*, rather than *mindless* journey

4. **Our understanding** of the value of *critical thinking* and *authentic dialogue* in communicating more effectively with others

5. **Our belief** in the value of *human progress* beyond our own time and lives

Another avenue for learning and deciding the *meaning* and *purpose* of our lives is to reflect on the issues and problems in our situational experiences, e.g. our physical location, our societal culture, our economic progress, our family safety, etc. What do we expect? What must change? Why?

1. Education – Expertise needed (STEM), decline in world ratings, cost increases, lack of degree completion, lack of critical thinking/knowledge/collaboration, cultural resilience/inflexibility

2. Economy – Unemployment (6.7%), national debt (17.0 t), foreign trade imbalance, middle class decline, home ownership decline, population/insufficient job growth, immigration rates, white collar scams

3. Health – Poverty (15%), obesity/Overweight (65%), addictions, food recalls, diabetes, cancer, heart Disease, HIV/AIDs, veterans physical/mental impairment, suicide, stress

4. Safety – Terrorism, urban violence, Incarceration rates, transportation accidents, robbery

5. Ecology – Global warming, air & water pollution, fresh water shortage, soil depletion, overfishing, energy production

6. Politics – Gridlock, polarization, demographic shifts, Executive/Congress/Supreme court prerogatives, public scandals

7. International – U.S. role/economy/Involvement, world political/culture/religion/territory conflicts

8. Technology – Explosion in data/Information/knowledge exchange, Identity theft, privacy loss, Internet lies/deception

If any of these societal issue areas are important enough to concern our thinking and emotions, then it might be that we already work to resolve some part of the issue or problem. If not, maybe we need to contribute to a social cause in order that we have the peace of mind that comes from taking action. In any case, should our meaning in life reflect the people, issues and events about which we have learned to care?

Process: Learning the HOW of Your Life

Meaning is only valuable if it results in meaningful outcomes.
A "Learnership" Maxim

At this point we could comment that finding our "meaning results from a process of learning and discovery followed its application." Mental activities such as reflecting on the past, observing the present and anticipating the future in a systematic manner are essential to learn relevant information, build new knowledge of ourselves and life, share our insights and intensions with others, and contribute to societal development.

Learning is a complex process with the object of knowledge creation and use in virtually all human affairs. And, learners are people with an ability to learn – although the development of this ability and willingness to use it varies widely across the general population. It follows, then, that there should be a term to describe people who are exceptional and influential learners; their capabilities and their influence on others. *Learnership* is the suggested term, and it is derived from: (1) learner – one who seeks to learn or to gain knowledge through experience or study, and (2) – ship (suffix) – to show or possess a quality, state, or condition. Additionally, *learnership* captures the essence and skill of *leadership* in which people are skillful in influencing others' thinking and behavior. (Reference Figure 2-3)

Learnership is about learning, and about being a learner. More importantly, it's about the journey or *process* that begins when we learn to become a skilled and purposeful learner and make a lifelong commitment to create and realize our individual potential. Learnership is intended to inspire the same generative perspective towards personal development, higher performance and social contribution expressed in such seminal works as Carl Rodgers' *A Way of Being* and Peter Vaill's *Learning as a Way of Being*. The attempt, herein, is to establish a gestalt-like description of how our own cognitive development and personal performance can not only serve our own purposes, but also be an inspiration to others' growth and achievement as lifetime leaders.

Authentic Learnership (lifelong learning and leadership) Practitioners is the term used in this book to give distinction to a special class of artful learners – those who immerse themselves in a lifelong quest for relevant learning, meaningful knowledge, and personal achievement. These are people who systematically increase their understanding of life's opportunities and challenges; develop their skills through questioning and learning; and produce products and services of value to themselves and others. Learnership practitioners have historically been contributors to societal development due to their innovation and problem-solving proclivities. They are people who have eclectic learning interests, enjoy rapid learning within both formal and informal social networks, and acquire the skills and technologies to become trustworthy leaders of others toward greater achievement.

A "Learnership" Architecture and Process Methodology

Figure 2-3 is a high level illustration of the *learnership development process* supported by the perspectives and models presented and advocated in this book. The perspectives, knowledge and skills implicit in the learnership philosophy, the learnership architecture, and the learnership process are available to everyone who wishes to significantly optimize his or her life and career performance across a wide range of topics and issues.

The use of a system/process model is particularly germane to the structure and application of this holistic concept.

Figure 2-3 introduces five interdependent human reasoning competencies (*social system inputs*) that enable an integrated development process. Additionally, it illustrates that four integrated *social system processes (domains)* are energized to produce *social system outputs* identified as self-fulfillment, high performance, the common good and human enlightenment. The result is the beginning of a comprehensive human development *learnership architecture* that when complete (later in this book) values personal and cultural meaning, authenticity, integration, inspiration and their reflection in a personal legacy.

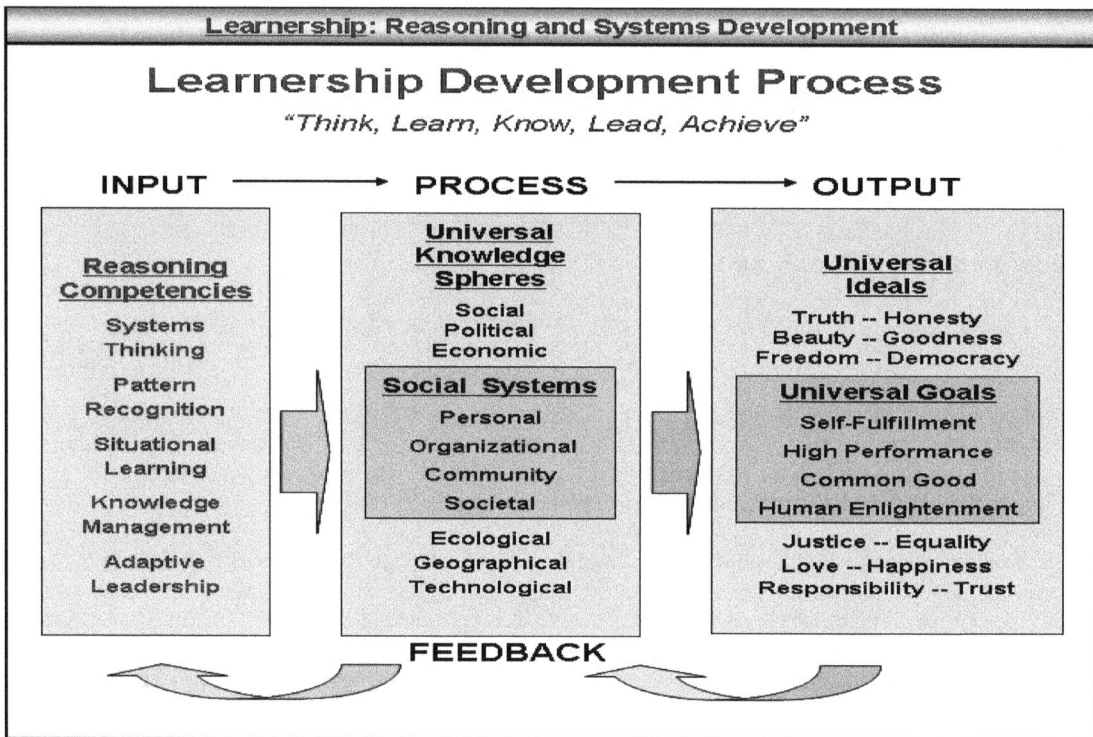

Learnership: Reasoning and Systems Development

Learnership Development Process
"Think, Learn, Know, Lead, Achieve"

INPUT → PROCESS → OUTPUT

Reasoning Competencies

Systems Thinking

Pattern Recognition

Situational Learning

Knowledge Management

Adaptive Leadership

Universal Knowledge Spheres

Social
Political
Economic

Social Systems

Personal
Organizational
Community
Societal

Ecological
Geographical
Technological

Universal Ideals

Truth -- Honesty
Beauty -- Goodness
Freedom -- Democracy

Universal Goals

Self-Fulfillment
High Performance
Common Good
Human Enlightenment

Justice -- Equality
Love -- Happiness
Responsibility -- Trust

FEEDBACK

Figure 2-3

[**Author's Note:** A detailed list of *Authentic Learnership Practitioner Characteristics* is provided later in this section 1.]

Universal Goals and Ideals

Universal Goals (Human Desires) (Figure 2-3)

1. Self-Fulfillment – Achieving one's foremost purpose; obtaining major needs, wants and desires; maximizing advancement potential in the cognitive, affective and psychomotor aspects of ourselves; attaining positive recognition.

2. High Performance – Achieving the organization's greatest efficiency and effectiveness; business and/or mission accomplishment; satisfying constituents, customers, workers and owners

3. Common Good – Achieving community institutional synthesis and consensus; satisfying community members' service expectations; and providing opportunities for meaningful citizenship

4. Human Enlightenment – Adding to the human capacity for fact-based learning and emotional maturity; improving worldwide thinking, learning, knowing and action; raising the standards of human conduct.

[**Author's Note**: These four goals are conceived as temporary placeholders for each social domain described below. Each reader is encouraged to define a more specific objective after further reflection and study.]

Universal Ideals (Aspirations) (Figure 2-3)

1. Truth & Honesty – Conforming to facts; displaying integrity and sincerity.

2. Beauty & Goodness – A quality that delights the senses; being positive and desirable in nature.

3. Freedom & Democracy – Not bound or constrained; government by the people, and majority rule

4. Justice & Equality – Due reward and punishment; fair treatment and value.

5. Love & Happiness – Deep affection and concern; receiving enjoyment and pleasure

6. Responsibility & Trust – Having personal accountability; reliance on the integrity and ability of a person or thing.

[**Author's Note**: These ideals are representative of the higher order values and behaviors offered by numerous spiritual prophets and cultural leaders over millennia. In this book, these topics are considered to be essential properties of people whom are regarded as being "authentic" with themselves and others. Authenticity is demonstrated when one's character depicts genuineness, honesty, dependability, realism and trustworthiness.]

Reasoning Competencies (Knowledge and Skills) (Figure 2-3)

Learnership is based on five foundational reasoning competencies. These competencies represent different aspects of how individuals have come to understand and focus on themselves, their social organization, their physical environment, and the situational factors that influence their lives and that of others.

Most often, people are not purposely cognizant of the thinking, learning, and resulting behavior that has become both programmatic and predictable about their selves. However, once aware of the choices that are available, and the relative priority and utility of the competencies that have proven to be associated with better thinking and decision making, most people attempt to acquire and apply these skills:

1. System Thinking (ST) A system perspective on social matters that illustrates the interdependency and mutual support among the personal, organizational, and community subsystems within which we learn, develop, and strive for success.

The system thinking competency helps us develop a broader, more integrated outlook, and to expand the contextual environment of our thoughts and decisions. The use of system thinking inspires us to be integrative thinkers and discover opportunities to synthesize our learning for better understanding. *Systems Thinking (ST) and Pattern Recognition (PR) combine to assure more effective Situational Learning (SL).*

2. Pattern Recognition (PR) By definition, a pattern can be an archetype, a model, an ideal worthy of imitation, a representative sample of something, or a composite of traits or features characteristic of individuals. All biological life forms maintain and exhibit patterns of activity; and, the social development of humankind is inextricably anchored to our thought processes as revealed in our behavior.
The cultural expectations, documented methodologies, and established practices that form our human experience and interpersonal and organizational relationships are the artifacts of inherited tendencies and learned values, beliefs, and experiences previously programmed into our computer-like minds.

The pattern recognition competency focuses on our ability to recognize those preprogrammed aspects of ourselves and others, and on the need for us to better manage our reasoning based on the why and how we think, learn, know, lead, and pursue certain objectives in all our societal endeavors. *Pattern Recognition (PR) combines with Systems Thinking (ST) to ensure more effective Situational Learning (SL).*

3. Situational Learning (SL) A major life activity is dealing with the wide variety of situations we encounter on a daily basis. Some situations are routine and need little attention while at the other end of the continuum they may be significantly life and/or career threatening. What is important to understand is that every situation we encounter requires some amount of information gathering and analysis followed by decision making and action. And, every situation is a potential learning opportunity.

The situational learning competency is a significant element in human capital development and in becoming a learnership practitioner which makes it a foundational anchor in the practice of learnership. *Situational Learning*

(SL) benefits from the support provided by Systems Thinking (ST) and Pattern Recognition (PR) – and, it is an essential foundation for the practice of Knowledge Management (KM).

4. <u>Knowledge Management (KM)</u> Human development can only proceed as far as our combined knowledge will allow. Whether we view ourselves as individuals, organizations or communities, we are both empowered and constrained by our current knowledge, and our willingness and ability to acquire additional knowledge. Contemporary studies and writings indicate that knowledge may be systematically created, managed and used to enhance human development and to produce the products and services we need and desire.

The knowledge management competency is the core element in becoming a learnership practitioner. It is the knowledge repository for situational learning artifacts, and in turn, it is the storehouse for the tacit and explicit knowledge used by adaptive leaders in advancing personal and social initiatives. *Knowledge Management (KM) is enabled by Situational Learning (SL) which itself is supported by Systems Thinking (ST) and Pattern Recognition (PR).*

5. <u>Adaptive Leadership (AL)</u> No amount of knowledge has practical value until it is applied to human needs or concerns. Someone needs to articulate what is known, show relevancy to the situation or challenge at hand, and propose a course of action that can create a meaningful result. It is the work of leaders to craft visions and futures that inspire others to accept change and become participants in the journey forward.

The adaptive leadership competency is another foundational anchor in the learnership discipline because it moves knowledge into action. Theory is turned into practice, and practice leads to meaningful accomplishment for individuals and social organizations. *Adaptive Leading (AL) applies Knowledge Management (KM) which has been enabled by Situational Learning (SL) which is supported by Systems Thinking (ST) and Pattern Recognition (PR).*

Social System Domains and Universal Knowledge Spheres

Social System Domains (Figure 2-3)
Learnership is a lifelong learning and development process through which people are able to pursue progress and achieve success in terms of their relevant personal, organizational, community, and societal domains of social activity and interpersonal relations. A social system framework is the most convenient and best understood approach for establishing interpersonal concepts and suggesting cause and effect relationships.

1. <u>Personal Systems Development (PSD)</u> PSD is social synthesis at the *micro-cognitive level*, and is the starting point for managing the quality of our individual lives. Priority at this level is focused on continuous improvement of our <u>health</u>, <u>character</u> and <u>ability</u>. The universal goal selected for individuals is *self-fulfillment,* and the key role to be played is that of *fellowship*. Learning, knowing, and leading inform and activate PSD.

2. <u>Organizational Systems Development (OSD)</u> OSD is social synthesis at the *macro-cognitive level*, and uses recognized benchmarks for achieving highly efficient and effective organizational performance. The organizational elements selected for intense management focus are the organization's <u>direction</u>, <u>operations</u> and <u>performance</u>. The universal goal selected for organizations is *high performance*, and the key role to be played is *leadership*. Learning, knowing, and leading inform and activate OSD.

4. <u>Community Systems Development (CSD)</u> CSD is social synthesis at the *mega-cognitive level,* and is conceived as the pathway for experiencing a rewarding community life. The community elements under development at this level are the institutions of <u>government</u>, <u>education</u> and <u>business</u>. The universal goal selected for communities is *the common good*, and the key role to be played is *citizenship*. Learning, knowing, and leading inform and activate CSD.

5. <u>Societal Systems Development (SSD)</u> SSD is social synthesis at the *meta-cognitive level*, and consists of fully integrated reasoning and development across all four levels of social synthesis. SSD strives to capture the spirit of John Sullivan's *To Come to Life More Fully* (1990), and suggests milestones for our timeless journey towards holistic personhood. The universal goal selected for the societal level is *human enlightenment*, and the key role to be played is *statesmanship*. Learning, knowing, and leading inform and activate SSD.

Universal Knowledge Spheres (Figure 2-3)

Learnership builds upon the *social systems framework* within which all human growth and development depends. Since the dawning of the human species people have had to communicate, coordinate, and collaborate with one another in order to secure their own survival and that of their families. Human history indicates that more interdependent arrangements and increasingly complex relationships were created as the evolutionary process of human development proceeded through the centuries.

Learning and knowledge leading to human development has been organized in many ways over the ages. Over the last 20 years, a number of useful approaches for categorizing knowledge have been suggested. One of these is the concept of six knowledge spheres. These knowledge spheres are defined in Learnership in a manner that respects the uniqueness of each sphere while emphasizing the integrative context we all must embrace as we go about our business of life.

1. Technological Knowledge Sphere – The technological knowledge sphere concerns the application of scientific methods and tools to societal activities. Emphasis here is on the study, development, and application of scientific methods and materials to achieve societal objectives. Major focus is on biotechnology, information technology, and materials technology.

1. Geographical Knowledge Sphere – The geographical knowledge sphere concerns the preservation of geographical, physical and continental regions of the entire earth. Emphasis is on international issues and relationships concerning nation-states' territorial boundaries and conflicts, population and immigration challenges, and property ownership and resource rights.

2. Political Knowledge Sphere – The political knowledge sphere deals with the study, structure, or affairs of government, politics, or the state. Focus is on citizenship, governance, foreign policy, political and cultural choices, and national defense.

3. Economic Knowledge Sphere – The economic knowledge sphere concerns the production, development and management of income and wealth. Focus is on the production and distribution of goods and services. Primary emphasis is on business management, financial management, and social systems economic development.

4. Social Knowledge Sphere – The social knowledge sphere addresses the associations   and living arrangements among individuals and groups in society. Focus is on the social activity dynamics among individuals, organizations and institutions. Major emphasis is on education, learning, culture, human relations, and interpersonal communication and media.

5. Ecological Knowledge Sphere – The ecological knowledge sphere concerns the relationships between organisms, their environments, and the goal of sustainable habitats. Emphasis is on the life processes and characteristic phenomena of living organisms. Focus is on bio-system management, energy production, population and demographics, and the availability of food and health services.

Learnership Process Feedback (Corrective Action) (Figure 2-3)

System feedback is an essential process model component that illustrates the need for continuous review and evaluation of performance to assure steady progress. A purposeful effort toward incremental improvement is necessary for societal development. At a summary level, learnership is both a personal and interpersonal capability distinguished by:

1. A synthesis of learning and leadership process skills in which the patterns of reasoning and behavior demonstrated by "learning-leaders" guide and motivate the performance of individuals in their pursuit of personal, organizational, community and societal accomplishment.

2. A focus on the what, why, and how of societal knowledge creation and application so individuals may (a) take responsibility for their own lifelong learning and knowledge creation, and (b) be motivated to achieve extraordinary results by discovering their unique purpose and crafting their journey so as to apply their increasing knowledge toward meaningful personal and social objectives.

3. A desire to participate and lead the development and implementation of a comprehensive strategy for lifelong societal learning, knowing, and leading that leads toward holistic and integrated human social systems development.

Learning Personal Life Meaning and Transition

Figure 2-4 that follows, encapsulates the fullness of our social development choices, restrictions and opportunities. What is being shown is that all through our respective adult life spans each of us is presented with, and experience, direct and indirect stimuli that influence both our near and longer term development. The rate of our maturation e.g. changes in our growth trajectory, may range from minimal to significant at any point along our pathway.

There are *three widely recognized life stages* in which personal issues have been well studied and warrant extra attention. These three transition points involve special challenges. However, we do have more knowledge and opportunities today for applying the ALF reasoning concepts, practices and tools presented earlier in this book.

Personal Benefits from Learning and Development

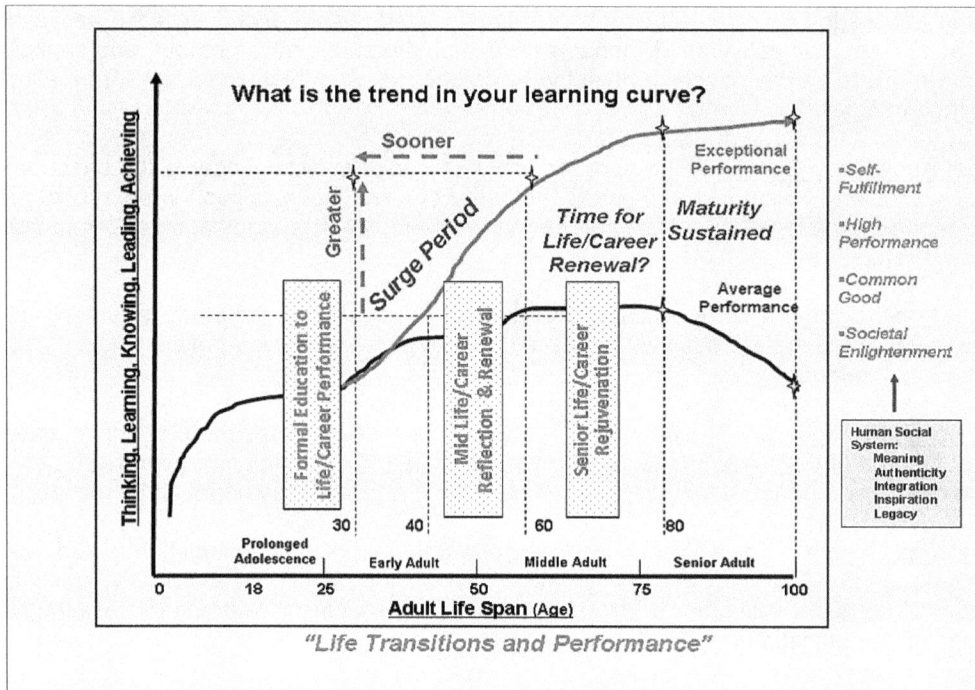

Figure 2-4

1. Formal Education to Life/Career Performance – The period of time during our 20s is a time for making a major investment in ourselves as to the type of adult we will become – but only if we take the time to consider:

    a. What ideals and values emerge as essential guides to our thinking, learning and behavior?

    b. What fields of education and career work skills will we need to learn and demonstrate?

    c. What commitment to marriage and family is appropriate now? Or, may be later?

    d. What social, political, economic and technological responsibilities and events should we embrace in this early period of adult personal growth and development?

    e. Can we find the thoughts and words that express the objectives we will attempt to accomplish, the manner in which we will participate in community and society, and the aspirations that loom large at this life stage. And, will our preferred rate of learning, knowledge, leading and achieving follow the Figure 2-4 choice of *growth* curves: AVERAGE PERFORMANCE or EXCEPTIONAL PERFORMANCE as our lives proceed toward completion?

Just knowing that we have this early adult responsibility and opportunity is not sufficient to build a foundation for future life and career growth and development. We also need a comprehensive "*thinking framework*" and a "*systematic learning*" process that together help us reason and take concrete action that we may build upon on a yearly basis. ALF products and services are designed with this foremost in our minds.

2. Mid-Life/Career Reflection and Renewal – The timeframe roughly between our ages of 45 and 65 is often when we find that many of the plans, dreams, aspirations and choices we made earlier in life have not been realized.

We also find the events and people we have experienced and trusted have not been sufficiently helpful – and even that our own choices and actions have led to inadequate effort or downright inept performance. When this occurs, a sense of being stalled or suppressed becomes persistent, thereby causing us to become tense, resentful, stressed and sometimes angry at the ties that bind us.

With reference back to once again, we find ourselves in the Mid-Life/Career Transition period of life with questions in mind like:

a. What has happened to what was supposed to be the best years of my life?

b. What has gone wrong in my personal life, and my career, and my work life?

c. What should I have done or not done before now? Is there time left?

d. Should I make changes in my personal objectives and situation, and also in my life purpose and career expectations?

e. Am I prepared to enter retirement at an appropriate time in the near future?

f. Am I becoming the person I now realize I really want to become?

g. How much time do I have, and can I afford to make significant changes in where I now find myself? And, What about the lives and careers of my family?

This transition event is as important to each of us as much as our *Early Adult Life Transition* back in our 20s. In most cases our lives are one-half completed by this time, and what many of us want this time is a chance for a "do-over."

A glance at the two competing life curve trajectories in Figure 2-4 should be informative. What is shown is that for most people they fail to realize what is occurring to them intellectually, emotionally or physiologically. They are slowing down to cope with what life has so far given them, and they continue to hope for a better situation without knowing what to do. Or, if they do know, the changes indicated may simply be too hard, too costly, or too risky. Their lives, careers, and societal contributions will always be constricted because their minds have been fully programmed to accept life as it is.

For some others (on the higher, "enhancement" curve), they come into their mid-life/career transition phase hoping to understand their current situation. They learned that they need to correct certain attitudes and behaviors; knowledge and skills; and/or family and work relationships that have not been helpful to their life aspirations. These people have learned how to collect relevant information, assess the facts of their situation, determine their choices and preferred changes, and be motivated to take sustained action for their own betterment and social worthiness. Their accomplishments, future potential, and self-satisfaction can be expected to grow more fully for most of their remaining years.

Once again, ALF products and services are designed with this period of life being a major focus. ALF training, coaching and mentoring classes and webinars are designed to unlock the challenges of this period so that everyone can come to understand, plan, take action, and experience personal growth and rewards.

3. Senior Life Rejuvenation and Legacy – The last of three periods of adult self-reflection and opportunity for planned life change is the age 65 plus timeframe. Gone are our early adult and mid-life/career adult transition opportunities. Our personal life growth and success has been firmly etched into who and what we have become in terms of our family relationships (*fellowship*), organizational performance (*leadership*), community participation (*citizenship*) and society at large (*statesmanship*). Questions we might want to ask ourselves, as objectively as we can, include:

a. Where am I located on the ALF graphic Adult Life Stages (Figure 2-4)?

b. How have I been doing over the last 50 years? Am I satisfied with the person into whom I have evolved?

c. What personal, organizational and community system issues and challenges remain obscure or unfinished?

d. What resources are available to assist me in reflection and future planning as I conduct the remainder of my life?

e. What aspirations are still unfulfilled, and how can I continue to pursue them?

f. What expectations should I have in terms of life expectancy? Live until age 80 wherein approximately one-half us will have died. Or, do I expect to live past age 80 like the other the other one-half who will continue on with growing impairment?

g. What new opportunities for my personal, organizational or community development still remain? Can I take action to immediately engage others outside myself and achieve success one more time?

h. Should I take the time to organize and write my own story and legacy for those I want to help, or for those close to me who would appreciate for me to bring closure to matters only I can accomplish?

 [**Author's Note**: The *Learnership: Personal Benefits from Learning and Development* graphic (Figure 2-5) is used as a foundation for emphasizing three major life/career transition opportunities: Early adult, mid-life adult and senior adult periods for reflection and renewal. Our belief is that everyone can benefit from a purposeful life review during these three periods of adult life in order to maximize our own performance, accomplishments and happiness.]

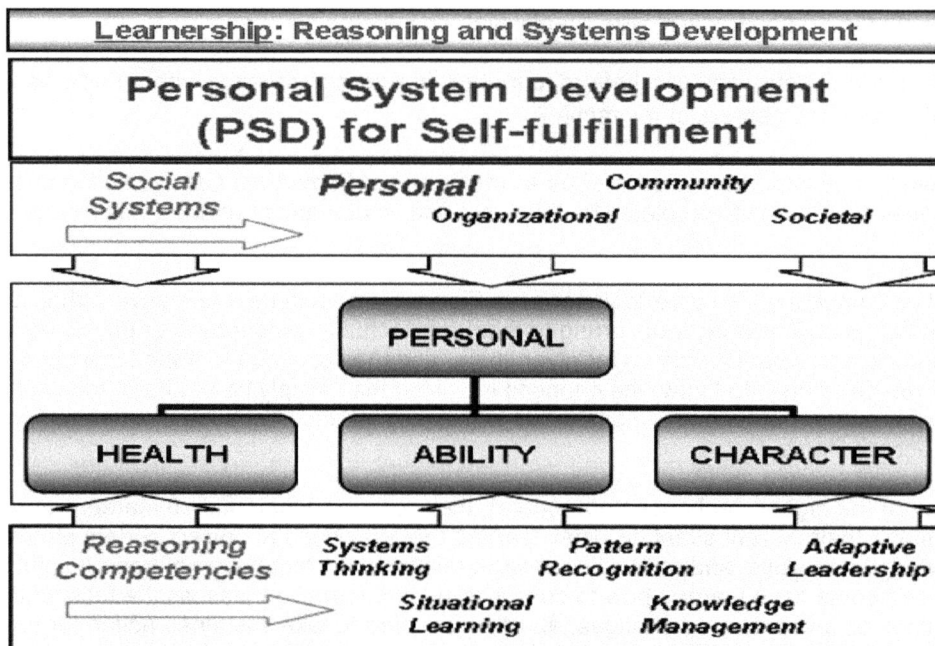

Figure 2-5

Learning Social System Meaning and Transition

As we have learned, all of us are part of system-of-systems with at least four domains of interdependent rights, responsibilities and activities. And, during our lifetimes there are intensive timeframes in which we may need to stop, reflect and redirect our interests and efforts to refine our purpose and ultimate legacies.

The section that follows suggests a four model set of graphics, one for each social system domain in which we need to have a clear understanding of the social system purpose, functions and people we need to consider and embrace during periods of continuous change.

1. Personal Systems Development for Self-Fulfillment (Figure 2-5)

On the *Personal Level*, this is the time to learn all about *Learnership Reasoning Competencies* as they relate to your own personal system development in the primary areas of Health, Character and Ability. What does self-fulfillment really mean in your life? And, can you regularly gather updated information for analysis and modify your developmental strategy for adaptive growth?

Can your *social system* engagement and performance include multiple perspectives and open-minded analysis; critical thinking and dialogue for interpersonal effectiveness; the building and use of fact-based knowledge without overly emotional bias; and the application of *fellowship* and *leadership* skills adapted for the events and people with whom you are involved – throughout your whole life experience? Are you becoming a *lifelong learner*, and maybe even a *learnership practitioner,* in pursuit of *a mindful way-of-being*?

2. Organization Systems Development for High Performance (Figure 2-6)
On the *Organization Level*, this is the time for considering and selecting employment locations, identifying key professions and supporting productive industries. Learning organizational objectives and capabilities in terms of the firm's Direction (Strategy), Operations (Processes), and Performance (Requirements) are significant functions you will need to learn and apply to demonstrate your competence and commitment to organizational goals and results. What does *high performance* really mean in your organizational life? And, can you regularly gather updated information for analysis and modify your developmental strategy for adaptive growth?

Your personal domain knowledge and contributions (from above) will now need to be continuously developed as you progress up the organizational ladder, or move occasionally to new positions with greater responsibilities and remuneration. *Leadership* and *citizenship* will become primary development concerns as you move to higher organization levels. However, your personal knowledge, skills and abilities applied on the job will need to expand as you expand your circle of professional contacts. Are you becoming a *lifelong learner*, and maybe even a *learnership practitioner* in pursuit of *a mindful way-of-being*?

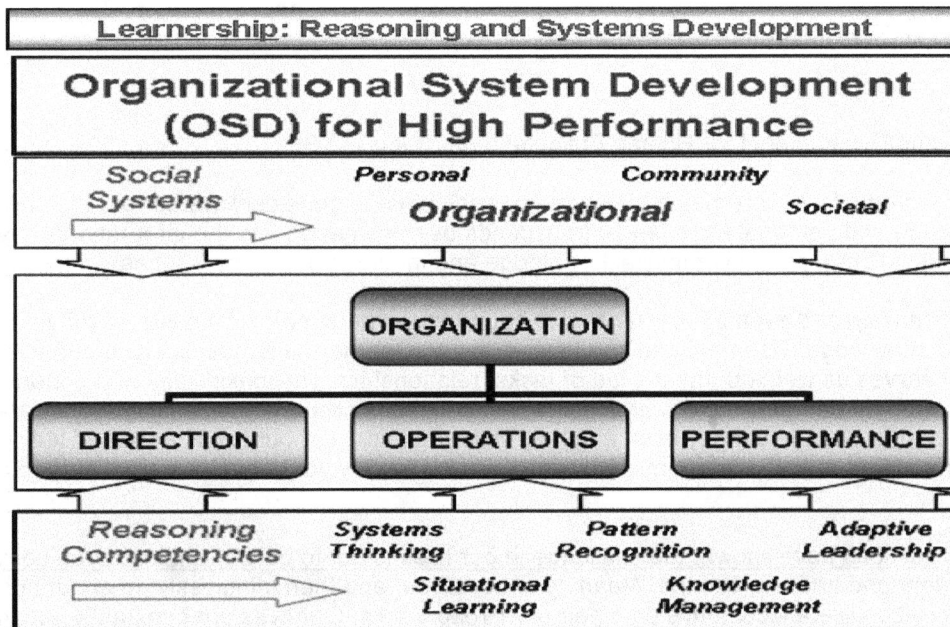

Learnership: Reasoning and Systems Development

Organizational System Development (OSD) for High Performance

Social Systems — Personal — Community — **Organizational** — Societal

ORGANIZATION

DIRECTION — OPERATIONS — PERFORMANCE

Reasoning Competencies — *Systems Thinking* — *Pattern Recognition* — *Adaptive Leadership* — *Situational Learning* — *Knowledge Management*

Figure 2-6

3. Community Systems Development for the Common Good (Figure 2-7)

On the *community level*, this is the time for participation in your local community in such areas as charitable fundraising, community service projects, and other not-for-profit activities that demonstrate your interest and willingness to assist others as well as enhance your personal and professional *citizenship*. What does working for the *common good* really mean in your community life?

Your personal and organizational perspectives and skills will continue to serve you well in this domain. It could have a reverse synergistic effect on your "*Being and Presence.*" Your knowledge, skills and abilities applied for the benefit of your community might need to advance as you expand your circle of social contacts. Are you becoming a *lifelong learner*, and many even a *learnership practitioner* in pursuit of *a mindful way-of-being*? And, can you regularly gather updated information for analysis and modify your developmental strategy for adaptive growth?

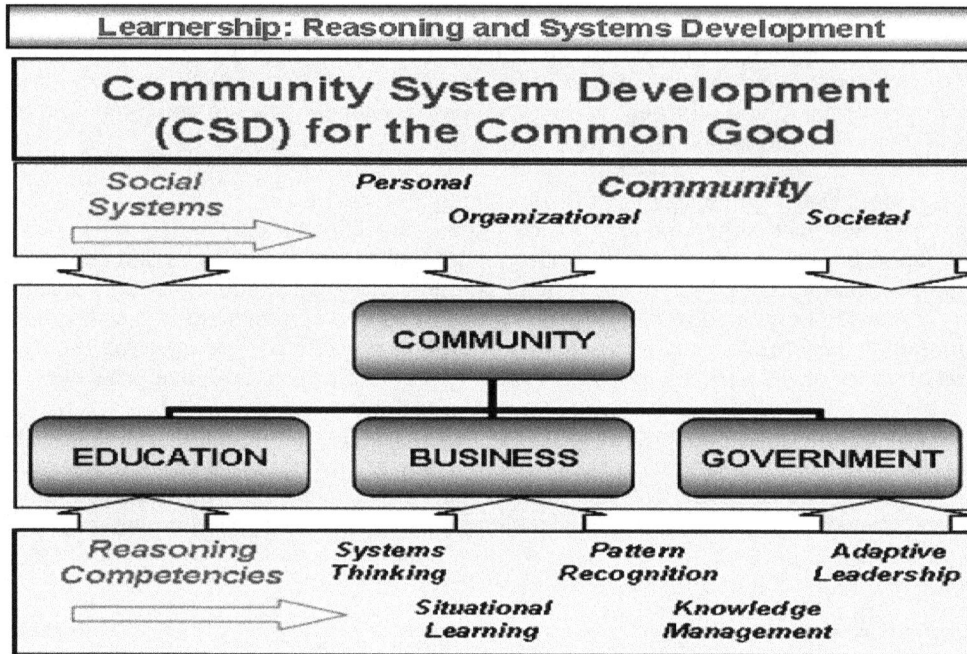

Figure 2-7

4. Societal Systems Development for Human Enlightenment (Figure 2-8)

On the *societal systems level*, this may be the time for each of us to consider whether our life philosophy, acquired knowledge and personal experience, transcends our own nation into the international system of nations and cultures. And, is it grounded in empirical knowledge and intellectual common sense.

Our sense of *citizenship* and even *statesmanship* is bound to our personal worldviews, which in turn are based on our learning and knowledge. Open-minded and flexible lifelong learners are most likely to attain "grounded knowledge" that serves us well with the myriad of tasks, relationships, responsibilities and opportunities we must engage with equilibrium and balance. What does human enlightenment really mean in your societal life? Are you becoming a *lifelong learner*, and many even a *learnership practitioner* in pursuit of *a mindful way of being*? And, can you regularly gather updated information for analysis and modify your developmental strategy for adaptive growth?

As the previous sections have shown, the challenge in our lives is not to quickly think about a convenient, short-hand way to understand and express the *"Meaning of our Lives"* and then mindlessly go about our regular business and activities like a locomotive on a pair of railroad tracks. Our lives are constantly accumulating new knowledge, skills and motivation to discover the next trail to explore in hopes of discovering a rewarding experience. While uncertainty and change abounds, we still engage and take action toward greater meaningfulness, self-actualization – and even, maybe, toward self-transcendence.

Personal Development and Meaning

Being in search of an "actionable meaning of life" entails having a foundation of beliefs and values, knowledge and skills, and motivations and goals that lead toward real outcomes for us and others with whom we live and work. In this pursuit of meaningfulness the researchers, educators and leaders in the discipline of personal development have been prolific in suggesting the procedures, attributes and skills that enable higher versus lower satisfaction and performance.

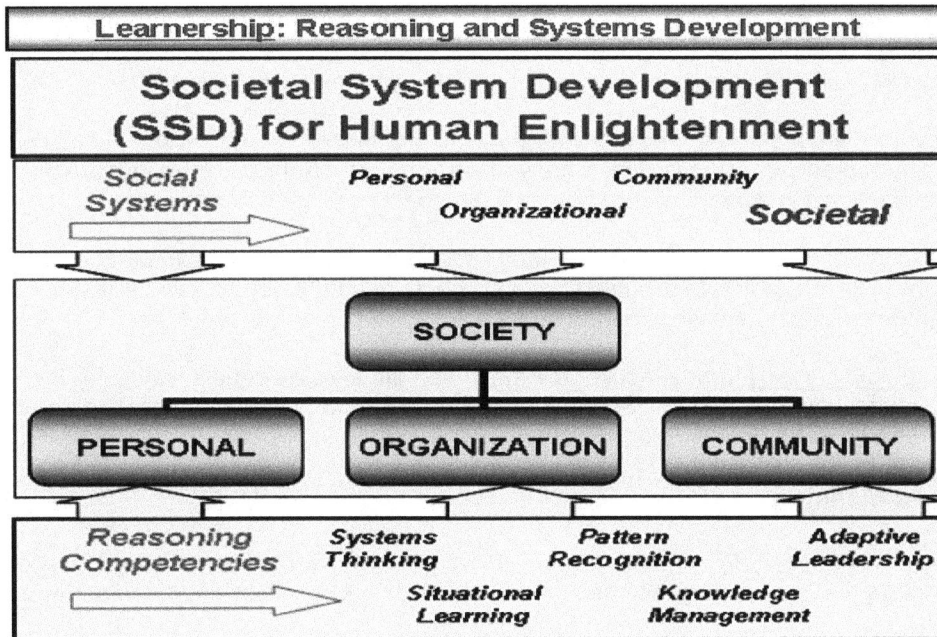

Figure 2-8

Learning Personal Development and Personhood

A useful reference is Steve Pavlina and his book entitled" *Personal Development for Smart People: The Conscious Pursuit of Personal Growth* (2008). His approach was to create a set criteria of desirable qualities; qualities that were universal, complete, irreducible, congruent and practical. Next he indentified seven seminal principles, supported by the criteria, and which would have significant influence on basic areas of life management, these were truth, love, power, oneness, authority, courage and intelligence. The principles, in turn, were essential factors in optimizing positive outcomes in six practical areas of applications: habits, career, money, health, relationships, and spirituality. (Table 2-2)

Personal Growth and Development

Fundamental Principles	Practical Application
Truth	Habits
Love	Career
Power	Money
Oneness	Health
Authority	Relationships
Courage	Spirituality
Intelligence	

Table 2-2

In summarizing the core message of his book, Steve Pavlina suggests:

1. "Seek truth with open eyes. Courageously accept your discoveries and their consequences. Rid your life of falsehood, denial, and fear of what is. Make truth your ally, not your enemy. This isn't easy, but it is correct.

2. <u>Share your love openly</u>. Connect with yourself and others by tuning in to the connection that already exists. The risk of rejection is overshadowed by the rewards of loving connections. Whenever you feel disconnected, reach and connect with another human being. Remember that you're always loved.

3. <u>Fully develop your human abilities</u>, and use your power in honorable service for the highest good of all. False power corrupts, but true power elevates. The more you resonate with truth and love, the greater your ability to wield power wisely. No one is served by your refusal to shine.

4. <u>Embrace your unique path of growth</u>. Use your intellect and emotions to guide you in the conscious pursuit of truth, love and power. Invest in creative expression, service and contribution and you will suffer no scarcity. Your greatest gift to the world is to share who you really are.

5. <u>Enjoy your incredible human journey</u>. Accept the highs and the lows as equally valuable. Recognize that your deepest sorrows reveal your greatest joy. Share your stories with others, and know that you're not alone. Be grateful for your time on earth."

Personhood and Meaning

Personhood: The Art of Being Fully Human by Leo F. Buscaglia. "If life's meaning is to be discovered, it is intrinsic in each stage that we assume the challenge of actualizing every moment of every day as we live it."

1. The Fully Functioning Mature Person

"Mature persons have a sincere desire to be productive and to give of that production to others. They desire to create and share their creations. They accept their lives and work with satisfaction and joy. They live their lives as an artist of life. They put their talents into each endeavor and their imagination into recreating their lives each day. The mature artists of life are spontaneous, accepting, flexible, receptive to new experience, suspicious of reality. They are harmonious with external forces, but autonomous, busy with the processes of inventing their own lives. They see existence as a series of choices, the selection of which they must determine, and for which they are singularly responsible. They care about, respect an appreciate t he world and society in which they live and the others who cohabit it, even though they may not wholly agree with them." Leo F. Buscaglia

2. The Fully Functioning Old Person

"Fully functioning old persons do not have the time to sit back and wait for death. They are faced with working through and actualizing two new stages – their old age, and their personal death. They must build confidence and give their limited time on earth purpose; they must make peace with the knowledge that some day they will be outgrown or even forgotten, but that the experience with life will have been enough. To ignore this task is to miss the opportunity for personal continued life in dignity through the pursuit of experiences which only old age can offer. They can choose themselves as unrealized potential, and in so doing, they can choose actualization." Leo F. Buscaglia

Questions on the Meaning of Your Life

An initial process for thinking, learning and committing to specific capabilities a person might consider in gaining a clear focus on who we are, and who we think we are, is at Figure 2-9. This handbook proposes that every reader and personal life project manager commit considerable time discovering their emerging selves. And, that readers understand that while it is human nature that the personal and organizational system domains may be given priority everyone has a responsibility to be an informed and contributing member of the community and societal domains.

How do these surrogate goals work for you right now? (Figure 2-9)
Can you venture a guess as to what might evolve as you continue to reflect and learn?

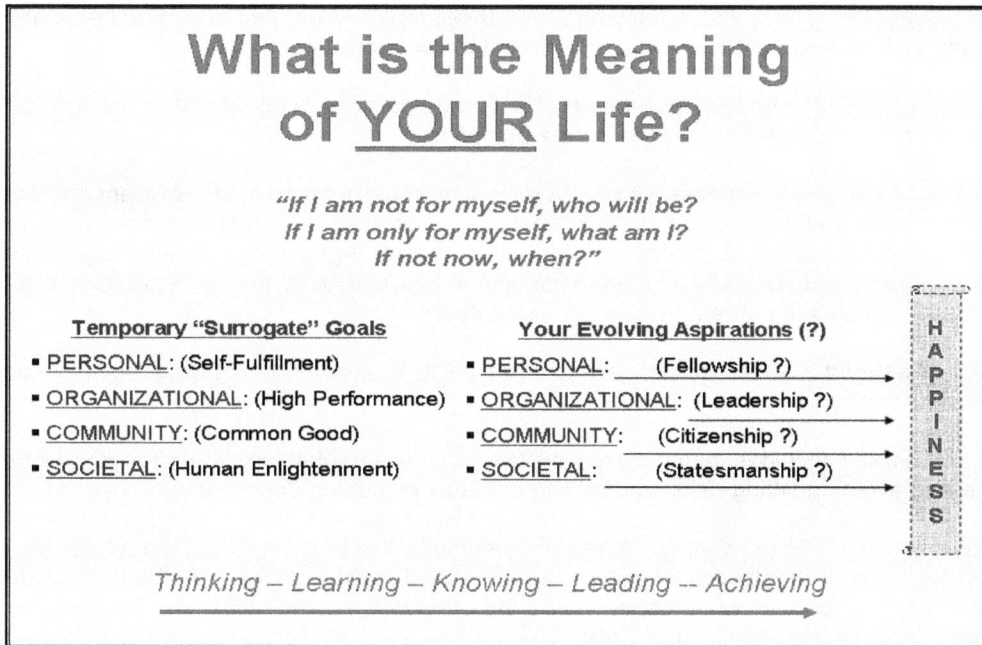

What is the Meaning of <u>YOUR</u> Life?

"If I am not for myself, who will be?
If I am only for myself, what am I?
If not now, when?"

Temporary "Surrogate" Goals	Your Evolving Aspirations (?)	
• <u>PERSONAL</u>: (Self-Fulfillment)	• <u>PERSONAL</u>: (Fellowship ?)	H A P P I N E S S
• <u>ORGANIZATIONAL</u>: (High Performance)	• <u>ORGANIZATIONAL</u>: (Leadership ?)	
• <u>COMMUNITY</u>: (Common Good)	• <u>COMMUNITY</u>: (Citizenship ?)	
• <u>SOCIETAL</u>: (Human Enlightenment)	• <u>SOCIETAL</u>: (Statesmanship ?)	

Thinking – Learning – Knowing – Leading -- Achieving

Figure 2-9

Author's Note 1: An important take away from this section is that when we seek to understand *"the meaning of our lives"* we should think in terms of a set of definable objectives or outcomes that can occur as the result of our purposeful decisions and actions. In our personal domain we can use a placeholder such as *self-fulfillment*, in the organizational domain *high performance*, in the community domain the *common good*, and in the societal domain *human enlightenment*. We recognize that each person, in time and learning, may want to choose more specific objectives in place of these temporary placeholders, Parts II, III, IV of this book provide frameworks for continued life and career learning, wealth building and legacy creation.]

[**Author's Note 2**: At this juncture, an open-ended question might be useful. How well does the lifelong learning personal and social assessment process described in this section align with Maslow's higher order self-actualization and self-transcendence needs listed back in Table 1? Is this information potentially helpful as you continue your lifelong learning journey?]

Wealth Generation and Financial Security

While the previous topic emphasized human "qualitative aspirations" it is essential that financial or "quantitative aspirations" be given equal consideration. This chapter is the first of many following chapters that consider the importance in everyone's life of earning money and acquiring wealth. For some, this is the overarching purpose to which they are committed and the one that assists them in measuring and quantifying the ultimate value of their lives. However, significant research on the lives of the most successful and wealthy people does not show that having significant wealth negates the desire for success -- and the happiest people are most often people of ordinary financial means.

How we think about financial security, acquired wealth, and their importance in achieving prosperity is significant in much of our personal and work lives. Our conscious and unconscious attitudes which were learned from early experiences with family, community and culture establish how we deal with others and make choices when acquiring and managing money. If we have thought about our purpose, success and happiness in terms of our personal, organizational and community relationships we are likely to maintain a balanced perspective in which money and the ownership of property and assets are mutually desirable but with due respect for the interests of others the larger social system.

In the *Psychology of Wealth* (2012), author Charles Richards PhD advises people to review their principles and values to assure that their personal beliefs and behaviors demonstrate the positive side of wealth instead of the negative side of wealth:

1. The <u>Negative Side of Wealth</u> is illustrated when fear, insecurity, anxiety and stress make us appear to be miserly, arrogant, self-serving, restrictive and judgmental towards others.

2. The <u>Positive Side of Wealth</u> is depicted when higher human purpose is on display in the form of generosity, proficiency, creativity, and discerning or considerate behavior.

According to Dr. Richards the psychology of wealth is, in fact, a psychology of self-esteem and self-respect. And, it is a mistake to pursue wealth believing that first acquiring wealth leads to those important psychological objectives. Each of us should invest in ourselves by pursuing meaningful things, assuming self-responsibility and maintaining integrity similar to those illustrated in this text in Figure 2-9. Dr. Richards advises that personal development leads to high self-esteem versus low self-esteem:

1. Having *high self-esteem* includes: being open to other points of view, learning from mistakes, accepting others' differences gracefully, and living in the present.

2. Having *low self-esteem* includes: being hypersensitive to criticism, blaming others for your circumstances, fearing change and avoiding taking risks, and having difficulty in making decisions.

Dr. Richards advises that "The psychology of wealth is a simple and pragmatic call to nurture the qualities and attitudes within ourselves that will create a prosperous life," and that "We expect the best of ourselves, and we recognize that the golden path to true prosperity, to a life of happiness and fulfillment, begins by showing up and putting one foot in front of the others." (pp. 224-5)

[**Author's Note:** This topic on Wealth Generation leading to adequate Financial Security (Figure 2-9) begins in this chapter and is developed in greater detail, as appropriate, in Personal Project Management (Chapter 3) Authentic Branding (Chapter 4), Personal Development (Chapter 10), Organization Development (Chapter 11), and Community Development (Chapter 12) In each chapter, the theme of earning financial returns from productive activity serves to remind the reader that lifelong learning, knowing, leading, and achieving is a multi-functional responsibility in human progress.

Implications for Integral Knowledge Management This handbook uses a "social system-of-systems" perspective for understanding the thinking and behavior of human beings. Doing this recognizes the artifacts and relationships among the four principal social domains of personal (family), organization (business), local community and society (largest) that includes them all. Each of these domains creates a psycho-social set of accepted understandings or culture that defines them each as both individual entities and intergroup collaborators. The goals, boundaries, plans, resources and activities of are based on the human needs, wants, and desires of all members. The thinking, learning and knowledge capabilities established within these groups are both interdisciplinary and integral. Knowing this truism encourages all of us to improve our reasoning and decision-making to obtain more meaningful outcomes.

Personal Reflection. This topic appears at the send of each chapter and is meant to serve two purposes: (a) be a reader's guide to main points and "takeaways," and (b) to encourage everyone to take a moment to engage their mental cognition and intuition on what the chapter means to them – especially at this time in their lives. Questions for chapter reflection follow immediately below; and for those readers inclined to maintain a self-assessment, your thoughts may be recorded in your *American Learnership for Life, Work, Wealth, Health and Legacy Success form which is located at Appendix B.*

Questions for Discussion

1. Can you make a comparison between people who have a sense of purpose and meaning in their work and life and those who have not determined this for themselves?

2. What are some of the ways people might determine whether they have achieved self-fulfillment?

3. Are there some examples of local community activities where working toward achieving the "common good" is evident?

4. How would you rate the goal of wealth building as compared to other personal and social objectives?

Insights, Commitments and Skills

If you plan to participate in the *American Learnership Life, Work, Wealth, Health and Legacy Success* self-development project, it is suggested you record your Insights, commitments and skills to be developed here in this chapter, and again in Appendix B:

My learning in terms of new insights, changing priorities, new commitments or skills I want to acquire:

1. <u>Insights (Example)</u>: Remind myself that ...

2. <u>Commitments (Example)</u>: Continue to ask myself ...

3. <u>Skills (Example)</u>: Apply my knowledge and skills to ...

Conclusion

This chapter may be the most important to you, our reader. It follows Chapter One in which the foundational American Learnership architecture and process models were described, and where a meta-level mental model was offered as a comprehensive, integral and interdisciplinary approach for human learning and development. Having done that, Chapter Two makes our commitment to you that this handbook will provide the basis for your expanded thinking, reasoning and action so that a quantum leap in your personal life management and professional performance will be your experience.

The American Learnership Forum, Inc. believes that only a modest commitment on your part to the learning, knowledge and legacy topics in this Handbook will return significant value to your life and success. If you do not find that to be the case, please contact the author, Dr. Garrity at www.alforum.org, for a prompt return of your cost for this Handbook.

Chapter Three

Being the Project Manager of Your Life

Major Chapter Topics

Being the Project Manager of Your Life

Personal Life Trajectory

Figure 3-1 was introduced in earlier chapters. Here again it envisions the fullness of our lifetime social development journey – our growth and development, the choices we may have made, and the restrictions and opportunities we have randomly encountered. What is shown is that all through our respective adult life spans each of us is presented with, and experience, direct and indirect stimuli that influence both our near and longer term development and capabilities. The rate of our maturation e.g. changes in our growth trajectory, may range from minimal to significant at any point along our pathway – but we are always moving forward and upward.

There are three widely recognized life transition stages in which personal issues have been well studied and warrant extra attention. These three transition points involve special life management challenges. However, we do have more knowledge and opportunities today than ever before for using the concepts, social practices and communications technologies addressed in this handbook. The challenge for you, the project manager of your own life, is to recognize that only you can conquer the inevitable transitions and bend the growth curves to optimize your personal life experience and accomplishments. When and how that happens is up to you.

[**Author's Note**: Figure 3-1 has probably been experienced by many of our readers already, however, few have ever witnessed the trends in advance nor understood the power of knowledge and choice that is now before you. You are the project manager of your life. You can achieve your lifetime goals by working towards them systematically. You can bend your thinking, learning, knowing, leading and achieving curve upward and surge forth with greater purpose and energy whenever you take command of your rate of development.]

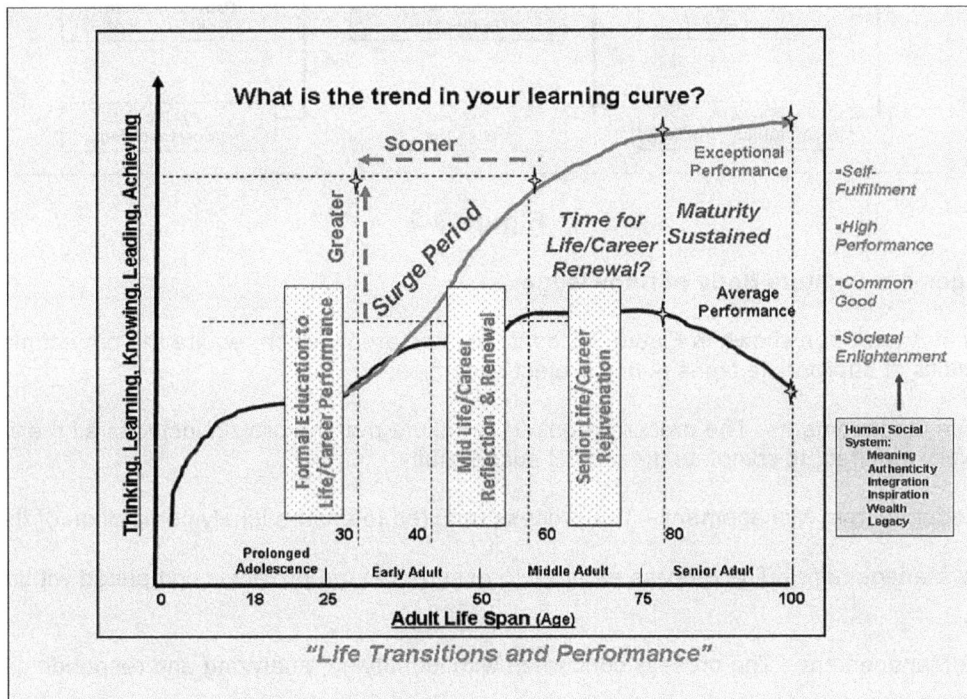

Figure 3-1

Project Management

The business management function known as project management has grown exponentially over the last twenty-five years. While its purpose and activities were fundamental for management of organizational improvement initiatives prior to 1990, the advent of the *organizational quality management* movement at that time and the popularity of *business process reengineering* and *technology innovation* methodologies made project management a core skill of business leaders and consultants.

As greater emphasis on organizational efficiency and effectiveness became a mantra for future organizational success after 2000, project management knowledge and skills were essential for *organizational learning, knowledge management, enterprise engineering* and all manner of organizational improvement programs.

Leadership in defining and codifying the project management discipline came from the U.S. Defense Department, large private sector industrial firms, and private associations such as the Project Management Institute that established the training and certification program entitled the Project Manager Professional (PMP). Today, many private and public sector organizations require that an employee or consultant be a certified PMP before being assigned to lead a major improvement project.

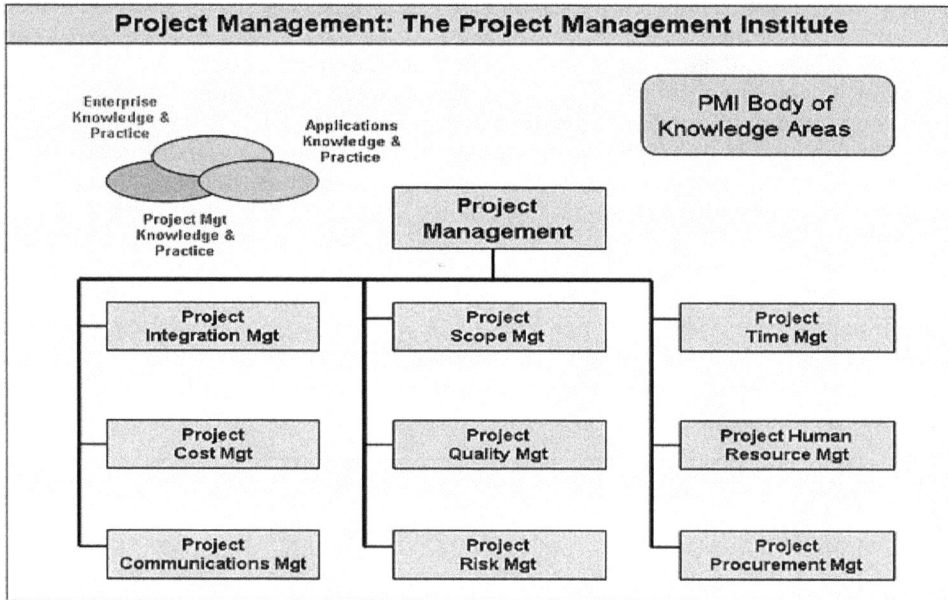

Figure 3-2

Project Management Institute Body of Knowledge

The PMI Body of Knowledge shown in Figure 3-2 contains nine areas which require the project manager's attention and skills at appropriate times during project execution:

1. Project Scope Management -- The process required to ensure that the project includes all the work required, and only the work required, to complete the project successfully.

2. Project Schedule (Time) Management – The process required to ensure timely completion of the project.

3. Project Cost Management – The process required to ensure that the project is completed within the approved budget.

4. Project Risk Management – The process concerned with identifying, analyzing and responding to project risk.

5. Project Quality Management – The process required to ensure that the project will satisfy the needs for which it was undertaken.

6. Project Integration Management – The process required to ensure that the various elements of the project are properly coordinated.

7. Project Human Resource Management – The process required to make the most effective use of the people involved with the project.

8. Project Communications Management – The process required to ensure timely and appropriate generation, collection, dissemination, storage and ultimate disposition of project information.

9. Project Procurement Management -- The process required to acquire goods and services from outside the performing organization.

Role of the Project Manager

Project management is the selection and systematic application of knowledge, skills, tools and technologies to achieve a planned objective. And, project management requires the sequential implementation of five work process phases: initiation, planning, executing, controlling and closing. The selected *project manager* is responsible for the overall integration and completion of all activities leading to project success. Three important tasks in managing projects are:

1. Define and *scope* the desired outcome or objective.

2. Establish time allotments and a *schedule* to accomplish all the activities that need to be addressed.

3. Estimate the *cost* and budget required to perform all the activities as they are scheduled to occur.

Together, these challenges are termed the "triple constraint" of project management. Two additional functions vital in keeping the project on-track are:

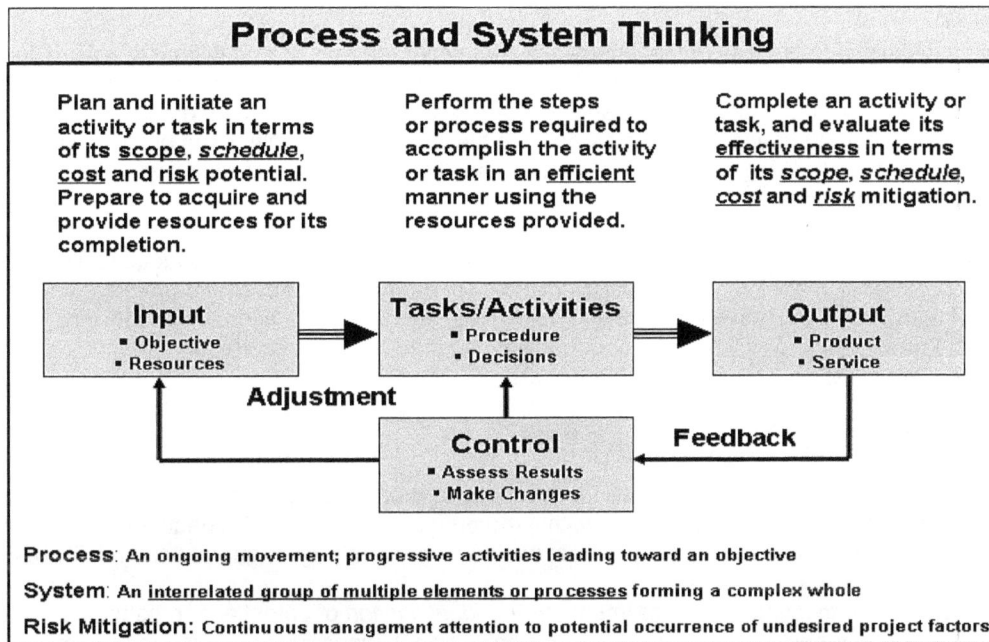

Figure 3-3

4. Be prepared for project changes. Some changes occur due to *unanticipated constraints* that need to be considered as the project proceeds, and other changes which result from *new project requirements* the project manager must incorporate into the original objective.

5. Conduct *risk* assessments at major decision points as the project proceeds in order to maintain triple constraint balance among *scope*, *schedule* and *cost*.

[**Author's Note**: Notwithstanding the organization or business emphasis traditionally used to teach and employ project management knowledge and skills, this methodology is now recognized as having broader application to any sizable social system improvement initiative whether in business, personal life or community improvement effort.]

Project Process, System and Risk Mitigation/Management

Project managers must have a foundational understanding of *systems thinking, process management* and *risk mitigation/management* (Figure 3-3). Even though projects are defined as having a specific beginning and end, it should be known that the project management methodology derives its features from the seminal concepts of recognizing the interdependent activities (systems thinking and analysis) and sequencing productive activities from an initial state to a final state (process planning and analysis).

<u>Process Management</u>

All human experience is ultimately involved with obtaining our needs, wants and desires from activities in our networks and relationships – and, those activities are mostly dependent on someone else deciding to provide a product or service by engaging appropriate processes and resources to do so. Virtually nothing of which we can conceive is at its very beginning – all human activity and products result from others' initiation, influence, work or social action. Functionally, the structure of process management includes a sequence of *activities* that are enabled through the use of *inputs* and work together to provide *outputs* that are desired or required by a person, organization or community. A *control* function is essential for corrective feedback to either the *input* or *activity* functions.

Once we understand the process-based environment in which we exist, we can learn how to work and succeed within recognizable boundaries. To make processes work efficiently, monitoring and control functions act to correct and improve what we plan to achieve. Earth itself is alive with predictable changes and events, and we may need to reflect on the damage we ourselves are causing.

<u>System Management</u>

A companion relationship to process management is system management in which smaller tasks support activities that are connected to form a process, and then multiple processes are grouped to enable more complex functions (e.g. humans, schools, railroads) to operate. The resulting interdependent functions are then able to form governments and societies to meet our human needs. From the smallest to the largest animal, plant and physical systems known, we can observe a social system-of-systems performing, evolving and even transforming itself if we take the time to observe the transitions and transformations.

Project management, consisting of process and system consideration, has been introduced to illustrate how essential they can be in organizing, planning, implementing, controlling enterprise improvement projects. These methodologies provide project team members with a purpose and objectives, sequential activities and resources, formal decision-making events, knowledge and skill building opportunities, and feedback and correction methods to manage necessary change in a timely manner.

<u>Risk Mitigation and Management</u>

Project management also necessitates assessing, mitigating and/or correcting risks (negative events or influences) that can impact the ability of the project team to stay within the project scope, cost or schedule while pursuing the desired outcome. Unanticipated problems have the potential to slow or prevent project operations and successful completion.

The primary areas for conducting risk assessment are the *identification* of potential or present risk factors, and the *probability* of the risk factor actually occurring. For example, if an unplanned change in the project scope appears on the horizon it is necessary to also assess the probability that the potential change will actually occur. Similar assessments should be considered for project cost/budget and project pace/schedule. There are two ways to combat risk, *mitigation* and *management*. The former requires the establishment of measures that deflect and reduce the likelihood of the risk creating a project problem. The latter employs direct action to prevent or eliminate the risk as it occurs.

[Author's Note: What is important for the purpose of *lifetime project management* is that these "organizational methodologies" are equally effective when used by individuals for planning, implementing and motivating themselves toward continuous personal and professional development.]

Personal Life Project Management

1. Lifetime Scheduling of Improvement Initiatives

An approach for scheduling and taking improvement action along one's own life cycle is notionally illustrated in Figure 3-4. Each person can choose appropriate times during their respective lives to pause, conduct a review of their progress, initiate a defined set of improvement actions and proceed to implement their learning, and commit to productive change and better results. Each *Life Project Task/Activity* represents an initiative such as: sign up for significant new education and skill building, change jobs to enhance one's career, move to a new location to gain for better experience, decide to move from an academic career to business or vice versa, or decide to retire early to pursue emerging interests. In each situation, the context and/or content of the person's life or career could be noted and recorded for later comparison.

This suggestion may be a challenge for people less experienced or less proactive people in two ways: (a) most people don't maintain the same energy for personal and career development throughout their lifetimes, and (b) quite often people fail to recognize the accretion of personal change already in their lives, or the disruptive change resulting from competitive sources outside their own control. Paying attention to social, economic, political and technological change is essential for continued personal, career and community development in all sectors of our social system of systems.

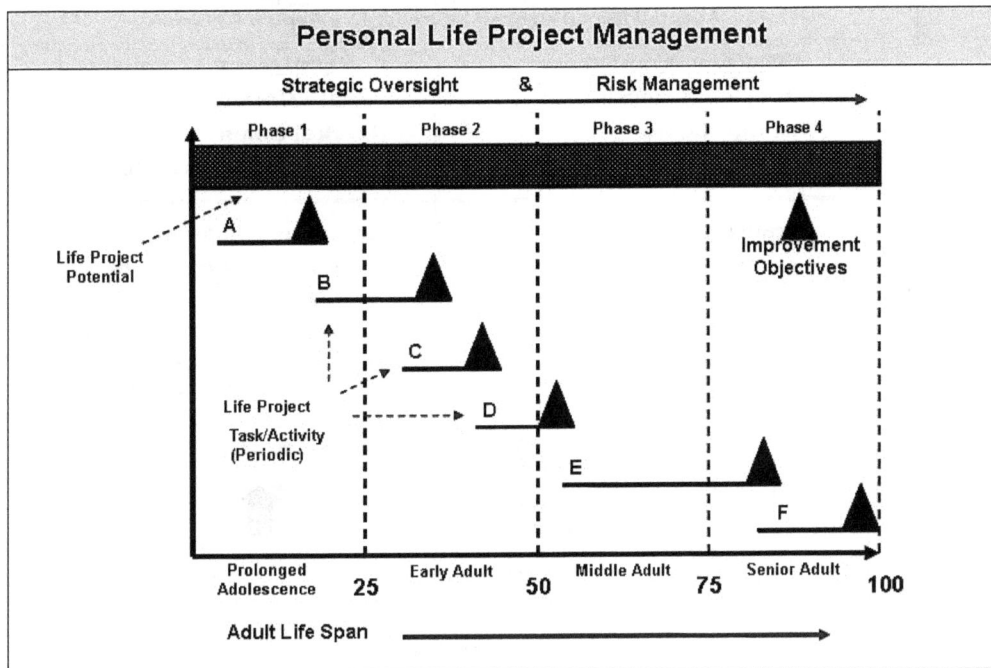

Personal Life Project Management

Figure 3-4

2. Supporting Project Management with a Balanced Scorecard

In their book *The Balanced Scorecard: Translating Strategy into Action* (1996), Robert Kaplan and David Norton presented a management system that enables organizations to clarify their visions and strategies and to establish a measurement system to evaluate organizational performance in the pursuit of those objectives. Kaplan and Norton state that: "The balanced scorecard retains traditional financial measures. But financial measures tell the story of past events, and were only an adequate story for industrial age companies for which investments in long-term capabilities and customer relationships were not as critical for success. These financial measures are inadequate, however, for guiding and evaluating the journey that information age companies must make to create future value through investment in customers, suppliers, employees, processes, technology, and innovation."

The Kaplan and Norton Balanced Scorecard uses a four perspective approach for assessing organizational performance: (1) Learning and Growth, (2) Business Process, (3) Customer Satisfaction, and (4) Financial Results. In each, stated objectives, measures, targets, and initiatives are identified and assessed as to their contribution to accomplishment of the organization's vision and strategy. The four perspectives are defined as:

1. (Employee) Learning and Growth. This perspective focuses is on the necessity for "knowledge workers" to be in a continuous learning mode. Learning is more than just training, and includes mentors and tutors, the availability of communications systems, and technological tools.

2. Business (Operational) Process. This perspective refers to internal business processes. Metrics based on this perspective allow the managers to know how well their business is running. Two kinds of processes may be identified: (a) mission-oriented processes, and (b) support processes.

3. Customer (Market Learning). This perspective emphasizes the important of customer satisfaction. Customers should be analyzed in terms of the kinds of customers and the kinds of processes that are used to service them.

4. <u>Financial (Revenue and Cost)</u>. This perspective continues the traditional emphasis on revenue and profit, but adds cost-benefit data and risk assessment to the criteria.

[**Author's Note**: The balanced scorecard approach has gained enormous popularity in the business community. Figure 3-5 presents a further illumination of the balanced scorecard concept as adapted from *The Personal MBA: Master of the Art of Business* by Josh Kaufman, 2010.]

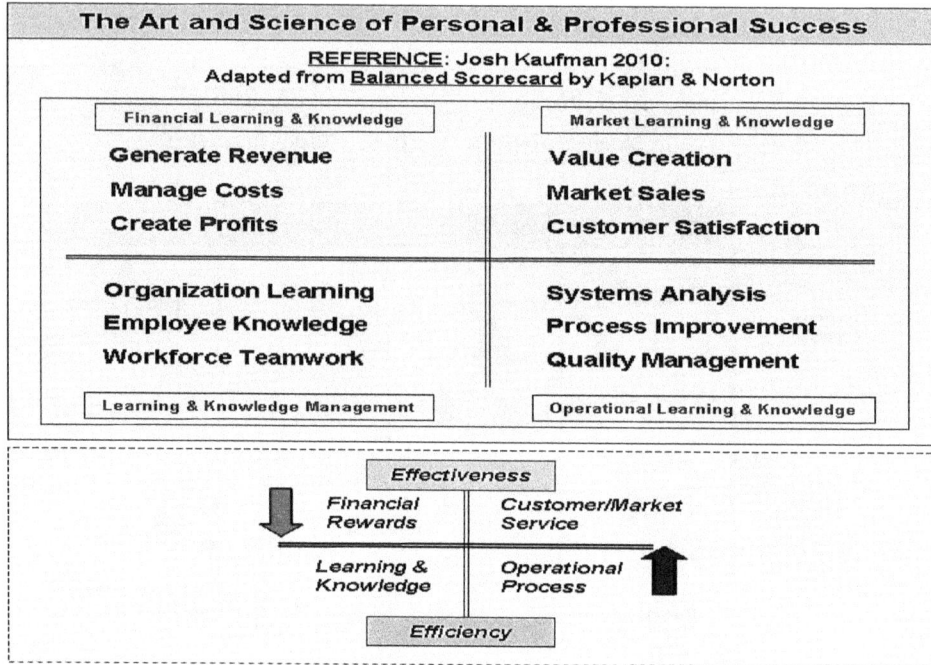

Figure 3-5

Kaufman argues in his *The Personal MBA* that the 2X2 matrix represents the highest level of executive management responsibility – and is therefore the highest level of guidance to which employees should aspire in assisting their firm's success. Given that perspective, the American Learnership adaptation in this Handbook is that the *project management* skill set and the *balanced scorecard* performance assessment are equally appropriate and effective when used together in a social system-of-systems (personal, organizational, community, societal) framework. With minor modification in description, the categories for management and performance assessment are:

a. **Learning** and Knowledge Management (Internal Focus) – What new learning and knowledge building should you pursue to increase both your personal and professional performance? [Efficiency]

b. **Operational** Learning & Knowledge (Internal Focus) – How can you improve the productivity of your personal and professional activities to save time and money? [Efficiency]

c. **Market** Learning & Knowledge (External Focus) – How can you better serve your needs and those of customers and clients in the various marketplaces? [Effectiveness]

d. **Financial** Learning & Knowledge (External Focus) – What results have you achieved to increase your income and reduce your cost of operations in the social system domains (personal, organization, community)? [Effectiveness]

3. Wealth and Financial Security Using an Integrated Balance Scorecard

The graphic at Figure 3-6 represents the American Learnership interpretation of the Kaplan and Norton model as a *Learnership Integrated Balanced Scorecard.* It begins with business *high performance* (HP) domain in the center, personal *self-fulfillment* (SF) domain on the left, and the community *common good* (CG) domain on the right. Simultaneously, it interlinks the balanced scorecard financial, customer, internal processes and knowledge and learning assessment factors to communicate a social system-of-systems framework. The result is an ambitious conceptualization of how future project managers, business leaders and social system architects can reflect and collaborate on interdisciplinary societal improvement and development in terms of the *planned and achieved financial management outcomes* for participants in all societal domains.

The efficiency and effectiveness of all domains can be best determined by reviewing systems performance in a counter-clockwise manner starting with the Knowledge Management domain, proceeding through the Operations Management and the Market Management domains, and ending at the Financial Management results domain:

    a. Personal Self-Fulfillment – From this viewpoint, an assessment that reviews an individual's personal level of learning and knowledge development, followed by how that development enables personal (family) operational efficiency, followed by the effectiveness in achieving personal (family) satisfaction, results in the near and longer-term accumulation of personal (family) income and capital assets. This process may be termed *personal (family) wealth and financial security* which is the result continuous review and learning in the other quadrants and is discussed in detail later in Chapter Ten.

    b. Organization High Performance – From this viewpoint, an assessment that reviews an organization's level of learning and knowledge development, followed by how that development enables organizational operational efficiency, followed by the effectiveness in achieving organization market satisfaction, results in the near and longer-term accumulation of organization income and capital assets. This process may be termed *organization (business) wealth and financial security* which is the result continuous review and learning in the other quadrants and is discussed later in detail in Chapter Eleven.

    c. Community Common Good -- From this viewpoint, an assessment that reviews a community's level of learning and knowledge development, followed by how that development enables community operational efficiency, followed by the effectiveness in achieving community citizen satisfaction, results in the near and longer-term accumulation of community income and capital assets. This process may be termed *community wealth and financial security* which is the result continuous review and learning in the other quadrants and is discussed later in detail in Chapter Twelve.

[**Author's Note:** Figure 3-7 has been modified to illustrate the wealth and financial security aspect of assessing the Meaning of our Lives as we continue through this Mindset Handbook.]

4. Lifetime Tracking of Improvement Initiatives

As the sequence of *Life Project Tasks/Activities* back in Figure 3-4 are accomplished, it is helpful to record the process and results of each improvement initiative as a milestone of that activity -- and as an information source for future reference. To be consistent with the *Learnership Methodology* advocated in this handbook, the three *Personal, Organization* and *Community* domains should be focused on moving forward to achieve their respective goals. A three

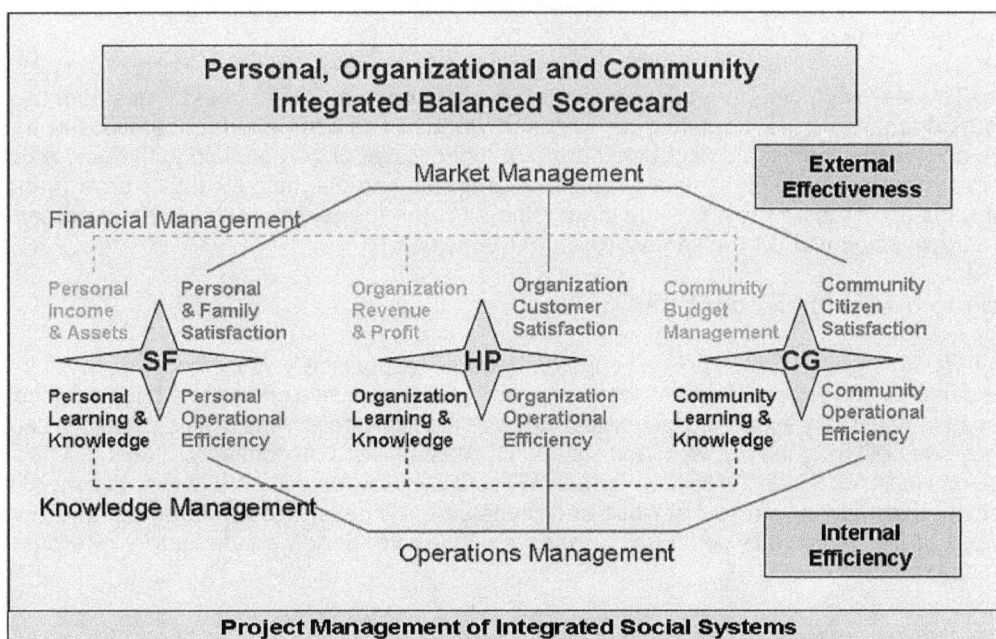

Personal Life Project Management

step analytical process that may be useful in organizing improvement efforts are: *Assess (previous) Progress, Plan Improvement*, and *Take action*. For each of the three domains four categories of *improvement initiatives* are recommended beginning with your *Personal* domain followed by your *Organization* domain and *Community* domain.

Project Improvement Initiative, Date: _____

|←————— **Personal Improvement Scorecard** —————→|

Project Task/Activity	Knowledge Management	Operations Management	Market Management	Financial Management	**Goals** to Achieve
Personal Health, Ability, Character	(Assess Progress, Plan Improvement, Take Action)	(Assess Progress, Plan Improvement, Take Action)	(Assess Progress, Plan Improvement, Take Action)	(Assess Progress, Plan Improvement, Take Action)	**Self-Fulfillment**
Organization Direction, Operations, Performance	(Assess Progress, Plan Improvement, Take Action)	(Assess Progress, Plan Improvement, Take Action)	(Assess Progress, Plan Improvement, Take Action)	(Assess Progress, Plan Improvement, Take Action)	**High Performance**
Community Education, Government, Business	(Assess Progress, Plan Improvement, Take Action)	(Assess Progress, Plan Improvement, Take Action)	(Assess Progress, Plan Improvement, Take Action)	(Assess Progress, Plan Improvement, Take Action)	**Common Good**

Table 3-1

To reiterate, Table 3-1 depicts three major *learnership domains* (personal, organization, and community) for systematically planning, implementing, improving, controlling and achieving personal knowledge, skills and personal progress. This method illustrates that the three major domains, while separately defined, may be treated as an *integral personal development responsibility,* That is, the three domains operating synchronously for one's lifetime could optimize lifelong learning, the assimilation of changes, and the accomplishment of life and career objectives. Notionally, the project could begin early in one's adult life wherein project *scope, schedule, cost* and *risk* could be formally recorded and then later reviewed and updated as significant life and career transitions compel reflection and renewal.

[Author's Note: The learning point here is not prescriptive such that everyone should implement this personal project management technique in a burdensome way. And yet, using this approach once, twice or three times during major life and career transitions might encourage a higher level of personal cognitive and emotional development. As a minimum, an assessment of personal progress and planning for future growth and development are advised at three main periods of transition: (1) the formal education to adult career transition, (2) the mid-life/career transition and (3) the senior/retirement transition.]

Questions on the Meaning of Your Life

Being the Project Manager of Your Life is both an opportunity and a responsibility. It is an opportunity in that it permits us to pursue our personal and professional development in an orderly, proactive and constant learning manner. It is a responsibility because many very successful people already use the similar practices discussed in this section, and they are outpacing their competitors in the life, work and community marketplaces. Accordingly, Figure 3-7 has been expanded to include *wealth and financial security across all social system domains*. While this aspect of our lives is not the only activity that makes living worthwhile and gives us happiness, it is fundamental that our knowledge, skills, abilities and accomplishments continue to improve so we experience a satisfactory rate of recognition and financial success.

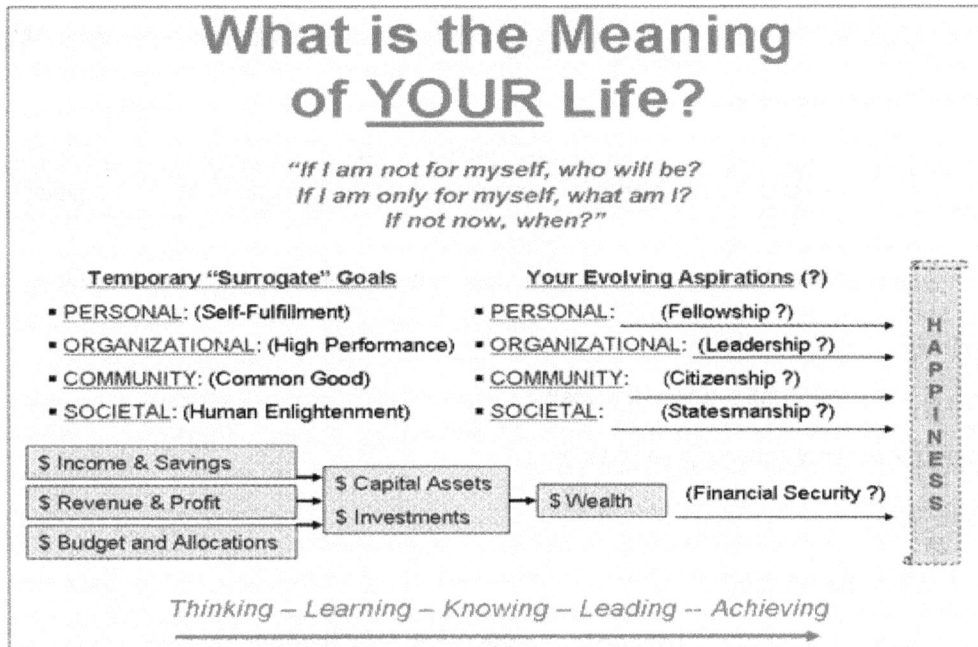

Figure 3-7

[**Author's Note**: It's the experience of this author that individuals trained in becoming Project Managers in their organizations have an affinity for focusing their knowledge and skills for operational improvement in all areas of their lives. The discipline of project management tends to reinforce the notion that having the will to persist against resistance builds the confidence that purposeful effort leads to better results.]

How do these surrogate goals work for you right now? (Figure 3-7)
Can you venture a guess as to what might evolve as you continue to reflect and learn?
Should your wealth and financial security goals and aspirations be included as areas for improvement?

Implications for Integral Learning and Knowledge Management. This chapter illustrates that Personal Life Project Management is a methodology that encompasses both the qualitative and quantitative aspects of human aspirations and financial security. It also cautions that a reasonable person would recognize that a thoughtful, balanced and holistic approach in setting goals and taking action is advisable. Because the quality and quantity of our learning
evolves – developed over a lifetime of experience – major changes can occur as new knowledge replaces that which no longer serves our needs and interests. And, as new learning and knowledge becomes influential, our goals will require modification within our already established mindsets and beliefs. An important feature that has been added in this chapter is that personal, organization, and community development and financial security is inextricably dependent on our willingness and ability to continuously learn and construct knowledge relevant to operational efficiency and external effectiveness within our social systems domains.

Personal Reflection. This topic appears at the send of each chapter and is meant to serve two purposes: (a) be a reader's guide to main points and "takeaways," and (b) to encourage everyone to take a moment to engage their mental cognition and intuition on what the chapter means to them – especially at this time in their lives. Questions for chapter reflection follow immediately below; and for those readers inclined to maintain a self-assessment, your thoughts may be recorded in your *American Learnership for Life, Work, Wealth, Health and Legacy Success* which is at Appendix B.

Questions for Discussion

1. Can you give an example of a potential life or career management situation in which project management might be useful?

2. Have you studied business process project management in the past? If so, how applicable is life project management to your personal development?

3. What project management aspect or function have you found to be most challenging to accomplish?

Insights, Commitments and Skills

If you plan to participate in the *American Learnership for Life, Work, Wealth, Health and Legacy Success* self-development program, it is suggested you record your Insights, commitments and skills to be developed here in this chapter, and again in Appendix B:

My learning in terms of new insights, changing priorities, new commitments or skills I want to acquire:

1. Insights (Example): Remind myself that ...

2. Commitments (Example): Continue to ask myself ...

3. Skills (Example): Apply my knowledge and skills to ...

Conclusion

A Section One review of this Handbook:

Chapter 1, An Introduction to American Learnership, provided an overarching summary of the foundational concepts and insights that make "Learnership" a distinctive trademark. The principles, graphics and practices advocated are meant to stretch readers' thinking and suggest new approaches for becoming successful – all within a logical social system-of-systems framework. Two foundational documents for this guidebook are the Learnership Integrated Systems Architecture (LISA) and the list of Twenty-Five Learnership Practitioner Characteristics.

Chapter 2, Discovering the Meaning of Your Life, offered a comprehensive method for reflection, learning and identification of one's own life objectives to create a sense of purpose and motivation. The learnership social system domains and guideline objectives used to organize this task were (a) Personal self-fulfillment, (b) Organization high performance, (c) Community common good, and (d) Societal human enlightenment. When pursued in an integrated manner, the learner is assured of achieving personal development and optimizing their life satisfaction.

Chapter 3, Being the Project Manager of Your Life, provided an introduction to a well-regarded business management skill with a description of how that tool could be used equally well in managing one's learning and life trajectory. The project management methodology adds value due to its use of process management and systems thinking techniques that require employing discrete steps in working towards a desired objective. Periodic review of project challenges and the updating of necessary project changes keeps the project (one's life) moving forward toward desired objectives at a reasoned pace.

The next chapter (4), Crafting Your Authentic Personal and Professional Brand, describes how everyone may responsibly learn more about themselves, and then use that learning to chart a course of action that enables their purpose and capabilities to be understood and valued by others in their network and field of business.

[Author's Note: Readers wishing to develop and publish their own *authentic personal and professional brand* e-book can obtain assistance from this handbook author. An example of how that document might look when completed is included in the following chapter and at *Appendix C.*]

Chapter Four

Crafting Your Personal and Professional Brand

Major Chapter Topics

- **Introduction 72**

- **Learning Objectives 73**

- **Hubert Rampersad's Authentic Branding Model 73**
  Authentic Personal Branding
  Alignment with Yourself:
  Authentic Corporate Branding
  Alignment with Your Organization

- **Criteria for Authentic Personal Branding 77**

- **Wealth Generation and Financial Security 78**

- **Questions on the Meaning of Your Life 79**

- **Implications for Integral Learning and Knowledge Management 79**

- **Personal Reflection 79**

- **Questions for Discussion 79**

- **Insights, Commitments and Skills 80**

- **Conclusion 80**

Crafting Your Personal and Professional Brand

Introduction

A brand is the expectation, image, and perceptions it creates in the minds of others, when they see or hear a name, product or logo. According to Randall Hansen (2007) "*Branding can be defined as a promise… a promise of the value of the product… a promise that the product is better than all the competing products… a promise that must be delivered to be successful*". For example, Volvo is differentiated from other car companies by its promise of safety and security and IBM stands for dependability. Branding isn't just for corporations anymore. There is a new trend called "*Personal Branding*". The reason for this is (Jane Tabachnick, 2007):

1. The technological revolution has changed the structure of careers today. It used to be that you went to work for one or two companies in your entire career. Today we will all have as many as four to eight jobs or careers in our lifetime. Personal Branding is essential to career development and an effective career tool because it helps define who you are, what you stand for, what makes you unique, special, and different, how you are great, and why you should be sought out.

2. The change in the way we communicate. The Internet has elevated each of us to the position of publisher. Email, newsgroups, bulletin boards, blogs, and online network and discussion groups afford all of us the opportunity to learn, network and get exposure for our businesses and ourselves. People want to do business with people they know or people they feel they can trust, with whom they feel some sort of connection, and with whom they relate. If you are a familiar, friendly, and consistent presence and brand online, people will have the sense that they know you and be more receptive to doing business with you. So Personal Branding is also essential to business development.

Being good and accomplished in your field is not enough. It's time to give serious effort to discovering your genius, passion, and your authentic dream, imagining and developing yourself as a powerful, consistent, and memorable person with your own specific brand, as you do related work you love. You can shape the market perception of your Personal Brand by defining your unique strengths, values, and personality, sharing it with others in an exciting, persuasive manner, and cultivating your brand continuously. It's something that you can develop and manage, which is essential for future employability and success in life. Everyone has a chance and should take the responsibility to learn, improve, build up their skills and be a strong brand.

There is no job security. Be independent and (re)define yourself by building, implementing and cultivating your authentic personal brand. Become a powerful brand as you attract and create new opportunities. According to Peter Montoya (2005), there are three categories of business that need personal branding:

1. <u>Independent service professionals</u> (actors, agents, artists, athletes, authors, advisors, consultants, designers, dentists, caterers, chiropractors, real estate professionals, etc.

2. <u>Personal service business</u> (owners of gyms, auto shops, cleaners, bakeries, computer repair shops, print shops, child care, painters, gardeners, etc.

3. <u>Value-adding product sellers</u> (auto dealers, bookstores, publishers, record stores, specialty retail, and so on. They need a personal brand in order to influence key people in their domain.

Everyone has a personal brand but most people are not aware of this and do not manage this strategically and effectively. You should take control of your brand and the message it sends and affect how others perceive you. This will help you to actively grow and distinguish yourself as an exceptional professional. Having a strong personal brand has benefits as it stimulates meaningful perceptions about the values and qualities that you stand for, and tells others: who you are, what you do, what makes you different, how you create value for them, and what they can expect when they deal with you. Additionally, it:

1. Influences how others perceive you.

2. Creates expectations in the mind of others of what they will get when they work with you.

3. Creates an identity around you which makes it easier for people to remember who you are.

4. Gets your prospects to see you as the only solution to their problem.

5. Puts you above the competition and makes you unique and better than your competitors in the marketplace.

Your personal brand is the synthesis of all the expectations, images, and perceptions it creates in the minds of others, when they see or hear your name. The underlying assumption of personal branding philosophy is that each of us has unique gifts and a distinct purpose and dream in life. By connecting these gifts, purpose and dream, we open ourselves up to greater happiness and success in life (Frost, 2003). Building your brand is clearly a life management enhancement function.

This new blueprint will help you to unlock your potential and build a trusted image of yourself that you want to project in everything you do. It must therefore be in harmony with your true values, beliefs, dreams, and genius. When your brand is combined with powerful tools, it will deliver peak performance and create a stable basis for trustworthiness, credibility, and personal charisma. This inside-out approach is durable, it differs from traditional methods and it is based on a passion for developing human potential. This new approach places more emphasis on understanding yourself and the needs of others. Meeting others' needs while staying true to your personal values, holistically improving yourself continuously, and realizing your personal growth will be outcomes of your new personal branding journey. This approach focuses on the human side of branding, and includes your reputation, character and personality. If you are well branded according to this approach, you will find it easier to convince others and will attract the people and opportunities that are a perfect fit for you.

The authentic personal branding process starts with determining who you are at your core authentic self. Rather than inventing a brand that you would like to be perceived as and to sell yourself to others, this one is based on your life philosophy, dreams, vision, mission, values, key roles, identity, self-knowledge, self-awareness, self-responsibility, positive attributes, and self-management. With an authentic personal brand, your strongest characteristics, attributes, and values can separate you from the crowd. Without this, you look just like everyone else. If you are not branded in an authentic, honest, and holistic way, if you don't deliver according to your brand promise, and if you focus mainly on selling, packaging, outward appearances, promoting yourself, and becoming famous, you will likely be perceived as inauthentic.

Learning Objectives

After learning this authentic branding methodology and applying its concepts, some of the many things you may learn to do are:

1. Build, implement, and cultivate an authentic, distinctive, inspiring, compelling, enduring personal brand.

2. Create positive perceptions and emotions in the mind of your prospects (that you are different, special, unique, and authentic) based on your personal brand.

3. Build a truly lasting and trusted relationship with your clients, make an emotional connection with them, and managing their expectations and perception effectively.

4. Manage and influence how others perceive you and think of you.

5. Stimulate meaningful perceptions about the values and qualities for which you stand.

6. Use your brand to communicate your unique service that provides a sense of value for your target audience, which is in line with your dreams, purpose in life, values, passion, competencies, uniqueness, genius, specialization, characteristics, and things that you love doing.

7. Position yourself strongly in relation to your competitors, built a strong reputation, and develop an effective image of yourself that you want to project in everything you do.

8. Communicate what you stand for in a unique way that is different from others in your field and that gets inside people's mind.

9. Provide value to others continuously, create visibility, build trust, and reinforce integrity, honesty, trustworthiness, credibility, transparency, and personal charisma.

10. Build a trusted image of yourself, which is based on your true values, beliefs, dream, and genius.

11. Make a difference in relationships throughout your life, find your passion, separate you from the crowd, be happy and attract success.

12. Differentiate yourself, set you apart from others, become authentic, and create an identity around yourself which makes it easier for people to remember who you are.

13. Enhance your brand equity and brand awareness.

14. Become known as a thriving and distinguished professional.

15. Eliminate the competition and make you unique and better than all your competition in the marketplace.

16. Manage yourself effectively as a business, develop self-esteem, unlock your potential, and enrich your relationships with others

17. Increase your personal effectiveness and deliver peak performance.

18. Align personal branding with corporate branding and get the optimal fi t and balance between these two activities in order to enhance labor productivity, to create a climate of trust, and to stimulate employee engagement.

19. Become an effective authentic personal brand coach.

> *A great brand taps into emotions ...Emotions drive most, if not all, of our decisions. A brand reaches out with a powerful connecting experience. It's an emotional connecting point that transcends the product. A great brand is a story that's never completely told. A brand is a metaphorical story that's evolving all the time. Stories create the emotional context people need to locate themselves in a larger experience.*
> -- Scott Bedbury

Hubert Rampersad's Authentic Branding Model

This section emphasizes Hubert Rampersad's organic, holistic and authentic branding model, which provides an excellent framework and roadmap to develop, implement, and cultivate an authentic personal and corporate brand in a sustainable manner. The Authentic Branding Model (Figure 4-1) consists of four phases which are the building blocks of sustainable personal and professional leadership branding.

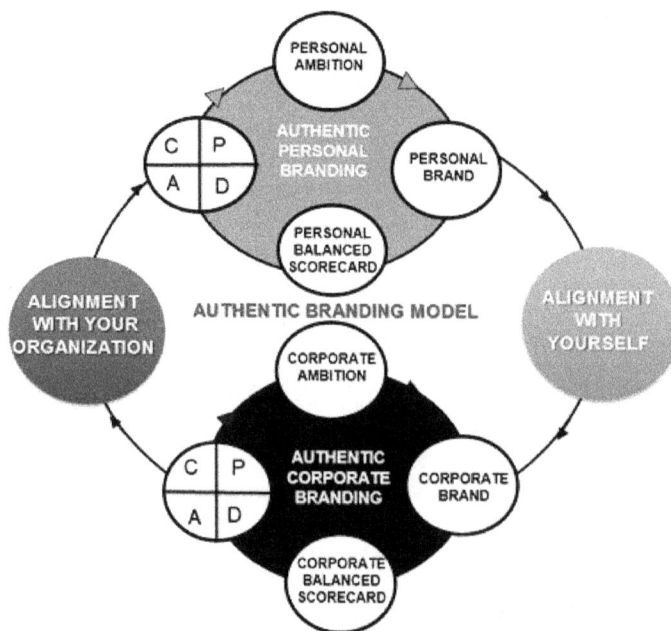

Figure 4-1

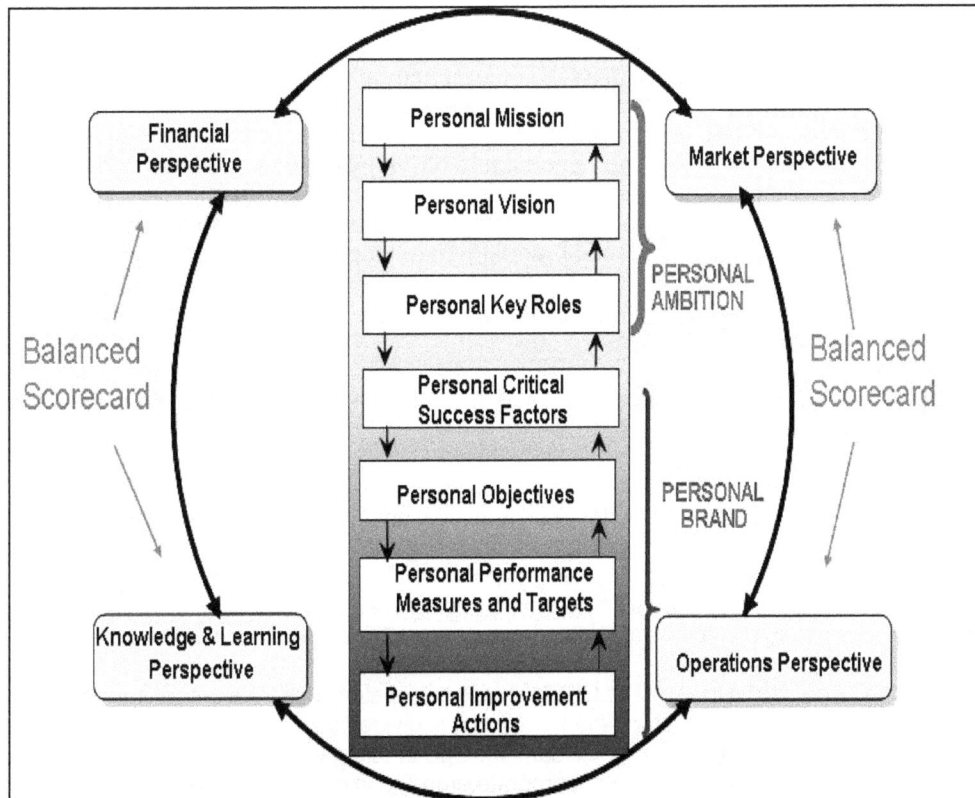

Figure 4-2

Phase 1: Authentic Personal Branding:

Personal Ambition: This phase involves a soul searching process based on thought, introspection, and self-reflection, supported by a breathing and silence exercise. Question which you can ask yourself are: Who am I, What do I stand for? What makes me happy? What do I live for? Why do I want to lead? What's the purpose of my leadership? The result of this phase is the formulation of your personal mission, vision and key roles. On the basis of insights acquired through this process, you develop self-awareness and self-regulation, which are the foundation of trustworthiness, integrity, and openness to learn.

Personal Brand: This phase involves defining and formulating an authentic, distinctive, and memorable personal brand promise, and using it as the focal point of your behavior and actions. This must be in harmony with your personal ambition. Personal ambition has no value unless you take action to make it a reality. Therefore the emphasis in this stage is developing an integrated and well-balanced action plan based on your personal ambition to realize your life objectives. It's about translating your personal ambition into action. Personal branding without continuous improvement of yourself based on your PBSC is merely cosmetic and will not lead to your sustainable growth.

Personal Balanced Scorecard (PBSC):. Your PBSC entails your personal critical success factors that are related to your personal ambition and your corresponding objectives, performance measures, targets and improvement actions (Rampersad, 2006). It is divided into two external facing perspectives (Financial, Market) and two internal focused (Knowledge & Learning, Operations) perspectives. Your PBSC translates your personal ambition into manageable and measurable personal objectives, milestones and improvement actions in a holistic and balanced way. Through your PBSC you can govern yourself effectively and become more disciplined, more effective, more responsible for yourself, and more ethical. (Figure 4-2)

Implementation and cultivation of your personal brand: Personal ambition and personal balanced scorecard have no value unless you implement them to make it a reality. Therefore the next step is to implement, maintain, and cultivate your ambition, personal brand and PBSC to manage you effectively. This focuses on your private life and business life.

Phase 2: Alignment with Yourself:

Aligning your personal ambition with your behavior and your way of acting is needed to develop personal integrity. You need to commit yourself to live and act according to your personal ambition and to keep promises that you make to yourself. Personal branding built on the person's true character is sustainable and strong. You should reflect your true self and must adhere to a moral and behavioral code set down by your personal ambition. This means that who you really are, what you care about, and your passions should come out in your personal ambition, and you should act and behave accordingly (you should be yourself) to build trust. Building trust starts with being true and authentic to you. When people find harmony between their personal ambition and their behavior/actions, they will not come into conflict with their conscience. This process will help you to become in harmony with yourself, which is the foundation of integrity, honesty, trustworthiness, credibility, transparency, and charisma. These two stages in the authentic branding model focus on personal leadership development by cultivating your inner compass.

Phase 3: Authentic Corporate Branding:

Corporate Ambition: This phase involves defining and formulating the shared corporate ambition. It entails the soul, core intention and the guiding principles of the organization and encompasses the corporate mission, vision, and core values. (Figure 4-3)

Corporate Brand: This phase involves defining and formulating an authentic, distinctive, and memorable corporate brand promise, and using it as the focal point of the organization's behavior and actions. This must be in harmony with the shared corporate ambition. The emphasis in this stage is developing an integrated and well-balanced action plan based on the corporate ambition to realize the corporate objectives. It offers a means to maintain balance between financial and nonfinancial measures and to connect strategic and operational standards.

Corporate Balanced Scorecard (CBSC): The CBSC entails the related corporate critical success factors, objectives, performance measures, targets and improvement actions It is divided into two external facing perspectives (Financial, Market) and two internal focused (Knowledge & learning, Operations) perspectives. The CBSC is needed to improve the business processes continuously based on the corporate ambition in order to add value to customers and satisfy them.

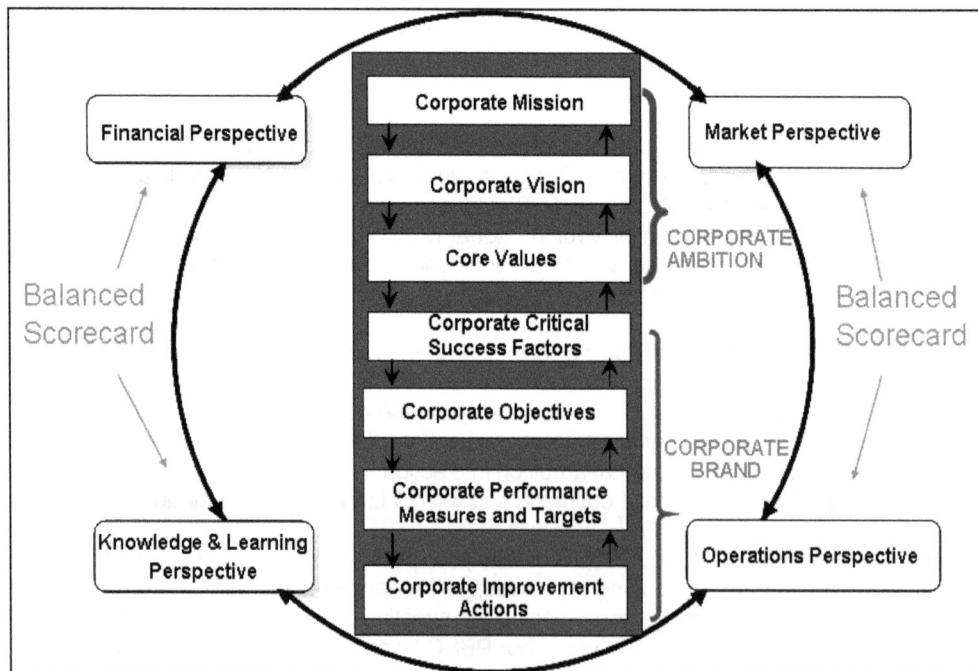

Figure 4-3

Implementation and Cultivation of the Corporate Brand: The next step is to implement, maintain, and cultivate the corporate ambition, the corporate brand and CBSC in order to govern your organization effectively, to deliver peak performance, and to create competitive advantage.

4. Phase 4: Alignment with Your Organization:

The emphasis in this final stage is aligning personal ambition with corporate ambition creating uniformity of personal and organizational values. It's about aligning personal branding with corporate branding and getting the optimal fit and balance between these two activities in order to enhance labor productivity, to create a climate of trust, and to stimulate engagement, commitment, integrity, and passion in the organization. This is needed because staff members don't work with devotion or expend energy on something they do not believe in or agree with. If there is an effective match between their interests and those of the organization, or if their values and the organization's values align, they will be engaged and will work with greater commitment and dedication towards realizing the corporate objectives. Identification with the corporate ambition is the most important motive for them to dedicate themselves actively to the corporate objectives and to maximize their potential (Figure 4-4).

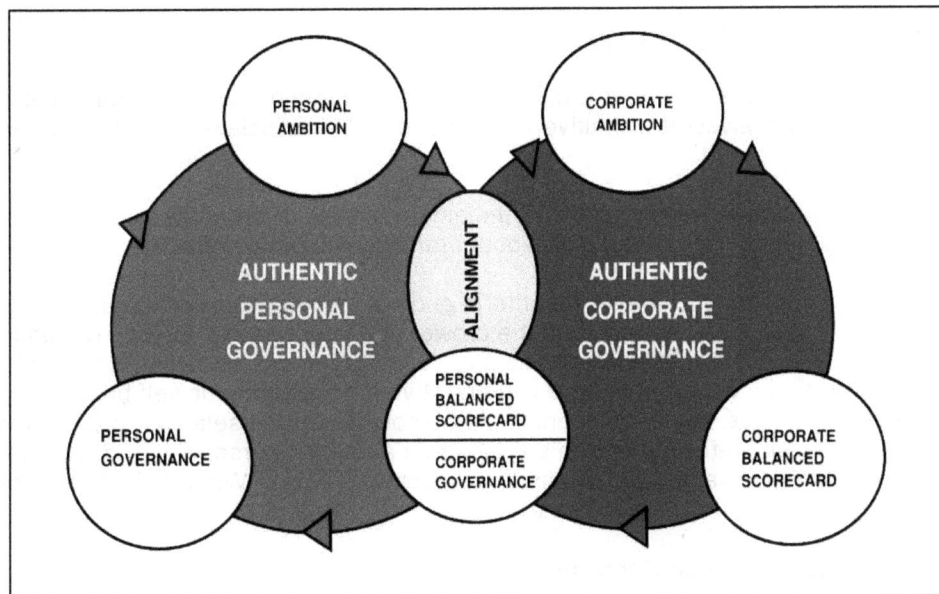

Figure 4-4

Aligning personal ambition with the corporate ambition has an impact on the organizational bonding of the employees. It energizes them and gives them the proud feeling that they count, that they are appreciated as human beings and that they make a useful and valuable contribution to the organization. Employees are stimulated in this way to commit, act ethically and focus on those activities that create value for clients. This will create a strong foundation of peace and stability upon which creativity and growth can flourish and life in the organization will become a harmonious experience.

The effective combination of all these four phases creates a stable basis for a high-performance and ethical organization. The authentic branding model gives us insight into both the way authentic branding can be developed effectively and the coherence between its different aspects. After the last phase is completed, the cycle is again followed in order to fine tune the elements with its surroundings on a continuous basis. By doing this you will constantly improve your personal performance, and continuously satisfy yourself and others on an ongoing basis. The organization will also constantly improve its performance and continuously add value to its clients.

Criteria for Authentic Personal Branding

Sustainable, authentic, consistent, and memorable personal branding is related to some important criteria:

1. Consistency; you need to be consistent in your behavior. This takes courage. Can others always depend and count on you? Are you doing relevant things again, and again, and again?

2. Specialization: focus on one area of specialization at a time. Be precise, concentrated on a single core talent or unique skill. Being a generalist without any specialized skills, abilities, or talents will not make you unique, special, and different in the near term – although this will be required later in more senior positions.

3. Authority; to be seen as a recognized expert in a certain field, extremely talented, highly experienced, and perceived as an effective leader.

4. Distinctiveness; distinguish yourself based on your brand. It needs to be expressed in a unique way that is different from the competition and needs to add value to others. It needs to be clearly defined that its audience can quickly grasp what it stands for.

5. Relevancy; what you stand for should connect to what your target audience considers to be important.

6. Visibility; it must be broadcast over and over again, continuously, consistently and repeatedly, until it's embedded in the minds of the audience. It's about repetition and long term exposure.

7. Persistence; your brand needs time to grow. It should be developed organically. You've got to stick with it, don't give up, believe in yourself, and be patient.

8. Goodwill; people do business with people they like. Your personal brand will produce better results and endure longer if you are perceived in a positive way. You must be associated with a value that is recognized as positive and worthwhile.

9. Performance; performance is the most important element after your brand has become known. If you don't perform, and improve yourself continuously, personal branding will not be effective.

When you are branded according to the above criteria and you commit yourself to act accordingly, your brand will be strong, you will distinguish yourself from the crowd, and your target audience will understand your brand much better. Building an authentic personal brand is a life management journey and an evolutionary and organic process. It starts with determining who you are at your core authentic self based on your dream, vision, mission, life philosophy, values, key roles, identity, self- knowledge, and self-awareness – rather than inventing a personal brand that doesn't reflect your true self. With an authentic personal brand, your strongest characteristics, attributes, and values can separate you from the crowd. Without this, you look like everyone else.

Wealth Generation and Financial Security

By the time individuals begin thinking about establishing their Personal Brand they have generally begun reflecting on who they are and what they hope to accomplish in their lives. For some, they may already been stimulated by thoughts of the level of income they are making, whether it is satisfactory at the current time of their lives, and if they want to equal or exceed that of those they see as competitors in achieving progress and respect. Once again, significant meaning in life may be attained by focusing primarily on the societal qualitative factors (personal, organizational, community, societal) without singular concern for personal wealth and financial security. And yet, without at least modest effort in this area one cannot assume sufficient income and wealth accumulation that will support them achieving all that they may hope to achieve.

The advantage of participating in the authentic personal and professional branding initiative in this Life Management Handbook is that its process blends the personal branding and the corporate (organization) branding initiatives to form a synthesis of ambition, branding, and balanced scorecard commitments toward integrated personal success and financial security (Figure 4-5). The required planning, documentation and execution of the project ensures a disciplined assessment of measurable progress. Setting wealth and financial security goals should be reviewed and action taken regularly.

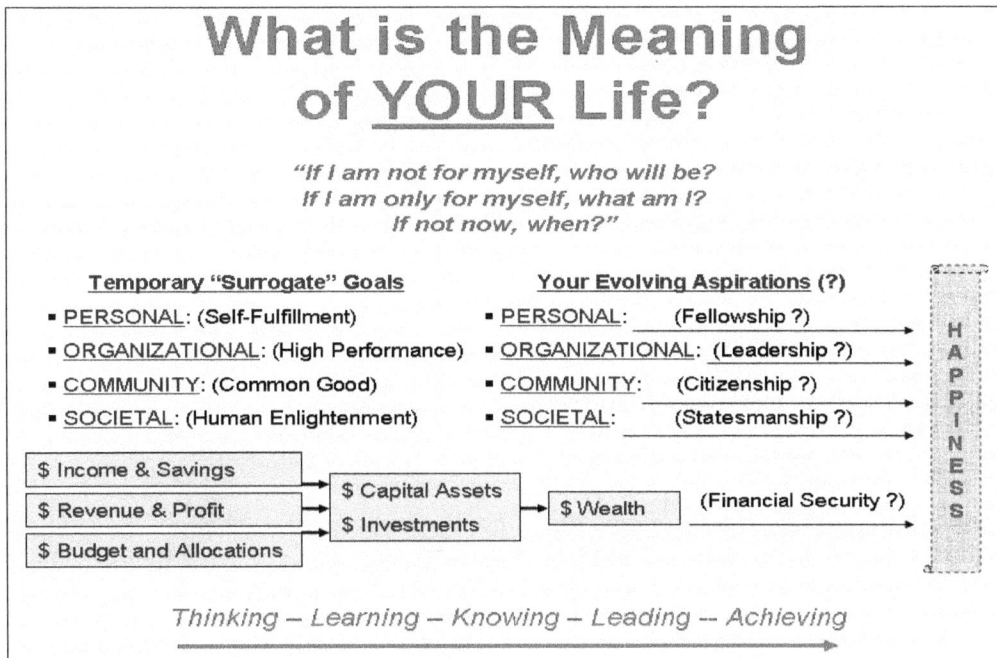

What is the Meaning of YOUR Life?

"If I am not for myself, who will be?
If I am only for myself, what am I?
If not now, when?"

Temporary "Surrogate" Goals	Your Evolving Aspirations (?)	
▪ PERSONAL: (Self-Fulfillment)	▪ PERSONAL: (Fellowship ?)	H
▪ ORGANIZATIONAL: (High Performance)	▪ ORGANIZATIONAL: (Leadership ?)	A
▪ COMMUNITY: (Common Good)	▪ COMMUNITY: (Citizenship ?)	P
▪ SOCIETAL: (Human Enlightenment)	▪ SOCIETAL: (Statesmanship ?)	P

$ Income & Savings
$ Revenue & Profit → $ Capital Assets
$ Budget and Allocations → $ Investments → $ Wealth   (Financial Security ?)   I N E S S

Thinking – Learning – Knowing – Leading -- Achieving

Figure 4-5

Questions on the Meaning of Your Life 79

How do these surrogate goals work for you right now? (Figure 4-5)

Can you venture a guess as to what might evolve as you continue to reflect and learn?

Do you recognize the importance of a *Wealth and Financial Perspective* when considering your potential financial security?

Implications for Integral Learning and Knowledge Management. The willingness and ability of people, organizations and communities to represent themselves as being authentic is based on the level of credibility they have accumulated in past and present encounters. To do so, they must have earned a reputation of being informed, open, honest and flexible in dealing with others in their family, business, community and marketplace. And, these characteristics are based, in part, on their intellectual, emotional and knowledgeable manner in conducting their relationships. Those who are multi-disciplinary and cross-trained in modern work practices and contemporary human relations are more valued and trusted by others. One's brand can be planned and improved by systematic reflection on who they are and how they want to be known.

Personal Reflection. This topic appears at the send of each chapter and is meant to serve two purposes: (a) be a reader's guide to main points and "takeaways," and (b) to encourage everyone to take a moment to engage their mental cognition and intuition on what the chapter means to them – especially at this time in their lives. Questions for chapter reflection follow immediately below; and for those readers inclined to maintain a self-assessment, your thoughts may be recorded in your *American Learnership for Life, Work, Wealth, Health and Legacy Success* which is located at Appendix B.

Questions for Discussion

1. What makes having an "authentic" personal brand a special accomplishment in today's social-economic environment?

2. Based on your experience, how common is it that a business or organization is able to accomplish an "authentic" relationship with their firm's own employees and customers?

3. Why is it likely that a firm committed to becoming authentically aligned and cohesive will become more efficient and effective in its operations?

Insights, Commitments and Skills

If you plan to participate in the *American Learnership for Life, Work, Wealth, Health and Legacy Success* self-development experience, it is suggested you record your Insights, commitments and skills to be developed here in this chapter and again in Appendix B.

My learning in terms of new insights, changing priorities, new commitments or skills I want to acquire:

1. Insights (Example): Remind myself that ...

2. Commitments (Example): Continue to ask myself ...

3. Skills (Example): Apply my knowledge and skills to ...

Conclusion

An example of a completed *Authentic Personal Brand book is included at Appendix C* as a detailed guide for you to accomplish personal growth and professional presence. Contact Dr. Garrity for assistance in writing your own *Authentic Personal and Professional Branding* e-book at rgarrity@alforum.org.

Once your Authentic Personal Brand has been established, your attention should turn to assisting your organization in establishing its own Authentic Corporate Brand. This is accomplished by corporate leaders collaborating in a procedure that reflects, learns and defines the organization's unique corporate ambition, corporate brand and corporate balanced scorecard. This topic is addressed more fully in Organization System Development (Chapter Eleven).

[**Author's Note**: Establishing both an Authentic Personal Brand and a Corporate Brand are functions critical in leading enterprise transformations, and are enabled by the next handbook sections on Reasoning Competencies and Social Systems Development.]

Section II

American Learnership:
Interdisciplinary Reasoning Competencies

Section II: This section on *American Learnership: Interdisciplinary Reasoning Competencies* describes the interrelatedness of five knowledge building skills that systematically enable meaningful thinking, learning, knowing, leading and achieving. These skills are *Systems Thinking*, *Pattern Recognition*, *Situational Learning*, *Knowledge Management*, and *Adaptive Leadership*. These competencies form an interdisciplinary and powerful methodology for driving social systems development.

Chapter Five

Reasoning Competency #1: Systems Thinking

Living effectively is best understood as living within a system-of-systems Decision making and problem solving that considers related system interdependencies almost certainly result in more complete solutions and fewer unintended consequences.

Major Chapter Topics

Reasoning Competency #1: Systems Thinking

Introduction to Systems Thinking

Systems Thinking. Systems thinking is the use of a systems perspective on social matters that illustrates the interdependency and mutual support among the personal, organizational, and community subsystems within which we learn, develop, and strive for success. The *systems thinking competency* helps us develop a broader, more integrated outlook, and to expand the contextual environment of our thoughts and decisions. The use of systems thinking inspires us to be integrative thinkers and discover opportunities to synthesize our learning for better understanding. *Systems Thinking (ST) and Pattern Recognition (PR) combine to assure more effective Situational Learning (SL).*

Blue Marble. Figure 5-1 (next page) is a picture of the earth from space – our own Blue Marble. Its purpose here is to significantly stretch our imagination and to lift us out of our own daily focus on ourselves and our material needs. From this vantage point, all the nations and people of the earth – whatever our differences in age, culture, race, nationality, etc. – are one.

System-of-Systems. The earth has been evolving over four thousand million years. Over that time, it has transformed itself, using electro-chemical means, from a totally inorganic array of chemical substances (basically water and rock) to become the organic garden of life we now know it to be. Originally, the earth was a relatively simple system, but it has developed into an extremely complex entity with millions of species of vegetation and animal life. And that life has formed and reformed not only itself but all manner of structures, tools, relationships and resources into streams of cause and effect activity. As humans evolved, they have learned-to-learn at an exponential rate and to use that learning to sustain themselves and their communities.

As we look carefully downward, we can see in our mind's eye the various physical, biological and social systems going about their respective life processes. On the physical level, we see the land changing in imperceptible ways as cycles of day and night systematically recur, and air and water temperatures change in nearly predictable patterns. Rivers flow to the sea, storms move through the sky, and earthquakes shake the land and mountains. On the biological (plant) level, we can observe the changing of the seasons with all the new life in the Spring, the growth and development in the Summer, the maturation in the Fall, and the death and/or hibernation in the Winter; followed by rebirth and/or renewal again in the Spring of the next year. On the biological (animal) level, we can see yearly cycles of growth and development and the increasing level of social interaction as each species pursues its respective life needs and motives. And for humankind, we observe continued development in the production and distribution of goods and services as communities and societies are formed to provide for the common good.

Global Commons. While it is in the nature of mankind for each individual and family to take primary responsibility for their own protection and sustenance, the vast majority of people have learned the social benefits that come from participation with others in matters of personal safety, economic production, and political representation. Wherever groups have formed into communities, states, and nations, we have understood our responsibility to care for resources and property in which there is a joint interest. At the community level, we might care for and share our parks; at the state level, we may have an interest in protecting our rivers and waterways; and at the national level, we might extend ourselves to implement controls on air polluting industries.

Whenever we take such interest and action, we are working to protect what we hold in common. So too, people and social groups at all levels have a responsibility to be stewards of the earth – this we hold in common for ourselves and posterity. We should always remember that we have a vested interest in the global commons: the rain forests in Brazil are equally as important to Americans as they are to Brazilians, and U.S. industrial plant carbon dioxide and air pollution can be inconsiderate behavior to other nations.

Ex-Body Objectivity. The reader should know at this juncture that organizing this book with the Blue Marble picture near the front has a dual purpose. Not only does this overarching view of the earth from outer space help us to appreciate the systems interdependency across all areas of our home planet, it also *challenges us as individual learners and leaders to occasionally step outside our prevailing mindset and take another, outside-in, more objective perspective* at the context within which many of our problems and decisions reside. Too often, the pressure of time or priority forces us to short change our thinking and to proceed with less than adequate information thereby failing our real or most important objective. We can do better. System thinking expands our understanding, develops our skills, and matures our reasoning.

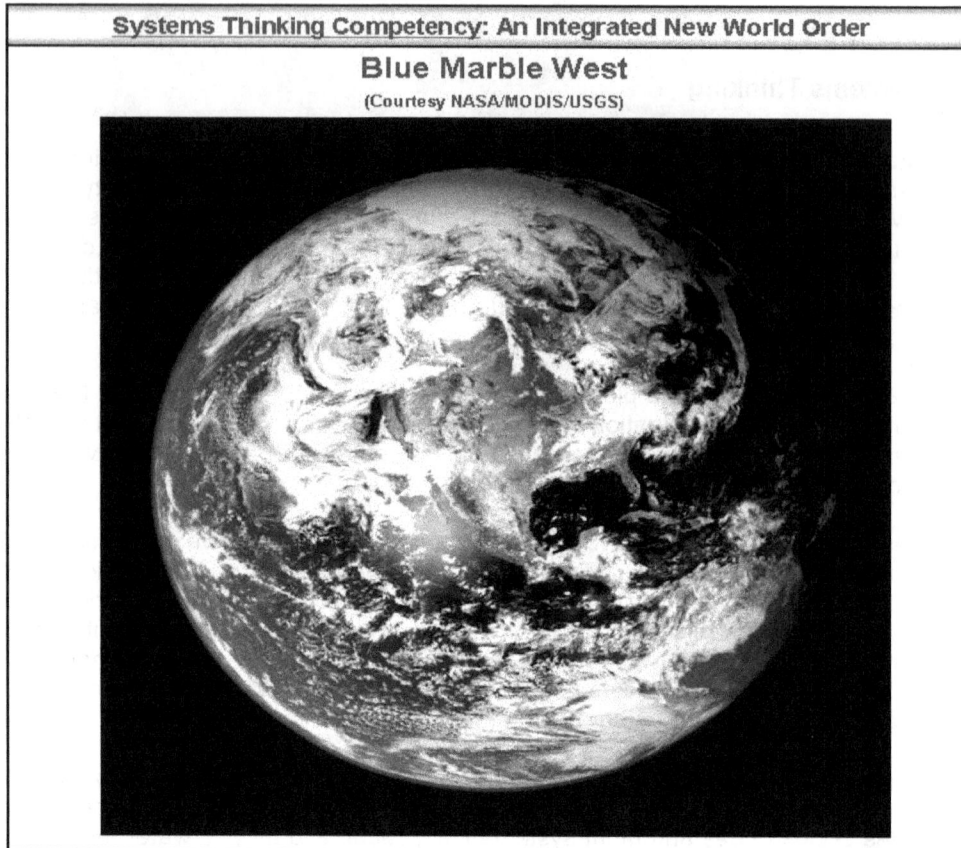

Figure 5-1

Flat New World. In his most recent book *The World is Flat: A Brief History of the Twenty-First Century* (2005), author Thomas L. Friedman brings new perspective on the worldwide, dynamic change that is engulfing us all. The following section contains extracts from what is surely to become a seminal commentary on U.S. international relations and responsibilities, and is herein viewed as a supportive corollary to the systems thinking theme of this section.

Friedman speaks of "globalization 3.0" in which a "triple convergence" of worldwide forces is already being experienced. The *first leg of the triple convergence* is a composite of his "ten flatteners," a series of technology and business-based innovations from the last decade that have broken through international boundaries and made all nations more interdependent and competitive. "The net results of this convergence was the creation of a global, Web-enabled playing field that allows for multiple forms of collaboration – the sharing of knowledge and work – in real time, without regard to geography, distance, or, in the near future, even language." (p.176) Major innovations he notes include: Worldwide Web, search engines, work flow software, open-sourcing, outsourcing, supply chaining, off-shoring, and others.

For the *second leg of the triple convergence*, Friedman says "But for the full effect we needed the emergence of a large cadre of managers, innovators, business consultants, business schools, designers, Information Technology (IT) specialists, CEOs, and workers to get comfortable with, and develop, the sorts of horizontal collaboration and value-creation processes and habits that could take advantage of the this new, flatter playing field. In short, the convergence of the ten flatteners begat the convergence of a set of business practices and skills that would get the most out of the flat world...We have gone from a vertical chain of command for value creation to a much more horizontal chain of command for value creation." (pp.178-179)

Lastly, for the *third leg of the triple convergence*, Friedman summarizes the explosion of people living in China, India, Japan, Russia, East Asia, and parts of Africa and Latin America that are now taking part in the global economy. He comments that "[It is] this triple convergence – of new players, on a new playing field, developing new process and habits for horizontal collaboration – that I believe is the most important force shaping global economics and politics in the twenty-first century. Giving so many people access to all these tools of collaboration, along with the ability through search engines and the Web to access billions of pages of raw information, ensures that the new generation of innovations will come from all over the Planet Flat. The scale of the global community that is soon going to be able to participate in all sorts of discovery and innovation is something the world has simply never seen before." (pp.181-182)

Learnership Universal Knowledge Spheres

The scope of Friedman's triple convergence, and the breadth and depth of the societal elements undergoing change provides us the opportunity to introduce the concept of learnership "knowledge spheres." Six knowledge spheres are presented to serve as a high level typology of interrelated societal topics and as a method for categorizing societal knowledge, relationships and activities. Definitions of these spheres along with comments from Friedman and others follow. Figure 5-2 (on the next page) is provided for reference and is an illustration of pervasive global connectivity and influence on the international stage.

Google and the internet make all data, information and knowledge available to all in over one hundred languages! This is your new brain, ready to be used for personal, organizational, community and societal growth and development.

Technological Knowledge Sphere. The technological knowledge sphere concerns the application of scientific methods and tools to societal activities. Emphasis here is on the study, development, and application of scientific methods and materials to achieve societal objectives. Major focus is on biotechnology, information technology, and materials technology.

Friedman and the writings of others contribute to a list of information technology innovations that depict the explosion of IT innovation over the last decade. Starting with a focus on networking, there is the huge expansion of the internet itself as a catalyst for web-based communications; improved communication transport protocols (e.g., HTML and XML); satellite and wireless communications; international fiber-optics as well as fiber optic to the desktop; encrypted communications protocols (SSLs); computer system identification certificates; and a significant increase in signal bandwidth to permit the transfer of very large files.

In the area of communication platforms, there is the worldwide increase in the quality and sophistication of PCs and laptops as well as other personal information tools such as cell phones, electronic games, palm pilots, and other PDAs. Applications such as MS Windows; search tools (e.g., Netscape and Internet Explorer); Virtual Private Networks (VPN); database management tools; instant messaging; digitalization and sharing of all previously hard to obtain information; and collaboration tools are proliferating. New work flow platforms, standard communications protocols, and huge free information stores (e.g., Wikipedia) are now available.

In the area of business process management, there are enterprise level applications for all types of support services; employee knowledge portals; e-business management tools; Radio Frequency Identification (RFID) microchips for physical in-process tracking; and horizontal workflow management tools. Additionally, there are virtual support tools that support open-sourcing, outsourcing, off-shoring, supply-chaining, in-sourcing, virtual production, Communities of Interests (COI), and personal in-forming (personal search techniques). The Internet and its associated technologies have become a distributed "global brain."

Culturally and politically, we continue to move closer to a global civilization and we continue to move from a bipolar toward a multi-polar world order.
— Yevgeny Primakov

The world has experienced considerable conflict and war during the last century. For the U.S., World Wars I and II, the Korean, Vietnam, and Persian Gulf I wars, and currently the U.S. wars with Afghanistan and Iraq, are significant. Also, Israel is in continual conflict with Lebanon, Syria, Egypt and Palestinians. Additionally, there has been the Serbian-Kosovo war, India-Pakistan war, and numerous conflicts among African states (Sudan, Somalia, Darfur, Ethiopia), and numerous other areas of continued intra-national hostility. These conflicts have been based on a variety of issues including political, economic, social, ethnic, religious, and national resource scarcities. But in every case, the cost has been large. In all these conflicts, the nations have committed huge sums of money, material and the lives of their citizens. Often, damage to the land as well as infrastructure has been notable.

The significance of this saga is that nations go to war as the result of strains in their international relationships and because of their economic and political deficiencies. Leaders and populations often strike out at those they perceive as their offenders. These extreme changes taking place (near chaos in some quarters) are sure to create new winners and losers in the world economy, thereby exacerbating current tensions. A flatter world is likely to create a preponderance of wealthy states, international businesses, and well- positioned billionaires that will be the cause for rebellion and conflict by those on the losing side. The unequal distribution of resources, talent, ambition and education could become untenable very quickly. Waves of immigration as currently being experienced in the U.S. and elsewhere will continue to burden some nations, while meliorating the tension and suffering in others.

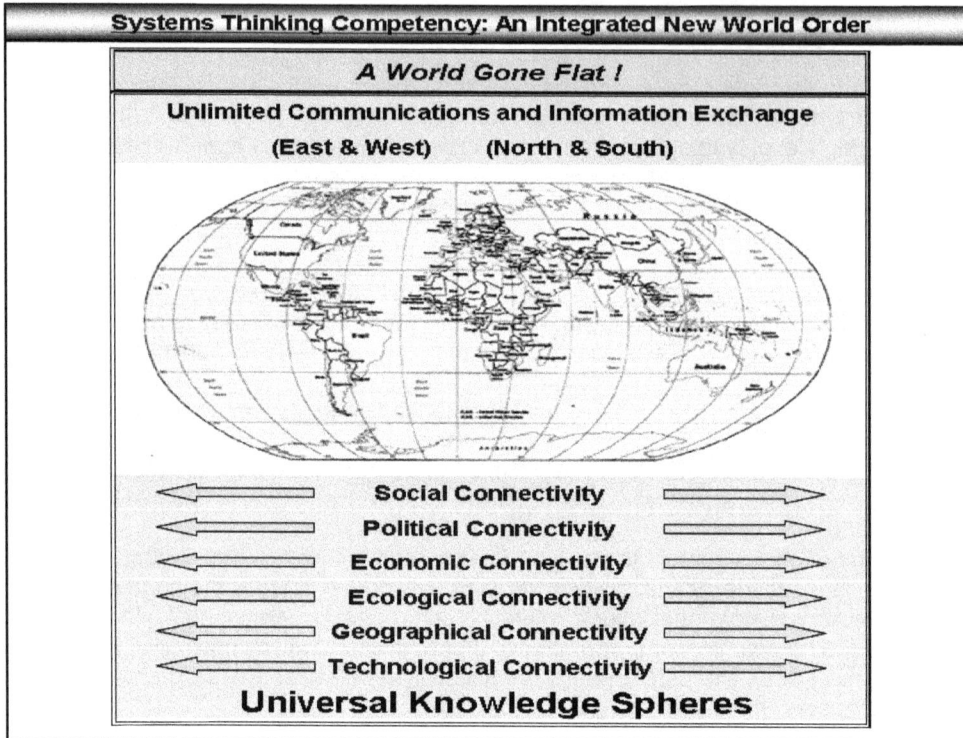

Figure 5-2

In terms of the management of physical and human resources, some nations are already far ahead in the game. The U.S., Japan, Australia, and much of Europe have productive economies, good natural resources and manageable populations. On the other hand, the billions of people in China and India as well as most people in Africa, Asia and some parts of South America survive on only a few dollars a day income. Often the land is barren and unproductive and the majority of the people have neither the knowledge nor education to move forward in increasingly competitive economies. Some will be helped by international businesses looking for cheap labor and resources, while most will continue to struggle. The elite in these nations will surely have the chance to survive and succeed, but the majority will not. The lesson here is that further inequality of education, ambition, knowledge, opportunity and income is likely as the earth churns with rapid political, economic and social change.

> *The emergence of a global economy and global society demands that we strengthen*
> *global governance. — Jack Straw, Former British Foreign Secretary*

Political Knowledge Sphere. The political knowledge sphere deals with the study, structure, or affairs of government, politics, or the state. Focus is on citizenship, governance, foreign policy, political and cultural choices, and national defense. Friedman and others express serious concern on the ability of the international community of nations to manage the period of change and chaos that has begun. Three major factors in play include: (1) the fall of communism in Europe and the end of the cold war – but, with the continued mixture of socialistic, democratic, autocratic, totalitarian and theocratic regimes conspiring for power and money regardless of the implicit social and international impact; (2) the rapid emergence of "political Islam" that threatens both Eastern and Western countries; and (3) the criminal conspiracies (e.g., international trade in drugs and human beings) being bred in many socially and economically deprived nations. The battle for national sovereignty and competitive international positioning will continue, but with the additional trend in which vertical politics and influence are challenged by economically-based horizontal shifts toward greater worldwide collaboration and production.

It is apparent that significant international responsibilities and issues are in need of United Nations leadership – but that is not likely to occur due to that organization's poor performance as the arbiter of conflict. The bottom line is that international political alliances may be coming apart as fast as new ones are established – a time of great uncertainty. Friedman suggests the time may be right for a new party system in the U.S. in which there would be a WALL party and a WEB party. The WaLL Party would focus on slowing down unacceptable change and globalization while the WEB Party would emphasize the exploitation of opportunities for outside/external contact and development.

The central challenge we face today is to ensure that globalization becomes a
positive force for al the world's people instead of leaving billions behind in squalor.
-- Former UN Secretary-General, Kofi Annan

Economic Knowledge Sphere. The economic knowledge sphere concerns the production, development and management of income and wealth. Focus is on the production and distribution of goods and services. Primary emphasis is on business management, financial management, and social systems economic development.

Friedman introduces his readers to David Ricardo (1772-1823) and his contribution to free trade and international exchange. Most notably, Ricardo's Theory of Competitive Cost Advantage which applies in international trade between nations is mentioned. His view was that nations should specialize in what they do best to drive down per unit costs of goods and services – and they should then trade with others for products that others can provide more cost efficiently. This supposedly benefits all nations that participate. However, that was before knowledge jobs were predominant and before pervasive worldwide communications and Web-based horizontal work processes allowed the inequitable distribution of efficiency that comes from the dispersal of knowledge, labor, and capital. The global partitions based upon national boundaries, languages, and monetary systems have been breached. We are coming to near free-fall wherein countries can race to the bottom cost-wise thereby reducing the average wage and economic well- being of most people – or, we can continue to strive for greater innovation and a larger economic "pie" in accordance with the belief of those who believe that humans have an unlimited desire for more and more products and services. At some macro-level, the planet's "carrying power" will need to be considered in either scenario.

Friedman also raises the issue of business' relentless attempt to eliminate sources of friction and inefficiency: "From the first stirrings of capitalism, people have imagined the possibility of the world as the perfect market – unimpeded by protectionist pressures, disparate legal systems, cultural and linguistic differences, or ideological disagreement." But, "some of these inefficiencies are institutions, habits, culture, and traditions that people cherish precisely because they reflect non-market values like social cohesion, religious faith, and national pride." (p.204) We can say with some certainty that investors in business do not care where or how profit is made on their capital investment – unless it impacts their own jobs, families, or community. How do politicians and other leaders decide what to do? It appears that we want Wal-Mart jobs and prices but we do not want Wal-Mart workers being a burden on our health and welfare system.

The global competitive playing field has flattened. Wage rates are changing significantly as businesses shop the world for the lowest resource costs. China and India have wage rates less than one-sixth of that in the U.S. for people with the same skill level. Japan outsources its lower value work to China as they strive to reserve higher value tasks for themselves. Friedman comments: "We don't know anymore where companies start and stop. Capitalists can sit back, buy up innovation, and then hire the best, cheapest labor input from anywhere in the world to research it, develop it, and distribute it." (p.209)

It ain't what you don't know that gets you into trouble. It's what you know
for sure that just ain't so. -- Mark Twain, Humorist/Author

Social Knowledge Sphere. The social knowledge sphere addresses the associations and living arrangements among individuals and groups in society. Focus is on the dynamics of social activity among individuals, organizations and institutions. Major emphasis is on education, learning, culture, human relations, interpersonal communication and media. Friedman and others predict continued and increased: economic, political, and social inequality; explosion of population and disease in poorer countries threatening to spread to advanced nations; media and popular culture expansion; cross-social boundary and culture communications; creation of "intelligence commons" for sharing information and knowledge; thousands of self-organizing communities of interest and the cross pollination of cultures and religions; and the establishment of "virtual modules" of trusted knowledge and experience that selected individuals and organizations can use in the pursuit of their personal objectives. In short, increased international integration is a certainty but with the probable downside that the disparity between the "haves" and "have-nots" will become even more pronounced due to the current spate of technological and economic innovations.

*The history of life on earth has been a history of interaction between living things
and their surroundings…Only within the moment of time represented by the present
century has one species acquired significant power to alter the nature of the world.*
-- Rachael Carson, Silent Spring

Ecological Knowledge Sphere. The ecological knowledge sphere concerns the relationships between organisms, their environments and the goal of sustainable habitats. Emphasis is on the life processes and characteristic phenomena of living organisms. Focus is on bio-system management, energy production, population and demographics, and the availability of food and health services.

In April 2007, the Intergovernmental Panel on Climate Change (IPCC) entitled "Climate Change 2007: Climate Change Impacts, Adaptation and Vulnerability" issued its Fourth Assessment Report saying that: (1) many natural systems are being affected by regional climate changes, particularly temperature increase, (2) warming has had a discernable influence on many physical and biological systems, and (3) other effects of regional climate changes on natural and human environments are emerging. Evidence provided includes: changes in the Arctic and Antarctic ecosystems; increasing instability of permafrost regions; warming of lake and rivers; shifts in plants and animal species; longer growing seasons – all of which are attributable to the increase in greenhouse gas concentrations and a rise in average global temperatures since the mid-20th century. And, they admonish that this occurrence is very unlikely to be to be due to natural variability in earth systems.

Future impacts from the same report include: (1) up to a 40% increase in average annual river runoff in high elevations concurrent with a decrease of up to 30% in an area already too dry; (2) reduced rain water where approximately one sixth of the world's people already live; (3) 20 to 30% of plant and animal species are in danger of extinction; (4) increasing acidification of oceans due to increasing atmospheric carbon dioxide; (5) decreases in crop productivity due to droughts and floods; (6) wholesale destruction of fish species due to warmer water; (7) increased glacier melting and ocean levels, coastal hurricanes and flooding; (8) devastation of poorer unprotected communities; (9) increased human death and social costs; (10) higher concentrations of ground level ozone; (11) increases in malnutrition, disease and death; (12) significant disturbances from pests, diseases and fire; and (13) a huge amount of coral bleaching and death to ocean species.

In his book *An Inconvenient Truth: The Planetary Emergency of Global Warming and What We Can Do About It* (2007), Al Gore makes the case for action by presenting data showing two major points. First, the earth's atmosphere is quite thin meaning that we are able to change its composition, and second that there has been an extraordinary and increasing, level of carbon dioxide in the global atmosphere in just the last few decades. The critical point is that average global temperature follows these increases very closely meaning that without an immediate effort to reduce carbon dioxide, the world's temperature will shortly rise a few degrees causing the aforementioned global warming, glacier melt, property and human losses like we have never seen before. The essential point here is that most of this problem is man-made; the whole planet is affected; the U.S. is the major contributor to the problem (but the Chinese and others with growing economies will contribute their share of the problem as they become more industrialized); our vulnerability can be mitigated and reduced; but we have to take action on the personal, organizational, community, and national level beginning now.

[**Author's Note**: The reader should appreciate that the book's developing undertone concerning Total Knowledge Management (TKM) is that TKM is possible when learning, knowing, and leading are being performed concurrently in both the six knowledge spheres and the four learnership social systems.]

Learnership Social Systems

Now that the six learnership knowledge spheres have been defined and described, it is important to note that in this book these spheres are viewed as having a support or contextual role in relationship to the "learnership social system" itself, which is part of the core content in the learnership architecture. The learnership social system is a dynamic, meta-system worldview that accounts for multiple social system levels of human goal-setting, development and accomplishment. The subsystems of the societal meta-system are the personal, organizational, community, and societal systems for which an optimal level of maturity and social achievement is desired. These systems are herein defined and described

Personal (Micro) Systems Development (PSD). PSD is social synthesis at the micro-cognitive level, and is the starting point for managing the quality of our lives at the personal, family and associates subsystem level. Our learnership *reasoning competencies* are focused on continuous improvement of our primary PSD domain elements: *our health, our character* and *our ability*. The universal goal selected for the personal level is *self-fulfilment*, and the key role for us to play is *fellowship*.

*I am inclined to attribute my good health, and that of my family, primarily to our
outlook on life, and to our philosophical approach to other people and to ourselves.*
— Harry Truman, 33rd U.S. President

Organizational (Macro) Systems Development (OSD). OSD is social synthesis at the macro-cognitive level, and uses recognized benchmarks for achieving highly efficient and effective organizational performance. Our learnership *reasoning competencies* are applied to the organizational domain elements selected for intense management focus: the organization's *direction*, *operations* and *performance*. The universal goal selected for organizational accomplishment is *high performance*, and the key role for us to play is *leadership*.

*America has become a society owned by corporations and a political system
dominated by corporate and special interests, and directed by the elites who are hostile –
or at best indifferent – to the interests of working men and women in the middle class
and their families.* — Lou Dobbs, Financial Commentator

Community (Mega) System Developments (CSD). CSD is social synthesis at the mega-cognitive level, and is conceived as the pathway for building a rewarding community life. Our learnership *reasoning competencies* at this level are applied to the community domain elements under development: the institutions of *government*, *education* and *business*. The universal goal selected for community accomplishment is termed the *common good*, and the key role for us to play is *citizenship*.

*We will do collectively, through our government, only those things we cannot do well
or at all individually and privately.* — Abraham Lincoln, 16th U.S. President

Societal (Meta) Systems Development (SSD). SSD is social synthesis at the meta-cognitive level, and consists of fully integrating our learnership *reasoning competencies* across all four levels of social synthesis. The universal goal selected for societal level accomplishment is *human enlightenment*, and the key role for us to play is *statesmanship*.

*The challenge, then, is to make sure that U.S. policies move the international system in the direction
of greater equity, justice and prosperity – that the rules we promote serve both our interests and
the interests of a struggling world.* — Barack Obama, 44th U.S. President

[**Author's Note**: This overview of the learnership *universal knowledge spheres* and *social systems* is noteworthy because when coupled with the learnership competencies previously described we have all the major components of the learnership process model. And as mentioned earlier, this model is also a depiction of a universal, Total Knowledge Management framework.]

Application of Systems Thinking

Open-System Dynamics. An essential capability in systems thinking is being able to visualize the myriad and interdependent factors and forces that could or should be considered in decision making or problem solving. Learning to ask the right questions – and having the courage to bring attention to those questions – when scoping the level of inquiry is often more challenging than coming up with an acceptable answer. Time available, issue priority, personnel involved, and cost impact are some of the risk management factors that need to be weighed and evaluated.

Whether the decision or problem exists within a closed or open system environment is another important consideration in framing our thinking and deriving well-reasoned solutions. If the choice is a closed system model the tendency is to de-scope the problem space, limit the number of variables, and use a zero-sum approach in evaluating the availability of solution aids and resources. When time is of the essence and situational complexity is minimal, adequate, albeit incremental solutions are often successfully achieved. All too often, however, this rapid and simplified approach becomes a standard and uniform practice which prevents individuals, organizations, and other social entities from becoming more knowledgeable, innovative and successful.

On the other hand, a more dynamic open system environment is chosen for framing thinking and conducting reasoned inquiry. This is the appropriate methodology when many factions and interests demand inclusion, complexity cannot be avoided, longer-term solutions are required, and the risks and costs of error are significant. In this situation, it is more productive to envision that sources of energy and resources currently outside the problem domain could be brought to bear on the issue, thereby expanding the range and depth of factors that may be used in achieving a holistic solution.

The learnership systems thinking reasoning competency is expressly designed to encourage greater use of open systems thinking. The exercises that follow are designed to demonstrate high level open systems thinking, and Figure

5-3 which illustrates the relationships among the learnership knowledge spheres and learnership social systems is provided as a reference tool.

Situation #1 – Illegal Immigration into the U.S. from and through Mexico:

Initial Impacts – Estimate is that there are at least 12 million illegal immigrants in the U.S. as of 2006 and many more are on the way. The vast majority is mostly welcomed by low skill level U.S. businesses to cut their operating costs and by low cost retail businesses to sell them services *(economic, organizational system, commerce)*; the U.S. borders are being illegally crossed *(territorial, political, social)*; many immigrants are being abused and exploited *(unanticipated consequences)*; most have minimal education, do not have IT skills, do not speak English *(economic, social, technological, knowledge limits)*; many politicians look to get the immigrant votes *(political)*; many U.S. communities have high concentrations of immigrants looking for housing, work and free education and medical care *(community system, social system, organizational system, tipping points, culture shifts, more unintended consequences)*; higher levels of gang activity, drug violations, petty crime *(economic, political, community system)*; tendency to have large families in the U.S. or on the way here, high birth rates due to religious views with children automatically becoming U.S. citizens *(feed forward effects, political, economic, social)*; inability of U.S. Congress, White House, and law enforcement entities to establish appropriate policies, enforce laws, solve crime in many affected communities *(uncertainty, chaos, feedback effects)*.

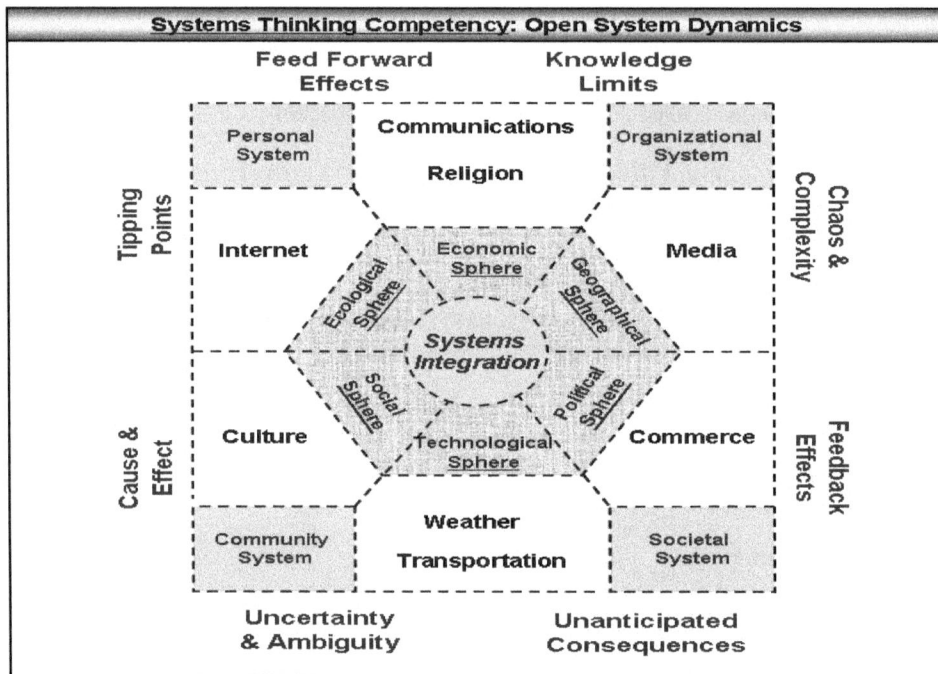

Figure 5-3

Comment – This is a multi-billion dollar a year problem that is steadily getting worse. While recognizing the human needs and aspirations of the immigrants themselves, this problem involves illegal and criminal behavior; huge economic costs to U.S. citizens; dubious political game-playing; corporate deception and tax evasion; and a myriad of social and cultural impacts involving all the learnership knowledge spheres and social systems.

The Solution – What would you do? What should be addressed, what should not, and how? Which issues and interest groups have priority? What open system insights might be appropriate? Can we learn to reason more fully and take mature action? The answer is certainly: "yes we can by using systems thinking."

Situation # 2 – Global warming and the U.S. responsibility to the international community:

Initial Impacts – Global warming and its derivative problems are caused in large part by the huge increase in carbon dioxide formation in industrial areas of the planet (ecological, economic, commerce, organizational systems, cause and effect); major studies and regional treaties place most of the responsibility for finding solutions on the leading industrialized nations and those rapidly modernizing nations with huge populations (economic, territorial, political, commerce, community and societal systems, tipping points); global weather patterns will change for the worse, fresh water flowing into the sea along with higher temperatures will kill hundreds of species and decrease organic sea life, deserts will become dryer while wet areas get wetter (economic, social, political, territorial, ecological, tipping points, chaos, knowledge limits); seas will rise flooding major cities worldwide, killing people, causing chaos and crime, costing billions, bankrupting insurance companies and financial institutions (economic, political, social, ecological, technological, unanticipated effects, feed forward effects, cultural disruption); transportation systems, petroleum refineries and petroleum-based fuels, and gas and electric production facilities are large greenhouse gas contributors and polluters (technological, economic, ecological, commerce, weather, feed forward effects); nations and regions across the globe are seeking cost-effective solutions without disrupting their own economic development or political influence (political, social, technological, economic, organizations, communities, uncertainty, feedback effects).

Comment – Within the next 50 years, the loss of life and cultural ties; disruption of plans and investments; elimination of thousands of plant and animal species; destruction of industrial and commercial facilities; international debates, arguments and threats; lack of stability in family life and careers; and general turmoil and anxiety could significantly reorder the economic, political, an social priorities of many nations and their citizenry. Some would say the issue here is overstated and that the planet is always going through change – and that we can and will incrementally adjust. Others would say we are late in recognizing this tremendous, negative impact on our nations and societies – we must immediately adopt risk mitigation strategies so as to minimize the disruption and damage to our common good and well-being.

The Solution – Similar to Situation #1 above, what are the facts; who should own which aspects of this problem; who will lead; who will pay; and how and when will we take action? There are dozens of "wicked problems" that can and should be addressed in the interests of the development and advancement of communities, nations and societies. In all cases, however, the recurring need is for greater systems thinking by those responsible for studying, advocating, leading and adapting to necessary change.

A Change of Perspective. Peter Senge, author of *The Fifth Discipline* (1990), comments that: "Today, systems thinking is needed more than ever because we are becoming overwhelmed by complexity. Perhaps for the first time in history, humankind has the capacity to create far more information than anyone can absorb, to foster far greater interdependency than anyone can manage, and to accelerate change far faster than anyone's ability to keep pace." The result is that: "Complexity can easily undermine confidence and responsibility…Systems thinking is the antidote to this sense of helplessness that many feel as we enter the age of interdependence." (p.69)

Systems Thinking about the Future

Another approach to systems thinking is to relate to subjects or issues in terms of chronological time (Past, Present Future). From a learning and knowledge standpoint, it should be easier to comprehend and discern what is useful if we focus on what has happened in the past. And, if we then add what we know to be accurate or true in the present, we should understand more thoroughly the full meaning of the subject or issue under consideration. An interesting question arises when discussion continues toward potential trends and future outcomes – how can the future be known when it has yet to happen? What evidence would be available? Still, isn't the movement of time defined in relation to the historical compounding effect of ongoing cause and effect of thousands of decisions and activities previously taken?

The art and science of "futuring" has rapidly proven its value over the last few decades. Futuring uses a process of scenario building (proposing alternative results based on current trends) and decision analysis (choosing among available alternatives using standard practices) to suggest what is more likely to change or happen in the future. This work is actively pursued around the world as individuals, organizations and even nations attempt to avoid problems and create opportunities through better prediction of trends and outcomes. On the international scene, one of the largest organizations that encourages and trains people in the futuring methodology is the World Future Society (www.wfs.org). Figure 5-4 is a snap shot of the Futures Magazine along with a taxonomy of major learning and knowledge categories the Society uses to provide a comprehensive overview of its domains: science/ technology, earth, governance, humanity, commerce, and futuring. Some examples of articles currently being shared are included.

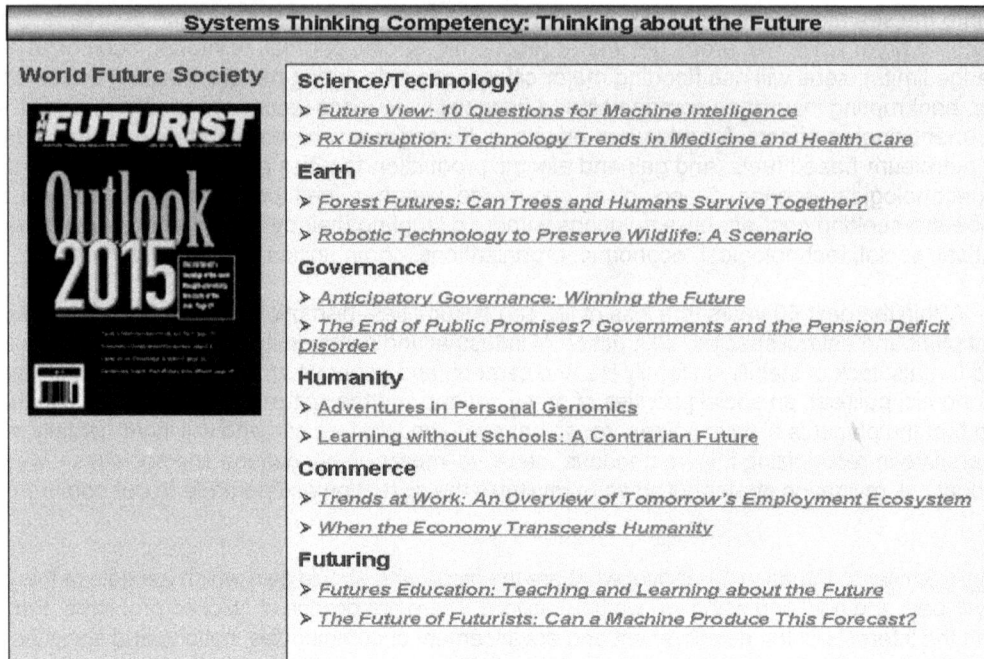

Systems Thinking Competency: Thinking about the Future	
World Future Society **THE FUTURIST** **Outlook 2015**	**Science/Technology** ➤ *Future View: 10 Questions for Machine Intelligence* ➤ *Rx Disruption: Technology Trends in Medicine and Health Care* **Earth** ➤ *Forest Futures: Can Trees and Humans Survive Together?* ➤ *Robotic Technology to Preserve Wildlife: A Scenario* **Governance** ➤ *Anticipatory Governance: Winning the Future* ➤ *The End of Public Promises? Governments and the Pension Deficit Disorder* **Humanity** ➤ *Adventures in Personal Genomics* ➤ *Learning without Schools: A Contrarian Future* **Commerce** ➤ *Trends at Work: An Overview of Tomorrow's Employment Ecosystem* ➤ *When the Economy Transcends Humanity* **Futuring** ➤ *Futures Education: Teaching and Learning about the Future* ➤ *The Future of Futurists: Can a Machine Produce This Forecast?*

Figure 5-4

[**Author's Note 1**: The World Futures Society, at an earlier stage of its development, employed a taxonomy that became the basis for the early research and writing of this book's author. Those context setting domains were and still are the social, political, economic, technological, ecological and geographical aspect of world human social development.]

[**Author's Note 2**: For purposes of the personal and professional development advocacy of this handbook, system thinking involves dutiful attention to the work of futurists as they research, propose, discuss and select future trends and likely outcomes. This work across the personal, organizational, community and societal domains – and then integrated into holistic perspectives of the future serve to stretch human thinking, learning, knowing, leading and achieving so that human prosperity can be systematic and intelligent as well as efficient and effective.]

Conclusion

Acquire new knowledge whilst thinking over old,
and you may become a teacher of others. — Confucius

Systems Thinking Competency: A Conscious Evolution? Barbara Marx Hubbard is a noted futurist whose extraordinary capacity for understanding the past-present-future continuum of human experience is reflected in her lectures and writings. The following excerpts from The Futurist Magazine interview with her entitled "Conscious Evolution: Examining Humanity's Next Step" (The Futurist, Sep-Oct 1993) are presented for the reader's contemplation.

1. On Societal Change – "Humanity is now learning the process of evolution and becoming consciously responsible for it…I believe that we as individuals are becoming part of a larger whole, both through our consciousness and through our electronic connections. Rather than it just being an individual or saint, it will be in a collective capacity, both technologically and spiritually. Traditionally, nature evolves through the formation of larger whole-systems – from atom to molecule to cell to humans, and now through Planet Earth to one interacting system. As the whole-system matures, its parts exercise synergy and become greater than they were when separated." (p.38)

2. Conscious Evolution Defined – "The capacity to be aware of the process of evolution and to guide that process for the good of all Earth life. Conscious evolution is based on three new conditions. One (1) is the new *cosmology*. Only recently have we learned that the universe had a beginning (the Big Bang), has a history, and is evolving now. Two (2) is our *new crises*. Never before has a species had the power to destroy the world. Three (3) is our *new capacities*. These capacities, social, scientific, and spiritual, indicate that we can transform the world – through deliberate intervention." (p.39)

3. <u>Fostering Conscious Evolution</u> – "We need images of social wellness to attract us forward. We need a mass media to communicate our evolutionary potentials. We need radical education at all levels in self-esteem, cooperation, and self-actualization. We need an expanded 'Earth-space human development process;' with the goal of restoring this Earth, emancipating human creativity, and exploring the universe." (p.41)

Implications for Integral Learning and Knowledge Management. Working in a complex world and a competitive marketplace tends to cause leaders and employees alike to reduce the scope of their thinking and attention in an attempt to become more efficient in accomplishing their life and employment responsibilities. Better, cheaper, faster can sometimes seem like an oxymoron; especially when "time is of the essence" or "the customer is on the phone." If we really learned from our not-so-positive experiences, why are we doing things over again so often? Part of the reason is that projects, problems, and workflow issues are being handled with minimal attention to the larger context, longer timeframe, or increasing risks associated with the status quo. Failure to take the time to observe, reflect, and consider all influential factors is the basis for attempting to solve the wrong problems and wasting time and resources on ill-conceived solutions. Effective knowledge management requires decision-making and problem-solving based on timely, accurate, and relevant information. Leaving out that which is relevant due to an unwillingness to pursue a larger, systems thinking approach is not wise personally or organizationally.

Systems thinking is an essential part of knowledge management, and is particularly important in that the six Universal Knowledge Spheres described in this chapter are essential elements in the construction of the Learnership Integrated Systems Architecture (LISA); and are contributing elements in building an Integral Knowledge Management (IKM) capability.

Personal Reflection. This topic appears at the end of each chapter and is meant to serve two purposes: (1) be a reader's guide to main points and "takeaways," and (2) to encourage everyone to take a moment to engage their mental cognition and intuition on what the chapter means to them – especially at this time in their lives. Questions for chapter reflection follow immediately below; and for those readers inclined to maintain a self-assessment, your thoughts may be recorded in the American Learnership for Life, Work, Wealth, Health and Legacy Success located at Appendix B.

Questions for Discussion:

1. Have you been able to experience some aspect of what Thomas Friedman calls the flat new world in your own life and career? Please explain.

2. Which of the universal knowledge spheres do you believe has the greatest likelihood of damage to the U.S. National interest in terms of worldwide acceptance of U.S. world leadership? Please explain.

3. Can you list two to three major learning points from this chapter that you want to keep in mind to improve your ability to manage your life and career?

4. What do you think the impact of this chapter's information might be on the personal, organizational, community, and/or societal systems to be discussed later in the book?

5. Can you identify two to three topics, models, or perspectives in this chapter you would like to learn more about?

6. Should you make an entry into your *American Learnership for Life, Work, Wealth, Health and Legacy Success* at Appendix B?

Insights, Commitments and Skills

If you plan to participate in the *American Learnership for Life, Work, Wealth, Health and Legacy Success* self-development e-book experience, it is suggested you record your Insights, commitments and skills to be developed in this chapter, and again in Appendix B:

My learning in terms of new insights, changing priorities, new commitments or skills I want to acquire:

1. Insights (Example): Remind myself that ...

2. Commitments (Example): Continue to ask myself ...

3. Skills (Example): Apply my knowledge and skills to ...

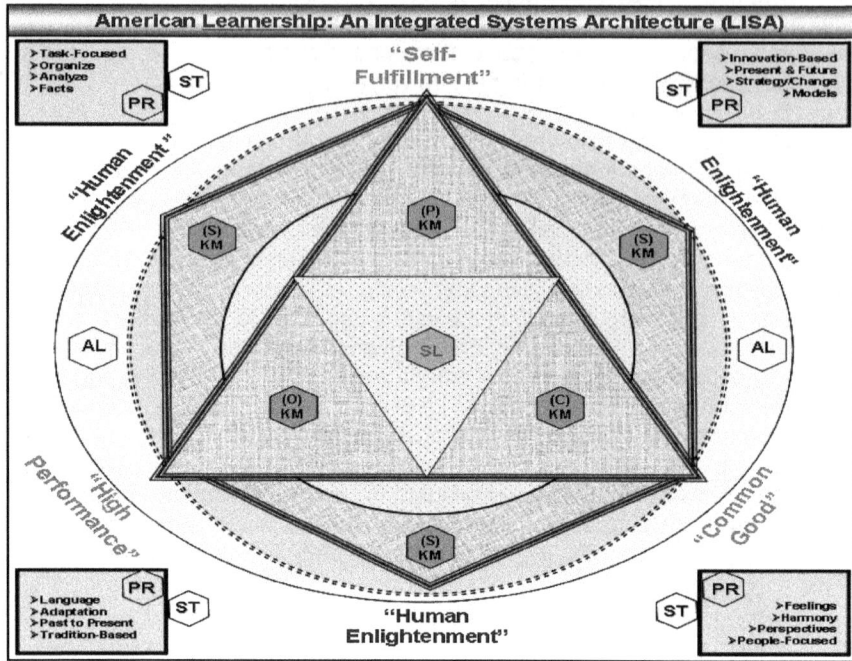

American Learnership: An Integrated Systems Architecture (LISA)

Chapter Six

Reasoning Competency #2: Pattern Recognition

Pattern making is a foundational brain function for creating human memory. The relationships, models and methodologies we comprehend and record precondition our understanding of everything we subsequently experience – positively or negatively.

Major Chapter Topics

Reasoning Competency #2: Pattern Recognition

Introduction to Pattern Recognition

Pattern Recognition. A pattern can be broadly defined as an archetype, a schema, a model, a script, a symbol, an ideal worthy of respect, a representative sample of something, or a composite of traits or features characteristic of individuals. All biological life forms develop and exhibit their structural patterns; and the social development of humankind is inextricably anchored to the patterns recorded in our minds and our use of them as revealed in our behavior.

The cultural expectations, established methodologies, and accepted practices that form our human experience and interpersonal and organizational relationships are the artifacts of learned values, beliefs, knowledge, skills, and inherited potentials programmed into our computer-like minds by our previous learning and experience. Unlike the *system thinking competency* in the last chapter used by the learnership practitioner to accomplish *integrated thinking and synthesis*, the use of the *pattern recognition competency* in this chapter emphasizes the need for *differentiated thinking and analysis*. This focus enables the learnership practitioner to be both cognizant of the intent and potential impact of others' attitudes and behavior, and to critically assess the contextual framing of social dialogue and situations. These are necessary skills in maintaining organizational dialogue and accomplishing situational learning.

Pattern Recognition (PR) combines with Systems Thinking (ST) to ensure more effective Situational Learning (SL). This chapter concentrates on helping learnership practitioners to understand and appreciate the human brain's amazing information processing, knowledge creating, and data storage capability – and what that means for personal effectiveness. Topics emphasized include understanding how:

1. The brain functions as an information processing and learning system

2. Brains are programmed (by patterns)

3. Brain programming leads to personal and group preferences (based on patterns)

4. Preferences lead to communication and behavioral styles (patterns again) that influence the context of social dialogue and relationships

5. We can further develop our cognitive skills and reasoning

6. We can learn-to-learn throughout our lives well into old age

7. We can recognize and use this pattern knowledge for better management of our social systems and achievement of our personal goals.

The section that follows presents an overview of human brain functionality through the eyes of three recognized experts – Elkhonon Goldberg, Matt Ridley, and Leslie Hart – each with their own unique research, experience, and perspective.

The first set of excerpts is from Elkhonon Goldberg, author of *The Wisdom Paradox: How Your Mind Can Grow Stronger as Your Brain Grows Older* (2005). The selections here provide insight on brain pattern making, language and cultural patterns in generic memory, competence and wisdom, and higher order executive functions in the brain's frontal lobes.

1. <u>Language and Culture</u> – Goldberg anchors the thesis of his book when he says that *language and culture are patterns* that are the basis for passing information and knowledge between succeeding generations: "What sets us apart as humans is the powerful capacity for transmitting the repertoire of these patterns from individual to individual and from generation to generation...Access to this knowledge automatically empowers the cognition of every member of human society by making it privy to society's cumulative, collective wisdom." He continues by referring to language as an important foundation that helps us categorize our experiences: "Language also shapes our cognition by imposing certain patterns on the world...By learning the use and meaning of words as children we acquire more than a communication tool. We also acquire taxonomy, a way of categorizing the virtual infinity of things, events, and impressions that *is* the world." (pp. 88-89)

Goldberg takes the opportunity to *challenge earlier modular theories* of brain functioning by stating that: "…contrary to some earlier assumptions, language does not sit neatly in one particular 'language-dedicated' part of the brain. Instead, various aspects of language are distributed throughout the neocortext by attaching themselves to different cortical regions, each in charge of representing certain aspects of physical reality." (p.95) His "distributed across the neocortext theory" is also described as overlapping neural networks processing elsewhere in his book.

2. Information Processing and Learning – According to Goldberg, "The brain comes pre-wired for certain kinds of pattern recognition but not for others…the more complex cortical regions, the so-called associative cortex, have relatively little pre-wired knowledge…their processing power is accomplished by the ability to forge their own 'software' as required by their survival needs in an increasingly complex and unpredictable outside world…the pattern recognition capability of these most advanced regions of the cortex is called 'emergent,' because it truly emerges in the brain, which is very complex but also very open-minded." (pp.104-105)

Noteworthy here is the proposed *self-organization capability of the brain* due to its being pre-wiring by *nature* in preparation for inputs from the external environment or *nurture*. Goldberg comments that: "…evolution carved out in the brain design a space for a tabula rasa, but one powered by an exquisite neural capacity for processing complexity of any kind and filling itself with any content." (p.105) Filling with content is accomplished because of the neural network's *attractor* capability, that is, "An attractor is a network, a group of closely connected neurons with a stable pattern of activity in the absence of direct stimulation from the outside…and this means the same attractor will be activated in its entirety, as a whole by activating any number of its various components." (p.144) Neural attractors seek and integrate appropriate information into their networks.

3. Generic Versus Singular Memory – These two kinds of memory are both distributed and stored primarily in the hemispheres of the neocortext. Singular memory works like a direct data store in that experience and factual data are directly recorded for possible recall as needed. Generic memory, however, is memory for a whole class of things (e.g., processes) as opposed to memory for specific facts that have been learned or detailed experiences that have been experienced. Generic memory has semantic and procedural components that are considered by Goldberg as *patterns* – the principle subject of this chapter. He states that: "…both language and higher perception are based on generic memories …language and higher perceptions are based on generic memories and are also resistant to the effects of normal aging." (p.134) Generic memory resides in the frontal lobes of each hemisphere which have been termed the brain's *executive function*. It is this area that contains the processing patterns we need to continue basic mental functioning even when other memory circuits are damaged or deteriorate due to aging. The executive function is resilient – resistant to aging and disease.

Goldberg continues: "Every new exposure to the same or similar thing in the environment – or for that matter, to the same or similar information conveyed through language or by some other means – will breathe new life into the reverberating loop supporting the formation of memory about it, and will increase the memory's chance of making it into long-term storage…The more generic a pattern is and the vaster the set of experiences on whose overlap it emerged, the more robust and invulnerable to the effects of brain damage." (p.123) He also comments that: "A typical pattern possesses a very interesting property. It contains information not only about the things you have already encountered, but also about the things you may encounter in the future." (p.125) In other words, generic memories are resident in the neural networks they established, they are self-organizing and energizing, and they have persistence if their experience was either repetitive or very powerful.

4. Competence and Wisdom – Goldberg provides a useful categorization of the qualities of human development in which people with *talent* that become exemplars in their trade are said to possess *genius*. And, he describes people who acquire *competence* in understanding and predicting social process outcomes can, over time, acquire a vast storehouse such that *wisdom* is the outcome. His comment is that: "…we have already established that such pattern-recognition capacity comprises a very important element of wisdom, which implies that a person endowed with wisdom has the ability to recognize an unusually large number of patterns, each encompassing a whole set class of important situations…The arsenal of these generic memories accumulates with age…Also accumulated with age is the facility for intuitive decision-making… intuition is the condensation of vast prior analytic experience; it is analysis compressed and crystallized." (pp.149-150) Competence leads to the development of intuition which leads ultimately to wisdom.

Goldberg's emphasis on competence and wisdom have particular value as they provide a foundation for the trove of information being collected, processed, and synthesized in the writing of this book. The initial part of the learnership architecture is based on the five reasoning *competencies* (system thinking, pattern recognition, situational learning, knowledge management, and adaptive leadership), and the latter part of the architecture leverages these competences for more mature and effective management of our social systems (personal, organizational, community, and societal) – an analogy to the competence to wisdom transition he describes.

To summarize Goldberg's contributions before moving on to other authors, we turn again to what he says about wisdom and competence: "To revert to the language of the brain, both wisdom and competence are attained through the accumulation of attractors allowing pattern recognition in important situations." And further, "The gift of wisdom is a reward, not an entitlement. It has to be earned. And likewise you have to work for your competence...Every human being accumulates a certain pattern-recognition capability in the course of his or her lifetime. But not every human being accumulates the patterns necessary for the solution of problems of genuine importance to a significant number of other people." (p.155)

The second set of excerpts is from Matt Ridley, author of *Nature Via Nurture* (2003). The selections here support and extend Goldberg's comments and provide further insight on the interdependence of nature and nurture in brain development, the role of genes in memory, and the influence of culture on human activities and development.

1. Nature Via Nurture – Ridley is an expert on the latest theories and discoveries in the field of evolution. He reports that the size of the neocortex determines potential brain power: "Gray matter consists of the bodies of neurons, and the new correlation implies that clever people may literally have more neurons, or more connections between neurons, than normal people." He also says that human development is currently thought to be approximately 50% nature and 50% nurture. Regarding intelligence, he says: "Unlike personality, intelligence does seem to receive a strong influence from the family...IQ is approximately 50 percent 'additively genetic'; 25 percent is influenced by the shared environment (twins studies); and 25 percent is influenced by environmental factors unique to the individual." (p.90) Ridley's comments are important in that he concurs with Goldman on the brain pre-wiring concept, and the belief that the pre-wiring is generic, thereby allowing the brain to await input from external stimuli to determine what will be recorded as knowledge and used to guide future action. Ridley states with confidence that: "By far the most important discovery of recent years in brain science is that *genes are at the mercy of actions as well a vice versa*...Nature versus nurture is dead. Long live nature via nurture." (p.280)

2. Role of Genes – DNA is a nucleic acid that consists of pairs of chromosomes. The chromosomes carry genes which have genetic information based on their locations on the DNA. Genes are able to self-replicate; to turn on and off at predetermined intervals; and to create proteins that trigger brain memory and body activity consistent with specific characteristics of the particular DNA and chromosome. Ridley reports that: "...different parts of the brain are pre-designed for different jobs, something that could come about only through genes. Genes are often thought of as constraints on the adaptability of human behavior. The reverse is true. They do not constrain; they enable." (p.64) Ridley comments on the role of genes after they have effectively discharged their obligation to implement human growth saying that: "Genes – those implacable puppet masters of fate that are supposed to make the brain and leave it to get on with the job. But they do not; they also actually do the learning...these genes are at the mercy of our behavior, not the other way around...memory is 'in the genes' in the sense that it uses genes, not in the sense that you inherit memories. Nurture is affected by genes just as much as nature is." (p.181) What we have here is a situation in which genes continue working at the behest of pre-wired chromosomal commands while simultaneously responding to stimuli in our external environment helping us to learn and to lock-in memories of that learning in our brain's neural networks. We must assume that when our genes are helping us remember *patterns we have learned* (semantics and cultural artifacts), our frontal lobe generic memory is reinforced expanding our executive function repertoire. Ridley reinforces Goldberg.

3. Imprinting the Brain – Ridley credits Piaget with discovering the time dimension of brain learning. He reports that: "Piaget...insisted that just as children will not walk or talk until they are 'ready,' so the elements of what the world calls intelligence are not merely absorbed from the environment; they appear when the developing brain is ready to learn them. Piaget saw cognitive development neither as learning nor as maturation, but as a combination of the two, as sort of active engagement of the developing mind with the world." (p.126) Furthermore, Ridley notes that it was Konrad Lorenz who "...realized that there was a narrow gap of time during which this imprinting could occur...formed the concept of the critical period – the window during which environment acts irreversibly upon the development of behavior...had discovered how the external environment shapes behavior just a much as the natural drive does." (pp.152-153) These findings confirmed earlier inclinations that chromosomes and their genes contained sequential timing characteristics that opened up specific learning opportunities for a limited period before closing the mental door and moving on to other developmental factors.

The importance here is that our early childhood imprinting period (followed by an adolescent socialization period) contributes a tremendous amount of pattern development which for the rest of our lives will influence our *perspective and preferences*. Again, Ridley's commentary aligns well with Goldberg's self-organizing capability of the brain in which attractor networks are prepared to be reinforced by external stimuli that are consistent with their current repertoire of data. To the learnership practitioner, this presents a challenge: how to countermand the pre-programmed "knowledge," biases, and potentially erroneous thinking of others when change is clearly required.

4. Brain and Culture – Following up on the role of genes and the reality of early life imprinting from above, Ridley reemphasizes the criticality of learning as a distinct result of external cultural imprinting: "And the only way that evolution can transmit such information from the past to the design of the mind in the present is via the genes. That is what genes are: parts of an information system that collect facts about the world in the past and incorporates them into good design for the future through natural selection…learning itself is an instinct." (p.194-195) Furthermore, speaking about all the knowledge, Artifacts and property acquired by people, he says: "They got all these things through culture, through their ability to accumulate ideas and inventions, generation by generation, transmit them to others, and thereby pool the cognitive resources of many individuals alive and dead." (p.209) And finally, Ridley declares: "To imitate, to manipulate, and to speak are three things that human beings are particularly good at. They are not just central to culture: they are culture." (p.220)

At this point, the reinforcing spiral of learning creating culture and culture influencing learning appears to establish, over time, impenetrable perspectives not amenable to new learning and change. Multiply this by hundreds, if not thousands, of learning-culture spirals as evidenced by the multitude of national and international languages, religions, nation-states and the wide range of ethnic, gender and age differences that have impact on social systems development and management and we can begin to understand why managing any type of personal, organizational, and community change is very difficult. Our *learnership practitioner* will need significant knowledge, skill and ability to succeed in this environment!

The third set of excerpts is from Leslie Hart, author of *Human Brain and Human Learning* (1983). The selections here add to and build on Goldberg's and Ridley's contributions to this book's themes. The particular areas of emphasis are pattern detection and recognition, living by programs, emotional downshifting, and learning through brain compatibility.

1. Pattern Detection and Recognition – According to Hart, real learning needs to take into account the natural forces and capabilities of the human environment. He presents his Proster Theory which argues that the process of learning is the extraction from confusion of meaningful patterns. His propositions are that the brain (a) is a pattern detection apparatus, (b) detects both features and relationships, and employs the use of clues and categorization, (c) uses negative clues as control factors, (d) uses innate probabilistic capabilities, (e) applies prior experience (preconditioning) which sets the stage for performance, and (f) memorizes patterns which can be revised to fit new experiences. (p.67)

Hart reinforces the idea that the brain works on a *probabilistic* basis. It compares incoming stimuli from its environment with the memories stored in its neural networks, factors in any disconfirming data, and makes a judgment on the appropriate response. He states that: "In practice our pattern-detecting ability depends on clues from vision, touch, or other senses, on the behavior and relationships, on the situation. In short, the ability depends heavily on what we bring to the act of pattern detection and recognition. The more experience tells us what we are likely to be looking at, or dealing with, the less detailed, feature-type of information we need to jump to a probably correct conclusion." (p.64) Hart attributes to Aldous Huxley: "What emerges most strikingly from recent scientific developments is that perception is not a passive reception of material from the outside world; it is an active process of selection and imposing of patterns." (p.61-62)

Significance of this to the learnership practitioner is two-fold: First, the positive – there is an ongoing need for subject matter experts to organize information, create processes, and establish methodologies so others can learn and apply improved approaches for achieving their objectives. This is *pattern making*, and by clarifying purpose, reducing uncertainty, sequencing activities, and increasing confidence of those who follow better outcomes can be attained. Second, the negative – pattern making has long been with us and has risen to an art form wherever there is a bureaucracy. Bureaucracies have so many locked-in policies and procedures in attempting to become highly efficient (pattern conformance) that they can no longer be adaptive and effective in a fast changing, integrated world. These two activities are in constant tension as those satisfied with the present culture, thinking processes, or methodologies resist suggestions by those who see change as essential for a better future.

2. Living by Programs – Hart introduces Proster Theory, which is a neologism from the compression of the words *program structure*. A Proster is a notional concept of how the brain is organized for storing and selecting programs. Hart reports that: "The key is the realization that we act very largely by *programs*…Clearly one of the reasons for our huge brain is that as humans we need and use a great number of programs to carry on our complex activities – thousands of times as many as the most intelligent of other animals." He continues saying that: "Present knowledge makes clear that programs can be acquired two distinct ways: by being transmitted with the genes, or by being learned after birth…". (pp.82-83) Hart obviously agrees with Goldberg and Ridley on the brain's dynamic "give and take" with its external environment, but he does not mention the role of genes locking-in external information as part of the nurturing process. He does, however, envision the brain's purposeful selection of a particular program from a repertoire of programs in an ongoing "conversation" with the external environment, and states: "To carry on activities, one must constantly select a

program from those that are stored in the brain, and implement it – put it to use…Each time, the program in use has to be switched off, and another selected and switched on. The brain does this so smoothly that we ordinarily are not aware of the switches being thrown." (p.83)

Hart comments on the difficulties in teaching/learning situations when there is the need to align the programs to be used. "He presents his evaluate, select, and implement cycle and indicates the respective challenges:

  a. <u>Evaluate</u> – Unless the learner can reasonably accurately evaluate the need or problem the situation presents…the cycle goes astray at the outset. The student simply does not know *what* to do.

  b. <u>Select</u> – Individuals can only use those programs they already possess. However much one may be coerced or urged, or motivated or rewarded there is no way to perform the program unless it has already been stored by that individual. He or she does not know *how* to do it.

  c. <u>Implement</u> – A student cannot implement a program unless given the chance to do so." (p.84)

What is particularly noteworthy to the learnership practitioner in Hart's commentary is the need to establish common ground among the programs in use. The transfer of information and knowledge cannot be efficiently or effectively communicated when the sender's perception and or perspective is very different than that of the receiver. The following chapter on "Situational Learning" addresses this concern and poses solutions.

3. <u>Emotional Downshifting</u> – Hart reports that: "The quality of brain – which to a large extent means the number of neurons – determines the degree to which patterns can be detected and discriminated" and determines the scope of program building." (p.103) He also comments that a major consideration in program building and learning is the quality of the learning environment. Given a triune brain structure consisting of a reptilian core (survival skills, fight or flight), within a limbic mid-brain (deeply held emotions and beliefs), within an outer neocortex (thinking, substantive memory, frontal lobe executive functions); the challenge is to exercise the memory and learning of the neocortex without unnecessarily creating a sense of danger or fear that disrupts the learning process. The presence of threat is detrimental to effective instruction/learning. Threat causes a sense of danger, the neocortex begins to shut down (down-shifting), and the limbic and reptilian brains react negatively. The effect is one of shock and interference with the ability to speak. Removal of the threat allows neocortex dominance (up-shifting) to occur and learning to continue. The learnership practitioner will need to be astute in evaluating whether the subject matter (content), reasoning framework (context), and tone of interpersonal communications is factual, open, and supportive of all participants.

4. <u>Learning through Brain Compatibility</u> – Hart comments on the current state of educational development and learning that courses are arranged for academic convenience, not on how learning occurs in the real world; and intimates that fragmentation introduced by courses (fields of study) focus on prescribed basic content but mostly fail to integrate well with material in other disciplines. He says that: "…the emphasis on patterns tends to unify, and to promote a natural transfer of learning." (p.136) Hart calls for learning in an open-ended, non time-constrained environment with an emphasis on mastery (mostly determined by the students), and with *overarching grand ideas* that provide a large context for deliberation and critical thinking. The ability of the students to have choice and sense of control, manipulate relevant materials, use language and written materials, obtain feedback, and link to grand ideas are all helpful for effective learning and development. Learnership practitioners are likely to agree that much of this perspective applies within their own adult lives and social systems.

Pattern Recognition Complexity

> *What emerges most strikingly from recent scientific developments is that*
> *Perception is not a passive reception of material from the outside world; it*
> *is an active process of selection and imposing of patterns.* — *Aldous Huxley*

University of the Mind. A major example of how life and work has been systematically divided and organized into units of knowledge and performance is illustrated in Figure 6-1. Shown is the approach used by a well known university to depict the various schools, departments, and programs that have a logical connection to the University's Knowledge Management Program. Two aspects of this taxonomy are important: (a) knowledge management practices and technologies are necessarily broad in scope and easily cross traditional educational and organizational boundaries; and (b) each of the departments and programs have their respective *knowledge and process patterns* by which they are distinguishable (e.g., Information Management has IT Architecture; Systems Engineering has SEI Methods and Practices; Business Administration has Leadership Development; Human Resources has Human Capital Development). The breadth of the university's educational program inspires this author to propose the concept of *University of the Mind – an* artifact that describes the similarity between a university and the human mind wherein their modular construct, breadth of knowledge, and responsibility to accommodate activities requiring both integration and differentiation. This perspective poses the challenge: How can we select, record, modify, apply, and share patterns of belief and information among individuals and social systems when and where they are needed?

Focusing on patterns of belief and information as a framework for social inquiry provides the analysis and understanding of individual preferences and mindsets. The *pattern recognition competency* focuses on our ability to recognize the pre-programmed aspects of ourselves and others, and on our need to better manage our reasoning based on why and how we think, learn, know, lead, and pursue objectives in our societal endeavors.

The development and application of these two fundamental competencies (pattern recognition in conjunction with system thinking) permits us to stretch the mental models that govern our thought and behavior in both hierarchical and lateral directions. This enables us to comprehend our environment and experiences more fully and expand our range of personal options and social action. Additional insight on this challenge is offered in the following paradox of integration and differentiation.

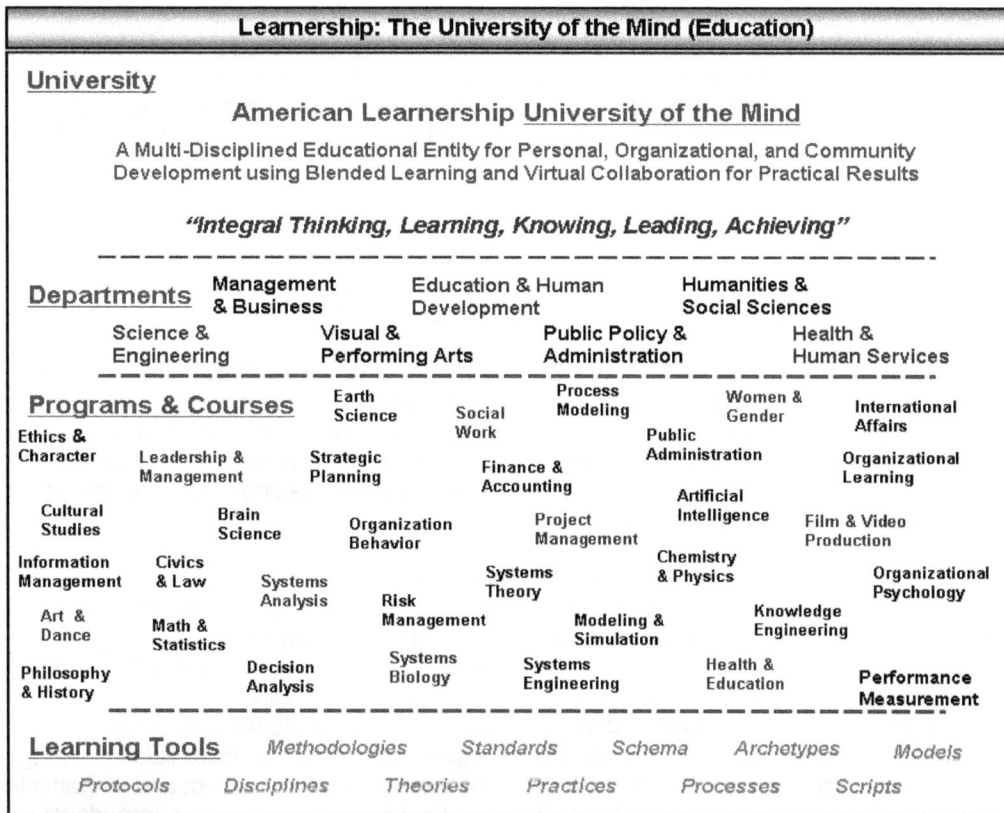

Figure 6-1

Paradox of Integration and Differentiation. Much of life comes at us with speed and complexity that defies our desire for orderly thinking and decision-making. Most of us find ourselves being pressured to live an *integrated* lifestyle in which a myriad of diverse objectives, issues, people, responsibilities, and personal preferences clamor for our daily attention – simultaneously! The societal subsystems (personal, organizational, community) that comprise our societal experience constantly compete for more of our time, resources and involvement. Stress and ill-health is the occasional result.

The other part of our lives demands that we narrow our attention and focus on the specific needs of the people and organizations, tasks and relationships we need to support or influence. We spend much of our time and life trying to simplify things and to make them understandable and predictable. Our language, culture, and educational systems are designed to *differentiate* our skills and knowledge. This places boundaries on our activities thereby making our tasks and functions more manageable. This also enables us to limit our attention to prescribed strategies for developing expertise and achieving efficiency.

In reality, we spend our lives cycling between the larger, broader, more inclusive system thinking activities discussed in the last chapter; and the narrowly focused, more deeply analytical issues and responsibilities that require our immediate attention. We are required to differentiate and then to integrate, to specialize and then to generalize, to serial-process and then to parallel-process, and to continually accept diverse factors impacting the achievement of our objectives.

The *university of the mind* archetype connotes a repository of patterns, an architecture of integrated themes and differentiated subjects, the use of symbiotic system thinking and pattern recognition, and a need to maintain an *overarching grand idea* that provides a meta-cognitive architecture for improving thinking, learning, knowing, leading, and pursuing achievement. This is the mindset of the <u>learnership</u> <u>practitioner</u> who relishes lifelong learning, adaptive leadership, and the pursuit of goals yet to be discovered.

Social Framing and Analysis. Framing is the term used to describe how people attempt to organize their social experiences and to influence others. Framing is mainly about how we strive to create patterns of communication and context interpretation that leaves preferred impressions, provides us with desired social leverage, and creates movement in the directions we favor. This effort involves designing the context or patterns within which a conversation or product/service discussion will take place so that subject matter content itself is perceived within the frame of interest of the initiator. The fields of marketing and advertising where sales and revenue are dominant are the most prevalent examples of communications framing; however, the purpose here is to focus on gaining better understanding of interpersonal communications on the personal level and in social relations.

In his seminal work entitled *Frame Analysis* (1974), Erving Goffman's definition is that frame analysis is the analysis of situations in terms of the organization of the interpersonal experience that was observed. That is, an observer using frame analysis is able to discern the "play" between two or more people in communication, and then organize the data collected into a commentary on individual intent and results. It is important to note that all of the involved parties could be attempting to "frame the dialogue" as might be expected in a situation of negotiation.

When viewed from a theatrical perspective, the phrase "staged production" is apropos in that the actors are following a script that leads to the formulation of specified assumptions and conclusions concerning the main theme or storyline. Goffman cites the Marilyn Chambers example: "In 1973 Marilyn Chambers, an uncontroversial personality was picked to be the mother figure on Ivory Snow laundry powder boxes – until the disclosure of her stardom in hard-core pornography films was learned. (p.277) Purposeful framing and production staging did not achieve the desired result when the obvious contradictions became known.

According to Berger and Luckmann (*The Social Construction of Reality*, 1967), we are all challenged to obtain knowledge and to "construct a reality" that rationalizes our preconceived experiences, personal objectives, educational learning, family cultures, and/or adopted biases. For a variety of reasons, many of us project a personality through language, body motion, and speech that is purposefully or inadvertently inconsistent with our self-interest or intent. At the duplicitous extreme, our psycho-social outlook could be that we could not care less about our impact on others as long as our personal objectives are achieved. Examples include: (1) we claim to be openly seeking information and input even while we are actually rejecting others and their suggestions, and (2) we have little knowledge or feeling about others or a situation while actually scheming to convince them of our commitment and empathy to their cause. In either case, the frames we project have little authenticity and cannot be the basis for long-term development and success.

These behaviors are part of human nature and provide a useful backdrop for movies and stage plays. Many times humor springs from these contradictions, while at other times the results are tragic. The point for our purposes is that dispassionate observers operating from an objective distance are better able to collect information and perform frame analysis when they temporarily step outside the immediate situation. In the previous chapter, this activity was referred to as "ex-body objectivity."

Finally, the question that may now be asked is: How should we deal with others' projected frames of reference when they are recognized? In approach one, a defensive posture may be employed which is to comment that the suggested (context setting) frame is an attempt to deflect attention away from the subject (substantive content) at hand, and to point out that the irrelevant and inaccurate frame being posed is essentially a red herring distraction. In approach two, a developmental perspective may be the best technique because the situation is one in which the initially established frame/context is, in fact, erroneous and a new mind-frame should be considered. In the latter case, an open-minded search for pattern alignment would be most constructive.

The learning here is that open and authentic dialogue that establishes common ground for collaborative problem-solving reduces misunderstanding. The discussion of issue content, within an agreed context, using open-minded collaboration is the preferred approach for achieving greater consensus and results. Learnership practitioners attempt to establish such conditions.

Mental Models. In his book *The Fifth Discipline* (1990), Peter Senge lists the development and use of "mental models" (or mindsets) as one of his five major learning organization disciplines. He states that: "Mental models are deeply ingrained assumptions, generalizations, or even pictures or images that influence how we understand the world and how we take action. Very often, we are not consciously aware of our mental models or the effects they have on our behavior." (p.8) Senge's mental model description, and cautionary observation of the potential impact of unknowingly applying mental models to social situations, aligns well with the pattern recognition discussion in this section.

Senge notes that: "The discipline of working with mental models starts with turning the mirror inward; learning to unearth our internal pictures of the world, to bring them to the surface and hold them rigorously to scrutiny. It also includes the ability to carry on 'learningful' conversations that balance inquiry and advocacy, where people expose their own thinking effectively and make that thinking open to the influence of others." (pp.8-9) This point is significant in that it challenges each of us to develop the courage to expose our deeper thinking and feelings to others in an effort to learn, to better understand, and to find common ground upon which we can agree so that issues and problems may be resolved. The reality in today's fast paced, dynamic environment is that few of us are willing to afford that level of commitment unless the issue or problem is very serious – and then only with a select few family and friends.

Personal Preferences and Behavior

> *Our attitude is not determined by circumstances, but by how we respond to circumstances. Our minds*
> *determine our attitude. We can respond positively or negatively. It's how we react to an event,*
> *not the events themselves that determines our attitude.*
> — *Wynn Davis*

A desirable outcome from understanding human brain learning and programming, and the fact that language, culture and experience has created such disparities among us; is developing a capability to apply our pattern recognition knowledge to individuals, organizations and communities with whom we live and work. Differences in our perception, perspectives and preferences affect our ability to live and work together.

This section introduces a selection of theoretical constructs developed over the last century that attempt to account for a wide range of psychological and behavioral variables observable in both individuals and social groups. Numerous studies have been conducted and books written that attempt to explain the uniqueness of each construct. Additionally, each construct has its own advocates and experts that suggest how practical use may be made from their respective concepts. Little has been done to overlay the theories and to explain areas of consistency and difference. In fact, when this is attempted strengths and weaknesses and the lack of 100 percent alignment becomes evident. Greater in-depth research is clearly indicated for those inclined to achieve definitive knowledge of the relationships. And yet, having an 80 percent, symbiotic understanding of what has already been discovered is information worth knowing. Our practical lives are full of patterns and concepts that are only 80 percent accurate requiring that we balance the risks of error and use our judgment to learn what we can and then move forward to the next learning opportunity.

The explanations that follow provide selected fundamentals on a number of personality studies and the information that has resulted from the use and interpretation of their respective personality instruments (surveys). The figures used below have been developed as conceptual reference models in an effort to construct a "notional" or general relationship among the psycho-social concepts so that an overarching tool might become available for our use in discussing our preferences and tendencies as we try to communicate and live a constructive social existence. Figure 6-2, Pattern Recognition Competency: Psychological Preferences, is the symbiotic model for relating brain dominance, personality types, learning styles, and cultural preferences.

[**Author's Note**: Readers will see that starting with Figure 6-2 reasoning competency abbreviations (ST, PR, SL, KM and AL) are illustrated within an octagonal-shaped figure. Figure 6-2 begins with System Thinking already inserted to allow for the preceding presentation in Chapter Five.]

Brain Dominance. *The Whole Brain Business Book* (1996) by Ned Herrmann links human preferences and capabilities to individual styles of thinking and learning. Herrmann uses brain physiology as a metaphor for illustrating four unique modes of thinking which, in turn, determine our individual personalities, acquired preferences and skills, and ultimately our behaviors. According to Herrmann, the adult personality represents the result of numerous choices and preferences that have synthesized to create the interests, skills, strengths, and limitations found in each person. A *Universe of thinking styles* exists within which each person has at least one, probably two, dominant capabilities. In group work and in business, it is theorized that a "Whole Brain" capability contributed by numerous team members is the best approach to encourage innovation and for problem solving.

In Figure 6-2 the brain is the conceptual illustration around which everything else revolves. The illustration notionally accommodates the left and right brain hemispheres – each with frontal lobe executive functions. It also shows that there is a new mammalian neocortex (cerebral outer brain) and an older mammalian (limbic mid-brain) both of which are split between the left and right hemispheres. Using a quadrant perspective, the brain can be said to operate in terms of its Cerebral Left (CL), Cerebral Right (CR), Limbic Left (LL), and Limbic Right (LR) pre-wired functionality, information storage, and personal preferences as indicated by the labels provided. Herrmann's *whole brain* concept is that all these regions have valuable contributions to make and should be developed and used more effectively. Ideally, a sense of balance would be achieved wherein the right thinking, capabilities and knowledge would be applied at the right place, at the right time, as needed.

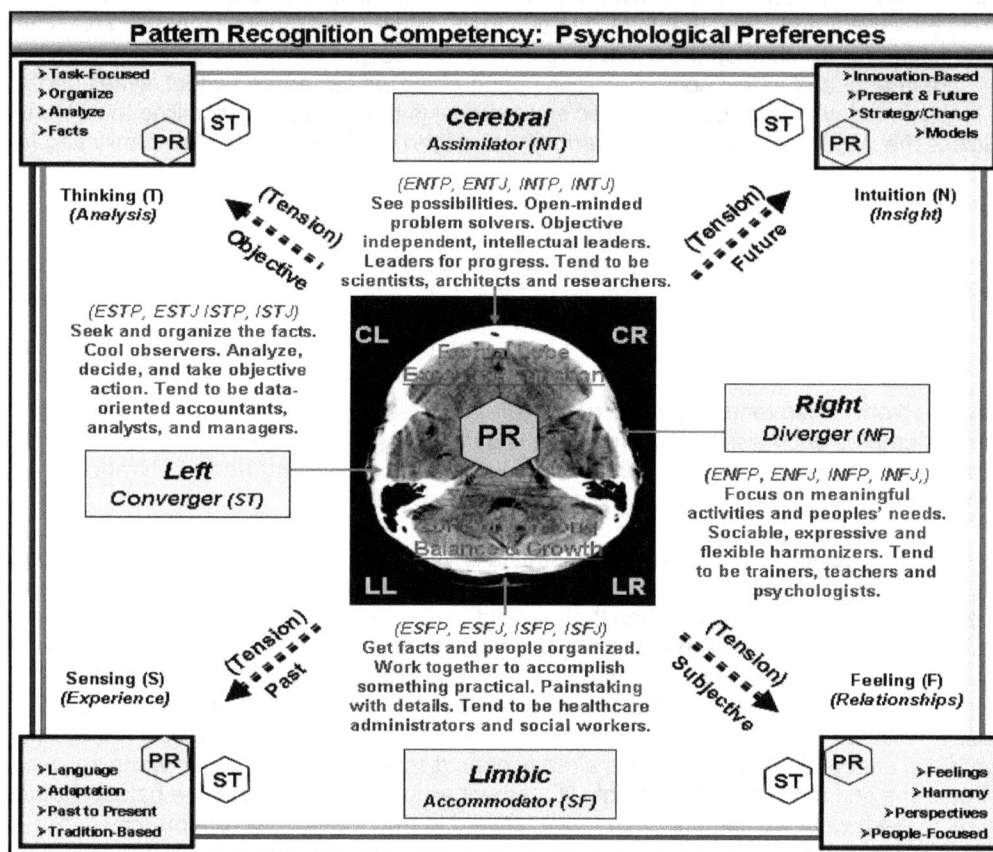

Figure 6-2

In the figure, the size of the cerebral brain is the distinguishing factor in permitting human information storage, thought, knowledge and development. And, the frontal lobe of the cerebral brain is the primary area for pattern development and recognition. The *Cerebral Left (CL) brain* area is pre-wired to record elements of culture and experience that enable the recordation and use of task-focused knowledge and skill that emphasize the analysis and organization of facts relevant to a situation or relationship. Moving our focus to the right side of the brain, there is the *Cerebral Right (CR) brain* area which is pre-wired to record and use information in the form of models and pictures to envision innovations, future possibilities, and strategies for change.

In reference to the limbic mid-brain – the area that records and attempts to sustain our values and relationships – the *Limbic Left (LL) brain* area is pre-wired for language, symbols and traditions developed in the past and thought to be equally applicable to the present. Adaptation to new concepts and experiences is slow and rapid change is actively resisted. For the *Limbic Right (LR) brain* area, pre-wiring is designed to record information for building harmony, encouraging people-focused relationships, respecting feelings and developing perspectives that put people first in communications and action.

An important point to recognize at this juncture is the natural brain tension that occurs between the diametrically opposite areas of the brain. The well-organized, task-focused CL brain area does not relish dealing with the people-focused, sometimes undisciplined LR brain area and its needs. Similarly, the tradition-based (LL) brain area is very resistant to the future and change oriented (CR) brain area due to its threat to limbic stability. Herrmann's whole brain concept recognizes values and builds on these differences and turns them into valuable insights for personal and organization development.

Whole Brain Theory postulates that everyone has a dominant brain preference, that is, left versus right and cerebral versus limbic which indicates that one, and probably two, quadrants are of strongest influence. To enable better thinking and communications in relationships and teamwork it is useful to have more rather than fewer people involved using their preferences and strengths. More useful information is acquired, considered and used in decision-making thereby providing a better result.

A typical collaborative process might proceed as follows: A situation arises in which some aspect of an organization's tradition has come to everyone's attention because proposals are being made to stop a planned activity that occurs the same time every year. Tension between those with strong LL brain tendencies and new team members with CR interests requires management attention. In a properly functioning organization, some time would be spent gathering relevant information (a CL activity) and relevant workforce information (a LR activity). These two areas also represent an opportunity for tension prior to proceeding into the expected cycles of discussion and decision-making. A whole brain solution should have involved more of the useful information and perspectives to make the final solution acceptable to all those involved due to the decision's inherent accuracy and fairness.

Learning Styles. In his book *Experiential Learning: Experience as the Source of Learning and Development* (1983), David A. Kolb created a Learning Style Inventory (LSI) that proposes that individuals with different kinds of personality styles prefer different mental approaches for engaging their minds and the world around them. Some learning abilities are emphasized over others. Four distinct approaches to learning are seen in childhood development: *accommodator behavior* leads to Concrete Experience (CE - "feeling"); *diverger behavior* leads to Reflective Observation (RO - "watching"); *assimilator behavior* leads to Abstract Conceptualization (AC - "thinking"); and *converger behavior* leads to Active Experimentation (AE - "doing'). This learning process yields four distinct "styles" of which two approaches are preferred by individuals. Figure 6-3 illustrates the childhood learning process and adults choose the one or two favorites for later life use.

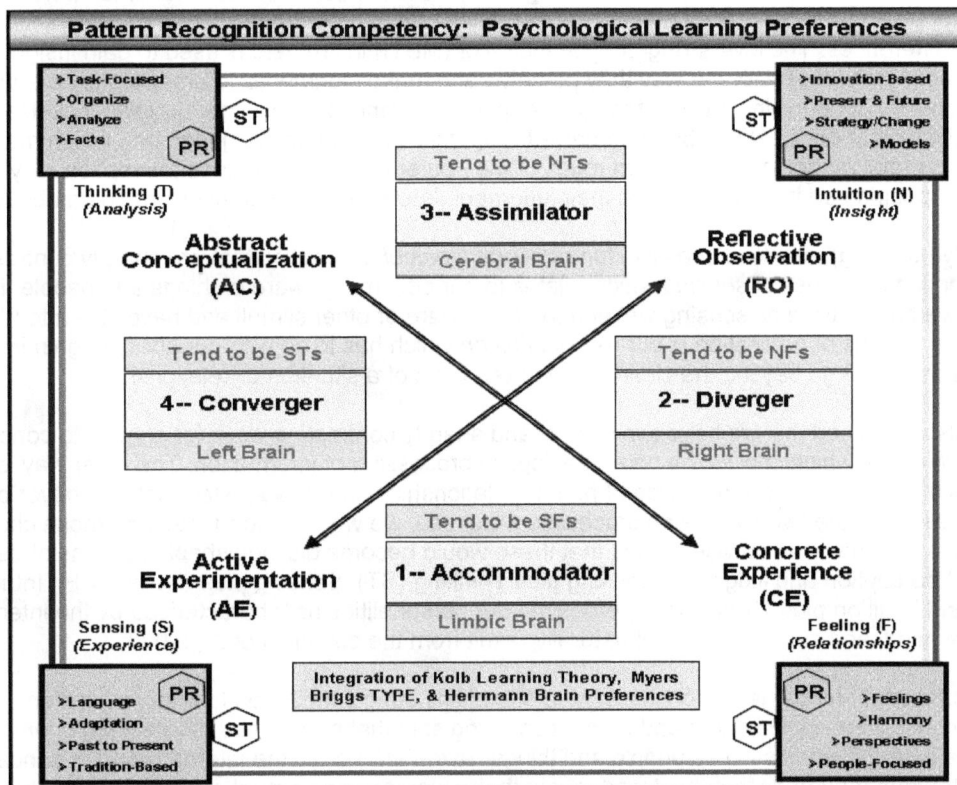

Figure 6-3

Accommodators (CE-AE) – Learners who are accommodators are opposite of the assimilators, and their strength lies in doing things and getting involved in new experiences. They are likely to be more of a risk taker than the others and tend to excel in situations requiring adaptation to immediate circumstances. They like to discard a "theory" or "plan" and tend to be impatient and "pushy." They like action oriented jobs like sales.

Divergers (CE-RO) – Divergers are opposite of convergers. Their strength lies in their imaginative capabilities and their ability to view things from multiple aspects. They are good at "brainstorming, and in dealing with people. They tend to be imaginative and emotional. They have broad cultural interests and specialize in the arts. They may have backgrounds in humanities and liberal arts and may work in personnel occupations.

Assimilators (AC-RO) – Assimilators are opposite of accommodators. Their strength lies in the ability to create theoretical models and the use of inductive logic to synthesize disparate observations. They are less interested in people and more focused on abstract concepts – even to the exclusion of a practical application of those concepts. Their interest is more in the basic sciences rather than applied sciences and is likely to be in the R&D and planning occupations.

Convergers (AE-AC) – Convergers are opposite of diverters. Their strength lies in the practical application of ideas. They excel in conventional intelligence tests in which there is one preferred answer and the use of hypothetical-deductive reasoning is paramount. They prefer to deal with things rather than people, are relatively unemotional, have rather narrow technical interests, and like the physical sciences. Their typical occupation is engineering.

Our learning styles affect how well we learn. What is useful in understanding learning styles is that when others' preferences are known the trainer, manager or colleague has a choice of methods for helping others learn either in classrooms or in organizational settings. Kolb's LSI has been shown to be useful in gaining appreciation of diversity and interpersonal differences, gaining insight on how to help others learn from experience, and in helping groups better understand collaboration and using strengths of participants. Lastly, these styles have a general correlation with the brain dominance preferences illustrated in Figure 6-2 which means that quality of learning preferences are consistent with brain studies, but probably not 100 percent aligned with Herrmann's conclusions and models.

Personality Type. *Gifts Differing* (1980) by Isabel Briggs Myers is the seminal work on human personality. It presents a classification of personality types through study of personal mental preferences based on Jung's studies of human similarities and differences. The Myers Briggs Type Indicator (MBTI) instrument is used to gain insight into how people prefer to use their minds, especially the way they perceive and make judgments. "*Perceiving* is here understood to include the processes of becoming aware of things, people, occurrences, and ideas. *Judging* includes the processes of coming to conclusions about what has been perceived. Together, perception and judgment, which make up a large portion of people's total mental activity, govern much of their outer behavior, because perception – by definition – determines what people see in a situation and their judgment determines what they decide to do about it." (p.1)

According to Myers (Jung), mankind uses two fundamental *types of perception* that are sharply contrasting. One means of perception is our use of *sensing* which relates to our becoming aware of things and people through our five senses. When we concentrate on sensing we tend to be unaware of other stimuli and have little attention left for other thoughts. Another means of perception is our use of *intuition* which has to do with our ability to gain insights from "hunches" or "trends' that go beyond the clearly recognized facts of a situation or relationship.

Myers (Jung) also proposed that we have two distinct and sharply contrasting ways for coming to conclusions. One way is through *thinking*, which implies the objective, logical processing of information. The other way is by using *feeling* which concerns the subjective, personal side of human relationships. Jung suggested that whichever of the two perception process, and the two conclusion processes we chose, we would tend to stay with those choices over a wide range of mental and behavioral activities – and that these would become distinguishable patterns of behavior. The combinations of perception and judgment: Sensing plus Thinking (ST), Sensing plus Feeling (SF), Intuition plus Feeling (NF), and Intuition plus Thinking (NT) produces our personalities as "characterized by the interests, values, needs, habits of mind, and surface traits that naturally result from the combination." (p.4)

In addition to Jung's four fundamental functions, Myers explains Jung's theory on four more functions or preferences: introversion and extroversion, judgment and perception. Jung said that people had different *life orientations;* more interested in the external world such as people and things (*extraverts*) or on the internal world of concepts and ideas (*introverts*). Extroverts tend to do their best work out in their external environment, while introverts do their best work by concentrating their perception and judgment on concepts and ideas. Both are needed for high levels of societal functioning and accomplishment.

Lastly, Myers explains Jung's judgment-perceiving preference as a "choice between the perceptive attitude and the judging attitude as a way of life, a method for dealing with the world around us…people shift back and forth between the perceptive and judging attitudes, sometimes quite abruptly." (p.8) Using perception we are open to additional and new information, but when using judgment we seek closure and conclusion.

Use of the MBTI allows individuals to select their personality type by choosing among Jung's four sets of functions. The result is that all of us fit into at least one of the sixteen types available – and often we can see ourselves partially in two or more of the other types. For purposes of this book, the MBTI concept has been included in Figure 6-2 in the following manner: First, Jung's four primary functions are aligned with the brain dominance model such that the *cerebral thinking* (value analysis) and *limbic feeling* (value relationships) preferences are at opposite corners. Similarly, the *cerebral intuition* (value insight) and *limbic sensing* (value experience) preferences are at opposite corners. This alignment is coherent with what has already been displayed in that NT types are associated with cerebral mental functioning, SF types are associated with limbic mid-brain functioning, ST types are associated with left brain functioning, and NF types are associated with right brain functioning. The symbiotic relation among brain dominance, Myers-Briggs Type, and Kolb's learning theories are beginning to be seen. Specifically, the four sets of MBTI types can now be distinguished and summarized:

1. **NT** *(ENTP, ENTJ, INTP, INTJ)* – NTs see possibilities. They are open-minded problem solvers. They are objective, independent, intellectual leaders. They are leaders focused on progress. Many scientists, architects and researchers are NTs.

2. **SF** *(ESFP, ESFJ, ISFP, ISFJ)* – SFs get facts and people organized. They work together to accomplish something practical. They are painstaking with details. Many healthcare administrators and social workers tend to be SFs.

3. **ST** *(ESTP, ESTJ ISTP, ISTJ)* – STs seek and organize the facts. They are cool observers. They analyze, decide, and take objective action. Many data-oriented people, accountants, analysts, and managers tend to be STs.

4. **NF** *(ENFP, ENFJ, INFP, INFJ,)* – NFs focus on meaningful activities and peoples' needs. They are sociable, expressive and flexible harmonizers. Many trainers, teachers and psychologists are NFs.

Once again, a new theoretical concept is introduced and compared with our Figure 6-2 model under construction. An 80 percent correlation and symbiotic relationship is easily observed, but perfection is not assured. Each noted expert (Herrmann, Kolb, Myers) established their respective theories with knowledge of Jung's work and that of many other researchers. However, each also constructed their own data collection plan, analyzed their findings, and published their conclusions – most often for slightly different purposes and audiences. Notwithstanding their efforts, our objective is to determine general correlations that can serve as the basis for higher level pattern recognition in human memory, thinking and behavior.

What should be observable at this point is that we and others have our preferred manner of thinking, learning and behaving – and those patterns can be discerned by those of us empowered with knowledge of the physiological and psychological basis for the mental models we all display through our language and behavior. As *learnership practitioners* we are encouraged to raise our personal antennas and be alert for others' preferences, styles and needs so we can become more efficient and effective in working with them. We should learn to recognize that some of those around us driven by their left brain desire for facts and organization will sometimes be in conflict with right brain people seeking new insights and better interpersonal relationships. The cerebral thinkers with their theories and complex models will certainly find themselves challenged when working with those whose limbic value system is threatened by perceived counterculture schemes. And, if we find ourselves in the position to plan and lead an organizational change initiative we should not be surprised at just how hard that turns out to be!

[**Author's Note**: For those readers interested in more information on psychological preferences or to do a self-assessment using the Myers-Briggs Type Indicator and/or the Herrmann Brain Dominance Indicator, the following web sites may be helpful: http://www.hbdi.com; http://www.humanmetrics.com; http://www.personalitypathways.com; http://www.spiraldyna mics.org.]

Introduction to Spiral Dynamics:

> *Spiral Dynamics presents a new framework for understanding the dynamic forces at work in human affairs – business, personal lives, education, and even geopolitics.* — Ronnie Lessem

Cultural Styles/Spiral Dynamics. Before leaving the personal preferences and behavior subject area, we turn our attention to the contemporary work being done in the field of Spiral Dynamics. We are interested to see what broad-based conclusions might apply to our psychological patterns effort. Authors Beck and Cowan, *Spiral Dynamics: Mastering Values, Leadership, and Change* (2006), report on, and further develop, the foundational work of psychologist Clare Graves. In introducing the work of Beck and Cowan, Ronnie Lessem comments that: "…a Meme reflects a worldview, a valuing system, a level of psychological existence, a belief structure, an organizing principle, a way of thinking or a mode of adjustment." Lessem also notes that "…a Meme is a discrete structure of thinking…[that it] can brighten or dim as the *Life Conditions* (consisting of historic *Times*, geographic *Place*, existential *Problems*, and social *Circumstances*) change." (pp.4-5)

[Author's Note: This description is nearly identical to the dictionary definition of culture in which values and behavior patterns, beliefs, intellectual activity, and products of a group's work and thought represents what they together have come to understand, value, trust, and advocate to others about themselves. Nonetheless, to the degree Memes are thought to be uniquely identifiable characteristics or archetypical subsets of social traditions that have distinct core knowledge and belief, Spiral Dynamics may be examined for a potential symbiotic relationship with the models of psycho-social preferences already illustrated in Figure 6-2.]

Beck and Cowan explain that there are eight identifiable Memes that (1) represent patterns of human thought and behavior over the ages; (2) that Memes change as individuals and social entities have "awakenings" and spiral forward to higher levels of cognitive and emotional development; (3) that the eight levels of Memes alternate between the Self-Expressive and Self-Sacrificing modes of being; (4) that multiple Memes may be present in the thinking and behavior of individuals and groups at any particular time and place in society; and (5) that each Meme is identifiable by a color and key words that mark its unique nature and impact. The authors say that: "What biochemical genes are to cellular DNA, Memes are to our psycho-social and organizational 'DNA'…they take us through the fascinating dynamics of spiraling human systems…These include the dynamics of change, leadership, complexity, alignment and integration." (p.4) Also, the authors state that: "Environmental factors (Time, Place, Conditions and Circumstance) awaken systems within people and societies designed to cope with and adapt to those specific *Life Conditions*." (p.288)

Memes already in societal relationships are organized into the six in the *first tier* which represent the *old management paradigm* (reference to organizational management and leadership), and the first two (Numbers seven and eight of six) already developing in the more socially advanced *second tier*. To align with the pattern recognition framework in this book, the Memes have been correlated with brain dominance and the MBTI below and are illustrated in reference Figure 6-2 as colored lines around the periphery of the model.

Tier 1:

Level 1. **(Bottom)** The Survival-Sense Meme – Color is **beige**, primary objective is survival, and behavior is seen as basic-instinctive. Level 1 is recognized as a strong limbic brain (SF) activity that emphasizes the use of MBTI Sensing during perception. The overarching goal is to "stay alive through innate sensory equipment."

Level 2. **(Bottom)** The Kin-Spirits Meme – Color is **purple**, primary objective is safety, and behavior is seen as magical-mystical. Level 2 is recognized as a strong limbic brain (SF) activity that emphasizes the use of MBTI Feeling during judgment. The overarching goal is to rely on "blood relationships and mysticism in a magical and scary world."

Level 3. **(Left)** The Power-Gods Meme – Color is **red**, primary objective is dominance/power, and behavior is seen as powerful-impulsive. Level 3 is recognized as a strong left brain (ST) activity that emphasizes the use of MBTI Sensing during perception. The overarching goal is to "enforce power over self, others, and nature through exploitive independence."

Level 4. **(Left)** The Truth-Force Meme – Color is **blue**, primary objective is meaning/order, and behavior is seen as purposeful-saintly. Level 4 is recognized as a strong left brain (ST) activity that emphasizes the use of MBTI Thinking during judgment. The overarching goal is to "maintain absolute belief in one right way and obedience to authority."

Level 5. **(Top)** The Strive-Drive Meme – Color is **orange**, autonomy/manipulation is the primary objective, and behavior is seen as strategic-materialist. Level 5 is recognized as a strong cerebral brain (NT) activity that emphasizes the use of MBTI Thinking during judgment. The overarching goal is to use "possibility thinking focused on making things better for self."

Level 6. **(Right)** The Human-Bond Meme – Color is **green**, primary objective is equality/ community, and behavior is seen as sensitive-humanistic. Level 6 is recognized as a strong right brain (NF) activity that emphasizes the use of MBTI Feeling during judgment. The overarching goal is to ensure "well-being of people and building consensus get highest priority."

Tier Two:

Level 7. **(Right)** The Flex-Flow Meme – Color is **yellow**, primary objective is flexibility/natural flows, and behavior is and seen as integrative-ecological. Level 7 is recognized as a strong right brain (NF) activity that emphasizes the use of MBTI Intuition during perception. The overarching goal is to use "flexible adaptation to change through connected, big-picture views."

Level 8. **(Top)** The Global-View Meme – Color is **turquoise,** primary objective is life/harmony, and behavior is seen as holistic-global. Level 8 is recognized as a strong cerebral (NT) activity that emphasizes the use of MBTI Intuition during perception. The overarching goal is to draw "attention to whole-earth dynamics and macro-level actions." (p.47)

Spiral Dynamics is a complementary overlay to the previously discussed psychological assessment tools. It provides a cultural dimension and context within which the other techniques may be better understood. Two examples showing the connection to the MBTI are provided:

Example #1 (Corporate Board Meeting) – Were we in a social service organization corporate board meeting, we might witness a cerebrally-centered ENTJ vice president making a strategically sound and materialistically-oriented (**Orange** Meme) argument for a course of action that is vehemently opposed by the limbic-centered INFJ corporate human resources officer on the grounds that the course of action proposed directly contradicts the firm's community and humanistic values as stated in the new employee handbook (**Green** Meme).

Example #2 (Program Review) – Were we involved in a program review meeting, we might observe a left-brained ISTJ financial manager, following standard financial practices (**Blue** Meme), dispute the right-brained ENFJ program manager's expenditures for team building conducted for the program's sponsors and clients (**Yellow** Meme). And, the INTJ CEO might just be frustrated by the inability of his subordinate managers to just do the "smart thing" (**Turquoise** Meme).

Universal Goals and Ideals

> *Experts are individuals who can recognize and make sense of more patterns than their peers.*
> *Sometimes, experts will "see" or recognize patterns that they may not be able to explain.*
> *They may even call it instinct or intuition. — B. Eugene Griessman*

Our attention is now directed to the inspirational thinking patterns that have influenced personal and social development throughout the civilization of humankind over the last millennium. The reader is invited to conduct a visual comparison between Figure 6-4 below and Figure 6-2 presented earlier in this chapter. The review will show the continuation of the basic brain dominance, MBTI, learning, and Spiral Dynamics concepts, but with the exchange of MBTI Type descriptions by a set of selected *universal goals and ideals*.

Learnership as a philosophy for successful living and working proposes a meta-system thinking pattern in which individuals pursue *self-fulfillment*, organizations seek *high performance*, communities focus on the *common good*, and societies aspire toward *human enlightenment* – a holistic, integrated, comprehensive, goal-seeking worldview. And to set the context for those achievements, six sets of ideals have been selected from the thoughts and writings of earlier sages and philosophers – the habits of mind that encourage our learning, leading, and being: striving to experience (a) *justice and equality*, (b) *truth and honesty*; (c) *responsibility and trust*; (d) *freedom and democracy*; (e) *beauty and goodness*; and (f) *love and happiness*. The summary level definitions used in this book for these goals and ideals are:

Universal Goals:

1. Self-Fulfillment – Achieving one's foremost purpose; obtaining major needs, wants and desires; maximizing advancement potential in the cognitive, affective and psychomotor aspects of ourselves; attaining positive recognition.

2. High Performance – Achieving the organization's greatest efficiency and effectiveness; business and/or mission accomplishment; satisfying constituents, customers, workers and owners.

3. Common Good – Achieving community institutional synthesis and consensus; satisfying community members' service expectations; providing opportunities for meaningful citizenship.

4. Human Enlightenment – Adding to the human capacity for fact-based learning and emotional maturity; improving worldwide thinking, learning, knowing and action; raising the standards of human conduct.

Universal Ideals:

1. <u>Truth & Honesty</u> – Conforming to facts; displaying integrity and sincerity.
2. <u>Beauty & Goodness</u> – A quality that delights the senses; being positive and desirable in nature.
3. <u>Freedom & Democracy</u> – Not bound or constrained; government by the people, majority rule.
4. <u>Justice & Equality</u> – Due reward and punishment; fair treatment and value.
5. <u>Love & Happiness</u> – Deep affection and concern; receiving enjoyment and pleasure.
6. <u>Responsibility & Trust</u> – Having personal accountability; reliance on the integrity and ability of a person or thing.

[**Author's Note**: This section is intended to encourage those aspiring to become learnership practitioners to undergo a period of self-reflection and to confirm those highest order goals and ideals that make learning and leading an essential part of our process of "becoming" our future selves.]

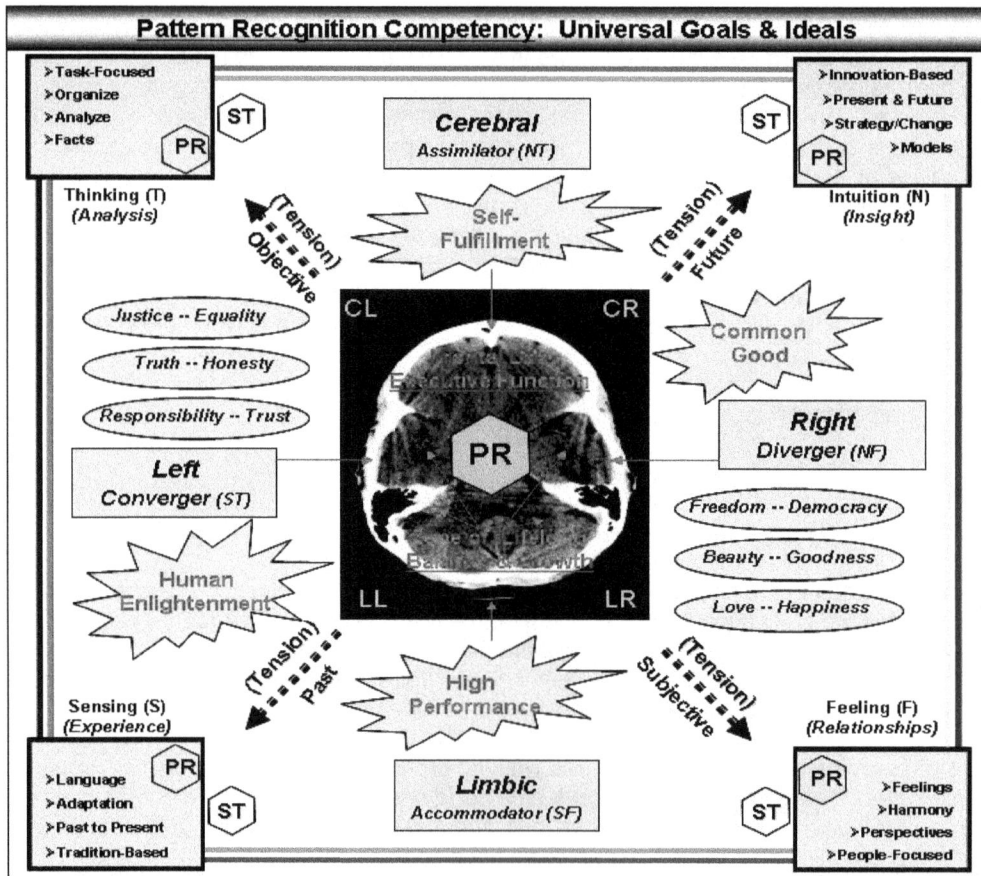

Figure 6-4

Ideals, Influences and Character

Much of what we in the American and European continents say we believe and value today are derived from the histories and cultures of hundreds and thousands of years ago. We are but the latest example of what previous people learned, thought and conjectured – the assumptions and traditions they established to protect and accommodate the influences in their respective physical and social environments. They established family routines and cultural commitments that met the needs and concerns of their particular in-group in order to create a degree of predictability and safety from other physical dangers and any encroachment from other tribes. People outside those groups were not so lucky back then, or even now.

Figure 6-5 displays a notional content and time relationship among the major religions using the concept of *Contemporary Influences*. And, from that center point we can recognize the emergence of the *Universal American Ideals* being suggested in this guidebook as well-supported guiding lights for the development of our culture. Concurrently, American *Character Development* is perceived to be at least partially founded on these influences and ideals. Significant economic, social and political angst is still present in today's diverse societies and cultures. This situation requires citizen and community effort to maintain a balance between these various group needs, desires and pronouncements.

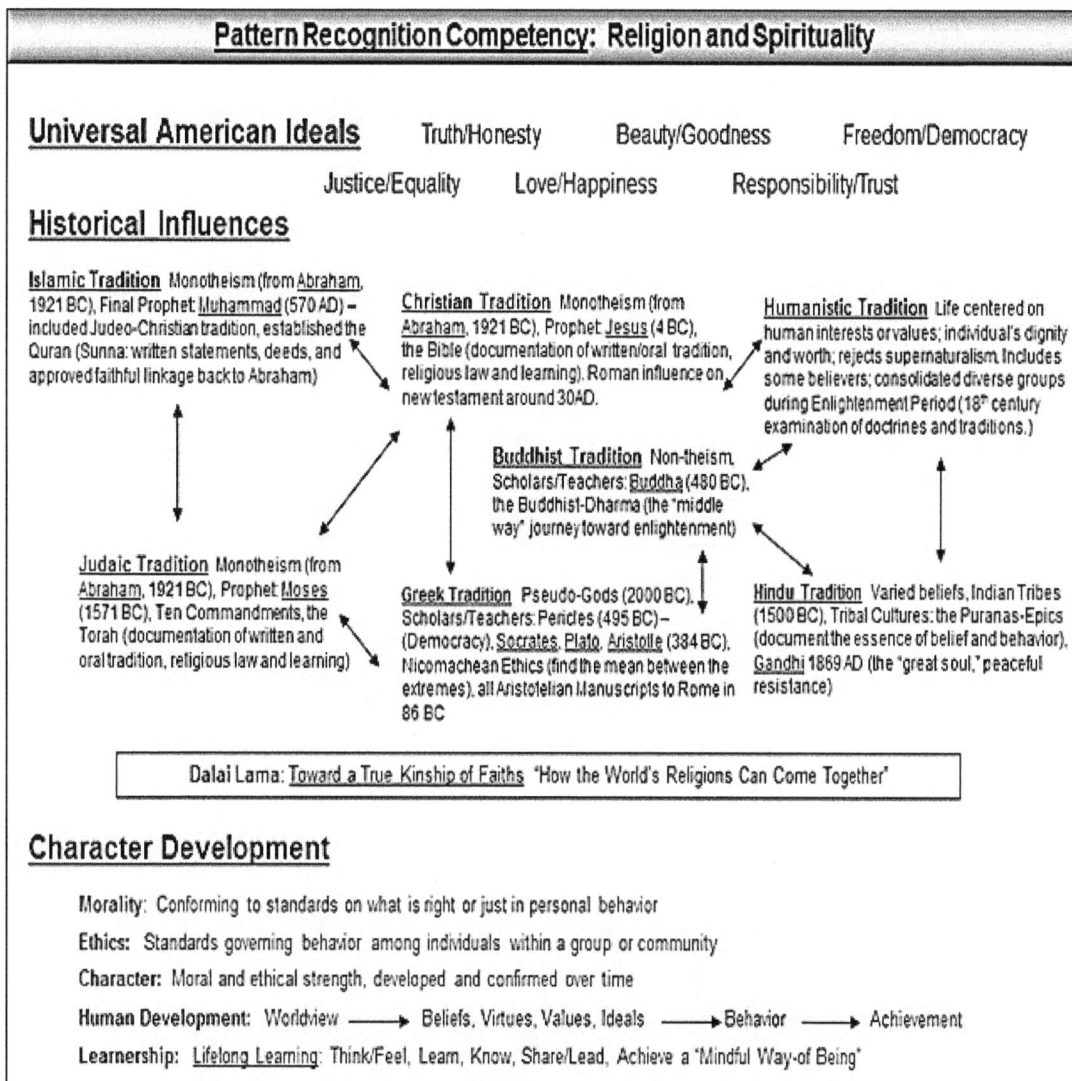

Pattern Recognition Competency: Religion and Spirituality

Universal American Ideals   Truth/Honesty   Beauty/Goodness   Freedom/Democracy

Justice/Equality   Love/Happiness   Responsibility/Trust

Historical Influences

Islamic Tradition Monotheism (from Abraham, 1921 BC), Final Prophet Muhammad (570 AD) – included Judeo-Christian tradition, established the Quran (Sunna: written statements, deeds, and approved faithful linkage back to Abraham)

Christian Tradition Monotheism (from Abraham, 1921 BC), Prophet Jesus (4 BC), the Bible (documentation of written/oral tradition, religious law and learning). Roman influence on new testament around 30AD.

Humanistic Tradition Life centered on human interests or values; individual's dignity and worth; rejects supernaturalism. Includes some believers; consolidated diverse groups during Enlightenment Period (18th century examination of doctrines and traditions.)

Buddhist Tradition Non-theism. Scholars/Teachers: Buddha (480 BC), the Buddhist-Dharma (the "middle way" journey toward enlightenment)

Judaic Tradition Monotheism (from Abraham, 1921 BC), Prophet Moses (1571 BC), Ten Commandments, the Torah (documentation of written and oral tradition, religious law and learning)

Greek Tradition Pseudo-Gods (2000 BC), Scholars/Teachers: Pericles (495 BC) – (Democracy). Socrates, Plato, Aristotle (384 BC), Nicomachean Ethics (find the mean between the extremes), all Aristotelian Manuscripts to Rome in 86 BC

Hindu Tradition Varied beliefs, Indian Tribes (1500 BC), Tribal Cultures: the Puranas-Epics (document the essence of belief and behavior), Gandhi 1869 AD (the "great soul," peaceful resistance)

Dalai Lama: Toward a True Kinship of Faiths "How the World's Religions Can Come Together"

Character Development

Morality: Conforming to standards on what is right or just in personal behavior

Ethics: Standards governing behavior among individuals within a group or community

Character: Moral and ethical strength, developed and confirmed over time

Human Development: Worldview ⟶ Beliefs, Virtues, Values, Ideals ⟶ Behavior ⟶ Achievement

Learnership: Lifelong Learning: Think/Feel, Learn, Know, Share/Lead, Achieve a "Mindful Way-of Being"

Figure 6-5

Religion and Spirituality. In the United States, there are currently twelve major Christian religions (together a large Christian majority) and significant numbers of Muslims, Jews, Hindus, Buddhists, Atheists and Agnostics. Studies show that notwithstanding peoples' tendency to self-report allegiance to Christian churches, there may be more than 20 percent "unchurched" – who Robert Fuller in *Spiritual, But Not Religious* (2001) reports are *pursuing spirituality without religion* or are not actually committed to religious activity.

According to Fuller, "Genuine spirituality, they believe, has to do with personal efforts to achieve greater harmony with the sacred. For them spirituality has to do with private reflection and private experience – not public ritual...Those who are 'spiritual, but not religious' tend to agree with Abraham Maslow's belief that there is a potential antagonism between the private realm of religious experience and the public realm of formal religious practice." (p.4) Furthermore, Fuller reports: "One survey showed that as much as 54 percent of the population has come to believe 'that churches and synagogues have lost the real spiritual part of religion." And, "One out of every three adults interviewed in this survey endorsed the still more radical conclusion that "people have God within them, so churches aren't really necessary." (p.5) To be spiritual, but not religious appears to connote a desire to personally connect with a power or reality larger than oneself in a manner that makes rational sense to those involved; in contrast to simply adhering to the formal rituals, dogma, and often coercive official denominational doctrines of religious organizations.

The *private versus public* aspect of this evolving dichotomy is particularly noteworthy in that this trend is symbiotic with the founders of the American Constitution emphasis on enforcing a *separation between church and state*. Authors Issac Kramnick and R. Laurence Moore write in *The Godless Constitution* (1996) that: "Deism was, as we shall see, a powerful force among the intellectuals of the founding generation, even among many of the delegates in Philadelphia. A non-doctrinaire religion, deism rejected a supernatural faith built around an anthropomorphic God who intervened in human affairs, either in answer to prayer or for other, inscrutable reasons. Instead, it posited a naturalistic religion with a God understood as a supreme intelligence who after creating the world destined it to operate forever after according to natural, rational, and scientific laws...Until 1787, 'there was never a nation in the world whose government was not circumscribed by religion." (p.34) The publisher of the Carlisle Pennsylvania "Aristocrotis" stated bluntly that: "...the new Constitution, disdains...belief of a deity, the immortality of the soul, or the resurrection of the body, a day of judgment, or a future state of rewards and punishments, because its authors are committed to a natural religion that is deistic non-religion." (p.35)

This thumbnail sketch of the pluralistic nature of American religious belief and spirituality demonstrates a broad range of individual and group perspective and another level of complexity in this chapter on Pattern Recognition. To illustrate how major religious and spiritual quests might be (notionally) symbiotic with human psychological preferences, the following inferences are provided to elicit discussion. It is clearly recognized herein that no definitive research on these relationships is likely to be available. Using Figure 6-6 for reference:

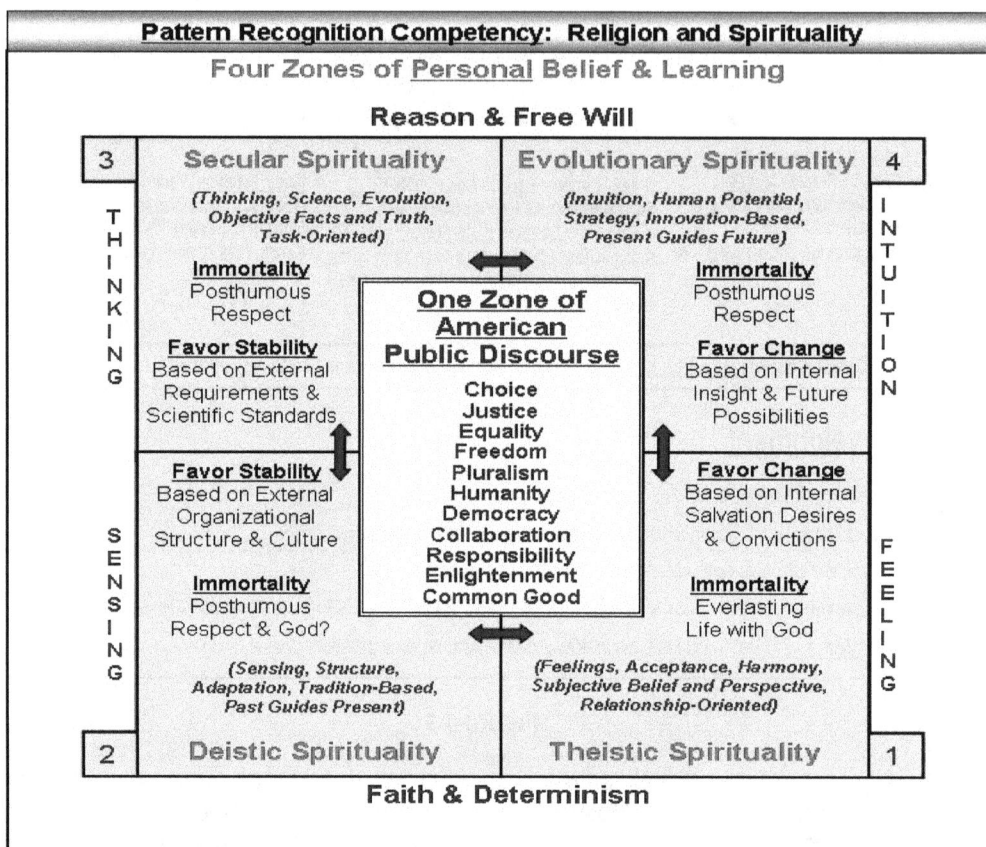

Pattern Recognition Competency: Religion and Spirituality

Four Zones of <u>Personal</u> Belief & Learning

Reason & Free Will

3	**Secular Spirituality**	**Evolutionary Spirituality**	4

T H I N K I N G

(Thinking, Science, Evolution, Objective Facts and Truth, Task-Oriented)

Immortality
Posthumous Respect

Favor Stability
Based on External Requirements & Scientific Standards

Favor Stability
Based on External Organizational Structure & Culture

Immortality
Posthumous Respect & God?

(Sensing, Structure, Adaptation, Tradition-Based, Past Guides Present)

One Zone of American Public Discourse

Choice
Justice
Equality
Freedom
Pluralism
Humanity
Democracy
Collaboration
Responsibility
Enlightenment
Common Good

(Intuition, Human Potential, Strategy, Innovation-Based, Present Guides Future)

Immortality
Posthumous Respect

Favor Change
Based on Internal Insight & Future Possibilities

Favor Change
Based on Internal Salvation Desires & Convictions

Immortality
Everlasting Life with God

(Feelings, Acceptance, Harmony, Subjective Belief and Perspective, Relationship-Oriented)

I N T U I T I O N

S E N S I N G

F E E L I N G

2	**Deistic Spirituality**	**Theistic Spirituality**	1

Faith & Determinism

Figure 6-6

1. <u>Monotheistic (Only one personal, and external God).</u>
   <u>Focus</u> – Religion and spirituality.
   <u>Organizational Construct</u> – Christianity, Judaism, Islam
   <u>Psychological Basis</u> – Strong limbic, feelings, SF/NF, relationship-focused; subjective belief in the "truth" taught by one's own prophet.
   <u>Achieving Immortality</u> – Life, after death, with God.

2. <u>Henotheistic (One main, mostly impersonal, external God).</u>
   <u>Focus</u> – Religion and spirituality.
   <u>Organizational Construct</u> – Deism, Hinduism, Buddhism
   <u>Psychological Basis</u> – Strong limbic, sensing, SF/ST, tradition-based; influenced by authoritarian culture.
   <u>Achieving Immortality</u> – Adherence to naturalism, spiritual guidance or God-figures.

3. <u>Non-Theistic/Secular (No God)</u>.
    <u>Focus</u> – Non-religion, possible spirituality
    <u>Organizational Construct</u> – Atheism, Agnosticism, Non-Religious
    <u>Psychological Basis</u> – Strong cerebral, thinking, NT/ST, task-oriented; objective analysis of scientific data.
    <u>Achieving Immortality</u> – Enduring reputation for personal and organizational achievement

4. <u>Humanistic (Humankind evolves internal, some God-like, capabilities)</u>.
    <u>Focus</u> – Non-religion, possible spirituality
    <u>Organizational Construct</u> – Evolutionary Enlightenment, Human Transformation, Ethical Humanism
    <u>Psychological Basis</u> – Strong cerebral, intuition, NT/NF, development-based; influenced by human potential literature
    <u>Achieving Immortality</u> – Enduring reputation for community and societal accomplishment

[**Author's Note**: The above extrapolation is presented to illustrate the existence of deeply rooted worldviews and situational complexity when human groups with wide variations in culture, knowledge, education, ethnicity, and experience attempt to resolve conflicts or plan community and societal initiatives. The willingness for group members to refrain from "wearing their religion on their sleeves" and to engage each other in respectful dialogue is essential for any kind of resolution and/or consensus to occur. The need is for a facilitated communication process in which the issue and its context are carefully defined, and a progressive and phased dialogue is conducted so a cooperative, if not totally collaborative, result is achieved. The themes and perspectives advocated in this book, due to the absence of the theistic dogma at the core of major religious beliefs, are acknowledged to be primarily of the secular humanistic tradition while respecting the other traditions.]

<u>Learnership practitioners</u> are skilled in recognizing patterns in play during social activities and in taking constructive action to validate and/or reset the frames of reference for better discourse. In a typical situation, it is sufficient to conduct high level psycho-social pattern interpretation that distinguishes among those participants who are bringing diametrically opposed viewing points to the conversation, such as: sensing versus intuition, thinking versus feeling, cerebral versus limbic, and/or left-brain versus right-brain. The resolution of these matters is not to select one perspective over another, but to acknowledge that all add value to the issue at hand; and that the best way to proceed is to use a sequential discovery process in which a number of viewing points are considered but only one at a time to reduce unnecessary conflict and confusion. In such a situation, the learnership practitioner's reasoning and facilitation skills enable constructive discussion.

> *"A firm sense of identity provides both a compass to determine one's course in life and ballast to keep one steady."* — Allen Wheelis

Self, Meaning, and Identity (Why Am I?). Obtaining a fundamental understanding of *self*, our own personhood, is a task we all have in common. However, few of us perform the data collection and analysis sufficiently well to construct a solid foundation for the "why" we are the way we are. This section summarizes expert insight on the topics of *self, meaning, and identity* which will serve as a basis for further discussion on universal goals and ideals.

In *Mind, Self, & Society (Works of George Herbert Mead)* (1934), the editor Charles W. Morris relates Mead's insightful conceptualization of the social character of the mind, and his conclusion that the emergence of what we term *self* and subsequent personality, is the result of the give-and-take between members of a social group or culture. Mead states that to have a *self* each of us must come to know ourselves in terms of both "I" and "me." He says that by way of socialization we come to know ourselves as individual members of the group or society within which we have been developed – the "me" self-consciousness of ourselves. Conversely, when we inculcate additional learning into our personal thinking and behavior, and act upon that new and different knowledge to impact our respective social groups and society – we recognize the "I" of our self-consciousness. The concurrent development of our individual "I" and "me" yields an evolving *self* that matures through our personal lifetimes. The significant contribution of this perspective to the learnership architecture presented in this book is the implicit challenge that we as individuals, as a developmental necessity, have to establish a multi-dimensional social context within which we conduct our lives. The Learnership Integrated Systems Architecture (LISA) that presents a personal, organizational and community social systems development schema that together drive societal systems development is meant to capture this imperative.

In *Man's Search for Meaning* (1959), author and holocaust survivor Victor Frankl explains his development of logotherapy (logos is Greek for "meaning") for counseling others in developing a will to live. He said that "striving to *find a meaning in one's life* is the primary motivational force in man." (p.99) Drawing on his experience in Auschwitz and what it took to survive when even one's dignity was taken away, he speaks eloquently on how "…each man is questioned by life; and he can only answer to life by answering for his own life; to life he can only respond by being responsible…logotherapy sees in *responsibleness* the very essence of human existence." [Italics added] (p.109) The conclusion here is that everyone is responsible for determining their own *will to meaning*, as contrasted with Freud's "will to pleasure" and Adler's "will to power." In fact, Frankl was known to comment when in America: "I recommend that the Statue of Liberty on the East Coast be supplemented by the Statue of Responsibility on the West Coast." (p.159)

Allen Wheelis, author of *The Quest for* Identity (1958) offers another perspective on the meaning of one's life by focusing attention on our ability to create *a sense of ourselves, our identity*. If we do not know who we are, it is difficult to aspire to having personal *meaning*. Wheelis says: "*Identity* is a coherent sense of self. It depends upon the awareness that one's endeavors and one's life make sense, that they are meaningful in the context in which life is lived. It depends also upon stable values, and upon the conviction that one's actions and values are harmoniously related. It is a sense of wholeness, of integration, of knowing what is right and what is wrong, and of being able to choose." (p.19)

Wheelis also comments that there is a distinct *diminishing of human will* in today's turbulent and ever changing society. He says: "When human affairs appear to be inexorably determined by forces over which man has no control, the concept of will has little significance. [but] When human affairs are characterized by a sense of freedom, when society concerns itself with the rights and dignity of the individual, the concept of will is of great importance." (p.43) It appears that restoration of *will* is essential to the formation of *identity* which is essential to ascertain one's *meaning* – *and* that these are basic human self-identity issues, responsibilities and opportunities with which we all must deal.

On the one hand, it appears that self-identity is a foundation upon which most every other thing in life we say or do depends. It is our true sense of being, it colors the way we think and do things. It is the point from which we develop our "leverage" in dealing with life's challenges and responsibilities. A strong identity makes decision-making easier because we know who and what we are and make our choices accordingly. A weak or illusive identity diffuses contrasts, makes decision making harder, increases anxiety, harms our health, and makes us generally less efficient. On the other hand, a self-identity that fails to learn, grow and develop as the context of our lives continues to expand and our experiences become more mature, we risk becoming an irrelevant relic in the evolutionary development of humankind. The solution to this apparent paradox lies in recognizing that human development is a lifelong learning-to-learn process in which the expectation is that new learning and knowledge leads to the continued reflection and refining of our core values and ideals. In fact, this must happen for us to discover, over time, who we are becoming (our identity) and what we should do with our lives (our meaning). And, lest we forget, every self-identity reflects a discoverable pattern of thought and behavior – the subject of this Pattern Recognition chapter.

> *"America must be a community where everyone can achieve personal*
> *freedom and basic security through hard work."* — David Callahan

"Being" and Ideals (What Should I?). Probably everyone by now has some knowledge of Maslow's hierarchy of needs proposed in his original 1943 paper entitled: "Theory of Human Motivation." The Hierarchy is often depicted as a five level pyramid starting at the bottom with psychological needs and progressing upwards to self-actualization needs as follows:

Level 1 <u>Physiological Needs</u> – Breathing, food, water, sex, sleep homeostasis, and an excretion.

Level 2 <u>Safety Needs</u> – Security of body, employment, resources, morality, of the family, of health, and of property.

Level 3 <u>Love/Belonging Needs</u> – Friendship, family, and sexual intimacy.

Level 4 <u>Esteem Needs</u> – Self-esteem, confidence, achievement, respect of others, and respect of others.

Level 5 <u>Self-Actualization</u> – Morality, creativity, spontaneity, problem solving, lack of prejudice, and acceptance of facts.

For Maslow, the first four levels were considered to be *deficiency needs* and the fifth level was for *growth needs*. Unless our lower level needs are sufficiently satisfied, it is difficult to focus on our growth needs. While some have criticized Maslow's theory, most find it to be a compelling framework for practical application. After Maslow's death, a compilation of his later writings were organized into a book entitled: *The Farther Reaches of Human Nature* (1971) in which his elaborations on such topics as transcendence, meta-motivation, and *being-values*. His thoughts on *being-values* are of particular interest in this study, and he says that: Self-actuating people are, without one single exception [in his own study], involved in a cause outside their own skin, in something outside themselves…They are working at something which fate has called them…the *being values*." (p.42) Maslow continues by stating that *being-values* occur in a meta-needs context and are experienced when self-actualizing people have "peak" experiences. (p.43) He provides eight illustrations in which a person can self-actualize which include some combination of:

1. The use of full concentration and total absorption
2. Establishing a sequence of progressive, positive choices
3. Listening to one's own impulse voices
4. Taking responsibility for honest actions
5. Having the courage to choose to disagree and goes one's own way
6. The willingness to prepare oneself for opportunities
7. Having had peak-experiences
8. Having done self-reflection in an effort to free one from unhelpful defenses (pp.46-47)

Lastly, Maslow asserts that: the result of having the capacity to enter into self-actualization is that one experiences selfhood, humanism, the far goals of all psychotherapies, and the characteristics of the *ideally good environment* and of the *ideally good society*. These higher order values or ideals are said to include truth, goodness, beauty, justice, wholeness and many other top tier guides to our personal and social performance.

Another contributor to the literature on higher-order personal and social values and ideals is Mortimer Adler. His book *Six Great Ideas* (1981) is a well-argued treatise on the ideas we judge by and the ideas we live by. Adler initiated his quest to determine the most significant or great ideas by starting with a prior effort in which 102 important words and concepts were selected by experts to enable a reasoned study of the great books of Western civilization. He then investigated the supporting relationships among those words/concepts to discern those that should be the best starting point for a reasoned and systematic study of those ideas. The result was his selection of *truth, goodness and beauty* as ideas we judge by, and *liberty, equality, and justice* as ideas we live by.

His reasoning for liberty, equality, and justice was that: "They represent ideals which a considerable portion of the human race has sought to realize for themselves and their posterity...Only in human society, in which the individual is associated both cooperatively and competitively with other human beings, is there any articulation of claims for liberty, equality, and justice, and only in society do individuals engage in the actions needed to support such claims." (p.23) In terms of his choices of truth, goodness and beauty, Adler says that: "Unlike the ideas we live by (liberty, equality, and justice), these three functions for us in our private as well as our public life. The solitary individual enabled to live comfortably by himself or herself would still have occasion to judge something to be true or false, to appraise this to be good and that evil, to discriminate between the beautiful and the ugly." (p.24)

> *You can't wait for somebody to make a path. You have to go in and*
> *make mistakes and create your own path.*
> —Robert Goizueta

Achievement Factors (How Can I?). Assuming for the moment that we have come to understand our *identity*, and are willing to seek our *meaning*, and we are motivated to *self-actualize*, and the *universal goals and ideals* are on our to-do list; the question still remains: How do I go about pursing my future success. Author B. Eugene Griessman offers to help us out in his book: *The Achievement Factors: Candid Interviews with Some of the Most Successful People of Our Time* (1987). Griessman defines "a high achiever as someone whose work and reputation is such that he or she cannot be ignored by people in their field. Their peers do not have to approve of their work, but they must reckon with it." (p.4) His analysis of his interviews indicates nine general principles that distinguish those who achieve the greatest success:

High achievers discover their vocation and their *specialty*. They find something they love doing, something at which they can become really proficient.

High achievers *develop a competency*. There is no long-term success without developing one's interest, or specialty, into a real competence.

High achievers value and manage what everyone starts out with: *Time*. They are aware that they live in a very time-constrained society and that they must learn to cope with its demands.

High achievers *are persistent*. They are not easily stopped – if they feel that they are on the right track.

High achievers *channel their needs* and wishes into their work. Individuals who are able to channel intense desire into focused, informed, and sustained effort often do attain significant goals.

High achievers develop the *ability to focus*. They possess the ability to tune out static and distractions and give absolute attention to the task at hand.

High achievers *function appropriately* in their situations. There is no denying the importance of being in the right place at the right time.

High achievers *perceive opportunities*. They are always learning, because they are inquisitive, questioning individuals.

High achievers *seize opportunities*. They recognize the existence and importance of trends and social forces, and they try to exploit than for their own purposes." (pp.241-251)

Griessman makes two noteworthy comments about the results of his study. The first is that his list is not comprehensive and there are certainly factors worthy of consideration from other studies. The second is that the personal characteristics of all those he interviewed were not always positive and that the price of success has occasionally been unsatisfactory outcomes in other areas of their lives. Notwithstanding these findings, it is clear that most successful people have a knack for rapid practical learning and an affinity for adaptive leadership to move others and resources toward the ends they desire. Our learnership practitioners will need a self-assessment of their own competencies and initiative to determine how they can further develop the knowledge, attitude and methodological patterns that will enable goal achievement.

Conclusion

Pattern Recognition Competency. The purpose of Chapter Six has been to introduce an array of topics that illuminate the many aspects of pattern recognition, and to explain why it is necessary to develop skills in determining how these patterns impact personal style and social discourse. Some of the major learning points for learnership practitioners are to:

1. Understand the brain as a data and information processor, database and a learning system

2. Develop our own cognitive and emotional reasoning skills.

3. Understand others' cultural programming, personal preferences, and styles of behavior.

4. Recognize and deal appropriately with contextual patterns in social affairs.

5. Appreciate the power of religious worldviews and people's need to sense spirituality.

6. Learn-to-learn a wide range of models and relationships useful in social system dialogue, making choices (exercising and opinion) and decision-making (having consequences).

Our ability to pause and reflect on the *system thinking* suggestions in Chapter Five and the *pattern recognition* observations here in Chapter Six will pay off significantly when we engage in the challenging social situations in the next chapter on *situational learning*.

Implications for Integral Learning and Knowledge Management. The inability to skillfully recognize similarities and differences among workgroup members and/or between various types of work assignments and methods directly affects the quality of team relationships and performance. In everyday life the factors that make us think and act somewhat differently from others are far more numerous than those that tend to make us similar. Differences in age, culture, gender, education, career fields, work assignments, social circles, experience, expectations, and other mental programming make organizational, community, and personal relationships very difficult when it comes to establishing the alignment and cohesion required for high performance.

Effective leadership and management are necessary as well as a willingness among those involved to increase their sensitivity and awareness of the situation. Their being open to the information and clues that help one to understand the roles, objectives, styles, and objectives always in play, but not always clearly expressed is valued. Effective knowledge management depends on understanding what is needed by whom and when; clarity and accuracy matter as well an efficient communication and coordination. Knowledge and skill in pattern recognition enables the accuracy and speed of information sharing, task learning, and issue resolution.

Personal Reflection. This topic appears at the end of each chapter and is meant to serve two purposes: (a) be a reader's guide to main points and "takeaways," and (b) to encourage everyone to take a moment to engage their mental cognition and intuition on what the chapter means to them – especially at this time in their lives. Questions for chapter reflection follow immediately below; and for those readers inclined to maintain a self-assessment, your thoughts may be recorded in the American Learnership Journal: Life, Work, Wealth, Health and Legacy Success located at Appendix B.

Questions for Discussion:

1. Have you ever participated in a work group and wondered to yourself: What is wrong with these people; why do they fail to understand how things get done around here? Can't they see that they are wasting everyone's time? Please consider the mistakes managers often make when attempting to get action in such a situation.

2. Do you agree that people from different cultures, upbringing, experiences, career fields, and age groups have been programmed to have different viewing points, objectives, priorities, and approaches to the same situation or event? What needs to be considered when managing within such diversity? Please explain.

3. Are you able to compare yourself with someone else you know well in terms of either the mental models or learning styles you each prefer? Please explain.

4. Can you list two to three major learning points from this chapter that you want to keep in mind to improve your ability to manage your life and career?

5. What do you think the impact of this chapter's information might be on the personal, organizational, community, and/or societal systems to be discussed later in the book?

6. Can you identify two to three topics, models, or perspectives in this chapter you would like to learn more about?

7. Should you be making an entry into your American Learnership for Life, Work and Legacy Success at Appendix B?

Insights, Commitments and Skills

If you plan to participate in the American Learnership for Life, Work, Wealth, Health and Legacy Success self-development e-book experience, it is suggested you record your Insights, commitments and skills to be developed here in this chapter and again in Appendix B:

My learning in terms of new insights, changing priorities, new commitments or skills I want to acquire:

1. Insights (Example): Remind myself that ...

2. Commitments (Example): Continue to ask myself ...

3. Skills (Example): Apply my knowledge and skills to ...

[**Author's Comment:** Chapters five (ST) and six (PR) just completed have laid a foundation for subsequent reasoning competency graphics that will continue to evolve through Chapters Seven (SL), Eight (KM) and Nine (AL). At that juncture Figure 6-7 below will be completed and become designated as the Learnership Integrated Systems Architecture (LISA). The LISA will then be continuously applied in the Learnership Social System of Systems descriptions Chapters Ten (PSD), Eleven (OSD) Twelve (CSD) and Thirteen (SSD).]

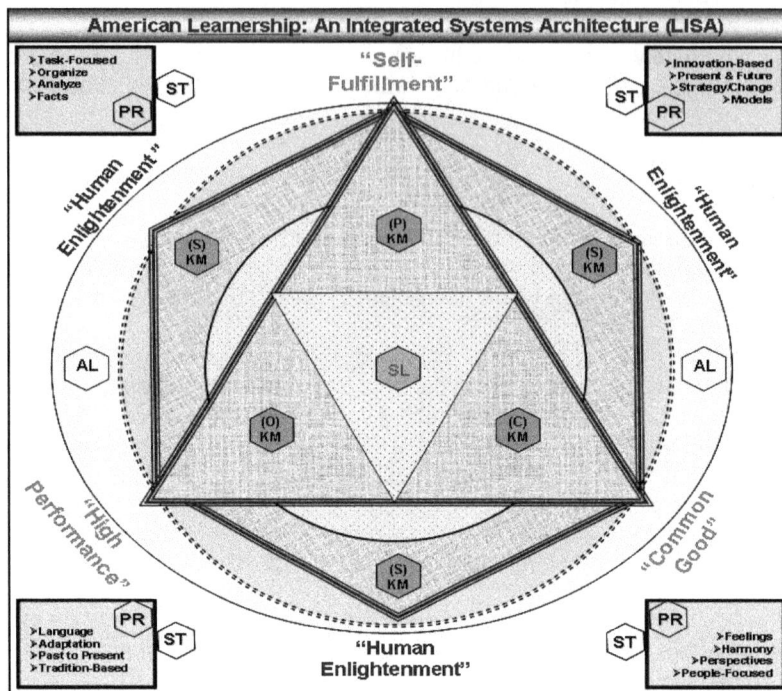

Figure 6-7

Chapter Seven

Reasoning Competency #3: Situational Learning

Major Chapter Topics

Reasoning Competency #3: Situational Learning

Introduction to Situational Learning

> It's almost impossible for a man to be President of the United States
> without learning something. – Harry Truman, 33rd U.S. President

A major life management activity is dealing with the wide variety of situations we encounter on a daily basis. Some situations are routine and need little attention while at the other end of the continuum they may be significantly life and/or career threatening. What is important to understand is that every situation we encounter requires some amount of information gathering and analysis followed by decision making and action – and every situation is a potential learning opportunity. The *situational learning competency* is a significant element in human capital development and in becoming a learnership practitioner which makes it a foundational anchor in the practice of learnership. *Situational Learning (SL) benefits from the support provided by Systems Thinking (ST) and Pattern Recognition (PR).*

Situational learning occurs through a sequential series of lifelong learning cycles in which aspiration, reasoning, action, and evaluation enable people in their roles as individuals, organization members, and community citizens to work toward the triple goals of self-fulfillment, high performance, and the common good. Clearly, learning is the process through which we strive to attain our aspirations. Learning is essential for human and social system development, learning results from resolving (albeit temporarily) the dynamic tension among societal issues, and learning is a precursor for system development toward a higher level-of-being. An ideal objective is to achieve *systems optimization* at the meta-system level, wherein people in their roles as individuals, and in organizations and communities, balance their respective developmental imperatives with consideration of the needs and interests of others. Improving on social system *information processing* (cognitive and emotional), *decision-making* (reasoning and judgment) and *action* (evaluation and feedback) provide a well-spring of new learning cycles, knowledge discovery, and insight into social development opportunities. Situational learning is depicted at the center of the learnership model to illustrate its catalytic potential for stimulating individual, organizational, and community system development.

Five Disciplines. Situational learning is informed by Peter Senge's five disciplines of the learning organization (*The Fifth Discipline*, 1990). All five disciplines are essential contributors to the use of critical thinking and interpersonal dialogue by individuals, organizations, and communities. Systems thinking and mental models (reference: pattern recognition) were introduced in previous chapters, and the other disciplines are also relevant to this topic. A high-level description of key learning-related features of the disciplines follows:

1. <u>Personal Mastery</u> – "Personal Mastery is the discipline of continually clarifying and deepening our personal vision, of focusing our energies, of developing patience, and of seeing reality objectively. As such it is an essential cornerstone of the learning organization – the learning organization's spiritual foundation." (p.6)

2. <u>Mental Models</u> – "Mental models are deeply ingrained assumptions, generalizations, or even pictures that influence how we understand the world and how we take action. Very often, we are not consciously aware of our mental models or the effects they have on our behavior." (p.8)

3. <u>Building Shared Vision</u> – "The practice of shared vision involves the skills of unearthing shared 'pictures of the future' that foster genuine commitment and enrollment rather than compliance." (p.9)

4. <u>Team Learning</u> – "Team learning is vital because teams, not individuals, are the fundamental learning unit in modern organizations. This where 'the rubber meets the road'; unless teams can learn, the organization cannot learn." (p.10)

5. <u>Systems Thinking</u> – "Systems thinking is a conceptual framework, a body of knowledge and tools that has been developed over the last fifty years, to make full patterns clearer, and to help us see how to change them effectively." (p.7)

[**Author's Note**: The learnership philosophy and architecture are constructed to fulfill the learning organization possibilities articulated by Peter Senge and colleagues at MIT.]

Double-Loop Learning. In his book *Reasoning, Learning and Action* (1982) Chris Argyris provides the seminal explanation of the paradoxes between what people say they do (theories espoused) and what they actually do in real situations (theories-in-practice). He explains that oftentimes when people find themselves in complex or conflictive situations wherein interpersonal relationships could be at stake, they *distance* themselves from being part of the problem and even from helping solve the problem. This behavior is replicated by others creating self-fulfilling prophecies in which problems are not solved; or attempted to be solved. Rationality is therefore subverted, mistrust grows among the members, and face-saving political games are played to avoid responsibility and blame. (pp.6-8)

Another dysfunction that may be observed in addition to *distancing* is *disconnecting*. This is a related occurrence in that when distancing is in progress, people – that research has shown are not cognitively aware of their reasoning processes – follow programs in their head that are not consistent with the very reasoning skills they believe they possess. Together, distancing and disconnectedness establish a paradox wherein they conduct themselves contradictory to what they would advise others to do, and resist any attempt to clarify the issues to the extent that they will not even discuss the undiscussables. Their mental processing and behavior are contradictory and they do not want to acknowledge that fact. This behavior has been studied and researched over and over in attempts to develop antidotes to their occurrence and methods to correct the pathology when it is evident.

Argyris argues that this issue is a significant obstacle in creating good learners and learning organizations, and that *double-loop learning* is a potential solution if thoughtfully adopted by organizations. The difference between single and double-loop learning is significant in that in the former problems are met with standard, predictable responses already tried in other situations and proven to be minimally acceptable within the organizational context and culture. Quasi-solutions are attempted with marginal results due to the group's reticence to obtain essential information, challenge inaccurate information, and recognize their own limiting attitudes and behavior.

If and when double-loop learning is understood and group leaders have the courage and skill to facilitate and support the double-loop learning and problem solving processes, the organization can become better informed, build trusted relationships, and take action applicable to multi–dimensional, complex systems and work environments. The double-loop learning process encourage leaders and clients to:

1. Go beyond the convenient, and usual responses and solutions
2. Take time to collect more extensive, relevant information
3. Enter into dialogue with insiders and outsiders to get a true reading on the issue or problem to be solved
4. Be willing to run tests of potential solution for better learning
5. Be willing to reframe issues and problems if new data and information indicate a need to do so

[**Author's Note**: The learnership concept places greater emphasis on double-loop learning rather than single-loop learning cycles. The reason is that the pace of life and work, the degree of complexity, and the rate of change are all increasing thereby ensuring that today's "ready-fire-aim" techniques are likely to miss their target much of the time.]

Learning-to-Learn. In *Workplace Basics: The Essential Skills Employers Want* (Carnevale et al, 1990), the authors attribute to Robert M. Smith of Northern Illinois University the view that: "Learning how to learn involves possessing, or acquiring, the knowledge and skill to learn effectively in whatever learning situation one encounters." They add that learning-to-learn skills should be acquired by individuals because the situations which they encounter are likely to be unpredictable and fraught with changing task demands, thereby requiring them to be *adaptive learners and leaders*. Early contributors to this theme were: (1) Benjamin Franklin who founded a discussion club, the Junto, which had rules to forestall dogmatism, minimize conflict, and foster productive inquiry; members who broke the rules were fined, (2) Arnold Toynbee who advocated that learners turn themselves into "self-teachers," and (3) John Dewey who suggested that schools be evaluated in terms of their success in causing students to desire "continual growth" and in providing them with the capability to do so.

The challenge in assisting individuals to acquire the learning-to-learn skill is to first help them identify their own developmental needs and to take responsibility for their learning and its progress. Next, the task is to enlighten them with the knowledge, resources, and techniques that make the process manageable. Learning-to-learn training designs strive to help trainers use, and learners take personal advantage of the following learning theory components:

Knowledge of Domains of Mental Activity. There are three spheres or domains of mental activity within which learning takes place. The first is the "cognitive (thinking/knowing) domain" which involves the skills people use to know, understand, or comprehend information. The second is the "psychomotor (physical) domain which involves neuro-muscular coordination and the skills people use to control their body movements. The third is the affective (behavioral/attitudinal) domain which involves skills in dealing with emotions and feelings, and focuses on valuing, organizing, and characterizing the human aspects of situations. Different people have different strengths in these areas, but all learners can strive to increase their attention and openness while experiencing a learning activity in each domain.

Knowledge of Learning Styles. Various learning-style inventories have been constructed to illustrate how individuals differ in perceiving and acting on information. The authors reference *Learning How to Learn* (1982) by Robert M. Smith as a resource of available instruments and explain that individuals who become aware of their unique styles of learning have greater self-awareness, and potentially, are better able to communicate and learn from others and their experiences. Examples given are Kolb's Learning Style Inventory, the Myers-Briggs Type Indicator (MBTI), and Herrmann Brain Dominance Inventory (HBDI).

Knowledge of Formal Learning Strategies. Both trainers who design learning experiences and learners who participate in them perform more effectively when they are aware of the range of techniques available to enhance learning. Five general techniques may be defined:

The first may be termed "rehearsal strategies" and includes activities to list, copy, or repeat items in order to commit them to memory.

The second technique may be called "elaboration strategies" and include mental imagery of the connections and relationships among items.

The third technique is termed "organizational strategies" that include grouping items that share certain characteristics or which can be arranged in a graphic diagram.

The fourth technique is called "comprehension monitoring strategies" in which individuals are aware of their learning process and are able to control their cognitive processes and change them as appropriate.

The fifth technique is termed "affective and motivational strategies" in which positive reinforcement and self-generated support is applied to maintain one's focus and progress.

When these strategies are understood and used in combination by the trainer and learner, the learner not only learns a subject better but *learns learning skills* transferable to other situations.

Knowledge of Informal Learning Strategies. Informal learning strategies occur outside formally planned learning activities, and are valuable experiences if the learner is aware that they are occurring and takes advantage of them. The techniques for using experiences for learning requires one to assume a questioning or inquiry stance towards an issue which includes:

1. Identifying the assumptions that underlay individuals' perspectives and test them for validity before proceeding

2. Generating and testing alternative interpretations of information in an effort to assess possible consequences of each choice. This approach improves a person's quality of learning by ensuring that misconstrued data or conclusions do not interfere with their reasoning.

Critical Thinking and Dialogue

Seized by an elemental togetherness, we touch the
genuine power of dialogue, and magic unfolds. — William Issacs

Critical Thinking Inquiry. M. Neil Browne and Stuart Keeley, authors of *Asking the Right Questions: A Guide to Critical Thinking* (2001) define their use of critical thinking by saying that: "Critical thinking consists of an awareness of a set of interrelated critical questions, plus the ability and willingness to ask and answer them at appropriate times." (p.3) The authors postulate two approaches to learning; the *sponge approach* and the *panning-for-gold approach*. In the sponge approach, the learner spends much time reading and listening carefully to information in the manner the writer or speaker chooses to present it – absorption is the passive technique. In the panning for gold approach, the learner is an active participant in *dialogue* seeking out the nuggets of knowledge he or she has decided to obtain. *Interactive involvement* is the technique used by the proactive panning-for-gold learner. Interactive involvement means careful pursuit of essential information for reasoning and decision-making, and engaging others through questioning that clarifies the information and/or motives of writers and speakers. The type of inquiries and direct questioning that gets to the essential information for contemplation are listed below and illustrated in Figure 7-1: (paraphrased)

1. Require facts and valid reasoning, reduce ambiguity, and challenge loaded language.

2. Request clarification and stronger reasons to support another's perspective.

3. Inquire as to the quality and appropriateness of research, observations and conclusions.

4. Build the impression that collaboration and inclusion are being pursued.

5. Convey a willingness to learn and accept new conclusions.

6. Present oneself as willing to suspend preconditions in the search for better information.

7. Voice critical questions with curiosity and a willingness to listen.

8. Constrain inappropriate emotions and concentrate on effective reasoning.

9. Encourage others to join in mutual examination of assumptions and factual information.

10. Restate what has been heard to assure others of being heard and respected.

Browne and Keeley understand that the use of critical thinking skills can be intimidating to those unaware of the usefulness of asking pertinent questions seeking better information and clarity of thinking. To alleviate possible resistance they advocate a few guidelines for use during dialogue:

1. Be certain to demonstrate that you really want to grasp what is being said. As questions that indicate your willingness to grasp and accept new conclusions.

2. Restate what you heard or read and ask whether your understanding of the argument is consistent with what was written or spoken.

3. Voice your critical questions as if you were curious. Nothing is more deadly to the effective use of critical thinking than an attitude of "Aha, I caught you making an error."

4. Convey the mindset that you and others are collaborators, working toward the same objective – improved conclusions.

5. Avoid critical thinking jargon that the other person would not understand.

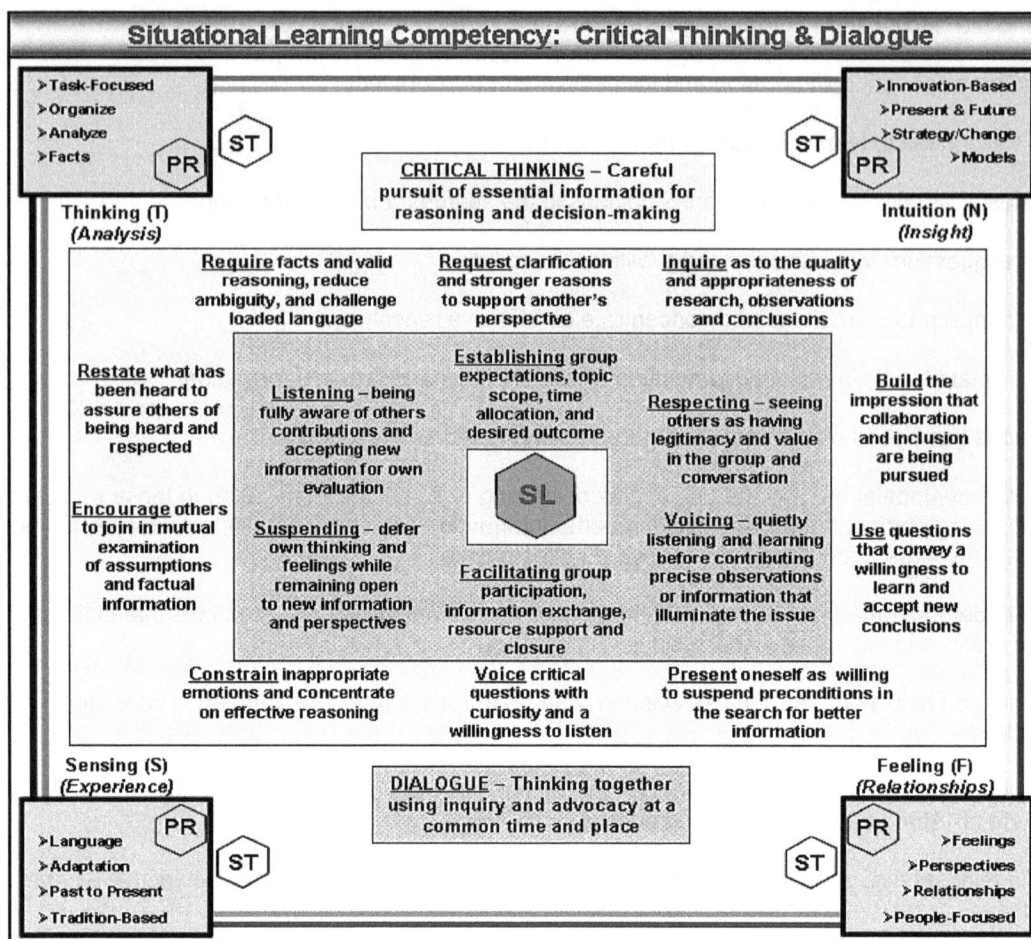

Situational Learning Competency: Critical Thinking & Dialogue

> Task-Focused
> Organize
> Analyze
> Facts

PR **ST**

Thinking (T)
(Analysis)

> Innovation-Based
> Present & Future
> Strategy/Change
> Models

ST **PR**

Intuition (N)
(Insight)

CRITICAL THINKING – Careful pursuit of essential information for reasoning and decision-making

Require facts and valid reasoning, reduce ambiguity, and challenge loaded language

Request clarification and stronger reasons to support another's perspective

Inquire as to the quality and appropriateness of research, observations and conclusions

Restate what has been heard to assure others of being heard and respected

Listening – being fully aware of others contributions and accepting new information for own evaluation

Establishing group expectations, topic scope, time allocation, and desired outcome

SL

Respecting – seeing others as having legitimacy and value in the group and conversation

Build the impression that collaboration and inclusion are being pursued

Encourage others to join in mutual examination of assumptions and factual information

Suspending – defer own thinking and feelings while remaining open to new information and perspectives

Facilitating group participation, information exchange, resource support and closure

Voicing – quietly listening and learning before contributing precise observations or information that illuminate the issue

Use questions that convey a willingness to learn and accept new conclusions

Constrain inappropriate emotions and concentrate on effective reasoning

Voice critical questions with curiosity and a willingness to listen

Present oneself as willing to suspend preconditions in the search for better information

Sensing (S)
(Experience)

DIALOGUE – Thinking together using inquiry and advocacy at a common time and place

Feeling (F)
(Relationships)

> Language
> Adaptation
> Past to Present
> Tradition-Based

PR **ST**

PR **ST**

> Feelings
> Perspectives
> Relationships
> People-Focused

Figure 7-1

Interpersonal Dialogue. In *Dialogue and the Art of Thinking Together* (1999) author William Isaacs asks:

1. How can we learn, as individuals, to take actions that might be conducive to evoke dialogue?

2. How can we create dialogue in settings where people may not have initially been willing to engage in it? [And]

3. How can we prevent retrenchment?" (p.29)

He offers that "dialogue is a conversation with a center, not sides" (p.17), and that dialogue builds interpersonal relationships and trust that leads to more effective communication and results in social situations. Specifically, the objectives of dialogue are to produce coherent actions, create fluid structures of interaction, and provide a wholesome space for dialogue." (pp.29-30)

A short definition of dialogue as used in this text is: *Dialogue is thinking and conversation using information inquiry and advocacy at a common time and place.* And, the view here is that situational learning is enabled whenever communications is based more on dialogue and less on debate or argument. Isaacs proposes four characteristics that distinguish dialogue from other forms of communication. These are paraphrased below, along with additional insight on the role of facilitators in the dialogue process. Dialogue characteristics listed below and in Figure 7-1 include:

1. Listening – Being fully aware of others contributions and accepting new information for own evaluation.
2. Respecting – Seeing others as having legitimacy and value in the group and conversation.
3. Suspending – Defer own thinking and feelings while remaining open to new information and perspectives.
4. Voicing – Quietly listening and learning before contributing precise information that illuminates the issue.
5. Facilitating – Assisting in group participation, information exchange, resource support, and closure.
6. Establishing – Group expectations, topic scope, time allocation, and desired outcome.

Facilitating Dialogue. Effective facilitation of group activity and dialogue brings people with different objectives, interests, knowledge, and preferences together to listen, learn and deliberate toward consensus and eventual action. When done well, individuals are empowered by the learning they acquire and the group organization benefits from the decisions that are made and supported. Figure 7-2 illustrates what occurs when a meeting facilitator provides a dialogue framework and coaches participants in systematic conversation. Assuming there is a spirit of mutual respect and trust among the participants, the facilitator obtains agreement for the group to hold two conversations, sessions 1 and 2 separated by a break period in-between.

The first session is used for participants to learn and reflect on the issue of problem under consideration. The obligation of the group is to use systems thinking and explore patterns of belief and mental models that may be relevant in session 2. Essentially, this is a period for getting increasingly open, absorbing contributed information and varying perspectives, and practicing dialogue skills so all are involved and committed to group success. Topics are discussed is a respectful manner, potential approaches and methods are explored, but no commitment is made other than some tentative clarification of the issue/problem space.

If the group is known to have significant interpersonal conflict on the topic being discussed or with one another, two extra initiatives may be useful:

1. Acknowledge the likelihood of different expectations and subsequent expectations, and

2. Request recommendations for corrective action and offer support for considerate communications.

The second session is used for participants to decide and act on what they now hold together in trust for one another – their understandings, contributions, and expertise. The facilitator, having done some prior organization of contributions during the break period, helps the group start to move toward closure. Continued dialogue (perhaps interspersed with occasional mild debate) focuses on alternative ways to organize and prioritize the group's thoughtful submissions. Eventually, a reasonable level of consensus becomes apparent wherein everyone acknowledges their views have been heard and considered, and that they can sign on to a final product. A plan of action and a communication strategy are prepared to communicate the group's decision.

Again, given a heightened amount of interpersonal attention the following actions may be beneficial:

1. Assert the value of working toward mutual respect and shared purpose, and

2. Recognize conciliatory comments and support for productive action.

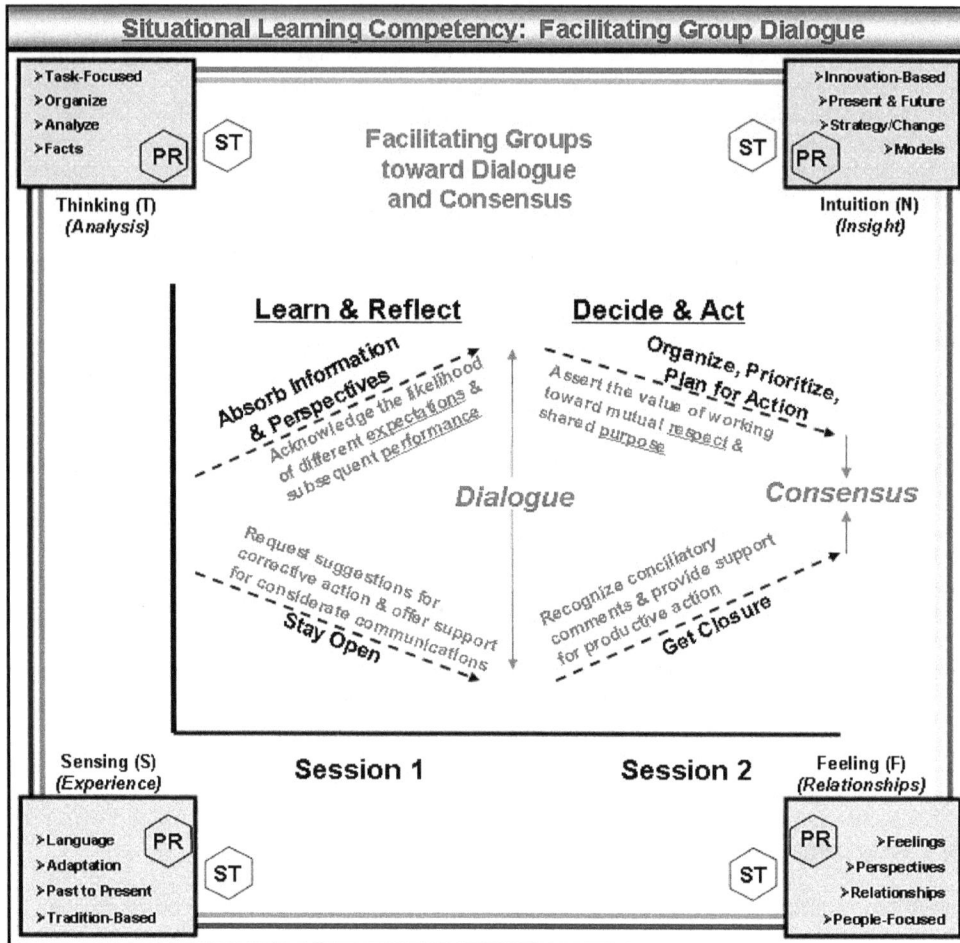

Figure 7-2

Reasoning, Learning and Knowledge

*To be adequate for our strange new world we must come to think
of learning as being the same as living.*
— *Malcolm Knowles*

Selected Perspectives.

Motives and Conditions for Learning. *In Understanding and Facilitating Adult Learning* (Brookfield, 1986), the author suggests that a society is able to realize its humanity through its ability to learn. It is through learning that we are able to both create and alter our beliefs, values, behaviors, and relationships which form our culture. He states: "The extent to which adults are engaged in a free exchange of ideas, beliefs, and practices is one gauge of whether society is open, democratic, and healthy. If adults of widely differing class and ethnic groups are actively exploring ideas, beliefs, and practices, then we are likely to have a society in which creativity, diversity, and the continuous re-creation of social structures are the accepted norms." (p.8) What is implied is that learning is a fundamental individual and collective function, and that the capability of a people to learn what they have in common and to forge agreements is essential for societal growth and development.

Brookfield emphasizes learning in adulthood as the basis for continued societal development, and addresses the importance of adult motivation, styles of learning, and conditions that facilitate learning. He offers six principles of effective practice (pp.9-10) in establishing a learning environment. These are paraphrased for general use in the context of this book as follows:

1. Learning should be voluntary – Better learning and commitment to what is learned is the result of voluntary participation wherein the learner's objectives create his or her own motivation.

2. Learning requires respect – Individuals whose self-worth is in doubt are limited in their ability to learn
.

3. Learning is collaborative – The teacher (leader) and learner are engaged in a cooperative enterprise in which objectives, roles, and responsibilities are discussed and renegotiated as required.

4. Learning is reflection upon experience – It is through collaborative analysis of actions and consequences that strategies for obtaining improved results are established for future use.

5. Learning should include critical reflection – Learners can develop further if they are able to recognize the underlying values, beliefs, behaviors, and ideologies that are culturally transmitted during their experiences, and if they are thereby able to appreciate the situational nature of their experiences.

6. Learning should be self-directed – Learners who take responsibility for what and how they learn are empowered adults in control of themselves, and to some extent, their environment.

Brookfield expands on his views by adding insights provided by C. Suanmali in an unpublished doctoral dissertation entitled: "The Core Concepts of Androgyny." Suanmali suggests that adults have enhanced capability to function as self-directed learners when they are able to:

1. Decrease their dependence on educators (leaders).

2. Identify and use learning resources.

3. Define their learning needs and objectives.

4. Organize what is to be learned in terms of their problems and level of understanding.

5. Improve their decision making and problem solving capability.

6. Develop and apply criteria for judging experience..

[Author's Note: An observation here is that human and social system learning is based on the same principles and practices advocated for adult learning. It appears that one who is motivated to learn, is willing to be responsible for his or her own learning, and is able to participate with those who can act as facilitators and sources of information, will experience growth and development commensurate with their personal capabilities and time investment.]

Orientations to Learning. In their book, *Learning in Adulthood: A Comprehensive Guide* (Merriam & Caffarella, 1991), the authors summarize major theories about the learning process into four orientations: behaviorist, cognitivist, humanist, and social learning. Each orientation poses a perspective on what happens during the learning process, and each offers insight into the multiple purposes and developmental outcomes from effective learning. They are:

1. The Behaviourist Orientation – Behaviorism focuses on the systematic design and delivery of instruction for the purpose of producing desired behavior change. Three underlying assumptions are held to be true. First, observable behavior rather than internal thought processes is the focus of study; in particular, learning is manifested by change in behavior. Second, the environment shapes one's behavior; what one learns is determined by the elements in the environment, not by the individual learner. And third, the principles of contiguity and reinforcement are central to explaining the learning process. "Stimulus-response" and "operant conditioning" theories hold sway in the behaviorist perspective as evidenced by the view attributed by the authors to B. F. Skinner that ". . . the ultimate goal of education is to bring about behavior that will ensure survival of the human species, societies, and individuals (Skinner, 1971).

2. The Cognitive Orientation – In contrast to the behaviorist viewpoint, cognitive orientation is based primarily on the Gestalt (German word for pattern or shape) or wholeness of a situation or event. The importance of individual perception, insight, and meaning are major contributions to cognitivism from Gestalt learning theorists. While behaviorists emphasize the environment as the locus of control over learning, the cognitivists (Gestaltists) place responsibility for learning with the individual or adult learning theory.

Cognitive psychologist Jean Piaget (1966) proposed a four-stage theory of cognitive development based on the view that one's internal cognitive structure changes partly because of maturational changes in the nervous system and partly because of the organism's experience with its external environment. Piaget explained that during childhood individuals pass through four stages of cognitive development that represent different ways of making sense, understanding, and constructing knowledge of the world. He suggested that the individual was capable of mature adult thought by the age of twenty. His four stages of cognitive development are:

a. Sensory-motor, in which thought is stimulated by innate reflex actions
b. Pre-operational, wherein concrete objects may be represented in symbols and words
c. Concrete operational, in which there is understanding of concepts and relationships of ideas
d. The formal operational, wherein the ability to reason hypothetically, logically, and systematically is fully developed

Others have built upon Piaget's foundational theory by adding their perspectives on various facets of cognitive learning and human development. Some of those directly applicable to this chapter include D. P. Ausubel's (1967) view that "meaningful learning" as opposed to "rote learning" occurs when it can be related to concepts which already exist in a person's cognitive structure and that "advance organizers" are necessary to prepare a person for new learning. Ausubel's work apparently stimulated research by others into *schema theory* wherein schemata – structures that organize the learner's worldview – in turn determine how new experiences are processed (Di Vesta, 1987; Greeno, 1980). The relationship of schema theory to learnership is discussed more fully later in this section under the subject of knowledge.

3. The Humanist Orientation – Humanist theories consider learning from the perspective of the human potential for growth, and include affective as well as cognitive dimensions of learning. Rather than accept that behavior is predetermined by environment (behaviorist) or subconscious (cognitivist), humanists see people in control of their own destiny, people that are inherently good and are striving for a better world, people that are free to act and whose behavior is a consequence of human choice, and people that possess an unlimited potential for growth and development (Rodgers, 1983; Maslow, 1970).

Maslow, with his theory of motivation based on a hierarchy of human needs (discussed in the section on personal systems development), is considered to be the founder of humanistic psychology. Maslow stated that the need to learn is intrinsic and that it emanates from the learner. He believed that among growth motivations could be found the need for cognition – a desire to know and understand. In addition to the primary goal of self-actualization, Maslow identified other goals related to learning and understanding (p.439) which (selectively) include:

a. The acquisition of a set of values
b. The attainment of peak experiences
c. A sense of accomplishment
d. An understanding of the critical existential issues of life
e. The control of one's impulses
f. Learning to choose judiciously.

Carl Rodgers is another major figure who writes from a humanist orientation. In his view, "client-centered therapy" conducted by psychotherapists and "student-centered learning" led by educators are similar in outcome – both are concerned with significant learning in which the client and student, respectively, achieve personal growth and development. The characteristics of such learning are: (a) personal involvement – the affective and cognitive aspects of a person should be involved in the learning event, (b) self-initiated – a sense of discovery must come from within, (c) pervasive – the learning makes a difference in the behavior (d) evaluated by the learner – the learner can best determine whether the experience is meeting a need, and (e) essence is meaning – when experiential learning takes place, its meaning to the learner becomes incorporated into the total experience. (p.20)

4. A Social Learning Orientation – Social learning theory takes the position that people learn from observing other people in a variety of social settings. Bandura (1976) observes that: "Virtually all learning phenomena resulting from direct experiences can occur on a vicarious basis through observation of other people's behavior and its consequences for the observer." He contends that what he calls "observational or social learning" may be characterized by the concept of self-regulation, and that "persons can regulate their own behavior to some extent by visualizing self-generated consequences." (p.392)

B. R. Hergenhahn (1988) adds the view that observational learning is influenced by the four processes of attention, retention or memory, behavioral research, and motivation. These processes are described as: (a) attention must first be given to someone who serves as a potentially worthy model for one's behavior modification, (b) information from observing the actions of the model and the consequences of those actions on the observer is set into the person's memory, (c) a rehearsal in which the learner imitates what has been modeled and compares the results received to the modeled experience, and (d) the modeled behavior is accepted as being useful and is stored for future use. Through this process, the interaction of the person with his or her social environment is described as a process of mutual influence, and learning is set completely within a social context.

[**Author's Note 1**: These orientations to learning are believed to be particularly relevant to the Learnership model and hypothesis of this book. Learning occurs with maximum impact when all four orientations are factored into the learning experience of the individual, organization, or community. When learning results in (1) desired behavior change in response to influences in the social environment (behaviorist); (2) the ability of persons to take responsibility for their learning and to reason maturely with relevant information (cognitivist); (3) increased motivation to create a better quality of social life (humanist); and (4) the willingness to learn from high-quality role models (social learning), significant social growth and development may be anticipated.]

[**Author's Note 2**: An observation in terms of this research project is that knowledge of learning theory and one's own preferred way of learning, coupled with an understanding of the strategies used by others, is likely to enhance the quality of social discourse. The willingness to explore issues with others while simultaneously making the process one of inquiry and learning contributes to the dignity and maturity of all concerned. This approach is linked directly to the quality of dialogue a group is able to achieve, and the range of social problem solutions they are able to develop for possible consensual action.]

Ordinary Knowledge and Problem Solving. In *Usable Knowledge: Social Problem Science and Social Problem Solving* (Lindblom & Cohen, 1979), the authors challenge the wide-spread view that social problems may be solved through scientific problem solving methodologies similar to those used in hard-science research. The authors opine that social problem complexity inhibits the effective conduct of social research, thereby invalidating much of the supposed evidence for the argument being made. In their view the formal technique of information gathering and analysis within defined, bounded, and controlled environments is impossible to achieve, and pretending to do so only minimizes the likelihood of problem solution and wastes resources. They point out that: "...a great deal of the world's problem solving is and ought to be accomplished through various forms of social interaction that substitute action for thought, understanding, and analysis." (p.10)

Lindblom and Cohen focus attention on the difficulty in handling "divergent problems," the importance of "social interaction and learning," the need for "political considerations" in problem identification and solution, the acceptability of "ordinary knowledge." They explain that *most social problems are diverging* rather than converging in nature. That is, they are *values-based* wherein increased deliberation often fails to bring the parties (with significantly different values) closer together on an issue. These issues require greater social interaction and learning by the participants, a desire to work for a political consensus, the admissibility of ordinary knowledge and experience as useful facts, and a willingness to take a series of iterative actions in the right direction with the expectation that a good solution will eventually be found. In their view, professional social inquiry can, at best, provide only modest new information that is both accurate and timely – the practical experience of informed people in the community must provide the bulk of the knowledge on an issue.

[**Author's Note**: This perspective is useful in that it reflects the need for participation of knowledgeable people in the affairs of their organizations and communities. There are no perfect scientific solutions to social issues that may be achieved without the involvement of those who are invested in the consequences of the decisions that are made. Divergent issues call for open inquiry and dialogue into values, assumptions, facts, objectives, and strategies relevant to the issue at hand. Individuals, organizations, and communities must engage one another and intelligently reason, learn, and act together for their common purpose.]

Knowledge, Learning, and Scheme Theory. In their book, *Learning in Adulthood: A Comprehensive Guide* (Merriam & Caffarella, 1991) explain that the ability to learn is based on an individual's previously developed cognitive structure and his or her skill at learning. They present the concept of "scheme theory" (plural of schemata) in which the way an individual packages knowledge and organizes his or her long-term memory establishes his or her perspective or worldview. This, in turn, influences how they interpret and assimilate new information. Two schematic types are distinguishable: *declarative knowledge* which are the facts one knows, and *procedural knowledge* which is one's knowledge on how to perform skills and tasks.

The authors identify three different modes of learning using scheme theory: *accretion*, in which there is a daily accumulation of facts, *tuning*, in which slow and gradual changes in the schemata occur, and *restructuring*, wherein new schemata are created and those already stored are reorganized. They state that the processes of tuning and restructuring are vital for adult learning, critical thinking, and problem solving. An important insight offered is that: "...in most problem-solving situations, we are trying to fit new ideas (declarative knowledge) and ways of thinking (procedural knowledge) into earlier patterns of thinking and doing (our current schemata). If we are unable to change our earlier thought patterns…our chances of being able to frame and act on problems from a different perspective is remote if not impossible." (p.171)

Another characteristic of prior knowledge and experience in learning is that novices and experts know things differently. Experts not only have a greater amount of knowledge, they also seem to have it organized differently. While novices organize their thinking in terms of the literal aspects explicitly given in a situation, experts are observant of underlying principles and abstractions that subsume the literal objects. Also, experts have knowledge on how to use or apply their knowledge. Finally, the authors speak to the importance of *dialectic thinking* in cognitive development. Dialectic thinking is thinking that recognizes alternative truths or ways of thinking about similar real-life phenomena. Whereas, *operational thinking* is focused on determining indisputable facts of a given situation, dialectic thinking seeks to recognize and understand the contradictory aspects of human thought and action. Some writers suggest that dialectic thinking is essential for the conduct of mature reasoning. The authors reference other writers' contributions on this subject, the highlights of which are useful in this work (bibliographic entries are provided for further inquiry). The highlights include:

1. Pascual-Leone (1983) offers that adult cognitive development continues past the formal operational thinking stage accepted by earlier writers, and suggests that there are four additional stages entitled: the late formal stage, the pre-dialectical stage, the dialectical stage, and the transcendental stage. It appears that it is only at these higher levels of thinking that societal contradictions, conflicts, and meta-developmental concerns may be understood.

2. Benack and Besseches (1989) have developed a "dialectical schemata framework" that illustrates the twenty-four moves in thought that dialectical thinkers can be construed to make. Apparently, *individuals with higher-order worldviews* are better skilled at turning existing knowledge into processes of inquiry aimed at attaining greater and more mature understanding.

3. Kramer (1989) indicates that the acceptance of contradiction and different worldviews are the hallmarks of adult thinking and believes that "*mature dialectic thought rarely appears before middle age*". (p.151) Merriam and Caffarella state that: "This mature dialectic thought is characterized by awareness that all thought processes are culturally and historically bound and therefore dynamic and constantly evolving." (p. 187)

[**Author's Note**: The significance of these views to the learnership model may be seen in the fact that they reinforce the notion that *pre-established paradigms or models for thinking affect the individual's capacity to learn and develop*. Improved thinking structures lead to improved reasoning, learning, and action. This is precisely what the learnership model is intended to demonstrate. Also, the idea of dialectic thinking for improved learning is a fundamental skill in the concept of dialogue developed earlier, and which is foundational in creating improved *societal dialogue*.]

Ten Philosophical Mistakes. In *Ten Philosophical Mistakes* (Adler, 1985), the author argues that modern reasoning and judgment are often poorly accomplished due to "*little philosophical mistakes*" that entered into the thinking of some noted philosophers of the seventeenth century – specifically Thomas Hobbes in England and Rene' Descartes in France. These mistakes continue in modern thought and are witnessed as erroneous premises persistently leading to false conclusions, inappropriate decisions, and failed consequences. In most cases when the little errors in the beginning are recognized, modern thinkers attempt to circumvent their impact further compounding the resulting difficulties. The ten philosophical mistakes (pp.xvi-xix) identified are:

1. Not recognizing that all of each person's ideas or viewpoints are *subjective interpretations* of his or her own knowledge and experience. Ideas, then, are not perfectly correct expressions of some objective reality.

2. The failure to distinguish between *perceptual thought* about sensible objects and *conceptual thought* about those things that are constructed through the mind's power of intelligence. Only humans can deal with the unperceived and the unimaginable.

3. Not recognizing that all *ideas are meanings*, and that they are the basis for all man-made words, signs, and symbols. Words, signs, and symbols cannot be said to be meaningless when they have referential ideas with which they are associated.

4. The failure to distinguish between *knowledge* and *opinion*. Having knowledge connotes being in possession of true information, the certitude of which is beyond reasonable doubt. Opinions on the other hand may be asserted with little basis in evidence or reason. Decisions in this case have to do with whether something exists or not and requires *descriptive judgment*.

5. The belief that there are no objectively valid and universally tenable moral standards or norms. The ability to distinguish and prefer human needs over human wants, and real goods over apparent goods, leads to a desire for knowledge and truth rather than opinion and the capacity to discern between "ought" and "ought not." Decisions in this case are said to be *prescriptive judgment*.

6. The identification of *happiness* exclusively with the psychological state of contentment. This notion contributes to the inability to distinguish between human needs and wants and between real and apparent goods – which undermines the development of a moral philosophy in which happiness also conveys attaining a *life well-lived* and in balance.

7. The misunderstanding of the relation between *free choice* and *moral responsibility*. Determinists argue that people do not have free will and choice and therefore should not be held fully accountable for their actions. The counterpoint is that moral virtue depends upon the freedom of will and choice in one's learning and development which necessitates moral responsibility and accountability.

8. The denial of common *human nature* among all people and cultures. Notwithstanding the deterministic characteristics common to species other than humans, and the belief that humans have no essential similarity because they each receive a different genetic beginning (nature), humans do have in common *potentialities* – man is a self-made creature who given a range of potentialities at birth may freely choose to develop him or herself within the guidelines of his or her culture (nurture).

9. The belief that the "social contract" theory of Rousseau and others explains the origins of a civil society and the state. Rather than the view that man moved from an independent "state of nature" to political association for protection, a better informed perspective is that human beings by nature are both socially- and politically-oriented and have a natural inclination to participate in government. As such, true *political community* may only exist in democratic, constitutionally based civil government.

10. The *fallacy of reductionism* – the assigning a much greater reality to the parts of an organized whole than to the whole itself. Notwithstanding the trends within the scientific community to differentiate entities and human existence into their respective parts for analysis and identification of their attributes, and the consequential tendency to reduce the value and responsibilities of the larger whole through this process; the potentialities of those entities and human beings that become present when viewed from a whole perspective are, from a common sense viewpoint, the predominant concern. Individual human beings are whole units with identifiable identities and the ability to choose patterns of growth and development. As such, "There can be no question about the moral responsibility that each of us bears for his actions." (p.190)

What may be derived from Adler's perspectives is that while empirical science and mathematics has resulted in breath-taking technological advances and knowledge of physical system reality (primarily in the last two centuries), the greatest achievements in philosophy occurred in Greek antiquity and the Middle Ages and should be the basis for an equally important knowledge of human system reality.

[**Author's Note**: The importance of this perspective, in terms of learnership, lie in recognizing the need for society to emphasize its willingness to enter into self-reflection, and to re-learn and apply those principles and practices of human common sense that underpin all human experience from the earliest of times. Reasoning, learning, and action informed by past wisdom, applied systematically to social issues, and focused on the quality aspirations of individuals, organizations and communities establish a tenuous but important foundation for societal learning and development.]

Critical Thinking and Reflection. In Developing Critical Thinkers (Brookfield, 1987), Brookfield says that: "When we become critical thinkers we develop an awareness of the assumptions under which we, and others, think and act …we learn to see our own actions through the eyes of others… we seek to exercise democratic control …and hold in check demagogic tendencies…". (p.ix) His fundamental purpose is to identify the primary capabilities individuals need to learn in order to become better at reasoning and making judgments. His themes (pp.5-9) are:

1. Critical thinking is a productive and positive activity. People learn to become open to possibilities, to appreciate social diversity, and to gain humility in understanding their own beliefs.

2. Critical thinking is a process, not an outcome. It is a process of continued inquiry into assumptions and healthy skepticism of universal truths and total certainties.

3. Manifestations of critical thinking vary according to the contexts in which it occurs. How critical thinking affects a person's thinking is seen either through the way he or she speaks and writes (internal effects) or in the change behavior exhibited (external).

4. Critical thinking is triggered by positive as well as negative events. Both tragedies and "peak" experiences may prompt scrutiny of past assumptions, beliefs, and abilities.

5. Critical thinking is emotive as well as rational. Emotions are central to the critical thinking process in that they respond to questioning of accepted values and behaviors and raise feelings of resistance and confusion.

6. Identifying and challenging assumptions is central to critical thinking. Once one's assumptions are identified, the accuracy and validity of those assumptions may be tested.

7. Challenging the importance of context is crucial to critical thinking. Being aware that habitual perceptions, understandings, and interpretations of the world frame our thinking structures.

8. Critical thinkers try to imagine and explore alternatives. Being open to new ways of thinking and perspectives on life for greater flexibility of thought and the adoption of new insights

9. Imagining and exploring alternatives leads to reflective skepticism. Critical thinkers understand that present methods of doing things are not automatically "right," and are suspicious of those with answers to all of life's problems.

Brookfield implies that critical thinking is not necessarily a rational activity; in fact, it is a means for breaking out of prescribed modes of thinking and action in favor of new learning and greater creativity. There are at least three alternative interpretations of the linkages of critical thinking to other modes of thinking and learning: *emancipatory learning, dialectical thinking,* and *reflective learning.*

1. Emancipatory Learning – "Emancipatory learning is that which frees people from personal, institutional, or environmental forces that prevent them from seeing new directions, from gaining control of their lives, and their society and their world".

2. Dialectical Thinking – "Dialectical thinking is viewed as a particular form of critical thinking that focuses on the understanding and resolution of contradictions... [it] welcomes them as a stimulus for development."

3. Reflective Learning – The process of considering the meaning of an issue or experience through internal examination of what the experience means to oneself, and which results in changes in one's conceptual perspective." (pp.12-14)

[**Author's Note**: Brookfield's viewpoint is significant for the learnership model because it recognizes the importance of understanding the context within which an issue exists, and identifies a strategy for reflective learning and deliberative development. The learnership construct is based on the notion of reflective learning from the experience of *being in* social dialogue and discussion. The premise is that applying learnership will lead to more effective societal development.]

Effective Reasoning. In *Clear Thinking* (Ruchlis, 1990), the author makes the case for the importance of clear thinking and reasoning. He notes that: "Reasoning power will be essential if we are to find workable solutions to the problems created by our own technology". (p.13) It is clear that human reasoning plus the ability to speak and to skillfully use our hands has brought society to its current level of development and dysfunctionality. If we are to make further progress, today's problems must at least be partially overcome or American society cannot achieve the potential imbued in its democratic founding. Ruchlis defines reasoning in terms of a general problem solving model which includes:

1. Identification of the *problem or issue* to be resolved.

2. *Mental searching* for facts that apply to the problem through recall of applicable information in one's memory.

3. Juggling facts to put together different possible solutions. This requires *thought experiments, correct reasoning,* and *drawing conclusions.*

4. Mental evaluation of each alternative solution and rendering a *judgment.*

5. Taking *action* to solve the problem.

At a more detailed level, the activities involve:

1. Obtaining appropriate facts,
2. Applying inductive reasoning (specific observations are used to create generalized theories)

3. Applying deductive reasoning (premises are established and used to deduce an outcome or conclusion)
4. Considering the applicability of intuitive insights
5. Using analogies for comparative analysis.

During the reasoning process it is essential that common errors in reasoning are avoided. Through elaboration on Ruchlis's thinking, the following cautions in reasoning may be articulated:
1. Keep an open mind and a spirit of inquiry.
2. Avoid jumping to premature conclusions.
3. Beware of overgeneralizations from limited data.
4. Don't confuse evidence with proof.
5. Beware of false analogies that don't fit the situation.
6. Consider conflicting opinions as opportunities to learn.
7. Avoid stereotypes, prejudice, and discrimination.
8. Be alert for illogical reasoning.
9. Use language accurately and with consideration of others' views.
10. Seek objectively obtained data versus subjective opinion.
11. Avoid being influenced excessively by emotional appeals.
12. Seek new knowledge from emerging contradictions.
13. Include the views of knowledgeable others.
14. Include those affected by the potential consequences of decisions.

[**Author's Note**: Ruchlis's work provides insight to the learnership emphasis on reasoned judgment. As previous writers have indicated, a major purpose in life is the pursuit of truth and happiness. The fact that this is accomplished in social units such as organizations and communities creates an imperative that scientific inquiry and interpersonal deliberations are open, informed, and constructive as viewed by the vast majority of society's members.]

Learning Systems: Cycles of Learning

One of the most important barriers to overcome is individuals'
unawareness of their own unawareness.
— Chris Argyris

Action Learning. David Garvin, in *Learning in Action* (2000) summarizes the three stages of the learning process and their potential disabilities. His recommended framework applies to organizational individuals and teams in the following manner:

Acquiring Information. "The real challenge for managers is to distinguish relevant from irrelevant information, while remaining open to unexpected, and occasionally unwelcome, surprises. Effective organizational learning demands clear signals and minimal noise, as well as the ability to share critical insights so that they do not remain isolated or unacknowledged." (p.21) (the disability = biased information). According to Garvin, data can be gathering in a variety of ways:

1. Search – Identification and look-up data/information from known sources.

2. Inquiry – Descriptive (closed-ended questions) or exploratory (open-ended questions) constructed and used to solicit data/information

3. Observation – Participate in and experience a situation, conduct interviews and take notes.

4. Reflection and Review – Reflect on experiences and develop lessons for the future after situations have occurred.

5. Experiential Learning – Reflect on experience and conduct reviews for alternating periods during the experience.

Interpreting Information. "Even if organizations were able to acquire all essential information, they would still have to interpret it…Unadorned facts and opinions are therefore of limited value. They become useful only after they have been classified, grouped, or placed with a larger context." (p.24) (The disability = illusion of information validity or causation). Garvin notes that unfortunately people "routinely develop interpretations, causal connections, and probability estimates that are seriously biased…some distinctive problems are:

1. Illusory Correlation – Viewing events as related simply because they have appeared together.

2. <u>Illusory Causation</u> – Ascribing causality to events that occur in sequence as seem to be linked.

3. <u>Illusion of Validity</u> – Increasing confidence in one's judgment, especially with larger and larger amounts of information, even though the accuracy of judgment remains unchanged.

4. <u>Framing Effects</u> – Different responses are identical, uncertain payoffs that have been framed as potential gains rather than potential losses.

5. <u>Categorical Bias</u> – The use and persistence of stereotypical categories for classifying people and events, even when faced with conflicting information.

6 <u>Availability Bias</u> – Assessing the probability of events by the ease with which examples come to mind, rather than their actual frequencies and likelihood

7. <u>Regression Artifacts</u> – Ascribing causality to actions that change a variable from an extreme (high or low) level to an average level, even though the change is really due to a chance (i.e., the greater likelihood that an average score will be obtained rather than an extreme value).

8. <u>Hindsight Bias</u> – The systematic biasing of probability estimates toward actual outcomes." (p.31)

<u>Applying Information</u>. Managers must translate their interpretations into concrete behaviors and must then ensure that a critical mass of the organization adopts the new activities…It is essential to eliminate unnecessary or outdated tasks as the same time that new ones are added. Otherwise, overload is inevitable." (p.27) (The disability = inaction). The shortcoming here pertains to passivity; an inability or unwillingness to act on new interpretations.

Garvin comments that "supportive learning environments" are essential to overcoming learning disabilities. He recommends four conditions for learning to flourish:

1. The recognition and acceptance of differences

2. The provision of timely, unvarnished feedback;

3. The pursuit of new ways of thinking and untapped sources of information

4. The acceptance of errors, mistakes, and occasional failures as the price of improvement

Situation-Handling. Karl Wiig, author of *People-Focused Knowledge Management* (2005) anchors his subject of knowledge management in a four stage process model with the following activities:

1. Situation Recognition

2. Decision-Making/Problem-Solving

3. Execution Method

4. Process Monitoring

While this approach works well for Wiig's purpose, it is in fact a restatement of the traditional learning cycle model advocated for decades by other researchers and authors explaining how *experiential learning* works. Of particular interest here is Wiig's emphasis on the fundamental need to understand the situation within which individuals and organizations find themselves – know the content and context of the situation – before attempting to determine a final solution or course of action.

According to Wiig, "People are required to act in all kinds of situations – large and small…The actions that are required depend upon the situation, its context and objectives, the person's understanding of the situation, and the person's capabilities. [And] Good situation-handling by people implies that the personal performance will be good. Personal situation-handling performance results from the quality of personal actions." (p.117) His emphasis on this topic is similar to others who have written that unless we know the real problem and its context, it is certain that we cannot determine the best solution.

[**Author's Note**: The learnership systems thinking and pattern recognition competencies addressed earlier in this text, as well as the specific perspectives provided on peoples' personalities and frames of reference demonstrate strong agreement with the information processing frameworks provided by Garvin and Wiig.]

Adaptive Learning Process. Stephen Haeckel, author of Adaptive Enterprise: Creating Sense and Respond Organizations (1999) contributes a contemporary view of how organizations' should continuously learn so as to be competitive in their marketplace. He argues that today's organizations need to be continuously adaptive, and to do so they have to increase to speed of their learning cycles – or if need be, short-change the time allowed for learning cycles to reach a conclusion. Basically, he says that the need is to move rapidly from sensing a situation to responding to the situation by reducing the time spent on interpretation and decision-making. He proposes that organizational strategy is traditionally treated as a strategy-plan activity, but in many industries it should now be understood as a strategy-design responsibility. That is, remake the organization by changing the operational structure and its locations through modularization of functions – and the corresponding management policies and procedures. This way greater effort is spent on preparing for client-stimulated action and providing the adaptive response that clients value.

[**Authors' Note**: The interpretation of Haeckel's recommendations in this text is that: (1) to the degree that significant learning has already occurred and is guiding client-focused organizational transformation, the recommendations are sound. And, (2) that learning cycles are, in fact, not eliminated but are streamlined and fine-tuned to operate more like a closed system which gains efficiency – however, a possible down-side is that narrowing opportunities for learning to gain speed may once again open the door to a "we don't do it that way" syndrome sometime in the future.]

Learnership Learning Cycles. A variation of both Garvin's learning process, Wiig's situation-handling approach, and Haeckel's adaptive learning process is advocated as the learnership learning cycle framework depicted in Figure 7-3.

The figure has two methodological features that illustrate the basic learning cycle concept. The first methodology is the traditional, sequential approach used for decision-making and problem-solving, which is: (a) Information Gathering; (b) Information Analysis; (c) Strategy Development; (d) Strategy Implementation; (e) Results Evaluation; and (f) Adaptive Action.

The second methodology is the use of basic human cognitive and feelings shown as three stages of mental activity: (a) Perception – use of sensing and intuition, (b) Judgment – use of thinking and feeling, and (c) Action – representing (hard) cognitive results or (soft) social developmental accomplishment. Together, these two contextual features convey the systematic and dynamic elements of the learnership learning cycle concept. [Note that these capabilities are based on the preferred styles of individual thinking and behavior discussed in chapter six. They are used here to create a sense of clockwise movement for understanding the recurring nature of learning cycles.]

The next area of learning cycle examination concerns the two developmental processes used in this book by learnership practitioners. First there is the cognitive, objective (fact based, hard) learning cycle consisting of the Assess, Decide, and Execute phases. Second there is the emotional, subjective (feeling consciousness, soft) learning cycle which follows the Sense, Adapt, and Renew phases of internal learning. (Figure 7-3)

Assess, Decide, Execute. This process is preferred when decisions and problems primarily require the acquisition and use of empirical facts and practical experience. The process requires the collection and Assessment of explicit information in accordance with standard and best practices. Data and information collected is then reviewed using further inquiry and dialogue in a decision-making or problem-solving process in which analysis, synthesis, prioritization, decision criteria, and risk management are considered. Decisions are then codified into implementation plans and Executed using good management practice. In practical experience individuals, organization and communities all need to use this approach on a daily basis.

Sense, Adapt, Renew. In this case, there are major tacit and/or feeling factors in play and the individual, using self-reflective intuition and/or emotional sensitivity, becomes aware or Senses the need to attend to the situation. Using a sorting process similar to the cognitive decision process, the individual considers how to Adapt to the new events or situation. Adaptation requires that new learning and knowledge be applied in the form of personal change or Renewal, which in turn, creates a new level of "being" or "personal realization." Again, practical experience indicates that everyone has the occasion to recognize their own personal dilemmas and treat them as learning opportunities.

Time, Change and Complexity. Lastly, the contextual setting within which the hard and soft learning cycles operate can either support or detract from learning cycle efficiency and subsequent knowledge building. When time for decisions and problem-solving is sufficient, change is desired and supported, and complexity is manageable;

learning cycles operated productively. At the other extreme, when *time*, *change* and *complexity* are not managed and supportive little learning and knowledge creation is possible.

[**Author's Note 1**: In both the hard and soft learning cycles, learning occurs as the outcome from the *Execute* or *Renewal* phase is evaluated, then *assessed* or *sensed* to begin another learning cycle. Also, the contextual impact of time, change, and complexity are significant variables that can pose major challenges and roadblocks to efficient and effective learning.]

[**Author's Note 2**: When coaching others through both the hard and soft learning cycles, the Adult Development Theory and Executive Coaching style of coaching may be most effective according to *Evidence-Based Coaching Handbook* by D. R. Stober and A. M. Grant, Jennifer Berger, Chapter 3, 2006)]

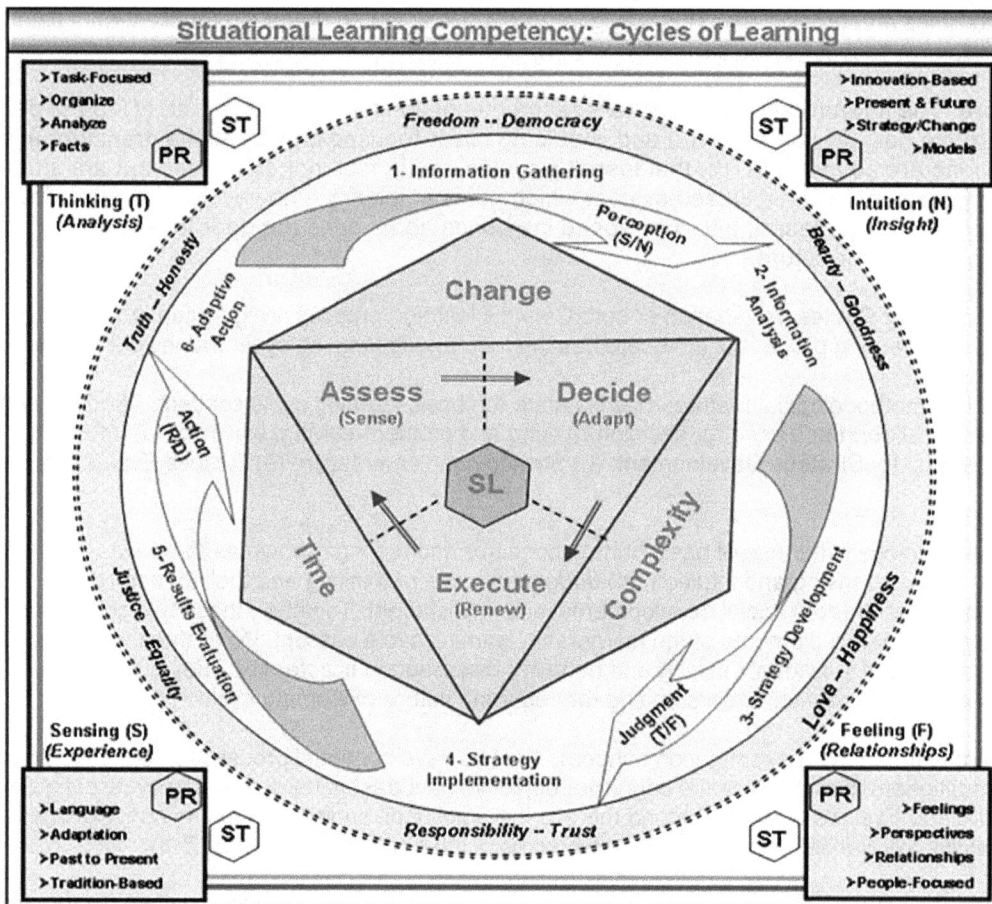

Figure 7-3

Learning-in-Action. Michael Marquardt, is the author of *Action Learning in Action* (1999) in which he proposes greater emphasis on the process of learning, itself. He argues that organizations that approach the learning process in a dynamic, reflective manner handle problem and decision content more efficiently leading to more effective outcomes. Marquardt says that: "...action learning is both a process and a powerful program that involves a small group of people solving real problems while at the same time focusing on what they are learning and how their learning can benefit each group member and the organization as a whole...Among the benefits, applications, and program components of action learning are: (pp.4-8)

1. Benefits:
    a. Shared learning throughout various levels of the organization
    b. Greater self-awareness and self-confidence due to new insights and feedback
    c. Ability to ask better questions and be more reflective
    d. Improved communications and team work

2. Applications:
   a. Problem solving
   b. Organizational learning
   c. Team building
   d. Leadership development
   e. Professional growth and career development

3. Program Components:

   a. A Problem – The problem should be significant, be within the within the responsibility of the team, and provide opportunity for learning.

   b. The Group – The group is composed of four to eight individuals who examine an organizational problem that has   no easily identifiable solution. Group characteristics include having an ability to listen, willingness to be open, respecting others, awareness of the need to learn, and a commitment to taking action.

   c. The Questioning and Reflective Process – By focusing on the right questions rather than [solely] on the right answers, action learning focuses on what one does not know, as well as on what one does know. It is essential that time be allowed for this activity.

   d. The Resolution to take Action – There is no real learning unless action is taken, for one is never sure the idea or plan will be effective until it has been implemented.

   e. The Commitment to Learning – There is equal emphasis on accomplishing the task and on the learning/development of individuals and organizations. Having everyone learn and grow through the process is an important outcome.

   f. The Facilitator – Helps the group members slow down their process, which will then allow sufficient time for them to reflect on their learning. Supporting attitudes and collaborative group behavior is required to aid the facilitation process.

The advantage of Marquardt's approach is that it establishes interpersonal relations and creates involvement while building long-term organizational capability to learn, know, and perform. Some *personal attributes* developed by participating in action learning teams include: critical inquiry, inquiry and questioning, openness and willingness to change, clear personal vision, personal mastery, empathy, active listening, courage and frankness, skills in advising and helping others, facilitation and presentation skills, wisdom and common sense, and self-awareness. Also, a person cannot lead or participate actively in a change program (personal, organizational, community) unless they themselves are changed in the process. The objective of action learning is to make good choices and grow in the process.

"Action learning creates conditions in which managers learn from their own experiences of real-life problems, helped by and helping others in similar or dissimilar situations. A manager actually changes the way he or she manages, on the basis of reality. The focus of action learning is on learning about the process of managing change by actually managing an organizational change." (p.123) Action learning develops leaders to be servants and stewards: finding answers to problems, learning from others' perspectives, challenging others and groups' assumptions, asking questions and improving reasoning, correcting mistakes and reframing learning experiences are all significant learning and development activities.

Dynamic Learning Environment: Perspectives on Time, Change, Complexity

Some problems are so complex that you have to be highly intelligent
and well informed just to be undecided about them.
— Laurence Peter

Wicked Problems and Social Complexity. In *Wicked Problems and Social Complexity* (2001) author Jeff Conklin addresses the all too familiar concern that the issues and problems modern society has to address are so dynamic and complex that they resist the thinking and efforts of even the most skillful of experts and leaders. Conklin states that wicked problems and social complexity are *forces of fragmentation* that challenge collective intelligence, doom projects, and make collaboration difficult or impossible. According to Conklin fragmentation is as "a condition in which the people involved see themselves as more separated than united, and in which information and knowledge are chaotic and scattered. The fragmented pieces are, in essence, the perspectives, understandings, and intentions of the collaborators…and can be hidden as when stakeholders don't even realize that there are incompatible tacit assumptions about the problem, and each believes that his or her understandings are complete and shared by all." (p.1)

Conklin attributes the definition of wicked problems to Horst Rittel, an early expert on the topic. Accordingly, problems are wicked when:

1. You don't understand the problem until you have developed a solution.

2. Wicked problems have no stopping rule.

3. Solutions to wicked problems are not right or wrong.

4. Every wicked problem is essentially unique and novel.

5. Every solution to a wicked problem is a "one- shot" operation.

6. Wicked problems have no solutions.

Conklin adds that when social complexity co-concurs with wicked problems the combination fragmentation is virtually certain to be the result. "Social complexity is a property of the social network that is engaging with the problem." (p.13) For example, when there are numerous organizations, experts, senior executives, and different skill sets actively involved there is sure to be social complexity. And, if technical complexity is a factor due to different levels of knowledge and experience, the situation becomes exacerbated.

Conklin advises that about the only way to proceed effectively is by "creating shared understanding about the problem, and shared commitment to the possible solution." (p.17) He says that this occurs when an "Opportunity Driven Problem Solving" methodology is employed. He indicates that the *antidote for fragmentation is coherence* and that can only occur when problems and solutions both become subjects for iterative thinking, design, and dialogue that leads incrementally, to clarification of what problems and solutions fit well together. Through iterative processing and learning *coherence* begins to take shape and consensus is possible because the group involved comes to believe something constructive has occurred. The caveat is that without leadership acceptance and support of the group's findings and suggestions improvement may not be achieved.

The Loss of the Stable State. In *Beyond the Stable State* (Schon, 1971), Schon presents a series of observations on human and social system striving for the *stable state*. He states that: "…belief in the stable state is belief in unchangeability, the constancy of central aspects of our lives, or belief that we can attain such constancy. We institutionalize it at every domain." (p.9) Evidence of this belief may be seen in our talk in which we identify ourselves in terms of our current state of being (e.g., "I'm a chemist," "I work for the government," "I live in Nebraska," and "I believe in the family"), rather than the directions toward which we are evolving. He finds that by believing that things will remain fairly stable, people are able to fend off feelings of uncertainty, personal inadequacy, and anguish. And, the more radical the change is likely to be, the greater the defense that is offered. Unexpected instability is even more of a concern because it creates larger "zones of uncertainty." Technological change is a major driver of change, not only in and of itself, but because of its interconnectivity and influence on human and social systems. All of this appears to apply to individuals, organizations, and communities.

People use various tactics to maintain a belief that relevant systems are stable. These include being selectively inattentive to new data, laboring vigorously to maintain the current system, and averting their attention to other areas of their lives to find compensatory constancy. The nature of the threat to the stable state is revealed by the actual and threatened dissolution of our previously stable organizations and institutions, our anchors for personal identity, and our system of values. According to Schon, trends may be seen that indicate a growing awareness and intolerance of economic imbalance, a growing dissatisfaction with the relative powerlessness of minority groups, and a general disenchantment with the values and goals of "social progress." He offers that: "No established institution in our society now perceives itself as adequate to the challenges that face it." (p.17)

Schon's view is that scientific activity and technology is accelerating at an exponential rate, and *implosive effects* are the likely outcome. That is, technology drives the very core of human systems by effecting the community's communications, its flow of goods and services, and its operating methodologies so as to exacerbate social inequities. The adaptation to large magnitude changes that used to be managed inter-generationally must now be accommodated within each person's own career and normal life span. The responses to the loss of the stable state tend to be anti-responses and may be identified as being in three primary forms: (1) *return* – the reaction that one should return to some previously better condition of life, or favoring some form of sustained isolationism, (2) *revolt* – the total rejection of all that was part of the past, a form of "reactionary radicalism," and (3) *mindlessness* – evading any form of self-consciousness to escape the anxiety, and as Schon suggests: "Mindlessness avoids the dreaded reality only by giving up awareness and humanity." (p.29)

The preferred strategy for dealing with accelerating change is to bring to the forefront new or modified institutions and methodologies that build human and organizational capacity to deal with growing instability in reasoned, constructive ways. The challenge is to maintain a healthy identity and self-respect while stable values and anchors are under review. It is preferred that transformations be accomplished through understanding of their causes and potential effects, and the taking of informed, collaborative action by those effected. Schon states that: "The task which the loss of the stable state makes imperative, for the person, for our institutions, for our society as a whole, is to learn about learning." (p.30)

[**Author's Note**: Schon's perspective articulated here is especially important to the "Learnership Integrated Systems Architecture (LISA)." A major premise is that all personal, organizational, and community development occurs in the context of a conflicted environment in which the current infrastructure or forces for stability are under attack from the ubiquitous forces for change. The capacity of each social domain to anticipate and accommodate this dynamic tension constructively, and to continuously learn and remain focused on long term goals is essential for balanced growth and development. This capability recently became known as *complexipacity*. Learning how to learn for a lifetime is what Schon argues for and is a *learnership practitioner* anchor.]

Adjusting to Turbulent Times. In *Rapids of Change: Social Entrepreneurship in Turbulent Times* (Theobald, 1987), the author describes the forces for change that may be seen impacting the society's current infrastructure. He observes that we live in a world of change: in ourselves, our culture, and our society. Because we are unable to slow down the pace of change we must learn to live with turbulence rather than letting it overwhelm us. He advises that we strive to see the world in its whole form rather than try to "analyze it apart." Contradictions, paradox, and diversity are embedded in our everyday experience requiring that we learn to deal with our affairs and social issues with balance and fairness. Regarding "balance," he recommends that we "seek dynamic balance and shun chaos and breakdown." (p.17)

Theobald identifies the following "driving forces" for change which need consideration in our policy and management discussions: the weaponry revolution, the computer and robot revolution, the environmental revolution, the human rights revolution, population growth, migration within and among countries, biotechnology, and knowledge systems. To deal with these forces, he advocates adopting the assumption that: ". . . *healthy* human beings want to grow and to help others to grow," and "we must change our thought and action patterns:

1. We must see conflict as a challenge to creative thinking, rather than as an excuse for violence both within and between countries.

2. We must learn to live within environmental and ecological limitations, rather than strive for maximum economic growth.

3. We must recognize that modern technology is freeing us from toil and will require profoundly different life cycles.

4. We must provide the possibility of dignity to all human beings, regardless of sex, age, race, or creed." (pp.16-17)

Particular attention is given to the complexity and interdependencies of today's problems. He notes that problems are often sets of interconnected issues and that tackling just one problem at a time can be very counterproductive. In other words, *system thinking* is required to understand and develop solutions to the more difficult social problems. Improving social dialogue and finding shared goals and solutions is also recognized when he offers that: "The bottom line of our [change agent] work is no longer converting others to a particular point of view, but encouraging commitment and will, so that we shall all learn how to search for positive changes." (p.44)

Theobald comments: "All societies must make arrangements to educate people, to get work done, to keep people healthy, to provide the necessities of life, and to make political decisions. The unique shape of each period of history emerges from the models used to meet those needs. We are at the point where we can state the basic models by which we shall live in our emerging era. When we create conditions suitable to our new realities; people, groups, and institutions will be able to be more effective." (p.55)

[**Author's Note**: An observation at this point is that the learnership is supported by Theobald's description of the forces for change that disrupt our level of comfort with the social status quo. The emphasis on *dialogue* and *balance* goes to the core of the learnership philosophy and is seen as an insightful understanding of how to help social change occur. His presentation suggests the need for new models for shaping our understanding of our world and our rights and responsibilities in it.]

Handling Discontinuous Change. In *The Age of Unreason* (Handy, 1989), the author agues that change is no longer the same as it used to be. Change is now discontinuous and not part of an easily identified pattern. Instead, it is random, unpredictable and is both confusing and disturbing. He notes that little changes may be seen making big differences, and that the way our work is organized is greatly impacting how we live our lives. His notion is that: "Discontinuous change requires discontinuous upside-down thinking to deal with it." Regarding current organizations and systems, he opines that: "For those in charge, continuity is comfort, and predictability ensures that they can continue in control. Revolutions . . . may be required in order to unblock societies and shocks, to galvanize organizations." (p.10)

Handy introduces the concept of *Triple I Organizations* of the future in which *Intelligence*, *Information*, and *Ideas* equal Added-Value (I+I+I = AV). He suggests that *quality is truth* in organizations, and that it takes "the right equipment, the right people, and the right environment to make quality happen." (p.145) Top management in these organizations will be dedicated to continuous learning, will focus more on the conceptual and human vice technical skills of management, and will learn to listen more willingly to subordinates rather than just talking at them. The new focus, he predicts, will be that organizations will stop trying to manage employees' careers, and instead, will help them develop their capabilities to take advantage of opportunities as they appear. In effect, education becomes as investment for future performance, and employees will be performing in teams and on projects in flatter organizations rather that the steeply hierarchical organizations of today.

[**Author's Note**: In terms of the learnership model, Handy's views are important in that they confirm the tension between the current infrastructure and forces for change, and illustrate that in order for organizations to cope they will need to focus on quality and adding value in their marketplaces. Continued quality learning, in terms of customer desires, need to become essential activities for managers and subordinates alike.]

Managing in Dynamic Environments. In his book *Beyond Rational Management: Mastering the Paradoxes and Competing Demands of High Performance* (Quinn, 1988), Robert Quinn offers that in order to manage in today's organizational environment, managers must deal with unprecedented levels of change, ambiguity, and contradiction. To do so they need the perspective of the *Master of Management*: "The people who come to be masters of management do not see their environment only in structured, analytic ways. Instead, they also have the capacity to see it as a complex, dynamic system that is constantly evolving. In order to interact effectively with it, they employ a variety of different perspectives." (p.3) Quinn offers three streams of research that address the thought processes and developmental approaches of high-performing managers:

1. How Managers Think – High-performing managers have developed greater *cognitive complexity* in thinking and problem solving, which means that they are better at both differentiation and integration of data and perspectives; they are able to handle more dimensions and relationships the issue environment. Also, they demonstrate "more moderated attitudes, openness to disconfirming information and adjustment in thinking, more effective discernment of the intents and strategies of others, better interrelationship of decisions, more appropriate strategy development, and more flexibility in consideration of distant goals." (p.5)

2. Torbert's Developmental Model – Using the psychological theories of ego development, Torbert (1967) argued that there were seven developmental stages and that as one moved between stages, a new worldview was needed. Manager competencies may be seen in stages three through six as follows:

   a. *Diplomat stage* where conformity to group norms is important.
   b. *Technician stage* where expertise is essential.
   c. *Achiever stage* where feedback and adjustment of behavior is valued.
   d. *Strategist stage* where paradox and anomalies are welcomed and various frames of thinking are employed.

An important insight by Torbert was that at the higher developmental levels, the capacity for *action inquiry* was a recognizable. This is the capacity to explore an issue while simultaneously framing and reframing the issue environment and maintaining focus on priorities.

3. Evolution of Mastery – Some researchers subscribe to a five-stage model for evolution from novice to master manager:

   a. *Novice stage,* able to understand and use facts and rules.
   b. *Beginner stage*, gaining experience and learning to see beyond stated facts and rules.
   c. *Competence stage*, able to appreciate the complexity of tasks and find important clues.
   d. *Proficiency stage*, able to "read" the evolving situation and gain an intuitive grasp of the nature of the issue.
   e. *Expert stage*, able to see beyond others' capabilities to recognize many dimensions of an issue and to reframe strategies as appropriate in terms of evolving clues.

According to Quinn, the high-performing, master manager must learn to operate in a "competing values" environment, and to do so require a *holistic* approach to skill development. A variety of continua are suggested, e.g., control/flexibility, long-term/short-term, task/people, internal/ external, etc., that define eight management perspectives and roles that may be used as situations warrant. These are: facilitator, mentor, innovator, broker, director, producer, monitor, and coordinator. Quinn says that beyond rational management means being able to see the polarities in given situations, evaluating the polarities for their respective strengths and weaknesses, and then moving one's perspective to a meta-level "to see the interpenetration and the inseparability of the two polarities…a simultaneous integration and differentiation." (p.165) Only those at the highest developmental levels are able to reason, learn, and act at this level.

[**Author's Note**: The significance in this perspective is in its support to the learnership concept of stages of adult development which are defined, in part, as the ability to deal effectively with complex, paradoxical and ambiguous issue environments. High quality learning occurs amid the tension between stability and change, in fact, it is probably accelerated by the ebb and flow of that tension. The resolution of social issues will depend in large part on the master manager capabilities of individuals, organizations, and communities to function with a high degree of cognitive complexity and action inquiry.]

Attaining Temporal Balance. In *Marking Time* (Rappaport, 1990), the author considers the impact of people's sense of time on their mental and emotional health, and their ability to attain a sense of balance within the social order. From childhood through adulthood, people's senses of time change from the infinite to the finite and they become aware that their time and their lives are passing by. They become more concerned with their identity and the directions in which they are tending as they reflect on their individual sense of past, present, and future. Rappaport refers to this aspect of human awareness as "temporal organization," and advises that human attention should be allocated to all three time dimensions of life for normal mental and emotional health. Apparently, fixation on the past or present with little thought for the future inhibits the development of a balanced sense of one's purpose and identity. The inability of individuals to develop this capacity often leads to a state of depression and social maladaptation.

Normal human and social development progresses from the period of childhood dependency, in which stability and predictability are essential, through periods of adolescence and adulthood in which achievement of the senses of independence and interdependency, denote maturity. Through this process, a greater understanding of one's purpose and history is obtained. The anticipation of the future and its potentialities creates the positive life force and necessary energy to pursue *a life well lived*.

The developmental challenge in modern society concerns our ability to sustain human and social system development amid the uncertainty, complexity, overload, contradiction and values differences so prevalent. Rappaport characterizes society today as being "…a culture struggling to find ways to cope with anxiety, depression, and addiction." (p.197) He says that a major reason for the situation is the breakdown of our value system, the lack of social ideals, and the lack of meaningful future images. From what Rappaport suggests, *the solution seems to be for individuals and society to redefine their purpose, establish common values, dream of future possibilities, and commit to working for their interdependent development.*

[**Author's Note**: This perspective is useful for understanding the learnership integrated systems architecture in that it establishes the need for human and social organization goals, recognizes the life-long process of learning and development, appreciates the dynamic nature of the social environment and the tension between the current infrastructure (past and present conditions) and forces for change (future potentialities), and alludes to the importance of attaining system balance for societal development.]

In summary of this section, it is useful to recapitulate the foundational themes of the learnership meta-system perspective: continuous learning in a dynamic environment. The construct proposes the idea that at the center of all human and social activity is the learning process. Through learning, individuals, organizations, and communities acquire the capacity for improved reasoning and action which supports the accomplishment of their respective goals. Learning occurs as new *information* is evaluated in terms of system *requirements* and *values* using current skills in *judgment* and *decision making*. The learning process is interactive and integrative, and all subsystem development is inextricably linked in a network of mutual influences.

The context for learning and systems development is one of continuous change and turmoil. The availability of information from the various *fields of education* (physical science, social science, mathematics, etc.) is growing exponentially, and unfortunately, toward greater differentiation as specialties are added and experts establish their paradigms of thought and action within the boundaries of their respective fields of endeavor.

Forces for change are colliding with the *current infrastructure* which has been established to protect past traditions and accomplishments. An explosion of values, viewpoints, and technological capability is being experienced at an increasing pace, and in a discontinuous manner that negates social comprehension. The result appears to be greater alienation, social upheaval, and the sub-optimization of the performance of most, if not all, societal systems.

The learnership architecture is a new mind-frame for contemplating society as a higher-order meta-system with the potential for optimization. The purpose of this inquiry so far has been to explicate those common themes and elements that provide the web of connectivity and interdependence among the various subsystems that form the model, and to establish the usefulness of the model for improving societal learning and development.

Communications and Culture

A major challenge for all of us is to understand the process of situational learning at its most subtle, but very persuasive level. That setting is at the intersection of social communications and societal culture. It is the place where daily information is dynamically exchanged between individuals, organizations and their communities – and it occurs continually day and night all year long. Figure 7-4 displays the fundamentals of social systems communications as they interface with social systems culture. The setting also recognizes the presence of people with different points of view and social preferences, albeit within a general adherence to established *universal ideals* and *spheres of knowledge*.

Social System Culture

Culture may be viewed dynamically as two social processes operating at three levels of depth or intensity. Over time, a culture tends to solidify and become predictable to both group members and others in their social arena. The paradox of culture is that provides group members with a sense of belonging, purpose and appreciation; but it can be seen by outsiders as a situation of groupthink, limited intelligence and purposeful exclusion. (Figure 7-4)

1. A learning (outside-in) process. Readily available Information and knowledge in a group moves from *Awareness*, to *Knowledge*, to *Understanding* as the group synthesizes a set of agreed perspectives they believe together e.g. purpose and worldview.

2. An action (inside-out) process. The group individually and together transcribe their agreed *Worldview* into *Principles* and *Values,* and than, take on others in more observable *Communications* and *Relationships*.

Social System Communications

The world of social media and international communications has exploded astronomically the last few decades. At any point in time or topic individuals and groups are correct in labelling the huge stream of *Data* and *Facts* as being true or false – determining one's opinion or options may be difficult to achieve. Because *chaos* is always at hand, people (in and out of the culture) construct mental filters to enable themselves to engage the *data/fact* stream in a useful manner. The mental filters are established when we make *choices* in how we accommodate data/facts. (Figure 7-4)

1. Incoming filters. These filters are applied when *data or facts* are assembled to form meaningful relationships known as *information*, which in turn, are then combined into *knowledge*. Not all knowledge is useful in all situations. The challenge for everyone is to separate the "*relevant*" knowledge for a situation from that knowledge that does not fit the situational context or issue.

2. Outgoing filters. These filters are pre-formed mental constructs or *mental models* that individuals or groups concoct when sending information, data and facts into the shared *data/fact* stream for others reading and learning. The content of the pre-formed mental models are often derived from the group culture all the way down to level 3.

Given the complexity of the communication and culture relationship, the rapid pace of information exchange across social groups and nations, and the proclivity for some in society to purposely deceive others for their personal gain, it is not surprising that misunderstanding and confusion are rampant in some locales and arenas.

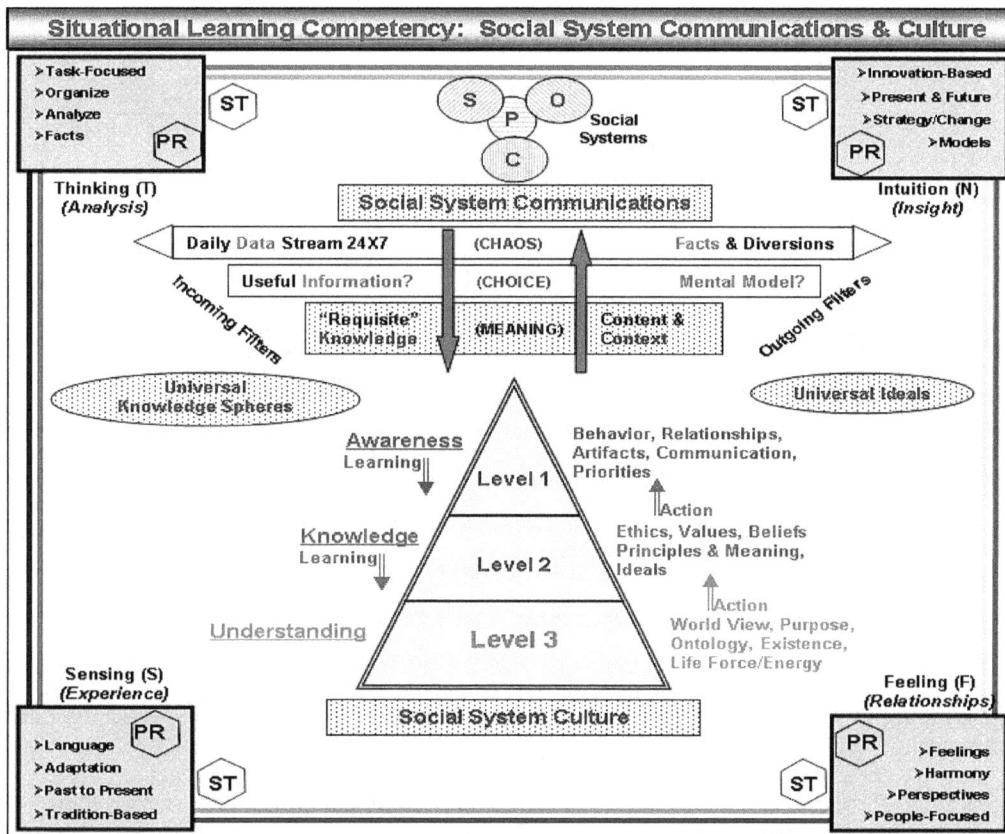

Figure 7-4

Thinking Straight

As if the communications and culture aspects of situational learning were not complex enough, we need to factor into consideration the relative thinking and communications skills of the people involved in our personal activities and business functions. Authors Gilliian Butler and Tony Hope in *Managing Your Mind* (1995) comment that "Becoming aware of the sources of error in thinking is the main resource we can draw upon to improve our thinking. The clearer we think, the better we will be at making decisions, at problem-solving, and also at keeping things in perspective." (p. 407) They identify and explain four common mistakes and four statistical rules everyone should take care to understand and avoid:

Common Mistakes

1. False assumptions – carrying unsupported prejudices and judgments tend to make people discount information that does not fit, or to distort and deflect certain information from being considered

2. What springs to mind – vivid or emotionally salient events people have experienced in the past tend to quickly come to mind at inappropriate circumstances

3. Influence of others – use of the "halo effect," scientific jargon, humor at presentations, and selected attribution of another's preferences at the moment tend to persuade our thinking

4. False associations – the willingness to associate something or someone with the same personal preferences of ourselves to be correct, or assume that the results we recognize in a situation must have come from the same category of causes we have witnessed before

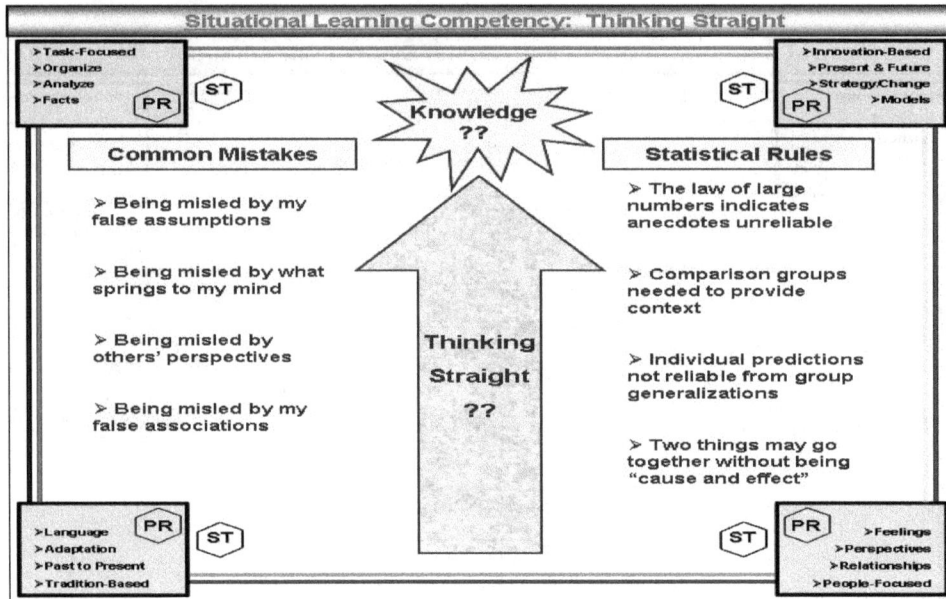

Figure 7-5

Statistical Rules

1. Law of large numbers – The larger the sample from a population the more likely it is to reflect the characteristics from which it is drawn.

2. Comparison groups – Value judgements are only reliable if a comparison group, (e.g. related topic, location or timeframe) is selected for consideration

3. Individual predictions – While predictions may be useful for groups, one cannot assume that a member of that group has those same characteristics

4. Cause and effect – Just because two things appear to be related in some manner they made not represent a cause and effect relationship. They may not be at all related or just occur in a symbiotic manner.

Conclusion

Man's mind stretched to a new idea never goes back to
its original dimensions — Oliver Wendell Holmes

Situational Learning Competency. Situational learning is the third of five life management competencies believed to be essential to the learnership philosophy, architecture, and practitioner way of being. The first competency, *systems thinking*, laid a foundation for expanding our awareness of related and mutually dependent people, organizations, and communities when resolving issues, solving problems, and taking on other personal and social system challenges. *Pattern recognition*, (similar to Senge's metal models) is the second competency and asks us to look for and cognitively inquire into the beliefs, processes, methods, styles, and perspectives embedded in our own and others' thinking and behavior. This allows us to "read" people and situations far better than when we are oblivious to the impact of such interpersonal strategies.

This chapter illustrated how the first two competencies play a useful role in the efficiency and effectiveness of personal and organizational learning. Learning cycles must be accurately "informed" at each stage of their activity. *Assessment and sensing* require collecting data that are accurate, relevant, and trustworthy; *Deciding and Adapting* cannot be efficient when there is a lack of factual information, use irrelevant criteria, and failure to discern appropriate priorities; and *Execution and Renewal* cannot achieve meaningful results if there is no buy-in to implementation plans and/or an unwillingness of key stakeholders and leaders to fulfill their responsibilities. Learnership practitioners are encouraged to develop the skills and heed the lessons from experts in personal and organizational learning.

Implications for Integral Learning and Knowledge Management. Unless there is efficient, effective learning, knowledge management will always be operating with too much decision-making risk. The reason is that required knowledge will often be inaccurate or too late thereby causing decisions to be made under excessive uncertainty and risk. Performance will be less than optimal and individuals and organizations will under-perform their objectives. Assertive learners cycling rapidly through numerous learning cycles are part of the remedy. So too, is an organization skilled in authentic dialogue and trusted collaboration wherein the parties involved know each other's needs, are committed to each other's success, and use critical thinking effectively without engaging in unnecessary game-playing or politics. Skills in Systems Thinking and Pattern Recognition support Situational Learning, which in turn, enables effective Knowledge Management.

Personal Reflection. This topic appears at the send of each chapter and is meant to serve two purposes: (1) be a reader's guide to main points and "takeaways," and (2) to encourage everyone to take a moment to engage their mental cognition and intuition on what the chapter means to them – especially at this time in their lives. Questions for chapter reflection follow immediately below; and for those readers inclined to maintain a self-assessment, your thoughts may be recorded in your *American Learnership: Life, Work, Wealth and Legacy Success* located at Appendix B.

Questions for Discussion:

1. Have you ever had an experience in which during a decision meeting the ranking person, the most talkative person, or the most emotional person dominates the discussion and rushes the group to a decision before many of the relevant facts and perspectives are even considered? Please explain the impact on you.

2. Do you now think you are able and willing to speak up professionally and point out that facts and perspectives essential for good decision- making are not being considered? In the future, will you be prepared to advocate effective decision-making based on collecting relevant information, deliberation and prioritization of alternatives, and assigning responsibilities to be performed by reliable and capable people? Please explain why or why not.

3. How would you rate yourself as a critical thinker? What do you do well, and not so well, when engaging in a difficult topic?

4. Can you list two to three major learning points from this chapter that you want to keep in mind to improve your ability to manage your life and career?

5. What do you think the impact of this chapter's information might be on the personal, organizational, community, and/or societal systems to be discussed later in the book?

6. Can you identify two to three topics, models, or perspectives in this chapter you would like to learn more about?

7. Should you be making an entry into your *American Learnership for Life, Work, Wealth, Health and Legacy Success* at Appendix B?

Insights, Commitments and Skills

If you plan to participate in the American Learnership for Life, Work, Wealth, Health and Legacy Success self-development e-book experience, it is suggested you record your Insights, commitments and skills to be developed here in this chapter, and again in Appendix B:

My learning in terms of new insights, changing priorities, new commitments or skills I want to acquire:

1. Insights (Example): Remind myself that ...

2. Commitments (Example): Continue to ask myself ...

3. Skills (Example): Apply my knowledge and skills to ...

Chapter Eight

Reasoning Competency #4: Knowledge Management

Integrating and managing knowledge enhances human mental potential. Human knowledge, when applied in goal setting and planning, sets the stage for enlightened action and achievement

Major Chapter Topics

Reasoning Competency #4: Knowledge Management

Introduction to (Total) Knowledge Management

Knowledge Management Competency. Human development can only develop as far as our combined knowledge will allow. Whether we view ourselves as individuals, organizations or communities, we are both empowered and constrained by our current knowledge and our willingness and ability to acquire additional knowledge. Contemporary studies and writings indicate that knowledge may be systematically created, managed and used to enhance human development and to produce the products and services we need and desire. The *knowledge management competency* is a core reasoning element in becoming a learnership practitioner. It is the knowledge repository for situational learning artifacts, and in turn, it is the intellectual storehouse for the tacit and explicit knowledge used by adaptive leaders in advancing personal and social initiatives. *Knowledge Management (KM) is enabled by Situational Learning (SL) which itself is supported by Systems Thinking (ST) and Pattern Recognition (PR).*

The previous chapters in this book have laid a foundation for us to engage in a full discussion of knowledge management. In fact, from this point on it is fair to say we are learning and investigating the subject of Integral Knowledge Management (IKM) – that meta-level application of knowledge management principles, practices and technology in which we identify, locate, acquire, organize, analyze, synthesize, apply, and share the knowledge we have obtained and decided to use. Systems thinking, pattern recognition, and situational learning have refined the manner in which we develop our knowledge; and now we are preparing to manage its use and application that will increase our performance and the performance of the organizations and communities we support. Finally, as we proceed it will become apparent that the Learnership Integrated Systems Architecture (LISA) is, in fact, an IKM artifact as well as a meta-cognitive framework for reasoning and a meta-system model for societal development.

Organizational Knowledge, Learning, and Intellectual Capital

In a time of drastic change it is the learners who inherit the future. The learned usually find themselves equipped to live in a world that no longer exists. – Eric Hoffer

Organizational Knowledge and Learning. In their book *Working Knowledge* (1998) Thomas Davenport and Laurence Prusak make notable distinctions between data, information and knowledge. They say that: "*Data is a set of discrete, objective facts about events in an organizational context, and data is most usefully described as structured records of transactions... Data describes only a part of what happened; it provides no judgment or interpretation and no sustainable basis for action...But data is important to organizations – largely, of course, because it is essential raw material for the creation of information. Information on the other hand, is meant to change the way the receiver perceives something, to have an impact on his judgment and behavior. It must inform; it's data that makes a difference. The receiver, not the sender decides whether the message he gets is really information – that is, if it truly informs him.*" (pp.2-3)

Knowledge, however, differs substantially from data and information. They comment that when it comes to knowledge: "Our definition expresses the characteristics that make knowledge valuable and the characteristics – often the same ones that make it difficult to manage well: *knowledge is a fluid mix of framed experience, values, contextual information and expert insight that provides a framework for evaluating and incorporating new experiences and information. It originates and is applied in the minds of knowers. In organizations, it often becomes embedded not only in documents or repositories but also in organizational routines, processes, practices, and norms.*" (p.5)

Davenport and Prusak also stress that knowledge is something that humans create between one another. Information must be analyzed in terms of making selected *comparisons*, assessing potential *consequences*, looking for important *connections*, and having interpersonal *conversations* concerning what others think in order to convert pieces of information into knowledge. Additionally, they note that "knowledge should be evaluated by the decisions and action to which it leads." (p.6) Key components of knowledge are:

1. Experience – Knowledge develops over time through experience. Experts – people with deep knowledge of a subject – have been tested and trained by experience.

2. Ground Truth – Experience changes ideas about what *should* happen to what *does* happen.

3. Complexity – Experience and ground truth result in knowledge that enables people to deal with complexity.

4. Judgment – Knowledge contains judgment and is able to refine itself to new situations by interacting with its environment.

5. Rules of Thumb – Shortcuts to solutions for new problems that resemble problems previously solved by experienced workers.

6. Values and Beliefs – The power of knowledge to organize, select, learn, and judge comes from values and beliefs as, and probably more than, from information and logic." (pp.7-12)

Knowledge may also be understood to be a personal or organizational asset a sustainable knowledge advantage can be achieved through continuously learning and developing new and relevant knowledge. Knowledge, in fact, may be understood as a commodity that is always undergoing replenishment and innovation – so much so that there is a knowledge marketplace in which there are sellers, buyer, and brokers. And, as in any marketplace, there are exchanges based on reciprocity and a sense of value which may be quantified in terms of price, or qualified in terms of personal repute. Altruism is often a motivational force, and trust is an essential qualifier for acceptance and participation. At the macro-level, the peripheral benefits of knowledge markets are:

1. Higher workforce morale
2. Greater corporate coherence
3. A richer knowledge stock
4. A stronger meritocracy of ideas.

The process of knowledge management rests on three fundamental activities: knowledge generation, knowledge codification, and knowledge transfer. The key features of these activities are:

1. Knowledge Generation – Knowledge generation includes the identification, acquisition, development, and/or rental of data and information that can be turned into knowledge. The use of especially dedicated human resources such as librarians, information specialists, and consultants assist in this activity.

2. Knowledge Codification – The acquired information is organized for analysis and synthesis in terms of the organization's goals, current knowledge stores, preferred taxonomies, and methods of access and distribution. Attention must be given to handling both explicit and tacit knowledge.

3. Knowledge Transfer – Transfers of knowledge may be accomplished either formally through the downloading or exchange of printed or computer files, or through person-to-person conversation and dialogue.

[**Author's Note**: A rather simple way to understand the difference between the creation and use of *information* and that of *knowledge* is that knowledge is not an absolute concept or artifact. People can have different knowledge about the same topic. It is appropriate to take the view that everything outside one's own cognition and reflection is still only information until that person thinks about it, and judges that information, which then makes it that person's knowledge. The corollary therefore is that not all "knowledge" is created equal.]

Organizational Knowledge. In Chapter 8 of his book *Knowledge in Organizations* (1997) Lawrence Prusak addresses "Learning by Knowledge-Intensive Firms (KIFs)" contributed by William Starbuck. Starbuck says that" The term *knowledge-intensive* imitates economists' labelling of firms as *capital-intensive* or *labor-intensive*...[And] implies that knowledge has more importance than other inputs." He continues by saying *human capital dominates* in KIFs as opposed to financial or physical capital. Starbuck offers five conclusions about KIFs: (paraphrased, pp.150-153)

1. A KIF may not be information intensive – *Knowledge* is the stock of expertise, not a flow of information. Thus, knowledge relates to information in the way that assets relate to income.

2. In deciding whether a firm is knowledge-intensive, one ought to weigh its emphasis on esoteric expertise instead of widely shared knowledge – To make the KIF a useful category, exceptional expertise must make an important contribution. One should not label a firm as knowledge-intensive unless exceptional and valuable expertise dominates commonplace knowledge.

3. Even after excluding widely shared knowledge, one has to decide how broadly to define expertise – One can acknowledge both the legitimatized expertise of people who have formal education and respected credentials and/or the uniquely hard to acquire skill set and understanding of people who have learned from hands-on experience.

4. An expert may not be a professional, and a KIF may not be a professional firm – Not all experts are a member of, or subscribe to "professional associations." For example, management consulting and software engineering have specialists with deep expertise, but do not qualify as professions because they do not have the ethical codes, collegial

enforcement of standards, assumed autonomy, and extra-organization cohesion most often a part of the professional practice.

5. KIFs may not be individual people – People convert their knowledge to physical forms when they write books or computer programs, design buildings, create financial instruments, etc. People also translate their knowledge into firms' routines, job descriptions, strategies and cultures.

Knowledge-intensive firms often have unique characteristics due to their effort to be knowledge, industry and marketplace leaders. *One way* this occurs is because of a peculiar emphasis on leadership of their special niche. Higher profits and longer-term survival come from successful competition and potentially monopolistic use of best practices. A *second* distinction is that KIFs are very effective in creating, applying and preserving knowledge and information from past successes to new problems and situations. They are skillful in research and learning, and in the adaptation of available information and knowledge into strategies, methodologies, and organizational improvement initiatives deemed to be valuable within their own firm and that of their clients. *Thirdly*, experts are usually aware that their expertise requires continual investment. According to Starbuck, "To learn, one must build up knowledge like layers of sediment on a river bottom. To learn effectively, one must accumulate knowledge that has long-term value while replacing the knowledge that lacks long-term value." (pp.158-159)

Organizational Knowledge Creation. In *Knowledge, Groupware and the Internet* (2000) David Smith presents "A Dynamic Theory of Organizational Knowledge Creation" by Ikujiro Nonaka (Chapter 1). Nonaka distinguishes between organizational information and organizational knowledge by indicating that: "…information is a flow of messages, while knowledge is created and organized by the very flow of information, anchored on the commitment and beliefs of its holder. This understanding and emphasis are an essential aspect of knowledge that relates to human action." (p.6) Nonaka stresses the fact that knowledge is only useful to the extent it has *meaning* to the values held by individuals involved, and that human beliefs and commitment to those beliefs are the basis for that *meaning*. Information that is incorporated into new knowledge is inherently valuable, however, information processing routines and technologies in and of themselves add little to the knowledge base of an organization – they can only support, but not guarantee improvement in organizational knowledge.

[**Author's Note**: This issue is prevalent in organizations wherein the CIO and IT specialists insist they "know" what the leaders and operational functions need to operate more knowledgeably, and proceed to provide them with IT gadgets without understanding how those gadgets might be used to improve actual work processes.]

Nonaka describes two dimensions of knowledge creation. One dimension is where a distinction is made between two types of knowledge: *tacit* knowledge and *explicit* knowledge. He says: "Explicit or codified knowledge refers to knowledge that is transmittable in formal, systematic language. On the other hand, tacit knowledge has a personal quality, which makes it hard to formalize and communicate. Tacit knowledge is deeply rooted in action, commitment, and involvement in a specific context." (pp.7-8) By way of further elaboration, tacit knowledge is considered to have both cognitive and technical elements. The *cognitive elements* pertain to the mental models, paradigms, and analogies the human mind uses to establish *perspectives* that help people define and operate in their perceived external world. The *technical elements* have to do with the concrete know-how, skills, and methods previously learned in order to successfully accomplish practical objectives in their real external world.

Nonaka makes a significant observation by saying that: "At a fundamental level, knowledge is created by individuals. An organization cannot create knowledge without its individuals. The organization supports creative individuals or provides context for such individuals to create knowledge. Organization knowledge creation, therefore, should be understood in terms of a process that 'organizationally' amplifies the knowledge created by individuals, and crystallizes it as a part of the knowledge network of the organization." (p.8) Nonaka continues by describing the synergistic individual-organization relationship in knowledge-building, and explaining that there exists in organizations a four-mode "knowledge conversion process" in which tacit and explicit knowledge is systematically exchanged. The four-mode process is paraphrased as:

1. Socialization – The *tacit to tacit* knowledge conversion/exchange between individuals who spend time together participating in shared experience.

2. Combination – The *explicit to explicit* knowledge conversion/exchange between individuals and groups who transfer codified knowledge claims and artifacts directly or indirectly to one another for sorting, re-categorizing, or re-conceptualizing.

3. Externalization – The *tacit to explicit* knowledge conversion/exchange in which individuals record their perceptions and understanding into documents and artifacts for use by others.

4. Internalization – The *explicit to tacit* knowledge conversion/exchange in which knowledge documents and holdings are used for learning by others.

The results of systematic, but mostly non-managed, information exchange and knowledge building among organization members should be continued organizational growth and development because the organization is able to maintain a competitive position in its industry and marketplace.

Another contribution made by Nonaka concerns his conceptualization of the Process of Organizational Knowledge Creation. The stages and activities Nonaka advocates (paraphrased, pp.17-27) are:

1. The Enlargement of an Individual's Knowledge – Individuals accumulate tacit knowledge through direct "hands-on" experience. High quality hands-on experience might, on occasion, required the redefinition of the nature of the "job." Also, the deep personal knowledge acquired is said to be "embodied" in the person when one's mind and body have been brought together.

2. Sharing Tacit knowledge and Conceptualization – The interaction of one's knowledge of experience and rational processes helps individuals build their own knowledge of the world. Allowing such individuals to associate in a "field" or a "self-organizing team" encourages collaboration built on trust and permits knowledge exchange and group acceptance of new knowledge. Dialogue directly facilitates this process by activating externalization at individual levels.

3. Crystallization – The process by which various departments within the organization test the reality and applicability of the concept created by the self-organizing team, and experience "dynamic cooperative relationships." To the degree that some overlapping knowledge exists between process activities shared functions exist which can expedite the implementation of new knowledge.

4. Justification and Quality of Knowledge – While organizational knowledge creation is a continuous process with no ultimate end, an organization needs to converge this process at some point in order to accelerate the sharing of knowledge beyond the boundary of the organization for further knowledge creation. This convergence may be defined as "justified true belief" in which the organization comes to trust as being accurate and useful. [Author's Note: There is no guarantee that what comes to be believed and trusted is in fact accurate and useful – which causes further correction and change to be extremely difficult unless learning is seen as a continuous process.]

5. Networking Knowledge – The realization of the new concepts just described represents a visible emergence of the organization's knowledge network which now becomes enhanced by the addition of the new learning and knowledge. As the knowledge spreads it becomes the basis for "how we think and work around here." This represents a change in organizational culture.

Nonaka comments that management of the above *organizational knowledge creation process* can follow one of three principle leadership strategies described below:

1. Top-Down – Top management becomes the agent of change in a large powerful headquarters operation, commanding what needs to be done and putting emphasis on communication and delegation. Hierarchy is respected and chaos is not allowed.

2. Bottom-Up – Organizational entrepreneurs are the agents of change operating in small organization and acting as sponsors of new ideas and methods. Emphasis is on self-organization, inefficiency and chaos are evident as well as autonomy and ad hoc teamwork.

3. Middle-Up-Down – A self-organizing team becomes the agent of change in a larger organization populated by a team-led culture. Leaders are catalysts for learning and action and contribute to organizational knowledge creation. Focus is on accumulating sufficient tacit and explicit knowledge, gaining upper management support for desired action, and spreading new knowledge and processes to others throughout the organization.

[**Author's Note**: Organizations lacking in cultural trust will find it difficult using anything other than the Top-Down approach because the level of voluntary person-to-person information exchange is low and politics and suspicion are high.]

Organizational Learning Systems. Another contribution by David Smith, in *Knowledge, Groupware and the Internet* (2000) is "Understanding Organizations as Learning Systems" by Edwin Nevis, Anthony DiBella, and Janet Gould (Chapter 2). The authors report their research and model based on the themes that

1. All organizations are learning systems

2. Learning conforms to culture
3. Styles of learning varies between learning organizations
4. There are generic processes that facilitate learning.

Given this perspective, Nevis et al, explain that their two-part model focuses first on seven *learning orientations* and then on ten *facilitating factors.* They say that diligent analysis and comparison of the *orientations* with the *factors* enables organizational leaders and consultants to rationally proceed with an effort to enhance the organization's ability to acquire, utilize, and disseminate information and knowledge. The orientations and factors for consideration are:

Learning Orientations:

1. Knowledge Source – Internal-External. Preference for developing knowledge internally versus preference for acquiring knowledge developed externally.

2. Product-Process Focus – What? How? Emphasis on accumulation of knowledge about what products/services are versus how an organization develops, makes, and delivers its products and services.

3. Documentation Mode – Personal-Public Knowledge is something individuals possess versus publicly available know-how.

4. Dissemination Model – Formal-Informal. Formal, prescribed, organization-wide methods of sharing learning versus informal methods, such as role modelling and casual daily interaction

5. Learning Focus – Incremental-Transformative. Incremental or corrective learning verses transformative or radical learning.

6. Value-Chain Focus – Design-Deliver. Emphasis on learning investments in engineering/production activities versus sales/service activities

7. Skill Development Focus – Individual-Group. Development of individual's skills versus team or group skills

Facilitating Factors:

1. Scanning Imperative – Awareness and curiosity about the external environment and its impact on the organization.

2. Performance Gap – Awareness of a gap between actual and desired state of operations.

3. Concern for Measurement – Discussion and use of metrics as a learning activity.

4. Experimental Mindset – Failures accepted not punished, but used as a learning opportunity.

5. Climate of Openness – Open communications throughout organization; debate and conflict accepted as ways to solve problems.

6. Continuous Education – On-going commitment and clear support for all members' growth and development.

7. Operational Variety – Appreciation of diversity of perspectives, methods, and competencies.

8. Multiple Advocates – New ideas and methods advanced by employees at all levels; multiple idea champions.

9. Involved Leadership – Leaders are engaged, interactive and assist in educational programs.

10. Systems Perspective – Ability to recognize interdependencies between problems and solution, organizational units, and company goals and customer needs.

[**Author's Note**: The creation and use of *personal knowledge* within an organizational context is of concern to individual employees because knowledge leads to competence and competence leads to performance – which should be related to remuneration. Also, the degree to which personal tacit knowledge is made explicit and exchanged with others in the organization to create *organizational knowledge* determines how well organizational leaders can build and retain meaningful marketplace relationships and produce the products and services that satisfy their customers' most deeply held needs. Organizations have a vested interest in becoming better at learning and knowledge creation. The learnership reasoning competencies of systems thinking, pattern recognition, and situational learning all impact the ability of individuals and organizations to generate, codify and transfer knowledge of greater quality and utility than would occur just by happenstance.]

Knowledge Management and Intellectual Capital

Intellectual Capital. In his book *Intellectual Capital: The New Wealth of Organizations* (1997) Thomas Stewart says that an ever-increasing percentage of people are becoming "knowledge workers." They work in knowledge-intensive companies in which a higher percentage of remuneration goes to the knowledge workers that make the largest contribution to the company's profitability. More and more knowledge workers are becoming the sought-after professionals in their respective workforces as they are the ones who plan, organize, and execute their own work in coordination with others essential to the accomplishment of their objectives. They are the ones who acquire, analyze, and use information to create new knowledge that empowers others to lead and operate the organization more efficiently and effectively thereby achieving marketplace success and rewards.

Intellectual capital is the term used to describe that special category of knowledge that is a foundational asset of the organization's existence and ability to provide marketplace value. Stewart says that the intellectual material or "smarts" that makes up intellectual capital, while *intangible*, needs to be formalized, captured, and leveraged to produce higher-valued assets, but that can only be done (1) when there is a purpose or strategy that requires the use of that intellectual capital, and (2) because much intellectual capital is tacit, that knowledge needs to be made explicit for others to learn and accept it into their tacit understanding. *Knowledge management techniques that provide tacit to explicit to tacit exchange of information and knowledge are essential for organizational learning to occur, and that in turn, creates the intellectual capital so valuable for development and success..* Stewart identifies three types of intellectual capital that provide sufficient purpose and focus for determining where management of knowledge creation can make a difference:

1. Human Capital – The source of creative energy, knowledge/skills, innovation, and renewal. "Human capital grows two ways: when the organization uses more of what people know, and when more people know more stuff that is useful to the organization." (p.87)

2. Structural Capital – The tools, methods, processes, and physical property needed to use, transport, store, or protect information and operations. Structural capital is particularly useful in that it can "codify bodies of knowledge that can be transferred…and connect people to data, experts, and expertise." (p.132)

3. Customer Capital – The value of an organization's relationship with the people with whom it does business. "You cannot own customers, any more than you can own people. But just as an organization can invest in employees not only to increase their value as individuals, but also to create knowledge assets for the company as a whole, so a company and its customers can grow intellectual capital that is their joint and several property." (p.155)

It is also worth noting that more effective organizational decision-making occurs when the three types of intellectual capital are applied to business process improvements focused on specific organization objectives.

The Wealth of Knowledge. Thomas Stewart continues his explanation of the important of knowledge management and intellectual capital in his book: *The Wealth of Knowledge: Intellectual Capital and the Twenty-First Century Organization* (2001). He comments that: "It has become standard to say that a company's intellectual capital is the sum of its human capital (talent), structural capital (intellectual property, methodologies, software, documents, and other knowledge artifacts), and customer capital (client relationships)." (p.13) Stewart also provide examples of business and industries that are relying more and more on intellectual assets in place of former strategic advantages such as geography, regulation, and vertical integration to expand their competitiveness and customer presence. He says emphatically: "You don't need physical assets to gain entry into a business. The specific asset – the differentiating asset – is not the machinery. It's the software and the wetware – the stuff between your ears. It's the knowledge, stupid." (p.18)

Stewart reiterates the view that success using an intellectual capital approach is tied directly to having a *strategy* for deciding what needs to be known and managed and an *implementation methodology* for accomplishing what needs to be done. He advocates a four step intellectual capital strategic intent (Chapter 4, paraphrased):

1. Identify and evaluate the role of knowledge in your business, as inputs, process, and output.

2. Match the revenues you've just found with the knowledge assets that produce them.

3. Develop a strategy for investing in and exploiting your intellectual assets.

4. Improve the efficiency of knowledge work and knowledge workers.

Concurrent with developing a knowledge strategy, an investment methodology should be implemented (Chapter 5, paraphrased)

1. Create knowledge leadership – Identify someone with clout in the organization to administratively lead knowledge enhancing initiatives.

2. Creating knowledge assets – Don't manage all your knowledge, just that which is critical.

3. Creating knowledge connections – Look to leverage knowledge. Ask "Who else can use this stuff?"

4. Managing in real time – Information moves at the speed of light, and business should learn to move as fast.

5. From plan to signal – "Traditional organizations are run like buses while real-time organizations are run like taxis responding to a waving are to voice on the radio." (p.96)

6. Haste eliminates waste – Apply just-in-time customer response; produce and deliver without large lead times or inventories.

7. Double the value of knowledge – Share information on customer forecast, order rates, order backlog, level of inventories, product availability, and delivery time with everyone in the supply chain – and optimize the interrelationships for reliable customer service.

8. Fly by wire – Information feedback rapidly provided enables immediate response.

[**Author's Note**: Stewart's articulate explanations are a powerful stimulant to modifying how organizations are both designed and managed. We are in an era of rapid change and extreme competition where being late to the game means not playing in the game. Organizations in most industries are finding that being *adaptable* to their environment – customer demands, supply sources, emerging technologies, etc. is not only useful, it is imperative. Knowledge management of rapidly growing human, structural and customer intellectual capital is what a "learning organization" looks like.]

Stewart takes a closer look at the nature of work and the change in workers in Chapter 12. The rise of the new knowledge worker has occurred as fast as the changes in organizations and their competitive industries. Today, an increasing number of employees are assertively managing their own careers, continuing education opportunities, and choices of work locations and environments. Whether their newly found semi-independence is being forced on them or by personal choice, they are in fact negotiating their terms of employment and seeing themselves as co-investors (human capitalists) in their employers along with other stakeholders and financial investors. Stewart speaks of a pattern of "...mobility across employers, stability across profession [and says that it] is one reason learning has taken on such psychic importance for human-capital-investing employees. Schooling, or at least credentials, partly replaces promotions, which flat organizations can't offer. Quasi-professional certification exams are showing up in all kinds of general management areas, such as project management, management consulting, and human resources management." (p.253)

The rise of the new human capitalist / knowledge worker requires organizations to modify the educational and training objectives of its employee development program. Emphasis now has to be on (1) *action learning* wherein learning by doing real work with others is most useful; (2) *just-in-time learning* for assistance on immediate learning needs; (3) training for today's job while at the same time training for increased flexibility and adaptability to change; and (4) focus on the key skills of the most productive professional knowledge workers.

[**Author's Note**: Each of us is personally building our stock of human capital so we can bargain more effectively with our employers for an appropriate return on our investment. Viewed from a learnership point of view, Stewart's development of the concept of intellectual capital is not only an essential feature in this chapter on the knowledge management competency, but also informative on the competencies of situational learning and adaptive leadership. Together, excellent learning, knowing and leading provide a strong foundation for the work of our learnership practitioners.]

Social Capital. In their book *In Good Company: How Social Capital Makes Organizations Work* (2001) Don Cohen and Laurence Prusak quote Robert Putnan, the Harvard political scientist saying that: "social capital refers to features of social organizations such as networks, norms, and social trust that facilitate coordination and cooperation for mutual benefit." (p.3) The authors own definition is that: "Social capital consists of the stock of active connections among people; the trust, mutual understanding, and shared values and behaviors that bind the members of human networks and communities and make cooperative action possible. They say that social capital bridges the gap between people and that this type of connection supports collaboration, commitment, ready access to knowledge and talent, and coherent organizational behavior." (p.4) Also, they comment that: "...without social capital, organizations simply cannot function...social capital can benefit organizations in particular ways...we explore those benefits throughout this book, and summarize them here as follows:

1. Better knowledge sharing, due to established trust relationships, common frames of reference, and shared goals.

2. Lower transactions cost, due to a high level of trust and a cooperative spirit (both within the organization and between the organization and its customers and partners).

3. Low turnover rates, reducing severance costs and hiring and training expenses, avoiding discontinuities associated with frequent personnel changes, and maintaining valuable organizational knowledge.

4. Greater coherence of action, due to organizational stability and shared understanding" (p.10)

Cohen and Prusak organize their book and argue their perspectives in six overarching topical areas which are herewith listed along with selected highlights:

1. Trust – "Social capital depends on trust. The relationships, communities, cooperation, and mutual commitment that characterize social capital could not exist without a reasonable level of trust." (p.29)

"Trust is largely situational: a particular person may be quite trustworthy in one set of circumstances but not in another, where particular pressures, temptations, fears, or confusion may make him unreliable." (p.30)

"A powerful sense of higher organizational purpose can sometimes foster trust. A sense of duty, patriotism, or idealism can help generate trust as well as commitment." (p.41)

2. Networks and Communities – "People do not always look for the optimum economic exchange, the best knowledge, or the greatest skill when they seek colleagues, partners, or suppliers. Their own past and the experience and norms of their organization or group powerfully shape their choices." (p.55)

"Though network building mainly happens between individuals, it contributes to an organization's social capital. Many of the benefits individuals derive from networks and communities – a sense of membership and purpose, recognition, learning, and knowledge – can also pay huge benefits to the organization." (p.61)

"...the very cohesion of commitment to a community can be a problem if that makes it clannish, insular, excessively idiosyncratic, or, in extreme cases, corrupt or destructive." (p.70)

3. Space and Time to Connect – "In walking, people become part of their terrain; they meet others; they become custodians of their neighborhoods. In talking, people get to know one another; they find and create their common interests and realize the collective abilities essential to community and democracy." (p.89)

"Speed matters, but not at the expense of everything else. In addition to damaging social capital, speed can limit the basic thoughtfulness that complex work requires...Trust, understanding, commitment, and the habit of reciprocity develop over time." (p.94)

4. Social Talk and Storytelling – "Conversation includes gossip, stories, the mutual discovery of meanings, the negotiation of norms and aims, expressions of sympathy and disapproval, bewilderment and understanding. It implies mutuality and a kind of engagement or relationship." (p.107)

"The ability of stories to make sense of events along with their ability to evoke the real-life feel of a situation and to illustrate rather that assert the values, norms, feelings that motivate people gives them tremendous power to communicate the richness and texture of a culture...When people can locate themselves in the story, their sense of commitment and involvement is enhanced." (p.117)

5. The Challenge of Volatility – "The forces driving volatility are real. Mobility, exciting opportunity, and extremely low unemployment tempt people to move from job to job. Organizations change their composition and even their aims and behaviors in the face of global competition, converging companies and technologies, new products and new customer demands." (p.135)

6. The Challenge of Virtuality – "The social capital implications of Virtuality are complicated, but the questions at least are fairly clear. To what extent can people develop and maintain social capital by electronics means? Can the trust-building, network-building meetings and conversations we have described as sources of social capital occur virtually?" (p.157)

[**Author's Note**: The concept of *social capital* adds another dimension to Stewart's human, structural, and customer intellectual capital of organizations by emphasizing the interpersonal and relational aspects of organizational work. One observation, however, might be that Cohen and Prusak are overly persuaded by the interests and needs of the extraverted and the NF and SF personality types to the exclusion of those people who are introverts or with ST and NT interpersonal preferences. Reference is made to Chapter Two on Pattern Recognition.]

Knowledge Management and Human Resource Management

Human Resource Management in the Knowledge Economy. Mark and Cynthia Lengnick-Hall, authors of a book similarly titled (2003), take on the challenge of describing the roles and responsibilities of HRM professionals in helping organizations adapt to the emerging knowledge economy. They talk about a new imperative for human resource management to assist organizations in building strategic capabilities in the use of their most important intangible assets, human beings. They discuss human capital and structural capital development in a manner similar to Thomas Stewart, but they introduce the term "Relationship Capital" that encompasses Stewart's customer capital and much of the social capital characteristics presented by Cohen and Prusak. They define relationship capital as: "...the interpersonal connections across members of the firm and relationships with suppliers, customers, and other firms that provide the basis for cooperation and collaborative action." (p.4)

The authors point out that the HR function in most organizations has evolved into a highly efficient employment bureaucracy that served the industrial world fairly well with its focus on conformance to government policies and intra-organizational strife between management and the workforce. They say, however, that: "Staying within the functional bureaucratic boxes that HRM has created for itself will only undervalue its impact on organizational effectiveness. Failure to change with the demands of the new economy will mean that formal HRM will become less important, whereas new challenges such as knowledge management and human capital management will be absorbed elsewhere within the organization." (p.14)

As far as defining HRM work, the authors note that: "HRM is no longer simply focused on 'managing people' in the conventional meaning of the phrase. Human resource management is now responsible for managing the capabilities that people create and the relationships that people must develop." And, they continue to say: "The rapid evolution of electronic-HR delivery systems is pushing more information in more usable formats to employees and managers who can use it directly for the benefit of their organizations." (p.30) Given this situation the authors suggest that there are new roles and challenges that the HRM careerists need to embrace and take action to transform HRM departments into influential contributors to organizational performance. They introduce four roles that properly educated and skilled HR professionals could learn to perform:

1. Human Capital Steward – The role requires accumulating, concentrating, conserving, complementing, and recovering the collective knowledge, skills, and abilities within an organization. (p.33)

2. Knowledge Facilitator – The new role for HRM is to facilitate organizational learning and knowledge sharing between employees, among departments, throughout the organization, and with external co-producers. (p.38)

3. Relationship Builder – The HRM function will create programs and practices that enable employees to encourage, facilitate, nourish, and sustain relationships among fellow employees, customers, suppliers, firms in complementary arenas, and at times even rivals. (p.39)

4. Rapid Deployment Specialist – The HRM function will be required to rapidly assemble, concentrate, and deploy specific configurations of human capital to achieve mission-specific strategic goals.

[**Author's Note**: The education, training and development of an organization's workforce have always been critical responsibilities in preparing to meet market competition and to deal with the changes being experienced in most industries. The HRM component of the Personnel Function should always have played a role in human capital strategic planning and in tactical skill development in the pursuit of greater organizational efficiency and effectiveness. The knowledge economy makes it even more important that this internal responsibility be recognized and acted upon. The learnership practitioner attitudes, skills, and behavior being advocated in this book are meant to incorporate the four roles just described, and to illustrate the development HR professionals may want to pursue.]

Managing Knowledge Workers. In his book *Thinking for a Living* (2005) Thomas Davenport says that: "Knowledge workers have high degrees of expertise, education, or experience, and the primary purpose of their jobs involves the creation, distribution, or application of knowledge." [And] "Knowledge workers think for a living. They live by their wits – any heavy lifting on the job is intellectual, not physical. They solve problems, they understand and meet the needs of customers, they make decisions, and they collaborate with other people in the course of doing their work." (p.10) His investigation into knowledge worker networks and learning activities indicted that that: "They tended to make good decisions in investing time and effort in developing new domains of expertise. They also seemed to get more learning out of a given experience and continually update their skills, expertise, and social awareness as a natural part of their work." (p.149) Davenport makes the following observations on the nature and process of the knowledge workers' work: (p.191)

1. From overseeing work, to doing it too.

2. From organizing hierarchies, to organizing communities.

3. From hiring and firing workers, to recruiting and retaining them.

4. From building manual skills, to building knowledge skills.

5. From evaluating visible job performance, to assessing invisible knowledge achievement.

6. From ignoring culture, to building a knowledge-friendly culture.

7. From supporting the bureaucracy, to fending it off.

8. From relying on internal personnel, to considering a variety of sources.

He also comments on what he terms *good management hygiene needed* in the knowledge age: (pp.203-206)

1. Putting the organization in context.

2. Brokering and learning from dissent.

3. Redesigning and improving knowledge work.

4. Orchestrating group decisions.

5. Harnessing good intent.

6. Enabling boundary-spanning.

7. Facilitating social networks.

In summary, high performing knowledge workers learned management from their experience, have had a wide variety of jobs from which to learn and integrate learning, have learned to see problems and opportunities from different perspectives, have built a diverse network of people to call upon, and have avoided unnecessary distractions when having chosen something important. They continue to invest in domains of learning where they are already competent while taking on additional knowledge areas, and they browse codified resources and then follow up by human contact to fill in the details.

[**Author's Note**: Management of this type of worker requires an open, collaborative goal setting dialogue in which what to do is discussed without too much focus on how to accomplish the task. Expertise is acknowledged, measures to be used are discussed, and feedback on issues and progress is expected. This style of management comes close to the full delegation mode of management advocated by many leadership experts. It is the style preferred by adaptive leaders in the next chapter of this book.]

Applying Knowledge Management in Organizations

> The only valuable knowledge is that which equips us for action, and that kind
> of knowledge is learned the hard way, by doing. — Karl Sveiby

Knowledge Management Strategy and Implementation

Organizational KM Practices and Initiatives. Karl Wiig, author of *People-Focused Knowledge Management* (2004) has written a comprehensive practical guide for understanding and implementing knowledge management. After the extensive descriptions in his text he provides an appendix that suggests five approaches for going about implementing knowledge management in organizations – anyone or all of which can have significant benefit in organizational performance. These are:

1. General Business Focus – "Manage knowledge effectively to make people – and the whole enterprise – act intelligently to sustain long-term viability by developing and deploying highly competitive knowledge assets in people and other manifestations." (p.299)

2. Intellectual Asset Management Focus – "Manage intellectual assets (intellectual capital) – people-based knowledge, products, services, patents, technologies, practices, customer relations, organizational arrangements, and other structural assets." (p.300)

3. Innovation and Knowledge Building Focus – "Build better knowledge assets to be available within the enterprise for improved competitiveness through personal and organizational innovation, organizational learning and R&D, and acquisition of outside knowledge, supported by motivators to innovate and capture valuable information." (p.300)

4. Knowledge Sharing and Information Transfer Focus – "Make available best available knowledge and facilitate its use at each point of action to allow knowledge workers to deliver quality work for all activities, operation, and plans throughout the enterprise; facilitate communications between individuals; facilitate locating relevant information; screen information for appropriateness; reformat and organize information to facilitate end-use." (p.301)

5. Information Technology-Based Knowledge Capture and Delivery Focus – "Organize, structure, store, and deliver information with IT and automation to the largest practical extent; effectively capture knowledge with IT support; obtain knowledge from unorganized databases; organize knowledge to facilitate its application; distribute knowledge to point of action." (p.302)

Additionally, Wiig provides a comprehensive list of KM initiatives and practices culled from the efforts of the world's best KM-based organizations: (pp.303-308)

1. Promote a knowledge-supportive mentality and culture.
2. Measure intellectual capital and create an intangible asset monitor.
3. Change and facilitate cultural drivers.
4. Create and foster collaborative practices.
5. Provide formal education and training.
6. Foster communities and networks of practice.
7. Conduct town meetings and conduct knowledge cafes.
8. Build and operate expert networks.
9. Capture and transfer expert know-how.

10. Capture and transfer expert concepts to other practitioners.
11. Capture and transfer expertise from departing personnel.
12. Capture and apply decision reasoning.
13. Capture and transfer competitive knowledge.
14. Create lessons learned systems.
15. Conduct after action reviews.
16. Provide outcome feedback.
17. Pursue knowledge discovery from data (KDD).
18. Implement and use performance support systems and knowledge-based applications.
19. Build and deploy knowledge bases.
20. Deploy information technology tools for knowledge management.

[**Author's Note**: Karl Wiig's book is recommended reading for anyone with a desire to understand the intricacies of knowledge management. His summaries, above, are particularly useful in this book because they provide the learnership practitioner with a thumbnail sketch on elements that should be considered when planning to knowledge-enable a business function, an organizational process, or the enterprise itself.]

The focus of attention now moves deeper into the subject of knowledge management as one of five reasoning competencies that together, empower individuals operating as learnership practitioners, to optimize their personal, organizational, and community social accomplishments. Two learnership architecture diagrams are presented and described to capture the essence of KM and to advance the ongoing construction of the summary level learnership model.

Knowledge Management Competency: Social Systems Integration

A core premise of this Life Management Handbook is that we as human beings have the opportunity and responsibility to manage our human social systems to the degree our genetic inheritances permit us to do so. As individuals and in groups of all sorts we have the cognitive and emotional capability to create much of what our futures hold in store for us. The corollary is that if we fail to do so humankind will self-select itself as being unfit in the evolutionary game of life.

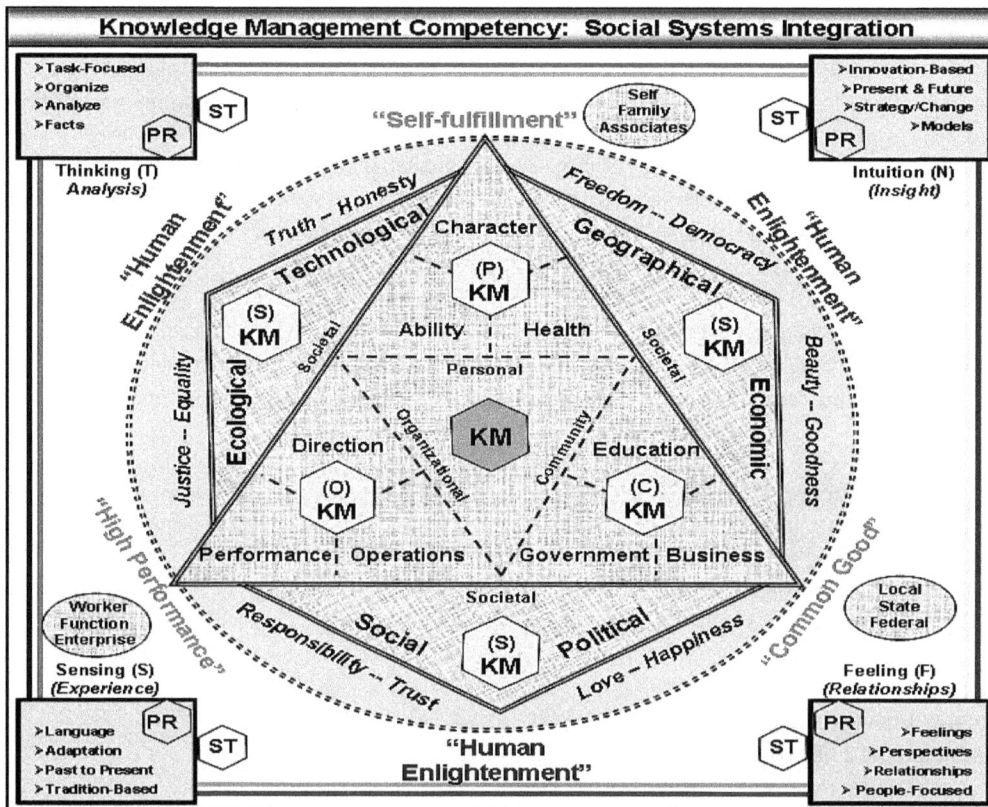

Figure 8-1

The KM competency is the one competency that bears the responsibility of visually depicting the integration of the learnership social systems under consideration – the personal, organizational, community, and societal social systems plus the context setting global knowledge spheres that cross-impact all the social systems. Figure 8-1 is an illustration of the KM competency superimposed on the Learnership Integrated Systems Architecture (LISA) that has been taking shape since Chapter Two on Systems Thinking and Chapter Six on Pattern Recognition. The KM social systems integration illustration has the following foundational features:

1. KM Knowledge Spheres – The six context setting global knowledge arenas with cross-impact on all levels of social system learning and development. These are the social, economic, political, ecological, technological, and territorial spheres of human participation and responsibility that overlay whatever system or structure we choose to use for understanding our joint human condition.

2. Personal KM – The use of KM for Personal (Micro) Systems Development (PSD) includes the three interdependent sub-processes of Character, Ability, and Health. An individual that knowledge-enables his or her Character, Ability, and/or Health sub-processes is in rapid pursuit of *self-fulfilment.*

3. Organizational KM – The use of KM for Organizational (Macro) Systems Development (OSD) includes the three interdependent sub-processes of Direction, Operations, and Performance. An organization that knowledge-enables its Direction, Operations, and/or Performance sub-processes is in rapid pursuit of *high performance.*

4. Community KM – The use of KM for Community (Mega) Systems Development (CSD) includes the three interdependent sub-processes of Education, Business, and Government. A community that knowledge-enables its Education, Business, and/or Government sub-processes is in rapid pursuit of the *common good.*

5. Societal KM – The use of KM for Societal (Meta) Systems Development (SSD) includes the combined, synergistic influence of the PSD, OSD, CSD and the KM knowledge spheres. Whenever progress is made by individuals, organizations, and/or communities society is enhanced and *human enlightenment* is advanced.

[**Author's Note**: Figure 8-1 visually describes the social system interdependencies that lead to the paradoxes, complexities, and uncertainty which we need to accommodate in our daily lives. The reader is reminded that a core premise of this book is that it is possible to organize and develop a framework for integrated social systems thinking and action using the knowledge being accumulated during our life journey. Having a cognitive mental model that reminds us of these relationships gives us the advantage of "choice" in how we engage the situations we experience.]

Knowledge Management Competency: Process, Practices, and Technologies

Knowledge management moves from theory to practice when procedures and methodologies are established to put it into service for people and organizations. Because KM inherits some of the knowledge and experience of previous organizational management practices and methodologies, it is accurate to state that KM is the practice of "knowledge-enhancing" or "knowledge-enabling" organizational functions or processes for better performance. The organizational improvement initiative requires a disciplined approach for integrating KM practices and technologies into the organization's design and workflow. And, the organization often employs project management techniques in which attention is given to the scope, schedule, and cost of accomplishing the required work. Figure 8-2 is a representation of the knowledge management competency's use of KM process, practices, and technologies:

KM Process. Knowledge associated with a particular organizational function or process is always at least partially unique to that discipline or subject. However, the methodology used to knowledge-enhance the function or process is a standard practice.

1. Identify – What information and knowledge is unique and essential?

2. Search – What are the best available sources for the information/knowledge?

3. Acquire – In what form can the information/knowledge be obtained?

4. Organize – How should the information/knowledge be prioritized and grouped?

5. Analyze – What can be learned by dissecting the information/knowledge?

6. Synthesize – What meaning can be projected by connecting disparate pieces of information/knowledge?

7. Apply – Where and how can the new knowledge be beneficially used?

8. Share – Are there others who could use the new knowledge?

9. Evaluate – Has the new knowledge been usefully applied?

KM Practices. The various ways in which individuals, groups, and organizations arrange to associate and communicate in an effort to acquire and share information and knowledge, and to build the trusted networks through which cooperation and collaboration occurs.

1. Community-Building – Bringing people together in electronic communities of interest or practice.

2. Social Networks – Tracking and building supportive interpersonal relationships.

3. Story-Telling – Using human interest situations to communicate information.

4. Learning Communities – Organizing communications and feedback around specific functions or areas of concern.

5. Best Practices – Acquiring and documenting highly effective techniques and methods of work.

6. Lessons Learned – Documenting, discussing and learning from past experience.

7. Expertise Location – Organizing and making available a locator of knowledgeable and skilled personnel

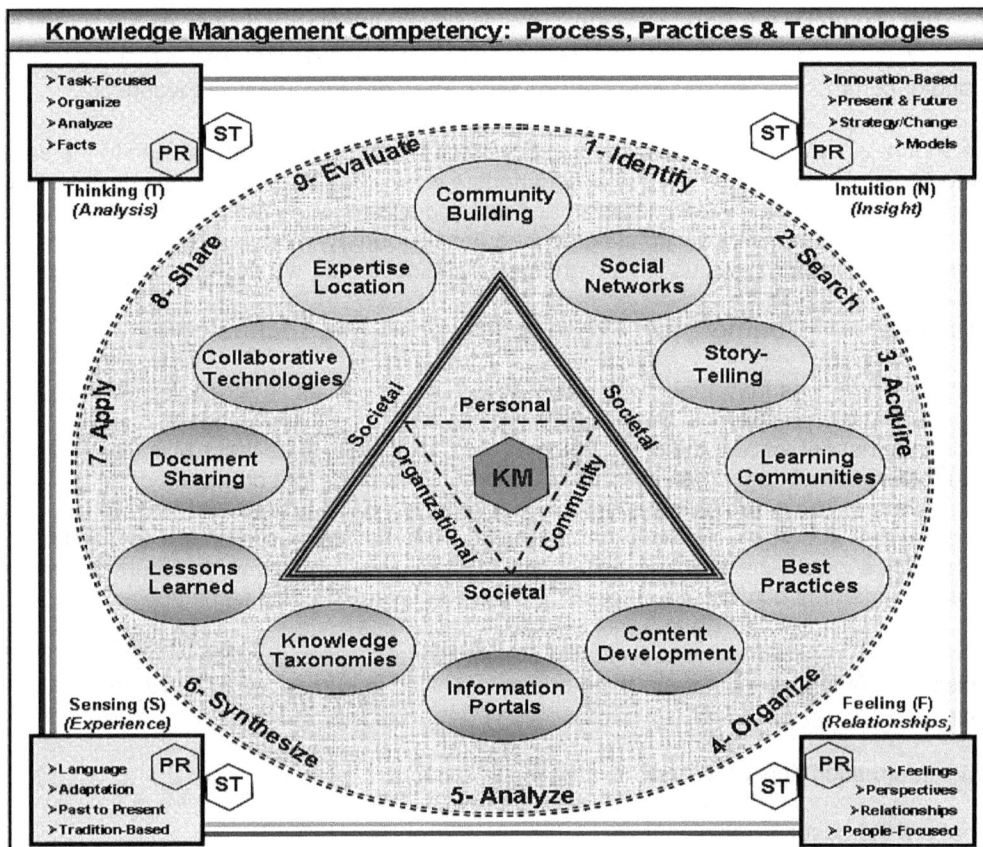

Figure 8-2

KM Technologies. KM practices are supported through the application of information technology and electronic tools that connect people at virtual locations, and integrate and support their workflows with software applications unique to the functions supported.

1. Information Portals – Organization web-sites providing single-point-of-access to stores of related and integrated information and services.

2. Content Management – The management of web site contents, capabilities, and information presentation. Also applies to the management of information stores accessible from web sites.

3. Knowledge Taxonomies – The logical organization of information and knowledge concerning a subject, methodology, or organizational function.

4. Collaborative Technologies – Computer applications that enable synchronous (same time give and take) communications among two or more people.

5. Document Sharing – Database applications that allow the storage, access, updating, downloading, and tracking of electronic documents.

[**Author's Note**: New KM practices and technologies continue to emerge as organizations innovate and implement new ways to communicate, coordinate, and collaborate with their employees, customers, and suppliers. From an enterprise-wide perspective, business to business relationships, business to government relationships, and business to stakeholder relationships are increasingly important in the growing global economy. The value of KM practices and technologies seems to be unlimited.]

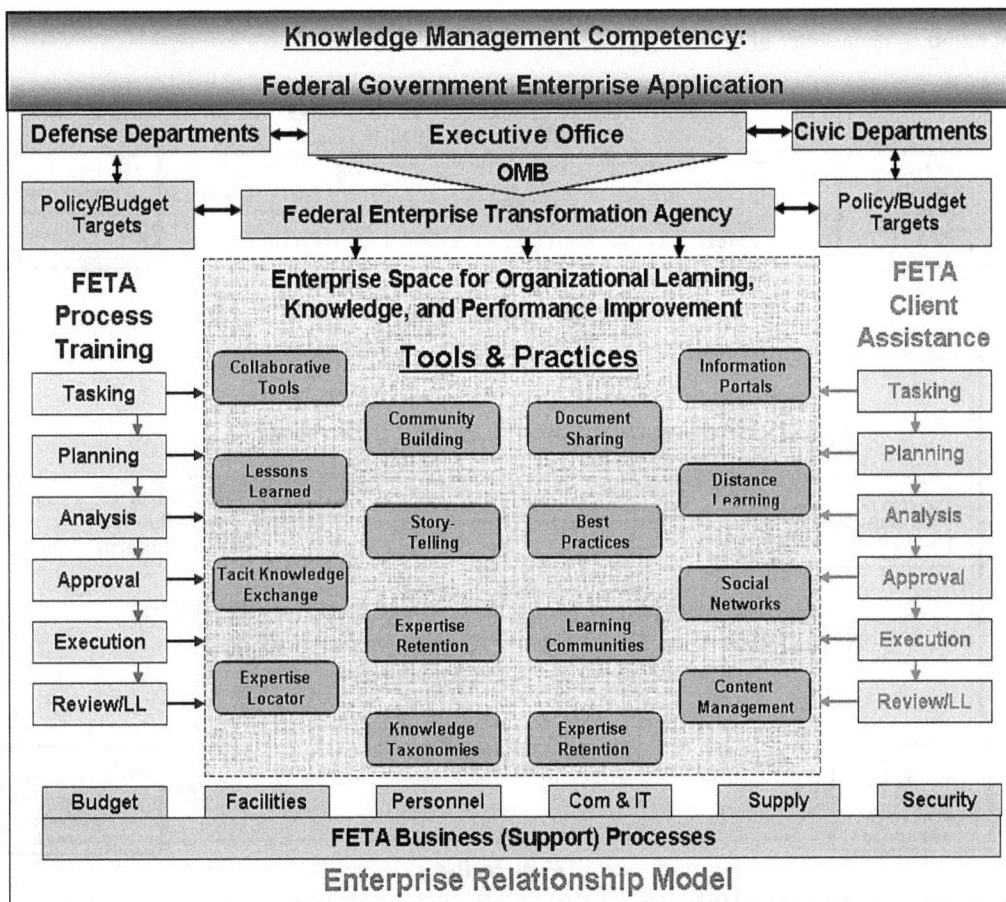

Figure 8-3

Enterprise Incorporation of Knowledge Management

Enterprise leaders or consulting teams are increasingly considering *where* and *how* knowledge management concepts and technologies may be employed to improve the organization's operational efficiency and/or market effectiveness. A useful approach for beginning that effort is to create a high level conceptual model that focuses the group's attention.

Figure 8-3 illustrates a recent consulting model (names changed) used with a government educational entity. The figure encourages useful conversation by having:

1. The executive functions at the top so important outward facing relationships can be considered.

2. The two primary core business processes on the sides so priority may be given to operational improvements.

3. The supporting internal business processes at the bottom so these critical functions can be readily considered.

4. The major knowledge building and management technologies in the center so comparisons may be made regarding the potential advantages and costs that may impact selecting one or more interventions.

Cultivating and Transferring Deep Smarts

Dorothy Leonard and Walter Swap, authors of *Deep Smarts: How to Cultivate and Transfer Enduring Business Wisdom* (2005) report that "throughout your organization are people whose intuition, judgment and knowledge both explicit and tacit, are stored in their heads, and – depending on the task – in their hands. Their knowledge is essential. They are, relative to others, expert. These are the people with deep smarts, and it is not an exaggeration to say that they form the basis of your organizational viability." (p.1) This is certainly true as most of us have been part of groups and firms where certain members appeared to have the ability to recognize both the *contextual environment* influencing important decisions as well as the *beliefs and social forces* directly impacting how tasks could be willingly accomplished. The authors comment that "we know we are in the presence of deep smarts when we see an expert size up a complex situation and come to a rapid decision – one that proves not to be just good, but wise…we think of that person of being really smart (at least in a given circumstance.)" (p.3).

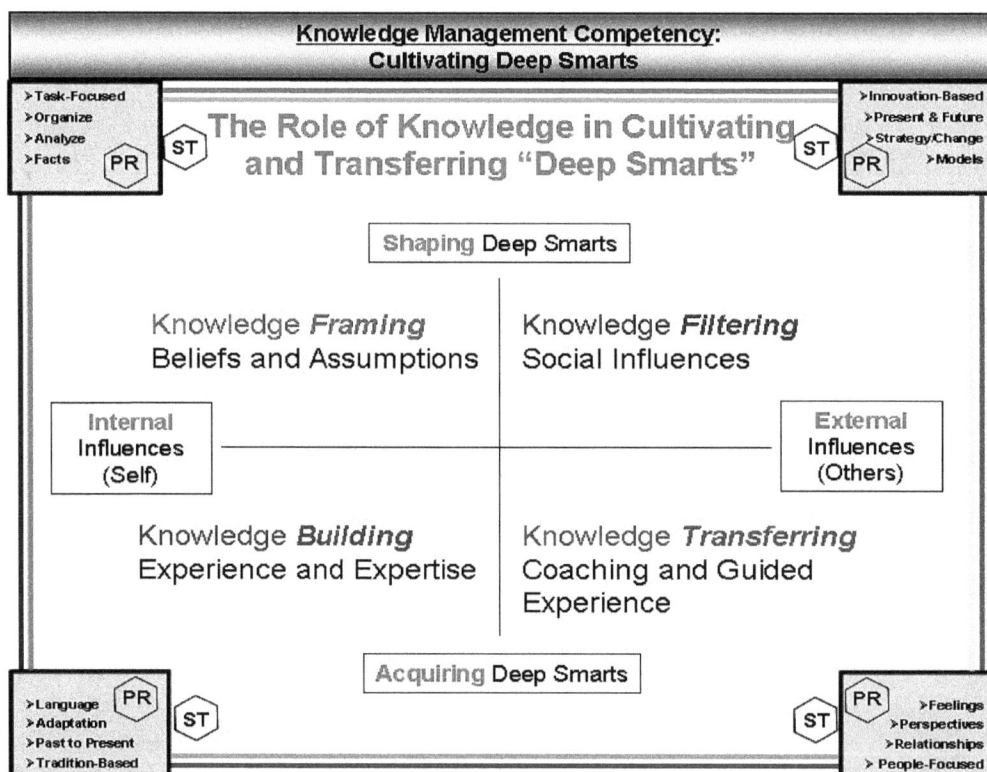

Figure 8-4

Figure 8-4 is a knowledge management adaptation of the authors' description of the skill sets involved in cultivating and transferring deep smarts:

1. Internal Influences (Self).

    a. Shaping deep smarts. A person or group is able to perform shaping (*knowledge framing*) by the way they agree to define what is knowledge based on their own beliefs and assumptions.

b. Acquiring deep smarts. A person or group is able to determine how acquiring (*knowledge building*) will be accomplished because once they have decided *what is knowledge* they are able to explain how to acquire more.

2. External Influences (Others).

a. Shaping deep smarts. Others are able to perform shaping *(knowledge filtering)* by the way they themselves choose to define what is knowledge through use of their incorporation of social influences.

b. Acquiring deep smarts. Others are able to determine how acquiring (knowledge Transferring) by the way they themselves choose to use coaching and guided experience in the acquisition.

What should be recognized at this juncture is that shaping and acquiring of knowledge destined to become, over time, deep smarts requires some definitional negotiation by the people designed the internals and the externals. The knowledge, skills and abilities that perfectly define a particular capability are not always agreed in actual practice which thereby allows slight differences in the minds of participants and observers. The content and context are now always agreed to by participants in a complex situation.

Knowledge Management Competency: Characteristics and Limitation of Deep Smarts			
	Experts	Novices	Limitations of Expertise
Speed of Decision Making	Make decisions swiftly, efficiently, without reviewing basic facts	Need to review all facts and choose deliberately among alternatives	Overconfidence; expert may ignore relevant data
Context	Take context into account; knowledge is "contextualized"	Rely on rules of thumb that minimize context	Difficult to transfer contextualized knowledge; novices prefer general rules
Extrapolation	Able to extrapolate from novel situation to find a solution	Lack of receptors limits basis for extrapolation	Mental set; expert may base solution on inappropriate pattern
Discrimination	Able to make fine distinctions	Use of rules of thumb obscures fine distinctions	May not communicate well to a novice who lacks receptors to understand distinctions
Awareness of Knowledge Gaps	Know when rules don't apply	Don't know what they don't know	Ignorance; expert may assume expertise where none exists
Pattern-Recognition Ability	Have large inventory of patterns drawn from experience	Limited experience constrains number of patterns	When no patterns exist, expert may perform no better than novice
Tacit Knowledge	Extensive tacit knowledge drives decision making	Knowledge is largely explicit	Difficult to access tacit knowledge, so difficult to transfer

Table 8-1

Table 8-1 provides the authors' comparison of the reasoning and behavior of people generally considered to be experts, novices or beginners with significant limitations of experience (knowledge and practice). The comparison illustrates that under most circumstances in the most complex situations it is better to employ knowledge and skill experts. However, in routine or less risky situations, novices and even those with limited knowledge and experience may temporarily be adequate. Still, when time, speed and quality are distinct organizational or community requirements, the use of experts is advised.

[Author's Note: It is useful at this point to direct the reader's attention back to the Chapter 3 discussion on the relationship between the project management and balanced scorecard relationship methods. The deep smarts discussion here is primarily applicable to the *internal knowledge and learning quadrant* of the Personal, Organizational, Community, and Societal system domains. And, in each case, it is this domain that applies human talent and capital to improve the performance of the other three domains.]

Conclusion

If you wish to know the road up the mountain,
ask the man who goes back and forth on it. — Zenrin

Knowledge Management Competency. Knowledge management is the fourth of five competencies believed to be essential to the learnership philosophy, architecture, and practitioner way of being. The first competency, *systems thinking*, laid a foundation for expanding our awareness of related and mutually dependent people, organizations, and communities when resolving issues, solving problems, and taking on other personal and social system challenges. *Pattern recognition*, (similar to Senge's mental models) was the second competency and asked us to look for and cognitively inquire into the beliefs, processes, methods, styles, and perspectives embedded in our own and others' thinking and. This allows us to "read" people and situations far better than when we are oblivious to the impact of such interpersonal strategies. *Situational learning*, the third competency introduced the need to pay attention to the learning process and learning environment within which we participate. Proactive management of our respective learning cycles increases the quality and speed of learning and the resulting knowledge available for our use.

This chapter focused on the core reasoning competency, knowledge management, which draws heavily upon systems thinking, pattern recognition, and situational learning for its accuracy and appropriateness in effecting reliable decision making and social systems outcomes. It is useful to know that KM as a discipline has become reasonably well described, researched, and applied so that best practices are becoming available – thereby enabling the development and use of organizational improvement methodologies and technologies. In the context of this book, learnership practitioners are encouraged to develop the learning, knowing, and leading skills necessary to become the knowledge architects and workgroup facilitators that knowledge-enable people, organizations, and communities in the pursuit of their respective objectives.

Implications for Integral Learning and Knowledge Management. The concept of IKM was introduced in Chapter One, has been developing through intermediary chapters, and has culminated here in Chapter Eight with a full, but high level explanation. All of the reasoning competencies and knowledge management capabilities described and discussed are now available for leader use in social systems development.

Notwithstanding the fact that knowledge management has been primarily discussed as an organizational capability in most management literature; all the issues, practices, challenges, and techniques discussed herein apply as well to personal and community social system development. Knowledge management is essentially a "personal" choice on how an individual chooses to learn and develop in the major domains of his or her life.

Knowledge always needed to be managed and those who acquired knowledge and applied it well were generally better rewarded and more successful. This is now true more than ever, and the future belongs to those who step up to the challenges of lifelong learning and knowledge management. Learning organizations applying knowledge management practices and techniques are the wave of the future whether they are the bricks and mortar operations of today or the virtual, networked organizations of tomorrow. And, the learnership practitioners are individuals skilled in the use of ILKM principles, practices, and technologies.

Personal Reflection. This topic appears at the send of each chapter and is meant to serve two purposes: (a) be a reader's guide to main points and "takeaways," and (b) to encourage everyone to take a moment to engage their mental cognition and intuition on what the chapter means to them – especially at this time in their lives. Questions for chapter reflection follow immediately below; and for those readers inclined to maintain a self-assessment, your thoughts may be recorded in your *American Learnership for Life, Work, Wealth, Health and Legacy Success* which is at Appendix B.

Questions for Discussion:

1. Have you worked in an organization in which information essential for your position and responsibility were not readily available, and others who may have had the information and/or knowledgeable expertise were not known to you? Please explain the impact on you.

2. Are workers in your career field considered to be knowledge workers? If so, in what way? If not, how would their work need to change to make them become knowledge workers?

3. What does the knowledge management competency have in common with the *Knowledge Management Competency; Social Systems Integration* concept in Figure 8-1?

4. Can you list two to three major learning points from this chapter that you want to keep in mind to improve your ability to manage your life and career?

5. What do you think the impact of this chapter's information might be on the personal, organizational, community, and/or societal systems to be discussed later in the book?

6. Can you identify two to three topics, models, or perspectives in this chapter you would like to learn more about?

7. Should you be making an entry into your *American Learnership for Life, Work and Legacy Success* at Appendix B?

Insights, Commitments and Skills

If you plan to participate in the *American Learnership for Life, Work, Wealth, Health and Legacy Success* self-development e-book experience, it is suggested you record your Insights, commitments and skills to be developed here in this chapter, and again in Appendix B:

My learning in terms of new insights, changing priorities, new commitments or skills I want to acquire:

1. Insights (Example): Remind myself that …

2. Commitments (Example): Continue to ask myself …

3. Skills (Example): Apply my knowledge and skills to …

Chapter Nine

Reasoning Competency # 5: Adaptive Leadership

Knowledge plus leadership equals action. The adaptive leader performs as a change agent *by facilitating him/herself and others in transition from the current state to a higher level-of-being.*

Major Chapter Topics

Reasoning Competency #9: Adaptive Leadership

Introduction to Adaptive Leadership

Knowledge plus leadership equals action. The adaptive leaders performs as a change agent by facilitating themselves and others in transition from the current state to a higher level-of-being

Adaptive Leadership. From a life management perspective no amount of knowledge has practical value until it is applied to human needs and concerns. Someone needs to articulate what is known, show relevancy to the situation at hand, and propose a course of action that creates a meaningful result. It is the work of leaders to craft future visions that inspire others to accept change and become participants in the journey forward. The *adaptive leadership competency* is another foundational anchor in the learnership discipline because it moves knowledge into action. Theory is turned into practice, and practice leads to meaningful accomplishment for individuals and social organizations.

Within the context of learnership philosophy and architecture in this book, it is the learnership practitioner who develops the systems thinking, pattern recognition, situational learning, knowledge management, and adaptive leadership skills (the learnership reasoning competencies) that prove instrumental in improving personal, organizational, and community social systems performance. Adaptive Leadership (AL) applies Knowledge Management (KM) enabled by Situational Learning (SL) supported by Systems Thinking (ST) and Pattern Recognition (PR). The targets for adaptive leadership are the four societal systems described in the *Learnership Integrated Systems Architecture* (LISA). Concurrently adaptive leadership incorporates the discipline of TKM when in action. That is, adaptive leadership is focused on transitioning from the current (As-Is) state to a future (To-Be) state-of-being. And, the full range of *Total Knowledge Management* principles, practices, and technologies are considered when attempting to enrich the capability and performance in the four social systems for development or the six context setting universal knowledge spheres. The TKM sub-theme is now ready for cross-disciplinary implementation.

The following descriptions, explanations, and selected references direct our attention to contemporary organizational issues, and the changes that surround them as they attempt to fulfil their respective public or private sector responsibilities. In doing so, the role of the leader as a knowledgeable, supportive, and adaptive facilitator of innovation initiatives, rational decision-making, work group collaboration, and organizational change management is described. After establishing this organizational context, explanation of the unique characteristics and skills of adaptive *leaders (our learnership practitioners)* are addressed and followed by selected perspectives that serve as "think pieces" for the reader's further consideration.

Organizational Context and Complexity. A selection of introductory perspectives follow:
Paradoxes and Competing Demands. In his book: *Beyond Rational Management: Mastering the Paradoxes and Competing Demands of High Performance* (1988) Robert Quinn addresses two areas of particular relevance to the subject of adaptive leadership. The first topic provides an overview of how leaders move from being a novice to a master of organizational management. The second topic describes the contradictions and paradoxes or organizational life that requires the most skilled of leaders.

Quinn introduces his subject by saying that: "In order to understand managerial effectiveness, we must first move beyond the theories of rational management and begin to better understand the dynamic, paradoxical, and competing forces that block us from creating high-performance systems...In running large organizations, there is no one way to manage effectively. Master managers understand this and develop the capacity to use several contradictory logics simultaneously." (p.xiv) Quinn's observations over 20 years ago have been confirmed by numerous studies and reports since that time, and we now find ourselves with much greater change and complexity than he probably anticipated.

On the subject of *mastery,* Quinn comments: "A primary characteristic of managing, particularly at high levels, is the confrontation of change, ambiguity, and contradiction. Managers spend much of their time living in fields of perceived tension. They are constantly forced to make tradeoffs, and they often find that there are no right answers." (p.3) Given this situation (remember our *situational learning competency*), he says that: "The people who become masters of management do not see their work only in structured, analytical ways. Instead they also have the capacity to see it as a complex, dynamic system that is constantly evolving." What this says to us is that the ability to understand a decision or problem's larger context (remember our *systems thinking competency*), and perhaps the assortment of personalities and competing mental models (remember our *pattern recognition competency*) is an essential learning skill in order to sort out viable alternatives and courses of action.

Quinn offers an excellent perspective on how managers think using the research terminology of *cognitive complexity*. This concept deals with how well people are able to *differentiate* between related entities when necessary, and *integrate* seemingly disparate entities when relationships are needed to be considered. Complexity results when a situation involves significant effort toward differentiation and integration within the same subject area or domain of consideration. Quinn continues to state that: "Researchers have found that cognitive complexity is associated with more moderated attitudes, openness to disconfirming information and adjustment in thinking, more effective discernment of the intents and strategies of others, better interrelationship of decisions, more appropriate strategy development, and more flexibility in consideration of distant goals. In general, they argue that highly complex individuals are more effective managers." (p.5) Quinn also adds that when a manager moves from being a novice to becoming a master manager he/she learns to "read cues from the situation, calls on both a task and process view…[which involves] that two contrasting domains are understood and woven together…the result it a much higher level of productivity – a level most managers never experience." (p.11)

[**Author's Note**: I suppose we have to become much more *cognitively complex* people if we are going to become learnership practitioners.]

On the subject of the contradictions of organizational life that requires the management skills just presented, Quinn indicates that a major cause of most managers inability to handle the situations they encounter is that they have become blinded by their own purposes, that is, they have prematurely settled on the facts, theories, methods, values, and motives that they prefer to use (remember our personality types and mental models) and have even developed moral positions that they use to resist any different thoughts, perspectives, or strategies. He further illustrates how through analysis of the research data, four distinct problem orientations can be discerned; and that a four quadrant *Competing Values Model* advocated. The two axes he uses to develop the model are

1. Manager preference for *decentralization and differentiation* as contrasted with a preference for *centralization and integration*; and

2. Manager preference for maintenance of the *current socio-technical system* versus support for a *competitive systems* position.

Quinn's model shows that managers can self-select themselves into one or more of the four stylized categories based on questions concerning their managerial thinking and behavior: (pp.26-38)

1. Rational Model/Style – The preference is for short time lines and high certainty in information use and action. Use of single purpose and focus predominates in decision making. Decisions are made quickly and seen as final. Focus is on logical direction and taking action. [An MBTI **ST** Style]

2. Human Relations Model/Style – The preference is for long time lines and low certainty and the need is for affiliation and mutual dependence. Major emphasis is on information processing and consensus. High tolerance is shown for individual differences and spontaneous behavior. Team harmony is an essential outcome. [An MBTI **NF** Style]

3. Open Systems Model/Style – The preference is for short timelines and low certainty in information use to allow time for variation, risk, excitement and growth. Decisions are made quickly but are able to be changed as new information is acquired. Adaptability and external legitimacy are major concerns. [An MBTI **NT** Style]

4. Internal Process Model/Style – The preference is for long time lines and high certainty, and the need is for predictability and security. Tendency is for systematic examination of externally generated facts and the focus is on maintaining present capability. Respect for standardization and preservation of the current order of things is desired. [An MBTI **SF** Style]

[**Author's Note**: Quinn's research and perspectives are major contributors to the learnership philosophy of social systems development and the reasoning competencies that drive the maturation of those systems. The critical learning is that we live and work in dynamic, changing systems filled with uncertainty and complexity – which means that there is no one right way to accomplish our objectives. Being multi-skilled and circumspect concerning our situational environment is needed for good decision making. Adaptive leadership contributes to this end.]

5th Generation Management. Author Charles Savage in his *5th Generation Management* (1996) offers at least three ways we will need to change organizational management. First, he introduces us to the idea that U.S. business environment is moving away from the Late Industrial Age focus on the use of capital in rather routine production processes to the Early Knowledge Age in which the focus is on organizational knowledge and the use of knowledge networks to manage and coordinate complex operations. He says that the new conceptual principles are:

1. Peer-to-peer networking
2. Integrative processes
3. Work as dialogue
4. Importance of human time and timing; and the essentials of
5. Virtual enterprising and dynamic teaming.

Together, this new way of internal and external teaming to include both suppliers and customers reduces the hierarchical vertical organizational structure in favor of a horizontal, more inclusive and collaborative way of doing business and delivering value. Second, Savage makes the important point that leaders in this new environment have to face the difficult task of transforming their visions, values, and strategies to align with this new way of working. They will face significant challenges in that they will need to:

1. Overcome the fragmentation of organizational functions currently in place
2. Figure out how to maintain a sense of accountability in the new flat, dynamic organization
3. Increase support for continued and rapid personal and organizational learning
4. Develop methods for focusing and coordination among the increasing number of cross-functional task teams that will be working collaboratively across organizational barriers.

Third, Savage suggests that today's businesses have to go beyond the typical "find out what our potential customer wants or needs, and then fulfill those requirements." He says that firms should be teaming with their suppliers to work together to determine not only the needs of the primary customers, but also the "aspirations" of the customer's customers. His belief is that horizontal knowledge networking will bring more business intellect to bear on the marketplace and that firms will be looking further downstream in the supply chain to better define what customers "wish for" and will then be able to "anticipate" the developing market and provide enhanced customer services.

Organizational Complexity and Chaos. In a recent book entitled: *Surfing the Edge of Chaos* (2000) the authors (Pascale, Millemann, and Gioja) discuss what they term a new scientific renaissance in how businesses of the future will compete and be managed. They review the fundamentals of *Complex Adaptive Systems* (CAS) and explain the implication for today's organizations. They define CAS as a "…system of independent agents that can act in parallel, develop 'models' as to how things work in their environment, and, most importantly, refine those models through learning and adaptation." (p.5) The authors explain that their work builds on the new science of complexity that considers the common properties of all living things. They attempt to distill what they term the "four bedrock principles that are inherently and powerfully applicable to the living system called a business:

1. *Equilibrium* is a precursor to *death*. When a living system is in a state of equilibrium, it is less responsive to changes occurring around it. This places it at maximum risk.

2. In the face of threat, or when galvanized by a compelling opportunity, living systems move toward the *edge of chaos*. This condition evokes higher levels of mutation and experimentation, and fresh new solutions are more likely to be found.

3. When this excitation takes place, the components of living system *self-organize* and new forms and repertoires *emerge* from the turmoil.

4. Living system cannot be *directed* along a linear path. Unforeseen consequences are inevitable. The challenge is to *disturb* them in a manner that approximates the desired outcome." (pp.5-6)

The authors point out that "*complexity* and *chaos* are frequently used interchangeably, even though they have almost nothing in common. The world is not chaotic; it is complex. Humans tend to regard as chaotic that which they cannot control. This creates confusion over what is meant by the term *chaos*. From a scientific point of view, chaos is an unlikely occurrence in which patterns cannot be found nor interrelationships understood." (p.6) The authors also emphasize that the "living systems" term is more than a descriptive metaphor – it is, in fact, exactly how human institutions operate.

The concept of *surfing the edge of chaos* is presented by the authors as a real life organizational adventure. They comment that: "The edge of chaos is a condition, not a location. It is a permeable, intermediate state through which order and disorder flow, not a finite line of demarcation…The edge is not the abyss…It's the sweet spot for productive change." (p.61) The potential impact of this philosophy in today's highly complex competitive and "flat" world is not only is there a compelling need to accept change, there is the need to go out to the organization's boundaries and create change if none is on the immediate horizon. In most organizations this thinking is still counterintuitive; however, the authors indicate they will not be content until organizations actually purposely move away from a sense of stability into a place of continued disequilibrium. That is, if a firm expects to succeed, over time, it needs to anticipate the future – even attempt to create an augmented future – in order to get a jump on the competition with products and services for which a desire is still somewhat subtle or unrealized. The organization management behaviors or disciplines suggested to help "sustain the disequilibrium driver for change are:

1. Infuse an intricate understanding of what drives business success. Establish a clear line of sight between a firm's overall strategy and each individual's performance; use deep (leading) indicators of desired outcomes.

2. Insist on uncompromising straight talk. Use frank, accurate, honest information. Conflict, reframed as 'fuel for organizational learning,' can contribute to an organization's long-term vitality.

3. Manage from the future. Establish a compelling goal, but difficult goal, that draws organizations out of their comfort zone – a key discipline to move to the edge of chaos.

4. Reward inventive accountability. Permit self-organization to operate at opportune moments; go beyond procedures and rules; use common sense and see the larger picture; and, take accountability for the outcome.

5. Harness adversity by learning from prior mistakes. Self-organizing units need to learn from their experiences and adapt; use after action reviews as systematic learning opportunities.

6. Foster relentless discomfort. Always seek to do better, to make a difference.

7. Cultivate reciprocity between the individual and the organization. Achieve a level of trust and mutual respect in which organization members receive consideration and compensation in balance with their innovations and contributions; create a good teamwork and working relationships." (Chapter 12 paraphrased)

[**Author's Note**: The notion of recognizing the complexity internal and external to an organization, and in confronting the apparent chaos that results from that uncertainty is pertinent to the practice of learnership. Having the time and skill to enter into and complete cycles of new learning is critical to organizational development and effective decision-making. And yet, there is the need to move toward the organizational edge, to anticipate the potential future, and to proactively create change before it is clear what change will be required. As a minimum, the learnership practitioner will need to be good at scanning the external environment using available communication tools (internet, industry websites, search services, etc.) and being well networked within the organization itself (strategies, supplier websites, employee Blogs and communities of interest).]

Adaptive Enterprise. In his *Adaptive Enterprise: Creating and Leading Sense-and Respond Organizations* (1999) Stephen Haeckel addresses the organizational challenge of keeping up with, and getting ahead of, the increasing pace of marketplace and socio-economic change. His message of "*adaptive enterprise* is that large, complex organizations must and can adapt systematically – and successfully to this kind of change." (p.xvii) Haeckel says that as important as speed-to-market, customer intimacy, operational excellence, and organizational agility happen to be – they are really subsets of a more pervasive issue: how well the enterprise can systematically adapt to its environment and remain successful.

Haeckel says that the make and sell organizations of the past industrial era will be replaced by the sense and respond organizations of the information and high technology age. The make and sell organization assumed that change was *predictable* and that the organizational goal was to become *efficient*. In contrast, the sense and respond organization assumed that change was *unpredictable* and the organization goal was to become *adaptive*. While the former used a closed system approach in which missions and strategies were planned in advance and implemented without much change, the latter situation is real-time sensitive and adapted to emerging customer requirements and change in the organization's environment. Figure 6-1 (adapted from Haeckel's work) provides a comparison of a number the organizational functions between the two approaches.

Haeckel comments on the changing role of leaders as organization transition to a sense and respond style of operations. He says "Transforming a system involves changing both its purpose and its structure. Leaders must anticipate the effects on the whole system of each change they make to any part of it. A system cannot be improved, much less transformed, by making isolated adjustments to individual capabilities." (p.21)

[**Author's Note**: Learnership practitioners will be expected to perform the roles required of them in assisting the creation of organizational flexibility and transition.]

MAKE & SELL compared to SENSE & RESPOND

Leadership & Strategy	MAKE & SELL	SENSE & RESPOND
-- Strategic Intent	Business as an _efficient mechanism_ for selling to predictable markets	Business as a _responsive system_ prepared to satisfy unanticipated customer requests
-- Profit Focus	Profit margins based on achieving _economies of scale_ – drive down fixed cost by increased production of the same product	Return on investment based on _economies of scope_ – re-use modular processes over a range of product components and customers
-- Articulation of Strategy	_Strategy as a plan_ to aim defined products and services at defined markets	_Strategy as an adaptive business design_ to sense earlier and respond faster to unpredictable change
Organ. & Process	**MAKE & SELL**	**SENSE & RESPOND**
-- Organization Priority	Focused on _planning and scheduling_ for greater predictability and efficiency	Focused on _building capabilities_ for rapid process response to customer needs
-- Process	Achieve _mass production_ using standard practices and repeatable processes	Build _modular capabilities_ for customized responses to customer requirements
-- Operational Concept	_Functional and sequential activity_: a predefined value-chain responding to centralized decision making	_Networked and parallel activity_: dynamically formed team participating in decentralized decision making
Technology & Tools	**MAKE & SELL**	**SENSE & RESPOND**
-- Information Architecture	_Functionally managed_ and optimized for each unit to achieve its own objectives	_Enterprise managed_ to create a unified view of the business environment and an integrated approach to service/product delivery
-- IT Architecture	_Host-centric_: Shadowing the hierarchical top-down command and control management system	_Network-centric_: Shadowing the dynamic network of people and teams
Learning & Knowledge	**MAKE & SELL**	**SENSE & RESPOND**
-- Know-How	Embedded in _products_	Embedded in _people & processes_
-- Decision Making	_Competitive strawmen_ proposed and defended using selective, known facts and personal appeal	_Collaborative inquiry and consensus seeking_ opened to unknowns, uncertainty, and a range of alternatives
-- Culture	Emphasis on stability, reliability, and _"tried and true" perspectives_ and methodologies	Emphasis on an _open and inquisitive approach_ to sources of new learning and experience
-- Communications	_Monologue_: Seek to persuade	_Dialogue_: Seek to understanding

Table 9-1

Managing Organizational Change

Since humans have limited processing capability, and the mind is easily overloaded and clings to its past experience and knowledge, "letting go" becomes as important as learning — Alex and David Bennett

Now that we have considered the challenges facing modern organizations in terms of their need to become adaptive enterprises able to deal with cognitively complex situations, fragmented organizational functions, and complex business environments; our attention is directed toward the knowledge, skills, roles, and methodologies of the *adaptive leadership competency* – basically, the job of our learnership practitioners. The figures that follow are a continuation of the evolving Learnership Integrated Systems Architecture (LISA) that contains artifacts from the previously addressed learnership competencies of Systems Thinking (ST), Pattern Recognition (PR), Situational Learning (SL), and Knowledge Management (KM). And, both figures support the four areas of learnership social system development: personal, organizational, community, and society.

Social Systems Change and Development. The specific emphasis, herein, is on two major adaptive leader responsibilities: developing a comprehensive methodology for organization change, and leading the change and development process.

Methodology for Organizational Change. After a decision has been made to proceed with an organizational change process and a target audience has been identified, an organization change methodology suitable to the effort should be developed. A comprehensive approach should identify and compare the pros and cons of the organization's *current system performance* with that of the newly defined and proposed *future system performance* (Figure 9-2). Additionally, the methodology should address the six critical business functions affected (strategy, structure, culture, process, technology, people) with sufficient explanatory information to gain the attention and support of those affected. Descriptions of these functions with examples of selected areas of emphasis are:

1. Strategy – An enterprise level view of the new goals and objectives to be pursued. Typical examples are: (a) Firm will become proactive, market-based, and adaptable to changing environment; (b) Customer and stakeholder satisfaction will be assessed and improved; and (c) Internal planning will focus on organization alignment and cohesion.

2. Structure – How the enterprise or business function will organize its authorities, locations and resources to accomplish its new goals and objectives. Typical examples are: (a) Workplace will be global, virtual, less hierarchical, and IT-enabled; (b) Governance will be participatory, democratic, and based on shared responsibility, (c) Leadership will be distributed, shared, and demonstrated through example; and (d) Community will be created through alliance with customers and suppliers.

3. Culture – Changes desired in terms of attitudes, priorities, relationships, and behaviors concerning internal operations and external contacts. Typical examples are: (a) Leaders and workforce should share a common vision and values; (b) Communication and collaboration will occur anytime, anyplace; and (c) Information and knowledge will be acquired, developed, coordinated, and shared.

4. Process – The standards, procedures and workflow changes that are implemented. Typical examples are: (a) Work will be knowledge-based, innovative, and value-driven; and (b) Processes will be reviewed, standardized, and continuously improved; and (c) Decision making will be informed, objective, and timely.

5. Technology – The information processing, new technologies and tools, and communication infrastructure changes that will be employed. Typical examples are: (a) Information technology will be digital, client-server, open-system, and include multimedia; (b) Workers should networked, collaborative, and empowered to act; and (c) IT networks are to be expanded and integrated to support virtual operations.

6. People – Changes planned in workforce knowledge, skill, competencies, work skills, responsibilities, and welfare. Typical examples are: (a) Learning is to be continuous, life-long, and integrated into work experiences; (b) Teamwork and individual initiative are to be valued and rewarded; and (c) Workforce well-being and satisfaction will be assessed and improved.

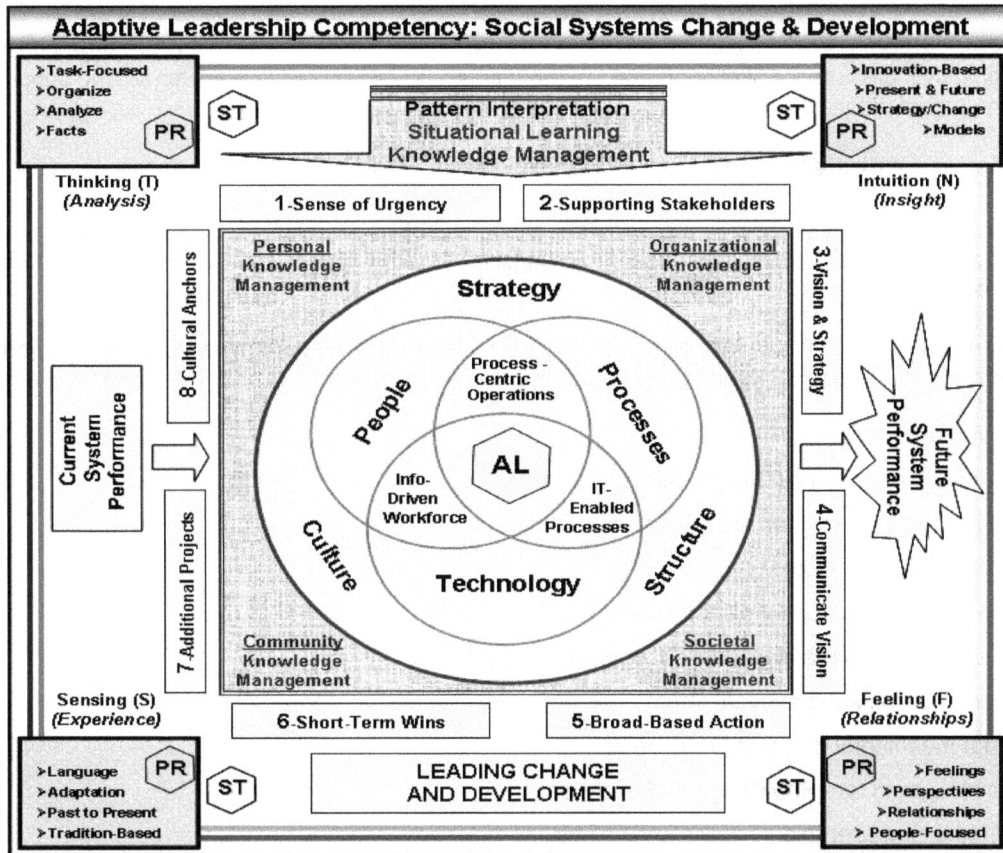

Figure 9-1

Leading Change and Development. The responsibility for leading organizational change and communications usually falls to those managers and workforce members with knowledge and responsibility for the functions and/or work processes being improved. However, executive involvement and leadership, as well as consultant and facilitator assistance, are often required when the initiative is complex or controversial. In his book *Leading Change* (1996) John Kotter presents a clearly written description of the challenges and techniques for leading major organizational change. Kotter comments that: "And those people at the top of enterprises today who encourage others to leap into the future, who help them to overcome natural fears, and who thus expand the leadership capacity in their organizations – these people provide a profoundly important service for the entire human community." (p.186) An adaptation of Kotter's overarching change management process and leadership activities is herewith summarized and illustrated in Figure 9-2:

1. Create a Sense of Urgency – Succinctly describe the potential crises or major opportunities that will result.

2. Identify and Involve Supporting Stakeholders – Organize a group of concerned and influential supporters.

3. Establish a Meaningful Vision and Strategy – Envision future benefits and a plan to achieve those results.

4. Communicate the Vision – Spread the word about the planned change and have leaders demonstrate their support.

5. Establish Broad-Based Action – Identify obstacles, risk management efforts, and advocates of initiatives to be implemented.

6. Achieve Short-Term Wins – Place priority on obtaining visible near-term results that contribute to the larger planned change.

7. Launch Additional Projects – Add additional projects and initiatives using outputs from the initial short-term wins.

8. Connect Success to Cultural Anchors – Identify the new attitudes and behaviors that contributed to more efficient operations and effective outcomes.

[**Author's Note**: The combination of a comprehensive change methodology and a well-led change and development process significantly increases the likelihood that the planned improvements will be accepted and supported by other leaders and the organizational workforce.]

Adaptive Leader Attributes, Roles, and Dialogue

The four areas of emphasis in this section are (a) leader attributes, (b) leader roles, (c) leader dialogue and (d) leaders manage attention. They are illustrated in Figure 9-3, which together with Figure 9-2, depict the core capabilities of organizational change agents.

Leader Attributes. A survey of literature on this topic yields a long list of leader characteristics or attributes associated with having positive influence and attaining high performance. A few of the most prominent factors are being or having:

1. Competent in one's field.

2. Objective in handling decisions and problems.

3. Reflexive in looking at one's own attitudes and behavior.

4. Trustworthy in dealing with other's interests.

5. Innovative in the pursuit of better performance.

6. Focused in an attempt to maintain efficient operations.

7. Open-minded in considering relevant information and perspectives.

8. Confident that meaningful outcomes may be achieved.

9. Intuitive in considering tacit knowledge and experience.

10. Character exhibiting exemplary morals and values.

11. Initiative and willingness to take action.

12. Courage to take a stand for principle.

Leader Roles. In order to accomplish his organizational objectives the leader may have to perform different organization roles at various times and places. In each situation he is charged with moving other's reasoning and behavior forward toward desired results. A number of roles have been identified for use during appropriate circumstances:

1. Listener – Considering the perspectives and suggestions of others.

2. Collaborator – Participating in the give-and-take of conversation in an attempt to find common cause and consensus.

3. Facilitator – Organizing and guiding the process of group communications and deliberations.

4. Steward – Caring for the thoughts and property of others.

5. Convener – Bringing people and groups together for thinking, learning, decision making and/or problem solving.

6. Learner – Being open to new issues, information and perspectives in an effort to understand situations more clearly.

7. Educator – Allocating time to help others understand information and situations more clearly using facts, logic and experience.

8. Tactician – Determining near-term courses of thought and action to achieve desired objectives.

9. Strategist – Determining longer-term courses of thought and action to achieve better marketplace and mission positioning.

10. Visionary – Becoming mentally aware of overarching missions, purposes, and possibilities and sharing that perspective with others.

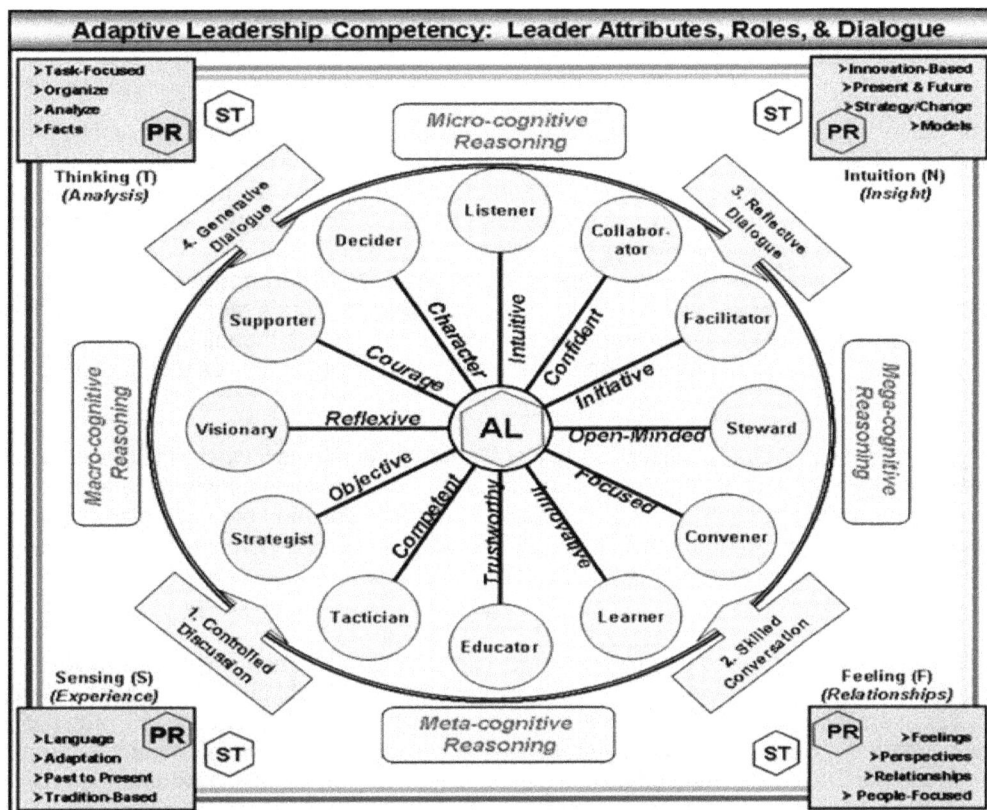

Figure 9-2

11. <u>Supporter</u> – Acting as a follower by assisting others to achieve their objectives.

12. <u>Decider</u> – Taking responsibility for choosing among alternative perspectives, objectives, methods, and course of action

Leader Dialogue. In his book *Dialogue and the Art of Thinking Together* (1999), William Isaacs explains how important it is to move much of group and organizational conversation away from being unproductive and defensive to

being skillful, reflective and generative. His research indicates that so often the Initial strategy in a conversation is for individuals to mentally *deliberate* on whether to *defend* against others' views and objectives by *advocating* one's own views and needs – or to *suspend* one's own interests and needs and *listen* to what others have to say. Taking the former tact leads to either to *debate* (least productive in terms of consensus), or possibly skillful conversation (analytic and reasoned problem solving). If the latter choice (suspending) is taken initially, there is the probability that *reflective dialogue* leading to *generative dialogue* can be the result leading to more inclusion and better long-term organizational alignment and cohesion. The stages of progressive leader dialogue are:

Stage 1 <u>Controlled Discussion</u> – Advocacy, competing, and abstract verbal brawling.

Stage 2. <u>Skilled Conversation</u> – Analytic, use data for answers, and explicit reasoning.

Stage 3. <u>Reflective Dialogue</u> – Exploring underlying causes, rules, and assumptions.

Stage 4. <u>Generative Dialogue</u> – Creates new insights, possibilities, and group "flow."

Leaders Manage Attention. Thomas Davenport and John Beck's book on *The Attention Economy: Understanding the New Currency of Business* (2001) is very timely in that it not only recognizes, but predicts major changes required to live and succeed in an information overloaded personal and business environment. They indicate that all aspects of business direction, operations, and performance will be impacted by the need for leaders and managers at all levels to keep their focus on essential business goals, objectives, functions, processes, outputs, and markets while wading through huge quantities of incoming communications (people, reports, articles, messages, decisions, problems, emails) demanding immediate attention. The overall effect will be to increase individual and organization stress, make building relationships and making informed decision-making difficult, and maintaining organizational cohesion and alignment an act of artistry.

On a daily basis, the dynamic, fast-paced work environment will be one that challenges the most experienced and skilled leaders. Add to this scenario the fact that the leader is often leading major organizational change and/or transformation to stay competitively positioned in the marketplace, we can see the need to employ techniques at filtering and control of incoming information while simultaneously employing multiple paths for outgoing communications that ensures necessary information sharing and direction to organizational officials, the workforce, investors, competitors, and other stakeholders. In their chapter on Command Performance, the authors say that: "The universe is available twenty-four hours a day at the click of a mouse, and there's more distracting information than we could ever absorb. Now, more than ever, leaders have to find innovative ways means of capturing and directing attention. With greater efficiency and creativity, leaders will need to secure the four elements of attention leadership:" (p.136) The elements are:

1. Focusing their own attention – Leaders need to monitor themselves and know where their own attention is being directed. "To manage attention well, we must be self-aware and believe passionately that the issues we focus on are the most important ones for our own careers, our company, our employees, and our customers. Employees throughout a company make decisions about what to pay attention to based on what their perception of what their leaders pay attention to. Consequently, leaders have to be more careful about how they invest their attention, for themselves and for their subordinates." (p.137)

2. Attracting the right kind of attention to themselves – Most senior managers and executives have risen up the corporate ranks by knowing when and how to get the right attention at the right time. Although the old methods of leadership – power and position – are still effective at getting attention, they are decreasingly effective at *maintaining* attention. Attention leaders influence behavior by creating a meaningful context for information – attention is awareness with meaning. Thus, selecting and contextualizing information – choosing what to focus on and how to focus on it – is essential to successful attention management." (p.141)

3. Directing the attention of those who follow them – "Leaders must work to shift the organization's attention from *faux work,* or the politics that consumes too much daily energy, to 'real work.' To lead effectively, you must create a corporate culture in which people get used to communicating clearly and directly. Since we pay the most attention to things that are ours, include employees in the decision process at every turn. When an individual has created something, the person feels a natural sense of ownership and belonging." (p.144-147)

4. Maintaining the attention of their customers and clients – "Even if you get 100 percent of your employees attention directed in the right ways 100 percent of the time, your company will still fail if you can't secure and maintain your customers' attention. Sometimes a firm might want their customers to keep the firm in a comfortable place in the *back of their minds* especially if the firm has a *captive relationship* with the customer. However, in other situations it may be more important to have the customers move the firm to the *front of their minds* because of a *voluntary relationship* that the firm needs to exploit." (p.149)

[**Author's Note**: The leader roles, attributes, dialogue and attention management practices of the adaptive leadership competency describe how a learnership practitioner goes about performing his or her personal, organizational and community social responsibilities – and getting action on the organization's goals and strategies.]

Additional Adaptive Leadership Perspective

> *To be a leader you have to have conviction – a fire in your belly. You've got to*
> *have passion. You've got to really want to get something done.*
> *— Lee Iacocca*

This section provides perspectives from a slate of additional writers. The perspectives offered are meant to "round out" the emerging panorama of adaptive leadership skills – with particular emphasis on how our learnership practitioners succeed as leaders in their own organizations or as professional management consultants.

Adaptive Leadership Skills. Four areas are presented for consideration and learning: An Intrapreneurial Spirit, Project Management, Action Learning, and Action Coaching.

An Intrapreneurial Spirit. In their book *Intrapreneuring in Action: A Handbook for Business Innovation* (1999) Gifford Pinchot and Ron Pellman encourage people working in organizations to become intrapreneurs. They say that

"*Intrapreneurs* is short for *intra*-corporate entre*preneur* …Within an organization, intrapreneurs take new ideas and turn them into profitable realities. Without empowered intrapreneurs, organizations don't innovate." (p.ix) And, regarding innovation Pinchot and Pellman say that: "Innovation is more than creativity. It is the creation of, and bringing into widespread use of, a new product, service, process, or system – from the first glimmer of an idea to successful implementation and exploitation." (p.1) Some examples of the type of innovations they consider are: new products and services, better ways of reaching customers, improved organizational systems and structures, techniques for doing more with less, and new approaches for gathering and using information and knowledge. Pinchot and Pellman identify what they call the crucial roles in innovation: (pp.16-20)

1. Idea People – Most people in organizations can contribute potentially useful ideas if encouraged to do so. Only a few ideas will have a chance of being used; and then only if they capture the enthusiasm and commitment of competent leaders.

2. Intrapreneurs – Not necessarily the person who comes up with a new idea, but the one who can provide thought-leadership and turn an idea into commitment and action.

3. The Intrapreneurial Team – Volunteers that form a core group of knowledgeable people who stay with the initiative from inception to implementation.

4. The Sponsor – Support intrapreneurs by asking tough developmental questions, protecting the initiative from the "corporate immune system," and assisting in obtaining limited resources.

5. The Climate Maker – Those at the executive levels that create a corporate climate in which suggestions and innovations get a fair hearing and an opportunity to show potential value.

The authors comment that their research on successful Intrapreneuring indicates the following learning and useful behaviors:

1. Be a courageous but moderate risk taker.
2. Be frugal, stay flexible.
3. Be creative about the pathway.
4. Build a team of enthusiastic volunteers.
5. Ask for advice before asking for resources.
6. Accept help when offered.
7. Express gratitude.
8. Under-promise, over-deliver.
9. Learn from everything.
10. Embrace barriers without losing optimism.
11. Develop business judgment.
12. Work for the good of the whole.

[**Author's Note**: The Intrapreneurial spirit should be alive and well in the mind of the learnership practitioner. Moderate risk taking, learning from every situation, working for the good of the whole, and expressing gratitude demonstrates the use of learnership reasoning competencies and social systems development objectives are the core of the learnership philosophy and architecture.]

Managing Projects. In his book *Building Project Management Competence* (1999), David Frame suggests that in today's increasingly competitive and changing world and work environment flatter organizations are required, middle management layers are being reduced, and organizational improvement is being accomplished by greater numbers of project teams. His argument is that the project management specialty is gaining more responsibility for improving, changing, and transforming organizations; and he identifies three levels of project competence that should be developed: the individual, the team, and the organization. Within the project team it is the project manager that bears ultimate responsibility for making things happen. He is the leader who is expected to balance the "triple constraints" of accomplishing the specified task (1) requirements, (2) within budget, and (3) in accordance with the project schedule. Frame comments that: "The *competent project manager* should do the following: (pp.46-48)

1. Be a *results-oriented*, can-do individual.
2. Have a *head for details.*
3. Possess a *strong commitment* to the project.

4. Be aware of the *organization's goals.*

5. Be *politically savvy.*

6. Be *cost conscious.*

7. Understand *business basics.*

8. Be capable of *understanding the needs* of staff, customers, and management.

9. Be capable of *coping with ambiguity,* setbacks, and disappointments.

10. Possess good *negotiation skills.*

11. Possess the appropriate *technical skills* to do his or her job.

[**Author's Note**: This list of practical traits and skills is significantly aligned with the learnership *philosophy, architecture,* and *practitioner* competencies presented in earlier Chapters. The list also contains knowledge and skill similarities (see italics) with many core capabilities addressed in the organizational and community systems development chapters that follow.]

Frame is astute at reinforcing a core tenet of learnership that lifelong learning, hard work, and strong teamwork are essential ingredients in the achievement of personal, organizational and community success. In fact, Frame integrates his own experience and perspectives with those of Peter Senge and Daniel Goleman (whose views we have already included elsewhere) so effectively that only a direct quote could do justice to the powerful comment he provides: (p.63)

1. "A review of the lives of successful people in all walks for life (including spiritual leaders) shows that one thing they have in common is that they work hard to achieve their success.

2. Peter Senge's *Fifth Discipline* (1990) identifies *personal mastery* as one of the five key disciplines that people should seek. Although Senge is not precise in defining personal mastery, a key component is continual learning. People who achieve personal mastery have an insatiable appetite for knowledge and understanding. They never let up in their attempt to learn. The payoffs to such a duty to learning are substantial.

3. In his study of what contributes to the effectiveness of people in the worlds of school and work, Daniel Goleman (1995) notes that mastery is a characteristic these people share. He also points out that the achievement of mastery entails a high degree of discipline and a long-term commitment to learning. Again the payoffs are substantial."

[**Author's Note**: Learnership practitioners operating in organizational and community social system development will need project management knowledge and experience into which they can anchor many of their other competencies and personal capabilities.]

Action Learning. Author Michael Marquardt in his book *Action Learning in Action* (1999) says "*action learning* is both a process and a powerful program that involves a small group of people solving real problems while at the same time focusing on what they are learning and how their learning can benefit each group member and the organization as a whole…The benefits of action learning are:

1. Shared learning throughout various levels of the organization.

2. Greater self-awareness and self-confidence due to new insights and feedback.

3. Ability to ask better questions and be more reflective.

4. Improved communications and teamwork. (p.4)

Marquardt indicates that action learning is a systematic methodology or program of activities that derives its power from six components:

1. A Problem – One that is within the responsibility of the team, and can provide an opportunity for learning.

2. The Group – Four to eight individuals from across various departments in order to maximize perspectives and fresh viewpoints.

3. The Questioning and Reflection Process – Cycles of focus on both what is known and what is not known which allow insight and learning.

4. The Resolution to Take Action – The group has the power to either take action themselves or a commitment that their recommendations will be acted upon.

5. The Commitment to Learning – Uses a dual focus in which learning from the process is valued along with determining the task solution.

6. The Facilitator – Manages the group process and helps them slow down their process, which allows them to reflect on their learning. (paraphrased, pp.7-8)

The action learning methodology is distinctly different from what most people experience in everyday organizational life. Instead of a "rush to judgment" by a few well-connected "leaders" serving their own interests before others can get involved; action learning values much more deliberative conversation – even dialogue – which by its very nature expands workforce involvement, seeks useful input, and encourages a sense of participation and being valued in all involved. Marquardt comments that: "Action learning creates conditions in which managers learn from their own experience of real-life problems, helped by and helping others in similar or dissimilar situations. A manager actually changes the way he or she manages, on the basis of reality. The focus of action learning is on learning about the process of managing change by actually managing an organizational change. It stresses the importance of learning about oneself and the influence that one's attitudes and assumptions have on how one leads and make decisions." (p.123)

[**Author's Note**: Marquardt states that modern organizations and communities need leaders that perform seven roles for a leader in the twenty-first century: (1) *systems thinker*, (2) *change agent*, (3) *innovator and risk taker*, (4) *servant and steward*; (5) *polychromic coordinator*, (6) *instructor, coach, and mentor*, and (7) *visionary and vision builder*. The same skills apply to our learnership practitioner.]

Action Coaching. Authors David Dotlich and Peter Cairo's book *Action Coaching: How to Leverage Individual Performance for Company Success* (1999) says that in today's organizations every manager is a coach and stresses the critical relationship between individual employee development and overall organizational performance. They note that quite often external coaches are brought into organizations to resolve development and performance issues that could have been handled by organizational leaders themselves – if they knew how to do effective coaching themselves. They comment that: "Action coaching is a process that fosters self-awareness and leads to the motivation to change, as well as the guidance needed if change is to take place in ways that meet individual and organizational performance needs…Action coaching has four clearly focused change goals:

1. Self-Awareness – A client gains a better understanding of his or her attitudes and behaviors, strengths and weaknesses.

2. Performance Improvement – A client improves his or her performance in a way that contributes to his effectiveness in growing a business.

3. Performance Breakthrough – A client raises his personal or job performance to an entirely new level, thereby benefiting themselves and the organization.

4. Transformation – A client makes a fundamental change in behavior, attitude, values, and basic emotional intelligence that serves them for the longer-run." (p.2)

The authors clearly establish that in action coaching the unit of analysis and improvement is the *employee within the needs and context of the organization*. That means that the *client* to be coached is most often an individual whose performance requires improvement for the benefit of the organization within which he or she works. The action coach follows a general problem solving methodology that proceeds from data collection and analysis to action planning and performance evaluation:

Step 1 Determine what needs to happen and in what context
Step 2 Establish trust and mutual expectations
Step 3 Contract with client for results
Step 4 Collect and communicate feedback
Step 5 Translate talk into action
Step 6 Support big steps
Step 7 Foster reflection about actions
Step 8 Evaluate individual and organization progress

Lastly, Dotlich and Cairo caution that when leaders, managers, and consultant's attempt to motivate change in other people's performance care must be taken to stay on target. That is, seek to understand and improve those individual behaviors with clear linkage to organizational performance. Some motivational mistakes that are often made when attempting to "close a gap" between individuals and their organizations include: (pp.118-120)

1. Closing the gap between who someone is and where he wants to be in his career. The action coach must distinguish between areas in need of strictly personal development and those that have organizational performance impact.

2. Closing the gap between who someone is and what personal bias dictates he or she should become. Action coaches must recognize their own biases and preferences and not allow them to become part of the client's issue.

3. Closing the gap between who someone is and an illusory business requirement. Find out from organizational leaders exactly what they need to accomplish, and use that information as the framework for data gathering and recommendations.

4. Closing the gap between who someone is and the new behavior everyone wishes he or she would develop. Attempt to change only those behaviors that really impact organizational performance.

[**Author's Note**: *Learnership practitioners* may perform their skills as a member of an organization or as an external consultant hired to assist an organizational change effort. In either function, they are astute observers of the situation on the ground – the issues, the players, the desired outcomes – and can fashion an approach for bringing disparate sides together using action coaching reasoning, interpersonal dialogue, and change management interventions.]

Organizational Consulting. In the book *Internal Consulting for HRD Professionals* (1994) the authors Jerry Gilley and Amy Coffern argue their case for using internal HRD professionals as organizational performance consultants to improve operational efficiency and effectiveness. They list eight areas in which the HRD office could perform consulting functions similar to what is often provided by external organizational consultants. In order of increasing organizational impact, these are:

1. Providing information.
2. Solving problems.
3. Conducting an effective diagnosis.
4. Providing recommendations.
5. Implementing change.
6. Building consensus and commitment.
7. Facilitating client learning.
8. Improving organizational effectiveness.

The authors also state that for those HRD professionals wishing to develop into internal consultants will need to embrace the increased knowledge, skills, and responsibilities that come with being a trusted consultant. "To be successful, you must have a set of values that guide your day-to-day activities. Each of the following is a value that can help you improve your efforts":

1. Credibility as a focus.
2. Responsiveness as an attitude.
3. Competence as a standard.
4. Value-added as a method of operation.
5. Professionalism as a goal.
6. Performance improvement as a given.
7. Organizational effectiveness as a way of life.
8. Quality as a standard.
9. Communication as the key to success.
10. Involvement as an ongoing effort.

[**Author's Note**: On the face of it one would think that the HRD office should play a significant role in accomplishing the list of improvement functions presented, it is important to recognize that in most organizations middle and senior level managers prefer, instead, to hire external subject experts for most important and large scale organizational improvement projects. The reasons for this include: (1) deeper subject matter expertise; (2) knowledge and experience with best industry practices; (3) non-involvement with organizational politics; (4) greater objectivity in information interpretation and recommendations; (5) ability to use temporary contract employees rather than building up own staff; and (6) perception of easier application of authority using contract provisions.]

[**Author's Note:** You, the reader are reminded that just like in all the previous graphics presented in this guidebook, the Systems Thinking (ST) and Pattern Recognition (PR) reasoning competencies preferred by the people considering our topics – leads to unpredictable influences and outcomes. Becoming an adaptive leader is essential for success in today's rapidly changing and complex world.]

Complex Decision-Making

The rapid change, ambiguity and complexity of today's social and work environment places a premium on having senior managers adept at systems thinking, situational learning and adaptive leadership. Time pressure and lack of sufficient information are often at odds with the demands for decision-making and problem-solving. And due to the nationwide and international scope of many organizations, leaders may often be tempted to easy their stress level by taking action without considering the involvement of all the topics and people that have responsibility or essential knowledge that should be factored into assessments, decisions and subsequent actions.

Previous discussions in this chapter focused on leader dialogue, action learning and coaching, and project management competence have argued for leaders and teams to take care in their strategic and complex planning processes to allow for increased information gathering and knowledge building – as well as greater dialogue and expert participation – to ensure all the necessary content and context factors and best people are invited to share their insights and expertise.

Scoping the Issue or problem

Figure 9-3 illustrates the holistic American learnership approach that begins with Ten Team Scoping Discussions that address the four social system domains and six universal knowledge spheres in terms of their (1) degree of impact on the issue at hand, and (2) on the weighted priority that each should be given as discussions proceed. This Adaptive Leadership (AL) process establishes a "decision space" in which most major influences and risk considerations are acknowledged. Doing this permits everyone to articulate their expectations, to participate in critical thinking, and to experience authentic dialogue which, in time, may be key to obtaining their subsequent support when the final actions are decided.

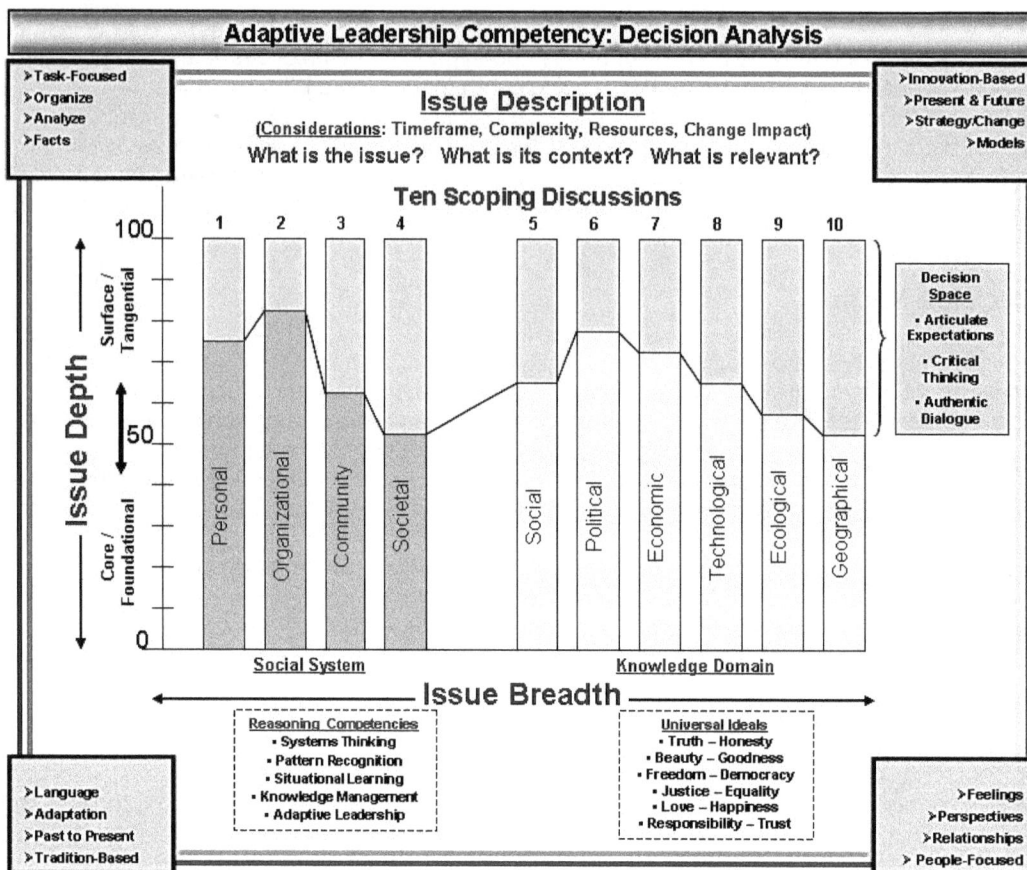

Figure 9-3

Using a systematic process

Once the Adaptive Leadership (AL) content deliberation and context setting effort of Figure 9-3 has been conducted and recorded for further use, the deliberation process in Figure 9-4 can proceed using the information already required on an as-appropriate basis. Through cycles of systematic learning and knowledge crafting, the team should acquire sufficient Knowledge (KM) factors that can be organized into alternative solutions for selection and action by the team and its adaptive leader (AL). Two major caveats that should be employed during the deliberation process are:

1. The deliberations will require an experienced strategic leader, subject matter experts and a skilled facilitator. This ensures structured meetings and conversations where substantive knowledge is exchanged and recorded.

2. Agree that "nothing is agreed to unless all is agreed to." This will allow better information sorting because some items can be deferred until more appropriate times in the process.

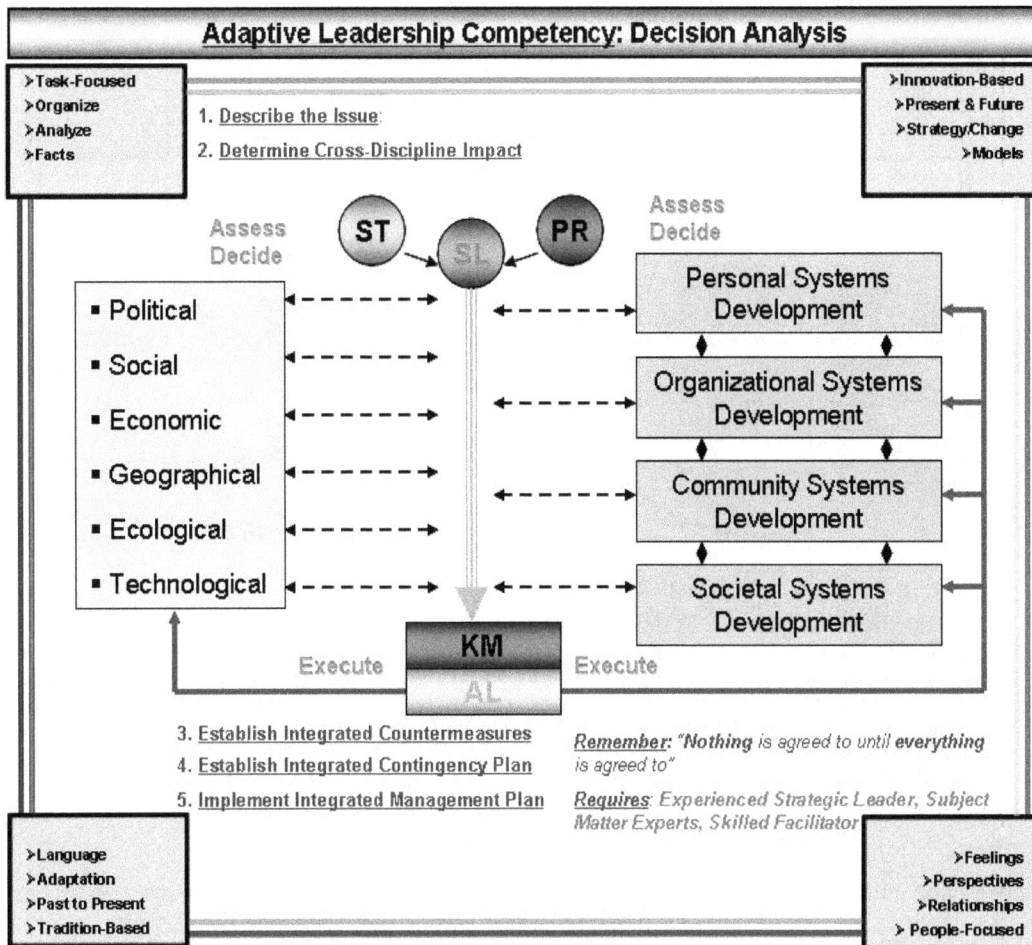

Figure 9-4

Phases of Change Management

An insight on adaptive leaders is that they maintain a continued awareness of the influencing factors in their respective lives, organizations and communities. In the external arena of personal and social system goals and mission requirements they are aware of emerging challenges that threaten the effectiveness and success of their initiatives. In the internal arena of operational productivity and workforce performance they pursue opportunities for increased efficiency to build competitive capacity. In fact, requirements for proactive and/or reactive change management are always ongoing or on the agenda.

Figure 9-5 is a dynamic illustration of the phases of change management. It is important to recognize that accomplishing change within ourselves, our companies and our communities is hardly ever an easy task. The nature of human change is that whatever the social domain change efforts are considered to be external initiatives that disrupt the status quo or comfort zone of the participants. The graphic suggests that people generally do not embrace change until they first become *aware* and have an *understanding* of why they should comply. Only when that occurs will our *attitudes* and *behavior* begin to accommodate the new requirements being presented and desired *results* have a chance to be achieved. Conceptually the change process is easy to understand, but in practice many obstacles tend to make the process less than satisfactory all along the way:

1. The lack of clear, continuous, and convincing communication from leaders makes getting started slower than anticipated.

2. Failure to assess and confront obvious or potential negative consequences stimulates active personnel resistance to the effort.

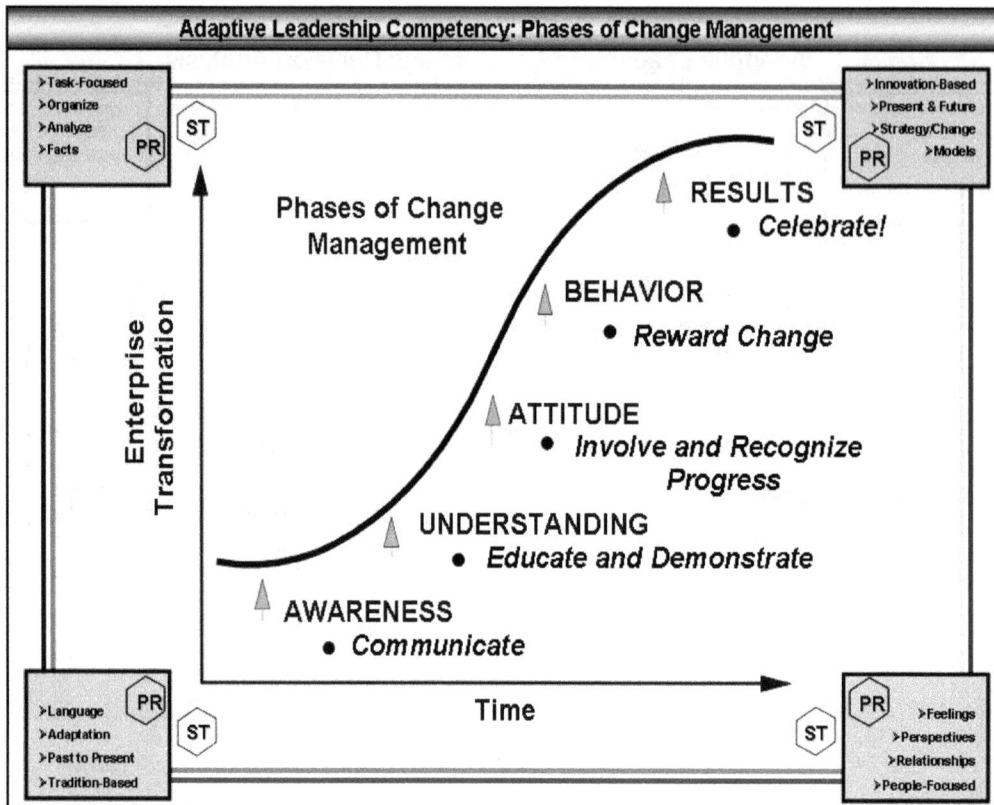

Figure 9-5

3. In the process of gaining support regarding 1 and 2 above, tradeoffs and compromises are agreed which may derail the expected results or cause unanticipated issues and cost to restrict progress and the outcome.

4. Slowing the process down allows inertia to build which becomes compounded if other related change efforts are begun that impact the availability of resources from the first initiative.

For the adaptive leader, the best course of action is to:

1. Prepare and implement a change management initiative concurrent with the improvement project itself.

2. Ensure needed resources are identified and prepared for usage as soon as they are needed for support.

3. Build a constituency of other leaders and subject matter experts to assist in building and maintaining communications and support.

4. Provide substantive information on project progress, and address questions and issues as they emerge.

Conclusion

The final test of a leader is that he leaves behind him in other men
the conviction and the will to carry on. — Walter Lippmann

Adaptive Leadership Competency. This chapter has taken a wide-ranging journey through organizational life; its challenges and complexities; and the kind of initiatives, skills, and people required to maintain a high state of efficiency and effectiveness. The *adaptive leadership* competency has now been added to the previously developed competencies (systems thinking, pattern recognition, situational learning, knowledge management) to round out the *set of five reasoning competencies critical for individuals to manage the effectiveness of the four social systems of their lives* – their personal, organizational, community, and societal social systems. These social systems are described and developed in the following chapters in a manner that exploits the advantages of using the five learnership competencies (represented by the *Learnership Integrated Systems Architecture* (LISA), the stock in trade of *learnership practitioners.*

Implications for Integral Learning and Knowledge Management. Adaptive Leadership principles, practices, and technologies are of little use in an organization that does not take implementation action. Concurrent with the design and change of work processes and procedures and the addition of IT technology and tools; leadership is essential to communicate the business case for change, arrange for training and mentoring, and to advise everyone in the enterprise of the improvements and what they mean to both internal units and external customers and constituencies. Adaptive leadership is the critical skill at this juncture because more than likely the changes being implemented will be based on greater distribution of organizational functions and people, and might even require an increased flexibility in the performance of tasks. Organizational changes require experienced, competent management by those well suited to stressful and oftentimes conflicted situations.

The wide range of practices and technologies available for today's leaders means change is continuous and adaptability to new circumstances is a regular requirement for those in leadership positions. The learnership social system domains addressed in chapters ten through fourteen will all need a strong infusion of Integral Learning and Knowledge Management (ILKM) to achieve their growth potential and universal goals (Self-Fulfillment, High Performance, Common Good, Human Enlightenment).

Personal Reflection. This topic appears at the send of each chapter and is meant to serve two purposes: (1) be a reader's guide to main points and "takeaways," and (2) to encourage everyone to take a moment to engage their mental cognition and intuition on what the chapter means to them – especially at this time in their lives. Questions for chapter reflection follow immediately below; and for those readers inclined to maintain a self-assessment, your thoughts may be recorded in your *American Learnership for Life, Work, Wealth, Health and Legacy Success* at Appendix B.

Questions for Discussion:

1. Have you worked for a manager who was often confused by the chaos surrounding her responsibilities and unwilling to see the true complexity of her job? What was the effect on your job performance?

2. Why is it so important in tomorrow's workplace to not only be skilled in one's field, but also to have the capability to continuously learn, to apply new methodologies, and to adapt to changing events and in getting the job done differently?

3. What are two to three differences between the predominant *make and sell* organizations of the past and tomorrow's need for more *sense and respond* organizations?

4. Can you list two to three major learning points from this chapter that you want to keep in mind to improve your ability to manage your life and career?

5. What do you think the impact of this chapter's information might be on the personal, organizational, community, and/or societal systems to be discussed later in the book?

6. Can you identify two to three topics, models, or perspectives in this chapter you would like to learn more about?

7. Should you be making an entry into your *American Learnership for Life, Work and Legacy Success* at Appendix B?

Insights, Commitments and Skills

If you plan to participate in the *American Learnership for Life, Work, Wealth, health and Legacy Success* self-development e-book experience, it is suggested you record your Insights, commitments and skills to be developed here in this chapter, and again in Appendix B:

My learning in terms of new insights, changing priorities, new commitments or skills I want to acquire:

1. Insights (Example): Remind myself that …

2. Commitments (Example): Continue to ask myself …

3. Skills (Example): Apply my knowledge and skills to

First Interlude

Transition from Reasoning Competencies to Social Systems Development

The very substance of the ambitious is merely the shadow of a dream.
— William Shakespeare

Overview of Learnership Artifacts.

The Chapter One Introduction to this book provided a foundation for the development of a new concept: *"Your Integral Life Matters: Create a Life and Legacy Management Mindset for Personal, Organizational, Community and Societal Success in the American Tradition."* A *learnership philosophy* and *learnership architecture* were defined and developed, and a social role for *learnership practitioners* was described. This role has been evolving in this Handbook from chapters one through nine as personal desires and reasoning competencies were developed and advocated for use in the new knowledge economy. Five Reasoning competencies – *systems thinking, pattern recognition, situational learning, knowledge management,* and *adaptive leadership* – were featured as an interdisciplinary set of knowledge, skills, and abilities that operate in a mutually enhancing manner. These competencies are believed to empower people and social entities to plan, manage, and improve their respective capabilities and responsibilities so that four Integral Social Systems domains may be achieved in support of higher levels of human performance.

The *Learnership Integrated Systems Architecture (LISA)* (Figure I-1) is a montage of selected elements of the five reasoning competencies, and serves *learnership practitioners* as a graphical model and University of the Mind (Mindset) in which reasoning competencies are harmonized and comprehensively applied at each level of social system responsibility, e.g. in the personal (*self-fulfilment*), organizational (*high performance*), community (*common good*), and societal (*human enlightenment*) domains of human system development and performance. Concurrently, an Integral Training and Knowledge Management (ILKM) capability has evolved as a major part of the systems architecture, and knowledge management practices and technologies are positioned to support performance improvement at all levels of social system activity.

Additionally, the Figure I-2 individual personal preference model should be considered as a symbiotic concept to Chapter Two Figure 6-2 in ensuring that human personality factors are given sufficient attention when designing and implementing social system development initiatives. The wide variety of personal styles and cultural factors to be addressed make Change and Culture Management a topic worthy of advanced planning.

Beginning with the next chapter, our task is to apply the learnership concepts and practices discussed so far in this Handbook for even greater social system-of-systems development. Chapters ten through thirteen explore a broad range of topics and issues of importance for personal, organizational, community and societal integral learning, meaningful living, personal branding and a memorable way-of-being. Our ultimate goal is to demonstrate the interdependence and viability of lifelong learning – and to specify how almost everyone can craft a productive way-of-being, experience happiness and establish a memorable living legacy.

The LISA appears again in Figure I-3 as the major component in the *Learnership Architecture and Collaboration Instrument (LACI).* Here it is presented as a tool for observing and assessing the quality of discussion among people charged with problem solving, opportunity finding and/or associated decision-making. The graphic may be copied and used as a template by individuals during meetings and decision-making to track the breadth and depth of conversation leading up to a conclusion. Participants are encouraged to make a copy of the LACI and a copy of the instructions on the page following Figure I-3. Then, follow the instructions provided wherein colored markers are used to track meeting deliberations, and to remind the group when important areas are not being given sufficient integrated social systems consideration.

The Learnership Integrated Systems Building Blocks presented on three slides (Figures I-4, I-5, and I-6) are matrixes of 78 distinguishing features (building blocks) each, relevant to the learnership concept and practice. The dynamic relationship among these activities and concepts is meant to convey the breadth and depth of the foundational "University of the Mind" insight – and to encourage a thoughtful review. Their arrangement allows easy identification of each specific block (e.g., B4 = "Continuous Change") in preparation of practical exercises that support the Handbook's use in training exercises. Readers are encouraged to make copies of these graphics and create team exercises for reinforcement of concepts under discussion.

The Learnership Practitioner Characteristics presented on two slides (Figures I-7 and I-8) are offered as a summary of the attitudes and behaviors our learnership practitioners have acquired as part of their professional development. Each characteristic is useful in its own time and place – and when used in combination with the other positive characteristics; a personal and professional demeanor devoted to total learning, knowing, and leading for life, work, wealth, health and legacy may be reinforced. Readers are encouraged to make copies of these guidelines for weekly reference.

Application of Learnership Artifacts. The artifacts just summarized are major contributors to a proposed methodology for successful group/team dialogue and decision-making. The primary component in this approach is the expanded use of the LISA not only as a static conceptual model, but as a *Learnership Architecture and Collaboration Instrument* (LACI) that may be used during meetings and conferences to keep track of the efficiency and effectiveness of ongoing communications and deliberative activity. This technique for facilitating and monitoring the quality of conversation and information exchange incorporates the building block features in Figures I-4 to I-6 and the practitioner characteristics in Figures I-7 and I-8.

The proposed life management methodology borrows reasoning processes and social communication skills from various perspectives offered throughout this handbook, such as: the five reasoning competencies, techniques for interpersonal dialogue, strategies for handling wicked problems, use of cycles of learning, application of whole brain deliberation, effort toward integration versus differentiation, use of critical thinking, and many others. These objectives and challenges for significantly improving group/team decision-making, problem-solving, and opportunity-finding may be achieved in this manner.

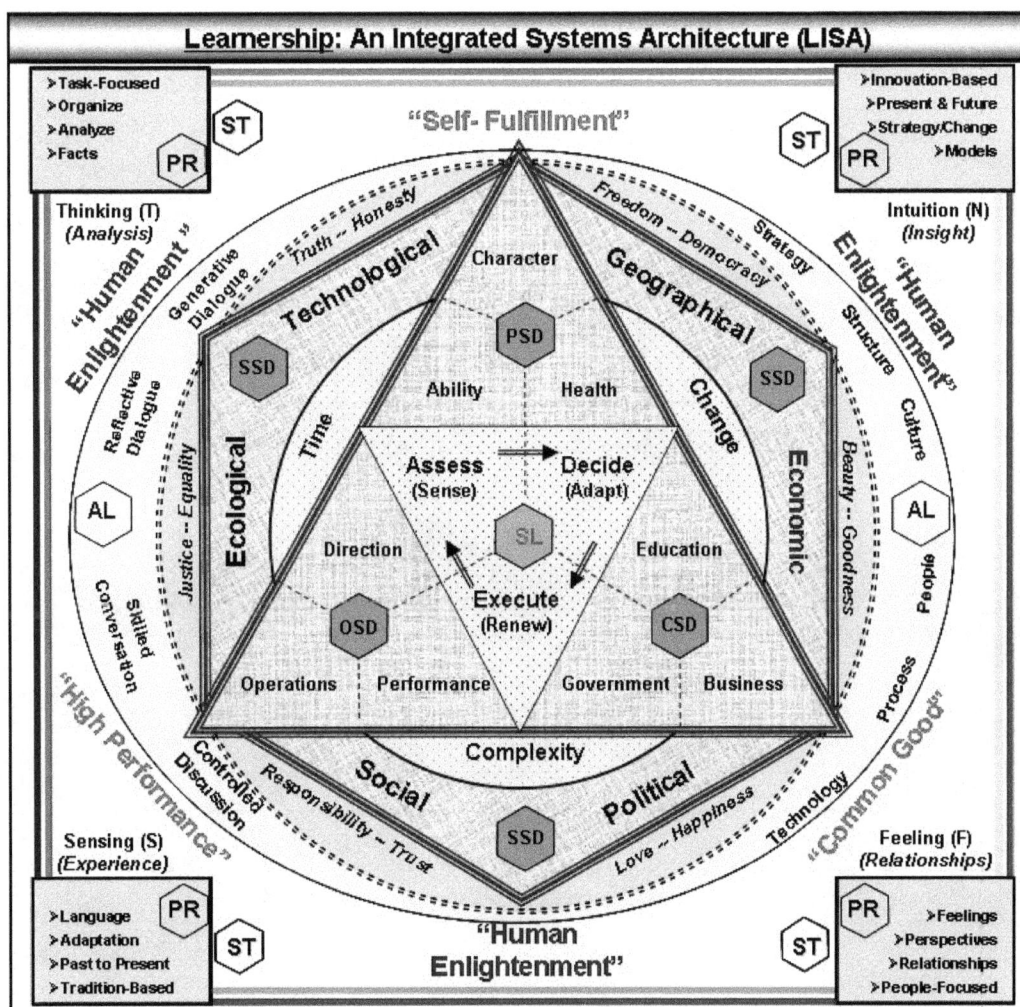

Figure I-1

Personal Preferences

The subject of Pattern Recognition back in chapter two is addressed here again in Figure 1-2 as reinforcement of the notion that all people have both similar and different characteristics, preferences and styles of psycho-social self-awareness, cognitive thinking and emotional tolerance. The American Learnership University of the Mind (brain training) approach used in constructing this Handbook includes concepts, graphics and practices that appeal to our mind's cognitive and emotional, left and right, language and pictures, and analysis and synthesis interests and capabilities.

[**Author's Note**: At this point in time, the American Learnership Learning Process, Interdisciplinary Reasoning Competencies, and Integrated Knowledge Management benefits derived from systematic inquiry reflection and learning have been positioned to deliver holistic social systems development in the personal (family), organizational (business), and community (societal) domains. Figures I-1 and I-2 together are American Learnership tools for achieving total learning, knowing, leading and legacy fulfilment in the next chapters.

Additionally, Figure I-2 is submitted as another illustration of how personal psychological patterns or preferences are prevalent across a group or human population so that at any point of time or situation a variety of mindsets may be operating and generating supportive or non-supportive group thinking, learning, knowing, and leadership when addressing objectives, decision alternatives or chosen courses of action. Achieving agreement on the relevant content or context on any issue or opportunity is often a tedious activity.

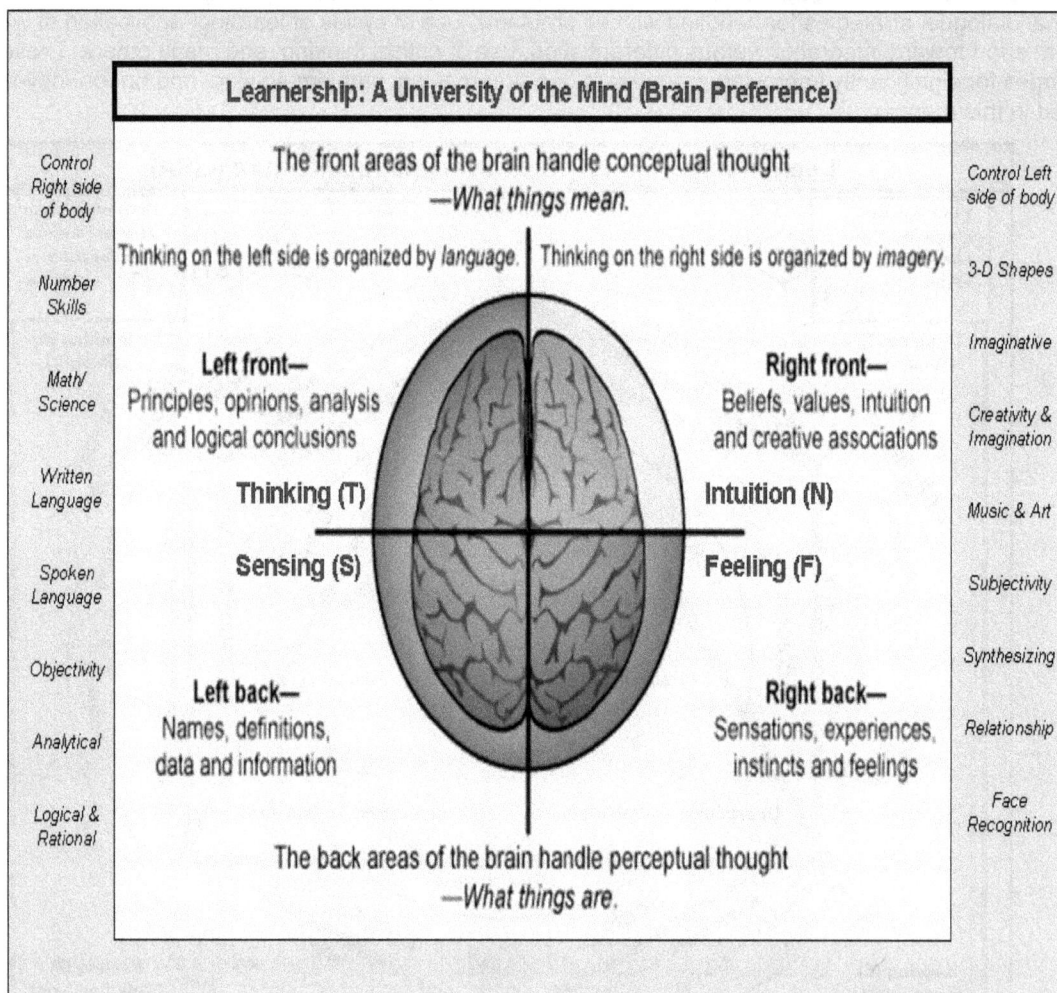

Figure I-2

Learnership Architecture & Collaboration Instrument (LACI)

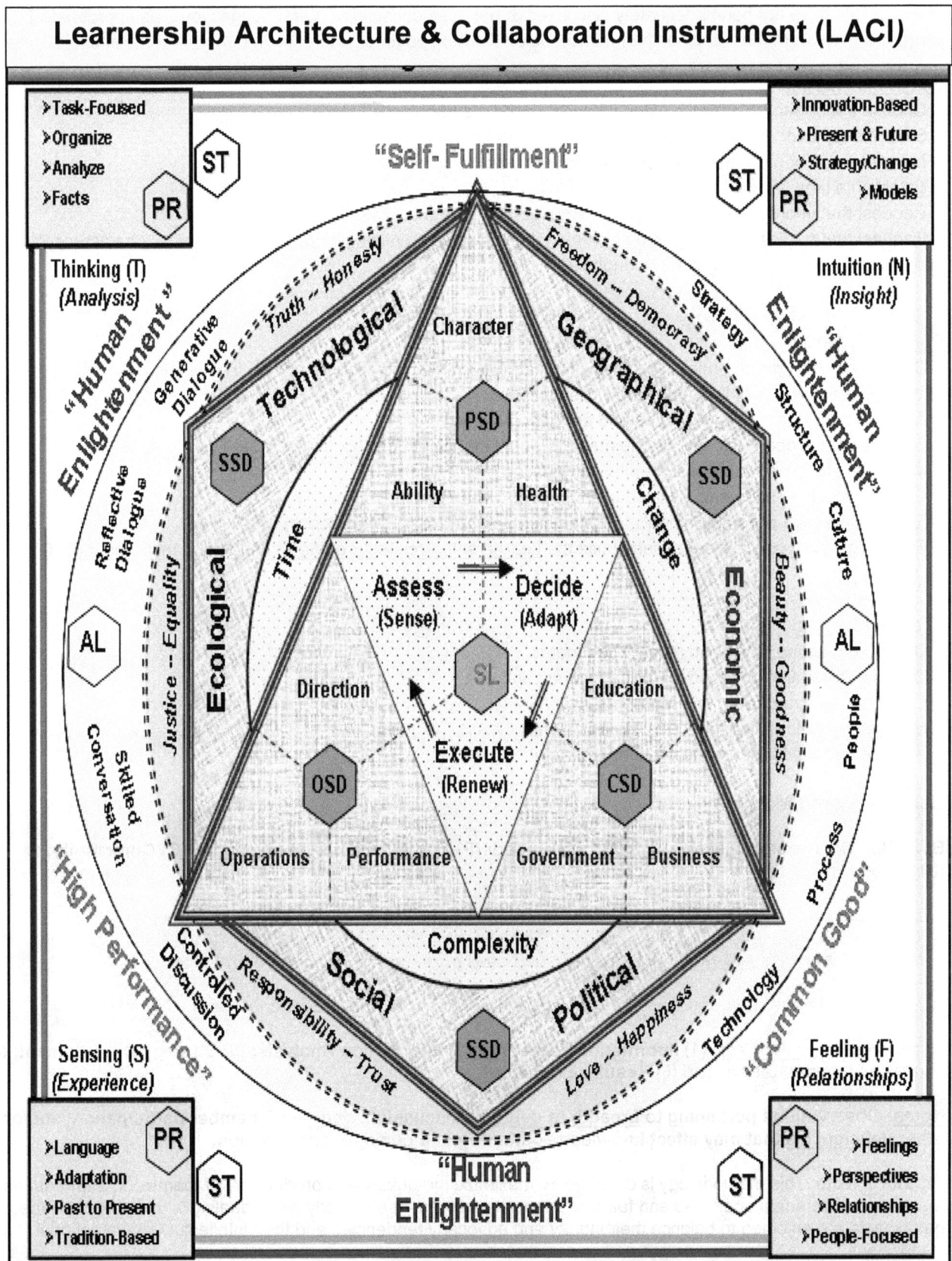

Thinking (T)
(Analysis)

> Task-Focused
> Organize
> Analyze
> Facts

ST PR

"Human Enlightenment"

Generative Dialogue
Reflective Dialogue
Skilled Conversation

Truth -- Honesty
Justice -- Equality
Responsibility -- Trust

"High Performance"

Sensing (S)
(Experience)

> Language
> Adaptation
> Past to Present
> Tradition-Based

PR ST

Intuition (N)
(Insight)

> Innovation-Based
> Present & Future
> Strategy/Change
> Models

ST PR

"Human Enlightenment"

Freedom -- Democracy
Beauty -- Goodness
Love -- Happiness

Strategy
Structure
Culture
People
Process
Technology

"Common Good"

Feeling (F)
(Relationships)

> Feelings
> Perspectives
> Relationships
> People-Focused

PR ST

"Self- Fulfillment"

AL

AL

Technological   Geographical
Ecological   Economic
Social   Political

Character
Ability   Health
Time   Change
Complexity

Assess (Sense) → Decide (Adapt)
Direction   SL   Education
Execute (Renew)
Operations   Performance   Government   Business

PSD   SSD   SSD   OSD   CSD   SSD

"Human Enlightenment"

[**Author's Note 1**: To make your meeting discussions more complete and to obtain better decisions and outcomes that include ALL relevant factors and viewing points, copy the above graphic on a piece of paper. Then use the colored

pencils/markers as explained on the next page to markup your graphic in such a way as to identify what relevant topics or viewpoints have not been adequately discussed or not even considered. Offer suggestions, as appropriate.]
[**Author's Note 2:** Make a copy of the instructions on the next page for reference in performing the above]

Before the Meeting:
-- Choose a facilitator to assist in using the learnership methodology.
-- State the topic for discussion – in writing.
-- Indicate if one or more meetings are planned on the subject
-- Establish a time limit for the meeting and the desired outcome.
-- Request that information to be shared is acquired and brought to the meeting.
-- Request that participants prepare by scanning the learnership building blocks and practitioner characteristics information provided in Figures I-2 through I-7.

During the Meeting:
-- Set conversation ground rules: Specificity, Non-attribution, Participation, Learning, Time Limits, One Speaker, Mutual Respect, Rules of Dialogue, and Collaboration.
-- Assign a recorder to take key notes and assigned actions.
-- Discuss what a good outcome for the meeting would be. What does "done" look like?
-- Identify the information to be shared by contributing members.
-- Commit to getting everyone involved in an open and sharing dialogue.
-- Evaluate meeting accomplishments: substantive (task) and learning (process).
-- Encourage everyone to independently use the Learnership Architecture and Collaboration Instrument.(LACI)

After the Meeting:
-- Distribute meeting notes and request comments.
-- Obtain additional information for further sharing and use.
-- Complete assigned tasks and report results.
-- Maintain cordial relationships among participants.
-- Prepare agenda for next meeting (if appropriate).

Use of Colored Markers:

BLACK = The major subject/issue being addressed: (P) Personal, (O) Organizational, (C) Community, (S) Society

BLUE = Sub-topics under discussion. Content, context, and dialogue process is balanced.

GREEN = Sub-topics adequately discussed and being prioritized for inclusion and closure.

RED = Sub-topic not being addressed. Negatively impacts blue and prevents green.

Decision-Making Process: (1) Information Gathering; (2) Information Analysis; (3) Strategy Development; (4) Strategy Implementation; and (5) Results Evaluation

Notes: Observations pertaining to breadth or depth of discussion, degree of member participation, and/or other deficiencies that may affect knowledge gathering and commitment to action.

[**Author's Note**: This methodology is designed to maximize the quality and productivity of teamwork, and requires a foundation of personal openness and fairness in social relations – particularly when dealing with divergent issues. All participants are enjoined to balance their inquiry and advocacy tendencies and their intellectual and emotional dispositions.]

Learnership: Integrated Systems Building Blocks

	A	B	C	D	E	F
1	Intrapreneurial Spirit	Systems Thinking	Knowledge Management	Wicked Problems	Adaptive Leadership	LISA
2	Life, Work & Legacy	Fight & Flight	Dynamic Convergence	Meaningful Presence	Competitive Capacity	Situation-- Handling
3	Psychological Preferences	Universal Goals/Ideals	Evolutionary Development	Constructed Reality	Mental Models	Inquiry & Advocacy
4	Flat New World	Continuous Change	Multiple Intelligences	Organizational System	Mid-Life/Career Transition	Cycles of Learning
5	Nature & Nurture	Critical Thinking	Chaos & Complexity	Whole Brain Learning	Cognitive Dissonance	Societal System
6	Meta-cognitive Reasoning	Ex-Body Objectivity	Lifelong Learning	Perception & Judgment	Human Enlightenment	University of the Mind
7	Community System	Double--Loop Learning	Rights & Responsibilities	Efficiency & Effectiveness	Contextual Understanding	Integral Learning
8	Adaptive Enterprise	Secular Spirituality	Knowledge Management	Generational Differences	Reflective Reasoning	Intellectual Capital
9	Way-of- Being	Integration vs Differentiation	Balance & Moderation	Sensing & Intuition	Self -- Renewal	Thinking & Feeling
10	High Performance	Self- Fulfillment	Common Good	Best Practices	Personal System	Meta-System Development
11	Personality TYPE	Communities of Practice	Time & Stress Management	Social Dialogue	Emotional Maturity	Organizational Teamwork
12	Communications & Collaboration	Facts & Feelings	Tradition & Innovation	Life Transitions	Quest for Identity	Future Orientation
13	Pattern Recognition	Leader Attributes	Learnership Practitioners	Courage & Persistence	Adaptive Technologies	Situational Learning

Figure 1-4

Learnership: Integrated Systems Building Blocks

	G	H	I	J	K	L
1	Conflict Resolution	Sense of Order	Rational Living	Personal Reflection	Meaning of Life	Enterprise of the Future
2	Decision Making	Free Agent Learners	Emotional Health	Adult Generativity	Professional Presence	Corruption & Terrorism
3	Workforce Versalists	Posterity & Immortality	Optimal Experience	Psychological Archetypes	Intelligent Organization	Human Capital
4	Organizational Assessment	Enterprise Architecture	Project Management	Objectivity & Subjectivity	Total Quality Management	Workplace Competencies
5	Intuition & Emotion	Customer Satisfaction	Business Processes	Cultural Cohesion	Learning Organization	Five Reasoning Competencies
6	Responsible Individualism	Public Administration	Enterprise Leadership	Psychological Traps	Maturity Models	Distance Learning
7	Sense of Purpose	Moral Development	Risk Management	Spiral Dynamics	Shared Power World	United Nations
8	Practical Ethics	Responsive Communities	Sense of History	Virtual Operations	Performance Management	National Defense
9	Learning & Education	Managing Attention	Age of Enlightenment	American Revolution	Social Saturation	Constraints & Trade-offs
10	Global Commons	Theory of Everything	The Human Prospect	Communities of Interest	Authentic Branding	Personal Development
11	Social Saturation	Self-Transcendence	Employability & Security	Class in Society	Necessary Losses	Answering Your Call
12	Unity of Knowledge	Sustainable Habitat	Second Acts	Senior Legacy	International Statecraft	Learnership Journal
13	Sense of Consequences	Longevity Revolution	Human Rights	Learnership Forum	Bill of Rights	Four Social Systems

Figure I-5

American Learnership: Integrated Systems Building Blocks

	M	N	O	P	Q	R
1	Walk your Talk	Information Sharing	Systems Development	Pluralistic Gridlock	Global Warming	Citizen Obligations
2	Knowledge Economy	Expertise Location	Personal Ambition	Core & Support Services	Encore Opportunities	Purposeful Life
3	Balanced Scorecard	Secular Reasoning	Financial Security	Meta-Cognitive Reasoning	Lessons Learned	Public Discourse
4	Life Passages	Organization Alignment	Brain Training	Customer Capital	Mission and Vision	Temporal Balance
5	A Hopeful Realist	Phases of Change	Mindful Meditation	Basis for Spirituality	Learning Curve	My True Calling
6	Diseases of Adaptation	Project Risk Management	Psychology of Wealth	An American Experiment	Living by Programs	Collaboration Tools
7	Wealth Generation	Operation Processes	Decision Analysis	Tipping Points	Legacy Planning	Responsibility And Trust
8	Cerebral vs Limbic	LISA & LACI	Senior Rejuvenation	Open— Minded	Body of Knowledge	Deep Smarts
9	Professional Presence	Learning by Immersion	Cultural Intelligence	Facilitating Dialogue	Surge Period	Triple Constraints
10	Self— Actualization	Senior Transitions	AS-IS and To-BE	Executive Capability	Pursuit of Happiness	Theories and Practices
11	Achievement Practices	Estate Planning	Value of Unification	Knowledge Spheres	Action— Learning	Requisite Knowledge
12	Technology & Innovation	Character Development	Building your Reputation	Sense and Respond	Corporate Ambition	Self— Ambition
13	Personal Bias	Needs vs Wants	Brain Dominance	Personal Finance	Social Capital	Professional Branding

Figure I-6

Learnership: Practitioner Characteristics (1 of 2)

1. A desire to understand and appreciate the fundamental theories in their fields of interest and education.

2. A capacity for good cognitive and reflective skills. But unlike their more academic counterparts, those skills are valued to the degree they align with their need to turn knowledge into action in a timely manner.

3 A capacity for "learning-to-learn." They get psychological rewards from the process of learning, and do it all their lives.

4. A desire to operate as "free agent learners," and to be distinguished from many others that they are not bound by the limitations of the traditional educational curricula taught in formal school and classroom settings.

5. A capacity for curiosity concerning the world around them that enables them to achieve important career and life objectives through all phases of their adult lives.

6. An enthusiasm to fully absorb their experiences and to learn from them. They also become influential through their ability to put their knowledge into action.

7. A willingness to embark on humanity's journey toward mindful growth and an understanding of life's mysteries and human purpose.

8. A desire to motivate themselves and others to discover life's opportunities, pursue a unique purpose, confront personal challenges, develop enlightened perspective, and attain a higher level-of-being.

9. An appreciation for interpersonal dialogue based on open inquiry, rapid learning, interpersonal understanding, and reasoned decision making.

10. A capacity to improve human relations by exemplifying the principles of leadership, followership, stewardship, citizenship, fellowship, and statesmanship.

11. An enthusiasm to participate in issue resolution in the political, economic, social, technological, geographical, and ecological domains of societal knowledge and endeavor.

12. A developmental perspective on how individuals, organizations and communities progress through their respective phases of development – each with its own objectives, challenges and rewards.

13. A systems perspective on societal learning and development that balances the human need for both stability and change to achieve higher levels of societal development and performance.

Figure I-7

Learnership: Practitioner Characteristics (2 of 2)

14. A focus on personal learning and knowledge management as key capabilities in the development of social systems: personal, organizational, community, and society.

15. A personal commitment to learning reasoning competencies that improve systems thinking, pattern recognition, situational learning, knowledge management, and adaptive leadership.

16. An expectation that personal development depends primarily on being responsible and responsive to the ever-changing political, economic and social forces occurring locally or on a global scale.

17. A desire to replace differentiation with integration as a lifelong practice – and the ultimate foundation for a mindful journey through life.

18. A commitment to use knowledge, science, and practical experience to challenge over-reliance on mysticism, superstition, and supernatural intervention.

19. An advocate of the means between the extremes – weighing personal rights with social responsibilities in order to negotiate adequate, inclusive outcomes.

20. An appreciation for balancing inquiry and advocacy in all one attempts to accomplish. No one knows all that could be known in life to reduce potential risk and to guarantee success.

21. A capacity to perform multiple roles such as consultant, coach, facilitator, student, mentor, thought leader, and project manager as situations require.

22. Are people who systematically increase their understanding of life's opportunities and challenges; develop their skills through questioning and learning; and produce products and services of value to themselves and others.

23. Have historically been contributors to societal development due to their "innovation and problem-solving" proclivities. They are people who have eclectic learning interests and acquire the skills and technologies that enable their achievements.

24. Are "knowledge managers" in their own right in that they continually identify, acquire, organize, use and share new found knowledge within their respective social systems.

25. A willingness to apply the Learnership Integrated Systems Architecture (LISA) model at all levels of personal and social systems development.

Figure I-8

Section III

American Learnership:
Integral Social Systems Development

Section III: This section on *American Learnership: Integral Social Systems Development* provides a comprehensive explanation of how we citizens can function within four interdependent knowledge building social system domains to become exceptionally successful. These are *Personal Systems Development*, *Organization Systems Development*, *Community Systems Development*, and *Societal Systems Development.* These competencies increase the speed and quality of knowledge building.

Chapter Ten

_Personal System Development (PSD)

I find the great thing in this world is not so much where we stand as in what direction we are moving. To reach the port of heaven, we must sail, sometimes with the wind and sometimes against it — but we must sail, and not drift, nor lie at anchor. — Oliver Wendell Holmes

Major Chapter Topics

An Introspective Overview of Personal System Development

Personal System Development (PSD). PSD concerns human growth and development throughout one's lifetime. And for the learnership practitioner using the Life Management Handbook, it represents a thinking, learning, knowing and leading maturation process. The goal of self-fulfillment satisfies the ontological need for a "sense of purpose," and is best attained through interdependent growth and development in our character, ability, and health subsystems. The *character subsystem* highlights continuous refinement of our values, morals, ethics, and civic standards that establish how one relates with others in families, organizations, and communities. The *ability subsystem* concerns what we are able to accomplish in terms of applied knowledge, skill, and experience. And, the *health subsystem* focuses on our development of substantial mental, emotional, and physical capacity to perform desired human and social functions. Ideally, these three subsystems operate over time in a mutually reinforcing manner enabling us to learn and express the meaning and direction of our lives. Our life management objective is to achieve personal   self-fulfillment.

Achieving Self-Fulfillment. The desired synergy among the subsystems is thought to increase a person's capacity to achieve fulfillment. Self-fulfillment is the term used, herein, to represent a desired end-state such as self-actualization, personal mastery, peak performance and other similar expressions of our self-described highest level of experience, satisfaction, or *being*. As experiences and goals evolve throughout our life journey, changes in what we consider to be fulfilling occur also.

While self-fulfillment is uniquely determined by each individual, it is accomplished within the values and expectations of the larger community. Many writers have studied human growth and development within the context of what the relevant community comes to view as esteemed attitudes and behavior. From this research, recognized *patterns* have emerged which establish the predominant attributes of self-fulfillment; those human characteristics that are well regarded by the community. These *patterns* are most often in evidence in individuals who have attained their highest maturity, which usually occurs later in life. These people are highly respected within the community because of their higher level of understanding, wisdom, and personal accomplishment.

A number of authors' perspectives, whose writings contribute to an understanding of the process of self-fulfillment, are considered in the succeeding section. It is noteworthy, however, to first observe the *objective* and *process* dimensions of self-fulfillment that are recognizable. As an objective, or end-state, self-fulfilment is seen as *achieving sought after personal objectives*. And, when viewed as a process, self-fulfillment is seen as resulting from *being fully in the experience*. Together, they convey the wholeness of self-fulfillment and the notion of a *higher level-of-being*. Further consideration of this chapter's topics and supporting perspectives from contributing authors are anchored in the Personal System Development (PSD) for self-fulfillment model in Figure 10-1. Illustrated are the following features:

1. Micro-Cognitive Reasoning. Illustrated are the *four learnership social systems* with this chapter's emphasis being at the *personal micro-level*.

2. Personal Health Subsystem. The health subsystem emphasizes physical, cognitive, and emotional development.

3. Personal Ability Subsystem. The ability subsystem focuses on knowledge, skills, and aptitude development.

4. Personal Character Subsystem. The character subsystem applies to values, morals, attitude, and behavioral development.

5. Micro-Systems Development. Illustrate the five reasoning competencies that can be used to maximize personal social system development.

6. Information Processing Model. Illustrates a general approach to problem solving and decision making throughout one's personal life: Gather and analyze information, develop a strategy and implement it, observe and take corrective action, if required

[**Author's Note**: A significant point to make at this juncture is that during Part One (Chapters 5 through 9) the Five Learnership Reasoning Competencies have been integrated into a comprehensive Total Knowledge Management (TKM) framework. That "total learning, knowing, and leading" framework has been embedded in the Learnership Integrated Systems Architecture (LISA) and all the principles, practices, and technologies of TKM are conceptually available, and should be appropriately applied, for full personal social systems development.]

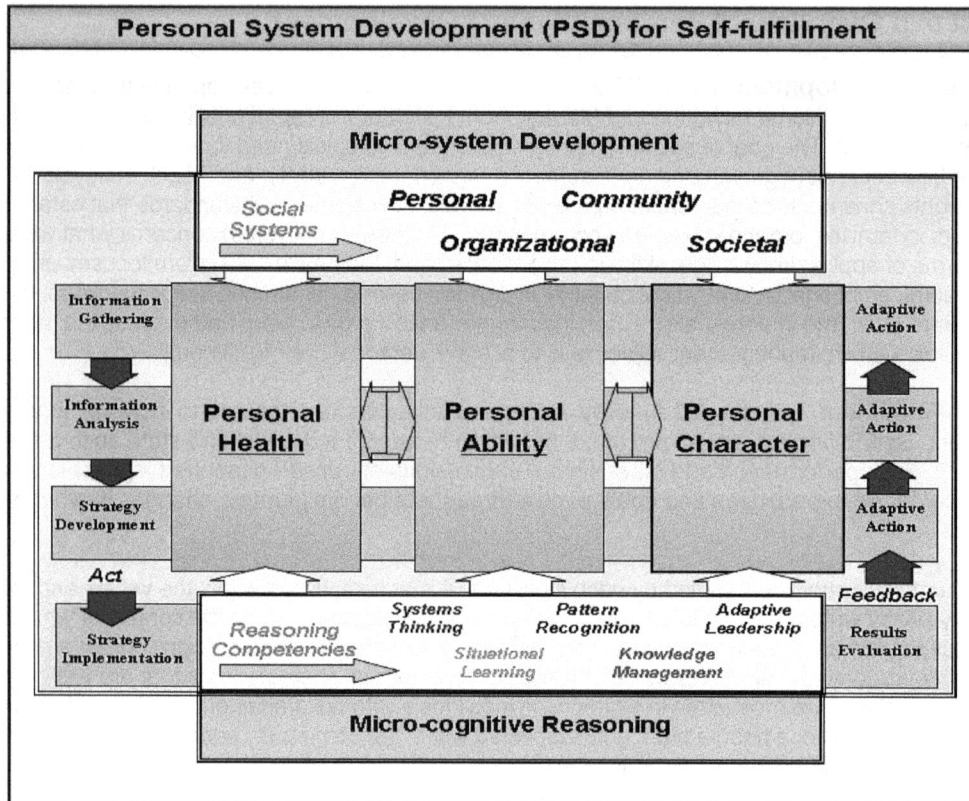

Figure 10-1

Attention now focuses on selected perspectives that enrich this topic. Each offers unique insights to an important psycho-social aspect of human growth and development, and it is recommended that that readers return regularly to Figure 10-1 to reflect on new insights offered by the authors selected. The following list of professional perspectives is provided as an overview of the more detailed concept summaries that follow. The summary at the end of this chapter will serve to integrate these perspectives into a cohesive framework for understanding the *Learnership Integrated Systems Architecture* (LISA) construct for personal system development:

1. Self-Image Perspectives:
    a. Structural Ontology for Social Systems
    b. One's Self-Image – self-images develop and mature over time
    c. A Mutable Self – an adaptable self that accommodates social change

2. Personal Development Perspectives:
    a. Stages in Adult Development – stages and sequence of ego-development
    b. Power Orientation and Development – power orientation and ego-maturity
    c. A Maturity Continuum – from dependence to interdependence
    d. Discipline and Human Evolution – from discipline to spiritual competence

3. Human Aspiration Perspectives:
    a. Experiencing Flow or Optimal Experience – being *fully in* an experience
    b. Man's Place in the Universe – foundations for spirituality and religion
    c. Achieving Self-Actualization – achieving full humanness and self-fulfillment

Self-Image Perspectives

> *It's not the most difficult thing to know oneself, but the most inconvenient*
> *– Josh Billings*

A Structural Ontology for Social Systems. Louis Gawthrope, author of *Public Sector Management, Systems, and Ethics* (1984) proposes that it is a basic issue for every individual to develop an understanding of their social ontology (basis for being). He suggests that having a sense of identity (What do I stand for?) and a sense of faith (What can I hope for?) are essential elements of healthy social adjustment and development. In the context of this book on learnership, our task concerns the establishment of senses of purpose, consequence, history, and order:

1. The first concept concerns a *sense of purpose* which has to do with have a value-based goal or objective that creates purposefulness in the life of the individual, organization, or community. Without a purpose, most activity will appear to be disconnected and random causing a high degree of uncertainty about directions in which to head and procedures needing to be followed. The perspectives that follow abundantly illustrate this concern.

2. The second concept, a *sense of consequence*, acknowledges that all actions yield consequences. Ideally, all chosen courses of action should aid in accomplishing desired purposes, and responsibility for behavioral consequences should be attributed to those initiating action. The perspectives that follow indicate that higher levels-of-being are attainable through motivation and commitment to action.

3. The third concept, a *sense of history*, recognizes the historical linkages between past, present, and future, and establishes the perspective of a "steady evolutionary flow of time." This tends to provide a feeling of movement towards chosen objectives, and a belief that progress is being made. The perspectives that follow describe levels on a developmental continuum wherein individuals learn from experience and seek achievement.

4. The last concept is a *sense of order* which relates to the orderliness of individual and social life that allows choices to be made with partial predictability of likely outcomes. A sense of order includes an understanding of the relatedness (e.g., lower/higher) of phenomena and the recognition of system interrelationships. The perspectives that follow articulate essential relationships and a process for achieving higher levels of performance and self-fulfillment. The essence of Gawthrope's thesis appears to be that individuals (organizations and communities herein included) who establish self- awareness in terms of these ontological concepts frame their respective identities and place a foundation under their faith in what is yet to come.

One's Self-Image. In *Change and Continuity in Adult Life* (Fiske, 1990), the author focuses on the many ways in which adults view themselves and how their self-images change over time. She offers that: "Each of us carries around a self-image, or set of images about the self, that makes up what we see as the self. While these images may appear highly individualized and perhaps chaotic, certain patterns do emerge. These patterns constitute the individual's personality, the self-concept as viewed from outside the self." (p.20)

Her work suggests that each of us regularly review our self-image as it evolves from our personal histories, unique experiences, and the consequences of our choices to determine if what is revealed is satisfactory. In other words, what we stand for and where we are headed is our continuous concern, and is likely to become a personal issue should our self-critique yield less than satisfactory results. It is probably safe to conclude that greater self-esteem, and achieving self-fulfillment are interrelated.

Fiske's longitudinal study of individuals over a 12 year period also revealed common patterns of goals and values that indicate what people typically seek in their life. The list (p.216) includes:

1. Achievement and Work. Competence, economic rewards, success, social status

2. Good Personal Relations. Love and affection, happy marriage, having good friends, belonging to groups

3. Philosophical and Religious. Living a spiritual life, doing God's work, having a philosophy of life, seeking the meaning of life, being wise, being morally good

4. Social Service. Helping others, serving the community, contributing to human welfare

5. Ease and Contentment. Freedom from hardship, security, self-maintenance, peace of mind, health, simple comforts

6. Seeking Enjoyment. Recreation, exciting experiences, entertainment, seeking pleasurable sights, sounds, feelings, and tastes

7. Personal Growth. Self-improvement, being creative, learning new things, knowing yourself, meeting and mastering new challenges

According to Fiske, most people are able to achieve some of their objectives, but a select few individuals (usually later in life) attain the ability to *function at the fullest* in terms of their goals and values. She associates the concept of *generativity* with them which may be defined as having full understanding of cultural tradition and the ability to dispense wisdom for the continuity and growth of the community.

A Mutable Self. In *The Mutable Self: A Self-Concept for Social Change* (Zurcher, 1977), the author poses the notion that there are four key components of self-concept: *physical self*, *social self*, *reflective self*, and *oceanic self*. He suggests that the pace and uncertainty of modern life tends to disrupt the needed balance among these selves causing individuals to focus disproportionately on one or the other resulting in self-limiting consequences. His thesis is that: "It is possible for people to develop *mutable selves* in which all four components are balanced and synthesized, purposely and productively for the individuals and for society" (p.14).

According to Zurcher, two aspects of the *self* must be recognized: (1) the self as process, and (2) the self as object. He states that: "In every day life the individual is engaged to a greater or lesser degree in a dialogue with social structure. The person may elect to minimize the dialogue (for reward, for simplicity, for certainty) by identifying closely or entirely with some specific piece of social structure (e.g., the church). Or the person may elect to maximize the dialogue with social structure, standing apart from it (though perhaps participating in it), reflexively, autonomously, continually evaluating the relationship. This again is a distinction between *self* as process and *self* as object." (p.27)

A conclusion that may be made from this view is that when the locus of the individual's identity is based on external social structures (a stabilized or closed-issue approach), the *self* is understood objectively as being defined by those structures. On the other hand, when the individual moves the locus of his or her identity inward for subjective inquiry (an open-to-change and learning approach), the self is seen as accomplishing a needed transition in the human growth process, and is considered to be undergoing development.

Zurcher's concept of mutability is one in which flexible and resourceful individuals are able to move skillfully among their physical, social, reflective, and oceanic selves to achieve an appropriate, integrated, and balanced response to social situations. He notes that: "…though the motivational basis for the evolution of the Mutable *Self* may be survival, the definition of survival becomes increasingly more complex, increasingly more sophisticated, and increasingly more encompassing of a mutual understanding of the dignity of others' survival." (pp.218-219).

[**Author's Note**: The usefulness of these views within this study is notable in the dynamic tension between *stability and change, communality and individuality and between rights conferred and responsibilities accepted.* The latter item in each pair indicates movement away from the primacy of the "social external" to the growth of the "personal internal." Choices are required in the individual's developmental journey towards self-fulfillment.]

> *I guess the essence of life for me is finding something you really enjoy doing*
> *that gives meaning to life, and then being in a situation where you can do.*
> — *Isaac Asimov*

Personal Development Perspectives

Stages in Adult Development. In "The Psychological Development of Adults: Implications for Public Administration" (Schott, 1986), the author correlates the work of a number of adult development researchers—Jung, Erikson, Gould, Levinson, and Valliant (Table 10-1). He suggests that there is a great deal of consistency in their findings, and that two major themes are recognizable. The first is that the adult psyche is continually unfolding, apparently seeking a greater level of self-understanding, individualization, and maturation. The second theme is that as psychological maturation proceeds, various stages of development are definable, each with its own characteristics. Schott quotes Erikson as suggesting that there are crucial turning points or moments of decision that provide transformation between developmental stages.

Successful growth and development appear to depend on the reconciliation between internal psychic events and forces in the external social environment. At the highest levels of maturity and personal development, terms such as integrity, authenticity, meaning, wisdom, generativity, and dignity appear as representations of what the individual has been able to achieve. These are the objective results of *life span learning*—an iterative process of acknowledging one's capabilities, confronting life's challenges, and resolving major life issues.

[**Author's Note**: An observation might be that those who complete the transformations between developmental stages—and do so with increasing competence and social grace—experience fulfillment both through participation in the process and reflection on capabilities attained. The *learnership practiti*oner must work through these stages of development.]

Power Orientation and Development. Power may be thought of as the capability to control the manner in which one's needs and objectives are satisfied. According to David McClelland in *Power: The Inner Experience* (McClelland, 1975), there are four modalities of experiencing power and each represents a level of ego-development. The four modalities are established via a matrix in which two *sources of power* (from either inside or outside the self) and two *objects of power* (either the self or someone other than the self) are the axes. The result is that four orientations to power emerge as sequential and distinct phases of personal development which may be summarized as follows:

Comparison of Adult Life Cycle Stages
Adapted: Richard L. Schott, "The Psychological Development of Adults"

Jung	Youth, Middle Age, Old Age
Erickson	Early, Middle, and Later Adulthood
Valliant	Intimacy, Career Consolidation, Generativity, Meaning, Dignity
Gould	Leaving Parent's World, Nobody' Baby, What's Inside? Mid Life, Die is Cast, Search for Meaning
Levinson	Early Adult Transition, Entering Adult World, Age 30 Transition, Settling Down, Mid Life Transition, Age 50 Transition, Middle Adult Culmination, Late Adulthood Transition

Table 10-1

Phase I. The objective is for the self to feel stronger which is achieved when *others provide what is needed by the self*. This is seen as the oral stage of development in which the focus is on being supported, and the pathology of the stage might be hysteria due to denial of support. Adult behavior representative of the stage may be the reading of power-oriented material.

Phase II. The objective is for the self to feel stronger which is achieved when the *self takes responsibility for itself*. This is seen as the anal stage of development in which the focus is on autonomy and free will, and the pathology of the stage might be obsessive-compulsive neurosis. Adult behavior representative of the stage may be the practice of accumulating prestige possessions.

Phase III. The objective is for the self to feel stronger which is achieved when the *self is able to influence the action of others*. This is seen as the phallic stage of development in which focus is on assertive action, and the pathology of the stage might be criminal activity. Adult behavior representative of the stage may be a willingness to argue and compete.

Phase IV. The objective is for the self to feel stronger which is achieved when the *self becomes a conduit for others to influence others*. This is seen as the genital mutuality stage of development in which the focus is on principled assertion and duty, and the pathology of the stage may be a messianic complex. Adult behavior representative of the stage may be a desire for organizational membership and participation.

McClelland provides a number of conclusions from his studies and his power orientation typology. These include:

1. The acquisition and proper use of power is a grave concern of societies. Its use is best legitimized when associated with acts undertaken for others rather than for the self.

2. Power is learned sequentially from Stage I to Stage IV. However, the successive phases are best understood as enlargements of one's power orientation rather than the substitution of one orientation for another.

3. Maturity is achieved when one is capable of choosing the specific power orientation that is right for the situation encountered.

4. It appears that people who achieve a Stage IV expression of power are more fully actualized.

[**Author's Note**: The applicability of this reference to the *learnership architecture* is seen in its emphasis on the power orientation aspects of human learning and development. Through this process, individuals become *empowered* to pursue their respective needs and objectives. It may well be that those who evolve to become most empowered establish ever higher goals for themselves and attain a higher order of self-fulfillment. Of particular importance in this book is the *Adaptive Leadership Competency* as a Phase IV capability that is essential for social systems synthesis.]

A Maturity Continuum. In his popular book, *The Seven Habits of Highly Effective People* (Covey, 1989), the author offers the view that human growth and development occurs in an incremental, sequential, and highly integrated manner as one's personal and interpersonal effectiveness improves over time. It is his view that reaching full maturity should be the individual's objective and doing so consists of concurrently attaining three dimensions of maturity – physical, emotional, and mental. Development is seen as occurring along a continuum in which there are stages of dependence, independence, and interdependence in all three dimensions. While in the *dependent stage*, the individual looks to others as the sole source of responsibility or blame for his or her life condition or situation. When in the *independent stage*, the individual takes responsibility for his or her choices, actions, and the resulting consequences.

This is the stage of development in which it is important to distinguish ourselves from others and to understand the self more clearly. At the highest level of development or personal maturity, is the *interdependent stage* in which strong connectivity to others is deemed important. The individual's need to combine talents and abilities with others to form mutually supporting relationships is emphasized and seeking cooperation gains greater importance. This stage of development concerns learning to see oneself as being both a separate entity and as part of a larger, complex life system. For Covey, the objective of life is personal effectiveness and success. This is achieved when a person becomes fully interdependent with others in the community. At this point, physical, emotional, and mental maturity is realized and synergistic relationships are possible.

[**Author's Note**: An observation at this point is that a person's self-fulfillment should be judged not only in terms of his or her own needs and perspectives, but within the context of community expectations. It may be that we may only achieve mature self-fulfillment when interdependency is recognized and celebrated. On the other hand, if we are unable to establish an intellectual life beyond our reference social group—and get beyond their average level of expectations and self-imposed limitations—how can we possibly achieve our own potential? Learning often means leaving in order to actualize our human capacities.]

Discipline and Human Evolution. In *The Road Less Traveled* (Peck, 1978), the author presents a psychiatrist's perspective on the relationships among (self-) discipline, love, growth, and spirituality. He speaks of a human evolutionary process in which the process of confronting and solving problems is the foundation for learning and personal development. One's capacity to absorb the pain associated with difficult problems and decision making, and to work through these situations successfully is seen as "learning and growing in the process" (p.18). The individual acquires self-discipline through experiencing pain constructively and learning to use the techniques of delayed gratification, acceptance of responsibility, dedication to reality and truth, and focusing on achieving balance.

The willingness to confront one's "reality maps" or fixed frames of reference through open communication and self-examination is a critical skill in becoming more knowledgeable, responsible, and psychologically balanced. Peck uses the term "bracketing" in reference to one's becoming balanced: "Bracketing is essentially the act of balancing the need for stability and assertion of the self with the need for new knowledge and greater understanding by temporarily giving up one's self ...so as to make room for the incorporation of new material into the self" (p.73). An observation here is that individual learning occurs as a result of distinct tension between stability and change. To learn, the individual must reconsider what it is that they already believe in the light of any new, and potentially more influential, viewpoints and concepts.

Peck explains that it takes the force of love to make becoming disciplined desirable. Love is defined as: "The will to extend one's life for the purpose of nurturing one's own or another's spiritual growth." He continues with the notion that love requires work and that: "The principle form that the work of love takes is attention," and "When we love another we give them our attention; we attend to that person's growth" (p.81).

[**Author's Note**: Peck's writing suggests a continuous learning and evolutionary aspect of personal growth and development which focuses on the attainment of "spiritual competence" which may be interpreted as achieving great understanding of our purpose within a larger universal context. In the context of this study, spiritual competence equates to the self-fulfillment anchor in personal system development.]

> *Try not to become a man of success, but rather*
> *try to become a man of value.*— Albert Einstein

Human Aspiration Perspectives

Experiencing Flow or Optimal Experience. In *Flow: The Psychology of Optimal Experience* (Csikszentmihalyi, 1990), the author describes occasions of personal experience "in which attention can be freely invested to achieve a person's goals, because there is no disorder to straighten out, no threat for the self to defend against...the flow experience" (p.40). He says that "Flow helps to integrate the self because in that state of deep concentration consciousness is unusually well ordered." The suggestion is that a degree of self-fulfillment, or realization of potential, is achieved during flow because of the alignment of attention and focus of energy that occur in attempting to achieve a specific objective. The result is that the person wins a battle "against the entropy that brings disorder to consciousness…(and wins) a battle for the self" (p.40).

Additionally, Csikszentmihalyi notes that through flow, or optimal experience, the person achieves growth of the self in terms of *complexity*. The self becomes more complex (synonymous with greater maturity and capability). He offers that the two broad psychological processes of *differentiation* (movement toward uniqueness, separation) and *integration* (movement toward union with others, ideas, and entities beyond self) are experienced, resolved within the self through deep concentration and consciousness, and result in greater self-confidence and capacity for skill development and societal contribution. His theme is expanded to suggest a plethora of positive results such as the enhanced ability to cultivate purpose, forge resolve, establish harmony, unify life themes, and achieve meaning in life so that the "individual's purpose merges with the universal flow" (p.240).

[**Author's Note**: It may be that self-fulfillment occurs temporarily when we are *fully in* an experience, but does not last. An objective might be to develop the capacity to function at our fullest capability as often as possible.]

Man's Place in the Universe. In *Basic Teachings of the Great Philosophers* (Frost, 1962), the author reviews the philosophical development of the concept of "man in the universe." This quest for understanding the meaning of man's existence and relationship to what is unknown is the basic for spiritual belief and the establishment of religion. Frost comments that: "…throughout the history of human thought man has endeavored to understand the universe in relation to himself. Some philosophers have arisen to tell him that the universe is like him and is his friend; that in the universe are forces which are concerned with his welfare. Indeed, the philosophic God is very often a Being whose concern is for man. But there are other philosophers who find the universe, and man included, a vast system of laws and consistencies in which human values have little or no place. Man lives his little day and is forgotten" (p.78).

Frost defines a continuum in which the extremes in belief are the "religious position" and the "scientific position." The religious position appears to be one in which a values-based explanation of man's relationships to others, a belief that which is eternal is given, and that one's attitudes and behavior are guided by the tenets of the particular religion to which one belongs. The quality of one's life is dependent on "proper living" which connotes living in accordance with chosen values and becoming more closely connected to God.

On the other end of the continuum is the scientific position which is based upon the scientific laws discovered through inquiry into the nature of practical experience with the physical environment, and the acquired attitudes and behavior that are guided by the laws and relationships that govern known aspects of the universe. While some have tried to reconcile the extremes, no arguments have been convincing to the majority of Americans to uniformly adopt one particular point of view; in fact, an effort to do so would violate basic American principles respecting diversity, pluralism, and tolerance.

Achieving Self-Actualization. The foundation for a concept of self-actualization was first developed by Abraham Maslow in his 1954 work entitled *Motivation and Personality*. In his later book *Toward a Psychology of Being* (Maslow, 1968), he elaborated on the concept, taking care to acknowledge the controversies surrounding his earlier views. The placement of Maslow's perspective at the end of this series of perspectives is because his work proceeded the others cited and was often acknowledged by others' when developing their views. Another reason is that Maslow's conceptual explanations tend to be more comprehensive than those of others, thereby serving to integrate this section's various perspectives. Self-actualization for Maslow is the term used to capture the notion of *full-humanness*. His view is that all individuals, regardless of time, place, or culture have a natural need to experience the fullness of the human experience—they seek self-fulfillment. *Fulfillment*, however, is a psycho-social accomplishment and is therefore a construction both of individual cognition and social influence. Maslow acknowledges *the being-psychology* (end-state) and *becoming-psychology* (process-experience) aspects of psycho-social growth and development, and establishes their part in an individual's capacity to become self-actualized or *self-fulfilled*.

To appreciate the breadth of his view, one needs to understand self-fulfillment in Maslow's own words: "…any person in any of (his or her) peak experiences takes on temporarily many of the characteristics which I have found in self-actualizing individuals…these are moments of greatest maturity, individuation, and *fulfillment*…What seems to distinguish those individuals I have called self-actualizing people, is that in them these episodes seem to come far more frequently, and intensely and perfectly than in average people" (Maslow, 1968, p.97). The behaviors leading to self-actualization or *self-fulfillment* are listed here to anchor the theme of this chapter. (Maslow, 1971):

1. Self-fulfillment means experiencing fully, vividly, selflessly, with full concentration and total absorption

2. <u>Self-fulfillment</u> means seeing life as a process of choices, some progressive and some regressive—and choosing the progressive course

3. <u>Self-fulfillment</u> means "letting the true self emerge," being free from cognitive constraints imposed by others

4. <u>Self-fulfillment</u> means that when in doubt, be honest rather than not

5. <u>Self-fulfillment</u> means listening to one's previous experience and learning, and daring to be different, unpopular, and a nonconformist if necessary

6. <u>Self-fulfillment</u> is not only an end-state, but also the process of actualizing one's potentialities at any time and mount

7. <u>Self-fulfillment</u> occurs as transient moments of peak experiences for which conditions may are pre-selected /arranged

8. <u>Self-fulfillment</u> means opening oneself up for examination, identifying one's defenses, and finding the courage to give up those defenses

Description of PSD Life Cycle Model

> *I have learned that success is to be measured not so much by the position*
> *that one has reached in life as by the obstacles which he has to overcome*
> *while trying to succeed.* — *Booker T. Washington*

Personal Systems Development Life Cycle Model. Our attention now turns to a discussion of the progressive nature of our lives. Research has shown that while each of us are uniquely different in our experiences, decisions and actions; we still appear, fundamentally, to travel a very well worn path that others have traveled before. Figure 10 - 2 and the selected perspectives that follow are a compilation of symbiotic developments many of us experience as we move through our (hopefully) self-fulfilled lives. First, however, an overview of the illustration is in order.

The horizontal axis is a non-linear depiction of the adult lifetime constructed to emphasize certain patterns of activity. Age 18 is the starting point for adulthood, and age 30 is selected as the average end of *prolonged adolescence*– a period of time in modern times in which youthful thinking and behavior extends far longer than what was previously expected when economic times were less prosperous and personal time for formal education and entertainment was more limited. The other ages and times are notional boundaries for the *early adult*, *middle adult*, and *senior adult* periods of our lives, and serve as a measuring stick against which other topics and trends may be displayed and considered. A time period for mid-life transition/crisis is placed in the late 40s in order to accommodate two trends: (a) the occurrence of what might be termed "delayed adolescence" and, (b) the longer lifetimes now becoming the norm. For many of us mid-life issues are experienced later or longer than they used to be, in part due to advances in medicine and the healthier lifestyles that permit some of us to live significantly longer lives.

The vertical axis is used to display the thinking, learning, knowing, leading, and achieving (reasoning) processes that enable us to learn and understand ourselves and our external world, and to devise the knowledge and methods needed to influence the world's potential and trajectory. Five sets of developmental activities are presented below.

Cognitive Priorities. The *Learnership Integrated Systems Architecture* (LISA) envisions four levels of social systems development, each one requiring its own level of personal cognitive activity in which we come to understand our unique purpose and our relationship with others in society. We realize both the breadth and depth of our interrelationships as we sequentially shift our mental energies from (a) *personal micro-cognition* when it is "all about us" as we pass through prolonged adolescence; (b) through *organizational macro-cognition* when we take on the responsibility of family and career, (c) through *community mega-cognition* as we invest additional time to help manage and guide the future of our local communities (city, county, state); and lastly (d) to *societal meta-cognition* when we have lived the majority of our lives and begin to take measure of our larger world (our nation, the world's nations) and our place in it–our search for a *sense of wholeness and completion*.

Learning Cycles. The vertical scale identifies five major categories of activities that generally unfold in an overlapping, but systematic manner. As each of these activities moves through the sequential time periods, other opportunities for lifelong learning and development are presented, but of course are optional. The *reflect-reason-renew cycle* inserted in each age period is a reminder that there are distinct cognitive and emotional insights available to each of us as we continue to grow and develop.

Psychological Objectives. As we move through our adult time periods, we experience psycho-social changes. In the prolonged adolescence period our *identity* and personal *ego* are foremost in our attention. Who are we; what is our purpose; and how will our needs be satisfied are the questions that need to be answered. When we move to the early adult period our concerns expand to include getting in touch with ourselves (*soul*) and others (*intimacy*) at a deeper level. In middle adult life we evolve again as we attempt to gain a full understanding of what we really have become (*self*) and how we can begin to share with posterity (*generativity*) the best of our knowledge and insight. Lastly, if we are healthy and lucky, we transition into the level of psychological *integrity* when our interests, knowledge and accomplishments converge into mindfulness and *self-fulfillment.*

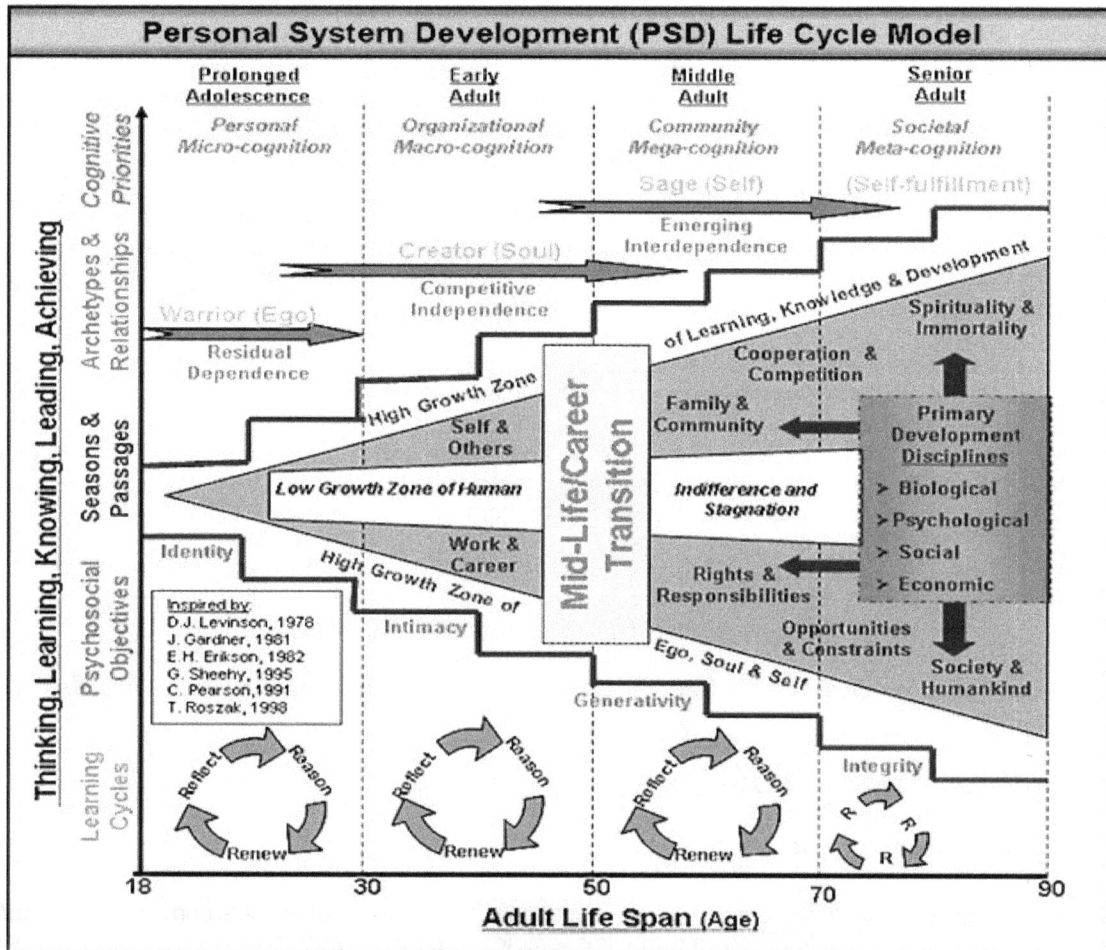

Figure 10-2

Archetypes and Relationships. Four distinctive periods of growth are recognizable across the human life cycle in terms of representative archetypes, psychological drivers and levels of dependence. The first three symbiotic relationships are: Warrior (*Ego*) Dependence; Creator (*Soul*) Independence; and Sage (*Self*) Interdependence. In the last stage personal *Self-fulfillment* is the culmination of a life well-lived.

Seasons and Passages. Running horizontally through the model is a conceptual vision of how each of us could hopefully become self-fulfilled. This vision is the space between the *High Growth Zone of Human Knowledge and Development and the High Growth Zone of Ego, Soul and Self.* Our ever-expanding acquisition of learning, knowledge and skills permits us to master the challenges in each time period, refine and maintain our focus, and experience a well-lived and successful life. It is important, however, to acknowledge the reality that given the unequal allocation of knowledge and resources among most social groups, a significant portion of each population will enter what is termed the *Low Growth Zone of Human Indifference and Stagnation.* Once in this zone, an immense effort is required to re-emerge and get back onto the road of development of life success.

The main contributors to the Figure 10-3 conceptualization through their writings are Erik Erickson, Daniel Levinson, Gail Sheehy, and Carol Pearson. Selections from their insightful and symbiotic comments follow:

Childhood and Society. Following his association with Freud and Jung in the early 20th century, Erik Erickson posited a view of the human life cycle which he subsequently described in *Childhood and Society* (Norton, 1950) and "Identity and the Life Cycle" in *Psychological Issues*, 1 (1959), 1-171. He chose four stages:

1. Childhood and Adolescence, age 1-17

2. Early Adulthood, age 17-45

3. Middle Adulthood, age 40-60

4. Late Adulthood, 60 and onward.

According to his thinking a major component of these life cycle periods was the individual's need to resolve a sequence of eight "ego issues." The first four "issues" were in childhood and the others applied to the adolescent through the adult period. Specifically, he found that the issue to be resolved in the adolescent to Early Adult transition was *Identity vs. Identity Confusion*; the issue to be resolved in order to transition into Middle Adulthood was *Intimacy and Isolation*; the issue to be resolved in order to transition into Late Adulthood was *Generativity and Stagnation*; and lastly once in the last stage the issue of *Integrity and Despair* needed to be resolved in order to complete the human life cycle successfully. Figure 10-3 uses the positive aspects of resolving these challenges (Identity, Intimacy, Generativity, Integrity) and aligns them vertically with the major cognitive priorities of the learnership integrated systems architecture social systems (personal, organizational, community, society).

[**Author's Note**: It is useful to understand at this juncture that Erikson's work in the 1950s, was studied and further developed by Levinson in the 1960s and 70s, and further studied and developed by Sheehy in the 1980s and 90s. Their views, however, attempt to account for the changes in Western societies—particularly the U.S.—in which cultural shifts and expanding life spans require a rethinking of the appropriate age boundaries. Pearson's theory of archetypes is also an extrapolation of original research by Freud and Jung, and serves to integrate many of the others' concepts. Figure 10-3 is this author's consensus position of the four authors' writings.]

> *In the longer run, our further progress in fostering adult development may*
> *be a part of a transformation of human society and personality, and thus contribute*
> *to a new epoch in human evolution. — Daniel Levinson*

Seasons of Life. In his *The Seasons of a Man's Life* (1978), author Daniel Levinson examines each of the adult eras from three contrasting perspectives: "

1. Changes in biological and psychological functioning
2. The sequence of generations
3. The evolution of careers and enterprises.

Levinson points out that: "The *instinctual energies*, too, pass their maximal level and are somewhat *reduced in middle adulthood*...He can be more free from the petty vanities, animosities, envies and moralisms of early adulthood...he develops greater capacity for intimacy and integrates more fully the tender, 'feminine' aspects of his self...possibility of becoming a more responsive friend...more facilitating parent...more caring son...more compassionate authority and teacher." (pp.24-25) From these comments we can begin to envision ourselves learning to manage two related, but separate mini-life cycles—one growth period up to middle adulthood (mid 40s), and then a short period of correction and renewal followed by the possibility of another 45 years of growth and development before death.

Levinson recounts that Jung conceived the term "individuation" to account for a person's development up through age 40, and again for the second occurrence that continues to death. Individuation is described as a "developmental process through which a person becomes more uniquely individual. Acquiring a clearer and fuller identity of his own, he becomes better able to utilize inner resources and pursue his own aims." (p.33) However, as he eventually moves to and through his *late adulthood* (Figure 10-3 Senior Adult) into his 70s he must deal with the issue of *Integrity vs. Despair*. Levinson states that: "As a man enters late adulthood he feels that he has completed the major part—perhaps all—of his life work. His contribution to society and to his own mortality is largely completed. He must arrive at some appraisal of his life. The developmental task is to *gain a sense of the integrity of his life*—not simply of his virtue or achievement, but of his life as a whole. If he succeeds in this, he can live without bitterness or despair during late adulthood. Finding *meaning and value* in his life, however imperfect, he can come to terms with death." (p.37)

> *Let's refer to successful aging as saging—the process by which men and*
> *women accumulate wisdom and grow into the culture's sages. — Gail Shehy*

Life Passages. In her *New Passages* (1995), Gail Sheehy states: "People today are leaving childhood sooner, but they are taking longer to grow up and much longer to die...Puberty arrives earlier ...Adolescence is now prolonged...true adulthood doesn't begin until 30...Middle age has already been pushed far into the fifties...Everything seems to be moving off by a decade." (p.4) She continues with the thought that 80 percent of people in American can expect to live past their 65th birthday, that mid-life crises are now more common in the mid to late 40s and that a whole second adulthood of 45 more years are truly possible after the new mid-life period. She speaks of the flaming 50s, serene 60s, sage 70s, uninhibited 80s, and the nobility of the 90s.

Sheehy comments that: "Baby boomers in their forties, as they run out of rungs to climb in middle management, will be obliged to find other ways to redefine personal success. Men in their fifties will have to face the fact they have peaked professionally, rather than a gentle, stepped-down transition to honorable retirement in their mid-sixties, they may be handed a take-it-or-leave-it package." (p.16) It is going to be extremely important that most of us experiencing similar career or psychological road-bumps learn to adapt to our new circumstances and get prepared for the second half of our lives. Sheehy indicates that we will be expected to live new cycles of learning within our longer primary life cycle— perhaps as many as three full renewal cycles. Figure 10-3 reflects her insights by illustrating repetitive *learning cycles* (reflect, reason, renew); a *mid-life transition/crisis* zone approaching age 50; the possibility of a second life after age 50; and the challenges that await many of us as we choose the *high growth zone of human learning, knowledge & development* in contrast to the alternative *low growth zone of human indifference and stagnation.*

A major portion of Sheehy's attention is on a period she terms "*middlescence,*" which is when we come through the late 40s mid-life transition/crisis with (hopefully) new found energy and focus to craft a *second life* that complements and completes our first life. She speaks of moving from a period of *survival* to a period of *mastery*—in terms of Figure 10-3 this is a transition from *competitive independence* and *intimacy* to *emerging interdependence* and *generativity.* She says: "The transformation of middle life is to move into a more stable psychological state of mastery, when we control much of what happens in our life and can often act on the world, rather than habitually react to whatever the world throws at us." She also comments that we need to create and manage our way to a second life: "...we must construct our new *second identity.* Sooner is better than later. It means throwing off all the old stereotypes, letting go of outgrown priorities, and developing real clarity about what is most relevant in our lives for the future." (pp.142-143)

Another aspect of the second life is the emerging *meaning crisis.* "The search for meaning in whatever we do becomes the universal preoccupation of <u>Second Adulthood</u>. It could well be called the <u>Meaning Crisis</u>. It is based on a spiritual imperative: *the wish to integrate the disparate aspects of ourselves, the hunger for wholeness, the need to know the truth.* Women are more likely to develop their rational thinking functions and enjoy extending their powers into a broader arena, while men are often drawn inward, from thinking to feeling." (p.148) This is the period when our genders begin to move closer as we awaken to our own mortality, and the fact becomes prevalent in our minds that our lives are not ready to be finished. We become more conscious that our individual lives are part of something much larger and we develop the need to understand and fully align ourselves with the past and the future.

Sheehy refers to further transformation into the 60s and beyond as: "Passage to the Age of Integrity."(p.345)*Integrity* is the time in which we become ready for our *prime time.* The combination of good health, a successful career with a retirement program, and fewer family obligations often leads those in their 60s and 70s to continue to learn, grow and contribute significantly to their families and communities. Research shows that our brains are still able to learn and develop as we take on the responsibility of completing our self-development and achieving full integrity. Sheehy says that there is a "hunger for harmony" in this time period, and that she thinks of "...integrity as the work of integration. One of the overarching desires by men and women I have interviewed in late middle age is for balance—being able to bring all the parts of one's life into harmony, as opposed to incongruity." (p.355)

As Sheehy assesses her research and experience she comments prophetically that: "People with positive outlooks, who continue to connect themselves to the future and marshal their energies to defeat creeping depression or entropy, are far more likely to extend their Second Adulthoods into healthy and satisfying later lives...To engage in successful aging is actually a career choice. Your job is to revive your life energy to make the next passage. That life force is then ready to be applied to whatever current challenges you face or the life accidents that may occur ahead. Successful aging must be a conscious choice with a commitment to continuing self-education and the development of a whole set of strategies." (pp.419-420)

"The issue for us today is not simply to create the unified self—connecting Ego and Soul, heart and head, male and female—but also to express this self in the everyday business of living our lives." — Carol Pearson

Heroes Within. Carol Pearson is the author of *Awakening the Heroes Within: Twelve Archetypes to help Us Find Ourselves and Transform the World* (1991). Her research and writing explain how a selected number of well defined archetypes can be used to help us better recognize and understand recurring patterns in personal situations and social activities. The term "archetype" as used in this context refers to the controlling paradigm, metaphor or *controlling mind pattern* that has influence on human thinking and behavior.

Pearson's basic theme, building off the work of Joseph Campbell's *The Hero with a Thousand Faces* (1949), is that a part of everyone's life journey has to do with navigating through certain psycho-social transitions to higher levels of personal development. Through these transitions we develop an *ego* (a boundary between our self and the world), a *soul* (connects us with the transpersonal), and a *self* (our sense of genuine identity). She indicates that while this pattern is basically linear over our live time, it operates more like a spiral in which each new learning cycle falls back to reflect on previous learning cycles for renewal and subsequent emergence to higher levels of learning and knowledge. This process synchronizes well with the *reflect-reason-renew* function in Figure 10-3 and also with the Spiral Dynamics concept discussed in Chapter 6. Three developmental stages are considered:

1. Ego Level. The relationship between ourselves and others changes as a function of our age and stage of development. The childhood and adolescent years are committed primarily to developing our *ego* wherein we concentrate on becoming socialized and fitting into our culture. "Me" as the receiver of cultural direction is the primary focus, and this is a time of *dependence* (*residual dependence* if this continues through our 20s.) The *ego archetypes* of this stage include the *Innocent*, the *Orphan*, the *Caregiver*, and the *Warrior*—with the *Warrior* being perhaps the best representative of action we take to "change the world to meet our own needs."

2. Soul Level. Our emerging sense of who we are turns to taking responsibility for ourselves and others who belong to us. We focus on becoming *competitively independent.* "I" the sender, becomes assertive and tries to influence the external world. The *soul* emerges and develops as our ability to make decisions and take action grows. Obtaining clarity on meaning, value and purpose becomes more important. Family, career and winning become a major emphasis in our lives into the mid 40s. Quite often, as we rush through this period, we crash right into our mid-life transition/crisis—our opportunity to rethink much of what we have done, become, and could be. The *soul archetypes* include the *Seeker*, the *Destroyer*, the *Lover*, and the *Creator*— with the *Creator* being an example of this stage as we use "our imaginative potential to create lives that emerge out of the truth about who we are." (p.48)

3. Self Level. The *self* signifies our achievement of a sense of genuine identity as we close in on completing our "individuation process." Our emphasis is on our *emerging interdependence*. The "I" and "Me" synchronize to form a more complete sense of *self*. In the *self stage* we become fully conscious of the world that has revealed itself to us, and we accept the "burden of consciousness" in which newly acquired wisdom creates new responsibilities and an "urge to know" what we still might need to know. The *self archetypes* include the *Ruler*, the *Magician*, the *Fool*, and the *Sage*—with the *Sage* being the most comprehensive example of this stage in that it "helps us face whatever is true in our lives and transcend our smaller selves to be one with cosmic truths." (p.59)

Notwithstanding Pearson's three stages of psycho-social development just described, she speaks of a period of time *beyond individuation* in which Hal Stone's *Embracing Our Selves* concept comes into play. Stone provides a practice for helping people to re-experience the richness of the plurality within themselves...to speak and move from these other selves...to move from one identity to another..." (pp.67-68) Pearson comments: "It is the Wise Fool who can move past the illusion of a unified self, to express the diversity of his or her wholeness in the world." (p.68)

Furthermore, Pearson states: "Rulers and Magicians work hard to redeem and heal the planet. Sages struggle and strive to attain truth. Only the Fool simply trusts the moment and savors life in its fullness, without judgment, appreciating not only life's joys but also its sorrows." (p.68) Accepting these views leads this author to conceive of a life cycle period of *senior adulthood* in which *"differentiated holism"* is possible. In Figure 10-3 this is illustrated as a period of *self-fulfillment and integrity* in which multiple archetypes, methodological *patterns*, and styles of personal and social behavior are understood, integrated into ageless wisdom, and applied for the resolution of societal meta-system problems.

This compilation of studies and perspectives makes a strong case for the existence of human life cycles that have distinguishable common factors that may be described and analyzed. The conclusion is that there are eras of human maturity that apply in all societies as the result of their common biological, social, psychological, and economic needs. Each of us has the opportunity to learn and manage our own development across the phases of adult life, and doing this well helps us become who we want to become. However, for personal life cycle management to effectively contribute to Personal System Development (PSD) it must do so in a minimum of three PSD subsystems: the health, character and ability subsystems. These subsystems operate in a synergistic manner and each has its own life cycle attributes and contributions in optimizing the *learnership practitioner's* learning, leading and performance.

Three PSD Subsystems

> *And remember friends, it's better to look good than to feel good.*
> *-- Billy Crystal*

Health Subsystem. The Personal System Development (PSD) health subsystem is the first of three areas of learnership practitioner assessment, learning, and development. And they are all interdependent.

Physical Health. This section addresses disease prevention, diet and exercise, and being a smart patient. Together they offer topics for consideration and action, as appropriate.

1. Disease Prevention. Mark Hyman and Mark Liponis are authors of *Ultra-Prevention: The 6-Week Plan That Will make You Healthy for Life* (2003). Their emphasis is the practice of holistic, health-based medicine. Their action plan has five major health initiatives designed to conquer what they term the five forces of illness: sludge, burnout, heat, waste, and rust. An overview:

  a. Sludge (malnutrition) – Focus is on poor *nutrition, digestion and absorption*. Over 80 per cent of Americans are malnourished. They are not getting the recommended daily allowance of vitamins, nutrients and minerals. The major cause is improper digestion (breaking food down into components), and absorption (getting nutrients from the gut into the blood stream). Stomach and intestinal tract functioning is of concern here.

  b. Burnout (impaired metabolism) – Focus is on improving *metabolism*, the creation of energy at the cellular level in our bodies. After the stomach and intestinal tract do their work, the metabolism process creates Adenosine Tri-Phosphate (ATP), the usable energy for all bodily functions. ATP is stored in fat for use as needed by the body, but poor eating affects the quality of this energy store. Improper Insulin production, mitochondrial dysfunction and thyroid dysfunction are all related to insufficient metabolism.

  c. Heat (inflammation) – The signs of inflammation are: redness, swelling, heat, pain, and loss of function. Localized inflammation as the body seeks to defend against an unwanted invader is evidence of good health. However long-term, systemic, generalized inflammation throughout much of the body is destructive to health and longevity. The consumption or absorption of unhealthy foods, allergens or toxins and/or physical entry of microbes and poisons are causes for inflammation, that uncorrected, lead to rapid aging, disease and eventually death.

  d. Waste (impaired detoxification) – "Detoxification is the process of breaking down and eliminating anything that shouldn't be in it…also eliminates foreign, potentially toxic compounds often unavoidably ingested with our food." (p.208) The waste products of metabolism, used hormones, and other cellular discards must all be removed to maintain health. The process requires making these products water soluble for excretion. The kidneys and liver receive attention here. Also, the exchange of oxygen and carbon dioxide by the lungs is also an area for medical review.

  e. Rust (oxidative stress) – "Rusting indicates the damage incurred by exposure to oxygen…Every one of us has and needs millions of oxidants in our body. However, oxidant molecules can cause injury to our tissues whenever they are present in excess, becoming a source of illness, causing oxidative stress." (p.216) Use of oxygen in metabolism yields high-energy oxygen molecules know as "free radicals." These radicals cause cellular destruction, inflammation, and are associated with various diseases. Countering free radicals through proper eating and appropriate vitamins is good proactive behavior.

2. Diet and Exercise. *You, On a Diet: The Owner's Manual for Waist Management* (2006) is a book by Drs Michael Roizen and Melmet Oz associated with The Joint Commission, a medical community oversight group. They provide factual, albeit humorous, advice on taking control of our most important asset—our health. A selection of useful topics that readers might find informative is:
  a. The Ideal Body. What your body is supposed to look like

  b. Can't Get No Satisfaction. The science of appetite

  c. Taking a Fat Chance. How fat ruins your health

  d. Make the Move. How you can burn fat faster

  e. The Chemistry of Emotions. The connections between feelings and food

  f. The YOU Activity Plan. Physical strategies for waist management

  g. The YOU Diet. The waist-management eating plan

h. <u>The Extreme Team</u>. What to do if your weight is out of control

We have one life to live and it takes significant time for us to discover are unique insights and skills. How unfortunate it would be if we fail to accomplish some of our goals and make our social environment just a little bit better for having been here. Diet, exercise, and disease prevention is a responsibility for each of us.

3. <u>The Smart Patient</u>. Michael Roizen and Mehmet Oz are medical doctors Their book: *You, The Smart Patient: An Insider's Handbook for Getting the Best Treatment* (2006) advises readers on how to ensure ourselves a safe and successful experience when dealing with health care providers and hospitals. Their prescriptions for preparing, participating and completing interactions with the medical community are both numerous and humorous. Not to be underestimated, however, is the life enhancing and lifesaving advice they dispense. Topics addressed include:

a. Find the right medical practitioner

b. Be smart in the use of prescription drugs

c. Always get a second opinion

d. Know your rights

e. Manage your health insurance

f. Know your alternatives and choices

g. Select the right hospital

h. Understand medical jargon

i. How to get through an operation successfully.

Learning this information is a complementary effort to the physical health perspectives discussed earlier in this section. Considered together, we should be able to manage our medical affairs with some degree of efficiency and expertise.

> *Life is a comedy for those who think, and a tragedy for those who feel.*
> — Horace Walpole

Emotional Health. Author Daniel Goleman's book *Emotional Intelligence: Why It Can Matter More than IQ* (1995), focuses attention on the role of emotion in human intelligence. He explains that while we depend on the rational mind for so much of our thinking, development and progress, it is the emotional mind that adds "heart' to any situation or relationship. In fact, the emotional mind often beats the rational mind into action leaving the rational mind to figure out what to do next. The learning here might be that systematically developing the emotional mind could do much more for human progress because of the social relationships that may be improved.

1. <u>Emotion and the Emotional Mind</u>. While the Oxford English Dictionary defines *emotion* as: "any agitation or disturbance of mind, feeling, passion; any vehement or excited mental state," Goleman suggests some refinement: "I take emotion to refer to a feeling and its distinctive thoughts, psychological and biological states, and a range of propensities to act." He says that some theorists propose basic families, though not all agree on them. The main emotions at the top of each family are: anger, sadness, fear, enjoyment, love, surprise, disgust, and shame...He also addresses derivative terms that move outward from emotion as if in concentric circles. These are: (1) *moods* which tend to be more muted that emotions but last for longer periods of time, (2) *temperaments* which are the willingness to evoke a given emotion to affect one's demeanor, and (3) *disorders* of emotion in which one finds themselves in a perpetual toxic state." (p.289-290)

2. <u>Rational and Emotional Minds</u>. According to Goleman, "In a very real sense we have two minds, one that thinks and one that feels. These fundamentally different ways of knowing interact to construct a mental life. One, the rational mind, is the mode of comprehension we are typically conscious of: more prominent in awareness, thoughtful, able to ponder and reflect. But alongside that there is another system of knowing: impulsive and powerful, if sometimes illogical—the emotional mind. The emotional/rational dichotomy approximates the folk distinction between "heart" and "head;" knowing something is right "in your heart" is a different order of conviction—somehow a deeper kind of certainty—than thinking so with your rational mind." (p.8) The important point to realize is that these two minds are interconnected and are constantly working together in our perception, reasoning, decision making, and behavior. The mid-brain or limbic system evolved much earlier in human development thereby providing the emotion and feelings that supported continued survival and progress through the millennia. The human neocortex that developed during more recent history is the largest in the animal kingdom and is the storehouse for cognition and purposeful mental processing—rational thinking. To the degree there are common attitudes, beliefs, values, and behaviors among a group of people we say that there is a culture that they share.

Goleman states that: "Ordinarily there is a balance between emotional and rational minds, with emotion feeding into and informing the operations of the rational mind, and the rational mind refining and sometimes vetoing the inputs of the emotions. But when passions surge the balance tips: it is the emotional mind that captures the upper hand, swamping the rational mind." (p.9) Goleman also refers to work by Paul Ekman (head of the Human Interaction Laboratory at the University of California, San Francisco) and Seymore Epstein (clinical psychologist at the University of Massachusetts) in which they offer a basic list of qualities that distinguish emotions from the rest of mental life. These are:

a. <u>A quick but sloppy response</u>. The emotional mind is far quicker that the rational mind, springing into action without pausing even a moment to consider what it is doing. Its quickness precludes the deliberate, analytic reflection that is the hallmark of the thinking mind.

b. <u>First feelings, second thoughts</u>. Because it takes the rational mind a moment or two longer to register and respond that it does the emotional mind, the "first impulse" in an emotional situation is in the heart not the head.

c. <u>A symbolic, childlike reality</u>. The logic of the emotional mind is associative; it takes elements that symbolize a reality, or trigger a memory of it, to be the same as that reality. That is why similes, metaphors, and images speak directly to the emotional mind, as do the arts—novels, film, song, theater, opera.

d. <u>The past imposed on the present</u>. When some feature of an event seems similar to an emotionally changed memory form the past, the emotional mind responds by triggering the feelings that went with the remembered event. The emotional mind reacts to the present *as though it were the past*.

e. <u>State-specific reality</u>. The working of the emotional mind is to a large degree state-specific, dictated by the particular feeling ascendant at a given moment. How we think and act when we are feeling romantic is entirely different from how we behave when enraged or dejected.

What has also been learned is that the whole brain is limited by its level of prior learning derived from study and experience, and everyone has their own preferences and insights concerning what they currently sense and experience. We should not be surprised at the social difficulty that arises as individuals and groups who basically agree from a rational standpoint still find roadblocks to harmonious collaboration when the emotions and feelings associated with an effort are not aligned. And, that if those same people lead with their feelings it is unlikely they can get focused enough to arrive at a rational conclusion.

3. <u>Social and Emotional Learning</u>. A topic of interest that arises from the above information concerns: What are the specific emotional skills and competencies we might want to teach people? What examples might be useful? Goleman provides examples from community early learning programs devised for primary and secondary level students. We should be able to draw the parallel that the same topics apply to adults.

In Example #1 he provides a Self-Science Curriculum developed by Karen F. Stone and Harold Q. Dillehunt entitled: "Self-Science: The Subject is Me," from Goodyear Publishing Company, Santa Monica, 1978) The curriculum proposes the following topics for instruction: (p.302)

a. Self-awareness
b. Personal decision-making
c. Managing feelings
d. Handling stress
e. Empathy
f. Communications
g. Self-disclosure
h. Insight
i. Self-acceptance
j. Personal Responsibility
k. Assertiveness
l. Group dynamics
m. Conflict resolution

In Example #2, Goleman provides a list of results from the design and evaluation of a social problem solving program by M.J. Elias and J. Clabby: Building Social Problem Solving Skills: Guidelines form a School-Based Program (San Francisco, Jossey-Bass, 1992). The result obtained and reported from the schools were: (p.309)

    a. More sensitive to others' feelings
    b. Better understanding of the consequences of their behavior
    c. Increased ability to "size up" interpersonal situations and plan appropriate actions
    d. Higher self-esteem
    e. More pro-social behaviour
    f. Sought out by peers for help
    g. Better handled the transition to middle school
    h. Less anti-social, self-destructive, and socially disordered behavior, even when followed up into high school
    i. Improved learning-to-learn skills
    j. Better self-control, social awareness, and social decision-making in and out of the classroom

Could it be that some adults have still to learn to take responsibility for their negative impact on others in person-to-person situations? If so, can we reflect on that now?

> *Anyone can become angry – that is easy. But to be angry with the right person,*
> *to the right degree, at the time, for the right reason, and in the right way – this is not easy.*
> *— Aristotle*

The Stress of Life. Stress is a major subject of concern in today's fast changing modern world. People everywhere complain that we do not have the time and energy to accommodate all the situations and people clamoring for our attention and assistance. If only we could get our sense of stress under control. Maybe if our lives were more organized, our living conditions more reasonable, and social relations more meaningful we could feel better about ourselves and others. There is little doubt that understanding the stress mechanism and how we might eliminate or at least accommodate the stress we feel would be immeasurable helpful. Dr. Hans Selye, at the University of Montreal did much of the seminal research on understanding the biologic impact of stress. His landmark book, *The Stress of Life* (1976), is used herein to communicate some foundational information on the topic.

General Adaptation Syndrome (G.A.S.). Selye's operational definition of stress is: "Stress is the state manifested by a specific syndrome which consists of all the nonspecifically-induced changes within a biologic system. Thus, stress has its own characteristic form and composition but no particular cause. The elements of its form are the visible changes due to stress, whatever its cause. They are additive indicators which can express the sum of all the different adjustments that are going on in the body at any time." (p.64) This definition encompasses the many biologic features and relationships that Selye recognized as an interdependent system to which he gave the name: General Adaptation Syndrome (G.A.S.). The deconstruction of this definition is useful for better understanding of what we term "being stressed. "The major elements are:

1. Stress is a state manifested by a *Syndrome*. When we are under stress (biologic tension) there are many physiological indicators that may be witnessed and measured. These indicators are the result of biological interactions and they are very much the same in everyone although not to the same degree or intensity. Technically, biologic stress is not the same as nervous tension.

2. Stress shows itself as a specific Syndrome yet it is *nonspecifically induced.* The body's reactions are very common and specific, but the *causes* that initiate the onset of the Syndrome are many, therefore *nonspecific.*

3. Stress is the nonspecific response of the body to any demand. That is, the demand placed on the body can be from a pleasant or unpleasant event or condition—and, the genesis of the event or condition can be from a wide variety of physical, emotional, or environmental sources.

4. Stress is a biologic Syndrome caused by demands known as "*stressors.*" If the body categorizes the demand as a harmful or threatening experience the stress induced is termed "*distress,*" however, if the demand is considered to be desirable or pleasant experience the stress induced is termed "*eustress.*" The mental component is an important factor because *how we choose to perceive a demand* affects the strength, within limits, of its impact on us.

5. Stress response of the body can be understood and demonstrated as occurring in three stages. The stage when a stressor is first recognized is termed the "*alarm response*" and the body immediately takes defensive action in the form of hormonal changes—G.A.S. begins. The second stage is when the full range of biologic actions takes place to either

resist or adjust to the effects of the stressor. This is the stage of "resistance" and lasts as long as the body's health and energy reserve remains supportive. The third stage of "*exhaustion*" occurs when the body gives up struggling against the stressor (or the stressor is removed) and the G.A.S. is ended.

6. Stress uses and consumes the body's store of "*adaptive energy.*" Everyone has a level of health based largely on heredity and an investment is a healthy lifestyle. If we are able to ameliorate the degree to which we permit stressors to turn into an internalized stress syndrome we are able to control the "wear and tear" on our bodies. Distress, in particular, consumes more of the body's adaptive energy thereby affecting our overall level of health and rate of aging.

Diseases of Adaptation. Selye says that: "An ever increasing proportion of the human population dies from the so-called wear and tear diseases, diseases of civilization, or degenerative diseases, which are primarily due to stress." (p.430) His research shows that our biological processes inevitably contribute to the increasing accumulation of waste products that are either insoluble or hard to remove from our bodies. In time, certain bodily functions and/or specific organs become weakened or incapacitated leading to malfunction. As this situation progresses to a stage not correctable through medical procedure, death is often the result. He says these are diseases of adaptation which include: "…high blood pressure, diseases of the heart and of the blood vessels, diseases of the kidney, eclampsia, rheumatic and rheumatoid arthritis, inflammatory diseases of the skin and eyes, infections, allergic and hypersensitivity diseases, nervous and mental diseases, sexual derangements, digestive diseases, metabolic diseases, cancer, and diseases of resistance in general." (pp.169-170)

Philosophic Implications. Selye tells us that " physiologic aging, is not determined by the time elapsed since birth, but by the total amount of wear and tear to which the body has been exposed. There is, indeed a great *difference between physiologic and chronologic age*…Vitality is like a special kind of bank account which you can use up by withdrawals but cannot increase by deposits. Your only control over this precious fortune is the rate at which you make your withdrawals…the intelligent thing to do is to withdraw and expend generously, but never wastefully for worthless efforts." (pp.428-429) "Apparently there are *two kinds of adaptation energy*: the superficial kind, which is ready to use, and the deeper kind, which acts as a sort of frozen reserve. When superficial adaptation energy is exhausted during exertion, it can slowly be restored from a deeper store during rest… [and] Life is a continuous series of adaptations to our surroundings and, as far as we know, our reserve of adaptation energy is an inherited finite amount, which cannot be regenerated." (p.429)

What we learn here is each of us should act responsibly in the use of our personal bank account of inherited mental and physical energy. Some of us may have more and some will have less, but in every case our reserve should be tapped at a rate than allows systematic personal development without unnecessarily limiting our lifespan by squandering our life force. Man's ultimate aims according to Selye can be achieved within the context of his *philosophy of altruistic egoism*. This philosophy "advocates the creation of feelings of accomplishment and security through the inspiration in others of love, goodwill and gratitude for what we have done or are likely to do in the future." (p.452)

> *The power to fulfill our dreams is within each of us. We alone have the responsibility to shape our lives. — Wynn Davis*

Rational Living. Rational Emotive Therapy (RET) is a method for practicing psychological well-being that advocates that individuals, themselves, have a *choice* in all aspects of their reasoning and behavior and that "others do not make them" think or act in self destructive and/or unsocial ways. In fact, if we always recognize that we have *alternatives*, tell ourselves what some of the more constructive alternatives are in challenging social situations, and choose a course of communication and action that moves us forward in our personal growth we will be inoculating ourselves against the irrational, sometimes destructive, elements in society.

In their *A New Guide to Rational Living* (1961), authors Albert Ellis and Robert Harper describe "…the humanistic educative model which asserts that people, even in their early lives, have a great more choices than they tend to recognize; that most of their conditioning actually consists of *self*-conditioning; and that a therapist, a teacher, or even a book can help them see much more clearly their range of alternatives and thereby choose to reeducate and retrain themselves so that they surrender most of their serious self-*created* emotional difficulties." They present the view that: "…unlike lower animals, people tell themselves various sane and crazy things. Their beliefs, attitudes, opinions, and philosophies largely…take the form of internalized sentences or *self*-talk." (p.x) The authors make the critical point that we can choose more *sane self*-talk than crazy self-talk once we take the time to reflect on what we think and why we think that way.

Ellis and Harper believe that everyone can lead themselves through a moderate level of self-analysis in which we consider the mental scripts that we ourselves and others have programmed into us. We can rationally decide if those beliefs, attitudes and subsequent actions are moving us in directions we prefer. And, we can do this throughout our lifetimes so that as we gain experience and learn more we can make adjustments in our perspectives and choices. They provide a list of perspectives and scientific conclusions for review by those willing to expend energy and time on *self-management* and able to take responsibility for their own personal development. Some thoughts for further consideration based on the authors' commentary are:

1. Try to be *rational* in our thinking and in how we appear to others. Excessive rationalizing, intellectualizing, and overgeneralization indicate excessive use of personal opinion, an unwillingness to obtain relevant data, and an attempt to influence through intimidation. Ellis and Harper state that: "When you think rationally, (a) you derive your thought primarily from objective fact as opposed to subjective opinion; (b) your thinking, if acted upon, most likely will result in preservation of your life and limb; (c) it will help you define your personal life goals more quickly; (d) it will produce in you a minimum of inner conflict and turmoil; and (e) if you act on it, it will prevent you from getting into undesirable conflict with those whom you live and associate." (p.73)

2. Understand that we have *choices* in life as long as we avoid absolutist thinking and behavior. Applying semantics to ourselves such as: "I need" or "I must" or "I have to" gives the appearance of over-emotionalizing, being too ego-involved, or being dogmatic. When we think about it the only thing we ever have to do is die—everything else is optional! Say instead, "I would prefer" or "I am hopeful" or "I would like to consider some options."

3. Avoid *perfectionism* as an objective for ourselves and others. In reality none of us can achieve absolute perfection wherein we are always right and never wrong. Even when we strive to be the very best we can be there will always have room for improvement—especially in the short run. When others annoy us or are unfair to us we should consider our own bottom line interests and proceed without excessive emotion to demonstrate tolerance, understanding and even some degree of acceptance consistent with that most admirable characteristic—humility.

4. Attempt to be *objective* in both reasoning and behavior. Feelings and emotions add a desirable flavor to human existence as they serve to inspire us and bring us pleasure. However, the advancement of humankind has been most significantly driven by the large cerebral cortex in our evolving brains. We can contribute most effectively to life situations through reasoning that emphasizes the factual, accurate and timely use of data and information. Try to see all sides of an issue, and to avoid the use of preconceptions and prejudices.

5. Strive for continuous, reasonable *improvement* in ourselves and others. However, be aware that there are few perfect solutions to complex issues so we should be prepared to understand others' frames of reference, expect to accommodate others' reasonable desires, and try to achieve a level of consensus among informed, well meaning people.

The value of this section on personal health is that it reaffirms the need for everyone to pay more attention to the one system that must work well for all other systems to be of any importance—our bodies. Learnership practitioners understand that we are inside the systems-of-systems we advocate. Because of this, we look to demonstrate our willingness to maintain and advocate good health practices.

No person was ever honored for what he received;
honor has been the reward for what he gave. — Calvin Coolidge

Character Subsystem.

The Personal System Development (PSD) character subsystem is the second of three areas of learnership practitioner assessment, learning, and development. And they are all interdependent. Character is considered herein to be the distinguishing attributes of individuals that occur over time as we choose, acquire and demonstrate the personal values and socially encouraged virtues that frame our system of ethics. These individual attributes tend to both underpin and overlap the universal societal goals and ideals presented earlier in this chapter. We begin this section with a discussion on thinking as it relates to the purposeful activity of character development, and then continue on with two perspectives that focus primary on the attributes of moral character—the right way to deal with others in a good society.

Thinking and Character. According to John Maxwell, author of *Thinking for a Change* (2003), "Those who embrace good thinking as a life style understand the relationship between their level of thinking and their level of progress. They also realize that to change their lives, they must change their thinking." (p.3) Maxwell is a lifelong student of good thinking skills, and has written many books on personal development on such topics as attitude, motivation, and leadership which are based on his knowledge of good thinking.

Maxwell's book presents a well-structured, easily understood challenge to all of us who want to improve our lives by being able to think, learn, know, lead, and pursue our goals more effectively—a fundamental learnership theme. Maxwell comments on the need to understand the value of good thinking by saying: "If you are willing to change your *thinking*, you can change your *feelings*. If you change your *feelings*, you can change your *actions*. And, changing your *actions*—based on good thinking—can change your *life*."[Italics added] Further, he provides three reasons everyone should value good thinking: (Chapter 1)

1. Good thinking creates the foundations for good results. He quotes James Allen, philosopher of the human spirit, as saying "Good thoughts and actions can never produce bad habits; bad thoughts and actions can never produce good results."

2. Good thinking increases your potential. Quoting James Allen again, "You will become as small as your controlling desire, as great as your dominant aspiration."

3. Good thinking produces more good thinking if…you make it a habit. Maxwell says "Every person has the potential to become a good thinker. I've observed that: unsuccessful people focus their thinking on *survival*, average people focus their thinking on *maintenance*, and successful people focus their thinking on *progress*." [Italics added]

Maxwell comments that as a motivational speaker he needed to learn that no one can change someone else—everyone is responsible for their own change and improvement. He advises people to realize the potential impact of changed thinking:

1. Changing your thinking changes your *beliefs*. People will only attain what they can see themselves doing.

2. Changing your beliefs changes your *expectations*. A belief is not just an idea that you possess; it is an idea that possesses you.

3. Changing your expectations changes your *attitude*. Negative expectations are a quick route to dead-end thinking.

4. Changing your attitude changes your *behavior*. He quotes author LeRoy Eims as saying "How can you know what is in your heart? Look at your behavior."

5. Changing your behavior changes your *performance*. Don't be too impressed with goal- setting; be impressed with goal-getting.

6. Changing your performance changes your *life*. When you change your performance—that is, what you do on a consistent basis—then you have the power to change your life. Clearly, good thinking has to be a prerequisite for determining the values and beliefs that contribute to the formation of our character; which in turn, affects our ability to establish ourselves as constructive and valued members of our social communities. John McCain and William Bennett have suggestions on the attributes that are most desirable.

Character is Destiny. The first selection is from U.S. Senator John McCain's *Character is Destiny: Inspiring Stories Every Young Person Should Know and Every Adult Should Remember* (2002). McCain presents thirty-four vignettes of individuals noted for their demonstration of high level social principles as a way of encouraging personal reflection and development by both adolescents and adults. McCain says: "Even a long life is a brief experience, hard as that is to believe when we are young. God has given us that life, shown us how to use it, but left it to us to dispose of as we choose. Our character will determine how well or how poorly we choose. [And] It is your character and your character alone, that will make your life happy or unhappy…Others can encourage you to make the right choices or discourage you. But you must choose." (p.xi) He continues on to introduce people that illustrate one or more of the attributes (values, virtues, ideals) he has chosen and comments that: "Most are people of exceptionally good character. All, no doubt, had flaws. Everyone does. But they all exemplify one or more essential attributes of good character." (p.xii) McCain's book focuses on thirty-four attributes arranged in seven primary groups: *Honor, Purpose, Strength, Understanding, Judgment, Creativity, and Love.*

Book of Virtues. The second selection which overlaps well with McCain's presentation is William Bennett's *The Book of Virtues: A Treasury of Great Moral Stories* (1993). Bennett also appeals to adolescents and adults to spend time learning "the do's and don'ts of life with others." He comments that: "Aristotle wrote that good habits formed at youth make all the difference. And, moral education must affirm the central importance of moral example…For children to take morality seriously they must be in the presence of adults who take morality seriously." (p.11) Bennett organizes the stories, poems and essays written by hundreds of other notable writers into ten primary groups, each represented by a particular virtue: *Self-Discipline, Compassion, Responsibility, Friendship, Work, Courage, Perseverance, Honesty, Loyalty, and Faith.*

Upon review, the character attributes presented by McCain and Bennett in their respective books are nearly identical. Such a positive correlation is indicative of significant agreement in the American culture on desired attitudes and behavior, regardless if the categorization is virtues, values, or ideals. The only area around which dispute is likely is the *inclusion of God, religion or faith* as one of the required attributes. Approximately one-third of U.S. adults who do not subscribe to religious guidance or formal organization, but value a sense of higher purpose would likely prefer a non-binding term such as "*spirituality*" to describe humankind aspiration. The difference here is not inconsequential in that the belief, and the non-belief, in a form of an "intelligent guiding hand" outside rational human contemplation are opposing world-views for eternal debate. Some additional thoughts on the non-belief perspective follow.

Spirituality and the Secular Quest (1996), edited by Peter Van Ness is a review of European Enlightenment (1700s) and American philosophical perspective (1800s and early 1900s) concerning the movement from religious to secular based thinking about "*spirituality*." According to Van Ness "…most enlightenment thinkers thought of *reason* as a broad and generous power for intuiting innate and universal truths that spell out the ends of humankind in relation to government, ethics and religion…[and that] becoming a *self* is a proleptic project of the whole person; for that reason, we can say that such a project contains a *spiritual*, if not always religious dimension." (p.96) Van Ness also summarizes the characteristics of the *American Secular Quest* as framed by writers such as William James, John Dewey, and George Santana that speak to a "*aesthetic spirituality*:" "Spiritual life in the secular world consists in the progressive integration of even more complex feeling, thoughts, and habits by which one reacts to an ever larger portion of the world and relates oneself to the whole of reality. This mode of *spirituality*, like art, is therefore a matter of maximizing complexity and intensity in some degree of harmony." (p.107)

[**Author's Note**: An observation at this juncture is that the vast majority of people, regardless of their religious or non-religious worldview, can agree on the majority of ethical principles upon which they would choose to advocate and manage the interpersonal relationships among citizens and for the common good of society. Differences of opinion on the source of these principles – sectarian intervention or secular construction – should not be the determining factor on the worthiness of the principles as guidance in human affairs. All cultures and societies need to agree on an overarching set of standards to guide their moral affairs and to achieve their potential. This author and owner of the "learnership" concept is currently a fan of the "progressive integration of even more complex feeling, thoughts, and habits" perspective offered herein]

Ethics and the Quest for a Good Life (1990). Another avenue for the consideration of character and ethics is presented by William Gellermann et al, authors of *Values and Ethics in Organization and Human Systems Development.* The authors discuss the professional code of conduct for human systems developers in organizations, and make a distinction between *ethics as morality*, wherein a code of conduct establishes basic obligations among people, and *ethics as a quest for a good life*. The latter view was ascribed to Aristotle who conceived that all objects had natural ends toward which they strive, and which determine the course of the object's natural development. This natural end was termed the object's *telos*, which for human beings was the *good life*. The *good life* was to be achieved through development of the individual's full capacity (*fulfillment*) within the context of the society of which they were a part. Society's role is to foster conditions under which individuals could attain the *good life*, or happiness, which at the highest degree consisted of achieving *virtue*. And, *virtue* was thought to be the ability to maintain in all things a point of moderation, somewhere between the extremes of deficiency and excess. In terms of the *learnership architecture* in this book, the quest for our telos is seen as a quest for *self-fulfillment* which is achieved through life-long *personal system development*.

Character and Social Class. While character is often thought of in terms of the conformance of something or someone to pre-established standards—as we have discussed so far—character also has the dimension of uniqueness in which it might be said that something or someone has certain distinctive traits or features. And, in many cases those things or people can be subject to classification. This is the situation when we turn our attention to the degree to which Americans have similar and dissimilar values, attitudes, interests, capabilities, influence, and accomplishments. The importance of social class in this book on learnership is that the social class we are currently in, or plan to join, has great influence on what we choose to value, learn, and accomplish during our lifetimes. Our personal levels of aspiration and motivation are affected by the context of our experience. Our exposure to fields of education, cultural artifacts, economic opportunities, social responsibilities, and accomplished leaders determine what we think is possible and desirable for ourselves.

According to the Wikipedia summary of research and information on "Social Class in America," social class is the hierarchy in which individuals find themselves. The social class system is mainly a description of how society has distributed its members among positions of varying importance, influence, and prestige." Reference is made to *Society in Focus* (William Thompson and Joseph Hickey, 2005) in which they say: "It is impossible to understand people's behavior...without the concept of social stratification, because class position has a pervasive influence on almost everything...the clothes we wear...the television we watch...the colors we paint our homes in and the names we give our pets...Our position in the social hierarchy affects out health, happiness, and even how long we will live." Clearly, each of us should reflect on our relative positioning in our careers, communities and society's and decide how to invest the time of our lives. In other words, where do we want to be? And how are we going to get there?

The section that follows is a compilation of social class characteristics from two sources:. *Society in Focus* (2005), (William Thompson and Joseph Hickey), and *Popular Culture and High Culture* (1999) (Herbert Gans). The five categories and percentage of Americans in those categories are stratified using U.S. government data on income, education, culture, and taste preferences (Gans). The reader is encouraged to contemplate his or her own positioning in the categories, and to reflect on whether there are opportunities for additional personal growth that he or she might want to pursue. It is important to remember that social class mobility and ascendancy is always possible over time—particularly in American—and is being accomplished everyday.

1. Upper Class (1-5%). Have a disproportionate amount of societal influence and income ($150,000+). Tend to be prominent government officials, CEOs and successful entrepreneurs. Top 1.5% with incomes over $250,000 (many that do not work), includes old (inherited) money "blue bloods," and "nouveau riche." *Tastes*: Prefer exclusive pursuits; original and abstract art, music, literature; relies on critics and experts for professional input and opinion; only top tier clothes, homes, furnishings, and cars; high culture TV (when available); foreign movies and cars.

2. Upper Middle Class (15%). Tend to be white collar salaried management and professional employees with advanced college degrees. Household income commonly above $100,000, but may be considerably less for one income earner households or lesser paid professionals, active in politics and social issues. *Tastes*: Selectively interested in Upper Class worldviews and consumption; interested in TV and film plots rather than moods and in activities, ideas, and feelings relevant to own careers and endeavors in social and civic organizations. Like Broadway shows, prints of original art, news magazines like Harpers, New Yorker, Vogue; like public TV/radio, network documentaries, museums, concert halls; high quality clothes, homes and cars; some foreign movies and cars.

3. Lower Middle Class (33%). Bachelors degree from state universities and smaller schools. White collar employees have considerably less autonomy than upper middle class professionals. Incomes are commonly between $30,000 and $75,000 depending on the number of income earners. Emulate consumption patterns of the more affluent Upper Middle Class. Tend to be overworked, little leisure. *Tastes*: Value wholesome TV plots, heroes and traditional values, institutions, and religions; major mass media consumers, get advice from TV and friends/neighbors; read Life, Look, Saturday Evening Post, Readers Digest, homemaking and hobby magazines; art and entertainment tends to be romantic and common to own experience; few foreign films or cars.

4. Working Class (30%). Blue collar and clerical workers, work often in uncomfortable environments, and have little or no college education. Little job security, prone to outsourcing, closely supervised. Household income commonly between $16,000 and $30,000, pride themselves in doing "real work." *Tastes*: Often support church, police, and government efforts to censor erotic materials, albeit that they themselves prefer action, often violent, and melodramatic entertainment; aesthetic standards of low culture stress substance, little concern for form; little interest in fictional accounts of contemporary social problems and issues.

5. Lower (Under) Class (17%). Less than high school completion. Prone to job loss, often work multiple jobs. Household income is likely to be less than $16,000. *Tastes*: Typically tabloids and comic books; prefer church and street festivals; TV soap operas, folk culture, and low culture street art.

The Wikipedia summary also includes cultural study data by Dennis Gilbert from his book The American Class Structure (2002). Commentary based on Gilbert's data states: "Parental views are perhaps the most essential factor in determining the socialization progress which shapes new members of society. The values and standards used in childrearing are commonly related to the parent's occupational status. Parents from the professional class tend to raise their children to become curious independent thinkers, while working class parents raise their children to have a more communal perspective with a strong respect for authority. Middle Class parents tend to emphasize internal standards and values while Working Class parents emphasize external values. A comparison between Middle Class and Working Class norms follows, and the reader is encouraged to assess how his or her values currently align with their peer group.

6. Middle Class (48%). Consideration of others, self-control, curiosity, happiness, honesty, tolerance of nonconformity, open to innovation, self-direction.

7. Working Class (30%). Manners, obedience, neatness, cleanliness, strong punishment of deviant behavior, stick to old ways, people not trustworthy, strict leadership

In-Group versus Out-Group. Author Matt Ridley provides a different perspective on the establishment of social character in his book *The Origin's of Virtue: Human Instincts and the Evolution of Cooperation* (1996). He argues that through the evolutionary process human genes direct people's behavior in a manner likely to achieve their ultimate objective—the continued propagation of their unique species (Richard Dawkins: the "selfish gene"). As such, "cooperation is a frequent feature of human society; trust is the very foundation of social and economic life." (p.57) Cooperativeness, however, has a significant downside in that it generates self-seeking "groupishness" among people attempting to manage and control their social environment for their own selfish purposes. Groups form to seek and protect their own interests, develop their own values and character, and create rituals to reinforce conformity within, and distance from, other groups. As an example he refers to the development of varying cultures, ethnicity, religions, and states that seek to emphasize how they are different (and better) than the others—which often results in hostility and war. Ridley quotes anthropologist Lyle Steadman saying that: "…ritual is about more than demonstrating the acceptance of tradition; it is also specifically about the encouragement of cooperation and sacrifice." (p.189)

Ridley continues with the observation that religious teachings, in particular, have always been about identification of those who were part of the in-group (the adherents) and the out-group (the enemy). He says: "Religion teaches its adherents that they are a chosen race and their nearest rivals are benighted fools or even subhuman. There is nothing especially surprising in this, given the origins of most religions as beleaguered cults in tribally divided, violent societies." (p.191) He points out that the Old and New Testaments of the Bible are full of *rules of morality that apply to the in-group at the expense of the out-group.* Enemies may be slain e.g., God's instructions to the Jews (Joshua) and the authority to Christians to conduct the Crusades, the Inquisition, and killing in Northern Ireland and Bosnia. Similar contradictory rules for moral character and acceptable conduct may be ascribed to virtually all religions even in today's contemporary world; therefore, religion cannot be the only source of ideas regarding virtue and character formation.

Given this state of affairs, and the compelling evidence of evolutionary selection Ridley says that: "Human beings have social instincts. They come into the world equipped with predispositions to learn how to cooperate, to discriminate the trustworthy from the treacherous, to commit themselves to be trustworthy, to earn good reputations, to exchange goods and information, and to divide labour…this instinctive cooperativeness is the very hallmark of humanity and what sets us apart from other animals." (p.249) Ridley sums up his view with "Trust is as vital a form of social capital as money is a form of actual capital…[And] Social contracts between equals, generalized reciprocity between individuals and between groups—these are at the heart of the most vital of all human achievements: the creation of society." (pp.250-251)

[**Author's Note**: The Learnership philosophy and architecture has as its integrated social systems goal: personal self-fulfillment, organizational high performance, the community common good, and societal human enlightenment. This meta-system construct exists on the basis of democratic pluralism in which human reasoning and rational action combine to encourage critical thinking, informed dialogue, and collaborative consensus. To accomplish this outcome requires a marketplace for innovative ideas and moral expression without undue censorship or social intimidation.]

American Moral Character. A useful way to bring closure to the character subsystem overview may be to consider the perspective of Alan Wolfe in his book *Moral Freedom: The Search for Virtue in a World of Choice* (2001). He comments that there is an underlying moral philosophy of Americans that may be perceived and that it can be understood in terms of the following framework:

1. Moral Agreement. His observation is: "A pluralistic liberal democracy committed to equality and respect for difference ought to appreciate the fact that no one conception of the right or wrong way to live has the power to drive out all others. [And]…we should not confuse differences over how and why virtues ought to be applied [global warming, abortion, capital punishment] with differences over the underlying moral philosophy that guides people's understanding of the world." (pp.167-168)

2. Human Nature. His research shows that: "When is comes to human nature, our respondents know what they think and the overwhelming majority of them think the same way. They believe that people are not born with a predisposition to do evil. Although some are convinced that human beings are innately good, most think that we are shaped by our environment and that we can be taught to do the right thing…when things go wrong, and even when they go right, they also ought to be viewed as responsible for the decisions they make." (pp.177-178)

3. Character Formation. His data indicated that: "Character in American is no longer viewed as preformed, as if it were a quality known in advance…rather, [it] is a base from which children can obtain the confidence to discover rules of

right conduct that apply best for them...[and are] capable of discovering meaningful values by which they ought to lead their lives." (pp.186-187)

4. Beyond Good and Evil. People who lack a radical sense of evil may not be capable of grasping the full complexity of the human condition; they may be ill prepared for evil when it shows its face and they may even, in rare cases, be unable to recognize the evil existing inside them. Yet compared with radical evil, radical niceness is worth appreciating...[And] It may also represent a fairly realistic assessment of what it takes to make a society function smoothly." (p.192)

Wolfe continues to describe the emergence of "moral freedom" – its presence and its challenges. He says: "The defining characteristic of the moral philosophy of the Americans can therefore be described as the principle of moral freedom. Moral freedom means that individuals should determine for themselves what it means to lead a good and virtuous life...Schooled in the language of self-fulfillment and convinced that words like "maturity" and "growth" are preferable to "sin," they find themselves quite comfortable with the idea that a good society is one that allows each individual maximum scope for making his or her own moral choices." (p.195) Wolfe sums up his perspective with the following observations:

1. Americans have become comfortable with the idea of moral freedom because its optimistic theory of human nature makes more sense to them than the one [Victorian or Puritan] it replaced.

2. Americans would rather assume that human beings are born good, thereby giving them a standard to which they can aspire.

3. There is a moral majority in America. It just happens to be one that wants to make up its own mind." (p.197)

The significance of this section on personal character is that we are all participants in a variety of social systems, and the degree to which we can accommodate our own purposes and needs while collaborating with others on their personal desires, and on what we have in common, the better it is for all involved. There is little doubt that most people prefer working and socializing with others of good moral character, a positive outlook on the meaning of their lives, similar values and social class, and an aspiration to live a life that includes doing something constructive for their community. Fundamentally, however, we need to consider both our rights and responsibilities and strike a balance that is realistic and socially supportable.

> *When we say that high achievers have priorities, we mean they have rank-ordered their goals...By means of persistence they translate goals, arranged by priorities, into action.* -- B. Eugene Griessman

Ability Subsystem.

The Personal System Development (PSD) Ability Subsystem is the third of three areas of learnership practitioner assessment, learning, and development. And they are all interdependent. Ability herein addresses not only the knowledge and skills required for career success in a fast changing world, but also the inter- personal dimensions of each of us as we fulfill our personal, community and societal roles. Starting with the assumption that we have positioned ourselves well in terms of the Health and Character Subsystems already discussed, this section presents the reader with a variety of topics that allow us to jointly envision a person who *has their physical and emotional act together* as they present themselves to associates, colleagues, and citizens in their communities.

Multiple Intelligences. Howard Gardner, author of *Frames of Mind: The Theory of Multiple Intelligences* (1983) is the starting point for this section. His well framed but often controversial theory tells us that "intelligence," that well advocated concept focused on the depth of human knowledge, is not one but a number of "extraordinary potentials" within human beings. These potentials are believed to be primarily inherited capabilities (nature) that can be further developed in the right environment (nurture) and are consistent with the either the modular or network theories of brain functioning. Gardner states that: "I argue that there is persuasive evidence for the existence of several *relatively autonomous* human intellectual competences ...the frames of mind of my title" (p.8) He continues to say: "To my mind, a human intellectual competence must entail a set of skills of problem solving—enabling the individual *to resolve genuine problems or difficulties* that he or she encounters and, when appropriate, to create an effective product—and must also entail the potential *for finding or creating problems*—thereby laying the groundwork for the acquisition of new knowledge." (pp.60-61) Garner proposes that there seven types of intelligences or extraordinary potentials that are often distinguishable in early in childhood; and are positioned for further development within a supporting environment. These are:

1. Linguistic intelligence. Is one's skill in expression through the use of language, and Expertise in the semantics (meaning) of words used in speech and writing.

2. Musical intelligence. Is one's understanding and skill in the pitch (melody), rhythm, and other characteristics of music construction and performance.

3. Logical-mathematical intelligence. Is the ability to understand and apply the principles of logic and the highly structured relationships of mathematics to problem solving and decision making.

4. Spatial intelligence. The ability to perceive the visual world accurately, perform transformations and modifications upon one's perceptions, and to be able to re-create aspects of one's visual experience. Having a sense of the whole; seeing all relationships.

5. Bodily-kinesthetic intelligence. Is one's skill is the use of the body to convey meaning, demonstrate thoughts and feelings, and elicit sensitivities and behavior by others.

6. Personal Intelligence (Self). Is the ability to assess one's own needs and feelings and to make discriminations among those findings. This provides a learnership opportunity to *learn*.

7. Personal Intelligence (Social). Is the ability to notice and make distinctions concerning the underlying purpose, feelings, and behaviors of others, and this provides a learnership opportunity to *lead*.
The usefulness of being able to understand and appreciate the existence of different intelligences are threefold: (1) to help us assess whether we have unique talents that should be further developed, (2) to help us recognize others' skills and interests in an effort to build constructive working and social relationships, and (3) to help us interpret and appreciate the richness of the human knowledge and culture for improved social development. In particular, the identification of *personal intelligences* (self and others) reminds us that Personal System Development (PSD) is critically dependent on our willingness to play constructive roles in the social systems in which we participate.

Learning and Leading. Peter Vaill's *Learning as a Way of Being* (1996) is a foundational reference in this book. In it, he explains the "permanent white water" within which most of us exist, and provides strategies for understanding and succeeding in this turbulent social and career environment. "Vaill's central thesis is that:

1. Our continual imaginative and creative initiatives and responses to systems are, in fact, *continual learning*; in other words, continual learning is what we are seeing as we observe people acting in complex situations.

2. We need to consider carefully what we need to learn about continual learning to live productively and comfortable in our macro-systems.

3. We need also to consider whether we are prepared to engage in continual learning as we need to be, and if so, how we go about engaging it." (p.5)

"There are five intertwining characteristics of "Permanent White Water" (PWW). (a) PWW conditions are full of surprises, (b) Complex systems tend to produce novel problems, (c) PWW conditions feature events that are "messy," (d) white water events are often extremely costly, and (e) PWW conditions raise the problem of recurrence." (pp.10-13) Conditions such as these make continual learning an essential Personal System Development (PSD) responsibility.

Vaill provides a definition of learning: "Changes a person makes in himself or herself that increase the know-why and/or the know-what and/or the know-how the person possesses with respect to a given subject." (p.21) He explains that he is not talking about institutional learning in which students are busy absorbing previously selected subject matter as a means to achieve an objective not necessarily needed or desired by the student. Instead, Vaill suggests "that learning as a way of being has real substance, that it is an authentic way of living and working, thinking and feeling, in the world of permanent white water." (p.42)

In terms of a leader's role in learning, Vaill coins the term "leaderly learning." "His main hypothesis is that *managerial leadership is not learned; managerial leadership is learning*." His says that: "The ongoing process of learning is occurring all the time in executive life. The word *leaderly* is an adjective modifying learning. Thus, *leaderly learning* is the kind of learning that a managerial leader needs to engage in as an ongoing process in the job." (pp.126-127) Vaill suggests that: "Instead of memorizing "subject matter" [in management courses] would be managerial leaders can learn about learning processes in general by becoming immersed in the seven qualities of learning as a way of being. These are:

1. Pre-programmed Assumptions. Learn how to surface and examine our assumptions about human being—assumptions that derive from our past experiences and also assumptions that are built into any specific principles we have been employing.

2. Accurate and Useful Information. Learning about human behavior requires the confrontation of much literature which needs to be reviewed for accuracy and applicability.

3. Personal Synthesis. There is a need to achieve a personal synthesis about human behavior in organizations that balances and integrates all the kinds of data and concepts that are available.

4. Frame of Mind. The learner needs to discover and recognize the temptations to become a passive spectator and contemplator or a detached critic and skeptic.

5. Objectivity and Subjectivity. The learner should achieve a balance between objectivity and subjectivity, between one's personal perspective and…a more objective stance that takes in account other points of view.

6. Micro and Macro Continuum. Human behavior exists on a continuum from the deep intrapersonal to the macro-sociological. Learners need to appreciate the need to understand this range of knowledge.

7. Variety of Contexts. Learners should be willing to grasp the huge variety of contexts to which the basic idea can be applied.

Vaill summarizes the above leaderly learning description by noting that a one-time learning event is not sufficient exposure to adopt this leadership skill. The requirement is for *lifelong leaderly learning* and an extended program would be necessary to allow for training and development to have its effect over time. Lastly, the educational program content should address leaderly learning from seven aspects which are: self-directed, creative, expressive, feeling, online, continual, and reflexive leaderly learning." (pp.128-146)

Lifelong Learning. In *Wise-Up: The Challenge of Lifelong Learning* (1999), Guy Claxton comments that "learning is living." "To be alive is to be learning. Learning is not something we do sometimes, in special places or at certain periods of our lives. It is a part of our nature. We are born learners." (p.6) Claxton also makes a useful distinction between learning itself and the developmental process of "learning-to-learn;" he says: "Learning, in the way I am using the term is what you do when you do not know what to do. Learning to learn, or the development of learning power, is getting better at knowing when, how and what to do when you don't know what to do." (p.11)

Claxton provides a comprehensive overview of traditional beliefs about learning, but with insightful extensions to make his points. He does this in terms of beliefs about learning (Chapter 1) and feelings about learning (Chapter 2), each of which are paraphrased below for easy review. Concerning *beliefs about learning*:

1. The outcome is knowledge, but is more importantly an ongoing life process.
2. Knowledge is thought to be the truth, but it is really a provisional assumption.
3. Learning is considered to be for the young, but is really life-long for everyone.
4. Learning is simple in concept, but it can be difficult to do.
5. Learning involves teaching, but learning and the learner is for a lifetime.
6. Learning can proceed calmly and steadily, but may be just the opposite.
7. Learning results in explicit understanding, but much is tacit and not easily explained.

We can see here that learning requires diligent effort, and our self-esteem is often tied to our ability to learn. How well we learn is considered to be a function not only of the learning tools we posses, but of the implicit beliefs which we have acquired. Additionally, our beliefs help provide resilience, that is, we have learned to believe in ourselves and that our ability is expandable. We know we can overcome difficulties. However, we do need to stay aware for "articulate incompetence" wherein someone is clever in rationale and presentation, but wrong in the substance of what they say.

Concerning feelings about learning, Claxton says that:

1. Learning may be experienced as a journey or adventure and we may sometimes feel like withdrawing to protect ourselves.

2. We need to have the courage to persevere based on our innate tenacity or practical experience. This comes from emotion (desire or drive) and might be coupled with excitement.

3. We often need to choose between staying with the current situation and the possibly that new experiences might be beneficial; there is always some uncertainty and risk.

4. Inattention and detachment can be feigned to avoid the pressure. Anger and shame may occur over time if learning and success are not achieved.

Another aspect of learning is that it takes many years to become fully competent at using both *thinking* (hard reasoning) and *intuition* (soft reasoning). *Learning to think* requires rational thought, critical thinking skills, valid arguments leading to well thought-out conclusions. Pieces of information must be aligned, hypothesis created, alternatives considered, and choices made leading to effective decision-making and problem solving. A limitation to this process occurs when those involved have a tendency to rely on sources of unsubstantiated belief (clairvoyance, horoscopes, spirits, etc) that reduce the quality of their reasoning. Claxton quotes David Perkins: "Despite their ability to do better when reminded, people's thinking generally tends to be *hasty* (impulsive, coming to premature conclusions without examining all the evidence); *narrow* (failing to challenge assumptions and explore alternative points of view); *fuzzy* (careless and imprecise, tolerant of ill-defined and ambiguous concepts); and *sprawling* (generally disorganized and unfocused, not adding up to a coherent argument)." (David Perkins, "Post-primary Education has Little Impact on Informal Reasoning," *Journal of Educational Psychology*, vol. 77, pp.562-571)

In the area of *learning to use intuition* (soft reasoning), it is known that some situations require the reframing of the problem and viewing it from other perspectives. This is may be achieved by freeing our minds to allow for hunches and insights. Being able to shift our minds between a tight focus and a broad focus, and to being able to adjust to the timing and the amount of information perceived is a useful skill that can be developed. Claxton credits philosopher George Spencer Brown as recognizing that: "The ability to hold a problem in mind without activity, purposely deliberating on it—perhaps even for years—is one of the keys to soft thinking." (p.155) He also quotes Arthur Combs and Charles Taylor with reporting that: "Some individuals, because of past experiences with frustrating situations involving delay of need satisfaction, become generally incapable of tolerating frustrating situations...the inevitable consequence is *behavioral rigidity*." ("The Effect of Perception of Mild Degrees of Psychological Stress on Performance," Journal of Abnormal and Social Psychology, vol. 47, pp.420-424)

Claxton addresses the subject of reality and perception by noting that: "...people's learning depends not so much on the challenges and uncertainties that their world contains, but on how these are *perceived*." (p.180) He maintains that perception has two distinct aspects: the in-take activity (sense, context and personal filters) and the out-take activity (imposed worldview, rules, methods). If we perform well we are said to be *mindful* in our activity, if not we are then said to be *mindless*. In terms of our learnership theme, our ability to balance *open-minded inquiry* with *closed-minded advocacy* and action creates cycles of learning and determines the efficiency and effectiveness of the actions we take. When we perform well, we demonstrate our mindfulness.

The *learnership theory and practice advocated in this book* is based on the premise that there is a select set of sequential *reasoning competencies* (thinking, learning, knowing, and leading), when skillfully applied to an integrated set of *social systems* (personal, organizational, community, societal), empowers individuals to optimize their life accomplishments in the form of self-fulfillment, high performance, the common good, and human enlightenment. At the very core of this proposal is the idea that individuals are well informed in the logic of reasoning, and they are willing to apply the knowledge acquired through thinking and intuition to various personal and social situations.

[**Author's Note**: At this juncture it is significant to recognize the mutual support relationship between Claxton's focus on *lifelong learning* and Peter Vaill's *concept of learning as a way of being* in the previous section. Together, they represent two main pillars in understanding the dynamics of learnership, and the distinctive characteristics of the learnership practitioner.]

Learnership Practitioners. The operative agent in the learnership philosophy is the learnership practitioner. All the espoused effort toward thinking, learning, knowing, and leading does not amount to much unless there are catalysts for change and development. Learnership practitioners are meant to be those catalysts. The nature of their knowledge, skills and abilities is that they have been lifelong learners who have sufficient experience with the continua of failures and accomplishments that affect individuals, organizations, and social communities. A high degree of maturity is incumbent in the behavior of the learnership practitioner. They typically experience the need for reinvigoration and self-renewal as well as the desire to communicate and share their learning (cognition and feelings) with others. Learnership practitioners, regardless of their career specialties, are drawn to the social role of facilitator, mentor, coach, and consultant. They have knowledge, experience, and concern for the betterment of human relationships and performance.

Frederic Hudson, author of *The Adult Years: Mastering the Art of Self-Renewal* (1999), brings unusual insight into this subject area. In the preface of his book, Hudson observes that: "Abundant research describes and explores aspects of adult life but precious little wisdom for how adults can design and manage their own lives. " He then expresses the purpose of his writing: "This book is an effort to provide both guidance and wisdom. We will explore ways an adult today can establish a life course, construct durable life chapters, manage life and career changes and transition, engage in lifelong learning and training, live an anticipatory life rather than a reactive one, master the art of self-renewal, and contribute to planetary renewal." (p. viii)

After presenting a systematic review of the adult life experience, he ventures into an explanation of the need for "A New profession of Adult Mentors and Coaches" in Chapter 13 of his book. He proposes the concept of the mentor-coach, saying: "A mentor is a trusted role model, adviser, wise person, friend, mensch, steward, or guide. A mentor-coach is someone trained and devoted to guiding others into increased competence, commitment, and confidence. Coaches play their roles to achieve future-oriented results—fostering career paths, facilitating personal and professional renewal, training high-performance teams, and providing informal leadership for transition management." (pp.253-254) Hudson continues with "a five-point description of a mentor-coach in action:

1. Models mastery in professional arenas that others want to obtain
2. Guide others to high achievement in emerging scenarios
3. Advocates, criticizes, and extends corporate culture and wisdom
4. Endorses and sponsors others without having power or control over them
5. Facilitates professional development and organizational system development"

Hudson comments that: "for at least eight reasons, mentoring-coaching is important as this time, not only in corporate America but throughout society. These are:

1. To help adults manage change effectively
2. To model mastery
3. To provide ongoing training in technical abilities
4. To elicit core values and commitments
5. To renew human systems
6. To sponsor future generations
7. To model collaboration and consensus building
8. To tap the genius of older workers" (pp.254-261)

Hudson's mentoring-coaching construct adds value by its focus on the learnership practitioner's ability to maintain interpersonal credibility based upon his or her continuing accomplishments, and generative outlook when working with others. The text that follows adds three additional insights to the competency and demeanor needed by learnership practitioners: *Reflection-in-Action, Self-Renewal*, and *Generativity*.

1. Reflection-in-Action. The seminal book on self-reflective, learning-in-action is *The Reflective Practitioner* (1999) by Donald Schon. His concept of reflection-in-action pertains to those individuals and circumstances in which a person (the reflective practitioner) approaches a complex issue or problem differently than most others. Instead of taking the problem statement as a "given" and proceeding to the selection of one of the available solutions that they have embedded in their minds from previous, and most likely easier situations, they hold the issue or problem in mental suspension while they test other possible definitions of the problem or frameworks for thinking about the problem.

Then, through dialogue with others and the testing of their pat solutions against the problem, they go through cycles of experimentation and learning from which they evolve toward a restatement of the original problem and/or the solution of the original problem with discoveries and appreciations not known at the start of the deliberation. This trial and error approach, while somewhat eclectic, is not without structure. There is a period of assessment, data gathering, testing of potential or partial solutions, review of likely consequences, and re-cycling through the process again until a preferred, if not optimal, path becomes clear.

Schon is particularly insightful when he considers implication for professionals in formal organizations which maintain a premium on stability and predictability of organizational life. Coaching such organizations is difficult because by its definition learning requires new experiences and new perspectives on those experiences which usually interject surprise and complexity. The organization and its leaders are primed to reject such incursions and thereby prevent the very organizational learning they require to meet their constantly changing environment.

2. Self-Renewal. The preeminent author on the subject of self-renewal is John Gardner. His book *Self-Renewal: The Individual and the Innovative Society* (1963) is perhaps the most referenced intellectual resource on this subject. On the topic of self-renewal, Gardner states: "No one knows why some individuals seem capable of self-renewal while others do not. But we have some important clues to what the self-renewing person is like, and what we might do to foster renewal. For self-renewing men and women the development of their own potentialities and the process of self-discovery never end. It is a sad but unarguable fact that most people go through their lives only partially aware of their abilities." (p.10) As budding learnership practitioners we are encouraged by Gardner's straightforward acknowledgment that "most" people are not thinking like us, which means, of course, that some of us will be often misunderstood while the professionals among us will be resisted when they attempt to make significant change in their community or work environments.

Gardner is also astute as he cautions us to acquire *self-knowledge* to go along with our willingness for *self-renewal*; together they cooperate in our *self-development*. He says that for many of us it appears to be inconvenient to get to know ourselves. He comments that: "More often than not, we don't want to know ourselves, don't want to depend on ourselves, don't want to live with ourselves. By middle life most of us are accomplished fugitives from ourselves." (p.13) Again, as learnership practitioners we seek to know and understand ourselves and open-up our minds and hearts for greater learning, higher performance, and memorable service to others.

3. Generativity. Most people who have reached middle age and survived their mid-life transition and/or crisis begin to see new terrain on the horizon. This is the time when a combination of nature and nurture introduce the fact that at least half of our lives is irretrievably behind us and we realize that others in our families, organizations, and communities could benefit from a bit more of our guidance and attention. The generativity stage of life is calling, and if we were not thinking about "renewal" maybe this is the time we did. The question is what should we do with the (hopefully) second half of our lives? Stephen Berglas, author of *Reclaiming the Fire: How Successful People Overcome Burnout* (2001), tells us that a large percentage of super successful people eventually face the end of their meteoric social and economic rise, and have to deal with psychological burnout. They become stagnant in their lives and careers, overextended in attempting to maintain feelings of accomplishment, and uncertain on what to do next to sustain a meaningful life. Very often they are candidates for transitioning into a *generative stage of life*—if they are ready and able to seize that opportunity. Doing so leads to personal development and greater maturity.

Berglas says that: "People who aim to achieve generativity utilize their wisdom or mental excellence in ways that allow them to realize their dreams while enabling successive generations to prepare to realize theirs." He provides a caveat, however, in that: "...the essence of generativity ...[is] ceasing self-absorptive thoughts and actions in order to nurture or give yourself to others." (p.171) An ancillary point is that people in the generative stage stop trying to gain recognition and reward simply for what they now do, and instead focus on coaching others on their way to success. About the best they can hope for is a legacy formed by how they have positively aided others – not a bad deal for most people in their post-career years.

At this juncture we are able to articulate specific attributes of the learnership practitioner. He or she has good personal *intelligence skills* (H. Gardner), is a *leaderly learner* (Vaill), is a *lifelong learner* (Claxton), is a *mentor-coach* (Hudson), is a *reflective practitioner* (Schon), practices *self-renewal* (J. Gardner), and is a *generative mentor* (Berglas). The reader is now invited to consider three additional learnership practitioner skills: (1) Conversational Skills, (2) Future Work Preparation, and a (3) Focus on Excellence.

1. Conversational Skill. In the book *Crucial Conversations: Tools for Talking When Stakes are High* (2002), authors Kerry Patterson et al, explain that: "When stakes are high, opinions vary, and emotions start to run strong, casual conversations become crucial. Ironically, the more crucial the conversation, the less likely we are to handle it well. The consequences of either avoiding or fouling up crucial conversations can be severe. When we fail a crucial conversation, every aspect of our lives can be affected—from our careers, to our communities, to our relationships, to our personal health." (p.16) Building on extensive research and practical observation, Patterson and team caution us to *work on ourselves first* before becoming too entangled trying to bring others around to our point of view; they say: "More often than not, we do something to contribute to the problems we're experiencing. People who are best at *dialogue* understand this simple fact and turn it into the principle "Work on me first." (p.29) [Italics added] The key self-management techniques advocated are: (a) maintain the right motive, (b) be willing to listen, (c) replace *either/or* thinking with *both/and* thinking, and (d) remember that *dialogue* is an option.

An abstract of the authors' model for successful conversation begins with establishing a *pool of shared meaning* through the use of dialogue techniques coordinated by the person (primary discussant) most concerned about the direction or meaningfulness of a conversation. This requires:

First, taking responsibility for assessing where the conversation needs to be focused and in determining what he or she needs to have happen

Second, the primary discussant looks to see when a conversation becomes crucial and *reduces anxiety and stress* without agreeing to premature either/or thinking or to the typical silence or violence emotional response often employed.

Third, the primary discussant works to establish the sense of *mutual purpose and mutual respect.*

Fourth, all parties to the discussion *share their perspectives and experiences* on the situation or issue with the expectation that others listen carefully.

Fifth, the primary discussant seeks to *determine points of agreement* and reach consensus for action.

Sixth, the primary discussant or group leader helps the group decide to decide, schedule action, and commit to following up on results.

While this methodology does not guarantee successful results, particularly in tough situations, it does give the high road of maturity to the primary discussant in terms of skill, courage and demeanor – a reaffirmation of his or her developmental progress.

Patterson and team offer many tips on managing our conversational styles and building successful communication habits. Their suggestions tend to remind us that:

a. Our ability to pull ourselves out of the *content* of a conversation and to focus on the *process* is inversely proportional to our emotional involvement in the subject,

b. We have learned to carry *scripts* around in our heads that may not really apply to the situation at hand,

c. The more we know about the subject under discussion the better off we are in helping others think more clearly

d. Good conversation is enabled by a combination of rational thinking and emotional moderation.

Finally, Table 10-2 is comparison of conversations on the basis of a person's desire to move others to immediate action and results, or to build relationship and capabilities. The reader is invited to identify his or her own preferences (style, objective, process) when working with others. Is there a best way? What are the positive and negative aspects of each? What learning might you take from your reflection?

2. Future Work Preparation. Barbara Moses, in "Career Intelligence: The 12 New Rules for Work and Life Success" (The Futurist, World Future Society, Aug-Sep 1999) explains that becoming a *career activist* is one of the key principles of career intelligence. The ability to define ourselves independently from our organizations and taking change of our career choices is a direction for more and more of today's workers. She says (paraphrased) that Our responsibilities include:

a. Writing our own script. Rather than having someone write it for us

b. Being vigilant on our own behalf. Identifying and preparing for opportunities rather than expecting anyone else to guide us along or do reconnaissance

c Becoming an independent agent. Defining ourselves in terms and concepts that are independent of our job title, our organization, or what other people think we should be

d. Being entrepreneurial. Looking for opportunity, undertaking enterprises that provide opportunities (as well as risks)

Comparative Conversations

Concern For:	Move to Immediate Action and Results	Build Relationships and Capabilities
Time	Tactical View	Strategic View
	Impatience/Immediate	Patience/Ongoing
Knowledge	Advocacy of Facts	Inquiry into Facts
	Deliberate/Know Enough	Contemplative/Know More
Feelings	Fear of Failure	Confident of Success
	Impersonal Style	Personable Style
Others	Followers/Resources	Partners/Assets
	Dismissive Toward Others	Appreciative of Others
	Monologue/Directive	Dialogue/Collaborative
	Win/Lose	Win/Win

Table 10-2

The twelve new rules for career success are:

a. Ensure our marketability. Think of our boss as our client; know ourselves, our skills and strengths; know our market

b. Think globally. See the entire world as our marketplace; use technology to keep connected

c. Communicate powerfully, persuasively, and unconventionally. Capture our listener's attention, make information vivid, communicate clearly, translate concepts into value propositions

d. Keep on learning. Stay current in our fields; take time off for course work; read books, journals, and practice new skills

e. Understand business trends. Stay aware of key trends in business, society, and politics; know our competition

f. Prepare for areas of competence, not jobs. Titles and nature of work is changing, keep up on the latest skills and roles being sought

g. Look to the Future. Stay on top of emerging "hot" career fields and innovative practices; develop new skills that will be needed

h. Build Financial Independence. Work to get ahead of our bills and put six month's income in the bank; plan for our own health care and retirement

i. Think lattice, not ladders. Track our career progress by the type of jobs not our step on the corporate ladder; keep networking and seek horizontal advancement

j. Be a generalist with a specialty, or a specialist who's a generalist. The requirement is for both. Become competent in two or more specialties while also broadening our cross-organizational integration skills.

k. Be a ruthless time manager. No one has enough time to do everything they could do so set priorities that have long term strategic implications for growth and success. Avoid just being busy with routine matters.

l. Be kind to ourselves. Set realistic objectives and celebrate even small accomplishments. Being less than perfect on some things allows time for excellence on the right things.

Wherever we look; change, complexity and chaos are all challenging the status quo. Issues of war, illegal immigration, terrorism, white collar crime, growing national debt, gang activity, illegal drugs, rampant consumerism, a decline in school performance, unfunded pension plans, pandemic threats, middle-class decline, global warming, Medicare deficits, and dozens of other trends are straining the traditional safety nets of family, government and society. Workers in all occupational specialties face uncertainty within their current organizations, which in turn, seek to stay competitive in an expanding world marketplace that seeks to reallocate resources more efficiently across the globe. The only way to assure long-term employability and sustain personal progress is for more and more workers to become business entities of their own. Learnership practitioners are not immune to these trends. However, the flexible, adaptable, lifelong learning and competent business entities that they are; learnership practitioners should do well by themselves as they assist others in their strategies for development and performance.

3. Focus on Excellence (Relationships, Personality, Professional Presence). Here are three topics of great importance to those of us committed to growing professionally and emotionally.

a. The Importance of Relationships. In *Managing Your Mind: The Mental Fitness Guide* (1995), Gillian Butler and Tony Hope reflect on the value of social relationships. They say that: "We are, to a great extent, social animals. Our happiness, our self-esteem, our moods, our capacity to flourish, all are influenced enormously by our relationships. [And] In order to improve relationship we can only work on ourselves, and then others will change the ways in which they relate to us." (p.119) Their point is clear from a psychological perspective, but surely we know how hard this is for many of us to do. Drs. Butler and Hope anticipate this difficulty and suggest four specific techniques to assist us in improving this area of our personal system development initiative:

(1). Looking for Patterns. (Addressed in Chapter 3 of this text) Do a comparison of our feelings between when We find ourselves separated or excluded from others, and when we are communicating and socializing with those whom we know a lot about.

(2). Focusing on Specific Areas of Difficulty. Separate and review our relationship problems into disputes (hostile relations with others), role changes (choosing a perspective or persona that fails to have desired effects), and loneliness (inability to maintain friendships).

(3). Learning to Pilot Our Own Ships. Instead of focusing on our outward appearance and activities, focus on what we really need and desire from relationships in order to be happy. What should the outcomes be?

(4). Noticing How Others Change in Response. Pay closer attention to the social outcomes that result from our change in purpose and behavior.

b. Pastiche Personalities. In *The Saturated Self: Dilemmas of Identity in Contemporary* Life (1991) author Kenneth Gergen reviews many contemporary topics of concern in today's life and work environment. In particular, he identifies a personality type that seems to becoming more prevalent—*pastiche personalities*. He crafts a scenario in which the chaos and rate of change affecting our thinking and behavior tends to move us away from the traditional moorings we once relied upon. He says: "It becomes increasingly difficult to recall precisely to what core essence one must remain true. The ideal of authenticity frays about the edges and the meaning of sincerity slowly lapses into indeterminacy. As the guilt and sense of superficiality recede from view, one is simultaneously readied for the emergence of a pastiche personality." (150)

Gergen continues to develop his thesis by saying: "The pastiche personality is a social chameleon, constantly borrowing bits and pieces of identity from whatever sources are available and constructing them as useful or desirable in a given situation...[And] interest in "true character" and disgust with "false advertising" diminish...[And] we learn that "seeming" rather than "being"...becomes the most reasonable orientation to daily life." (pp.150-151). Having proposed this controversial perspective, Gergen adds that Zurcher (*The Mutable Self* earlier in this chapter) also discovered that his concept of human social adaptation could give rise to a form of narcissism indicating that: Daily life becomes suffused with the search for self-gratification...[In which] Others merely become the implements by which these impulses are served." (p.154)

[**Author's Note**: While the learnership practitioner is encouraged to continually develop his or her mental, emotional and physical capabilities through a lifetime of learning, adjustment and development; the learnership philosophy is a rejection of self-centered extremism characterized by the concept of "pastiche." Instead, coming to know and evolve our "better selves" consistent with the *universal goals and ideals* introduced in Chapter 1 of this book is what we seek to accomplish.]

3. Professional Presence. Professionals in all fields of endeavor are people who have built a personal and career *presence* that has aided in their development and success. The best practices in relating to others, and influencing those others to seek out personal and business relationships with these professionals have been amply documented. Because we, as learnership practitioners, may be knowledgeable and experienced in any academic discipline or career field, we are responsible to ensure our professional image and behavior is exemplary. Research has yielded two sources of good advice that are herewith identified and used to provide an overview of topics everyone should use to conduct a self-review of their personal professional presence. The sources are *Your Executive Image* (Victoria Seitz, 2000) and *5 Steps to Professional Presence* (Susan Bixler and Lisa Scherrer Dugan, 2001). Integrated excerpts are:

a. Image. "Our executive image is our total persona. Mastering it is like packaging a product...but one appropriate for our chosen profession." (Seitz) Areas for review and improvement include: good posture, pleasant facial expression, firm handshake, purposeful eye contact, appropriate dress, and awareness of personal space and positioning.

b. Communications (Verbal, Non-Verbal, Virtual). The sound of our voice and how we use it has significant impact. It can reveal what kind of person we are, warm and friendly or cold and distant. It can also excite or bore our audience." (Seitz) Areas for review and improvement include: choice of words, tone and volume, rate of speaking, and frequency of speaking. Important non-verbal communications include: appropriate use of gestures, supportive facial expression, and inclusive body positioning. And, good virtual communication includes the use of appropriate written products (letters, invitations, emails) and verbal tools (phone, email. conference calls).

c. Etiquette. "Genuine good manners and a working knowledge of professional behavior are essential and productive business skills. Good manners are a show of respect. They humanize and harmonize business relationships, and promote a powerful spirit of cooperation in our work environment." (Seitz) Areas to pay attention to are: introductions and greeting, table manners, gift giving, active listening, avoidance of smoking and excessive drinking, use of others' time and attention, background noise reduction, and avoidance of gossip and rumors.

Learnership is a capability integral to all other personal abilities: The thinking, learning, knowing, and leading *reasoning competencies* developed in Chapters 5 through 9 enable us to proactively influence our own *personal systems development* by their support to the health, character and ability subsystems described in this chapter. And, the learnership practitioner is the idealized representative of learnership in action.

Brain Learning and Change

Our ability to perform all human functions is based on the quantity and quality of our brains' capacity to sense, record, store, recall, reclaim and utilize the information and knowledge we have acquired. Virtually all the inputs our brains have received during and since birth have been recorded somewhere in our brains even if we are unaware as to the location. That which is first learned tends to set a baseline and framework for what comes later, but very often that which occurs later is most useful when it assists us in un-learning things of questionable accuracy so that more relevant education, skills and maturity may be attained later in life.

Figure 10-3 illustrates the psychological impact of *"significant emotional experiences"* (SEEs) that have the greatest influence and long-term impact on what we think, believe and say that "we know." Our challenge in *"lifelong learning and development"* is to regularly test the validity of our new learning against the accumulated knowledge from our past. As we continue to experience new impacts and influences we need to use our evolving intellectual and emotional capabilities to determine what we should replace and deactivate (Red) to be replaced by what we select and accentuate (Green). On Figure 10-3 we can see that as our brains gain greater capacity to serve us we should expect reduction in the past (Red) as the current (Green) helps us to *"change our minds."*

[**Author's Note**: As we know, however, there is very little stability in life over time. What was once new becomes "the old" only to be replaced again by the "current new." Normal human life grows exponentially in the early years but slows down as we accumulate huge volumes of more trustworthy information and knowledge. The paradox we need to accommodate is that as life appears to move faster and become more complex we must increase our energy and learning pace to stay up with our contemporaries and juniors.]

Personal Wealth and Financial Security (Observations and Recommendations)

As explained starting back in Chapter Two, our Personal (Family) System Development can be evaluated on how well we make progress on achieving our meta-level life goals – specifically, how well we contribute toward self-fulfilment, high performance, the common good and human enlightenment. However, all of these qualitative socio-economic measures are enabled by the productivity of our knowledge and skills in growing personal wealth and attaining financial security. Figure 10-4 is a comparative illustration of the major income and expenditure categories during a typical adult lifetime. Points for consideration are:

1. **Employment** – A lifetime of career work and development that provides the income necessary for expenditures. Primary approaches to save for future needs are pensions, IRAs, 401(k)s, and payroll taxes. Part time work is often considered to accumulate sufficient income even through the retirement years.

2. **College (Savings)** – Lifelong learning is essential for successful career growth and retirement. It is recommended that we save and pay for part of our own education. And then, if children are a responsibility, begin a 529 savings or other investment account for their education.

3. **Insurance (Family)** – Insurance is needed primarily for family health and financial security upon our own death, and should be term life only. Long term insurance is recommended for our retirement period when other income and assets are insufficient to pay for group residential expenses. Medicare is federal government health insurance assistance starting at age sixty-five after federal Social Security is being received.

4. **Homes (Equity)** – Saving early and purchasing a starter home with equity growth potential can start an advantageous series of sell and buy transactions ending in the ultimate purchase of a final home that can be paid off by the owner's retirement.

5. **Investment (Near Term)** – Either saving or near term investments (5-8 years) may be a good way to acquire the money needed for a large purchase such as a house down payment. If funds are available when getting close to retirement, that surplus can be transferred to increase the value of the retirement account.

6. **Investment (Retirement)** – In today's financial environment when so many are underfunded for their retirement years it advisable that retirement investments are begun much earlier in life than was previously recommended. Starting by age 30 – and concurrently with near term investments – would not be too soon.

7. **Estate Planning** – While having a written will is advisable as soon as one has assets that need to be distributed after death, one should not wait past their mid-life period (age 45-50) to prepare a more detailed expression of the their wishes once they have a family situation wherein accumulated money, physical assets and other personal matters

must assuredly be addressed. Professional estate planning is recommended to ensure legal and administrative processing is achieved.

8. **Consumption** – The amount of income allocated for all the above items still needs to be allotted in a manner that all weekly and monthly expenses can be comfortably accommodated. In reality, for most people their early life/family budgets are not sufficient and some serious trade-offs are required.

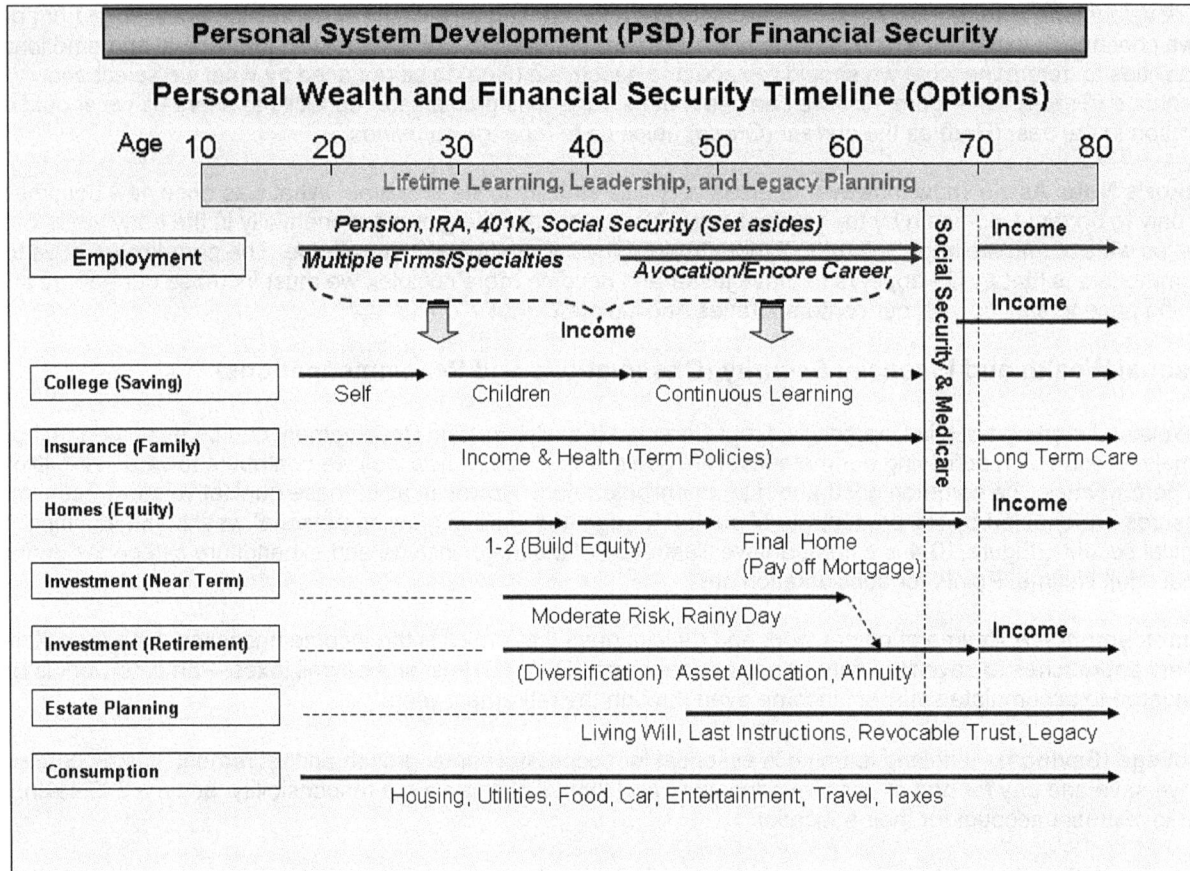

Personal System Development (PSD) for Financial Security

Personal Wealth and Financial Security Timeline (Options)

Figure 10-4

[**Author's Note:** Figure 10-4 is a notional reference model of the many areas each of us will need to engage during our financial management lives. The combination and degree of our incomes, interests, age and responsibilities will make certain areas more of a priority than others. The intent here is to understand the personal situations before us and to select an appropriate life wealth and financial security strategy that optimizes our future progress. Conversation with others in our class and personal networks should be informational, and seeking the guidance of local experts is certainly a smart option.

Going forward, a sample of expert observations and recommendations are provided to enrich our discussions in terms of this Handbook's informational structure. We suggest you purchase these books for detailed advice.]

1. ***A Guide to the New Rules of Personal Finance,*** Dave Kansas, 2011, The Wall Street Journal, Harper-Collins Publishers, New York, NY. To paraphrase a small sample of his thoughts:

a. Banks have been chastened and have to deal now with more stringent regulations. But they are aggressively arguing for their operational freedom – be careful with their new products and services.

b. The stimulus bill and healthcare bill have stabilized the economy and consumer demand but the costs, over time, have not been completely determined.

c. Thrift is getting more attention by businesses and consumers. Businesses are buying back own stock rather than offering new risky products, and consumers are delaying satisfaction to reduce personal risks which diminishes overall market demand. Saving to build a "rainy day fund" is gaining popularity.

d. Consumer loans should be limited to family *needs* not simply *likes* – and only for products that hold or increase their value over time. Avoid buying rapidly depreciating products.

e. Save and invest much earlier than in the past for long run needs such as *emergencies and retirement*. Never sacrifice one's own long term financial program for family short term needs. Use only low cost investment providers.

f. Use stock market investment for long run needs, but diversify as personal and market conditions change.

g. Delay taking Social Security payments past age 62 up to 70 to maximize retirement funding. Sign up for Medicare at age 65 or Medicaid when the conditions apply.

h. Consider annuities which include initial investments and guaranteed lifetime pay-outs during retirement. However, deal only with the highest rated organizations due to the complexity of these instruments and the many unscrupulous sales practices in this arena.

2. *The Money Class,* Suze Orman, 2011, Spiegel and Grau, Random House Publishing Group, New York, NY. To paraphrase a small sample of her thoughts:

a. We need to move beyond materialism to *actual happiness* in life. Put your finger on what is authentic to you.

b. Having lasting security requires standing in your own truth. Recognize, embrace and trust what is real for you and use that to *understand the choices you make and the real needs you have.*

c. Create *your own balance sheet.* Review your income and expenses. Get your FICO score. Balance your short term and long term needs and choose to live below your means.

d. Recognize the *power of cash.* Spend what you have today not what you hope to have in the future. Plan to have an eight month reserve for income emergencies. Get extra years out of cars, houses and appliances.

e. Use term insurance, not whole life insurance. Take advantage of all employer savings and investment benefits.

f. Always use Roth IRAs, federal loans not private loans for college loans. Do not co-sign loans, sacrifice retirement savings for others, and plan to create experiences for grandchildren rather that leave large cash inheritances.

g. Use estate planning in addition to a will to protect and allocate resources that remain after death. Consider the benefits of a "revocable living trust."

Conclusion

> *[If we] can include everything coherently and harmoniously in an overall whole*
> *that is undivided, unbroken, and without a border, then…from this will flow*
> *orderly action within the whole.* — *David Bohm*

Pursuing Self-Fulfillment. In closing this chapter on personal system development, it may be useful to recap the various aspects of cognition, emotion and behavior that contribute to our understanding the concept of self-fulfillment. It appears that our search for fulfillment progresses at an uneven pace along a maturity continuum containing stages of learning and development. We seek various forms of optimal experience and achievement, with the goal of becoming self-actualized (Maslow) and attaining a higher level-of-being (Schumacher, 1977). It is likely that as we pursue our objectives, we achieve temporary states and degrees of self-fulfillment; and that the greater the variety and intensity of our achievements over time, the greater our total sense of self-fulfillment in a life well-lived. Self-fulfillment has two major dimensions and may occur through participation in an experience (a process dimension) and/or by obtaining end results (an objective dimension). In either case, we experience a sense of accomplishment uniquely suited to our own needs, wants, and desires.

It is important to note, however, that our pursuit of self-fulfillment is inextricably linked to the social networks to which we belong. Through an iterative process of socialization and re-socialization within the community, each of us constructs our own reality, and therefore, our own personal meaning for fulfillment. In *The Social Construction of Reality* (Berger & Luckmann, 1967), the authors introduce the notion of two realities which we, the developing individuals, must consider and accommodate. One is termed the "objective reality" which is the social-structural nature of society as it exists outside the individual, and the other is the "subjective reality" which represents reality based on the our own perspectives and current level of learning. They state that "successful socialization…[is] the establishment of a high degree of symmetry between objective and subjective reality (as well as identity)," and that "*Identity* is a phenomenon that emerges from the dialectic between individual and society" (pp.173-174). The conclusion that may be drawn is that we are hardly ever isolated from the social effects of the community to which we belong, and we spend a good deal of time reconciling our respective views of reality, meaning, and identity. For this reason, self-fulfillment is better understood as a psycho-socially defined concept which leads to the establishment of a range of desirable experiences and objectives acceptable both to the community and to the majority of the community's members.

In terms of the ability, character, and health subsystems that shape our *personal system development*, it is reasonable to assume that each of us must participate in a dialectic that is specific to our learning and purpose. In each, there is need for us to define our current capabilities, estimate our potential capabilities, and develop strategies for closing the gap between the two. For the *ability subsystem*, we receive societal feedback that indicates a continuing need to increase our capacity to use physical and mental skills focused mostly on our technical, rather than human, interests. This is achieved through continuous career learning and skill improvement. For the *character subsystem,* we receive feedback on social relations that indicate a continuing need for increasing our capacity to conduct ourselves within accepted societal standards. And lastly, for the *health subsystem*, we receive health and safety information which may be used to assure the full utilization of our physical, emotional, and mental potential. Higher levels of personal development and self-fulfillment are obtainable when the three subsystems achieve a synergistic relationship. Optimization of the larger personal system is preferred over maximization of any of the individual subsystems, that is, it does us little good to become highly educated if we allow deterioration in our character and health subsystems.

Pursuing self-fulfillment can be a journey without end, a process of personal growth and development throughout our whole lifetime. For most of us, development occurs as the countervailing forces between stability and change, between individuality and community, and between differentiation and integration are rationalized allowing a socially acceptable self-image and sense of identity to emerge. In these situations, a high degree of maturation is attained which may be characterized as each of us developing a multidisciplinary understanding of our interdependence, generativity, authenticity, integrity, and an overall belief that we are connected to something larger and more important than ourselves. Within the context of this study, we might say that we have used meta-cognitive thinking to achieve a meta-system perspective in which the locus for reasoning and judgment is flexibly distributed across the personal, organizational, community, and societal systems of social activity. For the learnership practitioner, the personification of the learnership philosophy as an integral part of the personal micro-system should now be more clearly understood and appreciated.

Application of Learnership Reasoning Competencies. A fundamental goal of learnership is to enable most readers of the book to gain a fuller understanding of how their personal lives and careers are progressing in terms of the larger social systems of which they are a part. This book provides a beginning baseline for this assessment by presenting a philosophical viewpoint, an architectural framework, recommended practices, and a methodology for immersing the reader horizontally into numerous knowledge disciplines, while exposing them vertically into greater depth in topics they never knew they wanted to know more about. The long-term objective is for those individuals who desire to rapidly develop their skills in this arena—and to begin to train and consult with others—to become accomplished learnership practitioners. A little theory can go a long way once we start to appreciate the benefits of becoming holistic thinkers, lifelong learners, and adaptive leaders.

This section is presented at the end of each chapter on social system development (personal, organizational, community, and societal). A little effort is now required from readers desiring to exercise their evolving understanding of learnership. Your task: using Table 10-3 below and a separate piece of paper, write down some examples of how the five learnership competencies influence, drive, support, or otherwise have a powerful effect on the personal social system discussed in this chapter.

Reasoning Competency	Personal Social System
Systems Thinking	Impact on you?
Pattern Recognition	Impact on you?
Situational Learning	Impact on you?
Knowledge Management	Impact on you?
Adaptive Leadership	Impact on you?

Table 10-3

Implications for Integral Learning and Knowledge Management. We now arrive at the *social systems domain* where the result of our knowledge building, with the assistance of the five learnership reasoning competencies, may be reviewed. The major determination for **PSD** is whether the knowledge recently created is "relevant" to the inquiry, study, problem or issue being considered. *Quite often a paradox occurs* at this juncture in which the conclusion reached appears to be inconsistent, conflicting or incompatible with what the individuals involved anticipated or desired. When analyzed, questions arise as to whether the Systems Thinking, Pattern Recognition or Situational Learning competencies have been utilized in an open, factual, unbiased, timely and convincing manner. That is, is the knowledge really correct and integral when considering the obvious limitations in people's minds and personal preferences – and their cultures, education, and beliefs are sometimes entirely in conflict. Effective and valued knowledge will need to be judged by the *PSD Health, Character, and Ability* domains of thinking and behavior as interpreted by skilled and experienced leaders.

[**Author's Note**: *Are the knowledge and skills you have acquired and using so far in your life sufficient for you to achieve your current goals, a meaningful life and a memorable legacy?*]

Personal Reflection. This topic appears at the send of each chapter and is meant to serve two purposes: (1) be a reader's guide to main points and "takeaways," and (2) to encourage everyone to take a moment to engage their mental cognition and intuition on what the chapter means to them—especially at this time in their lives. Questions for chapter reflection follow immediately below; and for those readers inclined to maintain a self-assessment, your thoughts may be recorded in your *American Learnership for Life, Work, Wealth, Health and Legacy Success* which is located in at Appendix B.

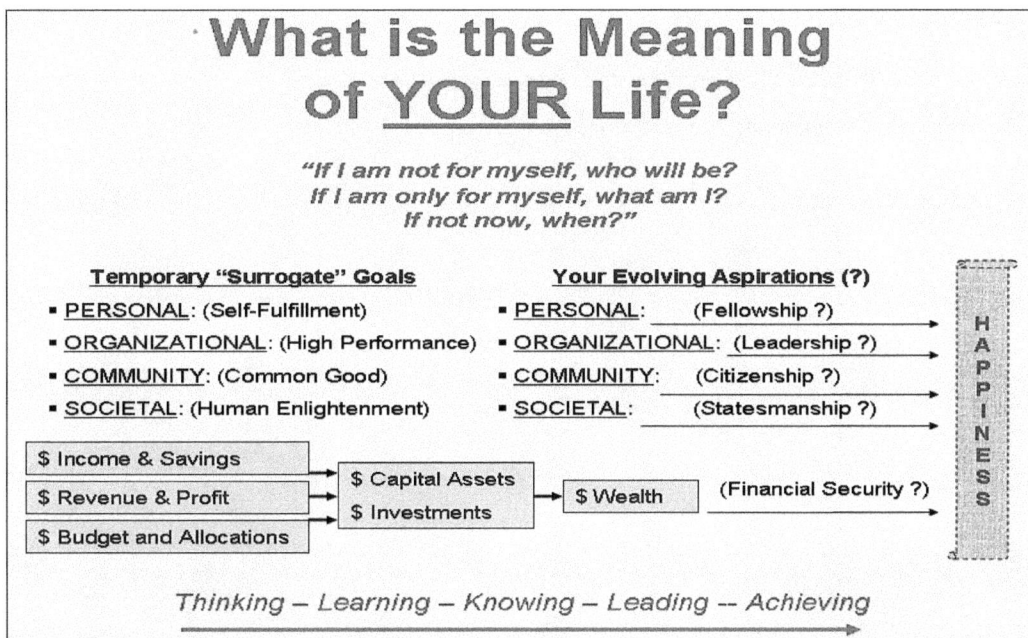

Figure 10-5

Questions on the Meaning of Your Life (Figure 10-5)

How do these surrogate goals work for you right now?

Can you venture a guess as to what might evolve as you continue to reflect and learn?

Questions for Discussion:

1. Where are you positioned in the Table 10-3 adult life cycle model? What influences are you experiencing that cause you to feel the need to change direction or build capability?

2. To what degree do you believe *good thinking* enables people to modify their behavior and better achieve their goals? Have you had such an experience?

3. The theory of *multiple intelligences* recognizes that there are many different ways for people to excel. What would be a lesson everyone could learn from knowing this?

4. What are the similarities and differences between *soft reasoning* and *hard reasoning*?

5. Can you list two to three major learning points from this chapter that you want to keep in mind to improve your ability to manage your life and career?

6. Can you identify two to three topics, models, or perspectives in this chapter you would like to learn more about?

7. Should you be making an entry into your *American for Life, Work, Wealth, Health and Legacy Success* at this time at Appendix B?

Insights, Commitments and Skills

If you plan to participate in the *American Learnership for Life, Work, Wealth, Health and Legacy Success* self-development e-book experience, it is suggested you record your Insights, commitments and skills to be developed here in this chapter, and again in Appendix B:

My learning in terms of new insights, changing priorities, new commitments or skills I want to acquire:

1. Insights (Example): Remind myself that ...

2. Commitments (Example): Continue to ask myself ...

3. Skills (Example): Apply my knowledge and skills to ...

Chapter Eleven

Organizational (Macro) System Development

Complexity thinking suggests that leaders and knowledge workers should take a new perspective on their organizations, develop new competencies, and take different action to create and maintain high-performing organizations.— Alex and David Bennett

Major Chapter Topics

- **Overview: Organizational System Development (OSD) 2397**
  Organizational System Development (OSD)
  Macro-Cognitive Reasoning
  Organization Direction Subsystem
  Organization Operations Subsystem
  Organization Performance Subsystem
  Macro-System Development
  Information Processing Model
  Achieving High Performance
  Competing for the Future
  Enterprise of the Future
  Complex Adaptive Systems
  Intelligent Organizations
  Phases of Organizational Growth

- **Organization Direction 244**
  Overview: Transformation Leadership
  National Baldrige Award Criteria
  Change Management Criteria
  Knowledge-Enabled Organizational Improvement
  Organizational Leadership
  A Contingency Approach to Leadership
  Learning from Experience
  Strategic Management and Planning
  Organization Development and Change
  Corporate Culture and Character

- **Organization Operations 249**
  Overview: Process Transformation
  Total Quality Management
  Business Process Reengineering
  Process Transformation
  Organizational White Space (Systems Management)
  Benchmarking Company Performance

- **Overview: Workforce Transformation 254**
  Workplace Learners
  Federal Human Capital Development
  Software Competency Development
  Workplace Competencies
  Self-Initiated Followership
  Employee Involvement and Teamwork

- **Overview: Decision-Making 260**
  Rational Thinking and Management
  Managing Our Minds
  A Role for Intuition and Emotion
  Making Better Decisions
  Ethical Business Decisions

Organizational (Macro) System Development

Overview: Organizational System Development (OSD)

This Life Management Handbook chapter contains a broad overview of insights and perspectives designed to assist the reader in learning to think holistically about his or her organizational responsibilities and contributions. Specialists will learn to see the larger, enterprise level complexity of which they are an important part. Leaders and managers will come to understand their roles more clearly and gain new perspectives leading to opportunities for systematic innovation. Learnership practitioners, in particular, will learn to grasp the comprehensive array of managerial topics and techniques relevant to their roles as adaptive leaders, workgroup facilitators, and project managers.

Organizational System Development (OSD). OSD concerns the long-term development of organizations and enterprises. And, for the learnership practitioner, it represents the integrated *learning* and *leading* required from teams, groups, and other social entities that exist within and external to the organization itself. The goal of high performance satisfies the ontological need for a "sense of purpose", and is best attained through interdependent understanding and growth in the organization's strategic direction, operations, and performance subsystems. Figure 11-1 provides an overview of key concepts and relationships to assist the reader in building an OSD mental model as he or she proceeds through this chapter. These major features are:

1. Macro-Cognitive Reasoning. Illustrates the *four social systems* with this chapter's emphasis being at the organizational macro-level

2. Organization Direction Subsystem. The *organization direction* subsystem highlights executive level effort in the areas of leadership support, strategic alignment, structural organization, and cultural cohesion

3. Organization Operations Subsystem. The *organization operations* subsystem concerns how work is accomplished by focusing on workforce development, process development, technology utilization, and decision making.

4. Organization Performance Subsystem. The *organization performance* subsystem provides information on measurement data, customer satisfaction, and business/mission results.

5. Macro-System Development. Illustrates the *five reasoning competencies* that can be used to maximize organizational social system development

6. Information Processing Model. Illustrates a general approach to problem solving and decision-making throughout the organization: Gather and analyze information, develop a strategy and implement it, observe results and take corrective action, if require

[**Author's Note**: A significant point to make at this juncture is that during Part Two (Chapters 5 through 9) the Five Learnership Reasoning Competencies have been integrated into a comprehensive *Total Knowledge Management (TKM) Social Systems Framework*. That "total learning, knowing, and leading" framework has been embedded in the *Learnership Integrated Systems Architecture (LISA)* and that all the principles, practices, and technologies of TKM are conceptually available, and should be appropriately applied, for full organizational social systems development.]

Achieving High Performance. Ideally, the three subsystems operate over time in a mutually reinforcing manner enabling individuals and the organization itself to learn and take action consistent with its purpose and strategy. When this occurs, it can be said that the organization has optimized its capabilities and has achieved a *high performance* end state. High performance is used herein to represent the synergy that occurs when organizational performance measures indicate desired levels of operational efficiency, and effectiveness measures e.g., customer satisfaction, and business or mission results are at all-time highs.

Competing for the Future. Authors Gary Hamel and C.K. Prahalad's book on *Competing for the Future* (1994) sets the standard for managing modern corporations aggressively. The authors take inventory of the past and current industry leaders, the major management initiatives being employed, and the marketplace performance being achieved. They view the traditional efforts at organizational improvement in a rather placid manner (the price of near-term sustainability), and they regard creating new markets and customer niches as the route to increased profitability and continued market presence and viability.

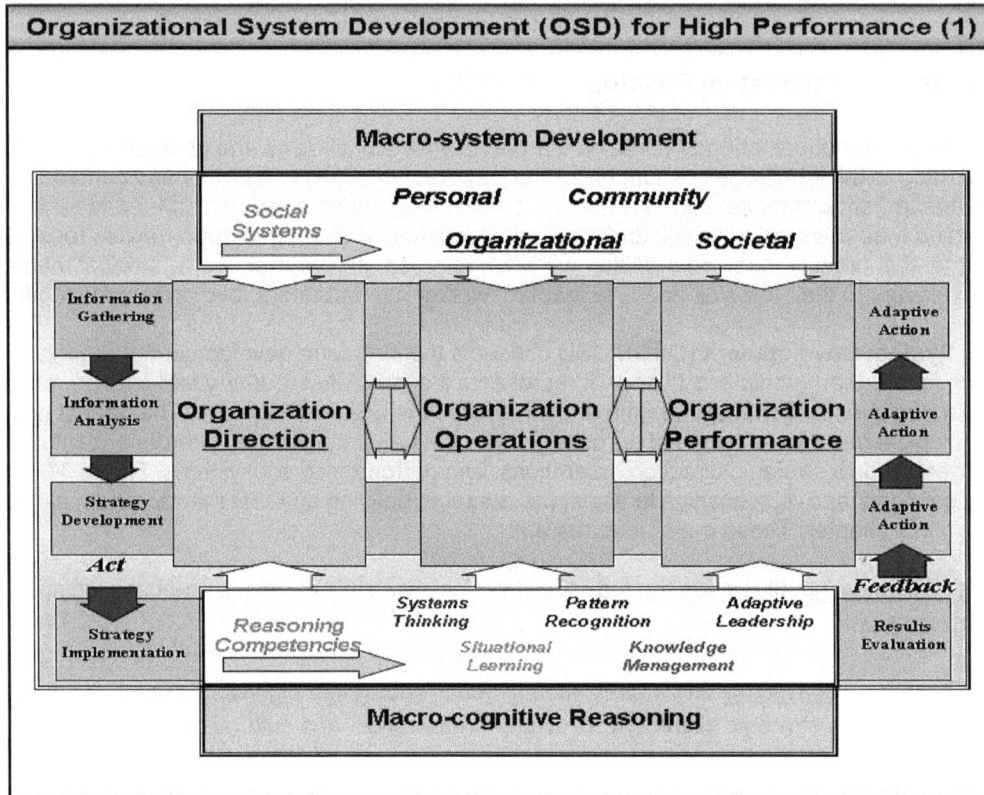

Figure 11-1

They comment that many of the market leaders of the past have faded from the scene, and that their replacements have become dominant due to their creativity, ability to reframe their industries, and willingness to forget much of their past thinking and establish new strategic architectures with the intuition to reach beyond traditional customer needs and management practices. A couple of examples of the new management thinking and areas for future focus follow (excerpt, pp.2-3). A lack of equal attention to (b) as to (a) indicates a lack of preparedness the future.

1. How does senior management's point of view about the future stack up against that of competitors? (a) Conventional/Reactive, or (b) Distinctive/Far-Sighted

2. Which issue is absorbing more of senior management's attention? (a) Reengineering Core Processes, or (b) Regenerating Core Strategies

3. What percentage of our advantage-building efforts focus on catching up with competitors versus building new advantages new to the industry? (a) Mostly Catching Up to Competitors, or (b) Mostly New to the Industry

4. To what extent am I, as a senior manager, a maintenance engineer working on the present or an architect designing the future? (a) Mostly an Engineer, (b) Mostly an Architect

Another way of assessing an organization's readiness for the future is to consider whether too much effort is on today's immediate business needs as compared to 5-10 years out in the future. For example, in comparison to today's concern and focus, have the following questions received adequate attention by management? (Excerpt, pp.16-17)

1. Which customers are you serving *in the future?*
2. Through what channels will you reach customers *in the future?*
3. Who will your competitors be *in the future?*
4. What will be the basis for your competitive advantage *in the future?*
5. What skills or capabilities will make you unique *in the future?*

Hamel and Pralahad's use of trend data and insight into developing markets is a compelling call-to-action for anyone still in early to mid-career level employment. They address such topics such as:

1. Crafting a strategic architecture
2. Strategy as leverage
3. Shaping the future
4. Building core competence
5. Thinking differently–all focused on preparing for the workplace and market-space of the near future.

Even those later in their careers and wishing to remain knowledgeable and involved—and maybe put retirement off for a while might want to make the necessary adjustments.

Enterprise of the Future. In their article: *Building the Enterprise of the Future* (2006), Arthur Murray and Kent Greenes researchers at The George Washington University, Institute for Knowledge and Innovation comment: "Whether public sector, private industry, or non-profit association, all organizations are facing an ever-increasing number of challenges. Some of the more serious of these challenges are: expanding globalization; intellectual property theft/piracy; proliferation of open sources software; massive disintermediation; compressed cycle times; increasingly mobile and less loyal knowledge workers; growing complexity; disastrous consequences of poor decisions; pressure to do more with less; pricing power erosion; reduced barriers to entry for competitors; shifting workforce and consumer demographics/preferences; and low knowledge worker productivity." (p.39) The authors argue that to overcome these challenges will require increased rates of workforce learning, innovation, and transformation entailing significant attention to four areas business:

1. Business Renewal. "By business renewal we mean completely rethinking strategy in order to achieve high performance in a flat world (Thomas Friedman, 2005). In other words, co-creating entirely new business ecosystems" (p.39)

2. New Organizational Designs. Industrial age, even information age, organizational structures are inadequate for achieving high performance in a flat world. Hierarchies and matrices need to be replaced by fluid, agile, social networks and communities." (p.39)

3. Enterprise Infrastructure Nexus. Despite the widespread adoption of enterprise software and the like, the level of integration needed for high-speed, anticipatory planning and response in complex, rapidly changing environments has not been reached." (p.40)

4. High Performance Transformation. We recognize as a key driving force the notion of shifting organizations from the mindset of "make and sell" to "sense and respond." (Haeckel, 1999). Learning, innovating and transforming at the speed of change requires rethinking of the whole notion of enterprise." (p.40)

Murray and Greenes take the view that knowledge worker performance will be a defining factor in these future enterprises, and that attracting, retaining, and developing these knowledge workers will be a critical success factors. They say that: "Knowledge workers must have one seamless environment for managing individual and organizational knowledge, and enhancing productivity." (p.40)

Complex Adaptive Systems. In their book *Organizational Survival in the New World* (2004), Alex and David Bennett comment that "Many current top organizations have made changes in the way they do business in the past decade and have been able to create performance through change management and deliberately develop the fundamental characteristics that support success." And, "Creativity and innovation have come to the forefront as key success factors with many organizations striving to develop and unleash these capabilities throughout their workforce, using a combination of management, the workforce, and their customers." (p.7) The spirit of this book on learnership is to support and confirm the viewpoint of the Bennett, and to go beyond their explanations by highlighting the perspectives and techniques that make working in this new world a practical accomplishment. The Bennetts introduce the concept of the *Intelligent Complex Adaptive System (ICAS)* which integrates much of the literature on dealing with organizational complexity in a manner that illustrates a number of emergent organizational properties occurring within a rapidly changing environmental context. Their effort is an innovative accomplishment given the level of intellectual reflection required to understand and ameliorate general confusion concerning creating organizational alignment and spirit de corps amid organizational downsizing and outsourcing.

The Bennetts comment that an ICAS is an enterprise in which "...*organizational intelligence is taken to be the ability of an organization to perceive, interpret, and respond to its environment in a manner that simultaneously meets its organizational goals while satisfying its stakeholders, that is, its employees, customers, investors, community, and environment...the organization's capacity to exhibit intelligent behavior.*" In their description, the authors state that the reality of organizational life today is constant and rapid *change*, high levels of *uncertainty*, and pervasive *complexity*. The way to deal with this unrelenting situation is to understand and balance the "emergent characteristics of the evolving ICAS." (pp.30-31) The eight characteristics they identify and link into an operating model are:

1. Organizational Intelligence. As defined, above. This capability results from the inter-action and mutual support among the other seven characteristics.

2. Shared Purpose. The coordination and unification of resources to gain maximum situational understanding, operational knowledge and innovative opportunity

3. Optimum Complexity. Ability to achieve coherence between organizational elements desiring maximum independence and those organizational functions requiring synchronized alignment of intent and use of resources.

4. Multidimensionality. Development of competencies in the use of a variety of thinking styles, perspectives, and methods to address issues and problems.

5. Knowledge-Centricity. The aggregation of critical data, information, and knowledge that informs strategic direction and action

6. Selectivity. An ability to determine patterns of information and to filter out those of particular interest and utility

7. Flow. Flow enables knowledge-centricity in that it accommodates the movement of people and information into and out of the enterprise to provide maximum access for thinking and decision-making.

8. Permeable Boundaries. In virtual, porous organization environments, the flow of information and intelligence crosses boundaries with little or no delay or resistance.

The dynamic Intelligent Complex Adaptive System the Bennetts describe requires continuous scanning of the organization's external environment so as to be aware of and act on emerging threats and opportunities. The primary ways that organizations prepare for and take action for survival and prosperity are to employ creativity, problem-solving, decision-making, and action implementation–proactively.

[**Author's Note**: The five reasoning competencies developed and advocated in this book: *systems thinking, pattern recognition, situational learning, knowledge management, and adaptive leadership*, are likely to be right at home when used in the ICAS.]

Intelligent Organizations. In *The End of Bureaucracy and the Rise of the Intelligent Organization* (1993) (Pinchot & Pinchot), the authors describe the changing nature of work which requires a revolutionary change in the structure of contemporary organizations. Whereas bureaucracy once provided the stability and control necessary for effective and efficient operations, the need is for a less hierarchical, more flexible structure to accommodate the complexity and pace in today's marketplace. Major changes include moving away from work that is unskilled, repetitive, individual, functional, and single skilled, to work that requires greater knowledge, innovation, teamwork, project focus, and multiple skills. The power of bosses and coordination from above is being replaced with the power of customers and coordination among peers and colleagues.

According to Gifford and Elizabeth Pinchot, organizations (and their members) must be able to learn efficiently what needs to be done and how to take action most effectively. They provide a thought-provoking delineation of the seven necessary conditions for organizational intelligence based on the perennial social paradox of trying to balance individual *rights* and *responsibilities*. Three of the conditions are grouped under a category entitled Freedom of Choice (herein considered to be *rights*). The right to have freedom of choice refers to the basic human need to be self-directed, and to choose one's own approaches to reasoning, learning, and action. The following organizational principles are indicated:

1. Widespread Truth and Rights. Well informed teams of people need accurate, timely information on customer needs, financial results, new product development, organization strategies and a host of other operational details to correctly assess situations and take action.

2. Freedom of Enterprise. Freedom of action is needed for knowledgeable teams to take those steps indicated by their information and analysis of situations. The focus should be on the customer, and the legitimacy of action comes from them, rather than the welfare of the bosses.

3. Liberated Teams. Teams need to learn and take action through knowledge-based collaboration which is embedded in shared mission, vision, and values. Self-responsibility and management are essential for this to be accomplished necessitating a reduction in bureaucratic direction and control.

Another three conditions are grouped under a category entitled "Responsibility for the Whole" (herein referred to as *responsibilities*). These conditions concern the need for people to connect, collaborate, and give each other support—to operate as a community in which the community's needs are sometimes superior to those of the community's members. The organizational principles include:

4. Equality and Diversity. Individual members of the organization are required to treat all others with equal respect as to essential human rights and privileges. Opportunity for learning and development should be provided to all members to improve their team contribution and performance.

5. Voluntary Learning Networks. The power to decide should be distributed so that all individuals and teams may pursue network building for purposes of learning and taking action in the areas for which they are responsible. A continually changing network of connections is anticipated as situational needs change.

6. Democratic Self-Rule. Participative democracy rather than representative democracy is indicated which provides for full rights and responsibilities for all individuals and teams. A fully participative organization provides the means for self-management.

Lastly, 7. Limited Corporate Government as a condition for organizational intelligence. This condition applies to the superstructure under which the first six conditions are framed. The Pinchots state that: "…the role of the center [corporate government] is to create the conditions that empower others to build effective intraprises" (p.73). Centrally established rules and procedures should be kept to a minimum to insure safe, efficient, and externally compliant operations. This would allow organization teams the maximum flexibility in internal operations and encourage self-management. The goal should be to enhance freedom and community and displace bureaucracy and hierarchy to the largest degree possible.

[**Author's Note**: This perspective contributes insight into the learning anchor. In order for an organization to be high-performing in terms of its customers' needs and expectations, it must continue to learn and increase its store of knowledge. It must maintain a rate of development that equals or exceeds that of its competitors if it is to remain effective. Achieving this capability requires balance in the manner in which the organization operates. Individual and team rights and responsibilities must be emphasized in a democratically managed environment to assure both personal (PSD) and organizational (OSD) growth and development.]

Phases of Organizational Growth. In *Evolution and Revolution as Organizations Grow* (Greiner, HBR, Sep 22, 2007), the author presents a social-systems-development model which suggests five phases of organizational growth. The model's horizontal axis depicts the age of the organization (young to old), while its vertical axis depicts the size of the organization (small to large) yielding a growth curve illustrating alternate periods of evolution and revolution. The overview of each phase is as follows:

Phase 1: Organization is Young and Small. Focus is on the technical, not the managerial aspects of the organization. This is the phase of evolutionary *growth through creativity* followed by a *leadership crisis* and a revolution leading to the next phase.

Phase 2: Organization a Bit Older and Larger. Focus is on leadership and organization direction and management. This is the phase of *directed* evolutionary *growth* followed by an *autonomy crisis* and a revolution leading to the next phase.

Phase 3: Organization is Much Older and Larger. Focus is on loosening the reins and empowering employees for greater performance. This is the phase of *growth through delegation* followed by a *crisis of control* and a revolution leading to the next phase.

<u>Phase 4</u>: Organization is Much Older and Larger. Focus is on work unit result, but organization size and complexity creates inefficiency and frustration. Focus is on *growth through coordination* followed by a *bureaucracy crisis* and a revolution to the next phase.

<u>Phase 5</u>: Organization at Highest Maturity and Very Large. Focus is on organization participation through employee development, teamwork, and other behavioral-oriented techniques. Focus is on *growth through collaboration* followed by (perhaps) a *psychological saturation crisis* leading to an undefined revolution.

Greiner suggests that each phase of growth presents a unique development challenge and requires a particular approach to management; and that the actions taken by management affect the direction and rate of organization growth.

[**Author's Note**: An observation here is that organizational system development may be aided or constrained by management's capacity to learn of emerging structural and social tension and take appropriate action.]

Organization Direction

> *It is only in respect to knowledge that a business can be distinct; and can produce something that has value in the marketplace.* — Peter Drucker

Overview: Transformation Leadership

National Baldrige Award Criteria. The development of the NIST Baldrige National Quality Award program early in the 1990s led to over 15 years of successful evaluation, recognition, and reward of U.S. organizations that have developed exceptional performance practices in the areas of business, health care, education, and not-for-profit services. During that time variations of the same seven criteria have been used which is testimony to their organizational importance and acceptance by knowledgeable professionals in the participating industries. These criteria are:

1. <u>Leadership</u>. How the organization's senior leaders address organizational values, direction, and performance expectations.

2. <u>Strategic Planning</u>. How the organization develops strategic objectives and action plans.

3. <u>Human Resource Development</u>. How the entire workforce is enabled to develop their full potential.

4. <u>Process Management</u>. How the organization systematically examines its processes for continuous improvement of quality and operational performance.

5. <u>Information and Analysis</u>. How the organization examines the scope, management, and use of data and information; and how that information drives operational performance.

6. <u>Business Results</u>. How well does the organization achieve and improve on its market and financial performance.

7. <u>Customer Satisfaction</u>. How well does the organization know its customer's requirements, and to what extent does it develop relationships with its customers.

Change Management Criteria. Since the 1980s various forms of organizational change methodologies have been developed and used. One of the most comprehensive was advocated by leaders at Massachusetts Institute of Technology; and subsequently applied in a number of variations by businesses and consulting firms since that time. The theory is that all six of the following criteria need to be addressed when building a full scale organizational change management program.

1. <u>Leadership</u>. Executive and middle management communications and support for activities and projects designed to change what work is done and how it is accomplished.

2. <u>Structure</u>. Organizational design and functional changes in how the organization arranges itself in terms of responsibilities, authorities, locations, and resource management

3. Culture. How the organization intends to change and/or modify its basic operating assumptions, work relationships, and workforce usage.

4. Process. How workflow is accomplished within and across organizational functions and boundaries.

5. People. The organizational workforce: its knowledge, skills, abilities; remuneration and work methods; management and employee expectations and relationships.

6. Technology. The tools and information technology used to expedite communications, workforce collaboration, and work process management

Knowledge-Enabled Organizational Improvement. The Knowledge Management discipline received a significant boost when in 2003 The George Washington University initiated a KM curriculum under the auspices of its Department of Engineering Management. The George Washington University curriculum for Knowledge Management includes an introductory KM course, four core courses in organizational leadership, organizational learning, organizational operations, and information technology; and a seminar in KM systems engineering and management. The program, recognized internationally as one of the leading programs in KM, is available to students seeking a certificate in KM and those wishing to make KM a major for their masters or doctorate programs in engineering management.

In 2004, this author established a comprehensive organizational assessment tool by integrating the Baldrige Award Criteria, MIT Change Management Criteria, and GWU Knowledge Management Education criteria into an *Enterprise Systems Excellence Model (ESEM)*. This Model has subsequently been used by GWU students and private consultants to conduct assessments of public and private organizations with very satisfactory results. Two additions were made to the criteria to ensure a more comprehensive analysis could be conducted. One was to establish a *decision-making criterion* to ensure the organization made timely and accurate use of the information they generated and received concerning their current levels of performance, and the second was to include a *learning and knowledge management criterion* to reflect the ubiquitous impact learning and knowledge have on the other criteria. An illustration of the ESEM criteria and their supporting relationships is at Figure 11-2, OSD for High Performance.

[**Author's Note**: The twelve criteria shown in Figure 11-2 are believed to be one of the most comprehensive set of topics by which organizations may be evaluated for use of best management practices, and for the achievement of high levels of management performance. They can be used for independent assessment of performance such as with the Baldrige Program, or they can be used, as appropriate, as part of an organizational change management strategy. In either case, they are knowledge-enabled through the use of KM practices and technologies which make them more integrative and broad-based than most similar techniques.

Organizational Leadership. In *Managing for the Future* (Drucker, 1992), the author recounts the Japanese view that there are only two demands of leadership: One is to accept that rank does not confer privileges; it entails responsibilities. The other is to acknowledge that leaders in an organization need to impose on themselves the responsibility for congruence—between deeds and words, between behavior and professed beliefs and values—that which we call personal integrity (pp.116-117).

Drucker builds on this point by stating that what distinguishes the leader from the misleader is: (1) his goals and standards—does he hold to them fairly well for the benefit of the organization while experiencing the constraints of reality? (2) his willingness to be ultimately responsible– does he accept the inevitability that things often go wrong in organizations and resist blaming others? (3) his comfort with strong associates and subordinates—does he encourage them and participate in their success? (4) his trustworthiness—does he earns others' respect through his integrity and consistent behavior? (pp.121-122). This viewpoint focuses on the importance of instituting a sense of purpose, responsibility, order, and integrity in the organization—an ontological infrastructure upon which operational processes and activities may be based.

Another perspective on modern leadership is offered in *The Leadership Challenge* (Kouzes & Posner, 1987) in which the authors include a comment by news commentator Edward R. Murrow on what followers want from their leaders: "To be persuasive we must be believable; to be believable we must be credible; to be credible, we must be truthful." From this they build the case for the following behavioral commitments from leaders:

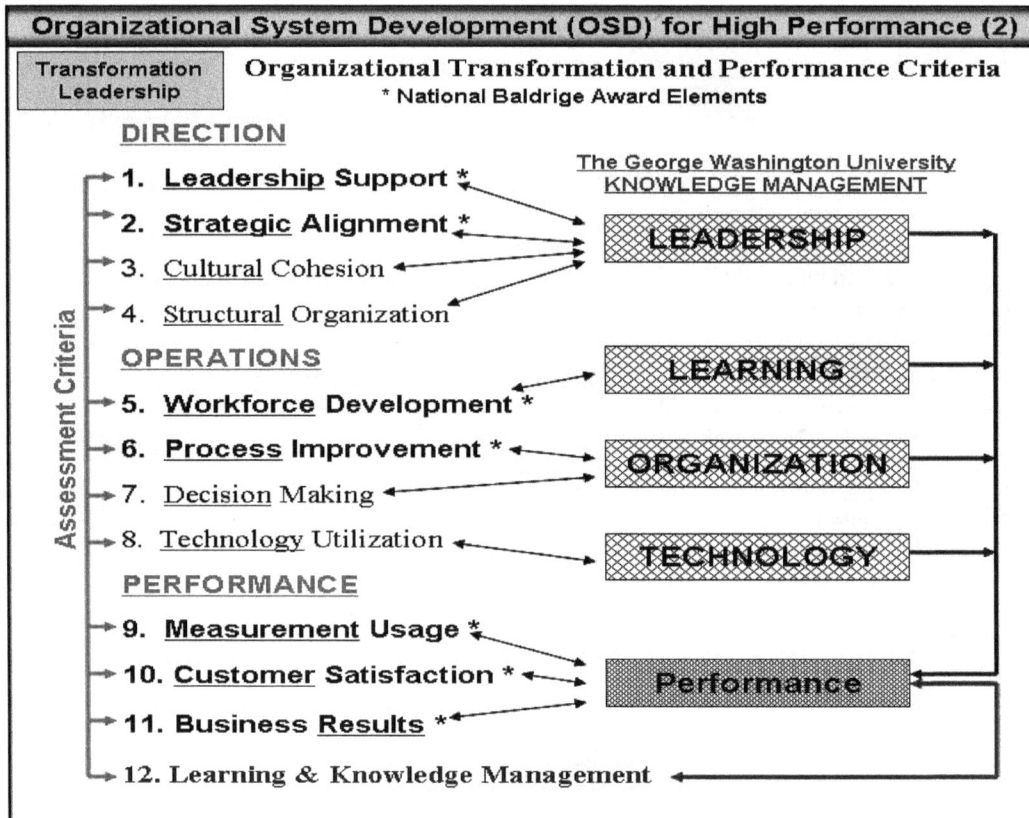

Figure 11-2

1. Challenging the Process. Search for opportunities, experiment, and take risks

2. Inspiring a Shared Vision. Envision the future and enlist others

3. Enabling Others to Act. Foster collaboration and strengthen others

4. Modeling the Way. Set the example and plan small wins

5. Encouraging the Heart. Recognize individual contributions and celebrate accomplishments.

The view here is one of leader pro-activity in which cognitive and affective engagement of others in the business or organization leads to greater inquiry, learning, and collaborative decision-making to improve processes and achieve better quality and operational results.

From a learnership perspective, leaders have a primary responsibility in establishing the vision, mission, values, strategies, and motivation to move the organization forward. Without their customer focus, strategic insight, organizational understanding, and personal commitment and integrity, the organization's human resources and operational processes may tend towards fragmentation because of insufficient alignment and cohesion. When leaders emphasize customer satisfaction, and support the workforce in learning how to better serve their customers, individual and organizational learning is encouraged which results in business process improvement, higher organizational performance, and greater customer satisfaction.

[**Author's Note**: In terms of the learnership organization systems construct, the social subsystem conveys the leader-follower relationship required for communication and coordination of the organization's strategic and operational capabilities. Leadership may be thought of as the social catalyst that creates future vision, fosters organizational dialogue, and forges participative strategies for organization high performance and customer satisfaction.]

A Contingency Approach to Leadership. In his book entitled *Management* (Stoner, 1982), the author comments on research for leadership effectiveness and says that: "...effective leadership seemed to depend on a number of variables, such as organizational climate, the nature of the tasks and work activities, and managerial values and experience. No one trait was common to all effective leaders; no one style was effective in all situations" (p.477). Apparently, the dynamic and fluid set of circumstances that surround organization decision makers prohibit a one-approach-fits-all approach to management. The leader's personality, past experience, and expectations; the expectations and behavior of his or her superior; and the subordinates' characteristics, expectations, and behavior are all important factors that frame the decision environment and must be accounted for if the decision requires others' action and support. A contingency approach to leadership requires that relevant factors be weighted in terms of organizational objectives and that a leadership style best suited to effective action be chosen. This leadership strategy requires flexibility in reasoning and action on the part of the leader, and the capability to adjust his or her perception and understanding of the decision environment. The more knowledgeable, experienced, and skilled leaders are thought to be more perceptive, open, and proactive in moving their agenda forward amid prevailing obstacles, complexity, and ambiguity.

Particularly noteworthy is the work of Hersey and Blanchard in suggesting *The Life Cycle Theory of Leadership* (Hersey & Blanchard, 1979). They hold that the appropriate style of leadership employed should be determined by the leader's perception of a subordinate's *maturity*, which in turn is a measure of his or her:

1. Desire for achievement

2. Willingness to accept responsibility

3. Task-related ability and experience.

The leader-subordinate relationship in their model is offered as a developmental strategy that correlates well with other theories of human psycho-social learning and development. Their model relates two dimensions of leader behavior (task behavior and relationship behavior) to derive a two-by-two matrix that illustrate four potentially effective leadership styles. These are:

1. High Task, Low Relationship. Appropriate when the subordinate is new, inexperienced, or not motivated. The perceived level of maturity is low.

2. High Task, High relationship. Appropriate when the subordinate somewhat more experienced and better motivated. The perceived level of maturity is moderate.

3. Low Task, High Relationship. Appropriate when the subordinate is experienced and motivated, and desires to participate in decision making in matters that concern his or her work. The perceived level of maturity is high organizational maturity.

4. Low Task, Low Relationship. Appropriate when the subordinate becomes a competent, confident, and highly motivated contributor.

[**Author's Note**: The applicability of these perspectives to the learnership Organization Systems Development construct is seen in the learning that both leader and subordinate experience as shared perspectives and increased performance develop. A transformation from dependence, through independence, to interdependence may be theorized—with all the attendant aspects of ego development presented earlier in the inquiries on Personal System Development. A reasonable expectation might be that improving the effectiveness of leader-subordinate relationships would improve the efficiency of organization operations and increase customer satisfaction.

Learning from Experience. In *The Lessons of Experience: How Successful Executives Develop on the Job* (McCall et al, 1988), the authors report on their research on the kind of experiences that have the greatest impact in developing competent general managers. The purpose served by this reference, in the context of this book, is to illustrate the essentiality of experiential learning for the development of managers—and for that matter, all members of the organization. Classroom and textbook learning are not sufficient methodologies for helping employees to develop the confidence and competence required for reliable and high levels of performance of their organization responsibilities. McCall et al. report that the managers they studied experienced a variety of *assignments* (learned: confidence, independence, knowledge, relationships, and toughness), *bosses* (learned: values and politics), and *hardships* (learned: humility and perspective) that led to thirty-two lessons in five major areas of development. The developmental areas are:

1. Setting and Implementing Agendas. Thinking broadly, accepting responsibility, and finding alternative ways to accomplish desired outcomes.

2. Handling Relationships. Developing a variety of interpersonal skills appropriate to the variety in the types of people and situations faced.

3. Basic Values: Accommodating established organization values that play out in organizational situations.

4. Executive Temperament: Coping with the demands and ambiguities of executive jobs through flexibility and adaptation.

5. Personal Awareness. Becoming self-aware and knowing one's strengths and weaknesses.

The advice given by experienced managers for others' development include: "Take advantage of opportunities, aggressively search for meaning, and know yourself," and "Ultimately we each are responsible for our own development...development boils down to the same 'do it, fix it, try it' philosophy found in excellent companies" (pp.123-124).

McCall et al. recognize the contradictory and paradoxical nature of organizational life and managerial responsibility, and emphasize the *need to achieve balance*. Examples provided (p.144) include:

1. Acting alone *and* working with others

2. Making tough decisions *and* treating people with compassion

3. Having the confidence to act *and* the humility to know there are other views

4. Seizing opportunities *and* planning for the future

5. Taking control *and* accepting the inevitable

6. Persevering in the face of adversity, *yet* changing direction when wrong.

An observation within the context of this study is that while the examples given above are meant to be specific to the management function, it may clearly be seen that most employees in the workforce are also challenged to achieve a similar state of balance in terms of performing their respective functions, and in maintaining cohesive interpersonal relationships.

[**Author's Note**: The importance of this experiential learning perspective in terms of the learnership OSD construct may be understood by recognizing that it is through daily, practical, personal and organizational experience that situational learning occurs. And, that situational learning is the foundation for OSD organizational subsystem (Direction, Operations, Performance) development.]

Strategic Management and Planning. Effective long-term survivability and prosperity for private and public sector organizations is significantly dependent on their respective capacities to discern future opportunities and threats and to develop strategies to succeed. In their book *Thinking Strategically: A Primer for Public Leaders* (Walter & Choate, 1984), the authors state that strategic management is equally important to private and public sector organizations and would include: " (1) a systematic analysis of pivotal long-term trends and issues, and (2) a comprehensive analysis of the institution's capacity to respond to those trends." An effective framework would include the use of foresight, goal setting, strategic planning, operational management, and evaluation of performance. A complementary viewpoint is offered in *Applied Strategic Planning* (Goodstein et al., 1992) in which the authors emphasize the need for organizations to conduct values scans, performance audits, and gap analysis in order to establish meaningful action plans and implementation strategies.

Implicit in these management recommendations is the need for organizations to learn about their external environments and to conduct evaluations of their capacities to respond to market pressures and customer needs. It is clear that strategic management contains elements of continuous learning and process improvement which are at the core of quality management.

[**Author's Note**: Once again, learning emerges as an underlying factor in achieving customer satisfaction, and this occurs within the ontological web of purpose, history, order, and consequences that provides the organization its sense of identity and faith.]

Organization Development and Change. In *Organization Development and Change* (Cummings & Huse, 1989), the authors define Organization Development (OD) as "a systematic application of behavioral science knowledge to the planned development and reinforcement of organizational strategies, structures, and processes for improving an organization's effectiveness." OD efforts begin with the assumption that the organization can learn to improve its ability to solve its own problems and take better advantage of available opportunities. The objective is to increase the organization's capacity to perform and to improve the quality and desirability of its products and services. Any organization subsystem: strategic, operations, or performance may be the focus of the improvement effort, however, interpersonal and team effectiveness (social subsystem) is usually part of most problems, and therefore, part of their solution. The typical OD practitioner is an external consultant or internal manager/specialist who knows how to frame organizational issues, structure data gathering and analysis, and assist management in making appropriate decisions. The process used is sometimes referred to as "action research" which connotes the idea of linking research closely to action when the objective is to effect near-term organizational change.

Today's organization's continued interest is in some aspects of quality management—and now focused on organizational learning, may be considered an elaboration on the organizational development methodologies that experienced acceptance in the 1970s and 1980s. What quality management emphasized was customer focus, managing with data, employee participation, and continuous process improvement in developing the organization; while organizational learning theory focuses on systems thinking, team learning and dialogue, and the attainment of shared visions of the future. Both offer a strategy to achieve the alignment and cohesion thought to be necessary for increasing the organization's capacity to perform.

[**Author's Note**: The *learnership philosophy and architecture* are designed to incorporate the OD features and activities learned through this writer's personal study and practical experience in these areas. In particular, the *learnership practitioner* has many of the skills of an experienced OD facilitator.]

Corporate Culture and Character. In *Gaining Control of the Corporate Culture* (Kilmann et al, 1985), the author says that: "Culture may be defined as the shared philosophies, ideologies, values, assumptions, beliefs, expectations, attitudes, and norms that knit a community together. Culture is manifest in behavioral norms, hidden assumptions, and human nature; each occurring at a different level of depth" (p.5). He views the culture of an organization as having significant impact on how well the organization performs and suggests that there are three interrelated aspects of the impact of culture: direction, pervasiveness, and strength. "Culture direction" pertains to the course the culture is causing the organization to follow; "culture pervasiveness" concerns how widespread or shared are the beliefs among the members of the organization; and, "culture strength" has to do with the level of pressure the culture exerts on the organization members. Taken together, organization culture may significantly aid or limit progress toward achieving desired goals and objectives.

A related cultural concept is that of *Corporate Character* (Wilkins, 1989). Corporate or organizational character has as its central premise that a mutually reinforcing relationship exists among three organizational culture components: shared vision, distinctive skills, and motivational faith. Wilkins regards motivational faith as the foundation of corporate character, and states that "If people believe that they will be treated fairly and have confidence that the organization can become competent, then they are willing to cooperate on developing shared vision and appropriate execution skills" (p.25). Motivational faith depends on *fairness* (of the leaders and of others) and on *ability* (personal and organizational). Wilkins refers to the faith ingredient as "social capital," that creates workforce resilience which may be drawn upon by the organization when it faces complexity and unexpected challenges. He suggests that leaders have a responsibility to build and maintain social capital in order to sustain the organization's adaptability, growth, and development.

[**Author's Note**: This inquiry into the organizational culture and character aspects of organizational development has been useful in that it helps explain certain foundational social beliefs and relationships with relevance to the OSD portion of the learnership model. An observation here is that when an organization's culture and character are aligned with, and supportive of, the organization's goals and objectives, the environment for learning and development and for quality improvement are appreciably enhanced. Under these conditions, the OSD social subsystem provides direct support to the direction, operations, and performance subsystems and creates the potential for optimization at the OSD level. Looking back at the Personal System Development (PSD) segment is also informative in that one may easily recognize that the degree to which an organization's social subsystem can succeed is dependent upon the level of development of the individuals' abilities (PSD ability subsystem) and character (PSD character subsystem).]

Organization Operations

Quality is never an accident, it is always the result of intelligent effort.
— *John Ruskin*

Overview: Process Transformation

Total Quality Management. Warren Schmidt and Jerome Finnigan in *The Race Without a Finish Line: America's Quest for Total Quality (1992),* state that: "Achieving a consistently higher quality of products and services for customers requires a significant difference in the way managers and workers view their roles, responsibilities, and relationships." (p.4) The authors trace the roots of TQM from quality of work life (1975), quality circles (1980) employee involvement (1985), employee empowerment (1990), and self-directed teams (1995). They say that "total" means *quality* and m*anagement*, and that there are six key factors evident in award-winning companies:

1. A high level of management commitment and leadership
2. Supportive organizational structures
3. Quality-oriented tools and processes
4. Tailored educational programs,(
5. Innovative reward strategies
6. Full and continuing communications.

Schmidt and Finnigan point out that: "TQM goes by many names, but it has a single goal: customer satisfaction…it is not a program but a way of organizational life." (p.33) They say that there are three qualities that distinguish TQM from other management theories and quality control programs:

1. It is company-wide in purpose and process. It is the way in which an organization carries on all of its activities, not just product delivery and functions.

2. It emphasizes steady, continuous improvements through the use of facts and the reduction of variability.

3. Its focus is on improving performance by turning the organization into an efficient engine for satisfying customer requirements." (p.34)

Research by the authors in public and private sector organizations in both service and manufacturing industries indicate that there are eight principles at work in these high performing organizations:

1. The Principle of <u>Customer Satisfaction</u>. The ultimate goal

2. The Principle of <u>Challenge</u>. The willingness to set an objective and go after it

3. The Principle of <u>Process</u>. Focus on process improvement to achieve better performance

4. The Principle of <u>Continuous Improvement</u>. Continuing to pursue and make small improvements toward the ultimate objective

5. The Principle of <u>Collaboration</u>. The willingness to work with others in goal achievement

6. The Principle of <u>Change</u>. The necessity of change in people as well as processes

7. The Principle of <u>Measurements</u>. A commitment to mange by operational facts

8. The Principle of <u>Persistence</u>. A marathon rather that a sprint

While there are proven benefits that result from transforming an organization with rather routine competencies and market positioning to one that emphasizes TQM throughout its operations, TQM is not for all firms. Schmidt and Finnigan state that organizational leaders need to assure themselves that they understand the degree of challenge before them and their readiness to embark on that journey. They recommend that the organization leaders:

1. Understand the dynamics of the organizational transformation they will need to lead.

2. Assess their organizations readiness for change.

3. Assess the management team's willingness to learn and lead change.

4. Review the leadership styles in use to ensure they support the TQM methodology.

5. Determine if there is a willingness to learn from other organizations' experience.

6. Establish a well thought out project plan for getting started.

[**Author's Note**: TQM started in the 1990s and notwithstanding its well documented successes there was a chorus of negative comments from those ill-informed or unable to muster the ability and persistence needed to achieve the benefits others had obviously accumulated. This is to be expected because no improvement initiative is fail-proof. Still, the principles of TQM remain embedded in today's management culture—customer focus, continuous improvement, measurement of performance, and improvement of work processes.]

Business Process Reengineering. In their *Reengineering the Corporation* (1993), Michael Hammer and James Champy broke from the continuous process improvement, incremental model of TQM to the break-it and change-it, quantum change model of process reengineering. Discontinuous thinking became the notion at the time and they stated that: "Reengineering capitalizes on the same characteristics that have traditionally made Americans such great business innovators: individualism, self-reliance, a willingness to accept risk, and a propensity for change." (p.3) Through their research with companies dramatically reinventing themselves and making great strides in their respective markets, the authors concluded that: "Reengineering… can't be carried out in small and cautious steps….It is an all-or-nothing proposition that produces dramatically impressive results." (p.5) Better, faster, cheaper became the bywords of the late 1990s as public and private sector organizations attempted to transform into market leaders and providers of above average financial returns.

Hammer and Champy's definition of reengineering was: "…it is the fundamental rethinking and radical design of business processes to achieve dramatic improvements in critical, contemporary measures of performance, such as cost, quality, service, and speed. The four key words were *fundamental, radical, dramatic,* and *processes.*" (pp.32-35) The emphasis on process-thinking was particularly notable because, just like in TQM, business processes often cut across formal business functions—across the organizational white space—where much of the inefficiency occurs. This more true for core production processes of organizations than their support functions, and this is exactly where effort and resources needed to be focused to get the best return from process reengineering.
Research by the authors of successful Business Process Reengineering (BPR) efforts in major U.S. corporations led them to identify four recurring themes that made the difference for firms willing to persist with reengineering efforts:

1. Process Orientation. A willingness to choose processes that cut across organizational function boundaries

2. Ambition. A commitment to achieve breakthroughs and not settle for anything less than huge returns (80%, not 20%)

3. Rule-breaking. An ability to overcome previous assumptions and ways of working and to abandon anything that did not fit into the new ways of work

4. Creative Use of Information Technology. Used modern IT as an enabler in creating new ways of doing work (p.47)

Concurrently, they discovered that reengineering was not:

1. The same as automation

2. Software engineering old work processes without change them along the way.

3. The same as restructuring or downsizing which often just reduces capacity to perform.

4. The same as reorganizing, delayering, or flattening and organization which may jus move things around without improving efficiency. (p.48)

Hammer and Champy summarized the new world of work after business process reengineering as having changed on multiple levels of responsibility and activity:

1. Work Units Change. From functional departments to process teams

2. Jobs Change. From simple tasks to multi-dimensional work

3. People's Roles Change. From controlled to empowered

4. Job Preparation Changes. From training to education

5. Focus of Performance Measures and Compensation Shifts. From activity to results

6. Advancement Criteria Change. From performance to ability

7. Values Change. From protective to productive

8. Organizational Structures Change. From hierarchical to flat

9. Executives Change. From scorekeepers to leaders (pp.65-79)

[**Author's Note**: In a manner similar to TQM, reengineering was proven to work well in many major reengineering efforts, but many in the mainstream media failed to become sufficiently informed and so reported that "reengineering had come and gone" when all that had happened was that TQM and BPR morphed together into the management consultant's toolbox of business improvement methodologies. Just another tool along with Organizational Change Management and many others that are now a staple of good management practices. Also worth noting is that the progressive development and use of TQM and BPR laid the foundation for latter management improvement techniques such as organizational learning and knowledge management which has good support today in knowledgeable circles.]

Process Transformation. The centricity of process analysis in organizational performance improvement is a notable fact for private and public sector managers and management consultants. Most attempts at performance improvement begin with an understanding that all organizations are an arrangement of processes and that these processes consist of workflows that can probably be improved. Processes are sometimes referred to as systems when the focus is primarily on the IT tools that contribute to process workflow.

Figure 11-3 is an illustration of a generic high level organizational process model that places emphasis on the core functions or processes of the organization. Core processes are defined as those processes that contain the fundamental purpose of the organization such as automotive manufacturing, newspaper production, intelligence gathering, and dry cleaning. All organizations require an executive level infrastructure that leads, directs, and supports *organizational management* interface with the external environment. These functions are represented by the executive leadership, research and development, legal and contracts, financial management, and sales and marketing functions. Functions focused on internal support to the core functions/processes are called *business support* and typically include program and budget, human resources, information technology, facilities and supplies, and security.

Within U.S Federal Government IT operations, the relationships in the figure could be the beginning of the development of an Agency or Department Enterprise Architecture (EA). Typically, there would be five sub-elements through which the enterprise would be described for IT management purposes: (1) business architecture, (2) performance architecture, (3) data architecture, (4) service architecture, and (5) technology architecture. Reference is made to Figure 11-5 for more information on the IT architecture and its contributions to enterprise systems engineering.

Organizational White Space (Systems Management). Rummler and Alan Brache are authors of the book: *Improving Performance: How to Manage the White Space on the Organization Chart* (1995). In it they say that organizations need to be managed as systems, and to do that process management is essential. In particular, however, they claim that: "…managers should concentrate as much or more on the flow of products, paper, and information *between* departments as on the activities *within* departments. Process management provides a methodology for managing this white space between the boxes on the organization chart." (p.xvi)

The authors are particularly concerned with the *silo mentality* in organizations where function set their own objectives and subordinate managers tend to perceive other functions as competitors. They say the: "The silo culture forces managers to resolve lower-level issues, taking their time away from higher-priority customer and competitor concerns. Individual contributors, who should be resolving these issues, take less responsibility for results and perceive themselves as mere implementers and information provides…This functional sub-optimization often contributes to the sub-optimization of the organization as a whole." (p.7) Instead, the authors advocate a systems (horizontal) view of the organization in which a high level picture of the business can be seen. This way, three important features can be observed: (1) the relationship between flow of work, the product, and the ultimate customer, (2) how work gets done across functional boundaries, and (3) the internal customer relationships that need to be managed.

Performance:

1. Organization Level. At this level the organization's relationship with its market be clearly seen. Executive level leaders focus on organizational goals, design, and management. This is the level at which the organization measures its performance effectiveness within its marketplace.

2. Process level. At this level the organization performance at the cross-functional process level is managed by mid-level managers. Their concern is measuring and managing the efficiency of their processes.

3. Job/Performer level. At this level of the organization the emphasis is on job goals, design, and performance. The concern here is that each contributor operates in a competent manner, and is recognized in doing so. (pp.15-19)

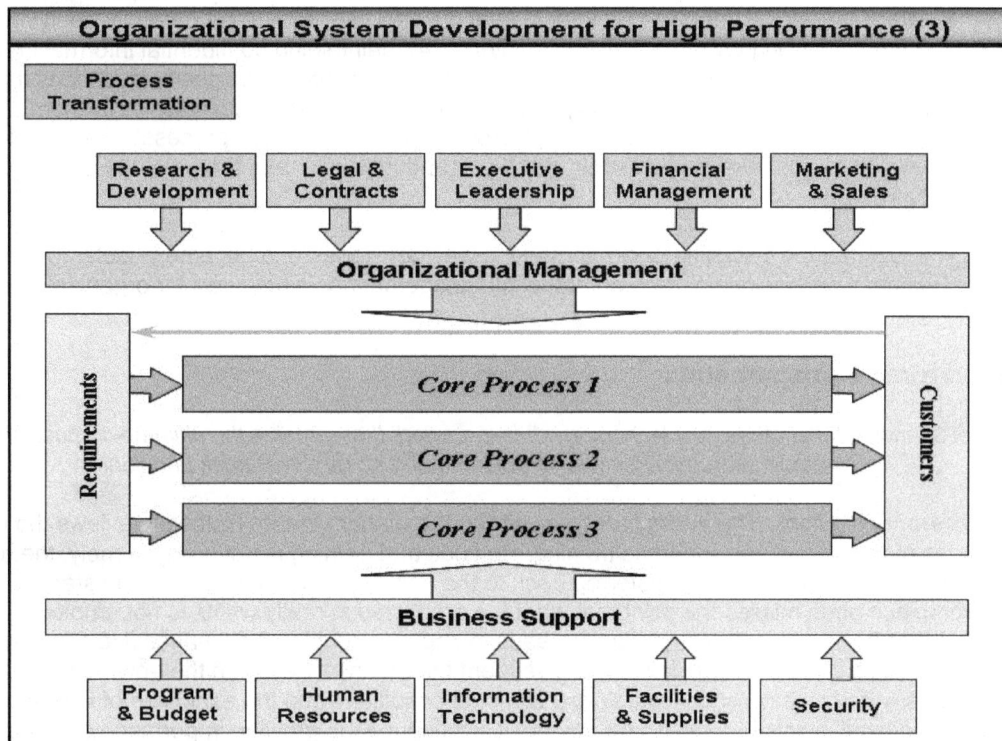

Figure 11-3

Rummler and Brache suggest a useful conceptualization of the enterprise or organization in terms of three levels of

[**Author's Note**: The Rummler-Brache approach to managing organizational performance improvement is significant in that it provides an easily understood framework that simplifies organizational complexity and allows effective communication and action. The Three Levels viewpoint enables the manager, consultant, or learnership practitioner to recognize important variables affecting performance and to systematically take corrective action.]

Benchmarking Company Performance. Gregory Watson's book entitled: *Strategic Bench-marking: How to Rate Your Company's Performance Against the World's Best* (1993), contributes to the process improvement emphasis of this section in that it describes a methodology for making comparisons between one's own organization and another organization already recognized for its expertise in a related aspect of process management and performance. Watson defines benchmarking as "A continuous search for and application of significantly better practices that leads to superior competitive performance." (p.2) The benchmarking process follows the well known Deming improvement cycle (plan, do, check, act) with plan the study, conduct the research, analyze the data, and adapt/implement the findings.

In explaining the important value-added contribution of benchmarking to organizations that use it, Watson mentions a study by GE by former CEO Jack Welch who wanted to position GE for the coming decade. The GE team discovered that the top competition placed great emphasis on leading top-down process improvement and increased productivity. In fact, they concluded that a world-class competitor:

1. Knows its processes better than its competitors know their processes

2. Knows the industry competitors better than its competitors know them

3. Knows its customers better than its competitors know their customers

4. Responds more rapidly to customer behavior than do competitors

5. Uses employees more effectively than do competitors

6. Competes for market share on a customer-by-customer basis (p.34)

According to Watson, the essentials of benchmarking start with recognizing the potential value of comparing functions and processes in order to improve how to perform the same or similar function. Doing so requires following certain accepted principles which include: (1) creating reciprocal relationships with others, (2) carefully applying analogy between process features, (3) using valid measurement criteria, (4) maintaining confidential information gained from others, and (5) using information only for purposes fully described in advance. The specific questions that should be answered in setting out to do a benchmarking activity are: (1) What should *we* benchmark? (2) Whom should *we* benchmark? (3) How do *we* perform the process? and (4) How do *they* perform the process? In each situation it is important to carefully review each other's processes, practices, and methods; and then the outputs, results, success factors that are involved.

[**Author's Note**: The fact that the discipline of benchmarking was developed and became popular is a strong indicator of the importance business professionals place on process management as a key area for organization performance improvement.]

Overview: Workforce Transformation

> *Not finance. Not strategy, Not technology. It is teamwork that remains the ultimate competitive advantage, both because it is so powerful and so rare. -- Patrick Lencioni*

Workplace Learners. In his book: *The Workplace Learner* (2002), author William Rothwell reviews the recent studies on the effectiveness of organizational workforce training. He finds that training is not always timely, the right solution, sensitive to individual differences, and/or transferred back to the one's job efficiently. In fact, he states that training away from the workplace often misses the point that what the organization really wants is not employee *training*, but employee *learning*–and particularly, that learning that leads to improvement in *performance*. He comments that: "A better approach is to focus on how people learn and give them the means to learn on their own. Only that way can individuals keep pace with dynamically changing organizational conditions and the explosion of information and knowledge." (p.25) Rothwell points to fourteen trends that will influence the growing importance of workplace learning:

1. Partitions between the workplace and other spheres of life are falling down.

2. Increasingly, individuals must take charge of their own learning.

3. Instructional technology will encompass all senses and will be paired with expert systems.

4. More workplace learning will occur in real time.

5. Workplace learning will assume broader definitions.

6. Advances in neurophysiology will yield new insights into the learning process.

7. Individuals will increasingly seek employers who encourage learning.

8. Organizations will increasingly seek individuals who are willing to take charge of their own learning.

9. Workplace learning program practitioners will increasingly become facilitators of learning, and their competencies will be dependent on learner competencies.

10. Organizations viewed as learning organizations will become synonymous with high performing workplaces

11. Links between learning and performance will become more apparent, more measurable, and more convincing to traditionalists

12. Work groups and teams will become one of many vehicles by which to organize and direct learning experiences

13. Learning ability, not educational attainment will become a measure of success

14. Cross-cultural differences in learning styles will become more widely explored"

Rothwell introduces the concept of Free Agent Learners (FALs) who will be those who "…take their own initiative to seek out knowledge skills, and attitudes to meet their needs without necessarily relying on support, or assistance from immediate supervisors or institutional provider. [And] The key challenge they face is sifting through the immense amount of information that is available to find useful knowledge that can be applied to solving the immediate work and life problems they face." (p.39) The characteristics of Free Agent Learners that distinguish them from other learners are:

1. They want information on demand, and they also want learning resources just in time to help them.

2. They are persistent. They are tenacious enough to wade through useless information on the Web to find what they need.

3. They are more highly motivated for their own purposes that most people or other learners. When they have a problem or sense a need, they jump into action.

4. They are problem-oriented. They usually do not learn just for fun, though they may occasionally learn out of curiosity.

5. They structure their own knowledge and skill acquisition. They willingly accept chaotic information, and are willing to piece it together like someone working on a jigsaw puzzle.

6. They are skilled in using technology. They may start researching a problem on the Web because of its accessibility, but they eventually branch out to find other technologies of use to them.

The author also explains why the traditional Instructional Systems Design (ISD) process, no matter how well done, still comes up short in term of the quality of performance improvement achieved from a training program. It's because all of the thinking and effort came from the trainer will little energy and commitment from the so-called learners. Instead, Rothwell says: "…as work settings become more dynamic and as the individuals become more aggressive in their pursuit of real-time learning to help them meet real-time needs, the ISD-model–which will always in some form remain useful to trainers – needs to be paired up with a corresponding model of the workplace learning process. When it is, training can be "pushed" while learning can be "pulled. The result can be a more powerful impact on individuals and groups." (pp. 41-42)

According to Rothwell's research, workplace learners go through the following sequence of activities and experiences when the learning process is working well. The learner:

1. Experiences a triggering circumstance.

2. Recognizes the importance of learning.

3. Experiences curiosity about the issue or circumstance that triggered learning.

4. Seeks information.

5. Processes the information.

6. Converts that information into what is useful to the individual and thereby internalizes it into short-term and/or long-term memory.

7. Applies the knowledge in the future.

8. Reflects on what was learned and may apply that newly acquired knowledge to new situations.

9. May experience a double-loop trigger, which means a stimulus to reflect on the learning process, and evaluation of the learning process.

[**Author's Note**: Learnership practitioners inculcate much of what Rothwell has advocated. They are lifelong learners who seek learning for its practical applications. They operate as free-agent learners across a wide variety of personal, organizational, and community venues always alert to new experiences and environmental factors that present additional information and knowledge. Double-loop learning is something they enjoy because they know that what they already think they know can be modified by new circumstances that push the boundaries of their comprehension.]

Federal Human Capital Development. In September 2000 the U.S. Government Accounting Office published a document entitled: "A Human Capital Self-Assessment Checklist for Agency Leaders (GAO/OCG-00-14G)." The GAO said that enhancing the value of employees is a win-win goal for employers and employees alike. The more an organization recognizes the intrinsic value of each employee; the more it recognizes that this value can be enhanced with nurturing and investment; the more it recognizes that employees vary in their talents and motivations, and that a variety of incentive strategies and working arrangements can be created to enhance each employee's contributions to organizational performance, the more likely the organization will be to appreciate the variety of employee needs and circumstances and to act in ways that will make sense in both business and human terms.

The GAO asked: Why Should Agencies Conduct a Human Capital Self-Assessment? And they answered: Self-assessment is the starting point for creating "human capital organizations"—agencies that focus on valuing employees and aligning their "people policies" to support organizational performance goals. The GAO's self-assessment focused on five organizational management responsibilities:

1. Strategic Planning: Establish the agency's mission, vision for the future, core values, goals and objectives, and strategies

2. Organizational Alignment: Integrate human capital strategies with the agency's core business practices

3. Leadership: Foster a committed leadership team and provide reasonable continuity through succession planning

4. Talent: Recruit, hire, develop, and retain employees with the skills for mission accomplishment

5. Performance Culture: Empower and motivate employees while ensuring accountability and fairness in the workplace

The GAO also conducted a symposium of leaders from many government organizations, and according to the symposium participants, the demand for faster, cheaper, and better service delivery led their organizations to develop new and more flexible ways of managing people. On the basis of the symposium proceedings, GAO discerned eight interrelated principles common to organizations that value their human capital:

1. Value people as assets rather than as costs.

2. Emphasize mission, vision, and organizational culture.

3. Hold managers responsible for achieving results instead of imposing rigid, process-oriented rules and standards.

4. Choose an organizational structure appropriate to the organization rather than trying to make "one size fit all."

5. Instead of isolating the *personnel function* organizationally, integrate human resource management into the mission of the organization.

6. Treat continuous learning as an investment in success rather than as a cost to be minimized.

7. Pursue an integrated rather than an ad hoc approach to information management.

8. Provide sustained leadership that recognizes change as a permanent condition, not a one-time event.

As GAO reported at the time, the sense of the symposium participants was that the eight principles should be treated as a whole and that effective human resource management and effective business practices are inseparable.

Software Competency Development. The continuous development of an organization's workforce is an imperative if the organization intends to remain competitive in its marketplace. This can be accomplished by continuing to educate and build the skills of the current staff and/or through the use of new hires, contractors, and/or partnerships that bring the required capabilities to the organization for integration and use. In the case of the U.S. Department of Defence and its need to build a more professional software development industry, the

DOD sponsored a study by the Carnegie-Mellon University Systems Engineering Institute to recommend and design an evolutionary approach for growing a high quality team of software engineers and project managers that could be used throughout the defence industry. An overview of the concept proposed and subsequently implemented is at Figure 11-4. At the strategic level of software systems management, progress occurs as individuals and organizations move upward from being part of *Initial* and *Repeatable* levels of systems performance through the *Defined* and *Managed* levels up to the *Optimized* level of performance. At the continuous improvement or *tactical level* of operations, daily cycles of learning and development recur as people, processes, and technology interact on software projects and in training programs. The results of this effort has been quite influential on the industry due to product improvements and cost savings.

[**Author's Note:** The concept of documenting knowledge, skills, and abilities required in the performance of employees in various professions and knowledge-based careers, and illustrating a timeline with benchmarks on progress, has proven to be helpful in personnel recruiting, development, and management.]

Workplace Competencies. In *Corporate Quality Universities: Lessons in Building a World Class Work Force* (Meister, 1994), the author collates the findings of a number of contemporary reports on the knowledge, skills, and abilities required of productive employees in today's increasingly competitive workplaces, industries, and the international marketplace. She suggests six skill groups that are essential areas for employee development in order that businesses and organizations maintain their capability to grow, compete, and prosper over the long run. The skill groups are:

1. Learning Skills. Learning skills rank high in importance because an organization's power to introduce change depends on workers' abilities to learn new roles, processes, and skills. "The goal is for continuous improvement to become a natural part of how an employee thinks and behaves on the job" (p.5)

2. Basic Skills (reading, writing, computation, and cognitive reasoning). These skills are more essential than ever in aiding workers to acquire and use information relevant to their positions. Cognitive reasoning appears to be particularly important in that more complex work environments and task interdependence make applying information correctly an important capability

3. Interpersonal Skills. Individual effectiveness is becoming increasingly linked to team effectiveness which is the driver for organization problem solving and high performance. Good communications skills and knowing how to work cooperatively with co-workers to successfully resolve conflicts and influence action are essential skills in flexible and adaptable organizations.

4. Creative Thinking and Problem Solving Skills. "Today's worker is expected to give constructive input on everything from how to ensure the quality of raw materials used to make a product to how to improve processes and procedures" (p.6). In order to do this, the workers must be capable of responding flexibly at their point of responsibility for production or sales, and be able to apply an acquired set of problem solving skills as difficulties arise.

5. Leadership (visioning) Skills. In today's flatter organization structures, direction will not always be from the top. Instead, all workers are expected to be cognizant of the organization's goals, vision, values, and strategies and be able to proactively elicit commitment from others to pursue shared visions and workplace improvement. Leaders are everywhere in the organization.

6. Self-Development (and self-management) Skills. Having command of basic skills is an essential starting point in today's workplace, but these should be used as a platform for the development of higher-order competencies and continued personal growth. Increased use of multi-skill positions, job rotation, and self-directed work teams within dynamic, changing workplaces require individuals that can think and act effectively within a context of greater responsibility and authority. And, ensuring that one's career security takes precedence over a focus on one's job security

[**Author's Note**: With reference to the *Learnership Integrated Systems Architecture*, Meister's skill set connotes a sense of purpose, order, learning, and development—an evolution of personal and organizational capability on the route toward higher performance. The mutual development of strategic, operational, and performance management skills may be expected as the organization and its employees make progress toward their respective higher levels-of-being. An observation is that when OSD and worker PSD occur in a mutually reinforcing quality learning relationship, the organization rapidly achieves greater internal and external satisfaction.]

Self-Initiated Followership. In *Beyond Participative Management* (Gilbert & Nelson, 1991), the authors describe the importance of followership as a corollary to effective leadership. Without the former, the latter could not occur. Also, good followership is likely a part of the good leader's behavior. In regard to the quality and customer service movement, they suggest that followership is the behavior that results when individuals think and behave in ways to fully assist and support their colleagues, supervisors, and others as "customers" as well as those normally thought of as the customers.

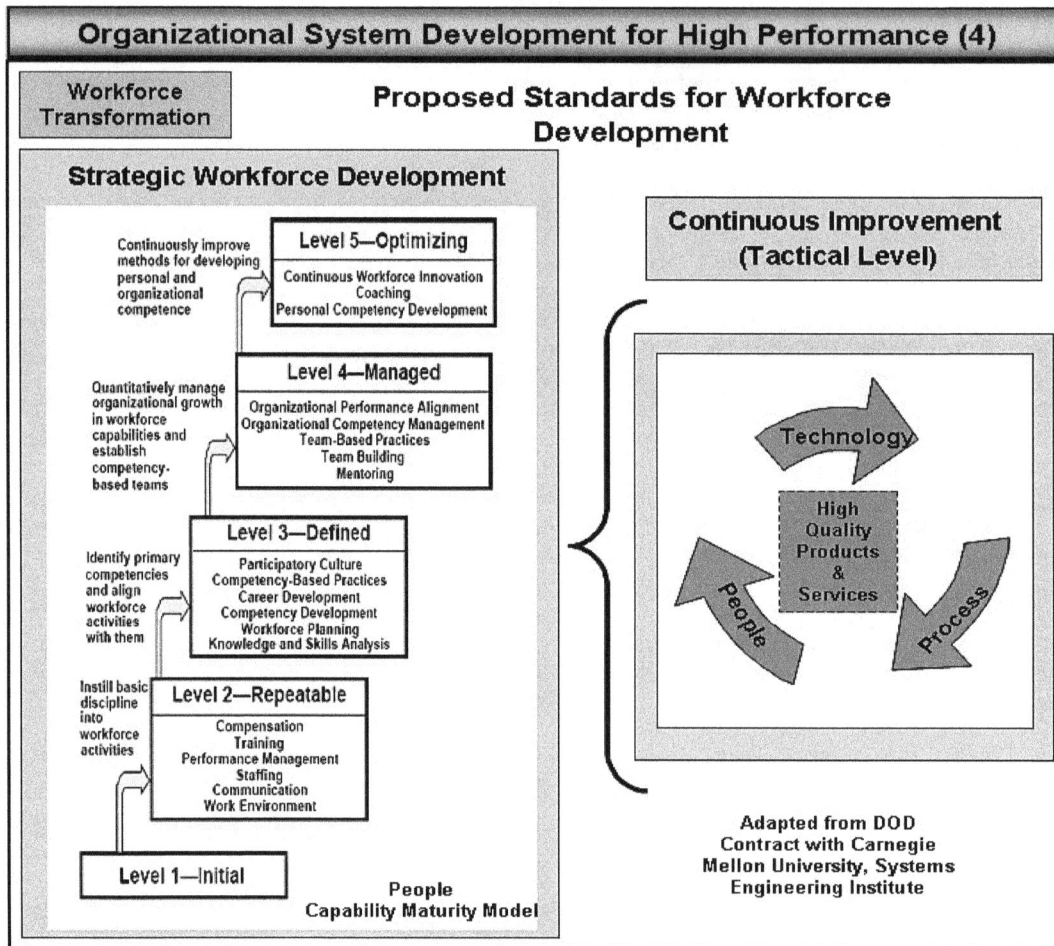

Figure 11-4

Gilbert's study of nearly one thousand people's outstanding behavior on the job led to the identification of eight notable characteristics of good followership:

1. Partnership. The willingness to create a partnership relationship with all customers so that their needs and objectives are assimilated and supported

2. Motivation. An enthusiastic attitude ("can do") toward work to satisfy whatever customers want or need

3. Technical Competence. The knowledge and ability to accomplish tasks with excellence, and a willingness to continue to learn

4. Dependability. The willingness to be counted on, be trustworthy, and make contributions

5. Professional Comportment. Presents oneself well in terms of manners, dress, speech, language, cleanliness, tact, and diplomacy

6. Sense of Humor. Demonstrates good cheer, smiles, and shares appropriate humor

7. Positive Working Relationships and Team Play. Avoids negative interpersonal behavior in favor of constructive and cooperative behavior

8. Speaking Up. Willing to share information and educate others for their improved understanding and action.

[**Author's Note**: This perspective relates well to the OSD construct in that it illustrates an often overlooked aspect of teamwork—the act of followership. It also emphasizes the idea that organizational quality may be defined through the goal of customer satisfaction—in this case, the satisfaction of all customers including one's colleagues and supervisors.]

Employee Involvement and Teamwork. In the book *High-Involvement Management* (Lawler, 1986), the author makes the case for greater use of participative management by U.S. organizations. He states that: "The societal, business, product, and work force changes that have occurred argue strongly for a change in management. Clearly, American organizations need to be more effective simply to be competitive...It is unlikely that dramatic improvements can come about through the use of traditional management approaches" (p.19). He believes that participative management suits today's technologies, work force, and social conditions because of its potential to create a knowledgeable, motivated, responsive work force with the capacity to handle the increasingly complex, challenge, and pace of change regularly experienced in the work environment. Greater employee participation in an organization occurs as:

1. Decision- making power moves downward

2. Information flows up and down more directly to those in need of it

3. Rewards are tied to contributions to organizational performance

4. Knowledge and skills of all employees are used more complete

5. More of the organization is involved.

A related perspective to employee involvement is offered in *Teamwork* (Starcevich & Stowell, 1990). The authors describe how organization groups become teams and how the dynamics of groups can be managed. The focus is on team process with the assumption that skilled team process management leads to effective team performance. The authors describe effective teams as follows: "Teams work at building spirit and commitment; they talk about how they are doing, and they are willing to invest time and money to protect and enhance the basic team fabric and integrity. In a team, people care about each other and are concerned about how their actions and attitudes affect each other" (p.12). A five-point Team Effectiveness Model is presented that delineates the interdependence among:

1. Leadership—is flexible and participative

2. Direction – goals, vision, values, priorities, and strategies are clearly defined

3. Structure/resources—responsibilities are defined, and supportive administrative procedures and resources are available

4 Atmosphere—cohesion and caring are emphasized, and (5) processes—team periodically evaluates its process, and effective communications and consensus decision making are encouraged.

[**Author's Note**: The significance of employee involvement and teamwork in respect to the learnership model may be understood by focusing on two aspects of organizational life. The first concerns the environment or context within which most organizations operate. For many private and public organizations, increasing turmoil is an apt description of their immediate environment. Rapid change in customer needs, markets, and competition, coupled with a general increase in situational complexity and information overload make maintaining customer focus and satisfaction an essential task for organization survival. The second area considers the hierarchical and typically bureaucratic internal structure of today's dominant public and private sector organizations. Organizations of this type are built for control in orderly environments, rather than speed and responsiveness in dynamic environments. What greater employee involvement and efficient teamwork do is encourage greater management delegation of problem solving and decision making, establish a foundation for greater employee empowerment, motivate employees through task responsibility and ownership, assure information and other resources are distributed more efficiently, and encourage employees to improve customer service and satisfaction. In the OSD portion of the learnership model, customer satisfaction is the determinant of organizational quality, and the process of learning what must be achieved and how it should be done is what well-led and cohesive teams are expected to accomplish.]

Overview: Decision-Making

Effective managers do not merely wait for problems to arise;
they actively look for problems and opportunities — James Stoner

Rational Thinking and Management. In their book *The New Rational Manager* (1981), Charles Kepner and Benjamin Tregoe argue for a rational, team-based approach for organizational change—a reality for all organizations desiring to stay competitive in a changing world. They state that: "A new idea or an expectation, in itself, will seldom bring about change. On the other hand, change can be very attractive if it is a product of a new idea or expectation that appears to be in the best interests of the people who are expected to adopt it, if it is accompanied by the means for its fulfillment, and if it results in recognition and approval. To improve an organization, we must introduce good ideas, establish the means for making them work, and provide a visible payoff for the efforts involved." (p.20)

The essence of the Kepner-Tragoe approach is to use effective teamwork and decision-making focused on four choice-making functions required in all organizations: situation appraisal, problem-analysis, decision analysis, and potential problem analysis. These may be summarized as follows:

1. Situation Appraisal. Four activities are involved which are: (a) Recognize Concerns–deviations, threats, and opportunities, (b) Separate Concerns–expand/combine and add sub-concerns, (c) Set Priority–decide on importance of concerns and order to be used, and (d) Plan for Resolution–select a process (PA, DA, PPA) for action and an implementation approach.

2. Problem Analysis (PA). Explain and fix a deviation from a plan: (a) Prepare a Deviation Statement, (b) Specify What Is and Is Not, (c) Develop Possible Causes, (d) Test for Probable Cause, and (e) Verify Findings.

3. Decision Analysis (DA). Follow five sequential steps for making choices: (a) Prepare a Decision Statement (purpose, level), (b) Establish Objectives, (c) Classify Objectives, (d) Generate Alternatives, and (e) Compare and Choose.

4. Potential Problem Analysis (PPA). Follow five steps to ensure success of problem resolution activities: (a) Action Plan Statement, (b) Anticipate Problems, (c) Anticipate Likely Causes, (d) Select Action, and (e) Provide for Information.

What is clear from the explanation of the Kepner-Tragoe approach for rational management is that it works best when organizational leaders embrace the recommended techniques and lead other managers and the workforce in their application. Individual teams and groups can make some progress on localized issues, but the real benefit comes from organizational-wide use of the methodology. At its core is the need for effective decision-making, the ability and commitment to use rational thinking when making choices in setting organizational direction, improving organizational operations, and evaluating organizational progress.

Managing Our Minds. According to authors Gillian Butler and Tony Hope of *Managing Your Mind: The Mental Fitness Guide*, (1995) "Thinking straight is not always easy: It is harder to think logically, and to avoid being led astray by illogical pitfalls, than it would seem...Far more frequently than we realize we use thinking strategies that are based loosely on fact, or we make one of a number of the standard mistakes studied and analyzed by psychologists." (p.400) In Chapter 33 on thinking straight they list four common mistakes in thinking are:

1. Being Misled by Theories, Beliefs, and Assumptions. They say that opinions can easily slip into becoming prejudices, and these prejudices tend to set up a mental framework that causes us to discount, distort, or deflect new information we encounter. They say that we should (a) look specifically for evidence that disconfirms our previous beliefs, (b) take note of new thinking and reflect on it to see if it should be the basis for changing our views, (c) be aware of our preferences and inclinations as guard against allowing their excessive intrusion, and (d) recognize that people's perspectives do change incrementally over time.

2. Being Misled by What Springs to Mind. The information that most readily comes to mind has a disproportionate effect on opinions and reasoning in general...The more recent an event, the more likely it is to influence our judgment. They caution to (a) avoid snap judgments, (b) keep feeling from being excessively engaged, and (c) allow room for other's views in our thinking.

3. Being Misled by the Influence of Others. There are pitfalls in the advice to consider the views of other–they make have too much influence on us because of our regard for the other people. Be aware of the "halo effect", the fallacious use of "scientific evidence", and being wowed by the "presentation skills" of others.

4. Being Misled by Associations. The fact that others use preconceived similarities or other associations to convince us of their views. The issues or problems may not really be similar and the results could be significantly different. We should do our own assessment of relationships, cause and effect, and analogies, and make sure our expectations are realistic whatever the situation.

Also concerning *thinking straight*, the authors advise their readers that the science of numerical facts and data is complex, but that everyone should know and avoid common errors by knowing four basic statistical rules:

1. The Law of Large Numbers. The larger the numbers on which information is based, and the more random the sampling involved, the more valid our judgment will be.

2. Comparison or Control Groups. In the absence of comparison groups and of knowledge of the total population involved, the more unlikely it is that that data and information can be trusted and useful in discussion and argument.

3. Group-Individual Predictions. The behavior of a group does not tell use with certainty the behavior of a particular member of that group.

4. Correlation and Cause. It is often assumed because two things occur together that one causes then other. This is particularly true when the subject has to do with social issues as compared to scientific factors.

On the subject of *making decisions* in Chapter 32, Butler and Hope state that: "In both our domestic life and at work, we need to make decisions, and in order to make good decision we need to be able to think clearly and weigh up evidence effectively…They say that it is impossible to make the 'perfect decision' as every course of action will lead to more choices and throw up some unexpected difficulties." (p.388) Six strategies to help in making decisions are offered:

1. The Balance Sheet. Make a list of the advantages and disadvantages concerning a course of potential action. Assign a weighting system to the items on each list, and draw some preliminary insights and conclusions on the data developed.

2. Trial Runs and Time Projection. Choose one course of action and build a scenario for some time in the future (e.g. 6 months) as to what the likely results could be. Do the same independently for the other options and then compare the results.

3. A Sounding Board. Select a few other people whose knowledge, experience, or similar concerns would enable them to willingly dialogue with us on the subject or issue. See what their views are and allow that information to become part of the decision data we apply to our situation.

4. Information Gathering and Sifting. Identify and collect available information concerning the most significant aspects of the issue to be considered or choice that needs to be made.

5. Dealing with Chain Reactions. Identify the relevant topics, issues, and timelines that pertain to the issue or choice. Time-phase them in the order they will probably occur, allow for unexpected consequences and alternative actions, and predetermine how future events will be decided and reconciled.

6. Keeping up the Energy Reserve. Recognize that fatigue and preoccupation are interfering factors that can drain our commitment and energy. Plan to allow the time and other resources necessary to stay on course.

[**Author's Note**: This section begins with a look at some human aspects of decision-making. How we choose to think, and the mental and emotional energy we apply to our decision-making effort, matters to the efficiency and effectiveness of our results.]

A Role for Intuition and Emotion. In "Making Management Decisions: The Role of Intuition and Emotion," (Feb 1987) Herbert Simon of Carnegie-Mellon University, argues that the development of decision-making tools such as operations research, management science, and expert systems have not diminished significantly the need for the use of intuition and emotion in the interpersonal, and face-to-face aspects of decision-making. Specifically, he addresses what may be termed the judgmental, illogical, and irrational aspects of managerial decision-making.

Simon credits physiological research on *split brains* (severing the corpus callosum between the two hemispheres) with showing that there is a division of labor between the left and right brain, and that each appears through study to have its own, but somewhat overlapping, mental and emotional capabilities. Intuition and emotion tend to be right brain capabilities and the source of non-logical thought that has been embedded, over time, and available to contribute to decision-making without have to go through the detained rational processing normally attributed to left brain sequential activity. Experts appear to have developed these right brain repositories of *judgment and knowledge* and have no need to exercise or use them in a planned and controlled manner.

Simon makes a major point by stating that the intuition used by the expert is very different than the intuition used by the emotionally-driven worker or manager. For the former, intuition has been developed over years of learning and experience and can therefore be trusted to contribute meaningfully to the problem at hand. For the emotionally-driven person, non-rational activity causes results that do not contribute, but actually undermine, the need to make appropriate decisions. This situation occurs with regularity when stress has become a factor in getting decisions made and problems solved. Simon advises that managers seek to become role models for effective decision-making and problem-solving by following these four principles:

1. Solving the problem takes priority over looking backward to its causes. Initially, backward looks should be limited to diagnosing causes; fixing responsibility for mistakes should be postponed until a solution is implemented.

2. The manager accepts personal responsibility for finding and proposing solutions instead of seeking to shift that responsibility either to superiors or to subordinates, although the search for solutions may, of course, be a collaborative effort involving many people.

3. The manager accepts personal responsibility for implementing action solutions, including securing the necessary authority from above, if required.

4. When it is time to look backward, fixing blame may be an essential part of the process, but the primary focus of attention should be on what can be learned to prevent similar problems from arising in the future.

[**Author's Note**: The reader is reminded that Chapter 3 on Pattern Recognition Competency addresses the left/right brain dichotomy and the value of having both a structured (sensing) and a relationship (intuition) based approach to thinking and behavior.]

Making Better Decisions. In a book entitled: *Smart Choices: A Practical Guide to Making Better Decisions* (1999), authors John Hammond, Ralph Lee, and Howard Raiffa present a general framework for decision-making. They say that everyone can learn to make better decisions and they offer and eight step process:

1. Work on the Right Decision/Problem (Chapter 2). Define the decision problem to solve the right problem. Determine the real objective to be achieved.

2. Specify the Objectives (Chapter 3). Clarify what you are trying to achieve with the decision. Determine the primary objective and those that only support that objective.

3. Create Imaginative Alternatives (Chapter 4). Create better alternatives to choose from. Keep an open mind and do own thinking before engaging others. Narrow the choices only after full discussion and consolidation.

4. Understand the Consequences (Chapter 5). Describe how well each remaining alternative meets the objectives. Make a list of likely consequences (pros/cons) for each alternative and compare the results.

5. Grapple with the Tradeoffs (Chapter 6). Be prepared to propose priorities and make tradeoffs between alternatives. Systematically compare tradeoffs that currently need to be made and those that may need to be made at a later time.

6. Clarify the Uncertainties (Chapter 7). Identify and act to reduce uncertainties that continue to be problematical. Prepare a risk profile based on the uncertainties concerning both the *impact* and the *likelihood* of occurrence of each major uncertainty.

7. Think Hard about Risk Tolerance (Chapter 8). Take time to review the group's and/or leader's degree of tolerance for dealing with risk factors. Determine how much risk to accept and mitigation strategies to reduce or avoid too much risk.

8. Consider Linked Decisions (Chapter 9). Plan ahead to effectively coordinate current and future decisions. Look for cross-cutting dependencies among the decisions and maintain flexibility on when certain decisions are needed to be made.

Hammond et al advise that certain psychological traps arise in decision-making and it is necessary to avoid the tricks our minds typically play. Their list of cautions include: (pp.191-212)
1. Over-relying on first thoughts – the *anchoring* trap.
2. Keeping on keeping on – the *status quo* trap.
3. Protecting earlier choices – the *sunk-cost* trap.
4. Seeing what we want to see – the *confirming-evidence* trap.
5. Posing the wrong question -- the *framing* trap.
6. Being too sure of ourselves – the *overconfidence* trap.
7. Focusing on dramatic events – the *recallability* trap.
8. Neglecting relevant information – the *base-rate* trap.
9. Slanting possibilities and estimates – the *prudence* trap.
10. Seeing patterns where none exist – the *outguessing-randomness* trap.
11. Going mystical about consequences – the *surprise by surprises* trap.

The authors advise that: "The only way to exert control over your life is through decision-making…Be proactive, take charge of your decision-making, strive to make good decisions and to develop good decision-making habits. You'll be rewarded with a fuller, more satisfying life." (p.234)

Ethical Business Decisions. According to Gerald Cavanaugh, author of *American Business Values* (1984), there are three prominent ethical models affecting business decisions: Utilitarianism, Theory of Justice, and Theory of Rights: Depending on the model one has in mind, significant differences exist in defining the problem, the alternative solutions to be considered, and the viability of the decision-making process.

1. Utilitarianism. Emphasis is on the greatest good for the greatest number. Advocated by Adam Smith and David Ricardo. *Strengths* include: justifies a profit maximization system; promotes a system of exchange beyond "this firm;" and encourages entrepreneurship, innovation and productivity. *Weaknesses* are: difficulty in quantifying all important elements; self-interest can dominate, may abridge a person's rights; and may neglect the less powerful segments of society.

2. Theory of Justice. Focus is on the equitable distribution of society's benefits and burdens. Advocated by Aristotle and Rawls. *Strengths* include: follows the democratic principle; prevents a society from becoming status or class conscious; and ensures that minorities, handicapped, and the poor receive opportunities and a fair share. *Weaknesses* are: can result in less risk, incentive and innovation; and encourages a "sense of entitlement."

3. Theory of Rights. Emphasis is on not violating anyone's freedom. *Strengths* include: ensures respect for others' property and personal freedom; and parallel's the political "Bill of Rights." *Weakness* is: it can encourage individualistic, selfish behavior.

Cavanaugh also proposes a flow diagram for ethical decision-making that follows the traditional data gathering, information analysis, and decision-making or judgment–and includes the three ethical criteria just defined. The process is:

1. If the act or policy suggested *is appropriate according to ALL three ethical criteria*, the act or policy *is ethical* and should be pursued.

2. If the act or policy suggested *is not appropriate according to ALL three ethical criteria*, the act or policy is *not ethical* and should not be pursued.

3. If the act or policy suggested *is not appropriate on one or two of the three criteria*, it is *probably not ethical*–unless the remaining criterion is overwhelmingly more important or there are no other incapacitating factors–then maybe it can be considered ethical.

[**Author's Note**: It is useful to recognize that the Utilitarian and Theory of Rights models closely parallel the socio-economic and political conservatism for which the American Republican Party is noted. On the other hand, the Theory of Justice model is more representative of the Democratic Party platforms of recent times. This means that problems are framed and alternative solutions chosen in accordance with these preexisting viewpoints–and decision-making cannot help but be biased, accordingly.]

Swampy Problem Contexts. Robert Biller's article entitled "Public Policy and Public Administration: Implications for the Future of Cross-Cultural Research and Practice" (Korean Journal, Autumn 1978) includes a useful two by two table on the relationship between organization type (*bureaucratic vs contingent*) and the context (*bedrock vs swampy*) within which a problem exists. In essence his research shows that there is no one right organization structure for every situation or contextual environment. For example:

1. "Bureaucracy can be described as that form of organization most likely to be used effectively when conditions of stability, certainty, and predictability either exist or can safely be assumed to proximately exist...the more surprise-free a problem and its context (extent to which predictions come true), the more likely bureaucratic decision rules are to prove effective." This is termed the 'bedrock' context which may be managed well within a bureaucracy." (p.257)

2. "Conversely, we are discovering that the more surpriseful a problem and its context are (extent to which predictions do not come true), the more likely contingent decision rules are to prove useful. This is termed the 'swampy' context which may be better "managed within a contingency organization structure." (p.257) The alternate decision rules that apply are compared in Table 11-1.

[**Author's Note**: The learnership practitioner described in this book will need to become more and more familiar with the issues, challenges, and workforce preferences that predominate in today's fast-paced, constantly changing organizations. The flat new knowledge-based world emphasizing horizontal relationships and boundary-spanning responsibilities requires adaptive management, virtual operations, and client responsiveness. More often than not, the decision context is likely to be quite "swampy."]

Vigilant Decision-Making. In *Crucial Decisions: Leadership in Policymaking and Crises Management* (Janis, 1989), the author presents a model for effective policy and decision making, and discusses the reasons why policymakers are so often seen to be deviating from moral, humanitarian, and rational principles in their actions. Janis focuses primarily on top-level policymakers, and his thoughts apply equally in the public and private sectors. His views have particular importance, however, in public sector deliberation and decision-making because of the complexity of social issues and their broad impact on large numbers of individuals and organizations in the community

Alternate Decision Rules

Management Variables	Decision Rules Bureaucratic for Bedrock	Decision Rules Contingency for Swampy
Planning - Scale - Scope - Time Horizon	Comprehensive General Long-Range	Incremental Specific Short-Range
Structure - Orientation and Strength - Nature of Organization - Key Value Amplified - Redundancy of Information	Maintenance Permanent Responsibility Minimize	Adaptation Temporary Responsiveness Maximize
Management Process - Preferred Management Strategy - Operational Processes - Major Presumed Risk - Key Intra-Organization Question	Exception Functional Inefficiency Consistency/Equity	Situational Project Catastrophic Error Issue Specific/Efficacy

Table 11-1

Janis builds on an earlier "Presidential decision-making model for foreign policy" by Alexander George to create his model entitled: "Constraints Creating Trade-Off Dilemmas in Policymaking." The features of the model are significant in that they illustrate the difficulty political leaders, in particular, have in legislating and implementing public policy. The model defines the policy making objective to be "the search for high quality decisions via *vigilant problem solving*." Three sets of constraints are identified which individually or together reduce the quality of decisions and policy. The constraints are:

1. <u>Cognitive Constraints</u>. Limited time, lack of expertise and other policy making resources for dealing with complex issues

2. <u>Affiliative Constraints</u>. The need for acceptability, consensus, and social support

3. <u>Egocentric Constraints</u>. The desire for prestige and other self-serving motives

Each leader has to weigh the impact of these constraints, to make compromises and trade-offs, and to take action that represents a majority view in the community. Unfortunately, the constraints are often substantial and the ability of policymakers rather limited, thereby causing the resulting policy to be less effective than the community requires. Janis presents a vigilant problem solving strategy to assist leaders in decision making and policy making. A summary of his problem-solving approach to decision-making framework, which focuses on the critical questions that must be answered, follows: (p.91)

1. <u>The Challenge</u>. What is the exact threat or opportunity? Clearly identify it.

2. <u>Initial Problem Assessment</u>
   a. <u>Formulating the problem</u>. What requirements should be met? What seems to be the best direction of solution?

   b. <u>Using information resources</u>. What prior information can be recalled or retrieved? What new information should be obtained?

   c. <u>Analyzing and reformulating</u>. Any additions to or changes in the requirements? Any additional alternatives? What additional information might reduce uncertainties?

   d. <u>Evaluating and selecting</u>. What are the pros and cons of each alternative? Which alternative appears to be best? Any requires Unmet? How can potential costs and risks be minimized? What additional plans are needed for implementation, monitoring, and contingencies?

3. <u>Ensure absence of following decision-making defects</u>.
   a. Gross omissions in survey of objectives
   b. Gross omissions in survey of alternatives.
   c. Poor information search.
   d. Selective bias in processing information at hand.
   e. Failure to reconsider originally rejected alternatives.
   f. Failure to examine some major costs and risks of preferred choice.
   g. Failure to work out detailed implementation, monitoring, and contingency plans.

4. <u>Move to Closure</u>.
   a. Internal consolidation of the choice – playing up advantages, refuting unwelcome information, and soliciting supportive information

   b. Social dedication to the choice – Announcing it to interested parties, and promoting it among implementers and evaluators who are uninterested or convinced.

[**Author's Note**: Janis's viewpoint is helpful for understanding the learnership model in that it provides insight into the conflicting and paradoxical environment of a major governmental function--policymaking. As elected representatives and public administrators pursue agendas for the benefit of the community and the common good, they must navigate among numerous personal, political, social, economic, and technical constraints that make the goal of optimizing social development extremely difficult to achieve. The objective, of course, would be to approach a policy or social issue with minimum constraints. To do so requires knowledge of issue factors, significant social consensus and support, and less concern for one's own interests.]

Decision-Making Model. The model at Figure 11- 5 illustrates selected aspects of the perspectives offered in this section. Shown in the center are the basic eight areas for making choices within the larger decision-making framework. On the left are five management activities that employ decision-making; on the right are eleven psychological traps that can derail effective decision-making; and on the bottom there are three constraints of which policymakers need to be aware to accomplish the trade-offs that accompany complex, governmental decision-making.

Overview: Information Technology Transformation

The successful companies of the next decade will be the one that use
digital tools to reinvent the way they work. — Bill Gates

Information Architecture. In *Managing Information Strategically (1993),* James McGee and Laurence Prusak explain that creating an information architecture is a fundamental business requirement. This is because the goals and priorities of the business are reflected in how business functions and processes operate, and the manner in which information flows through the business needs to be recorded, managed, and improved before any significant investment in an IT infrastructure is consummated. The information architecture addresses such topics as:

1. The Environment. Availability and quality of external data and information; universe of competitors and their activities; current knowledge about the global political and economic spheres; and knowledge about developing technologies

2. Human Capabilities. Short-term memory limits; information processing and decision-making styles; and long-term memory strengths and pattern matching skills.

3. Technology Limits. Database technology; communication networks; and group support technologies. (p.133)

According to the authors there are two audiences for the information architecture documents: (1) the *business client* who is concerned with the principles of information management that should be used, the budget involved, and the time it will take to accomplish improvements suggested in the information architecture; and (2) the *technical specialists* who will normalize entity relation diagrams and data models; and prepare data dictionaries, database management designs, and the data structures that will subsequently be used as a basis for the development and implementation of a IT architecture and an investment portfolio.

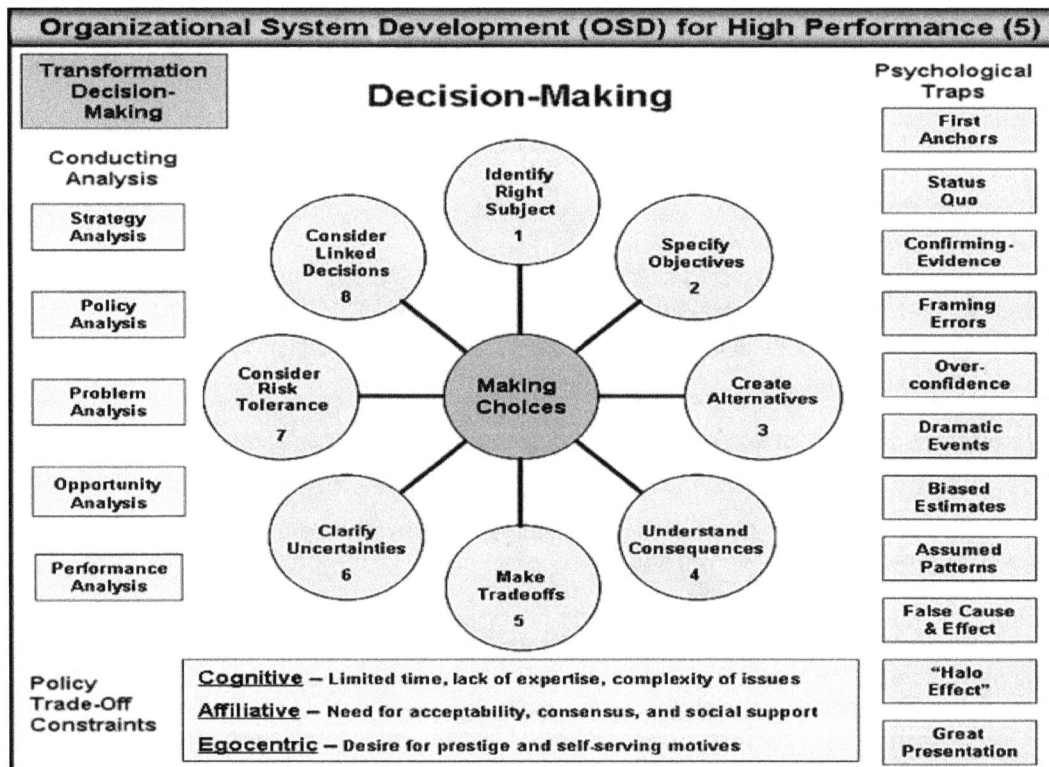

Figure 11- 5

Regarding the goals of an information architecture, they say that: "An information architecture articulates what information is most important to the organization. It becomes the information component of a strategic vision or an information vision." (p.136) It is significant here to note that the objective is not to define, access, and manage ALL organizational information—only that which is truly relevant, accurate, and timely that can serve management's need to be strategic, proactive, and customer responsive. The authors make the point that the information architecture is not:

(1) a technology architecture, (2) a data modeling effort, nor (3) an information system architecture. It is, in fact, a business management tool created and used by leaders and managers–not the CIO.

McGee and Prusak are astute to the challenge of creating the information architecture in that they recognize that: "The information architect must strike a balance between the organization's information needs and technology limitations. The architect must look to the business strategy to decide what information is important to the organization." (p.141)

[**Author's Note**: The information architecture work being described is the very work a knowledge architect or engineer might be doing in today's organizations. Conducting performance reviews of core organizational business processes– and paying attention to the prioritized information and knowledge needs of people working in those processes–should be part of the strategic planning initiative under the category of "strengths and/or weaknesses." Unfortunately, the information architecture function is either not accomplishes or thrown over the transom to the CIO organization wherein it is not usually seen to be as important as developing an IT architecture.]

Quality Assessment of IT Governance. The IT Governance Institute (www.itgi.org) was established to advance international thinking and standards for *directing and controlling an enterprise's information technology function.* Effective performance assessment by enterprise C-level executives of their IT governance function (often led by the CIO) helps ensure that the IT function:

1. Is clearly supporting stated business goals
2. Optimizes business investments in IT
3. Appropriately manages IT-related risks and opportunities
4. That value, risk, and control constitute the core of IT governance

To advance their purpose, the ITGI developed the *Control Objectives for Information and Related Technology (COBIT) 4.1* standard, and state that: "For IT to be successful in delivering against business requirements, executive management should put an internal control system or framework in place. The *COBIT control framework* contributes to these needs by: (1) making a link to the business requirements, (2) organizing IT activities into a generally accepted process model, (3) identifying the major IT resources to be leveraged, and (4) defining the management control objectives to be considered." (p.5) The specific *IT governance focus areas* through which the COBIT framework assures good IT governance are: (p.6)

1. Strategic Alignment. Focuses on *ensuring the linkage of business and IT plans*; defining, maintaining, and validating the IT value proposition; and aligning IT operations with enterprise operations.

2. Value Delivery. Is about executing the [IT] value proposition throughout the delivery cycle, *ensuring that it delivers the promised benefits against the strategy*, and concentrating on optimizing costs and proving the intrinsic value of IT

3. Resource Management. Is about the *optimal investment in, and the proper management of critical IT resources*: applications, information, infrastructure and people Key issues relate to the optimization of knowledge and infrastructure

4. Risk Management. Requires risk awareness by senior corporate officers, a clear understanding of the enterprise's appetite for risk, understanding of compliance requirements, *transparency about the significant risks to the enterprise*, and embedding of risk management responsibilities in to the organization.

5. Performance Measurement. *Tracks and monitors strategy implementation, project completion, resources usage, process performance and service delivery*; using for example, balanced scorecards that translate strategy into action to achieve goals measurable beyond conventional accounting.

Turning now to how COBIT meets the need for a control framework for IT governance, the COBIT was created with the main characteristics of being business-focused, process-oriented, controls-based, and measurement-driven.

1. Business-Focused: "The COBIT framework is based on the following principle: 'To provide the information that the enterprise requires to achieve its objectives, the enterprise needs to invest in and manage and control IT resources using a structured set of processes to provide the services that deliver the require enterprise information.'" And, that the information criteria used to rate the quality of the information being made available are: (pp.10-11)

   a. Effectiveness. Deals with the information being relevant and pertinent to the business process as well as being delivered in a timely, correct, consistent and usable manner.

b. <u>Efficiency</u>. Concerns the provision of information through the optimal (productive and economical) use of resources.

c. <u>Confidentiality</u>. Concerns the protection of sensitive information from unauthorized disclosure.

d. <u>Integrity</u>. Relates to the accuracy and completeness of information as well as to its validity in accordance with business values and expectations.

e. <u>Availability</u>. Relates to information being available when required by the business process now and in the future. It also concerns the safeguarding of necessary resources and associated capabilities.

f. <u>Compliance</u>. Deals with complying with the laws, regulations and contractual arrangements to which the business process is subject, i.e., externally imposed business criteria as well as internal policies.

g. <u>Reliability</u>. Relates to the provision of appropriate information for management to operate the entity and exercise its fiduciary and governance responsibilities."

While the information criteria (above) provide a generic method for defining the business requirements, defining a set of generic business and IT goals provides a business-related and more refined basis for establishing business requirements and developing the metrics that allow measurement against these goals. Every enterprise uses IT to enable business initiatives, and these can be represented as business goals for IT…The IT goals, in turn, define the IT resources and capabilities (the enterprise architecture for IT) required to successfully execute the IT part of the enterprise strategy." (p.11)

2. <u>Process-Oriented</u>: "To govern IT effectively it is important to appreciate the activities and risks within IT that need to be managed. They are usually ordered into the responsibility domains of plan, build, run, and monitor. Within the COBIT framework, these domains are called: (pp.12-13)

a. <u>Plan and Organize</u>. This domain covers strategy and tactics, and concerns the identification of the way IT can best contribute to the achievement of the business objectives.

b. <u>Acquire and Implement</u>. To realize the IT strategy, IT solutions need to be identified, developed or acquired, as well as implemented and integrated into the business process.

c. <u>Deliver and Support</u>. This domain is concerned with the actual delivery of required services, which includes service delivery, management of security and continuity, service support for users, and management of data and operational facilities.

d. <u>Monitor and Evaluate</u>. All IT processes need to be regularly assessed over time for their quality and compliance with control requirements. This domain addresses performance management, monitoring of internal control, and regulatory compliance."

3. <u>Controls-Based</u>. "Across the four domains (above) COBIT has identified all 34 IT processes that are generally used. The list is believed to be comprehensive and that it may be used to verify the completeness of activities and responsibilities. However, the need not all apply, and even more, they can be combined as required by each enterprise. Effective controls reduce risk, increase the likelihood of value delivery and improve efficiency because there will be fewer errors and more consistent management approach." These controls should be manages as part of the enterprises overall system of internal management controls; and they have impact at three levels in the enterprise: (pp.13-16)

a. At the *executive management level*, business objectives are set, policies are established, and decisions are made on how to deploy and manage the resources of the enterprise to execute the enterprise strategy.

b. At the *business process level*, controls are applied to specific business activities. Most business processes are automated and integrated with IT application systems, resulting in many of the controls at this level being automated as well.

c. To support the business processes, *IT provides IT services*, usually in a shared service to many business processes, as many of the development and operational IT processes are provided to the whole enterprise, and much of the infrastructure is provided as a common service."

4. <u>Measurement-Driven</u>. "Obtaining an objective view of an enterprise's own performance level is not easy. What should be measure and how? Enterprises need to measure where they are and where improvement is required, and implement a management tool kit to monitor this improvement. COBIT deals with these issues by providing: (p.17)

    a. *Maturity models* to enable benchmarking and identification of necessary capability improvements

    b. *Performance goals and met*rics for the IT processes, demonstrating how processes meet business and IT goals and are used for measuring internal process performance based on balanced scorecard principles

    c. *Activity goals* for enabling effective process performance"

A generic maturity model is provided that may be tailored for each COBIT IT process. Six levels of competency are defined, and performance is measured through review of the intent of the process and the actual level of accomplishment: (p.19)

Level 0 Non-existent
Level 1 Initial/Ad Hoc
Level 2 Repeatable, but Intuitive
Level 3 Defined Process
Level 4 Managed and Measurable
Level 5 Optimized

[**Author's Note**: The COBIT framework provides a way for internal and external leaders and stakeholders to evaluate whether the IT function is being professionally managed and performed using available best practices, and whether the results of that effort are, in fact, meeting the expectations and directions of enterprise business function owners. Considering the huge expense of IT investments, and the documented difficulty in determining the return on IT investments, this care by corporate level leaders should stimulate management attention and reduce unnecessary cost.]

Federal Enterprise Architecture. The U.S. Federal Government is one enterprise that has recognized the essential need for (1) a standardized management process for preparing, documenting, and implementing a set of standardized business and information technology architectures, and (2) the need to link its billions of dollars of IT investments to prioritized business goals and technology drivers. Computer Associates International (CAI) prepared a white paper entitled: "Federal Enterprise Architecture: Realigning IT to Efficiently Achieve Agency Goals" (June 2004) which provides an excellent summary of the purpose and contents of this federal program. The highlights are:

1. The goal of an EA is to create an IT architecture that helps map an organization's business processes with its IT systems.

2. The government's FEA initiative was designed to unify currently disconnected information "silos" that have taken up residence in virtually every federal agency over the last few decades, and therefore to make the delivery of agency services more efficient.

3. The gap between IT capability and Business needs cannot be allowed to continue–EA can build a critical bridge between technological and business strategies.

4. The greatest benefits being reported by federal agencies include: (a) lowers the cost of identifying technologies, (b) lowers the cost of complying with standards, (c) reduces redundant investments, and (d) promotes technology reuse.

5. Proponents say that EAs address key pain point in federal organizations such as: (a) speeding daily operational functions, (b) improving security, (c) taking the need for mobility, (d) enabling greater productivity, and (e) shrinking IT expenses.

6. EAs improve the ability to share data across agency networks. The current inability to share information and collaborate on specific IT projects, for example, is considered an enormous national security problem

7. EAs constructs can help by defining the processes and technologies to provide and secure trusted communities of interest by persons with proper security authentication, authorization and clearance levels.

8. To create a relevant, useable EA, and organization must consider three phases: Design (Build It), Implementation (Make it Work), and Maintenance (Realize the Benefits).

The core of any organization consists of its assets, which in addition to its people and capital also include processes, data, applications and technology. When designing an EA, an organization must create an architecture that enhances the relationships of these assets to each other.

Conceptual Overview of IT Office Functions. Understanding the IT function of any sizable organization, or even larger business enterprise, requires understanding the major responsibilities typically granted by the executive leadership board and *how those responsibilities are integrated and optimized to achieve alignment with enterprise goals and cohesion among enterprise functions.* Figure 11-6 illustrates the interdependent responsibilities and sub-functions performed by the Enterprise IT office if it is to maintain, if not actually transform itself into being a leading competitor in its market space.

1. Enterprise Leadership. Executive leaders are responsible for preparing the enterprise strategy consisting of goals and objectives, providing the policy and directives necessary for organizational components to conduct their respective functions, and directing the senior IT leader or Chief Information Officer (CIO) to prepare an IT strategic plan and update it as appropriate. The IT strategic plan must take into account all the sub-functions required to achieve the business and IT plans, and to follow the approved IT governance process. Management efficiency is directly related to the quality of the IT governance process and the return on IT investments.

2. Systems Integration. IT systems consist of the operational platforms (e.g., personal computers, remote communications devices), workload applications (e.g., workflow tools, portals), data/stores (e.g., databases, information taxonomies), security protocols (e.g., information classification, access management) and network hardware (e.g., telecommunication circuits, bandwidth).

3. Highly reliable, improvable, and maintainable state-of-the-art computer communications are necessary for today's complex, network distributed enterprises that strive to support the accomplishment of business goals and objectives.

4. Architecture Management. The enterprise architecture establishes the current status and approved future direction for the IT infrastructure. It does so in a manner that defines technical systems integration and ensures tight linkage among the interdependent IT sub-functions. In the Federal Enterprise Architecture a reference model framework is used that identifies the following five mutually dependent EA components, and directs that agencies and departments ensure their EAs address all five models.

   a. Performance Reference Model (PRM). Requires the establishment of performance indicators and measures to help track and improve IT performance and improvement.

   b. Business Reference Model (BRM). Requires the preparation of an inventory of business processes, their linkage to appropriate EA layers, and their use in influencing IT investment decisions

   c. Service Reference Model (SRM). Describes the types of IT supported services provided to the business, and is linked to other layers of the EA.

   d. Data Reference Model (DRM). Describes enterprise data at the data entity level, and their linkage to business processes and appropriate EA layers.

   e. Technical Reference Model (TRM). The inventory of deployed and approved technologies linked to other layers of the EA going and proposed IT investments. A generic five stage management process is applicable:

5. Portfolio Management. The process by which business information requirements and desired capabilities are met with are:
   a. Evaluate current IT assets in the deployed portfolio
   b. Assess It opportunities on the horizon
   c. Plan to adjust the future portfolio, (4) determine the cost of panned investments, secure and allocate IT funding for programs and projects.

6. Program/Project Management. Required is a systems engineering, acquisition management methodology for bringing new IT capabilities into the deployed infrastructure in terms of the evolving EA, and for using approved program/project management techniques to inculcate disciple and cost efficiency. The phase of project management activity includes:

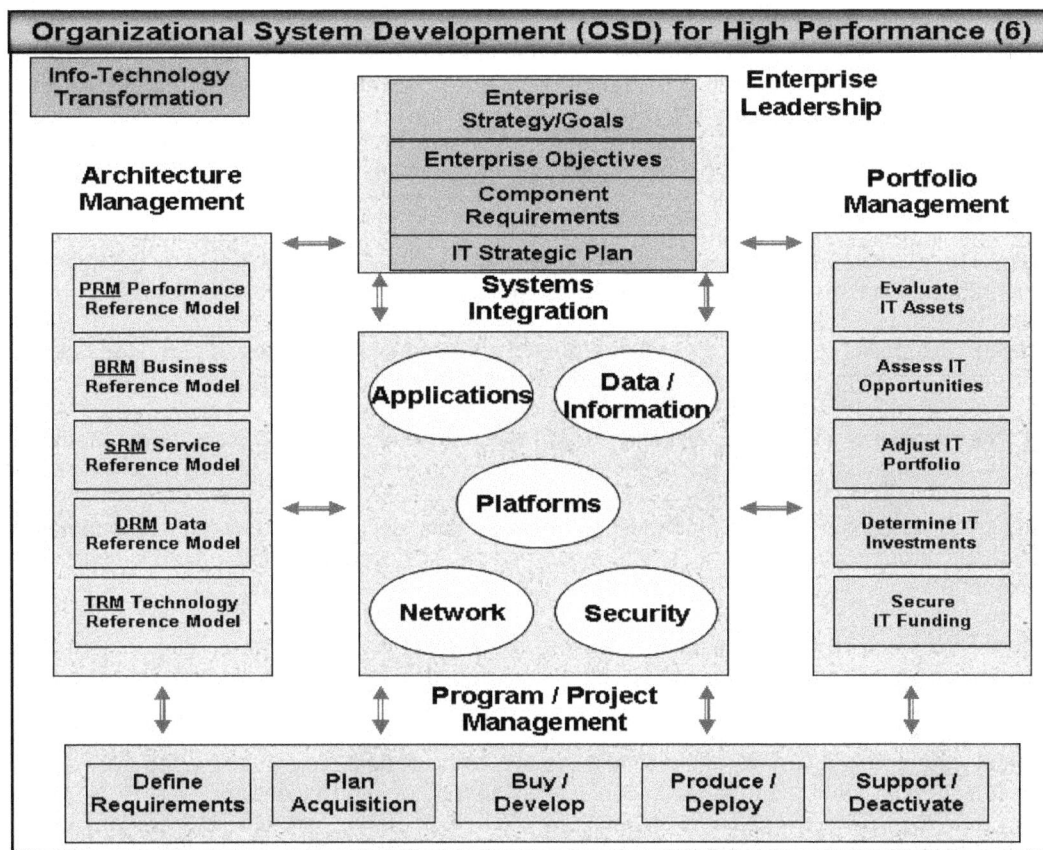

Organizational System Development (OSD) for High Performance (6)

Info-Technology Transformation

Architecture Management

Enterprise Strategy/Goals

Enterprise Objectives

Component Requirements

IT Strategic Plan

Enterprise Leadership

Portfolio Management

Systems Integration

PRM Performance Reference Model

BRM Business Reference Model

SRM Service Reference Model

DRM Data Reference Model

TRM Technology Reference Model

Applications

Data / Information

Platforms

Network

Security

Evaluate IT Assets

Assess IT Opportunities

Adjust IT Portfolio

Determine IT Investments

Secure IT Funding

Program / Project Management

| Define Requirements | Plan Acquisition | Buy / Develop | Produce / Deploy | Support / Deactivate |

Figure 11-6

a. Defining requirement
b. Planning the acquisition
c. Conducting a buy or develop process
d. Producing and deploying the new capability
e. Supporting and the eventually deactivating the system function and/or features.

[**Author's Note**: The ability of the IT leaders and/or the CIO to work cooperatively to ensure all aspects of a continuous IT improvement program, or of a major enterprise approved transformation, are executed efficiently and effectively is a determining factor on whether the enterprise business functions continue to perform as desired—poor performance almost certainly leads to decreasing productivity, customer satisfaction, and business revenue.]

Managing Interdependence (IT). The authors of "IT in the 1990s: Managing Organizational Interdependence" (Rockart & Short, 1989), argue that information technology (IT) is a partial solution to one of management's oldest problems: how to effectively manage organizational interdependence. By effective "management of interdependence," they mean causing the organization "to achieve concurrence of effort along multiple dimensions" (p. 8). They explain that organizational inter-dependence requires managers to focus on managing complexity, make greater use of teams, consider changing measurement processes, consider changing planning processes, and take action on establishing improved information technology infrastructures. They also note that as organizations continue to streamline their operations and integrate processes for greater efficiency, information technology can provide a vastly improved communications capability by wiring individuals and organizational units together.

The importance of this perspective is that it describes the increasingly complex, but manageable task of collecting, analyzing, and acting on selected management information. An efficiently constructed information distribution system capable of providing every manager, team leader, and specialist with information that is accurate, timely, and in the right amount is an important adjunct for organizational learning and development.

[**Author's Note:** In terms of the OSD framework, an information distribution system is seen as part of the operations subsystem. As such, it can be a catalyst for improving communication among individuals and teams and be an approach for the efficient exchange of technical information relevant to the organization's core processes.

Knowledge Management Technologies. IBM has been one of the leaders in the development of the field of Knowledge Management (KM). Their extensive research into the practices of tacit and explicit knowledge creation and transfer and into all aspects of IT services from information taxonomies and databases through tools for communication and collaboration to portals and networks has enabled their continued leadership in the IT industry. A study they conducted in the late 1990s illustrates their understanding of how IT innovation is an essential component when establishing corporate Knowledge Management systems. They identified twenty-two functional requirements desired by KM system users:

1. Agents/Push. The transparent delivery of relevant content   Agents are usually initiated by the information server rather than the information user. E-mail is a form of push technology.

2. Categorization. The classifying, indexing, and grouping of content according to pre-determined taxonomy hierarchies For example, tagging news feeds for distribution throughout an organization.

3. Clustering. The process of grouping collections of documents dynamically based on common themes or patterns. Clustering can extract dominant themes within documents and then group the documents according to those themes.

4. Collaboration. Transferring or sharing of "know-how" from e-mails, documents, drawings, data tables, multi-media between individuals, groups, or the enterprise independent of physical locations, and in both synchronous and asynchronous modes.

5. Communities. Enabling a self-organized, deliberate collaboration of individuals who share common practices, interests or goals and want to advance their knowledge. This can include communities of practice, interest, discussion groups, bulletin boards, etc.

6. Conferencing/White-boarding. Enabling the synchronous sharing of documents, text, video, with a group/team Conferencing can support both scheduled and spontaneous sharing of information.

7. Data Mining. Uses algorithms (usually proprietary) to analyze the aggregation of data and meta data across structured and unstructured repositories (often large volumes of data) to uncover relationships, patterns or visualizations.

8. Data Warehouse. A separate, centralized, or integrated repository for all or significant parts of the data that a enterprise's various business systems collect optimized for data retrieval and storage.

9. Distance Learning. Enabling learning technologies via various media and representations to allow for the absorption of tacit and explicit knowledge

10. Document Management. A family of applications which facilitate the management of compound documents, including storage/archiving, cataloging/indexing, search and retrieval, analysis, workflow, routing, aggregation, diffusion, and distribution.

11. Expertise/Skills Location. Enabling people/users to find the leading sources of expertise available to the organization – both internal and external–on a given subject   These systems can include expert/skills inventory databases, yellow pages or directories, project participation, or monitoring a person's activity.

12. Linguistic/Semantic Analysis. The break down of existing full text indexed repositories on the basis of word meanings and associations at the document, repository, and global levels.

13. Messaging. Enabling users to engage each other for synchronous dialog, file transfer or other forms of exchange in real time.

14. Meta-Data Management. The management of "data about data"   The process of capturing data like text, author, location, and date of creation to add context to the information being described.

15. Natural Language Inquiries. Enables users to ask questions to a system the way they think of issues.

16. Personalization. The subscription to information by a user based on their preferences and interests.

17. Search. Query based approach to discovering content across multiple sources. Search has evolved to include advancements in linguistic analysis, natural language queries, user profiles, contexts, etc.

18. Taxonomy/Mapping. The process of guiding, inventorying, and categorizing or associating complex documents (both internal and external), information or knowledge sources through hierarchies of words, meanings and associations

19. User Profiling. The chronicle, collection and administration of information about a user, such as a job title, department, skills, expertise, authorship, access rights, or role in process. This information is used to feed agent technology, document management systems, etc.

20. User Interface. The access capability, entry point and presentation of the corporate memory   Typically, access is offered through portals, intranets, extranets, etc.

21. Visualization. The graphical representation of massive volumes of information that link the interrelationships of content

22. Workflow Management. Enables the track/management of task-based work processes through an online, virtual community

[**Author's Note**: Knowledge management technology has become a staple in today's organizations, and all of the IT innovative tools and technologies listed herein are experiencing rapid implementation and improvement. The challenge, as always in the IT function, is to ensure IT strategies, architectures, and investments fully support business processes and enterprise objectives. *Learnership practitioners* will need to develop the IT knowledge and skills required for management consulting at the executive, process, and job/performer levels of enterprise responsibility.]

Fast Business   In his book *Business at the Speed of Thought* (1999), Bill Gates says that "business is going to change more in the next ten years than it has in the last fifty…These changes will occur because of a disarmingly simple idea: the flow of digital information." (p.xiii). He makes the point that: "The Internet creates a new universal space for information sharing, collaboration, and commerce. It provides a new medium that takes the immediacy and spontaneity of technologies such as the TV and the phone and combines them with the depth and breadth inherent in paper communications."

Gates continues to say "I've written this book for CEOs, other organizational leaders, and managers at all levels. I describe how a digital nervous system can transform businesses and make public entities more responsive by energizing the three major elements of any business: customer/partner relationships, employees and process. I've organized this book around the three functions that embody there three elements: *commerce, knowledge management,* and *business operations.*" To make digital information flow an intrinsic part of your company, here are twelve key steps: (pp.xix-xxi)

For Knowledge Work:

1. Insist that communication flow through the organization over email so that you can act on news with reflex-like speed.

2. Study sales data online to find patterns and share insights easily. Understand overall trends and personalize service for individual customers.

3. Use PCs for business analysis, and shift knowledge workers into high-level thinking work about products, services, and profitability.

4. Use digital tools to cerate cross-department virtual teams that can share knowledge and build on each other's ideas in real time, world-wide. Use digital systems to capture corporate history for use by anyone.

5. Convert every paper process to a digital process, eliminating administrative bottlenecks and freeing knowledge workers for more important tasks.

For Business Operations.

6. Use digital tools to eliminate single-task jobs or change them into value-added jobs that use the skills of a knowledge worker.

7. Create a digital feedback loop to improve the efficiency of physical processes and improve the quality of the products and services created. Every employee should be able to easily track all the key metrics.
8. Use digital system to route customer complaints immediately to the people who can improve a product or service.

9. Use digital communications to redefine the nature of your business. Become larger and more substantial or smaller and more intimate as the customer situation warrants.

For Commerce.

10. Trade information for time. Decrease cycle time by using digital transactions with all suppliers and partners, and transform every business process into just-in-time delivery.

11. Use digital delivery of sales and service to eliminate the middleman from customer transactions. If you're a middleman, use digital tools to add value to transactions.

12. Use digital tools to help customers solve problems for themselves, and reserve personal contact to respond to complex, high-value customer needs.

According to Gates, "The new horizontally integrated compute industry provides the best business and technical model for the future. The inexorable competition in each layer of the industry—chips, systems, software, solutions, and service—drives each area ahead independently of any other. This high volume model attracts more and more software developers who create packaged software that reduces the cost of business." (pp.436-437)

Organization Performance

> *Statistical Quality Control: A phenomenon will be said to be controlled when,*
> *through the use of past experience, we can predict, at least within limits,*
> *how the phenomenon may be expected to vary in the future.*
> *— W.A. Shewhart*

Overview: Organization Performance Management

Performance Management   Performance management is an aspect of organization improvement that is essential to quality management and customer satisfaction. In *Improving Government Performance* (Wholey & Newcomer, 1989), the authors focus on the performance management of government organizations. They state that "Strengthening government performance—improving the productivity, quality, timeliness, responsiveness, and effectiveness of public agencies and programs—is important to us all, as beneficiaries of public services and as taxpayers" (p.1). They suggest that in government there is greater difficulty in determining what constitutes high performance, not so much because the desires and needs of customers are not understood, but because the political and bureaucratic environment makes agreement over goals, priorities, budget, and performance measures difficult to achieve. They point out that customers are not only those who receive agency or program services, but other influential stakeholders and constituents that help determine policy and budget. The need for compromise among all interests tends to cause programs to have unclear goals, thereby making the collection and assessment of useful performance data a challenge. This being the case, they contend that effective and efficient agency and program management is more difficult to achieve than for the private sector. Notwithstanding this view, public sector organizations are accountable for their performance and must strive to align the interests of all those in their *customer set* who receive or are concerned with service delivery.

The authors state that "Public policy makers and managers face four leadership challenges:

1. Setting organizational goals
2. Ensuring that priorities among goals are clearly understood and agreed on
3. Providing continuous feedback on organizational performance in terms of those goals
4. Stimulating improved organizational performance" (p.2).

It should be noted that these challenges parallel the knowledge, quality, and learning themes of this book. Of particular interest, is the need to develop measurements by which organizational performance and results may be assessed and corrective action taken. To be acceptable, the performance indicators must be quantitative and qualitative measures that represent the goals and interests of all parties. In this regard, the notion of *acceptability* is an essential aspect of customer satisfaction. Acceptability may be defined as: "A term used to reflect approval by a consumer or a client of a product, service, or program. The term includes the notion of consumer or client satisfaction with services plus other relevant measures, such as clients' ratings of how well the program met their service goals, feedback about the process of service, records of complaints, and commendations" (Love, 1991). For public sector organizations, the concerns and objectives of all policy stakeholders and constituents also need to be considered.

[**Author's Note**: The above line of thinking is significant in that it elaborates on the performance measurement imperative to collect and manage with appropriate data and information, and emphasizes the product and service acceptability aspects of customer satisfaction. It also reinforces a quality management principle that being customer-focused is being quality-focused. From an ontological perspective, achieving customer satisfaction is the corollary to reaping the consequences of purposeful organizational order, knowledge, and action.]

Organizational White Space (Performance Measures). In their book *Improving Performance: How to Manage the White Space on the Organization Chart* (1990), Geary Rummler and Alan Brache advocate a high-level systems (horizontal) view of the organization in which three important process-based features can be observed:

1. The relationship between flow of work, the product, and the ultimate customer
2. How work gets done across functional boundaries
3. The internal customer relationships that need to be managed.

Their conceptualization of the enterprise or organization is in terms of three levels of end-to-end (input to output) performance:

1. Organization Level. At this level the organization's relationship with its market can be seen. Executive level leaders focus on *organizational goals, design, and management*. This level is where the organization measures its *performance effectiveness* within its marketplace.

2. Process Level. At this level the organization performance at the cross-functional work process level is managed by mid-level managers. Their responsibility is to focus on *process goals, design, and management*, and their concern is measuring and managing the *performance efficiency* of their processes.

3. Job/Performer Level. At this level of the organization the emphasis is on *job goals, design, and management*. The concern here is that each contributor operates with *performance competence*, accomplishes his or her tasks, and is recognized in doing so. (pp.15-19)

In Chapter 7, Linking Performance to Strategy, the authors say that: "Before performance at any level can be managed, the expectations for that performance need to be clearly established and communicated." (p.79) This is accomplished through strategic planning that includes (a) defining the desired end states, and (b) the preparation of a strategy implementation/monitoring plan. Subsequently, the diligent execution of the implementation/execution plan consists of multiple level performance reviews and the taking of corrective action at the organizational, process, or job/performer level. This concept has been adapted as shown in Figure 11-7. Illustrated are the three levels of organizational management slightly modified along a continuum beginning with *objectives* and moving through *improvement indicators* and *measures*, to *performance targets*. Organizational high performance occurs when the performance across all three levels is optimized, and the organization is recognized as being effective, efficient, and competent in achieving desired market results and customer satisfaction.

The Rummler-Brache performance improvement methodology is uniquely designed to integrate the three levels of goals/objectives, workflow analysis, improvement actions; and to follow-up with appropriate metrics to evaluate performance improvement. In Figure 11-7, continuous improvement is envisioned through the horizontal and vertical interdependencies among the organizational, functional/process, and job/performer levels of responsibility and accountability.

Customer Service. In *At America's Service* (Albrecht, 1988), the author offers a compelling view that serving customers more effectively and efficiently is the path to business success (in this context, the path to success for all organizations). He suggests that there is a service quality revolution occurring in American industry that will determine which businesses continue to grow and prosper. Albrecht's basic theme is that there are three major business factors that lead to customer satisfaction when they are well administered. These are:

1. "A Well-Conceived Strategy for Service. The outstanding organizations have discovered, invented, or evolved a unifying idea about what they do . . . [which] directs the attention of the people in the organization toward the real priorities of the customer.

2. Customer-Oriented Front-Line People. By some means, the managers of such organizations have encouraged and helped the people who deliver the service to keep their attention fastened on the needs of the customer.

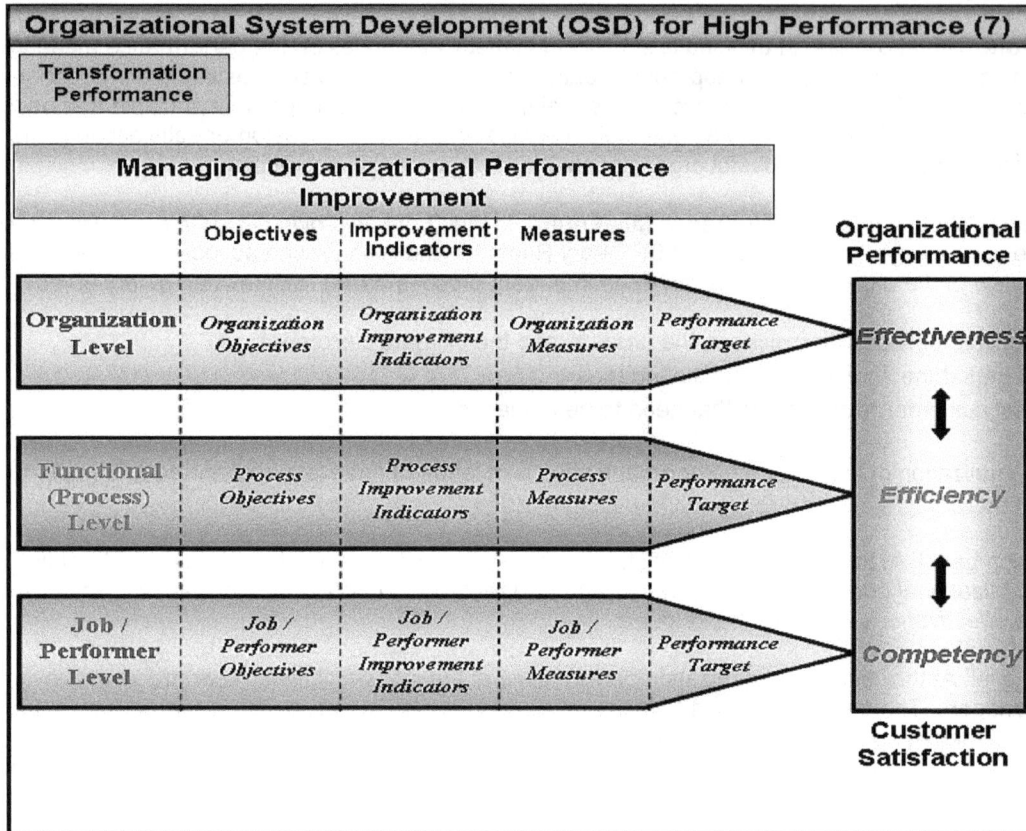

Figure 11-7

3. Customer-Friendly Systems. The delivery system that backs up the service people is truly designed for the convenience of the customer rather that the convenience of the organization" (p.32).
Albrecht's view is that the mission of all organizations is to satisfy their customers, and to do so require a focus on improving their respective systems, people, and strategies.

[**Author's Note**: An observation that may be made is that product and service quality results are determined by the organizations' customers, who typically have ever higher expectations making continuous improvement (through learning) an essential activity just to stay in business. Achieving high quality products and services, therefore, is a goal-inspired journey, rather than an end-state that may be permanently attained.]

Government Customer Services. The Federal government's National Performance Review of 1993 issued a number of reports designed to improve the effectiveness, efficiency, and economy of federal departments and agencies. One such report is entitled "Improving Customer Service" in which the stated objective was to have government focus more directly on the consumer of its services, the citizenry, than on its own internal operations. According to the report, customer and employee inputs should be used to set performance standards and that processes to collect, analyze, and take corrective action need to be established. This effort parallels the significant effort being made by private sector firms and organizations to "get in touch with their customers" as a means of increasing market share and financial performance. An Executive Order was issued that stated the following principles that govern the provision of customer service:

1. Survey customers frequently to find out what quality of services they want
2. Post service standards and results measured against them
3. Benchmark performance against the best in business

4. Provide choices in both source of delivery and means
5. Make information, services, and complaint systems easily accessible
6. Provide redress for poor service

7. Handle inquiries and deliver services with courtesy

8. Provide pleasant surroundings for customers

The intent of the Improving Customer Service initiative was to improve the quality of government product and service delivery, and this was to be done by learning what the customers and clients for these products and services need and want (their expectations). With this knowledge, the basis for improving the organization's strategies and processes was to be established and action taken to benefit the customers.

[**Author's Note**: An observation is that even the government should place more attention on service to its citizens. Whether that has happened to a large degree over the last decade is left to individual judgment, but this author thinks not.]

21st Century Measurement. In an APQC White Paper entitled: "Measurement in the 21st Century, (2004)" Lisa Higgins and Becki Hack present a thoroughly research perspective on contemporary activities in corporate performance measurement. They say that: "Successful organizations are marked by good planning, execution, and decision making in terms of corrective action and adjustments to strategic efforts. These actions stem from a strong measurement system. The key to marketplace longevity and competitiveness is finding the measurement framework that provides a balanced picture of organizational health by designing measures that are important to organizational strategic objects and actionable..." (p.8) Their recommended Performance Measurement Model (PMM) shows that strategy, goals, and objectives can be depicted in three levels of performance: (1) Strategic drives, and is evaluated by organizational performance measures, (2) Operational drives, and is evaluated by group performance measures, and (Tactical drives, and is evaluated by individual performance measures. Furthermore, they say that: "Ideally, measures should be reflected in a balanced, cascading scorecard...Organizations can achieve this balance by establishing measures in four quadrants that reflect key objectives:" (p.10)

1. Customers. Measures performance against expectations (e.g., satisfaction, loyalty, retention, acquisition, and profitability)

2. Financial. Measures economic consequences of actions already taken (e.g., income, return on equity, return on investment, growth, and cash flow)

3. Operational. Measures effectiveness, adaptability, and efficiency of internal processes

4. People. Measures employee skills, information exchange, and organization procedure

On the subject of measurement design, the authors state comment that: "APQC's research shows that organizations must begin by selecting measures that align with strategic objectives, demonstrate results, and focus on outcomes. They must also produce measures that (1) are meaningful, (2) respond to multiple organization priorities, (3) encourage operational improvements, (4) provide a complete, accurate, and believable picture of performance, and (5) blend leading and lagging indicators." (p.10) The recommended steps for setting up an effective measurement system are:

Step 1. Establish clarity around strategy and goals at the top

Step 2. Determine critical success factors

Step 3. Develop and assess effective measures

Step 4. Establish goals and baseline performance

Step 5. Assess performance

A cautionary note is provided that says: "Do not be tempted to think of measurement as an off-the-shelf solution. It first entails careful thought and planning concerning the organization's core strategies and the vital few measures that will adequately gauge performance and depict a comprehensive picture of organizational health. Then, the organization must implement and constantly monitor a performance measurement system using traditional change and management principles." (p.42)

[**Author's Note:** Readers are reminded that the APQC paper identities the same four quality performance focus areas of people, operations, customers and financial results, the ones that subsequently became the foundation of the Kaplan and Norton Balanced Scorecard introduced here in Chapter Three.]

Organizational Learning and Knowledge Management

There's a way to do it better…find it.
— *Thomas A. Edison*

Transformation Methodologies. There are many contemporary methodologies that may be pursued in an attempt to achieve significant change in organizational performance. Figure 11-8 illustrates a typical organization or business enterprise striving to stay competitive in its marketplace by working with its partners to overcome risks, achieve its mission, and satisfy its customers. To make progress, its *organizational direction* should be supported through *organizational positioning* in which business intelligence about the *competition* leads to improvement in its own operational *capabilities.* To do this requires a comprehensive *transformation strategy* that may include integrative improvements in its organization structure, processes, culture, workforce, and use of information technology. And, if the organization has been in business for more than just a few years, a number of improvement strategies may already be underway (e.g., supply chain management, process reengineering, e-business, etc.).

The addition of organizational learning and knowledge management practices and technologies will need to be carefully architected to reduce unnecessary disruption while at the same time bringing the proven benefits of these initiatives to the organization's workforce and leaders. If fact, the principles, practices, and technologies of organizational learning and knowledge management do not compete with other improvement efforts, they actually act as catalysts that enrich operational intelligence and promise even greater positive impact and results. The figure also illustrates that the five *learnership practitioner* competencies (system thinking, pattern recognition, situational learning, knowledge management, and adaptive leadership) already discussed in earlier chapters have a role to play in refining organizational organization direction and positioning, and in strategic planning and strategy implementation.

Learning Organizations. An important perspective on maximizing organizational performance is found in *The Fifth Discipline: The Art and Practice of the Learning Organization* (Senge, 1990). The author probes below the surface of most other contemporary prescriptions for improving organization performance to find important common ground—the ability of the organization to learn. According to Senge, there are five disciplines that require study and skill development if real growth and development are to occur. These are defined below.

Personal Mastery. "Personal mastery is the discipline of continually clarifying and deepening our own personal vision, of focusing our energies, of developing patience, and of seeing reality objectively…the learning organization's spiritual foundation" (p.7). Senge indicates that an organization can only learn as well as its individual members are able to learn. The implication is that the *LISA Model's* Personal System Development (PSD) feature is relevant in its focus on attaining self-fulfillment through individual quality learning and development. A mutual commitment between the organization and its members to heighten one another's learning is seen as a major first step in establishing a learning organization, and is an essential element in the OSD social subsystem.

Mental Models. "Mental models are deeply ingrained assumptions, generalizations, or even pictures and images that influence how we understand the world and how we take action" (p.8). Senge suggests that an individual's or organization's perspective on a situation may limit organizational learning, adaptation, and growth. This may be overcome by encouraging "learningful" conversations in which people balance inquiry (openness to others' views) and advocacy (willingness to expose one's own thinking). An appropriate observation may be that individuals who have optimized their personal development (reference PSD) have acquired the confidence and ability to engage in open, effective communication. The result should be better understanding, learning, and development which are important aspects of all OSD subsystems.

Team Learning. Senge says that "Team learning is vital because teams, not individuals, are the fundamental learning unit in modern organizations…unless teams can learn, the organization cannot learn" (p.10). Team learning occurs when team members are able to suspend assumptions and enter into *dialogue,* wherein thinking together causes free-flowing meaning to evolve from clear and authentic communication. The emphasis on dialogue is of particular importance in that it distinguishes the desired style of balanced, open, exploratory type of communication from the more common *discussion* in which competing viewpoints are often the at issue, and hidden agendas are often operating just below the surface. The conditions necessary to conduct dialogue include:

1. The participants' ability to suspend their respective "assumptions" so as to keep the exploration of new and related information and ideas flowing
2. The participants' regard for one another as colleagues worthy of being listened to and learning from

3. The participants' willingness to use a "process facilitator" to assure ownership of the process and the outcomes.

Senge offers that *dialogues diverge* and do not seek agreement, but attempt to achieve a richer grasp of complex issues. On the other hand, *discussions converge* on a conclusion or course of action. Used appropriately, dialogue and discussion improve issue understanding and encourage effective problem-solving and decision making. A reasonable conclusion is that fully developed and mature team members with a capacity to enter into dialogue provide a solid foundation for effective OSD social subsystem operation.

Shared Vision. A shared vision is important in that it is able to "bind people together around a common identity and sense of destiny…The practice involves the skills for unearthing shared 'pictures of the future' that foster genuine commitment and enrollment rather than compliance" (p.9). Whereas individuals pursue their visions of personal self-fulfillment, organizations need to create a common purpose that compels optimized results from the interplay among their respective strategic, operational, and performance subsystems. In the context of the LISA Model, customer satisfaction serves as the common purpose and is sought after as the goal with highest value or quality.

Systems Thinking. Systems thinking is the most important discipline (The *Fifth* Discipline) in that it provides the thinking framework for the other disciplines. Specifically, "Systems thinking is a conceptual framework, a body of knowledge and tools that has been developed over the past fifty years, to make the full patterns clearer, and to help us see how to change them effectively" (p.7). Senge notes that the overwhelming complexity, greater interdependency, and accelerated change of modern society makes it essential that we learn to see things in their wholeness. His view is that systems thinking allows us to understand, learn, and act more effectively: "…systems thinking is the cornerstone of how learning organizations think about the world" (p.69).

Senge's thesis is particularly significant when viewed within a quality and knowledge management context. Some examples include quality management's emphasis on: (1) customer satisfaction—which is accomplished through learning what the customer needs and how quality is determined before making product and service improvements, (2) quality planning—which requires learning external environmental threats/opportunities and organizational internal strengths/weaknesses which may be used for strategy development, (3) quality improvement of processes—which may be accomplished by learning how current systems perform and making selected improvements, and (4) human resource participation and development—which requires learning the degree to which employee knowledge, skills, and abilities are sufficient for task accomplishment and developing appropriate education and training.

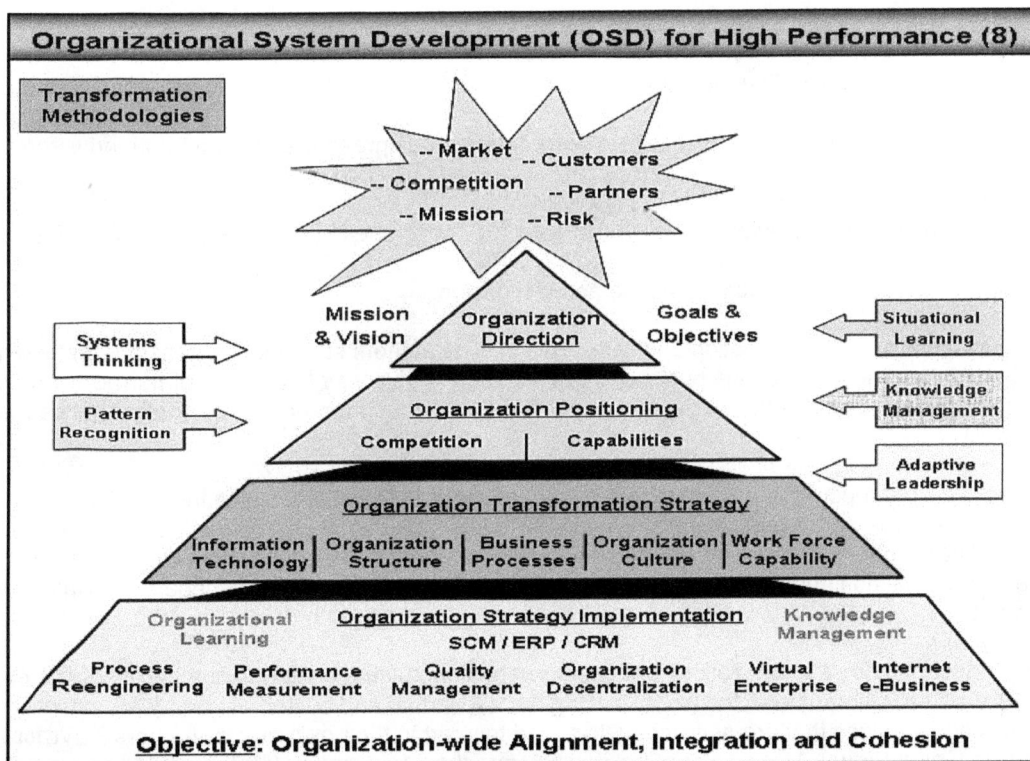

Figure 11-8

[**Author's Note**: It may be said with confidence that for organizations, just as for individuals, quality is a goal sought but never fully achieved, through a process of continuous learning. While the organization seeks learning to better satisfy its customers, its employees seek learning to achieve self-fulfillment. A strong case may be made that the goals and improvement processes for both an organization and its employees should be regarded as being mutually supportive.]

Learning Organization Principles. In *Ten Steps to a Learning Organization* (Kline & Saunders, 1993), the authors introduce the idea of "integrated learning" in which "The capacity for shared vision can be created as people learn to relate to each other in new ways that are both more intelligent and more humane" (p.14). They argue that it is possible to structure organizational workplaces to be more compatible with member needs. They also suggest that top management can model and guide changes in attitude and behavior, thereby building a foundation for increased individual and organizational learning—and improved personal and organizational performance. Their sixteen principles that promote learning in organizations (pp.16-17) are:

1. Prime the minds of individuals at every level to be self-directed.

2. View mistakes as stepping stones to continuous learning, and essential to further business growth.

3. There must be willingness to rework organizational systems and structures of all types.

4. Because learning is an emotional process, the corporate culture should be a supportive place to be.

5. Celebrate the learning process for its own sake, not just its end product.

6. Celebrate all learners equally.

7. Accomplish as much transfer of knowledge and power from person to person as possible.

8. Encourage and teach learners to structure their own learning, rather than structuring for them.

9. Teach the process of self-evaluation.

10. Recognize and accept as a goal the complete liberation of all human intelligence everywhere.

11. Recognize that different learning preferences are alternate tools for approaching and accomplishing learning.

12. Encourage people to discover their own learning and thinking styles and make them accessible to others.

13. Cultivate each employee's abilities in all fields of knowledge, and spread the idea that nothing is forever inaccessible.

14. Recognize that in order to learn something so it is easy for one to use it, it must be logical, moral, and fun.

15. Ideas can be developed best through dialogue and discussion.

16. Everything is subject to re-examination and investigation. The authors state that: "...tensions between management and labor and between the public and private sectors give way to a sense of harmony and community that satisfies the deepest needs of the whole commonwealth, and indeed for the first time fully defines the meaning of that term" (p.235)

[**Author's Note**: This perspective is notable in terms of learnership in that it articulates the need in human systems for meaningful and productive social relationships. When individuals experience shared goals and activities in a mutually supportive social atmosphere, their emotional and cognitive needs are satisfied leading to higher levels of performance. More detailed information on organizational learning and knowledge management may be found in Chapters 4 and 5.]

Going Virtual. Most of today's organizations are being swept along by the pace and complexity of the ever-changing marketplace. As we have noted here, the world is going flat and virtual and customers are demonstrating their bias toward products and services that are new, innovative, and tailored to their own needs. Authors Raymond Grenier and George Metes in *Going Virtual: Moving Your Organization into the 21st Century* (1995) provide some viewpoints and suggestions that are particularly useful in this chapter on Organizational Systems Development (OSD). A new set of mental models define the virtual operations culture. Here are just a few:

1. <u>Beliefs about Working with Networked Information</u>. These include (a) work in the network, not the office, (b) use electronic information versus paper documents, (c) seek needed information and knowledge, don't wait for it to come to you, (d) when in doubt, share–there is more power there, (e) start with the information you can get, don't wait for all of it.

2. <u>Beliefs about Work Processes</u>. These include (a) work in parallel, not serial mode whenever possible, and (b) plan and think about competencies, not geographies or organizations.

3. <u>Beliefs about Teaming</u>. These include (a) trust other stakeholders, they want the same results, b2) you are finished only when everyone else is done, and (c) recognition and rewards are based on the value the team creates, not the activity level of any individual in the team.

4. <u>Beliefs about Communication</u>. These include (a) this meeting's not over, its just gone to another medium, and b2) out of sight, but never out of mind.

5. <u>Beliefs about Learning</u>. These include (1) learn from everyone, everywhere, (2) failure is learning, and (3) learning is systemic, not episodic.

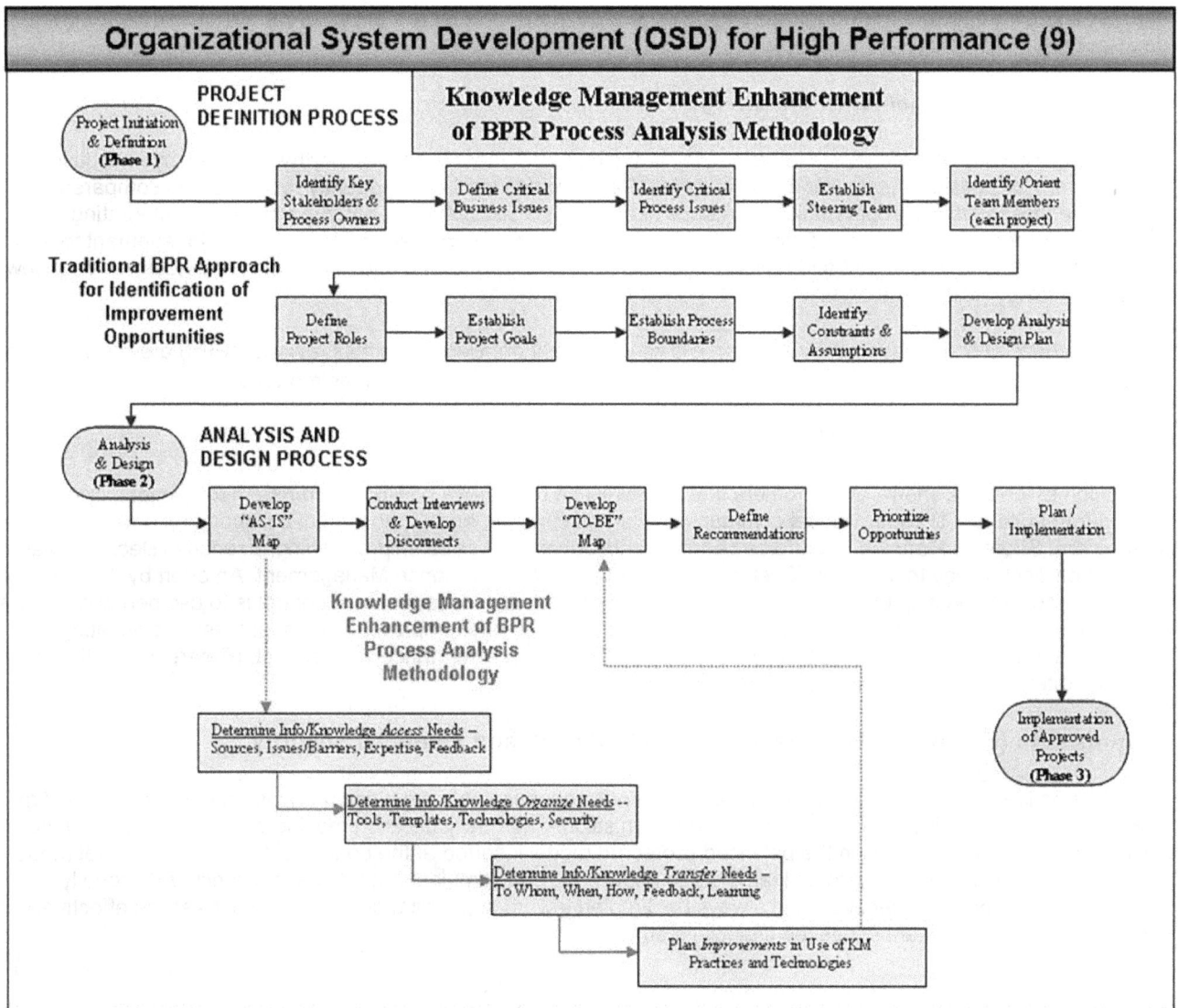

Figure 11-9

The authors comment that the term *knowledge worker* has now replaced *information worker*, and that the new title recognizes "knowledge" as the coin of the realm. Information is collaboratively built into knowledge which in turn is the basis for innovation in products and services. They say that: "The principal responsibility of the knowledge worker is to commit his or her knowledge, skills, experience and energy to create organizational value. In the virtual environment this means using the information infrastructure to support the development of knowledge as value." (p.87) This involves:

1. Understanding the organization's commitment to virtual operations

2. Understanding the virtual team's goals

3. Developing specialized and virtual operations competencies

4. Using the network to access information and knowledge in the network, and to integrate that knowledge with other knowledge/competencies in the team

5. Representing or embodying that knowledge in a product or service" (pp.88-89)

[**Author's Note**: Learnership practitioners will be responsible for understanding and consulting in all aspects of organizational systems development addressed in this chapter. Just as in the previous chapter, they will use the five learnership competencies as catalysts in framing their issues/problems and discovering the best solutions in the situation and context that presents itself. Additionally, they will need to expand their use of this chapter's knowledge and methodologies as they pursue work in selected areas of personal and community development.]

Organizational Management Consulting

In most organizations in competitive industries there are many business functions worthy of review by executive management for possible steam lining or elimination. Performance data are frequently reviewed and compared to identify the most significant opportunities. American Learnership Solutions has notable experience Integrating our (1) Project Management, (2) Business Process Reengineering and (C) Organizational Knowledge Management toolset to analyze, recommend, implement and review major "core" business functions and "supporting" services. An overview of that methodology is at Figure 11-9.

From an organization management viewpoint, it is essential that detailed *in process reviews* (IPRs) are conducted to keep key executives knowledgeable and available for assistance and redirection, as required.

Other Useful Leader and Consultant Tools

In addition to the tools shown above, others that are available to improve holistic enterprise management, operations and performance for (1) better vertical communications and control – and (2) horizontal collaboration and knowledge sharing are: Strategic Planning, Workforce Learning and Cohesion, Leadership Coaching, Executive Decision-Making, Information Technology Innovations, Customer Satisfaction and Performance Management. An effort by the firm that has been shown to be helpful in achieving greater efficiency, effectiveness and cost control is to use periodic surveys on the needs and observations of the organizations clients, customers, employees and suppliers. The resulting innovations tend to move the firm and its industry toward superior performance and respect. (Reference earlier figures in this chapter)

Organization (Business) Financials for Growth, Wealth and Financial Security

Organization leaders, chief financial officers and enterprise consultants have a common interest in assuring the firm's financial status is growing so as to achieve its stated mission. Their daily decision making activities must stay focused on improvements as illustrated in the balanced scorecard model inserted at the bottom of Figure 11–10. That model shows that improvement in workforce learning and knowledge can stimulate operational efficiency. Additionally, emphasis on business efficiency should always be directed toward supporting greater customer service effectiveness resulting in the achievement of desired financial results.

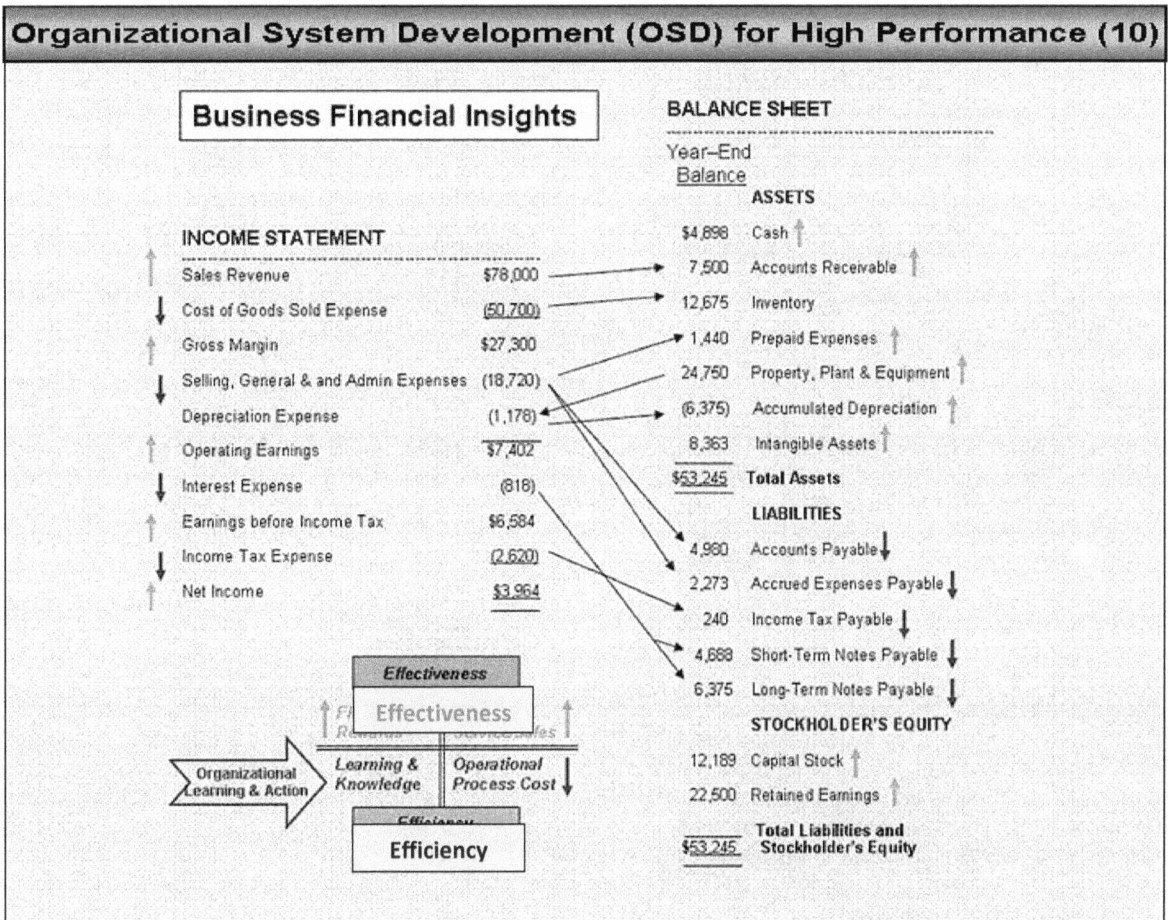

Figure 11-10

Conclusion

The first step in answering any hard business question is to take an objective, facts-based approach. This principle is easier said that acted on, — Bill Gates

Application of Learnership Reasoning Competencies. A fundamental goal of learnership is to enable most readers of the book to gain a fuller understanding of how their personal lives and careers are progressing in terms of the larger social systems of which they are a part. This book provides a beginning baseline for this assessment by presenting a philosophical viewpoint, an architectural framework, selected initial content, and a methodology for immersing the reader horizontally into numerous knowledge disciplines, while vertically driving that same reader into greater subject matter depth in topics they never knew they wanted to know more about. The long-term plan is for those individuals who desire to rapidly develop their skills in this arena—and to begin to train and consult with others—to become accomplished learnership practitioners. A little theory can go a long way once we start to appreciate the benefits of becoming holistic thinkers, lifelong learners, and adaptive leaders.

This section is presented at the end of each chapter on social system development (personal, organizational, community, and societal). A little effort is now required from readers desiring to exercise their evolving understanding of learnership. Your task: using Table 11- 2 below and a separate piece of paper, write down some examples of how the five learnership competencies influence, drive, support, or otherwise have a powerful effect on the organizational social system discussed in this chapter.

Implications for Integral Learning and Knowledge Management. We now arrive at the *social systems domain* where the result of our knowledge building, with the assistance of the five learnership reasoning competencies, may be reviewed. The major determination for **OSD** is whether the knowledge recently created is "relevant" to the inquiry, study, problem or issue being considered. *Quite often a paradox occurs* at this juncture in which the conclusion reached appears to be inconsistent, conflicting or incompatible with what the individuals involved anticipated or desired. When analyzed, questions arise as to whether the Systems Thinking, Pattern Recognition or Situational

Reasoning Competency	Organizational Social System
Systems Thinking	Impact on your organization?
Pattern Recognition	Impact on your organization?
Situational Learning	Impact on your organization?
Knowledge Management	Impact on your organization?
Adaptive Leadership	Impact on your organization?

Table 11-2

Learning competencies have been utilized in an open, factual, unbiased, timely and convincing manner. That is, is the knowledge really correct and integral when considering the obvious limitations in people's minds and personal preferences – and their cultures, education, and beliefs are sometimes entirely in conflict. Effective and valued knowledge will need to be judged by the *OSD Direction, Operations and Performance* domains of thinking and behavior as interpreted by skilled and experienced leaders.

[**Author's Note**: Are the knowledge and skills you have acquired and using so far in your life sufficient for you to achieve your current goals, a meaningful life and a memorable legacy?]

Personal Reflection. This topic appears at the send of each chapter and is meant to serve two purposes: (1) be a reader's guide to main points and "takeaways," and (2) to encourage everyone to take a moment to engage their mental cognition and intuition on what the chapter means to them—especially at this time in their lives. Questions for chapter reflection follow immediately below; and for those readers inclined to maintain a self-assessment and create their own e-book, your thoughts should be recorded here and in your *American Learnership for Life, Work, Wealth, Health and Legacy Success* format located at Appendix B.

Questions for Discussion:

1. Can you identify three to four characteristics of an *Intelligent Organization*?

2. What is the concept of *organizational white space*? Can you give a couple of examples of where organization White Space may be a problem?

3. Knowledge management provides a number of *practices and technologies* for organizational use. Can you name three of each?

4. Can you list two to three major learning points from this chapter that you want to keep in mind to improve your ability to manage your life and career?

5. Can you identify two to three topics, models, or perspectives in this chapter you would like to learn more about?

6. Should you be making an entry into your *American Learnership for Life, Work, Wealth, Health and Legacy Success* at Appendix B?

Questions on Meaning of Your Life (Figure 11-12)

How do these surrogate goals work for you right now?
Can you venture a guess as to what might evolve as you continue to reflect and learn?

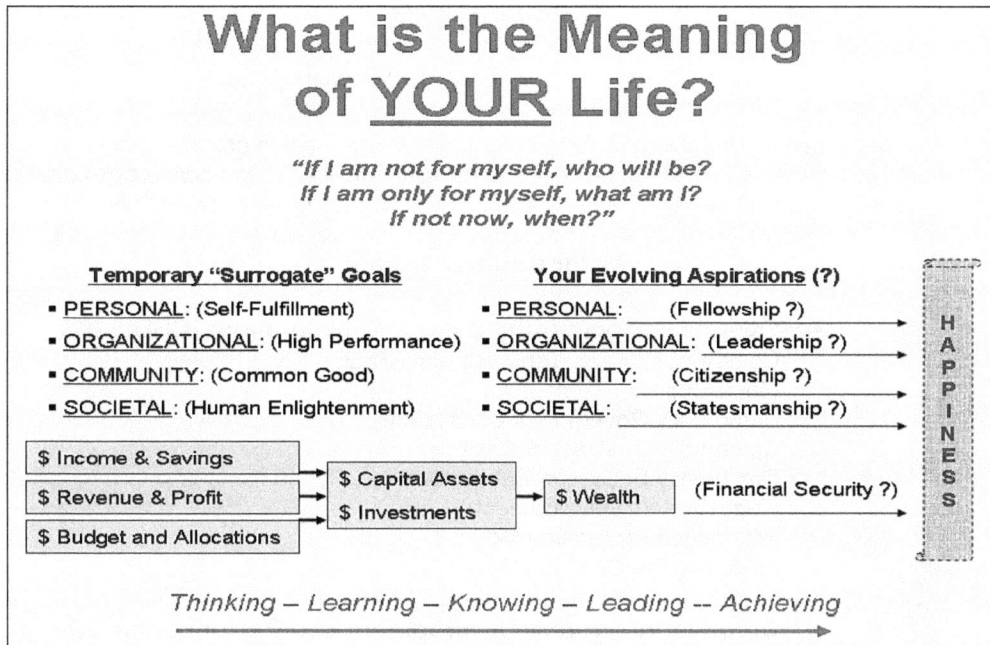

What is the Meaning of <u>YOUR</u> Life?

"If I am not for myself, who will be?
If I am only for myself, what am I?
If not now, when?"

Temporary "Surrogate" Goals	Your Evolving Aspirations (?)	
▪ <u>PERSONAL</u>: (Self-Fulfillment)	▪ <u>PERSONAL</u>: (Fellowship ?)	H
▪ <u>ORGANIZATIONAL</u>: (High Performance)	▪ <u>ORGANIZATIONAL</u>: (Leadership ?)	A P
▪ <u>COMMUNITY</u>: (Common Good)	▪ <u>COMMUNITY</u>: (Citizenship ?)	P I
▪ <u>SOCIETAL</u>: (Human Enlightenment)	▪ <u>SOCIETAL</u>: (Statesmanship ?)	N E S S

$ Income & Savings
$ Revenue & Profit → $ Capital Assets → $ Wealth (Financial Security ?)
$ Budget and Allocations $ Investments

Thinking – Learning – Knowing – Leading -- Achieving

Figure 11-12

Insights, Commitments and Skills

If you plan to participate in *the American Learnership for Life, Work, Wealth, Health and Legacy Success self-development* experience, it is suggested you record your Insights, commitments and skills to be developed here in this chapter, and again in Appendix B:

<u>My learning in terms of new insights, changing priorities, new commitments or skills I want to acquire:</u>

1. <u>Insights (Example)</u>: Remind myself that ...

2. <u>Commitments (Example)</u>: Continue to ask myself ...

3. <u>Skills (Example)</u>: Apply my knowledge and skills to ...

Chapter Twelve

Community (Mega) System Development

It now appears certain that a strong, local community is essential to psychological well-being, personal growth, social order, and a sense of political efficacy. These conclusions are now emerging at the center of every social science discipline. — Edward Schwarz

Major Chapter Topics

Community (Mega) System Development

Overview: Community System Development (CSD)

This Life Management Handbook chapter contains a broad overview of insights and perspectives designed to assist the reader in learning to think holistically about his or her responsibilities and contributions as a member of their local city or county community. Individual citizens will learn to see the larger complexity of which they are an important part. Community leaders and organizational managers will come to understand their roles more clearly and gain new perspectives leading to opportunities for public service innovation. *Learnership practitioners*, in particular, will learn to grasp the comprehensive array of community topics relevant to their roles as adaptive leaders, workgroup facilitators, and project managers.

Community System Development (CSD). CSD concerns the long-term development of geographically-based public and private sector entities. Community is considered to have two major aspects:

1. The view of community as a socio-political hierarchy of *local, state, and federal communities* to which most citizens belong

2. The view of *special purpose communities*, e.g., the scientific, ethnic, and social communities that may be found in most locales.

A significant trend we see more of is the impact of the internet, e-business, and globalization on community boundaries where what was once local can now be international.

The *Learnership Integrated Systems Architecture (LISA)* illustrates three major community subsystems through which inquiry into community objectives and processes may be pursued and understood:

1. Government/public administration subsystem – the primary means by which a community establishes the framework and authority for control and administration of its political relationships

2. Business/industry subsystem – the predominant source for the production and distribution of economic goods and services desired by the community

3. Education/academia subsystem – the fundamental educational resources for the community's intellectual and social development.

The principle here is that when government, business, and education are mutually supportive in their objectives and use of systemic processes, rapid community learning and development may be achieved. *The direction of that development, at the mega-system level, should be toward serving the public interest and the common good.* The goal of achieving the common good satisfies the ontological need for a "sense of purpose," and is best attained through understanding and cooperation among the community's governmental, educational, and private business institutions.

Figure 12-1 provides an overview of key CSD concepts and relationships to assist the reader in building a mental model as he or she proceeds through this chapter. These major features are:

1. Mega-cognitive Reasoning. Illustrated are the *five reasoning competencies* that can be used to maximize organizational social system development.

2. Community Government Subsystem. The *Community Government* subsystem highlights responsibility and effort at the public utilities, law enforcement, social services, fire and safety, and recreational levels of community activity.

3. Community Business Subsystem. The *Community Business* subsystem concerns licenses and registrations, trade and commerce policies and procedures, and economic and ecological operational responsibilities.

4. Community Education Subsystem. The *Community Education* subsystem focuses on the planning, construction, and maintenance of the public school system, and the oversight of all educationally based public and private organizations.

5. Mega-system Development. Illustrated are the *four learnership social systems* with this chapter's emphasis being at the *community mega-level*.

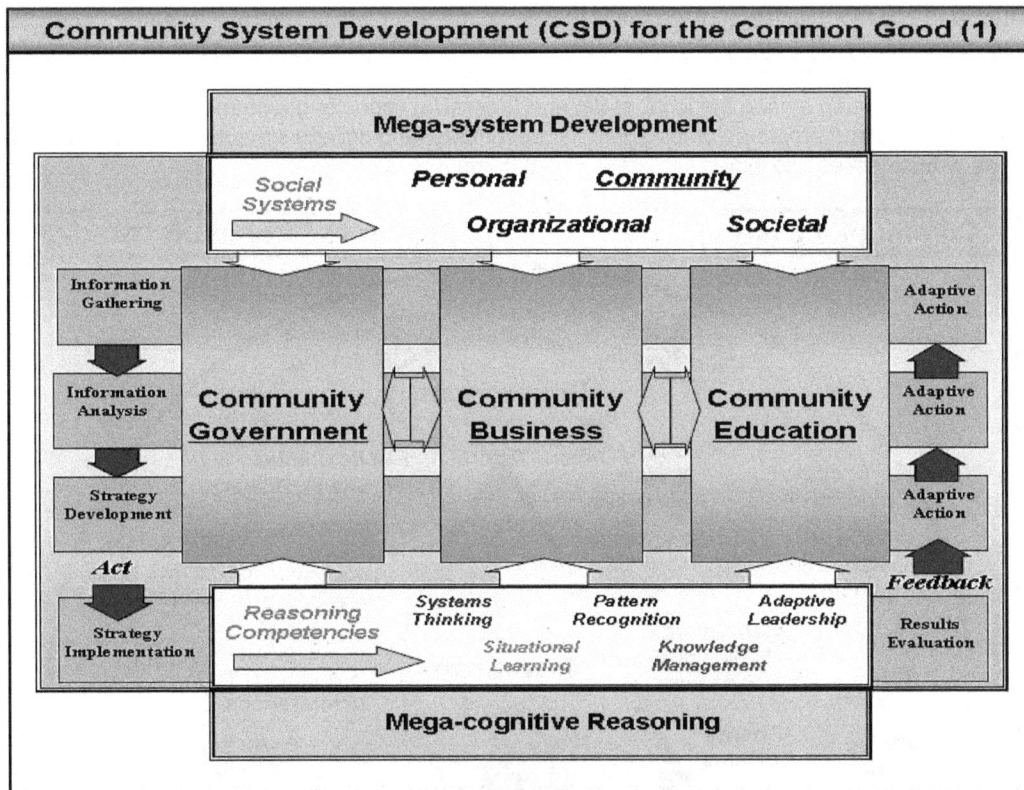

Figure 12-1

6. Information Processing Model. Illustrated is a general approach for problem solving and decision-making throughout the community: Gather and analyze information, develop a strategy and implement it, observe results and take corrective action, if required.

Ideally, the three CSD subsystems operate, over time, in a mutually reinforcing manner enabling individuals and the community to learn and take action consistent with their legal and publicized strategy and commitments – and, the public good is served.

[**Author's Note**: A significant point to make at this juncture is that during Part One (Chapters five through nine) the Five Learnership Reasoning Competencies have been integrated into a comprehensive *Total Knowledge Management (TKM) framework. That "total learning, knowing, and leading" framework has been embedded in the Learnership Integrated Systems Architecture (LISA)* and all the principles, practices, and technologies of TKM are conceptually available, and should be appropriately applied, for full community social systems development.]

Achieving the Common Good. The common good is conceived as being the combination of positive goals, ideals, attributes, and capabilities toward which a community strives, but never fully acquires. *The common good* is the CSD objective analog to the OSD *high performance* and the PSD *self-fulfillment* learning and knowledge objectives previously described. As conceived, herein, the spirit of *citizenship* acts as a catalyst for attaining the common good in a manner similar to that in which *leadership* fosters customer satisfaction and interpersonal *fellowship* elicits self-fulfillment. The common good relates to the building of a community's infrastructure and culture, and to the creation of peoples' capacity for full humanness and a life worth living.

The institutional contributions to the common good may be seen when:

1. Academia inculcates appropriate values, knowledge, and skills into the educational mainstream

2. Business provides value-added products and services that meet the developmental needs of an expanding population

3. Government improves the democratic processes that assure liberty and justice for all

4. All of this occurs with due consideration of the trends and implications of modern technology and the emergence of ecological concerns.

Figure 12-2 illustrates is a representation of the many functional areas for which community leaders and citizens are required to take responsibility. The ability of government, education, and business institutions to meld together the goals, strategies, and resources necessary to deliver required and desired services is a measure of the community's success. A mutually supportive relationship among the local, state, and federal functions of government; the exchange of learning and knowledge methodologies and programs among primary, secondary, and college schools; and the innovation and job creation activities of businesses and industry together make community happen.

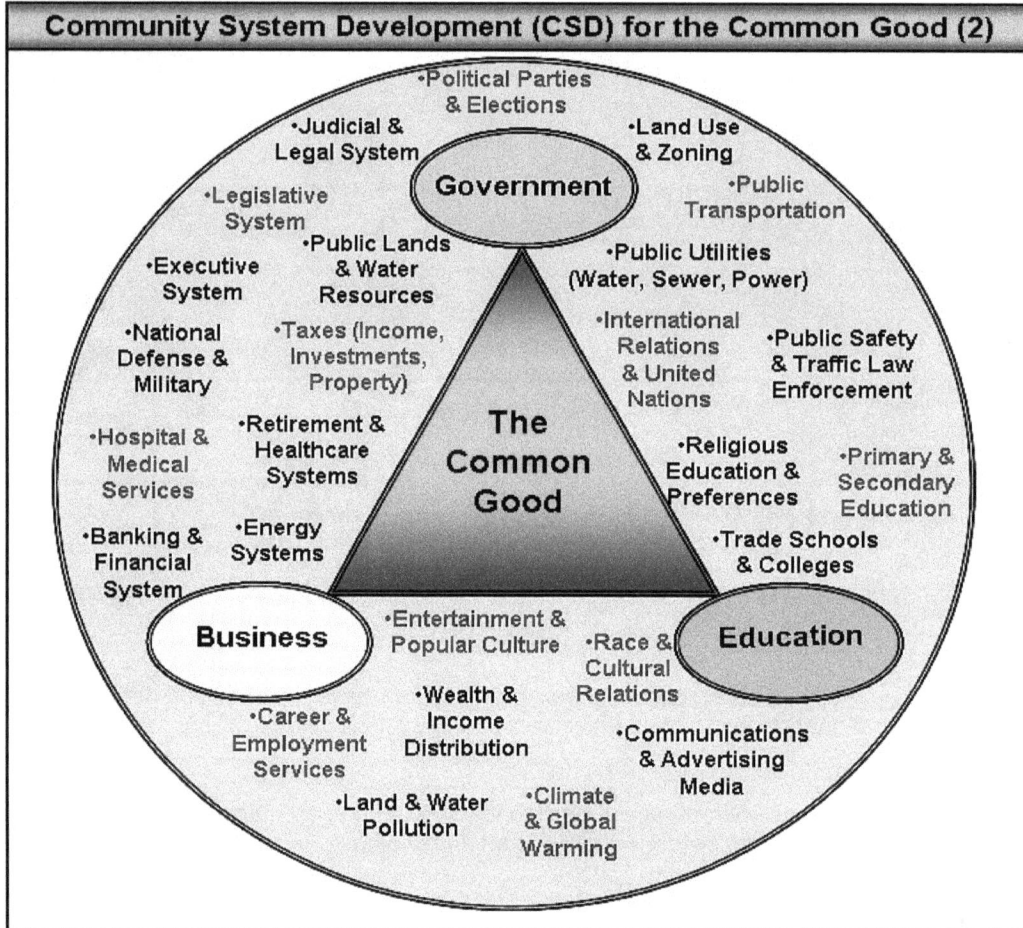

Figure 12-2

Community System Development and Performance

The first requisite of a good citizen in this republic of ours is that he should be able and willing to pull his weight — Theodore Roosevelt

General Observations. Some contemporary topics worth noting have be raised by academic experts and experienced leaders in community issue resolution and public management. These include the need to practice public sector stewardship, understand the unique American experience and responsibilities, set worthwhile goals and tackling public problems, build a responsive community, and create a spirit of participation and citizenship. These issues and observations are highlighted below, and set the stage for the additional perspectives provided in the sections on government, business, and education.

Stewardship for American Institutions. In his book entitled: *Stewardship: Choosing Service Over Self-Interest* (1993), Peter Block defines stewardship as "the holding of something in trust for another, and says that when we choose service over self-interest we build the capacity of the next generation" (p.xx). The elements of service include that: (1) there is a balance of power, (2) the primary commitment is to the larger community, (3) each person joins in defining purpose and in deciding what kind of culture will be developed, and (4) there is a balanced and equitable distribution of rewards (p.xxi).

Block argues that stewardship goes beyond the normal connotation in which one acts financially accountable or carefully develops and applies his or her talents. To him, stewardship has a political dimension in which power, when obtained, is used primarily for service to others rather than for one's own self-interest. He says that the best leaders in history were often religious leaders; they were able to integrate accountability and activism in service to their followers. In Block's view power is always granted from those below, and good leaders and stewards work to improve themselves through dialogue and learning with others.

[**Author's Note**: The LISA model's CSD construct envisions executive managers of business, government, and education transforming their institutions into service organizations capable of stimulating rapid Community Systems Development (CSD) in the quest for the common good. For this to happen, they (most likely their replacements) would need to change from being managers to being leaders; and then from being leaders to being stewards. Stewardship is a useful concept in capturing the essence of behavior for the individual who through personal development becomes self-fulfilled, the organization that through effective leadership achieves high performance, and the community that through participative citizenship accomplishes the common good.]

Tackling Public Problems in a Shared Power World. In *Leadership for the Common Good* (Bryson & Crosby, 1992), the authors "address the question of how public leaders can inspire and mobilize others in a shared power world to undertake collective action in pursuit of the common good" (p.xii). While it is clear that leaders in governmental and public administrative positions operate in a shared power world where no one is in charge, leaders in business and industry and in education also find formidable challenges in setting direction, establishing policy, and managing change. The higher the organization or community level at which one works, the more managing in a shared power environment becomes a reality. Sharing objectives, resources, and authority is essential to achieving any progress on collective goals. Bryson and Crosby suggest that public leaders need the following capabilities to succeed at their task in this difficult environment (p.xii):

1. Understanding the social, political, and economic "givens".

2. Understanding the people involved, especially oneself.

3. Building teams.

4. Nurturing effective and humane organizations, inter-organizational networks, and communities.

5. Creating and communicating meaning and effectively employing formal and informal forums as settings for creating and communicating meaning.

6. Making and implementing legislative, executive, and administrative policy decisions and effectively employing formal and informal arenas as settings for policy-making and implementation.

7. Sanctioning conduct that is, enforcing constitutions, laws, and norms, and resolving residual conflicts; and effectively employing formal and informal courts as settings for sanctioning conduct.

8. Practicing systems thinking; the ability to see the connectedness of people, groups, organizations, institutions, and communities.

[**Author's Note**: In terms of the LISA model's CSD construct, the role of elected government officials and senior public administrators in forging the public agenda, obtaining political support, establishing public policy, allocating public resources, and implementing consensually-supported public programs is now becoming evident. Systems thinking and consensus-building loom as monumental tasks as those selected to do the public's business struggle to frame contemporary issues within constitutional prescriptions, and to serve local communities and the whole of society. Knowledge, reasoning, learning, tolerance, and judgment are all needed in abundance as pluralistic forces debate what is in the public interest and for the common good.]

All Organizations Are Public. According to Barry Bozeman in *All Organizations are Public* (1987), all societal organizations have some aspect of "publicness," not only those that officially represent the public interest such as government organizations. His reasoning is that all organizations are based upon economic authority or political authority or some combination of the two, which are established by the society in which they reside. As he sees it, public sector organizations are created through political authority, but are influenced significantly by the society's economic practices. And, private sector organizations are established to meet economic needs, but are aided and constrained by the actions of those in political authority. Additionally, there are organizations designed specifically as hybrid private-public organizations further compounding one's ability to separate the two.

 This lack of clear delineation between the public and private sectors is at issue. While it has been traditionally thought that only public organizations are concerned with public awareness and the public's stake in the organization's activity, so too, private organizations have similar responsibilities for the health and development of their respective communities.

[**Author's Note**: The implications of this point of view on the LISA model is that business organizations should be considered to be purposeful contributors to the common good along with the academic and government organizations that traditionally carry this responsibility. "Business for business sake" as the old saying goes is an inaccurate description of the role of society's business community. Instead, business in the public interest and for the common good is a more appropriate conception wherein all of society's organizations take responsibility for planning and implementing desirable futures.]

America as a Construction of Mind. In his book entitled *Culture of Complaint: The Fraying of America* (Hughes, 1993), Robert Hughes expresses concern over the deterioration of American polity and culture. He views the contemporary fractionating of society as evidenced through the "political correctness" and "multiculturalism" movements, and numerous other politicization efforts, as tearing at the fabric of our traditions of tolerance and freedom. He observes strong *tendencies among individuals and groups to seek identification through separation from others in the society*, and to differentiate themselves at the expense of others, thereby causing resentment and despair.

According to Hughes, our ability and willingness to emphasize what we value in common while maintaining a posture of mutual respect for differences, appears to be diminishing in a wave of trivial political pursuits and nonnegotiable stands on smaller issues. Hughes comments that: "America is a construction of mind, not of race or inherited class or ancestral territory. [It] is a collective work of imagination whose making never ends, and once the sense of collectivity and mutual respect is broken the possibilities of Americanness begin to unravel" (pp.12-13). He suggests that present trends toward cultural separatism emasculate the larger culture Americans have in common, and that real self-esteem comes from discovering that which unites a community as well the special values of its diverse entities.

[**Author's Note**: This view supports the usefulness of the LISA model in that it stresses the need for communities, and society as a whole, to recognize and value those aspects of their common experience that melds them together and strengthens their capacity for human learning and development. Individuals, organizations, and communities are social system entities in need of one another's knowledge, skills, and caring while in pursuit of their respective quality objectives. A zero-sum approach to social relations and issues consigns the majority of citizens to less than satisfactory life and work experiences.]

Higher Goals for America. In *Higher Goals for America: Doing Better than the Best* (Nagel, 1989), the author suggests that what is often thought to be the optimum in public policy may in reality be a lot less than what should be desired. He suggests that *it is better to set society's goals very high and not achieve them, than to set them much lower and fully achieve them* (p.23). Essentially, when it comes to social policy, we should learn to think broader and aspire higher for the sake of our shared community experience. Nagel identifies eleven representative policy problem areas for which society could choose higher-level strategies in order to raise the quality of community life over the long-term:

1. Economic Problem: Unemployment. A goal of zero unemployment, plus a higher percentage of adults in labor force that are fully paid

2. Economic Problem: Inflation. A goal of zero inflation, plus increased benefits from prices paid

3. Economic Problem: Consumer Rights. A goal of zero fraud plus the availability of more useful information for decision making

4. Political Problem: World Peace. A goal of zero casualties, plus greater world cooperation

5. Political Problem: Free Speech. A goal of zero interference, plus greater support for innovative ideas

6. Political Problem: Government. A goal of zero waste and corruption, plus greater participation, equity, and due process

7. Social Problem: Crime. A goal of zero crime, plus zero civil and job wrongdoing

8. Social Problem: Poverty and Discrimination. A goal of zero poverty and discrimination, plus productive job satisfaction

9. Social Problem: Education. A goal of zero functional illiteracy, plus greater breadth and inquisitiveness in learning

10. Science Problem: Health. A goal of zero non-aging diseases, plus health robustness and greater longevity

11. Science Problem: Environment. A goal of zero pollution, plus reclamation and renewal

According to Nagel, the challenge is to achieve socially desired objectives through the appropriate analysis and establishment of public policy. He suggests a "general means for achieving desired goals" based on developing answers to a series of benefit/cost focused questions. The community's questions would be: How can we:

1. Increase the benefits of doing right

2. Decrease the costs of doing right

3. Increase the costs of doing wrong

4. Decrease the benefits of doing wrong

5. Increase the probability that the benefits and costs will occur (p.40)

Nagel calls this approach an *incentives approach* for encouraging socially desirable behavior. He also says that wherever possible this approach should be supplemented by a *structures approach* which focuses on eliminating the need, in many social problem areas, for individuals to even have to make benefit/cost decisions. A structures approach requires that the community evaluates and re-defines its common values and desired behaviors – essentially, a fundamental change in culture would need to be achieved.

[**Author's Note**: This perspective offers insight into the notion that a community can choose its path of development if it is willing to reflect on its current condition and culture, to create a vision for its desired future state, and is willing to take specific, rational action to close the gap between the two. The LISA model is structured to emphasize the need for communities to assess their internal strengths and weakness, and external threats and opportunities, so that quality-related features of their common good may be identified and pursued. Participants in this process would be individuals and organizations representing the government, academia, and business institutional domains.]

A Responsive Community. In *The Responsive Society* (Etzioni, 1991), the author presents his views on the need for social change, and the elements, structure, and ethics of that change. He offers the notion that: "...life is a train ride [that] should be led so that the ride is meaningful, which can be achieved not by Sisyphean pleasures but by dedication to service to transcendental causes, compelling values that serve the commons, not the transient self" (p.10).

Etzioni articulates the social-philosophical precepts of the *communitarian movement* in which *individual rights need to be balanced with the concern for the community as a whole*. The communitarian view is that contemporary liberal philosophies emphasize the rights of individuals within the community while neglecting the obligations to that community, its shared values, and its common purposes (p.127). When there exists a weak conception of community, the common good, and shared moral values, communitarians become concerned with the capacity of the community to avoid moral chaos and sustain development for the benefit of all in the community. Whereas some scholars hold that community responsibilities are discretional in nature and are secondary to an individual's human rights and self-interest, communitarians seek to equalize the scales by pointing out that all members of a community are socialized within the culture of that community and are thereby obligated to balance their rights and actions with what is good (the common good) for the whole community.

Regarding the notion of a "responsive community," Etzioni argues that communities influence every member's most inner drives, preferences, and moral commitments through a process of acculturation that establishes the basic human nature of its citizens. He states that: "One can determine that one's society is more responsive to human nature than another only if one assumes a basic underlying human nature (p.126). The social objective, according to this view, is to create social, political, and economic principles and practices that foster reasoning and decision-making that sustain the community's needs along with those of its individual citizens. Etzioni's comment is that: "Moreover, this notion of common good has a dynamic element: communitarians see the community and individuals as working toward a telos, a common purpose or goal, not fulfilled in society today" (p.132).

[**Author's Note**: In terms of the LISA model, Etzioni's viewpoint is exceptionally helpful. He establishes the anchor for the concept of "a common good" at the core of a community's acculturation of its citizens. To be raised in a community is to be a part of that community, and to have obligations to that community. These obligations are performed as a service to the community's common good, and are necessarily considered along with individual rights when determining how best to maintain societal development.]

Guideposts to Citizenship. In *Guideposts to Citizenship* (Finch, 1927) is a quaint little book that suggests an approach to school-based citizenship training for children. The goal is the rearing of children whose social development includes both the acquisition of the common virtues of good character and a willingness to display those virtues in support of their community's traditions. Finch summarizes the purpose of the book by saying that the intent is to help children "…cultivate the power to face real situations thoughtfully; to form clear and accurate judgments of desirable behavior; and to attain in a gradually increasing degree, conscious self-control. It provides for citizenship activities in that broad sense which includes character education. It stimulates effort along many lines, keeping in mind the usefulness to the community as the ultimate goal". (p.v)

The foundation for Finch's recommendations was The Code of a Good American, a winning essay written by William J. Hutchins for the 1916 National Morality Codes Competition sponsored by the Character Education Institution of Washington, DC. In abbreviated form, Hutchins' code of principles (pp.272-277) states the following: "Boys and girls who are good Americans try to become strong and useful, worthy of their nation, that our country may become ever greater and better. Therefore, they obey the laws of right living which the best Americans have always obeyed:"

1. The Law of Self-Control. Those who best control themselves can best serve their country.

2. The Law of Good Health. The welfare of our country depends on those who are physically fit for their daily work.

3. The Law of Kindness. In America, those who are different must live in the same communities. We are of many different sorts, but we are one great people. Every unkindness hurts the common life, every kindness helps.

4. The Law of Sportsmanship. Strong play increases and trains one's strength and courage. Sportsmanship helps one to be a gentleman, a lady.

5. The Law of Self-Reliance. Self-conceit is silly, but self-reliance is necessary to be strong and useful.

6. The Law of Duty. The shirker and the willing idler live upon others, and burden fellow citizens with work unfairly. They do not do their share for the country's good.

7. The Law of Reliability. Our country grows great and good as her citizens are able more fully to trust each other.

8. The Law of Truth. One should stand by the truth regardless of one's own likes and dislikes.

9. The Law of Workmanship. The welfare of our country depends upon those who have learned to do in the right way the work that makes civilization possible.

10. The Law of Teamwork. As we learn to work together, the welfare of our country is advanced.

11. The Law of Loyalty. If America is to become ever greater and better, her citizens must be loyal, devotedly faithful, in every relation of life.

[**Author's Note**: *This eighty year old perspective is included because of its simple message relating to personal character, organization teamwork, and community citizenship. Some might say that these notions are too simple, too prescriptive, and too limiting on individual rights. However, who would deny their value in a dialogue on American human and social system betterment in an era of general uncertainty, values conflict, information overload, and strident differentiation.*]

American Civic Documents. Before leaving this section it is useful to remind ourselves that the basis for the founding of the independent nation called the United States was the desire to wrest self-determination from the authority of the King of Great Britain. The leaders of the revolution, and subsequently the founding leaders of the American form of governance were careful to define what was not working, what was necessary for a democratic republic to operate, and what needed to be guaranteed for a better society to function. In this regard, they determined in their *Declaration of Independence* that: "We hold these truths to be self-evident, that all men are created equal, that they are endowed by their Creator with certain inalienable rights, that among these are life, liberty, and the pursuit of happiness."

This remarkable sentiment and action, leading as it did to the War of Independence, the establishment of the U.S. *Constitution*, and the first *Ten Amendments to the Constitution* was an innovation in nation building such that the nations and people's of the earth had never before seen. For over two hundred and thirty years this experiment in democratic governance and human development has persisted, cycling between moments of glory and those of nefarious behavior, to discern its purpose and meaning within a tumultuous environment of challenge and change. The reader is encouraged to once again review our *Declaration* (Appendix A) and *Bill of Rights* (Appendix A) to gain appreciation of what we have guaranteed to one another. It is our foundation, along with the Constitution itself, for achieving the common good to which we aspire.

Community Subsystem Development and Performance

There is no higher religion than human service. To work for the common good is the greatest creed.
— *Albert Schweitzer*

Government Subsystem.

Regime Values. In *Ethics for Bureaucrats* (Rohr, 1989), the author presents the concept of "regime values" which are defined as "…the values of that political entity that was brought into being by the ratification of the Constitution that created the present American republic" (p.68). He is speaking of the fact that through democratic and representative procedures the American founders created the Constitution to represent their collective interest. As such, *the Constitution represents the values of our society, and it is upon those values that public law is established.* Rohr's view is that people in public service are obliged to conduct their official affairs in terms of the law and their oath to uphold the Constitution – and in doing so they sustain the normative values of society. He observes that: "Thus the oath of office provides for bureaucrats the basis of a *moral community* [italics added] that our pluralism would otherwise prevent. It rescues pluralism from the downward plunge into 'an inharmonious melange of ill-assorted fragments' and presents it anew as 'an ordered dialogue of interesting viewpoints." (p.70)

While the primacy of the legislature, as the people's representatives, to make law is recognized, Rohr gives emphasis to the role played by the Supreme Court in instructing the citizenry on the character of the Republic. The fact that: decisions rendered by the judges are most often accompanied by explanations of the grounds for those decisions and include dissenting opinions, is represented as a source of valuable instruction for understanding the fundamental beliefs and attitudes of the regime. In terms of the responsibilities of those in public service, Rohr argues that they should frame their thinking and decisions with knowledge built on an *informed dialogue* with the political society they serve; and within that context, address contemporary problems with bold and creative applications of the traditional values of the people in whose name they govern". (p.85)

Every democratically-based society establishes its norms, codifies many of its norms into law, and enforces a standard of behavior acceptable to the majority. Through the Constitution, legislation, and their legal rulings, society establishes its guiding framework and manages its development.

[**Author's Note**: The usefulness of this perspective for understanding the LISA model is to recognize that civic values and ethics are a large part of the cultural framework within which individual, organizational, and community learning occurs. And, according to Aristotle (in *Politics*), "*The citizens of the state should always be educated to suit the constitution of their state."*

Constraints and Trade-Offs in Policy Making. In *Crucial Decisions: Leadership in Policymaking and Crises Management* (Janis, 1989), the author presents a model for effective policy making and discusses the reasons why policymakers are so often seen to be deviating from moral, humanitarian, and rational principles in their actions. Janis focuses primarily on top-level policymakers, and his thoughts apply equally in the public and private sectors. His views have particular importance, however, in public sector deliberations because of the complexity of social issues and their broad impact on large numbers of individuals and organizations in the community.

Janis builds on an earlier "Presidential decision making model for foreign policy" by Alexander George to create his model entitled: Constraints Creating Trade-Off Dilemmas in Policymaking. The features of the model are significant in that they illustrate the difficulty political leaders; in particular, have in legislating and implementing public policy. The model defines the policy making objective to be "the search for high quality decisions via *vigilant problem solving.*" Three sets of constraints are identified which individually or together reduce the quality of decisions and policy. The constraints are:

1. Cognitive constraints – limited time, lack of expertise and other policy making resources for dealing with complex issues,

2. Affiliate constraints – the need for acceptability, consensus, social support

3. <u>Egocentric constraint</u>s – the desire for prestige and other self-serving motives.

Each leader has to weigh the impact of these constraints, make compromises and tradeoffs, and take action that represents a majority view in the community. Unfortunately, the constraints are often substantial and the ability of policymakers rather limited, thereby causing the resulting policy to be less effective than the community requires. Janis presents a vigilant problem solving strategy to assist leaders in decision making and policy making.

[**Author's Note**: Janis's viewpoint is helpful for LISA model construction in that it provides insight into the conflicting and paradoxical environment of a major governmental function: policymaking. As elected representatives and public administrators pursue agendas for the benefit of the community and the common good, they must navigate among numerous personal, political, social, economic, and technical constraints that make the goal of optimizing social development extremely difficult to achieve. The objective, of course, would be to approach a policy or social issue with minimum constraints. To do so would require greater knowledge of issue factors, significant social consensus and support, and less concern for one's own interests. The vigilant problem solving model correlates well with the learnership learning and leading concepts, and will be discussed further in the section on societal dialogue.]

<u>Founding a Republic Through Public Argument</u>. In *To Run a Constitution: The Legitimacy of the Administrative State* (Rohr, 1986), the author presents his argument that the basis for administrative departments of government was established through the Federalist Papers debate of the framers of the Constitution. These papers were a dialogue among people who agreed that American governance was to be based on the principles of "popular government" and "individual rights." Within this fundamental consensus, the arguments over the particularities of government structures, responsibilities, and procedures ensued until documents could be written that resolved these arguments to the satisfaction of the participants, and another consensus was achieved. This process is referred to as the act of *founding a government*.

The American Constitution, along with the Bill of Rights that elaborates on it, are our *founding documents*. They establish an agreement among us citizens on the manner in which we will govern ourselves, and *they guide the cultural norms which bind us in common purpose*. The very nature of what we believe is in *the common good* may be seen in the preamble to the Constitution:

"We the People of the United States, in Order to form a more perfect Union, establish Justice, insure domestic Tranquility, provide for the common defense, promote the general Welfare, and secure the Blessings of Liberty, to ourselves and our Posterity, do ordain and establish this Constitution for the United States of America."

[**Author's Note**: The importance of this view to the LISA model's CSD construct is that it captures the very essence of government's role as the people's representative for achieving the common good – for which the nation was originally founded. As government serves its citizenry, it guides and responds to the people's needs and emerging desires through reasoning and action framed by the nation's founding documents. Public issues, and their debate, are part of an on-going dialogue in the continued refinement of the relationship between individuals, and their relationship with the community. The balancing of citizen and community rights and responsibilities is a continuous task as the volume and complexity of human and social system activity grows inexorably.]

<u>Creativeness of Public Administration</u>. In *The Enterprise of Public Administration* (Waldo, 1988), the author reflects on the historical and contemporary views concerning the administration of a government. The field of public administration is seen as a service-oriented, administrative technology legitimized in the nation's founding documents. Those who participate in conducting the public's business are at the same time accountable to the public for their performance, and are positioned to affect the quality of community life. Waldo quotes Abraham Lincoln who said: "*The legitimate object of government is to do for a community of people whatever they need to have done but cannot do at all or cannot do well for themselves in their separate and individual capacities.*" Waldo's view of the importance of effective public administration is based upon the following set of beliefs: (pp.17-24)

1. There is an intricate and intimate relationship between civilization and administration. Administration frames civilization, gives it a foundation, provides a stage.

2. Administration is conducted through bureaucratic structures which are neither the most or least effective form of organization. Government, in fact, is different than business and has no obligation to be judged solely on its efficiency.

3. There is no preexisting "state of nature" or human condition as suggested by Hobbs, Locke, and Rousseau. The rights and responsibilities of individuals to one another are *created* within the relationship they establish.

4. Private versus public sector effectiveness and efficiency is a meaningless comparison. Efficiency is not the main purpose of government, and political rationality and social rationality are as real as economic rationality.

5. Government without an administrative apparatus is an unknown entity. Public administration is a necessary function within government.

6. There is an "administrative technology" subset of social technology that contends with the legal and economic technologies for societal acceptance. It is this administrative technology that organizes and "controls concrete transformations" within a society.

7. The progress of social-science technology and physical-science technology are closely joined and rise and fall together. From the highest perspective, "all science is social science." (p.24)

Waldo argues that: "Historically, public administration has had an important role in every important field of endeavor: agriculture, mining and metallurgy, commerce and manufacturing, medicine, transportation, engineering, education." (p.25) The contributions of guidance, regulations, and subsidies are but a few ways by which those in administration have stimulated orderly and innovative societal development. In his view, good government is essential, and public administration is the operative element for taking action.

[**Author's Note**: The LISA model's CSD construct is supported by this perspective in that government is seen not only as representing the citizenry, but also conducting the public's business. If there is to be a common good, it must be achieved through continuous reasoning, learning, and action. Community system development is a notion that depends on a people's capacity to share visions and contribute support to that which they hold politically, socially, and economically in common.]

Responsible Conduct for the Public Administrator. In *The Responsible Administrator* (1982), Terry Cooper uses both descriptive and heuristic processes to discover and suggest a methodology to build an ethical foundation for administrators in the conduct of their public responsibilities. His issue is that the values and principles endemic to our democratic and Constitutional form of government administration are too general for practical application in specific issue areas. Ethical prescriptions have greater utility in well-defined situations where prior inquiry has illuminated necessary facts, alternative courses of action are understood along with their likely consequences, and applicable laws and norms are known.

Cooper refers to societal modernization as the socio-cultural context within which the public administrator works. Modernization is said to have the following traits:

1. Emphasis on functional rationality

2. The multiplicity and differentiation of roles

3. A separation of work and private life

4. A tendency toward relativism in values and roles

5. The pluralization of society.

It appears that the heterogeneity and interdependency that result from this situation cause a high degree of situational complexity and personal uncertainty as individuals and leaders realize that their respective fates are interwoven. Taking responsible action on controversial issues becomes a significant challenge.

Cooper addresses the implications of these characteristics of modern society for the public administrator's role by articulating the following propositions:
1. Public administration is inescapably political (small "p") making clear delineation from the politician's role difficult,

2. The multiplication and differentiation of roles; each with their own bundle of values, obligations, and expectations, creates an internal tension for the administrator

3. A conflict between these roles arises from antithetical obligations to oneself, and to the public. Cooper states that: "If the administrative role in modern society is inevitably political and heavily discretionary in nature, significant ethical consideration must be acknowledged" (p.32).

With this as background, Cooper offers "a matrix for responsible conduct." He says that the components of responsible administration include four major areas for emphasis: public participation, laws and policies, prescribed inner qualities, and requisite organization. Specific considerations include (pp.123-34):

1. Public Participation. Regularly confronting live human beings who expect things from government is a healthy reminder of one's service obligation and the sovereignty of the people in a democracy. It can also assist in clarifying and specifying the intent of laws and policies.

2. Laws and Policies. The *centrifugal forces of pluralism* in a large-scale heterogeneous society must be offset, to some extent, by the *centripetal influences of laws and policies*. The task in such a society is to arrive at a calculus of these opposing tendencies which maintains the necessary degree of cohesion and order, with the greatest opportunity for the expression of diversity.

3. Prescribed Inner Qualities. Inner qualities are personally cultivated guides and motivators, values and attitudes, that assist individuals in decision making. Suggested sources are John Rohr's (1989) "regime values," the American Society for Public Administration's handbook on professional standards and ethics for public administrators, and Stephen Bailey's (1965) three mental attitudes and three supportive moral values. Bailey's *three moral values* are: optimism, courage, and fairness tempered by charity. These are suggested as being supportive of *three appropriate mental attitudes*: (a) the recognition of the moral ambiguity of all men and of all public policies, (b) the recognition of the contextual forces which condition moral priorities in the public service, and (c) the recognition of the paradoxes of procedures – the need for order which restricts individual action.

4. Requisite Organization (attributed to Elliott Jacques, 1976). Hierarchical public organizations should be managed as "constitutional bureaucracies" in that participation, consultation, and negotiation imbue individuals with a sense of "*subjective responsibility*" for performance, while "*objective responsibility*" is achieved through clear delineation of authority and accountability. The result should be an integrated sense of "*administrative responsibility*" for guiding judgment and conduct.

[**Author's Note**: Cooper's perspective is particularly useful when considered along with Barry Bozeman's "all organizations are public" concept. It could be that all organization leaders and administrator – in business and academia, along with government – are public administrators. If so, *community system development and the common good occur as individuals attentive to regime values and community responsibilities balance their personal rights and responsibilities with those of the community*. The LISA model recognizes the substantive role of government in framing issues, establishing policy, and managing programs so that all community institutions, organizations, and individuals have the opportunity to reason, learn, and act constructively. Responsible citizen conduct is a moral imperative for community development.]

Transforming the Public Sector. In their popular book *Reinventing Government* (Osborne & Gaebler, 1992), the authors depict an American government unable to meet the expanding expectations of its citizenry because it is bureaucratically hobbled to outmoded methods of management and operation. They say they believe in government, that society cannot function without effective government, that the people who work in government are not the problem, that equal opportunity is essential for democratic societies to function, and that traditional liberalism or conservatism have little to offer in solving government's problems. The problem apparently is with the systems we use to administer government – the values, structures, reward systems, procedures, process, cultures, etc, that prescribe the way things are done. The authors offer examples of new approaches for reducing bureaucracy and administering government for the common good. Of particular interest is their notion of *community-owned government*.

Community-owned government emphasizes empowering citizens to accomplish their joint needs rather than focusing on providing service from outside sources. Osborne and Gaebler provide examples of successful community initiatives in which citizens stopped waiting for the nation's mega-institutions (big business, big government, and big labor) to solve their problems. They quote John McKnight, director of community studies at Northwestern University's Center for Urban Affairs and Policy Research as saying: "There is a mistaken notion that our society has a problem in terms of effective human services, our essential problem is weak communities" (p.66). His point is that *professional service delivery systems do not do as well as "associations of community"* such as the family, the neighborhood, the church, and the voluntary organization. The reasons for this are: (pp.66-70)

1. Communities have more commitment to their members than service delivery systems have to their clients.

2. Communities understand their problems better than service professionals.

3. Professionals and bureaucracies deliver service; communities solve problems.

4. Institutions and professionals offer "service;" communities offer "care."

5. Communities are more flexible and creative than large service bureaucracies.

6. Communities are cheaper than service professionals.

7. Communities enforce standards of behavior more effectively than bureaucracies or service professionals.

8. Communities focus on capacities; service systems focus on deficiencies.

[**Author's Note**: This perspective on community responsibility and action for problem solving correlates well with the LISA model in that for community system development to work, the community must own its problems and issues, it must participate in fact-finding and the generation of alternative resolution strategies, and for its chosen course of action, it must allocate resources and monitor their use. Through this process of involvement, quality goals are established, a learning process is followed, better results are achieved, and community development is positively managed.]

Business Subsystem

A Common Quality of Life. In *America's Future: Transition to the 21st Century* (Boyer, 1984), the author calls for a new standard by which economic development of the nation is measured. He opines that: "…we have obsolete indicators serving questionable purposes, and economics truly does become the 'dismal science" (p.90). Boyer states that a change in standards would account for a broader range of economic values. Included would be the "external costs" to society of economic decisions and activities, specifically, the social and ecological costs that are borne by the community while not being assumed by the producer or purchaser. The public interest and a *common quality of life would be factored into economic decisions*, and generational exploitation of the economy, without concern for posterity, would be unethical. Qualitative growth economics would be considered along with quantitative growth economics, and "People working toward contributions that serve human need, contribute to a peaceful world, and respect nature would have a form of 'payment' that the work of the 21st century should include" (p.98).

Boyer suggests that what is needed is a managed economy with *explicit ethical goals*. In his model, 21st century economics would be:

1. Compatible with nature.

2. Designed to produce goods and services that permit a high quality of life for everyone.

3. Accessible for employment so everyone can participate and everyone can benefit.

4. Reliable for delivery of basic needs: food, shelter, transportation, health, and education.

Boyer's goal is the transformation to an economy guided by the social cooperation of a people with a sense of control over the direction of that economy. He says that: "A new economics would treat human development the energies, the imagination, and the affirmation of life as central to economic enterprise" (p.112).

[**Author's Note**: The LISA model recognizes the government-business relationship in framing the community's economic and business activities. Together, they contribute to community system development and progress toward the common good. Boyer's view is a challenge to the predominantly quantitative objectives of that development, and suggests that the economic common good must consider the qualitative quality-of-life factors often treated as externalities to business operations. The implication here is that the businesses will be increasingly driven to become better corporate citizens of the community.]

Information Age Capitalism. In *The New Capitalism* (Halal, 1986), the author describes a changing business and economic environment for tomorrow's organizations. The old capitalism of the industrial age is giving way to the *new capitalism for the information age*. This emerging system of business and economics is seen as requiring a dramatic change in the way American businesses are managed and operated – and even in the way we think about goods and services, technology, social structures, power, and wealth. Halal offers six strategies for the future: (pp.79-319)

1. Smart growth. The inner domain of unlimited progress. The weighing of benefits against costs to improve the quality of life for all

2. Market networks. The flowering of creative enterprise. The decentralizing of control and the encouragement of autonomous business units that compete in markets inside of organizations

3. Participative leadership. Extending democracy to daily life. Sharing information and authority with employees and stakeholders to create forms of democratic governance and profit

4. Multiple goals. The strength of economic community. Bringing constituencies with multiple goals together to create win/win situation.

5. Strategic management. Converting threats into strategy. Integrating multiple goals into a strategic coalition of interests to identify issues and develop economic strategies.

6. Democratic free enterprise. A system of both cooperation and competition. Creating business-government partnerships in which democratic collaboration and free-market competition coexist.

[**Author's Note**: The value of this perspective for the LISA model is in its focus on the trends for change in American business, and how that change extends democracy and free enterprise throughout the workplace. Whenever a community's values and norms are embedded in its private sector activities, its political-economic bonds are strengthened; and, this results in more rapid community development which is the focus of this section of the book.]

Business Social Responsibility. The National Institute of Standards and Technology (NIST) administers the U.S. Baldrige National Quality Award Program, a competition for American companies to be recognized as being among the highest performing, most efficient and effective organizations in the nation. Since 1988 the Baldrige Assessment Criteria have been used by thousands of U.S. organizations to stay abreast of ever-increasing competition and to improve performance. The seven major categories for performance excellence and assessment are: Leadership; Strategic Planning; Customer and Market Focus; Measurement, Analysis and Knowledge Management; Human Resource Focus; Process Management; and Business Results. The criteria of particular relevance here is the Leadership Category with two sub-elements: Organizational Leadership and *Social Responsibility*.

Social responsibility requires that an organization addresses its responsibilities to the public, ensures ethical behavior, and practices good citizenship. Three areas are examined through written application by competing companies and by on-site review by Baldrige Award examiners. The questions asked are:

1. Responsibilities to the Public

   a. How do you address the *impacts on society* of your products, services, and operations?

   b. What are your key compliance processes, measures, and goals for achieving and surpassing regulatory and legal requirements, as appropriate?

   c. What are your key processes, measures, and goals for addressing risks associated with your products, services, and operations?

   d. How do you *anticipate public concerns* with current and future products, services, and operations?

   e. How do you prepare for these concerns in a proactive manner?

2. Ethical Behavior.

   a. How do you *ensure ethical behavior* in all stakeholder transactions and interactions?

   b. What are your key processes and measures or indicators for monitoring ethical behavior throughout your organization, with key partners, and in your governance structure?

3. Support of Key Communities.

   a. How does your organization actively support and *strengthen your key communities*?

   b. How do you identify key communities and determine areas for organizational involvement and support?

   c. What are your key communities?

   d. How do your senior leaders and your employees contribute to *improving these communities*?

[**Author's Note**: Nearly a hundred organizations have earned national recognition as Baldrige winners since the award's inception. Companies large and small across many fields of endeavor and industries have shown their willingness to systematically build their competencies and public participation. They have become exemplars in their respective counties, states, and nationally of what business can do to advance its own interest in a manner that contributes to the common good – business, government, and educational leaders – citizens together working to improve the quality of life and work in their communities.]

Principled-Centered Leadership. In *Principled-Centered Leadership* (Covey, 1991) says that: "When we *center our lives on correct principles*, we become more balanced, unified, organized, anchored, and rooted. We have a foundation for all activities, relationships and decisions. We also have a sense of stewardship about everything in our lives, including time, talents, money, possessions, relationships, our families, and our bodies. We recognize the need to use them for good purposes and, as a steward, to be accountable for their use." (p.22) Covey's characteristics of principle-centered leaders are: (pp.33-38)

1. They are continually learning. They read, they seek training, they take classes, and they are educated by their experiences.

2. They are service-oriented. They see life as a mission, not as a career.

3. They radiate positive energy. Their attitude is optimistic, positive, upbeat.

4. They believe in other people. They don't overreact to negative behaviors, criticism, or human weaknesses.

5. They lead balanced lives. They read the best literature and magazines, keep up with current events, and maintain good friendships.

6. They see life as an adventure. Their security lies in their initiative, resourcefulness, and creativity.

7. They are synergistic. They are change catalysts, able to improve almost any situation.

8. They exercise self-renewal. They regularly exercise the four dimensions of the human personality: physical, emotional, mental, and spiritual.

Covey continues by saying that principled-centered leaders apply the "seven habits" (The Seven Habits of High Effective People, Covey) for mature development:

1. They progress for a state of "dependence" to one of "independence" by achieving a private victory over themselves. To do this they:

   a. Are proactive. They learn to become self-knowing and self-aware. They take responsibility for their own thinking and behavior.

   b. Begin with the End in Mind. They develop a conscience to guide their behavior and a vision of who they are and want to accomplish.

   c. Put First Things First. They develop the discipline and willpower that comes with recognizing what is important and setting priorities.

2. They make progress by moving beyond "independence" toward "interdependence" by achieving a public victory by learning to work with others. To do this they: (pp.40-47)

   a. Think Win-Win. They understand the needs of others and are willing to share power and recognition.

   b. Seek First to Understand and Then to be Understood. They truly listen to others to understand them the way the want to be understood – before proceeding with their own point of view.

   c. Synergize. They go beyond negotiation and compromise to find a level of understanding to which everyone can become fully supportive.

3. Having sampled interdependence, they recognize their need for renewal, that is, they "Sharpen the Saw" through efforts at continuous improvement.

Covey relates his guidelines to the Total Quality Management (TQM) movement popular during the 1990s by saying that TQM, as an organizational management paradigm, is basically focused on helping leaders and people with their leadership and management skills. He says that Principled-Centered Leadership is a fundamental element in Total Quality Leadership. A summary of his thinking might be stated as follows: Transformational leadership builds *trusting relationships* which allow for *effective communication* which is required for *interpersonal commitment* that is necessary for *cohesive teamwork* which leads to *productive operations*.

[**Author's Note**: There is likely to be near unanimous agreement by readers from all backgrounds that Covey's sentiments, were they a major presence in our communities, would create the sense of inclusion, responsibility, and citizenship that most of us would favor. The fact that the business community spends huge sums developing the skills of their leaders should indicate that these skills could make a major contribution to the effectiveness of local, state, and national operations and performance – assuming the learning, knowledge, and skills of the individuals involved were "principle-based."]

Education Subsystem

School and Social Progress. In *The School and Society* (Dewey, 1915), John Dewey advises against looking at the school as a relationship solely between teacher and pupil or teacher and parent. It is his view that in a democracy, society accomplishes its objectives when schools place emphasis on the development of the individual within the community. He says that: "Only by being true to the full growth of the individuals who make it up, can society by any chance be true to itself" (p.7). In this regard, Dewey suggests that schools have social significance in that they are small communities in which community values of association, cooperation, and discipline may be learned.

Dewey encourages schools to participate in the larger social evolution by including the occupational, moral, social, artistic, scientific, and historical aspects of community, thereby fostering social progress. He states: "...*make each one of our schools an embryonic community life, active with types of occupations that reflect the life of the larger society and permeated throughout with the spirit of art, history, and science.* When the school introduces and trains each child of society into membership within such a little community, saturating him with the spirit of service, and providing him with the instruments of self-direction, we shall have the deepest and best guaranty of a larger society which is worthy, lovely, and harmonious". (p.29)

[**Author's Note**: An observation in terms of the LISA model is that community system development depends heavily on the ability and willingness of the community's school system to activity engage with its community and to encourage its faculty, administrators, and students to work toward community improvement. That which is good, and "of quality," needs to be recognized and learned for the betterment of all concerned – the individuals, the organizations, the whole community.]

General Learning for All Human Beings. In *The Paideia Proposal: An Educational Manifesto* (Adler, 1982), the author presents the results of the deliberations of the Paideia Group for which he was the director. The group's purpose was to advise educational experts and institutions on a strategy for renewing American education by providing a curriculum of general learning for all human beings. Their argument is that "...basic schooling ought to prepare every child to earn a living, live a good life, and preserve our free institutions." This is so because "*Those who are not schooled to enjoy the blessings of a good society can only despoil its institutions and corrupt themselves*" (p.77). The Paideia view is that academia is responsible primarily for the moral and civic education, and that all students are responsible for the same core knowledge and learning.

The Paideia Report advocates a one-track system with the same objectives and course of study for all students. It envisions remedial help for slower learners, multiple teaching strategies for greater retention, and emphasis on learning-to-learn approaches so schooling becomes but one source for education. *The goal is to emphasize the sameness, rather than differences, among students so they are better able to participate more effectively in their common life experiences – in social, political, and economic systems.* The three fundamental areas for development throughout the first twelve years would be: (a) personal growth and self-improvement – mental, moral, and spiritual, (b) citizenship and civic virtues, and (c) basic skills for future vocational training. Having built a strong base of general, liberal, and humanistic learning, specialized vocational training would be available after the first twelve years of schooling are completed. Additional study for a higher level of general learning would be available for continued adult social development.

[**Author's Note**: The importance of this perspective is that it challenges current notions on the content and structure of American education – a system generally acknowledged to have failed in its responsibility to educate a large minority of its students for their social, political, and economic responsibilities. It holds out a new approach which is endemic to the Model of this study. It integrates the need for focus on personal development (PSD), employee development within the organization (OSD), and citizen development within the community (CSD) – all-keyed to improved life-long learning. The same synergistic, social development goals are conceptualized by the group and in the model.]

<u>Universities for a Better Society</u>. In *The University and the Future of America* (Bok, 1990), the author acknowledges the multiplicity of social problems that predominate in contemporary American society. He says that the role for higher education is not to take on these problems directly, but to educate its students to fully engage the opportunities that exist for improvement. Bok states: ". . . the fact remains that our economy and our society are not likely to improve significantly without the benefit of greater knowledge than we currently possess and larger numbers of well-prepared teachers, business executives, engineers, and public servants ...universities have an essential contribution to make in improving our society along with corporations, government agencies, and other major institutions" (p.36).

Notwithstanding this responsibility, Bok makes it clear that progress by universities will be difficult. His criticism includes:

1. The lack of sufficient emphasis on moral education

2. Weak faculty performance in discovering emerging social issues,

3. Inadequate school response to defined social problems

4. Lack of faculty expertise, development, and focus in the areas of education and social work

5. Lack of focused leadership and integrated planning

6. Insufficient interest in community service programs

7. Inadequate funding of higher education

8. The lack of interest in hiring generalists with broad education for occupations such as public administration that obviously require that knowledge and skill.

He notes that these shortcomings are problematical because they occur when there is distinct need to handle issues and problems in an integrated, rather than fragmented, manner. He opines that: "*America's problems are sufficiently interrelated that we will be hard pressed to overcome any of them without attacking them all*" (p.121).

[**Author's Note**: The value of Bok's perspective for the LISA model is that he reaffirms the essential role of academia in educating a society to positively manage its own development, and that he emphasizes that societal problems cannot be solved other than through the implementation of systemic, informed, and integrated change strategies. A higher level of performance is obviously required from the nation's leaders, educators, and administrators in all sectors of the community.]

<u>Universities and the Public Interest</u>. In *The University and the Public Interest* (Giamatti, 1981), the author offers that the basic purpose of education in a democracy is for members of the community to learn to choose a civic role for themselves. A sense of citizenship is equally important as the learning of new information. Shared assumptions about individual freedoms and institutional needs establish an ethically-based civic sense which, in turn, usefully informs socially conscious action and serves the public interest. According to Giamatti: "*A civilized order is the precondition of freedom, and freedom of belief, speech, and choice – the goal of responsible order.*" (p.17)

Regarding the nature and purpose of the university within the community, Giamatti states that: "A university cannot expound these goals and expect a larger society to find them compelling, it cannot become a repository of national hope and a source of national leadership, unless it strives to practice what it teaches. If its goals are noble so must be its acts". (p.17)

[**Author's Note**: The value of this perspective is that, once again, the learning and leading anchors of this study are seen as being joined in academia. When academia assumes its responsibility for social development, the first order of business is to discern what is worth knowing, and the next is to determine how each topic should be taught. At the Community System Development (CSD) level of the LISA model, a liberal (meaning broad and balanced) education serves to both distinguish and interrelate the values, roles, and behaviors of individuals and organizations as part of a community. Universities, as do all schools, have opportunities to act as socially-relevant role models in the conduct of their activities. Doing so strengthens all institutional sectors (e.g., government, business, and education) and enhances the community's capacity for development and attainment of the common good.]

Moral Development as the Aim of Education. In *The Philosophy of Moral Development* (Kohlberg, 1981), the author establishes the view that *justice* is the most fundamental value upon which a society should base its moral development, and presents his concept of Six Stages of Moral Judgment: (pp.409-412)

Stage 1. The stage of *punishment and obedience*. Right is literal obedience to rules and authority, avoiding punishment, and not doing physical harm. This is an egocentric point of view in which physical consequences rather than others' interests are primary.

Stage 2. The stage of *individual instrumental purpose and exchange*. Right is serving one's own or other's needs and making fair deals in terms of concrete exchange. This is an understanding of individual's needs to pursue their respective interests with fairness.

Stage 3. The stage of *mutual interpersonal expectations, relationships, and conformity*. Right is playing a good role, being concerned about others, keeping loyalty and trust, and being motivated to follow rules and expectations. This is an awareness of shared feelings, agreements, and expectations which take primacy over individual interests.

Stage 4. The stage of social systems and *conscience maintenance*. Right is doing one's duty in society, upholding the social order, and maintaining the welfare of the group. This is an ability to separate oneself from interpersonal agreements or motives and take the viewpoint of the system within which one is functioning.

Stage 5. The stage of prior rights and *social contract or utility*. Right is upholding the basic rights, values, and legal contracts of a society, even when they conflict with the concrete rules and laws of the group. This is an ability to be objectively impartial and assure due process regardless of social attachments or contracts that may have been made.

Stage 6. The stage of *universal ethical principles*. Right at this stage assumes guidance by universal ethical principles that all humanity should follow. This is a commitment to respecting others as ends, not means.

A useful part of Kohlberg's perspectives, at this juncture, is the view that moral development is the main role of primary and secondary educational institutions. Kohlberg counters the often expressed notion that schools should not teach values because different groups have different values with the view that: "The problems as to the legitimacy of moral education in the public schools disappear, however, if the proper content of moral education is recognized to be the values of justice that themselves prohibit the imposition of beliefs of one group on another" (p.37). He continues by saying that public education has the responsibility to transmit the values of respect for individual rights and many of the other consensual values of society. Additionally, *Kohlberg equates knowledge of "the good" with justice and virtuous behavior, and observes that as one moves up the scale of moral development from stage one to stage six, this relationship is more fully understood.*

[**Author's Note**: An observation at this point is that Kohlberg's perspectives parallel the developmental processes addressed elsewhere in this report. His emphasis on schools as places for developing moral perspective reinforces the LISA model's identification of learning and knowledge. Also, the process of moving through stages of moral development while seeking what is good, just, and virtuous is consistent with the learning and development theme: Social Dialogue for Community Development]

> *We will have conversations, a break from Washington, where we are not having conversations now; we're having polarizing debate. — U.S. Senator Olympia J. Snowe*

Social Dialogue for Community Development

Seminal Viewing Points. The importance of the Learnership philosophy and the Learnership Integrated Systems Architecture (LISA) model in a social dialogue for community development strategy should be emphasized. The LISA framework not only illustrates the four integrated social relationships among the personal, organization, community, and societal systems – it also depicts the application of the five reasoning competencies that empower the thinking (systems thinking and pattern recognition), learning, knowing, and leading behaviors that add substance and context during communications. Dialogue is a communications process that needs rich content and context to be meaningful and to assist all participants to experience enlightenment and motivation to action. The seminal perspectives of Jurgen Habermas, Mary Parker Follett, and E.F. Schumacker provide insight on this subject. Their perspectives help incorporate the notions of "communication for action," "learning from participation within situations," and "striving for higher levels-of-being" into this topic.

First consideration is given to Habermas's "*doctrine of communicative action*." In *Coming to Public Judgment* (1990), Daniel Yankelovich argues against "a culture of control," and attributes profound insight to Habermas when he says:

"His doctrine of communicative action is based on his concept of rationality defined as the ability to reach mutual understanding even when interests, cultural frameworks, and languages conflict. The goals of communicative action are to permit us to comprehend each other well enough so that common goals and understandings are possible. In Habermas's view, communicative action is the key to building democratic consensus p.217) Apparently, *being able to find some common ground or basis for collaboration is useful as a foundation for effective communication.*

A second insightful perspective may be seen in Mary Parker Follett's "*law of the situation.*" Follett (*Creative Experience,* 1924) suggested that open, fact-based communication among individuals concerned with particular issues could provide the basis for solutions to those issues. For her, *learning by participating within the situation* was valuable social activity. Follett believed that people engaged in collaborative communication on issues of common concern would learn from one another within the context of the situation, and would thereby become informed of preferred courses of action.

A third useful perspective is that of E.F. Schumacher (*A Guide for the Perplexed,* 1977) who opined that facing divergent problems (problems rooted in value difference) of social life is the real challenge for societal development toward a higher level-of-being. *Striving for higher levels-of-being* is seen herein as being synonymous with seeking to attain integrated self-fulfillment, high performance, and the common good. An argument may be made that a common framework for effective reasoning encourages dialogue, enables the creation of shared values and visions, and provides a basis for social harmony and development.

Ten Principles for Effective Social Dialogue. This author's view is that the three foregoing viewing points may be used as catalysts to extrapolate a common set of principles and practices that better enable learning and social dialogue. In this book, the concept of *community or social dialogue* integrates the views of Habermas, Follett, and Schumacher and is offered as a metaphor for the reasoning, learning, and action that individuals, organizations, and communities engage in as they pursue their respective objectives and societal development. The concept of *societal dialogue* is herein presented as a special form of interpersonal communication in which the following ten principles for effective social dialogue are evident:

1. There is a spirit of inquiry and readiness to learn more about an issue or topic.

2. There is an effort to recognize hidden assumptions and bias that inhibit understanding.

3. There is tolerance, even exploration, of divergent viewpoints.

4. There is a willingness to discover common values and goals upon which all can agree.

5. There is an attempt to balance individual needs and concerns with those of the group.

6. There is effort to develop alternative scenarios and create choice.

7. There is attention given to the core values and ethics that bind the group together.

8. There is responsible, trustworthy behavior on the part of all participants.

9. There is hope for resolution by consensus rather than majority opinion.

10. There is an understanding of the social, physical, and biological systems interdependency that makes system optimization preferable to subsystem maximization.

These interpersonal and communication factors serve to emphasize how dialogue differs from discussion, debate, argumentation, and similar reasoning strategies in which these factors are either incidental or absent. And, the advantage of the LISA model is that it serves as both *a catalyst and a framework for dialogue* because it focuses communications on what society has in common, rather than on how its elements differ. The LISA model (First Interlude) offers common ground upon which reasoning, learning, and action may occur.

Collatéral Dynamics in Social Dialogue. To further develop this theme, there are often nine collateral dynamics or perspectives which are present during societal dialogue. These dynamics characterize social dialogue as a process for:

1. Maintaining face
2. Open-system reasoning
3. Finding common ground

4. Enhancing democratic processes
5. Promoting collective mindfulness
6. Creating public judgment
7. Conducting vigilant problem-solving
8. Assessing operative schema
9. Engaging in heuristic learning.

Perspective 1: In *On Dialogue, Culture, and Organizational Learning* (Schein, 1993), Edgar Schein refers to dialogue as "... a communication technology [that has] considerable promise as a problem-formulation and problem-solving philosophy and technology". (p.40) As he sees it, the increasing rate of change, the growth of technological complexity, and the tendency to break down into subunits and subcultures creates the need for greater skills in human relationships and communication. Of particular interest is *the need during communications for what he terms mutual maintenance of "face,"* meaning respecting the social value of all participants and working with them to prevent the infusion of "defensive routines" into conversation. To accomplish this, Schein emphasizes that: "All problem-solving groups should begin in a dialogue format to facilitate the building of sufficient common ground and mutual trust, and to make it possible to tell what is really on one's mind". (p.42)

Schein presents selected conditions for starting dialogue with a group and rules for *maintaining the dialogue* once it has begun. Starting dialogue requires paying attention to several important assumptions about new groups: (a) members should be made to feel as equal as possible, (b) everyone should feel a sense of guaranteed "air time," (c) the task of the group should be to explore the dialogue process rather than make a decision, and (d) members should feel that their personal experiences are legitimate and have value.

Maintaining dialogue requires that: (a) individuals be able to suspend their judgment and be patient as others express their views and more information is gathered, (b) facilitators be used to attend to group process matters, (c) a climate and set of explicit norms be established to help members handle "hot" issues, and (4) that dialogue not move into discussion before shared understanding and common ground are clearly established on the issue or problem. (pp.45-48)

[**Author's Note**: The MIT Center for Organizational Learning emphasizes action research on the use of dialogue for organization problem solving. What should be noted is that the term societal dialogue used throughout this book has had a more encompassing meaning that includes concern for including and balancing systems thinking, effective inquiry, group dynamics, rational decision making, intuitive decision making, heuristic learning, and social responsibility.]

Perspective 2: In *Uncommon Sense* (1983), Mark Davidson relates system theorist Bertalanffy's belief that a science of social systems was needed to offset the chaos and impending destruction of the present world. Bertalanffy argued for the application of General Systems Theory (GST) to the social order so that everyone could become aware of the interdependence of all societal entities and issues, and for recognition that opportunity for all persons could only be guaranteed if the social system's tendency toward chaos and fragmentation was countered by a structure that everyone understood. Bertalanffy suggested that social reasoning and action be based on a systems view of issues that takes into account their interdependencies. He also stressed the need to rehabilitate society's systems of values as an activity fundamental to all other efforts at societal improvement. *The implications here are that societal dialogue: (a) requires the use of a systems perspective to assure that relevant relationships are discovered, and b2) that the values of participants be understood and made part of the reasoning process.*

Davidson provides an example of a systems approach to the social problem of crime. He suggests that the problem of criminal violence will not be effectively managed by writing tougher laws – especially if the odds of getting caught are low and there are not enough prisons to incarcerate those convicted. He says that emphasis also needs to be placed on increasing the performance of law enforcement agencies, on reducing environmental contributors to criminal behavior, and on improving the society's system of values. Individually, these actions would show little progress, but together synergy is created that magnifies the impact of the effort. The lesson here is that dialogue on complex issues and problems require open-system reasoning and holistic strategies for improvement.

Perspective 3: In *Discovering Common Ground* (Weisbord, 1992), John Briggs relates his interview with philosopher-physicist David Bohm on the subject of "Dialogue as a Path Toward Wholeness." Bohm states: "I'm proposing that we need to learn to dialogue with each other because of all the fragmentation in the world. We need a type of social enlightenment to help that take place...a higher social intelligence". (p.116) He observes that individuals and social groups organize according to sets of rules which then prevent them from talking with one another about things that are really important. Intelligent communication is thereby prevented. Bohm argues that an important objective should be to find some common ground for resolution of the conflict. To achieve dialogue, he proposes: "To create a situation where we can suspend our opinions and judgments in order to be able to listen to each other . . . without a specific agenda or purpose to guide the proceedings . . . so that everyone's opinion will be held by everybody . . . [to obtain] a common pool of information". (pp.118-119) What is noteworthy in this perspective on *dialogue is the emphasis on suspending opinion and judgment in an effort to become fully aware of everyone's thinking before attempting to make decisions* or take action. Also, all parties are agreed that the more they emphasize why they are different, the more unlikely it is that any common ground may be discovered to assist in issue resolution.

In this book, societal dialogue is seen as a deliberative process in which emphasis is placed on inquiring fully into the nature and extent of a problem before attempting to solve the problem. This approach tracks with the management problem solving principle of finding the root cause of a problem. Additionally, societal dialogue includes the goals and values of the participants as part of the facts of the problem, and areas which need to be reconciled. An underlying feature of this process is that allowing participants to be heard and fully understood – in terms of their unique perspectives – often reduces conflict and encourages collaboration rather than debate.

Perspective 4: In *Reasoning, Learning, and Action* (Argyris, 1982), Chris Argyris reports on his research in attempting to increase the capacity of individuals and organizations to solve difficult problems. He argues for the use of *double-loop learning* in which complex problems are not simply acted upon by rote or preprogrammed response, but are considered from the standpoint of the underlying values, assumptions, and personal programs that direct or constrain effective decision making. He asserts that complex, un-programmed, diverse issues and problems require greater in-depth analysis of problem context to assure effective reasoning, learning, and action. Basically, he suggests that *using alternative ways of viewing problem situations often leads to greater understanding of relevant factors and better decisions.*

Argyris attributes the difficulty in increasing people's reasoning and learning skills to their inclination to avoid genuine participation in rational reasoning processes. Two dysfunctional human tendencies are examined: *disconnectedness* and *distancing*. Disconnectedness has to do with the failure to recognize that in the effort to work a complex problem, faulty premises and invalid data are being included. Distancing concerns the failure to take personal responsibility for staying actively involved in the reasoning process. Together, these *self-protective internal programs reduce the individual's willingness to learn new thought patterns* essential for dealing with the increasingly complex, dynamic, and divergent issues in today's societal environment.

What the process of dialogue can do to overcome these deficiencies is to establish interpersonal ground rules and explicit reasoning processes that assure these dysfunctions are overcome. A *willingness to both learn more about one's own assumptions and biases* along with actively participating in problem explication and resolution are essential traits of double-loop learners. Improving the quality of societal dialogue can be seen as an enhancement of the democratic process because its use demonstrates participatory management and governance in action.

Perspective 5: In *Taking Flight: Dialogue, Collective Thinking, and Organizational Development* (Issacs, 1993), the author reports on the MIT Center for Organizational Learning's Dialogue Project effort to promote collective learning for conflict resolution. He reports that: "Human beings everywhere are being forced to develop their capacity to think together – to develop collaborative thought and coordinated action . . . [and] the most important work in the new economy is creating conversations". (p.24) According to Issacs, these conversations are often focused on problem solving and are more effective when pursued using the process of dialogue. *The Center describes dialogue as "A discipline of collective thinking and inquiry, a process for transforming the quality of conversation and, in particular, the thinking that lies beneath it". (p.25)* The goal of dialogue is to consciously create shared meaning out of collective experience with the expectation that new and aligned action will result.
Building on Argyris's double-loop learning concept in which the question asked is: "What are the alternative ways of seeing this situation that could free me to act more effectively?" Issacs posits that dialogue creates *triple-loop learning* in which the question becomes: "What is leading me and others to have a predisposition to learn in this way at all?" (p.30) According to this view, being in dialogue causes participants to pay attention to their assumptions normally taken for granted, the degree to which polarization of opinions exists, the rules for acceptable conversation, and the methods for managing differences. What develops in this process is a *collective mindfulness* of being-in the experience and an ability to conduct *cool inquiry* without the defensiveness and competitiveness that inhibits effective communications and problem solving.

Perspective 6: In *Coming to Public Judgment* (1991), Daniel Yankelovich speaks about the need to transform public opinion into *public judgment*. In his view, public judgment is required so the complex and important societal issues of the day may be more effectively understood by the citizenry, thereby leading to better decision making. He is particularly concerned with "intellectual snobbery" in which expert views are judged to be superior to the values and views of ordinary people – those who have to live with the consequences of social policy and action. The term "public judgment" is meant to connote "a particular form of public opinion that exhibits:

1. More thoughtfulness, more weighing of alternatives, more genuine engagement with the issue, more taking into account a wide variety of factors than ordinary public opinion as measured by public opinion polls. Yankelovich presents three stages the public goes through to develop reasoned judgment on an issue:

2. More emphasis on the normative, valuing, ethical side of questions than on the factual, informational side" (p.5)

Stage 1. Consciousness Raising. The public learns about an issue and becomes aware of its existence and meaning.

Stage 2. Working Through. Having understood the issue fully, the public confronts the need for change.

Stage 3. Resolution. The public comes to closure on where it stands cognitively, emotionally, and morally on the issue.

Yankelovich expresses his conviction that unless the public is helped through these stages to acquire informed judgment, poor decision making is certain. He notes that lack of proper learning and deliberation on issues allows individuals to engage in wishful thinking, to gloss over important incompatibilities, and to overlook bases for collaboration. His goal is for society to move from top-of-the-head, ill-informed opinion-giving to critical thinking which includes information gathering, option development, open discussion, position polling, and committed action. He provides an example of facilitating a group's "working through" an issue by The Public Agenda Foundation and the Brown University Center for Foreign Policy Development. Through comparison of pretest and posttest responses they showed that facilitated deliberation led to more reasoned responses to the options presented. He comments that: (1) "the kind of compartmentalized thinking that permits people to hold onto incompatible ideas was broken through and a higher level of integration achieved, and (2) once pros and cons of each choice were clearly set forth, their drawbacks stood out and people's attitudes became more sober". (p.159)

In Stage Three, Resolution, Yankelovich offers ten rules as guidelines for those leaders who desire to engage the public in the kind of dialogue that develops public judgment. (pp.160-175) It is his view that it is as feasible to *teach these methods for improving leadership dialogue* with the public as it is to teach finance, marketing, or organizational development. The rules are:

1. On any given issue it is usually safe to assume that the public and the experts will be out of phase. To bridge the gap leaders must learn what the public's starting point is and how to address it.

2. Do not depend on experts to present issues.

3. Learn what the public's pet preoccupation is and address it before discussing any other facet of the issue.

4. Give the public the incentive of knowing that someone is listening…and cares.

5. Limit the number of issues to which people must attend at any one time to two or three at the most.

6. "Working through" is best accomplished when people have choices to consider.

7. Leaders must take the initiative in highlighting the value components of choices.

8. To move beyond the "say-yes-to-everything" form of procrastination, the public need help.

9. When two conflicting values are both important to the public, resolution should be sought by tinkering to preserve some element of each.

10. Use time as a factor and as a key part of the communication strategy.

Notwithstanding Yankelovich's use of the term "deliberation," the process he describes clearly conforms to the meaning of dialogue used in this book. The group was facilitated through a process that included the exploration of relevant information and the weighing of pros and cons for each available option before being asked to provide their view. Their pretest top-of-the-head opinions (regarded as ill-informed and contradictory by the Center) were converted to posttest *reasoned judgments* that represented the kind of thinking needed for effective democratic planning and decision making. The exploration into the interdependencies of related issues and the willingness to weigh alternative scenarios in coming to judgment supports the notion of societal dialogue herein presented.

Perspective 7: In *Crucial Decisions* (1989), Janis's perspective on *vigilant problem solving* in is elaborated here to explain its relationship to societal dialogue. At issue is the quality of policymaking evidenced in the policies formulated and implemented by leaders in business, academia, and government. Janis comments that despite the disagreements and chaotic lack of integration that currently characterize social science disciplines, the specific conditions may be articulated under which leaders use sound procedures to arrive at policy decisions more likely to have successful outcomes. (p.12) Vigilant problem solving leads to high-quality decisions when cognitive, affiliative, and egocentric constraints do not weigh too heavily on decision makers. The challenge then is to arm those participating in solving a problem with the knowledge, skills, and procedures to perform better at their task. This is where use of the LISA model and social dialogue skills may be helpful.

The LISA model can serve as an integrating tool to remind participants of relevant system interdependencies and the responsibilities they have as individuals, as members of organizations, and as citizens of the community to pursue an optimizing solution. And, it may help them to resist the three sets of constraints that tend to sub-optimize reasoning, learning, and action. More specifically, Janis's research indicates that there are *deliberation process errors* and *personal deficiencies* that hamper effective problem solving.

The *process errors include:*

1. Gross omissions in surveying objectives
2. Gross omissions in surveying alternatives
3. Poor information search
4. Selective bias in processing information at hand
5. Failure to reconsider originally rejected alternatives
6. Failure to examine major costs and risks of the preferred choice
7. Failure to work out detailed implementation, monitoring, and contingency plans.

Personal deficiencies include:

1. Lack of conscientiousness
2. Lack of openness
3. Chronic optimism or pessimism
4. Preference for use of "coping style" and being disconnected from problems
5. Excessive need for power, social approval, and status
6. Low tolerance for risk and stress
7. Ambivalence toward the organization
8. Chronic apprehensiveness of other power-holders in the organization.

The dialogue process acts as an antidote to these errors and deficiencies in that it is a process for opening up both the content and context of an issue or problem for examination. It is an inquiry and learning process that challenges participants to not only reflect on the problem, but also to reflect on their own assumptions, personal biases, and beliefs that contribute to the problem context. As mentioned previously, societal dialogue is a process of learning and development from *being-in an experience* (Follett).

Perspective 8: In *The Thinking Organization: Dynamics of Organizational Social Cognition* (Sims & Gioia, 1986), the authors describe the role of *cognitive schemas* (theories on how things are and work) and their impact on information processing and organizational behavior. Of particular interest in understanding the dialogue process is recognition that the schemas or thinking frameworks people use affect their perception of incoming information, their retrieval of stored information, and the inferences based on that information. Sims and Gioia relate that *there are four groups of schemas held by individuals:*

1 .Self-schemas – which concern one's beliefs about self

2. Person schemas – which concern beliefs about others

3. Script schemas – which concern beliefs about how processes work

4. Person-in-situation schemas – which concern interpersonal dynamics.

What is known from research is that people's schemas are helpful in expediting their responses to the events and stimuli they experience. However, *these schemas can be deleterious to social functioning when they restrict new learning and growth.* The dialogue process counters this tendency by making inquiry into these schemas part of the reasoning process. In dialogue, recognizing and evaluating the appropriateness of operative schemas serves to establish a basis for collaborative effort and assists the participants in determining their shared goals and values. Societal dialogue may be improved through the construction of new schemas and models that reflect the positive goals and values the society wishes to encourage.

Perspective 9: Schein perspective in Chapter Four, *Beyond the Stable State* (1979) on *loss of the stable state* is elaborated here to emphasize the heuristic learning aspect of dialogue (Chapter Seven). He explains that the rational-experiential model of public inquiry often fails to result in satisfactory approaches to social problems because the nature of the social environment is constantly undergoing change, and that time cannot be compressed sufficiently to assure that experimental results are highly predictive of outcomes that will be obtained in the general population.

Because of this conundrum, Schon encourages that reasoning and learning processes incorporate *systems analysis* and the use of *existential knowledge.* By systems analysis, Schon means that new models that account for the instability, uncertainty, and interconnectivity of social experience should be considered in issues analysis and problem solving. By using existential knowledge, Schon means that knowledge is continually being modified by the learner in terms of the conditions of the learning experience itself. He calls this an on-going, *heuristic process of learning* in which one thing grows out of another, but the circumstances and sequence of events causing it to do so are not completely known and cannot be replicated. This makes the knowledge obtained to have "projective" but not "predictive" value. Additionally, whatever knowledge exists is somewhat transitory because it is continually enriched by new learning.

Schon states that: "The loss of the stable state demands the invention of new professions. New bodies of projective models are required, or the revitalization of old ones by their translation across professional and disciplinary lines. The *learning agent* (italics added) must be willing and able to make the leaps required in existential knowledge". (p.235) He presents a *code for public learning* in which learning agents emerge to keep the development of projective models going. It appears that the learning agent can be a person, an organization, or even a community that nurtures its developing body of knowledge, goals, and values through use of an existential learning process. The skills of the learning agent include: (1) maintaining continuity over the learning process, (2) synthesizing theory to formulate new projective models out of his or her own experience, (3) carrying projective models to the next instance; and using the model as a basis for action while simultaneously regarding it as only one point of view, (4) confronting multiple, conflicting perspectives in situations of public action, and (5) being willing and able to use him or herself as an informational instrument within the learning situation. (pp.234-236)

[**Author's Note**: The importance of Schon's views in understanding societal social dialogue is that by its very nature, *dialogue is a learning process.* Any effort by participants engaged in the resolution of dynamic and complex issues:

1. To excessively restrict either the content, context, or process of their deliberations in order to prevent participation by others who are informed and concerned

2. To employ vociferous debate and other divide-and-conquer techniques, or

3. To speed the pace of deliberations so learning cannot occur; is likely to reduce the quality and acceptability of any resulting decisions.

The societal objective should be to create the conditions in which concerned and informed citizens at all organization and community levels can engage one another in dialogue on the critical issues of the day. The learnership contribution is the knowledge and skills of learnership practitioners – those people who practice learning and leading as a way of being when facilitating group deliberations.]

In this section, societal dialogue was shown to be a reasoning and learning process employed to bring members of the community together to establish mutual understanding and create communicative action. The LISA model helps the process by illustrating the *common ground* and *pooled knowledge* already in existence. The combination of the Learnership Model and the suggested societal dialogue process are offered as an important new practice for making progress on society's divergent issues and complex problems.

Confronting Complex Community Issues

Issues and problems at the U.S. national level (across state communities and boundaries) are particularly difficult to resolve because local and state laws are not always in common in the federal system. Previous discussions in this chapter focused on *coming to public judgment, discovering common ground,* and *crucial decisions* have argued for leaders and teams to ensure their strategic and complex planning processes allow for increased information gathering and knowledge building – as well as greater dialogue and expert participation – to enable the necessary content and context factors and best subject matter experts are invited to share their insights and expertise.

Figures 12-4 and 12-5 (the *scoping* and systematic *process graphics* from Adaptive Leadership, chapter nine) are engaged below to illustrate decision complexity at the Community System Development (Mega-Level) domain. The issue: Recent studies confirm the Global Warming threat to Washington D.C. is real. Major flooding begins in 5-8 years.

Scoping the Issue

Figure 12-3 illustrates the holistic American learnership approach that begins with Ten Team Scoping Discussions that address the four social system domains and six universal knowledge spheres in terms of their (1) degree of impact on the issue at hand, and (2) on the weighted priority that each should be given as discussions proceed. This Adaptive Leadership (AL) process establishes a "decision space" in which most major influences and risk considerations are acknowledged. Doing this permits everyone to articulate their expectations, to participate in critical thinking, and to experience authentic dialogue which, in time, may be important in obtaining their subsequent support when the final actions are decided.

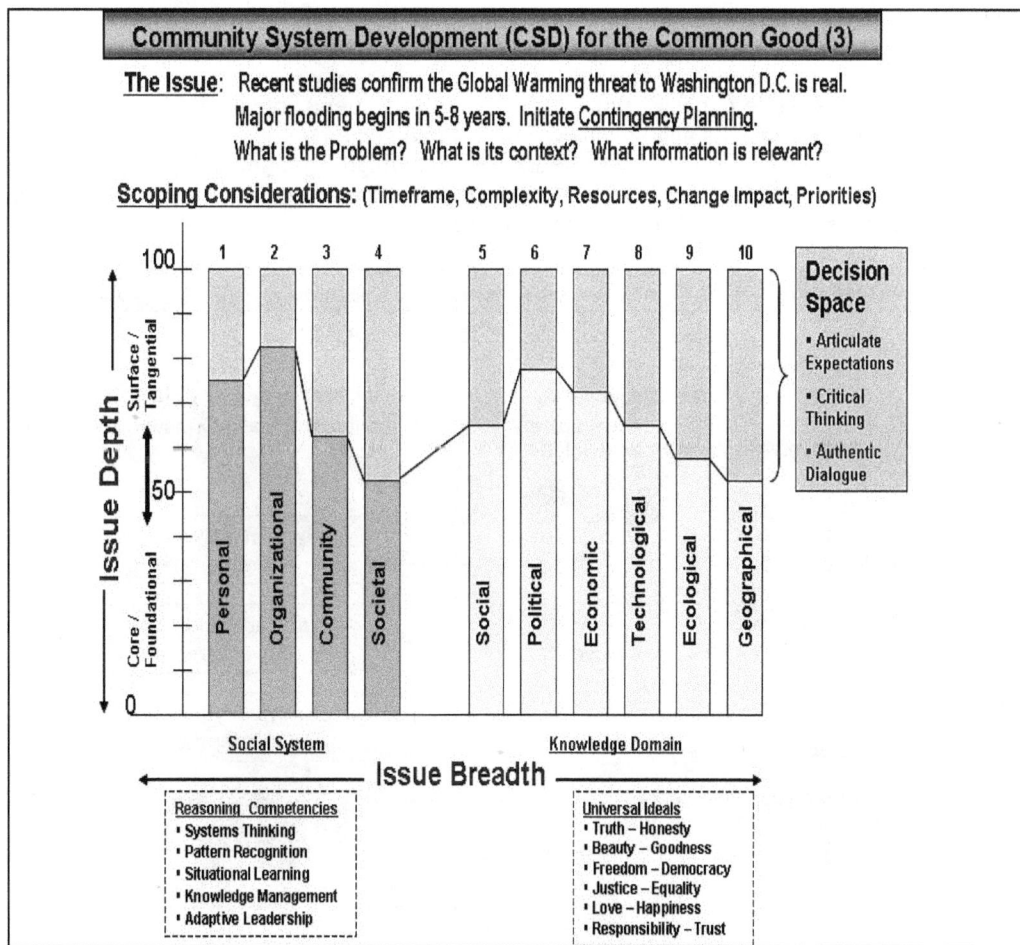

Figure 12-3

Using a Systematic Developmental Process

Once the Adaptive Leadership (AL) content deliberation and context setting effort of Figure 12-3 has been conducted and recorded for further use, the deliberation process in Figure 12-4 might proceed using the information already required on an as-appropriate basis. Through cycles of systematic learning and knowledge crafting, the team should acquire sufficient Knowledge (KM) factors that can be organized into alternative solutions for selection and action by the team and its adaptive leader (AL). Two major caveats that should be employed during the deliberation process are:

1. The deliberations will require an experienced strategic leader, subject matter experts and a skilled facilitator. This ensures structured meetings and conversations where substantive knowledge is exchanged and recorded.

2. Agree that "nothing is agreed to unless all is agreed to." This will allow better information sorting because some items can be deferred until more appropriate times in the process.

Leaders and other team members often have the opportunity to demonstrate their flexibility and adaptability when working
on fairly large and complex problems. An example of a challenging public sector issue is illustrated in Figures 12-13 and 12-14. The issue concerns government public policy making and strategic planning which important state and federal trends have all been heading in undesirable directions due to factors that are only partially under management and control of the government leaders. Government debt, consumer debt and private sector off-shoring have been increasing at the same time that consumer purchasing, middle class wages, and home buying have all been moving markedly downward.

Numerous local (content) and national (context) factors that are economic, social, technological and political in nature have combined to disadvantage citizen employment and family life. The complexity of the issue requires many cycles of data and information gathering, the development of alternative strategies for action, community participation in identifying community priorities, the development of new sources of business revenue and government taxation, and the choice of a sequence of initiatives that the citizens will need to approve.

Additional planning would need to emphasize turning the corner on some, if not all, of the related factors over the first few years, and then additional decisions and actions will need to be implemented, thereafter, to sustain positive movement. All along the way – even while the initial team members might change – integrated and supportive efforts will need to be made. Often, disruptive decisions and practices will ensue to limit (or maybe even enhance) the overall outcome notwithstanding previous expenditures in time and resources.

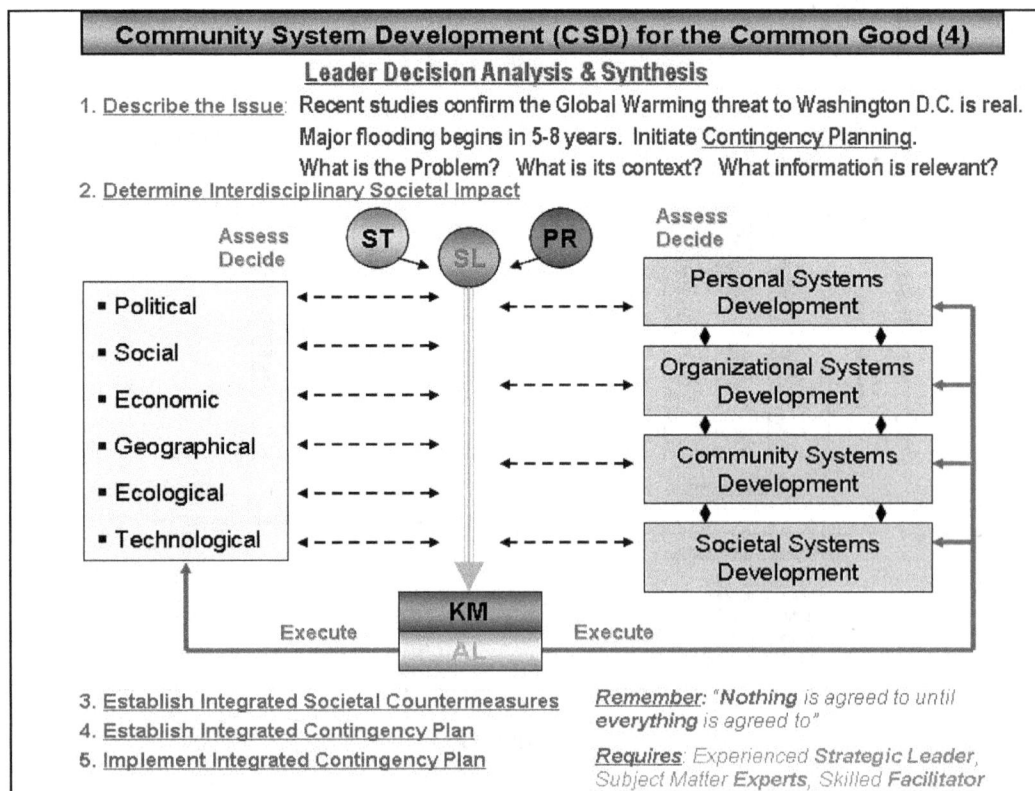

Figure 12-4

Community Wealth and Financial Security

Individuals and the organizations for which they work and support are inevitably members of local communities in which they and their families participate in shopping, recreation, school events, public associations, and the use of government services and school activities. Commercial and industrial businesses, government and non-government associations, schools for children ages 5 to 18 as well as those for whom colleges and private academies provide training for adult life interact in a myriad of communications and transactions that build both a sense of community and culture.

Using a balanced scorecard perspective (Chapters two to four) it can be illustrated that community wealth and financial security may be positively influenced (1) by the level of human knowledge and skill developed over time, (2) that stays within in the community and adds to public and private efficiency, and (3) is applied to effectively meet the needs and satisfaction of the community's citizens. When these factors and associated community values are present, well-intentioned leaders are able to collaborate to determine their community's priorities and desires, establish conservative and reasonable budgets, and gain consensus on an administrative process to collect operational income and to allocate and appropriate funding within budget guidelines – mostly through taxes and revenue from individuals, businesses and various levels of government administration.

Figure 12-5 illustrates approved budget limits for FY 2016 of one state county. It shows residents the result of numerous meetings and debates among community members prior to the beginning of the FY. Every member of the community who contributed their respective knowledge and skills to complete the deliberations and final budget – and those who will contribute their payment – are worthy of recognition for their commitment to finding the *Community Common Good.*

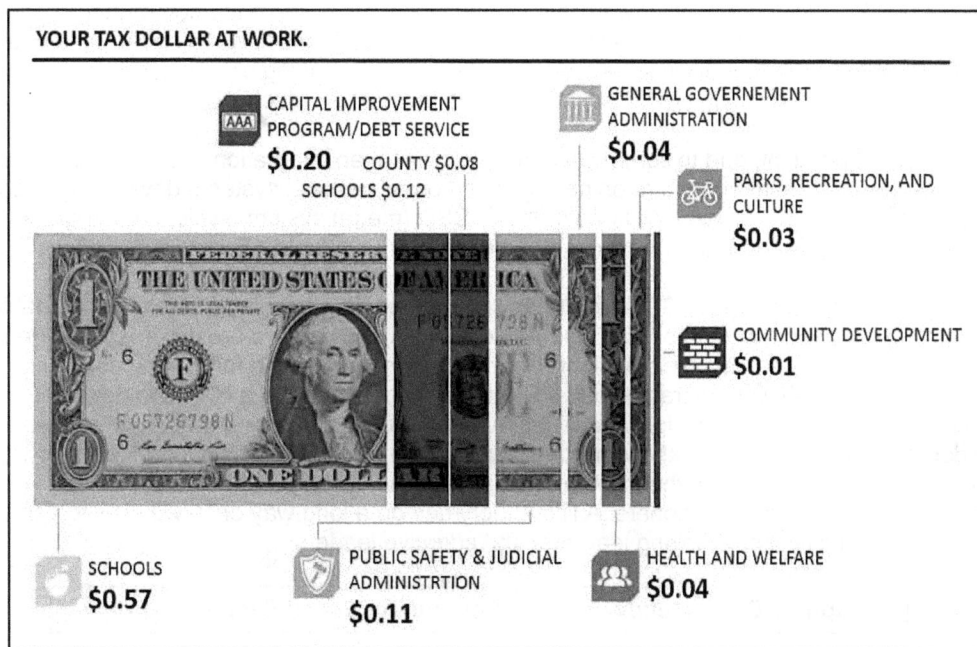

YOUR TAX DOLLAR AT WORK.

CAPITAL IMPROVEMENT PROGRAM/DEBT SERVICE
$0.20   COUNTY $0.08
SCHOOLS $0.12

GENERAL GOVERNEMENT ADMINISTRATION
$0.04

PARKS, RECREATION, AND CULTURE
$0.03

COMMUNITY DEVELOPMENT
$0.01

SCHOOLS
$0.57

PUBLIC SAFETY & JUDICIAL ADMINISTRTION
$0.11

HEALTH AND WELFARE
$0.04

Figure 12-5

The chart above shows how each dollar of real property tax revenue is allocated between the General Government and the Schools in FY 2016. The School system receives 69 cents of every tax dollar, with 57 cents going toward operating expenses and 12 cents toward capital improvements and debt service. The County receives 31 cents of every local tax dollar, 8 cents of which is devoted to capital improvements and debt service while the remaining 23 cents covers annual operating costs. The chart shows the distribution of the 23 cents in County operating costs across the five functional areas of County government. Operating expenses for the Public Safety and Judicial Administration function will require 11 cents of every tax dollar in FY 2016.

Conclusion

Apathy and lower motivation are the most widely noted
characteristics of a civilization in decline – John Gardner

In closing this chapter on Community System Development (CSD), it may be useful to recap the aspects of community that are central to the concept. Communities represent a composite of individuals and organizations living and working together for their individual and common purposes. Three major institutional domains or subsystems are identifiable: education/academia, government/public administration, and business/industry. Community progress is diminished whenever any of the major organizations in these institutional areas fails to perform in ways that are socially useful. *A useful national goal might be a greater level of cooperation among all individuals, organizations, and communities in pursuit of a shared vision of the common good.*

The common good is offered as the community (CSD) equivalent to the organization's focus on *high performance* (OSD) and the individual's desire for *self-fulfillment* (PSD). Each is presented as the major learning objective toward which the respective human and social systems strive. Achieving the common good can not be accomplished in isolation – individuals and organizations must all succeed for the community to succeed, and if any one sector attempts to maximize its accomplishments without regard for the others, all experience diminished returns due to the effects of system sub-optimization.

Some key community system development themes that emerged in this chapter include: (a) the LISA model as a catalyst for maintaining a sense of community, (b) the interdependence of community business, government, and education, (c) the community's need for purpose and faith in its future – a social ontology, (d) a concern for posterity and the future, (e) the need for balancing individual rights and obligations to the community, (f) the common good as a quality goal built upon a civic and moral ethic, (g) *education* as being primarily responsible for a community's social development, (h) *government* as being primarily responsible for a community's political development, (i) *business* as being primarily responsible for a community's economic development, (j) the challenge of policymaking in a shared power world, (k) the contribution of Constitutional government and responsible public administration in maintaining a sense of, and respect for, community, (l) the value of democracy and free-market practices in creating participative, productive workplaces, (m) the concept of stewardship wherein individuals serve the community interest along with their own self-interest, (n) the importance of "saving face," (o) the process of social dialogue, (p) the need for vigilant problem solving, (q) the impact of cognitive schemas, and (r) the understanding of dialogue as learning process in which the process of problem solving is almost as important as the problem itself.

These themes are interdependent, and to some extent they represent an integration of the fundamental principles and practices explained previously in the chapters on personal and organizational systems development. Systems at all three levels of analysis: the PSD (micro), OSD (macro), and CSD (mega) system levels, are integrated into and challenged by the *LISA model's societal system development (meta) system presented* in the next chapter.

Application of Learnership Reasoning Competencies. A fundamental goal of learnership is to enable most readers of the book to gain a fuller understanding of how their personal lives and careers are progressing in terms of the larger social systems of which they are a part. This book provides a beginning baseline for this assessment by presenting a philosophical viewpoint, an architectural framework, selected initial content, and a methodology for immersing the reader horizontally into numerous knowledge disciplines, while vertically immersing that same reader into greater subject matter depth in topics they never knew they wanted to know more about. The long-term plan is for those individuals who desire to rapidly develop their skills in this arena – and to begin to train and consult with others – to become accomplished learnership practitioners. A little theory can go a long way once we start to appreciate the benefits of becoming holistic thinkers, lifelong learners, and adaptive leaders.

Reasoning Competency	Community Social System
Systems Thinking	Impact on your community?
Pattern Recognition	Impact on your community?
Situational Learning	Impact on your community?
Knowledge Management	Impact on your community?
Adaptive Leadership	Impact on your community?

Table 12-1

This section is presented at the end of each chapter on social system development (personal, organizational, community, and societal). A little effort is now required from readers desiring to exercise their evolving understanding of learnership. Your task: Using Table 12-1 below and a separate piece of paper, write down some examples of how the five learnership competencies influence, drive, support, or otherwise have a powerful effect on the community social system discussed in this chapter.

Implications for Integral Learning and Knowledge Management. We now arrive at the *social systems domain* where the result of our knowledge building, with the assistance of the five learnership reasoning competencies, may be reviewed. The major determination for **CSD** is whether the knowledge recently created is "relevant" to the inquiry, study, problem or issue being considered. *Quite often a paradox occurs* at this juncture in which the conclusion reached appears to be inconsistent, conflicting or incompatible with what the individuals involved anticipated or desired. When analyzed, questions arise as to whether the Systems Thinking, Pattern Recognition or Situational Learning competencies have been utilized in an open, factual, unbiased, timely and convincing manner. That is, is the knowledge really correct and integral when considering the obvious limitations in people's minds and personal preferences – and their cultures, education, and beliefs are sometimes entirely in conflict. Effective and valued knowledge will need to be judged by the *CSD Business, Education, and Government* domains of thinking and behavior as interpreted by skilled and experienced leaders.

[Author's Note: Are the knowledge and skills you have acquired and using so far in your life sufficient for you to achieve your current goals, a meaningful life and a memorable legacy?]

Personal Reflection. This topic appears at the send of each chapter and is meant to serve two purposes: (1) be a reader's guide to main points and "takeaways," and (2) to encourage everyone to take a moment to engage their mental cognition and intuition on what the chapter means to them – especially at this time in their lives. Questions for chapter reflection follow immediately below; and for those readers inclined to maintain a self-assessment, your thoughts may be recorded in your *American Learnership for Life, Work, Wealth, Health and Legacy Success* which is at Appendix B.

Questions for Discussion:

1. How would you describe the concept of *business social responsibility*? Can you give two examples?

2. What does it mean when a community works together to achieve the *common good*? What are some examples where the common good has been achieved?

3. It has been said that "all organizations are public." What does that mean, and can you explain how a private sector organization can be referred to as a public organization?

4. What are the distinguishing characteristics of public administration, and what are the special requirements of public sector employees?

5. Can you list two to three major learning points from this chapter that you want to keep in mind to improve your ability to manage your life and career?

6. Can you identify two to three topics, models, or perspectives in this chapter you would like to learn more about?

7. Should you be making an entry into your *American Learnership for Life, Work, Wealth, Health and Legacy Success at Appendix B* ?

Questions on the Meaning of Your Life (Figure 12-6)

How do these surrogate goals work for you right now?

Are you able to achieve closure at this time on *Your Evolving Aspirations*? If so, please write them down for future use in this Handbook.

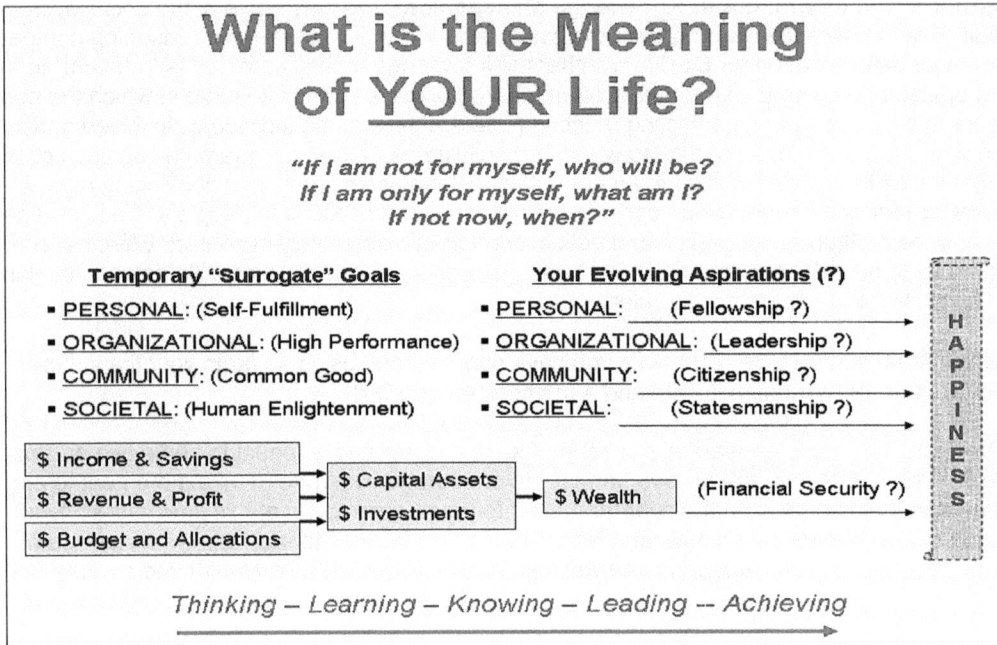

What is the Meaning of YOUR Life?

"If I am not for myself, who will be?
If I am only for myself, what am I?
If not now, when?"

Temporary "Surrogate" Goals	Your Evolving Aspirations (?)
▪ PERSONAL: (Self-Fulfillment)	▪ PERSONAL: (Fellowship ?)
▪ ORGANIZATIONAL: (High Performance)	▪ ORGANIZATIONAL: (Leadership ?)
▪ COMMUNITY: (Common Good)	▪ COMMUNITY: (Citizenship ?)
▪ SOCIETAL: (Human Enlightenment)	▪ SOCIETAL: (Statesmanship ?)

$ Income & Savings
$ Revenue & Profit
$ Budget and Allocations
→ $ Capital Assets / $ Investments → $ Wealth (Financial Security ?)

HAPPINESS

Thinking – Learning – Knowing – Leading -- Achieving

Figure 12-6

Insights, Commitments and Skills

If you plan to participate in the *American Learnership for Life, Work, Wealth, Health and Legacy Success* self-development e-book experience, it is suggested you record your Insights, commitments and skills to be developed here in this chapter, and again in Appendix B:

My learning in terms of new insights, changing priorities, new commitments or skills I want to acquire:

1. Insights (Example): Remind myself that …

2. Commitments (Example): Continue to ask myself …

3. Skills (Example): Apply my knowledge and skills to …

Chapter Thirteen

Societal (Meta) System Development

Social integration and teamwork are superior states of being over isolation and exclusion.
However, one should never trade their objectivity and sense of fairness for societal popularity and temporary gain.

Major Chapter Topics

Societal (Meta) System Development

Overview: Societal and Cultural Systems Development (SSD)

This Life Management Handbook chapter on SSD is dedicated to the final and comprehensive integration of all that has been written previously in this book. At this level of social systems integration, PSD, OSD, and CSD are viewed as being embedded into, and mutually interdependent with, the *six learnership knowledge spheres* from earlier chapters. These universal knowledge spheres – along with the learnership universal goals and ideals – are all brought forth, expanded, and used as mirrored reflections backward onto the five earlier learnership competencies and four learnership social systems that comprise the *Learnership Integrated Systems Architecture* (LISA).

For those learnership practitioners (the freelance learners, the versalists, the intrepreneurs, the facilitators) pursuing optimized learning and leading; their PSD *fellowship*, OSD *leadership*, and CSD *citizenship* knowledge and skills now fuse into SSD *statesmanship* wherein nations hold the fate of human existence. The overarching vision herein is that sometime before mankind destroys itself and this wondrous blue marble ecosystem; knowledgeable, compassionate, and truly wise leaders, citizens, and statesmen will rescue humankind from its ignorance and frenzy.
Understanding Social Intelligence and Cultural Intelligence

[**Author's Note**: Before considering the six universal knowledge spheres it is helpful to understand the wide variety of social and cultural factors that make understanding and integrating societal similarities and differences. When working within or across national boundaries, the worldviews, values, preferences and behaviors of groups of people can sometimes be misunderstood leading to poor communications and unsatisfactory relationship and outcomes.]

Social Intelligence

Dimension	Definition
Situational Awareness	The ability to read situations and to interpret the behaviors of people in those situations e.g. their emotional states, intentions, and proclivity to interact.
Presence	Verbal and nonverbal patterns of communications, voice quality, posture, and appearance that is non-threatening and respectful.
Authenticity	Others' social radars pick up signals from behavior that lead them to judge who is open, ethical, trustworthy and well intentioned.
Clarity	The ability to explain ourselves, to express ideas, share data accurately, and articulate our views with consideration so as to gain cooperation.
Empathy	Going beyond sympathy to where feelings are understood and shared between people. Achieving a degree of connectedness for positive interaction.

Table 13-1, Adapted from *Social Intelligence* by Karl Albrecht

"Social intelligence permits us to know and manage ourselves and to know others well enough to interact successfully with them. The better we know ourselves, the better we can develop, interact, and achieve success, by using our strengths and improving our weaknesses." *In Your Intelligence Makeover* (2005), Edward F Droge. Jr. explains that social intelligence is built on a foundation of intellectual intelligence (cognitive, rational, factual) and emotional intelligence (feelings, intuition, relations) and is positively correlated with higher skill levels in each of these basic human dimensions. From this two derivative personal abilities may be described:

1. Intrapersonal Intelligence – This skill relates to our personal capability in knowing ourselves, and to use that self-knowledge for our own efficiency and effectiveness. When we have learned to understand and manage ourselves in terms of our likes and dislikes, strengths and weaknesses, and intellectual and emotional preferences and priorities we are likely to have strong intrapersonal intelligence.

2. Interpersonal Intelligence – This skill considers our relationship with others, and how well know and relate to them

socially and in the workplace. When we are aware of their feelings and motivations towards us and others, and can understand their viewpoints and preferences, we are judged to have good interpersonal intelligence. Strength in this area is seen as individuals demonstrate the capacity to connect personally, analyze social situations, and provide situational leadership.

Another contributor is Karl Albrecht. In his book *Social Intelligence: The New Science of Success* (2006), he presents the view that developing social intelligence is an essential component of human success with others. To encourage practical conversation in this regard he offers the acronym "S.P.A.C.E.: Situational Awareness, Presence, Authenticity, Clarity, and Empathy. Table 13-1 above provides definitions and illustrates how an assessment tool might be created for individual and team discussion and learning. Coaches and consultants are encouraged to use this in their learning groups.

Cultural Intelligence

According to David Livermore in Expand Your Borders (2013), there is increasing worldwide pressure and expectations that travelers of all types e.g. business leaders, political leaders, academicians, technical specialists, and international travelers of all kinds to learn how to visit, live and work in cultures that are different from their own. Doing well often matters individually, socially and economically. He refers to the *GLOBE Leadership Project* conducted by Ronen and Shencar (1985) that used a seven factor set of criteria to establish "Ten Cultural Clusters" within which most countries worldviews, values and behaviors could be displayed (Table 13-2). In this text, their seven factors have been applied and organized into a table that illustrates a comparison of the strongest differences and similarities. No entry is made where there was no significant difference in a specific pair:

1a. Individualism: Individual goals and right are more important than personal relationship
1b. Collectivism: Personal relationships and benefiting the group are more important than individual goals.

2a. Low Power Distance: Status differences are of little importance; empowered decision-making is across all levels.
2b. High Power Distance: Status decisions should shape interactions; those with authority should make decisions.

3a. Low Uncertainty Avoidance: Focus on flexibility and adaptability; tolerant of unstructured and unpredictable situations.
3b. High Uncertainty Avoidance: Focus on planning and responsibility; uncomfortable with unstructured or unpredictable situations.

4a. Cooperative: Emphasis upon cooperation and nurturing behavior; high value placed on relationship and family.
4b. Competitive: Emphasis on assertive behavior and competition; high value place on work, task accomplishment and achievement

5a. Short Term: Values immediate outcomes more than long-term benefits (success now).
5b. Long Term: Values long-term planning; willing to sacrifice short-term outcomes for long-term benefits (success later).

6a. Low Context: Values direct communications. Emphasis on explicit words,
6b. High Context: Values indirect communication. Emphasis on implicit understanding.

7a. Being: Social communications and task completion are equally important; diffuse boundaries between personal and work activities.
7b. Doing: Task completion takes precedence over social commitments; clear separation of social and work activities.

Comparison of Cultural Preferences

Cultural Cluster	1a	1b	2a	2b	3a	3b	4a	4b	5a	5b	6a	6b	7a	7b
Nordic Europe	X		X		X		X		X		X		X	
Anglo	X		X		X		X	X			X			X
Germanic Europe	X		X			X	X				X			X
Easter Europe		X			X		X	X						
Latin Europe		X				X	X							
Latin America		X	X			X	X					X	X	
Confucian Asia		X				X	X			X		X		
Southern Asia		X	X				X					X		
Sub-Sahara Asia		X				X	X		X			X	X	
Arab	X		X				X		X			X	X	

Adapted from Expand Your Borders by David Livermore

Table 13-2

Education and international experience play a role in developing cultural intelligence; however, not everyone makes the right choices, has the right experiences, and works diligently to become fully adept at becoming culturally competent. Learning and adapting appropriately to what may be seen as unusual expectations and perspectives requires a systematic process through which additional skills at thinking and behavior are developed. David Livermore in *Leading with Cultural Intelligence* (2010), recommends a *Four Dimensional Model of Cultural Intelligence* that can guide the both visitors and business leaders alike in gaining competence and confidence. "The four sequential phases are:

1. CQ Drive: The *motivational drive* of CQ, and is based on the degree of interest, drive, and energy to adapt cross-culturally. The primary sub-dimensions are *intrinsic motivation*, *extrinsic motivation* and *self-efficacy*. The major question one should consider is: *Do I have the confidence and drive to work through the challenges and conflicts that inevitably accompany cross-cultural work?*

2. CQ Knowledge: The knowledge and *cognitive dimension* refers to the leader's knowledge about culture and its role in how business is done. An understanding of new roles and values in a cross-cultural environment is essential here. An important question is: *Do I understand the way culture shapes thinking and behavior between and among cultures?*

3. CQ Strategy: CQ strategy is the *leader's ability to strategize* when crossing cultures. The major sub-dimensions are: *awareness*, *planning*, and *checking* which are necessary to observe what is happening, create an acceptable approach for moving forward, and to evaluate the progress being made. A primary question at this point is: *Do I understand the way culture shapes thinking and behavior?*

4. CQ Action: By this phase the leader should have gained initial skills from their previous cross-culture experiences; and should be prepared to *take action* given the circumstances provided. Of importance here are successful communications in the areas of *verbal actions*, *nonverbal actions*, and *speech acts*. High skill in *social intelligence* can make a significant contribution for achieving a successful outcome. The major question to be asked here is: *Can I effectively accomplish my performance goals in this new and different situation?*"

[**Author's Note**: It would be easy given the pace and complexity of the lives and careers of the world's people to casually overlook the mistakes one makes in international affairs. Doing so, however, will certainly cause an unacceptable level of hard feelings and even occasional interpersonal anger which can serve no good purpose.]

Application of the U.N. Universal Declaration of Human Rights

The United Nations was established after WWII wherein the allied world leaders felt the need for a mechanism to help stop future wars and bring international peace. It was their belief that only through global collaboration could nations resolve their most serious interdependent issues.

In 1945 delegates from 50 nations (excluding the axis powers during WWII – Japan, Germany, Italy) met in San Francisco to agree on an organization and structure to preserve peace and build a better world. Subsequently, the excluded nations were invited to join the U.N. and over time the number of nations expanded to 193 as of 2012.

Major leadership from the United States came from President Franklin D. Roosevelt who was the first national leader to propose the need for such an international body. The land for use by the U.N. was provided by the U.S. and is in New York City. By charter, there are four areas specifically identified for permanent cognizance and potential action by the U.N. These are: (1) International Peace and Security, (2) Economic and Social Development, (3) Humanitarians Crises and Responses, and (4) Human Rights.

The Universal Declaration of Human Rights was adopted in 1948 after research and draft proposals were prepared by a committee headed by Eleanor Roosevelt, wife of the President. The document contains 30 articles that proclaim an extraordinary vision and resolve to protect and preserve the rights and freedoms to which every human being is equally and inalienably entitled.

United Nations Universal Declaration of Human Rights (Original Text)

Preamble

-Whereas recognition of the inherent dignity and of the equal and inalienable rights of all members of the human family is the foundation of freedom, justice and peace in the world,

-Whereas disregard and contempt for human rights have resulted in barbarous acts which have outraged the conscience of mankind, and the advent of a world in which human beings shall enjoy freedom of speech and belief and freedom from fear and want has been proclaimed as the highest aspiration of the common people,

-Whereas it is essential, if man is not to be compelled to have recourse, as a last resort, to rebellion against tyranny and oppression, that human rights should be protected by the rule of law, Whereas it is essential to promote the development of friendly relations between nations,

-Whereas the peoples of the United Nations have in the Charter reaffirmed their faith in fundamental human rights, in the dignity and worth of the human person and in the equal rights of men and women and have determined to promote social progress and better standards of life in larger freedom,

-Whereas Member States have pledged themselves to achieve, in cooperation with the United Nations, the promotion of universal respect for and observance of human rights and fundamental freedoms,

-Whereas a common understanding of these rights and freedoms is of the greatest importance for the full realization of this pledge

Now, therefore, The General Assembly,

Proclaims this Universal Declaration of Human Rights as a common standard of achievement for all peoples and all nations, to the end that every individual and every organ of society, keeping this Declaration constantly in mind, shall strive by teaching and education to promote respect for these rights and freedoms and by progressive measures, national and international, to secure their universal and effective recognition and observance, both among the peoples of Member States themselves and among the peoples of territories under their jurisdiction.

Article I
All human beings are born free and equal in dignity and rights. They are endowed with reason and conscience and should act towards one another in a spirit of brotherhood.

Article 2

Everyone is entitled to all the rights and freedoms set forth in this Declaration, without distinction of any kind, such as race, colour, sex, language, religion, political or other opinion, national or social origin, property, birth or other status. Furthermore, no distinction shall be made on the basis of the political, jurisdictional or international status of the country or territory to which a person belongs, whether it be independent, trust, non-self-governing or under any other limitation of Sovereignty.

Article 3

Everyone has the right to life, liberty and security of person.

Article 4

No one shall be held in slavery or servitude; slavery and the slave trade shall be prohibited in all their forms.

Article 5

No one shall be subjected to torture or to cruel, inhuman or degrading treatment or punishment.

Article 6

Everyone has the right to recognition everywhere as a person before the law.

Article 7

All are equal before the law and are entitled without any discrimination to equal protection of the law. All are entitled to equal protection against any discrimination in violation of this Declaration and against any incitement to such discrimination.

Article 8

Everyone has the right to an effective remedy by the competent national tribunals for acts violating the fundamental rights granted him by the constitution or by law.

Article 9

No one shall be subjected to arbitrary arrest, detention or exile.

Article 10

Everyone is entitled in full equality to a fair and public hearing by an independent and impartial tribunal, in the determination of his rights and obligations and of any criminal charge against him.

Article 11

1. Everyone charged with a penal offence has the right to be presumed innocent until proved guilty according to law in a public trial at which he has had all the guarantees necessary for his defence.
2. No one shall be held guilty of any penal offence on account of any act or omission which did not constitute a penal offence, under national or international law, at the time when it was committed. Nor shall a heavier penalty be imposed than the one that was applicable at the time the penal offence was committed.

Article 12

No one shall be subjected to arbitrary interference with his privacy, family, home or correspondence, nor to attacks upon his honour and reputation. Everyone has the right to the protection of the law against such interference or attacks.

Article 13

1. Everyone has the right to freedom of movement and residence within the borders of each State.
2. Everyone has the right to leave any country, including his own, and to return to his country.

Article 14

1. Everyone has the right to seek and to enjoy in other countries asylum from persecution.
2. This right may not be invoked in the case of prosecutions genuinely arising from non-political crimes or from acts contrary to the purposes and principles of the United Nations.

Article 15

1. Everyone has the right to a nationality.
2. No one shall be arbitrarily deprived of his nationality nor denied the right to change his nationality.

Article 16

1. Men and women of full age, without any limitation due to race, nationality or religion, have the right to marry and to found a family. They are entitled to equal rights as to marriage, during marriage and at its dissolution.

2. Marriage shall be entered into only with the free and full consent of the intending spouses.
3. The family is the natural and fundamental group unit of society and is entitled to protection by society and the State.

Article 17
1. Everyone has the right to own property alone as well as in association with others.
2. No one shall be arbitrarily deprived of his property.

Article 18
Everyone has the right to freedom of thought, conscience and religion; this right includes freedom to change his religion or belief, and freedom, either alone or in community with others and in public or private, to manifest his religion or belief in teaching, practice, worship and observance.

Article 19
Everyone has the right to freedom of opinion and expression; this right includes freedom to hold opinions without interference and to seek, receive and impart information and ideas through any media and regardless of frontiers.

Article 20
1. Everyone has the right to freedom of peaceful assembly and association.
2. No one may be compelled to belong to an association.

Article 21
1. Everyone has the right to take part in the government of his country, directly or through freely chosen representatives.
2. Everyone has the right to equal access to public service in his country.
3. The will of the people shall be the basis of the authority of government; this shall be expressed in periodic and genuine elections which shall be by universal and equal suffrage and shall be held by secret vote or by equivalent free voting procedures.

Article 22
Everyone, as a member of society, has the right to social security and is entitled to realization, through national effort and international co-operation and in accordance with the organization and resources of each State, of the economic, social and cultural rights indispensable for his dignity and the free development of his personality.

Article 23
1. Everyone has the right to work, to free choice of employment, to just and favourable conditions of work and to protection against unemployment.
2. Everyone, without any discrimination, has the right to equal pay for equal work.
3. Everyone who works has the right to just and favourable remuneration ensuring for himself and his family an existence worthy of human dignity, and supplemented, if necessary, by other means of social protection.
4. Everyone has the right to form and to join trade unions for the protection of his interests.

Article 24
Everyone has the right to rest and leisure, including reasonable limitation of working hours and periodic holidays with pay.

Article 25
1. Everyone has the right to a standard of living adequate for the health and well-being of himself and of his family, including food, clothing, housing and medical care and necessary social services, and the right to security in the event of unemployment, sickness, disability, widowhood, old age or other lack of livelihood in circumstances beyond his control.

2. Motherhood and childhood are entitled to special care and assistance. All children, whether born in or out of wedlock, shall enjoy the same social protection.

Article 26
1. Everyone has the right to education. Education shall be free, at least in the elementary and fundamental stages. Elementary education shall be compulsory. Technical and professional education shall be made generally available and higher education shall be equally accessible to all on the basis of merit.

2. Education shall be directed to the full development of the human personality and to the strengthening of respect for human rights and fundamental freedoms. It shall promote understanding, tolerance and friendship among all nations, racial or religious groups, and shall further the activities of the United Nations for the maintenance of peace.
3. Parents have a prior right to choose the kind of education that shall be given to their children.

Article 27

1. Everyone has the right freely to participate in the cultural life of the community, to enjoy the arts and to share in scientific advancement and its benefits.
2. Everyone has the right to the protection of the moral and material interests resulting from any scientific, literary or artistic production of which he is the author.

Article 28

Everyone is entitled to a social and international order in which the rights and freedoms set forth in this Declaration can be fully realized.

Article 29

1. Everyone has duties to the community in which alone the free and full development of his personality is possible.
2. In the exercise of his rights and freedoms, everyone shall be subject only to such limitations as are determined by law solely for the purpose of securing due recognition and respect for the rights and freedoms of others and of meeting the just requirements of morality, public order and the general welfare in a democratic society.
3. These rights and freedoms may in no case be exercised contrary to the purposes and principles of the United Nations.

Article 30

Nothing in this Declaration may be interpreted as implying for any State, group or person any right to engage in any activity or to perform any act aimed at the destruction of any of the rights and freedoms set forth herein.

Societal System Development (SSD).

All societies are concerned with their development; that is, they hope to realize their ontological purpose and objectives, and to achieve a higher level and quality of societal experience. This focus most often manifests itself as a drive toward economic growth and development, which is also the dimension of societal development most easily measured and evaluated. From a quality-of-life perspective, however, other dimensions of development need inclusion. Examples of the other dimensions are the improvements desired in the political, social, ecological, technological, and geographical arenas of community experience. The Learnership philosophy and architectural framework developed in this book illustrate this aspiration for growth and development by their emphasis on the meta-system goals of *self-fulfillment, high performance, the common good,* and *human enlightenment*. These goals are conceived as being fully achieved only when all dimensions of societal life are taken into account and meta-system optimization occurs. Common to all these dimensions are the civic and ethical values which bind a society – and societies together.

Figure 13-1 provides an overview of key SSD concepts and relationships to assist the reader in building a *"summative mental model "*as he or she proceeds through this chapter.

1. Meta-. Illustrated are the *four interdependent learnership social systems* with this chapter's emphasis being at the *societal meta-level*.

2. Personal Systems Development (PSD). PSD is brought forth from Chapter Ten. The objectives, challenges, and strategies concerning personal *health*, *character*, and *ability* are of primary concern in the pursuit of self-fulfillment. The major learnership practitioner trait in working for personal objectives with others is *fellowship*.

3. Organizational Systems Development (OSD). CSD is brought forth from Chapter Eleven. The objectives, challenges, and strategies are organization *direction*, *operations*, and *performance* in the pursuit of high performance. The major learnership practitioner trait in working for organizational objectives is *leadership*.

4. Community Systems Development (CSD). SSD is brought forth from Chapter Twelve. The objectives, challenges and strategies are organized as *education*, *business* and *government* in pursuit of the *common good*. The major learnership practitioner trait is *citizenship*.

5. Meta-System Development (SSD). SSD focuses on the objectives, challenges, and strategies of *personal*, *organization*, and *community* synergy in the pursuit of *human enlightenment*. The major learnership practitioner trait in working for societal objectives is *statesmanship*.

6. Meta-Cognitive Reasoning. Illustrated are the *five reasoning competencies* that can be used to maximize societal social system development.

7. Information Processing Model. Illustrated is a general approach for problem solving and decision-making throughout society: Gather and analyze information, develop a strategy and implement it, observe results and take corrective action,.

[**Author's Note**: A significant point to make at this juncture is that during Section II (Chapters Five through Nine), the Five Learnership Reasoning Competencies have been integrated into a comprehensive Total Knowledge Management (TKM) framework. That "total learning, knowing, and leading" framework has been embedded in the Learnership Integrated Systems Architecture (LISA) and all the principles, practices, and technologies of TKM are conceptually available, and should be appropriately applied, for full societal social systems development.]

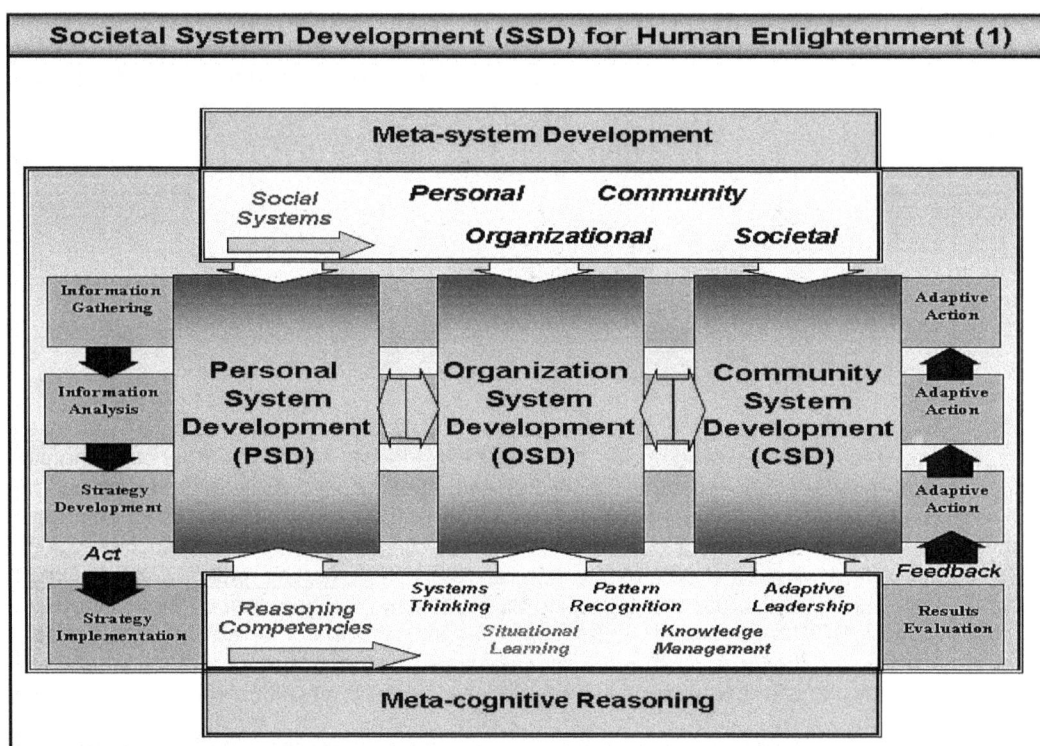

Figure 13-1

Aspiration for Human Enlightenment.

The theme of this chapter: "Aspiration for Human Enlightenment" is inspired by the unique relationship between the American founding and the legacy of the European Enlightenment during the period 1650 to 1800. An excellence summary of that period with the confluence of European and American knowledge and trends is stated in full from a document by Neil Janowitz, reference: Sparknote on The Enlightenment (1650-1800). 30 July, 2007, http://www.sparknotes.com/history/european/enlightenment.

The Legacy of the Enlightenment.

Events

1775 – American Revolution begins
1776 – Paine publishes Common Sense, Jefferson writes Declaration of Independence
1789 – French Revolution begins

Key People

1. Frederick II "the Great" – Prussian monarch from 1740–1786; instituted judicial reforms and created a written legal Code

2. Charles III – Spanish monarch from 1759–1788; weakened Church influence and implemented other reforms

3. Catherine II "the Great" – Russian empress from 1762–1796; improved education, health care, and women's rights, though continued to crack down on dissent

4. Benjamin Franklin – American thinker, inventor, and diplomat; transmitted many Enlightenment ideas between Europe and America

5. Thomas Paine – English-American political writer; pamphlet <u>Common Sense</u> influenced the American Revolution

6. Thomas Jefferson – American author of the <u>Declaration of Independence</u>; drew heavily from Enlightenment political philosophy

<u>Enlightened Absolutism</u> the later years of the Enlightenment, absolute monarchs in several European countries adopted some of the ideas of Enlightenment political philosophers. However, although some changes and reforms were implemented, most of these rulers did not fundamentally change absolutist rule.

In Russia, empress Catherine the Great, a subscriber to the ideas of Beccaria and de Gouges, decried torture while greatly improving education, health care, and women's rights, as well as clarifying the rights of the nobility. She also insisted that the Russian Orthodox Church become more tolerant of outsiders. However, she continued to imprison many of her opponents and maintained censorship and serfdom.

In Austria, monarchs Maria-Theresa and Joseph II worked to end mistreatment of peasants by abolishing serfdom and also promoted individual rights, education, and religious tolerance. An admirer of Voltaire, Frederick the Great, the King of Prussia, supported the arts and education, reformed the justice system, improved agriculture, and created a written legal code. However, although these reforms strengthened and streamlined the Prussian state, the tax burden continued to fall on peasants and commoners.

Spain had a great deal of censorship in place during the early Enlightenment, but when Charles III ascended the throne in 1759, he implemented a number of reforms. During his tenure, Charles III weakened the influence of the Church, enabled land ownership for the poor, and vastly improved transportation routes.

Enlightenment - Era Frauds
Not all the consequences of the Enlightenment were productive. Despite the advances in literacy, thought, and intellectual discussion that accompanied the Enlightenment, middle- and upper-class citizens often mistakenly carried this open-mindedness to an excessive degree. In many cases, this open-mindedness manifested itself in pure gullibility, as supposedly well-educated Europeans fell prey to "intellectual" schemes and frauds based on nothing more than superstition and clever speech.

For instance, during the eighteenth century, people who called themselves phrenologists convinced many Europeans that a person's character could be analyzed through the study of the contours of the skull. Likewise, the quack field of physiognomy claimed to be able to predict psychological characteristics, such as a predisposition to violence, by analyzing facial features or body structure. Similar medical hoaxes were common throughout the seventeenth and eighteenth centuries, some more dangerous than others, such as the continuing practice of bloodletting.

Although many of these misguided Enlightenment scientists believed that their methods could work, many were charlatans who knew exactly what they were doing. The world was wide-eyed and eager for new knowledge and, as of yet, lacked the fact-checking capabilities to separate real discoveries from pure deception.

The American Revolution
Across the Atlantic, the Enlightenment had a profound impact on the English colonies in America and ultimately on the infant nation of the United States. The colonial city of Philadelphia emerged as a chic, intellectual hub of American life, strongly influenced by European thought.

Benjamin Franklin (1706–1790) the consummate philosopher: a brilliant diplomat, journalist, and scientist who traveled back and forth between Europe and America, acting as a conduit of ideas between them. He played a pivotal role in the American Revolution, which began in 1775, and the subsequent establishment of a democratic government under the Thomas Jefferson–penned Declaration of Independence (1776).

The political writer Thomas Paine (1737–1809) also brought Enlightenment ideas to bear on the American Revolution. An Englishman who immigrated to America, Paine was inspired by America and wrote the political pamphlet Common Sense (1776), which encouraged the secession of the colonies from England. Later in his life, Paine's religious views and caustic demeanor alienated him from much of the public, and he died in somewhat ill repute.
In many ways, the new United States was the Enlightenment, for its leaders could actually implement many of the ideas that European philosophers could only talk idly about. Americans were exposed to, and contributed to, the leading works of science, law, politics, and social order, yet lacked the traditions and conservatism that impeded the European countries from truly changing their ways. Indeed, the Declaration of Independence borrows heavily from Enlightenment themes – even taking passages from Locke and Rousseau – and the U.S. Constitution implements almost verbatim Locke and Montesquieu ideas on separation of power. America was founded as a deist country, giving credit to some manner of natural God yet allowing diverse religious expression, and also continued in the social and industrial veins begun in Europe.

The French Revolution
Just a decade after the revolution in America, France followed suit, with the French Revolution, which began in 1789. Empowered by the political philosophies of the Enlightenment, the French citizenry overthrew the monarchy of Louis XVI and established a representative government that was directly inspired by Enlightenment thought. This harmonious arrangement, however, soon fell prey to internal dissent, and leadership changed hands throughout the years that followed. The instability reached a violent climax with the ascent of Maximilien Robespierre, an extremist who plunged the revolution into the so-called Reign of Terror of 1793–1794, beheading more than 15,000 suspected enemies and dissenters at the guillotine. (For more information, see the History Sparknote, The French Revolution.)

Distraught Frenchmen and other Europeans reacted to the tyranny of the Reign of Terror, as well as subsequent oppressive governments in France, by blaming the Enlightenment. These critics claimed that the Enlightenment's attacks on tradition and questioning of norms would always lead inevitably to instability. Moreover, many critics in the nobility saw the violence of the Reign of Terror as proof positive that the masses, however "enlightened," could never be trusted to govern themselves in an orderly fashion. Indeed, most historians agree that the French Revolution effectively marked the end of the Enlightenment. France itself reacted against the violence of the revolution by reverting to a military dictatorship under Napoleon that lasted fifteen years.

Long-Term Influence
Despite the brutalities of the French Revolution and the lingering resentment toward many philosophies, the Enlightenment had an indisputably positive effect on the Western world. Scientific advances laid an indestructible foundation for modern thought, while political and other philosophies questioned and ultimately undermined oppressive, centuries-old traditions in Europe. After several transitional decades of instability in Europe, nearly everyone in Europe – along with an entire population in the United States – walked away from the Enlightenment in a better position. The movement resulted in greater freedom, greater opportunity, and generally more humane treatment for all individuals. Although the world still had a long way to go, and indeed still does, the Enlightenment arguably marked the first time that Western civilization truly started to become civilized.

SSD for Human Enlightenment. Arriving at the Societal Systems Development (SSD) level of human activity, Figure 13 – 2. has been a complex and time consuming journey for this author. On the one hand it is a place toward which one systematically progresses moving from one's personal core, through organizational, to community levels of individual objectives, activities, and responsibilities. It is natural that one would seek to attain and understand the final, all-encompassing level of purpose, influence and integration. Only at this SSD meta-system level can any such ideas as universal knowledge spheres, universal goals, and universal ideals be fully valued for their overarching guidance and pervasive impact across all systems and domains. On the other hand, elements of what was "discovered" in the learning and writing process could already be seen as faint images etched on the fabric of one's own consciousness and quietly guiding the path of inquiry and architectural design. The use of review questions at the end of each chapter are expected to solidify the reader's learning and commitment to a learning and leading mindset as well as a way-of-being.

Societal Systems Development and Performance

The slenderest knowledge that may be obtained of the highest things is more desirable than the most certain knowledge obtained of lesser things. — Thomas Aquinas

General Observations.

Convergent versus Divergent Problems. In *A Guide for the Perplexed* (1977), E.F. Schumacher offered the viewpoint that much of life's growth and development involves problem solving, and that there are two types of problems – convergent and divergent. The nature of *convergent problems* is that they are fact-based and the more intelligently they are analyzed, the more that is known and may be agreed upon. This results in the potential for solutions to converge, thereby making the problems ultimately solvable.

Divergent problems, On the other hand, are values-based. For these problems, additional deliberation and logical analysis lead toward diverse or opposite conclusions for which there are equally supportable rationale. Schumacher suggests that the reason for the difference is that the co-existence of opposite values like *freedom* and *order* make problems divergent, while the absence of opposites with which to contend make problems convergent.

He suggests that it is human nature to study convergent problems because they are easier to solve, but that real growth results from engaging problems and issues that are divergent. He says that: "*While the logical mind abhors divergent problems and tries to run away from them, the higher faculties of man accept the challenges of life as they are offered, without complaint, knowing that when things are most contradictory, absurd, difficult, and frustrating, then, just then, life really makes sense; as a mechanism provoking and almost forcing us to develop toward higher levels-of-being.*" (pp.134-135)

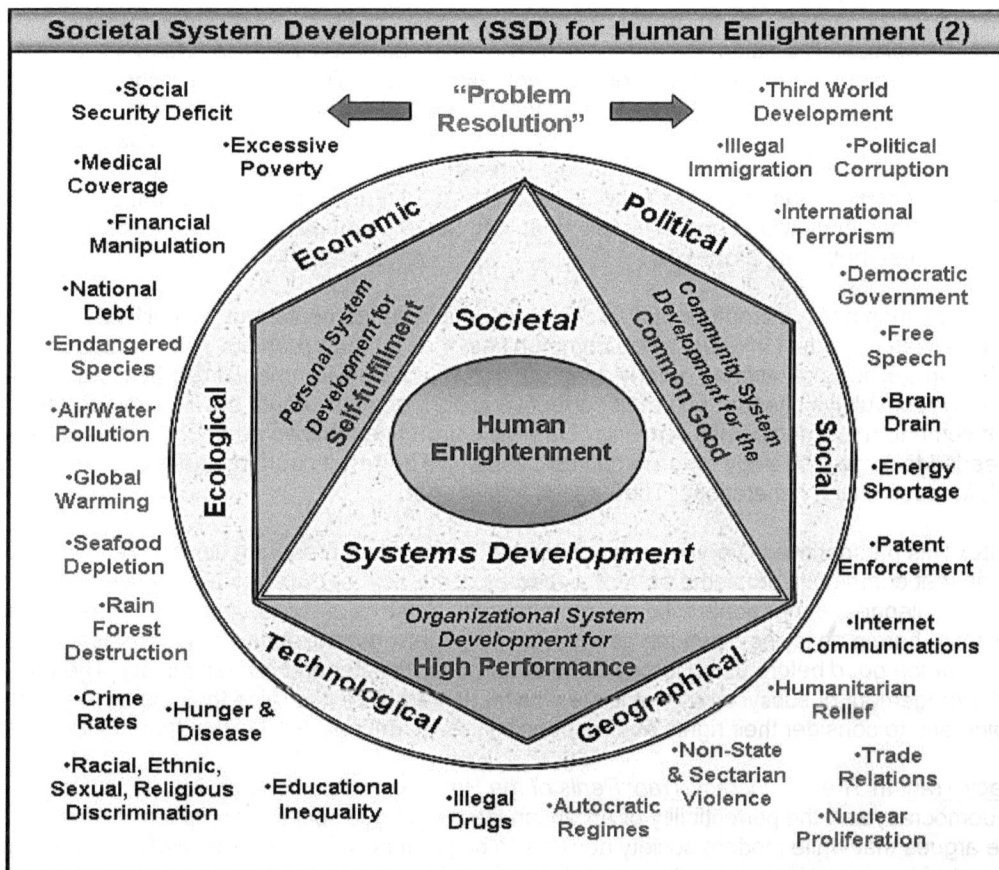

Figure 13-2

To Schumacher, the progress of human beings, and society at large, is tied to our ability and willingness to engage the more challenging divergent problems of life. By working through such issues, we are able to transform ourselves from stages of dependency and independency to interdependency and our highest level-of-being.

[**Author's Note**: This developmental process is considered, herein, to be the result of enlightened dialogue centered on learnership learning and leading. The LISA model is offered as an aid for thinking through (rather than thinking about) convergent and divergent issues, and is considered unique in its potential to frame social dialogue. To the extent that members of a society engage one another in social discourse and become cognizant of emerging trends and issues in terms of their mutual values and shared vision of the future, societal progress may be at least guided, if not managed.. Reference Figure 13-2]

<u>The Human Prospect</u>. In *An Inquiry into the Human Prospect* (Heilbroner, 1975), the author muses about what today's generation owes to those yet unborn. He reflects on the dilemmas of today's events and trends noting that there is every reason to have our confidence shaken by the levels of war, violence, crime, drugs, declining values, population increase, poverty, etc. *Heilbroner says that our sense of assurance and control is diminishing and civilization has entered a period of malaise.* The paradox of minimal learning, growth, and development in underdeveloped nations, concurrent with excessive growth and development in the advanced nations make him wonder whether solutions may be found – and, destruction of the ecological balance is occurring under any circumstances.

Taking a socio-economic position, *Heilbroner finds both capitalism and socialism wanting* in their ability to make the dramatic changes necessary to achieve a sustainable existence given the magnitude of today's challenges. *In capitalism,* he finds the excessive stress on personal achievement, materialistic acquisition, and relentless pressure for advancement in order to attain "the good life" to be the harbinger of the overuse of natural resources, environmental destruction, and an unsatisfying social ethos in which community health is sacrificed for individual betterment. *In socialism,* he finds the stultifying effects of intellectual oppression, bureaucratic ineptitude, and limitations on individual development and expression in favor of community prerogatives. Both focus on increasing industrial production as the way to progress, and neither are sufficiently concerned for the broader human and environmental implications of their policies and actions.

Taking a look at the political dimension and human nature, Heibroner states that: "For the exercise of political power lies squarely in the center of the determination of that [human] prospect. The resolution of the crises thrust upon us by the social and natural environment can only be found through political action". (p.100) He argues that *human nature leans opposite to directions necessary to forge the large, consensually-based decisions needed to positively affect the course of the future.* For one thing political power to act is reliant upon political obedience of those who follow. He does not see much of this occurring in the world's nations. Also, the human need for identification, particularly national identification, keeps the world divided and generally unable to find the common ground necessary for true progress against pervasive, cross-boundary problems.

Heibroner describes man as "...a creature of his socio-economic arrangements and his political bonds". (p.124) Given the degree of polarization evident in nations and communities, man's future problem-solving capacity is deemed to be very limited. The unlikelihood of rational, orderly adaptation to life and environmental realities causes Heibroner to conclude that only "convulsive change" can elicit corrective action, and that would not likely be correct or sufficient. He concludes that some form of *"democratic socialism,"* in which strong centralized authority exists with support of the citizenry, is needed to forge a strategy for societal improvement. The result could be that something of value could actually be left for succeeding generations. Then again, it might not.

[Author's Note: This perspective is very important because it provides a reasoned counterweight to any overly optimistic notion that community problems are not as bad as some say, or that they are certain to be resolved as others say. The challenges for our generation are monumental. In terms of the learnership concept, Heibroner's perspective is seen herein as laying down the gauntlet to individuals, organizations, and communities (and societies) to pursue *the common good* before being forced to do so through disaster and human misery. The LISA model depicts a hierarchical arrangement of subsystems that invite all who contemplate it to raise their sights to the next system level or viewing point, and to consider their rights and responsibilities for development within that higher order system.]

<u>The Democracy Trap</u>. In *The Democracy Trap: Perils of the Post-Cold War World* (Fuller, 1991), the author promotes the idea that democracy and the perfectibility of American life are unique social assumptions that may prove to be unreliable. He argues that while modern society appears to be plagued with problems, certain types of problems have always been part of human experience – danger, risk, grief, and death are inevitable and will always be so. He explains that the precursors of our American confidence come from the nature of our democratic founding and the cultural changes that have occurred through generations. He cautions against too optimistic a view of what is possible by noting that:

1. America was founded by moving away from state control and with a spirit of *"freedom-to-do."* This was a type of *responsible individualism* (my term) in which a willingness to accept life's risks was part of the social agreement.

2. America has moved to a mindset of *"freedom-from"* due to increasing government intervention and social engineering. Instead of the state being the last resource for the treatment of social ills, it now has become the first. It appears that with this transfer of responsibility and risk we now have a type of *selfish individualism* (my term) that pervades our culture.

3. America faces a contradiction in that our expression of "freedom-to-do" is fundamental to our capitalistic strivings while our concern for "freedom-from" underpins our collaborative tendencies. *Our challenge appears to be to negotiate a place of consensus* between the excesses of uncontrolled capitalism and those of paternalistic collectivism.

Given this scenario, Fuller argues that the larger issue for American society is to determine "freedom-for-what." That is, "as social problems seem to grow more intractable – and even less affected by application of money and goodwill – we are anguished by the thought that something deeper in fact may be wrong. We have not, after all, been able to escape those classic human problems of existence that the great literature of all cultures has dealt with." In his view, "We need the moral courage to recognize that many problems ultimately must be lived with rather than solved . . . [and that we should] find the inner resources to cope without despair and panic". (pp.145-146)

No matter what viewing point one chooses, it is obvious that much is yet to be done to build an American society that steadily approaches its potential. The need to engage all members of society in reasoning and learning processes that result in improved action on major issues of concern is clear.

[**Author's Note:** Fuller raises the undiscussables in contemporary American culture and society. Are democracy and capitalism the "best" way to achieve high quality health, welfare, and state-of-being for the nation's citizens? In a democracy, will the voting public secure the rights of the minority and the responsibilities of the majority? Will capitalism become unbridled and embarrassing while joblessness and poverty continue unabated from generation to generation? What does a society owe to its current and future members?]

Dysfunctions of Disciplines. In *For the Common Good* (Daly & Cobb, 1989), the authors take issue with what they term "*disciplinolatry*" which is the pervasive effort in the academic community to establish a disciplinary-focused organization of knowledge. They argue that there is an academic tendency to establish boundaries around the various disciplines (fields of education) through a process of successive abstractions which guarantees that the full understanding of the original subject is lost. The authors point out:

First, that disciplines are established through deductive processes in which the first step is to reduce connections to other parts of a subject – particularly those that don't yield to quantitative and scientific analysis

Second, to then develop a methodology for working in the discipline that uses only those features available to it

Third, dysfunction occurs when there is the failure to acknowledge the limitations in the assumptions that result because of the process of successive abstraction. The effect of this is that "misplaced concreteness" occurs in which too much credibility is given to conclusions made within the limits of one's information and discipline. This results in an inability to reason and act with genuine understanding of the fullness of a situation or problem.

[**Author's Note**: Human and social systems develop as knowledge and understanding lead to improved reasoning, learning, and action. The key, however, is to recognize that these systems are integrated and don't exist as separate disciplines (e.g., biology, economics, philosophy) as we actually experience them. To the extent that every field identifies its boundaries and offers ever greater amounts of information and knowledge from within those boundaries, societal complexity, conflict, and overload are certain to be exacerbated. The social challenge is to discover those core streams of knowledge interwoven among all disciplines and to rationalize a steady course of action that both holds to core values and accommodates informed change.]

Interdisciplinary Education. In *Uncommon Sense* (Davidson, 1983), the author offers the view that: "Our civilization seems to be suffering a second curse of Babel: just as the human race builds a tower of knowledge that reaches to the heavens, we are stricken by a malady in which we find ourselves attempting to communicate with each other in countless tongues of scientific specialization". (p.184) Davidson reveals the revolutionary thinking of Ludwig von Bertalanffy, and notes specifically, that he intensely stressed the need for the integration of education. Bertalanffy thought that only through an integrated perspective could the world be understood, and that his General Systems Theory (GST) could provide the basis for "... instigating the transfer of principles from one field to another [so that it would] no longer be necessary to duplicate or triplicate the discovery of the same principles in different fields". (p.185)

Regarding academia, Bertalanffy took a dim view of educational trends toward greater specialization. He railed against "*the tendency toward insularity among all disciplines,*" disliked the "*academic territoriality*" among departments, and reasoning that failed to see "the reality that all knowledge in interconnected". (p.187) Bertalanffy reasoned that even though people made their living as specialists, they needed to see the common elements that interconnected their fields and be able to regularly see the world in its wholeness. Only through this approach could issues be understood and correct action be taken.

[**Author's Note:** This view is relevant to the LISA model in that it reinforces the systems and interdependence themes which are essential to the learnership concept. Additionally it addresses the LISA model by illustrating the contemporary trend toward specialization and academic insularity which should be reversed. This is so because the trend exacerbates the negative effects of information overload, complexity, and uncertainty that threaten the social order and restrain societal development.]

Learnership Universal Knowledge Spheres

The most exciting way to cope with life requires that we cherish the courage to become,
the capacity to reason, and the ability to care for other human beings. — Paul Kurtz

The universal knowledge spheres represent a broad-based categorization of societal knowledge that applies to all learnership social systems: personal, organizational, community, and societal activity. Almost every topic worth learning and using can be associated within at least one or more of the six knowledge categories. Often, it takes two categories to properly describe a topic e.g., social-economic when considering a group of people's economic interests.

1. Social Knowledge Sphere. The social knowledge sphere addresses the associations and living arrangements among individuals and groups in society. Focus is on the dynamics of social activity among individuals, organizations and institutions. Major emphasis is on education, learning, culture, human relations, interpersonal communication and media.

Social Saturation. In *The Saturated Self: Dilemmas of Identity in Contemporary Life* (Gergen, 1990), the author devotes Chapter Three to the issue of "Truth in Trouble," and argues that there is "an emerging crises in the common conception of human understanding". (p.81) He suggests that there is an emerging crisis in academia (the bastion of our educational elite) and that it demonstrates itself as those in various disciplines acquiesce to the tendency toward the diminution of the traditional assumptions that undergird research and teaching. Gergen explains that: "...to part with the longstanding ideals of truth and understanding is to invite chaos, first in the world and then in society more generally". (p.82) He attributes the cause of this trend to be the "*social saturation*" that exists in today's society and its impact on rational inquiry and reasoning. At the most fundamental level for concern, Gergen states that: "...the crisis in the academy about beliefs in objective knowledge has profound implications for beliefs about the self...the social saturation of our personal existence leads to a breakdown in our sense of objective reality". (pp.82-83)

Gergen assumes a modernist's perspective as his point of departure with his perspective, and recounts that it used to be that natural scientists sought objective knowledge of physical matter, economists sought to articulate laws of finance, and that experts in other disciplines attended to discovery of those aspects of their field that were objectively verifiable, and there presumed to be correct and true until proven differently. Likewise in the social sciences, reflective discovery and truthful dialogue were the sources of what the society came to use as standards for thinking and behavior.

Gergen suggests that objectivity has traditionally been "achieved through a coalition of subjectivities" (p.84) providing society points of consensus and operational values. Counterpoised against this capability, however, is the condition of *social saturation in which excessive debate based upon mere opinion competes for individuals' rather limited attention.* In turn, this leads to a devaluing of what is a fact, a steadily accumulating sense of doubt, a general decline in social reasoning ability, and a concomitant decline in the individual's understand of the self and social relationships. One example of the dilemma is best expressed by the following quote: (p.83)

"Economics has...become so broad and so complicated that, within the fields one group of specialists barely speaks the same language as the PhDs across the hall. And so much of what is published seems more to proselytize for an ideology than to make sense of the chaotic world. . . . It's no wonder that a single economic development can be interpreted as a godsend or a disaster, depending on the interpreter's frame of reference."

Peter Passell, *Economics: Reading Your Way Out of Chaos.*

Gergen identifies three academic challenges to the modernist view of objective knowledge that contribute to the issue developed above:

1. Moving from Facts to Perspectives. The tendency, even in the physical sciences, to derive understanding not solely from empirical evidence of studies, but also from the informal notions that emerge from the network of social agreements that prevail among the scientific community. Facts are often "socially prescribed" thereby making "truth" dependent on the community within which one participates.

2. The Knower as Demagogue. Those who are the experts in a subject area are granted the power to decide on issues in that area. Their understanding reflects the realities of their own experience, and the power of their position allows them to serve their own interests in how they choose to recognize and apply truth and knowledge.

3. The Disappearance of the Knower. The tendency toward deconstructive analysis and textual debunking of knowledgeable writings undermines thought processes, debases real knowledge, and erodes the individual's belief in the availability of objective knowledge about individual mind, emotion, and intention. The belief in the individual as a participant in learning and knowledge creation is diminished.

[**Author's Note**: This perspective is extremely important in respect to the learnership concept. Whenever the owners of the academic disciplines, particularly in the hard sciences, create an exclusivity around their respective fields, and press on to higher levels of differentiation and specialization while redefining their own meaning of higher education in their fields, they contribute to the notion that life is lived in its parts and not in its wholeness. The greater societal need is for the social integration of learning already accumulated over years of historical development. This may be accomplished through broad participation in societal dialogue and collaborative decision making. Individual, organizational, and community "selves" need to emerge to strengthen social structures and to provide the basis for continued reflective learning and human systems development.]

A Universal Ethic. In *Practical Ethics* (Singer, 1979), the author reviews the diverse opinions on ethical reasoning and concludes that a case may be made for a "universal aspect of ethics." Singer offers that a broadly utilitarian position is most advised because it establishes a starting point from which all other ethical modes of reasoning have been derived. His reasoning is that: "In accepting that ethical judgments must be made from a universal point of view, I am accepting that my own interests cannot, simply because they are *my* interests, count more than the interests of anyone else. Thus my very natural concern that my own interests be looked after must, when I think ethically, be extended to the interests of others". (p.12) In terms of this perspective, an individual reasons and takes action in a manner that is likely to maximize the interests of those affected – the consequences they might experience are considered and balanced.

[**Author's Note**: Singer's argument appears to be a *self-interest within a relevant community* position that fits well into the learnership concept. A major premise of the LISA model is that the quality goals of individuals, organizations, and communities need to be pursued, *within balance*, to the point of meta-systems optimization. This goal and modality of reasoning is believed to be the manner in which society as a whole is best served.]

2. Economic Knowledge Sphere. The economic knowledge sphere concerns the production, development and management of income and wealth. Focus is on the production and distribution of goods and services. Primary emphasis is on business management, financial management, and social systems economic development.

Evolve or Become Extinct. Rosabeth Moss Kanter's book entitled *Evolve: Succeeding in the Digital Culture of Tomorrow* (2001) explains the impact of the internet on everyone's lives, the importance of partnership networks, and the new human skills and social evolution factors that are essential in transitioning into the electronic world of tomorrow. Kanter says that most of us will need to adapt to a new way of working because internet phenomena reshape markets and society itself in several ways: (p.16)

    a. Network Power. Everyone is potentially connected to everyone else. Network reach is more important than the size of individual components. There is greater reliance on partners in order to get big everywhere fast.

    b. Transparency and Direct Communication. Information access is rapid, open, direct. There is greater exposure and visibility.

    c. Fast Feedback and Easy Protest. Competitors can become partners, but there are opponents lurking everywhere that can mobilize quickly.

    d. Constant Change and Reliance on New Knowledge. There is a fierce competition for talent with the newest skills. New knowledge earns a premium. Rapid innovation creates the need for more change.

    e. Large Audiences and Crowd Behavior. Messages reach wider audiences. To coordinate complex networks, larger groups must share information and spread it further.

Kanter also comments that the star performers in her book continue to *personally evolve* by drawing on both analytical and emotional abilities which include: (p.288)

    a. They display curiosity and imagination that allow them to envision and grasp new possibilities as they emerge, to find new patterns in the kaleidoscope. They are adept at communications with others, near and far.

b. They work to make themselves understood and to understand people who have not shared their life experiences.

c. They are cosmopolitans who are not confined to a single world view, but are able to understand and create bridges of thought.

d.. They can grasp complexity – connecting the dots that make sense out of complicated multi-partner alliances. They can tune into the reactions of multiple audiences with conflicting points of view and chart a course that takes complexity into account.

e. They are sensitive to the range of human needs as well as to the messages conveyed by actions that create organizational culture. They care about feeding their team's bodies and spirits.

f. They work with other people as resources rather than subordinates, respecting what others bring to the table and listening to their ideas.

g. They lead through the power of their ideas and the strength of their voices more than through the authority of formal positions.

[**Author's Note**: In the electronic, networked society of the future those who engage change will witness opportunity. They will recognize that the status quo is not an option and to resist participating in new teams, organizations, and partnership arrangements will mean they will ultimately be relegated to lower priority tasks with less meaning and utility – with the concomitant impact on their personal, organizational, and community effectiveness.]

Building the Middle Class. In his book: *War on the Middle Class* (2006), Lou Dobbs details "How the Government, Big Business, and Special Interest Groups are Waging War on the American Dream and How to Fight Back." His depiction focuses primarily on the demise of the American middle class thanks to corporate profits and Washington's obsession with expanding global trade. However, the issue he identifies go beyond just this country's economic well-being, it is foundational for all societies that understand that a nation depends on its middle class to offset the polarization that historically occurs when a society becomes irretrievably divided between the wealthy (haves) and poverty stricken (have-nots).

The middle class categorization is based upon criteria that include: *income, education, occupation, wealth*, and *social class mobility* – this last one being of particular interest because good public education in the past permitted better job performance and income to move up the class ladder. By his description of the "War on the Middle Class," Dobbs provides the following information for reflection and counter-action: (pp.15-22):

1. The *middle three quintiles* consist of people making $26,000 to $150,000 per year – half of all Americans earn more than $44,000 and half less. Most people in the middle class come from families in which one or two parents worked, they went to public schools, and have attended some college. The *top quintile* averages $400,000 per year with over $1million per year going to those in the top 1% who are CEOs, Wall Street Bankers and brokers, many Hollywood actors and actresses, entertainers, professional athletes, and entrepreneurs. The *bottom quintile scrape by* on an average of $10,000 per year.

2. The *breakdown in the public educational system* means that the meritocracy in our society have been compromised, and in some instances eradicated. And without a strong public school system that serves all of us regardless of wealth or poverty, a class system will become ever more firmly entrenched.

3. Big government, big business, and big media have categorized the middle class by its consumption habits. Big business sees you as either a unit of labor or a consumer. Big media sees you as a consumer or as a unit of audience measurement for whatever message it is bombarding us with. And government sees you (if you are in the middle class) as just a taxpayer.

4. The middle class, the one that pays most of the taxes, are *increasingly at the mercy of institutions that only appear to serve the public interest*. These institutions are breeding grounds for the elite to enrich themselves at the expense of those who work for them and vote for them. They are the leaders of the class war and the middle class is their target.

5. Over the last 25 years, median family income has risen by 18 percent while the top 1 percent – the very wealthiest families – has gone up 200 percent. Only 30 percent of the Forbes 400 list of the richest people in the U.S. came from families who did not have great wealth of their own – 70 percent were born into wealth.

6. The business elite are the ones who've bought and paid for members of both political parties and who pursue so-called free-trade policies for the benefit of U.S. multinationals that remain uncompetitive in the global marketplace. They have put American middle-class workers in direct competition with the world's poorest workers.

7. The greed and self-interest in the nation's executive suites and boardrooms are major weapons in the war on the middle class, and have often led to outright criminality…They had no qualms about cooking the books, lying to their colleagues and friends, and defrauding investors.

8. You see the executives of a major airline increase their compensation by $2.5 million while the financially beleaguered airline attempts to slash the pay of its pilots, flight attendants, mechanics, and baggage handlers.

Dobb's "fight back" strategy for the American public includes a number of small, but potentially effective efforts if large numbers of people were to participate. Some of these initiatives to protect American sovereignty, security, and economic rights are: (pp.199-212)

1. Get personally involved in local public issues, and start voting in an informed manner in all elections. Let everyone and new voices be heard in the public domain.

2. Refuse to let politicians build a constituency based on "wedge" issues (school prayer, gun control, gay marriage, etc.), instead focus the common interests and services that everyone knows needs attention (better schools, crime management, health care).

3. Eliminate party affiliation and become officially an independent. Make the politicians and their corporate and lobbyist supporters redirect their focus on what the larger, independent middle class wants to get done.

4. Provide adequate public funding of campaigns. If a candidate chooses not to use only public funds, and take funding from private sources and lobbyists make sure the public knows what that probably means in terms of their interests being the candidate's top priority.

5. Use citizen activism to put referendums on their local ballots so that the citizenry can set the agenda and give up or down votes using direct voting, rather than representation, on topics with which they are concerned.

6. Any congressional trip should be paid for by the federal government. No elected official should be allowed to accept any gifts of any kind, shape, or size.

7. Prohibit any federal government official from working or lobbying back in their respective agencies and functions for five years after leaving or retiring from their public position. Similarly, prohibit senior military leaders from assisting businesses supporting U.S. defense in the areas of lobbying, contracting, procurement, or sales.

8. Eliminate "fast track" trade agreements, and ensure that all so-called "free trade agreements" be accompanied by an economic impact statement that ensures equal benefits to American workers, and does not encourage job outsourcing that harms American manufacturing employment.

9. Stop illegal immigration immediately through tight border control, and stop the exploitation of all immigrants and low income workers by raising the minimum wage significantly – and strictly enforce wage laws.

10. Protect the nation against terrorism by inspecting all containers, cargo, and products coming into the nation.

11. Develop and implement health care laws and program that make health insurance available to almost everyone. Use a mixture of Medicare, private insurance, and subsidized programs to provide at least a minimum of preventive and emergency care, and insurance more catastrophic illnesses that are often the basis for bankruptcy.

12. Institute better direction, guidance, and resource management for American schools. Cut through petty politics with a national core curriculum, standards for performance, and guidelines for class size, length of school year, teacher qualifications, and pay.

[**Author's Note**: This subject takes the Community Systems Development (business, government, education) subject of Chapter Twelve to a new and higher level because it not only applies to American society, it has significant implications on how this nation should engage other nations across the global. To the degree that this nation is still a beacon of hope to others we should be discussing these types of real life citizen concerns because a growing and prospering middle class around the world has major impact on reducing civil unrest, illegal immigration, poverty and illegal drug-based crime, and populations with health and disease problems.]

3. Technological Knowledge Sphere. The technological knowledge sphere concerns the application of scientific methods and tools to societal activities. Emphasis here is on the study, development, and application of scientific methods and materials to achieve societal objectives. Major focus is on biotechnology, information technology, and materials technology.

Arrival of the Cybercorp. James Martin, author of *Cybercorp: The New Business Revolution* (1996) defines cybercorps as "organizations designed using the principles of cybernetics. They are corporations with senses constantly alert, capable of reacting in real time to changes in their environments, competition, and customer needs. They are designed for fast change; and can learn, evolve, and transform themselves rapidly." (p.5) According to Martin "The cybercorp, like the jungle creature, should be constantly alert, electronically monitoring what is important to it, and constantly able to make adjustments." (p.8) Additionally, he points out that: (Chapter One)

1. *Inter-corporate networks and inter-corporate computing* are fundamentally changing worldwide patterns of commerce.

2. *Cybercorps are linked to one another electronically*, virtually, and as they make adjustment to their wealth-building processes they immediate affect their trading partners.

3. *Agility is essential* in adjusting inter-corporate core competencies and shifting patterns of markets, partners, and relationships.

4. The global reach of world-wide networks and markets ensures *brutally intense competition* that continually threatens profit margins.

5. *Corporations need a knowledge infrastructure* to capture and create knowledge, store it, improve it, clarify it, disseminate it to all employees, and put it to use.

6. The great rate of change means that *cybercorp work must be learning-intensive*. If employees have spent ten years doing routine work, they have probably lost the ability to do learning-intensive work.

7. Optimizing the parts of a corporation independently can be highly inefficient compared with optimizing the whole. It may be easier to totally build new cybercorp capabilities than attempt to reengineer the current infrastructure.

8. The new cybercorp *needs all the best management practices of the past – and has to build on them.* The cybercorp needs a different architecture, changed marketing, virtual operations, dynamically linked competencies from agile webs, and very fast evolution.

Martin explains that a critical success factor for the cybercorp is the capacity for rapid learning. He notes that the learning curves for employees will rise more steeply than ever before just to keep up with business needs and expectations. The barriers to rapid, experiential learning he cites are: (pp.268-269)

1. Insufficient Innovation. Cybercorps must have a strong urge to learn by innovation and to test new ideas.

2. Insufficient Capability to Act. Cybercorps need to reduce internal disincentives for innovation, and assist managers and employees to overcome their risk adverse behavior.

3. Insufficient Capability to Reflect. Too often action is a substitute for thought. Often reflection is overwhelmingly biased toward current practices and what employees have chosen to understand and do. Reflection is better done if it involves outsiders, who bring different perspectives and ignore current taboos.

4. Inadequate Recording of What is Learned. When insights are gained, they should be recorded; otherwise they will be lost. An external facilitator may be required to perform the recordation process if organizational members have no time or are disinclined to accomplish the recording process.

5. Inadequate Capability to Disseminate. When one group learns and improves its work process, the learning should be transmitted to other groups in the enterprise; otherwise the potential value of the learning is lost.

[**Author's Note**: The clear picture being described by Martin is of domestic and multinational corporations partnering on a global scale to maintain and grow their revenue and profitability. The question to be considered is "What happens to nations, societies, citizens and middle-class stability when businesses obliterate the traditional locations, cultures, and rules that have formerly encouraged them to be good corporate citizens of the communities and societies that nurtured their existence and development?" "Do they owe anything to the local workers, their domestic investors, the municipal infrastructure that supported their facility needs, the governments that gave them tax breaks?" The learnership philosophy and architecture focuses on the mutual support and interdependence needed among social, political, and economic entities to create the "social contract" that loosely binds all together.]

Upsizing the Individual. Given Martin's challenges to corporate leaders (above), what is the impact on individual workers – their families and communities when the most highly trained, skilled, and compensated corporate leaders work day and night to be proactive and adaptable in their respective industries and marketplaces/market spaces? Authors Robert Johansen and Rob Swigart's book entitled: *Upsizing the Individual in the Downsized Organization* (1994) comment that: "Business organizations are changing, whether they want to or not. The changes are chaotic…the pyramids of corporate strength have flattened into a web of organizational ambiguity. And, workers are trading their sense that they'll be taken care of for a realization that they'd better take care of themselves. Job security is a fragile hope that too often becomes a broken promise." (p.x) Current business trends with impact on employees work-life include:

1. Organizations are evolving from pyramid to fishnet structures as hierarchies collapse and broad, interwoven, flexible structure emerge.

2. Employees are increasingly turning from dependence on their corporations for health benefits and retirement and career planning to dependence on themselves and networks of co-workers and supporters for these needs.

3. Within organizations, individuals are less apt to work in big structures and more likely to participate in business teams and ad hoc alliances.

4. Businesses have shifted their attention from their competitors to their customers. Competitive analysis still plays an important role, but it has been overshadowed by an intense interest in customer needs and customer services.

5. Electronic networks are replacing office buildings as the locus of business transactions. You are where your network is; as a corollary, your network is your business.

6. Diversity is seen less as a problem than as a simple business reality in the global marketplace. Traditional us-versus-them mentality is yielding to the realization that then old majority is becoming a minority – and your customer is often a member of the new majority.

7. An orientation toward ongoing learning has succeeded one-time training for employees as companies realize that they must have a flexible workforce capable of continually acquiring new skills. Learning must be life-long, and it's for everyone.

For the authors, changing the expectations, focus, skills, and motivation of employees are necessary for those employees to become more valued and productive contributors in the workplace. The workers individually and as a team must become better aligned with the new business and global market realities; *they must become upsized* and better skilled at working in the current and future electronic marketplace. Some examples of what will be needed as nations and societies compete for desired opportunities and services are:

1. Knowing the difference between working on problems (obstacles to be overcome) and dilemmas (a balanced set of alternatives). The latter are more pervasive and require the skill of risk management in which the situation is assessed and a strategy developed and pursued that allows progress, but not total removal of obstacles and tensions that may still be in play over time. This requires *a high tolerance for ambiguity*.

2. Being *comfortable working in an anytime/anyplace environment*. Virtual work outside of contained workspaces, telecommuting and work-at-home, and being electronically connected outside normal duty hours are often required.

3. Being able to *work successfully in electronically-supported meetings*, even when face-to-face may not be possible, will be required. The use of electronic tools for brainstorming and participation in meetings using electronic support technology and other forms of groupware will be necessary for most knowledge workers.

4. Those who succeed in the global economy will follow Socrates' advise: "Know thyself." They will know who they are and what motivates them. They will have *"employability security" rather than "employment security."* This will be because they have proven themselves on work teams and will be called on again when their expertise, collegial behavior, and shared values can help another team succeed.

5. *The world, its culture, and its technologies are changing too rapidly for managers to depend on what they learned in the past.* Learning must be on time, in time, just in time, every time. Organizations and individuals need to create an environment in which they can continually renew their knowledge.

6. Recognize that time-driven urgency is a fact of life, but the ability to reflect on options and implications and not jump into decisions until it is really necessary is critical for successful managers. The need is to practice *"urgent patience."*

7. Greater focus will need to be given to the *building of communities*. Community should occur by reaching out to diverse groups, creating cross-cultural participation, building a common context for work and decision making, and establishing frames of reference hat are shared among all participants.

The authors sum up their recommendations by saying that: "The dynamic shift to global, interlinked, flexible fishnet organizations has brought with it anxiety and malaise. This is the sickness that threatens the land today. But everyone has the potential to become a hero in one way or another, voluntarily or involuntarily. This forging of new myths for our age is, very simply, a matter of survival." (p.167)

[**Author's Note**: American society, along with many other societies across the globe, has many of the same issues and opportunities with which to deal and take action. All nations with reasonable social, political, and economic goals and a desire for peaceful coexistence find themselves challenged by rapid economic change driven to a large extent by exploding technological innovation and development. In the end it is the workers, the employees in the lower to middle-class production and service jobs that may benefit significantly or experience the devastation of unemployment and economic exclusion from the increasing pace of change and international competition. Life-long learning, virtual operation, communities of interest and practice, employability, tolerance for ambiguity, and electronic connectivity and workflows are all part of the new workplace and work method. Individuals, managers, and employees must step up to the challenges and opportunities before them and their respective societies – otherwise, despair and lower standards of living may be in their future.]

4. Political Knowledge Sphere. The political knowledge sphere deals with the study, structure, or affairs of government, politics, or the state. Focus is on citizenship, governance, foreign policy, political and cultural choices, and national defense.

A Social Contract. Jean-Jacques Rousseau (1712-78), a product of the Enlightenment period, is the author of *The Social Contract* (or Principles of the Political Right). One of his most notable quotes is: "Man was born free, and is everywhere in chains." Rousseau describes the necessity of a social pact among men: "I assume that men reach a point where the obstacles to their preservation in a state of nature proved greater than the strength that each man has to preserve himself in that state. Beyond this point, the primitive condition cannot endure, for then the human race will perish if it does not change its mode of existence…How to find a form of association which will defend the person and goods of each member with the collective force of all, and under which each individual, while uniting himself with the others, obeys no one but himself, and remains as free as before. *This is the fundamental problem to which the social contract holds the solution."*

Rousseau is particularly eloquent on the topics of (1) democracy, and (2) the body politic. He is quoted as follows:

1. "Nothing is more dangerous in public affairs than the influence of private interests, and *the abuse of the law by the government is a lesser evil than the corruption of the legislator which inevitably results from the pursuit of private interests.* When this happens, the state is corrupted in its very substance and no reform is possible." Rousseau also adds this caution: "…*there is no government so liable to civil war and internecine strife as is democracy or popular government,* for there is none which so powerful and constant a tendency to change to another form or which demands so much vigilance and courage to maintain it unchanged."

2. "The constitution of a man is a work of nature; that of the state is the work of artifice. It is not within the capacity of men to prolong their own lives, but it is within the capacity of men to prolong the life of the state as far as possible by giving it the best constitution it can have." He continues to say that: "The principle of political life dwells in the sovereign authority. *The legislative power is the heart of the state, the executive power is the brain, which sets all the parts in motion.* The brain may become paralyzed and the individual still live. A man can be an imbecile and survive, but as soon as his heart stops functioning, the creature is dead."

[**Author's Note:** Rousseau's "social contract" accentuates Chapter Thirteen's emphasis on communities of organizational entities (education, business, government) collaboratively working to achieve the common good. In this chapter which is focused on the state or national society, we begin to understand the difficulty in holding together the democratic body politic. On the one hand, citizens will always attempt to influence and modify the principles and laws upon which the democratic state operates to suit their evolving needs and interests. On the other hand, stability and predictability are the cornerstones of a solid foundation necessary for forging foreign policy and building international relationships. The learnership contribution in these matters is the introduction of the meta-systems LISA model which illustrates the mutual dependencies among personal, organizational, community, and societal levels of social development and achievement. Optimization of these four integrated domains of experience requires balancing their individual influences on each other as well as balancing the total effect of their combination on international entities and societies. *The learnership philosophy and architecture propose a universal commitment to human learning and leading, which by design employs the balanced inquiry and advocacy principle so common in effective social dialogue*].

Democracy and Citizenship. In his book *The Assault on Reason* (2006), Albert Gore provides a review of the current state of a deteriorating American political system in which the quality of democracy and citizenship are being diminished. This is occurring, in large part, due to the lack of reasoned (truthful, fact-based, and considerate) dialogue, and the fact that politicians, lobbyists, and other self-seeking and one-issue groups want to win at all costs – even if that is based on using the public media to provide disinformation to the larger body politic. In his chapters on "Democracy in the Balance" and "A Well-Connected Citizenry" highlights recent destructive tendencies in federal governance that should cause the average citizen concern that they no longer live in a "reasonable" political environment and that they themselves have become marginalized in a nation built on the sovereignty of the people. In *Democracy in the Balance*, Gore cites the perverse accumulation of power by the Executive Branch which is intended to reduce the roles and responsibilities of the other two branches of government. For example:

1. Self-love versus reason. Gore explains that James Madison cautioned in Federalist No. 10 that reason must be separated from the "self-love" of the people using it, and focused instead on the *public good* – by ensuring it that no individual or small group can exercise power without entering into a negotiation with others who must be convinced that the proposed exercise of power meets the test of reason. Gore point out that "auxiliary precautions" were designed into the federal governance structure (three distinct branches of government) and Madison had these "checks and balances" in mind through the dialogue and oversight that would be necessary due to the separation of powers. Gore's accusation is that "President Bush had conflated his role of *commander-in-chief* with his roles of *head of government* and *head of state*." (p.219) And, that Bush has clearly used that integration of roles, with commander-in-chief in the lead during a self-determined war in Iraq, to extract exceptional power at the expense of the other branches of government.

2. Signing statements. Gore details how President Bush's chronic abuse of what are called "signing statements" – written pronouncements that the President issues upon signing a bill into law. He says that: "Throughout our history, these statements have served a mainly ceremonial function, extolling the virtues of the legislation and thanking those figures responsible for the enactment." (p.223) However, *the President has chosen to use the signing statements to point out what he and his administration will agree to and what they will not agree to do in terms of the law he just signed* – in effect, rewriting the law which is distinctly the responsibility of the Congress. Instead of an up or down choice by signing or not signing the legislation – the only choices allowed by the Constitution – the President has used this tactic over 1000 times to modify what he might think are the Congresses "suggestions."

3. Co-option of the Judiciary. Gore recounts President Bush's effort to make the Supreme Court simply an assistant in exercising the power and political will of the Executive Branch. He notes that even Alexander Hamilton in Federalist No.78 said that "the judiciary is beyond comparison the weakest of the three departments of power; it can never attack with success the other two; and that all possible care is requisite to enable it to defend itself against their attacks...It is in continual jeopardy of being overpowered, awed, or influenced by its co-ordinate branches." Gore points out that it is very hard for the judiciary to "call balls and strikes" when recent appointees by the President to the Supreme Court had been Chief Justice Roberts and Samuel Alito, long-time advocates of building the "unity executive" by increasing Executive Branch power at the expense of the other branches of government. Lastly, he said that Hamilton went on to comment that: "If the power of the judiciary were ever combined with the power of either the executive or the legislative branch, then liberty itself would have everything to fear."

4. Elimination of Oversight Hearings. Gore describes how Congress, being of the same political party as the Executive Branch, deliberately reduced its own Constitutional authority to conduct oversight of federal government operations at the behest of President Bush. He says that: "...oversight virtually disappeared during the first six years of the Bush-Cheney administration, because the party loyalty of the Republican congressional leaders outweighed their respect for the independent role that the legislative branch is supposed to play in out constitutional system." He also notes that: "In

the United States Senate, which used to pride itself on being 'the greatest deliberative body in the world,' meaningful debate was a rarity." (p.237)

A Well-Connected Citizenry. In the chapter on this topic, Gore comments: "*I believe that the viability of democracy depends upon the openness, reliability, appropriateness, responsiveness, and the two-way nature of the communication environment…*If democracy seems to work, and if people receive a consistent, reliable, and meaningful response from others when they communicate their opinions and feelings about shared experiences, they begin to assume that self-expression in democracy matters. [However] If they receive responses that seem to be substantive but actually are not, citizens begin to feel as if they were being manipulated. If the messages they receive feed this growing cynicism, the decline of democracy can be accelerated." (pp.248-249)

Gore makes the important point that it is not enough for the citizenry to be "well-educated" they must also be "well-connected." They must have the interest, willingness, and capability to connect with others in conversation so they are able to learn from experience and test their new knowledge for appropriateness and utility. He states: "The remedy for what ails our democracy is not simply better education (as important as that is) or civic education (as important as that can be), but the *reestablishment of a genuine democratic discourse in which individuals can participate in a meaningful way – a conversation of democracy in which meritorious ideas and opinions from individuals do, in fact, evoke a meaningful response.*"(p.254) Gore argues for:

1. Better electronic connectivity between the Congress and the American people

2. Real debates among representatives and senators in prime time

3. The disclosure of who is paying for the "political disinformation" that is often disguised in media presentations. In particular, he says that making the internet completely accessible by American citizens so that they may actually participate in communication by speaking and being heard instead of simply being on the receiving side of communications is an essential part of restoring democracy to the citizens.

[**Author's Note**: Learnership has a role to play in societal politics by the manner in which reasoning (better thinking, learning, knowing, leading, and achieving) is advocated, taught, and used. Developing learnership practitioners develops more effective citizens – the knowledge, skills, and abilities of the former are significantly beneficial for the latter. Additionally, learnership calls for a balance between information inquiry and advocacy which is the spirit of effective collaboration – the very thing Gore appeared to address.]

5. Geographical Knowledge Sphere. The geographical knowledge sphere concerns the preservation of geographical, physical and continental regions of the entire earth. Emphasis is on international issues and relationships concerning nation-states' territorial boundaries and conflicts, population and immigration challenges, and property ownership and resource rights.

International Statecraft, Sovereignty, and Multilateralism. When we consider the relationships among nations and their respective societies, the international assumptions and structures that legitimize each nation's right to be different from and independent of other nations must be factored into the conversation. In *Power and Responsibility in World Affairs* (2004) edited by Cathal Noland, selected writers discuss the foundations and trends in World Affairs as nations compete with or align with one another to accomplish their respective political, economic, and social objectives. The responsibilities of statecraft among nations are two-fold:

1. National Responsibility – National leaders can reasonably be expected to safeguard the national interest and specifically the national security of their nations

2. International Responsibility – national leaders can reasonably be expected to observe international law in their conduct of foreign policy, specifically the central provisions of the U.N. Charter which apply to the use of armed force in world affairs.

The U.N. Charter respects the sovereign rights of states to manage themselves and to not be accosted by other states wishing to impose their values on them. *These state or nation rights are viewed as superior to any perceived humanitarian rights of the people within these states who are assumed to be in agreement with, and supportive of, their own states leadership.* This was the current ethos of recognizing, tolerating, and coexisting with all other members of international society as long as they are doing the same in return. In this post-1945 world arrangement, nations are prohibited from attempting to interfere with other nations even in so-called humanitarian causes or to spread Western values of freedom, democracy and human rights.

The Blair doctrine (British Prime Minister) in 1999 called for a "*doctrine of international community*" which would require an activist role for the Great Powers as in the case of Yugoslavia (Kosovo and Bosnia) when acceptable standards were breached. Blair said: "We are all internationalists now, whether we like it or not." No longer was the 1945 notion of security the driving ethos, but *a more fully developed idea of human security; the universal goal was the safety of every man, woman, and child everywhere on earth regardless of their citizenship.* "The resulting outcome was that Western nations should generously make their 'values' available to the people of the world. They should be the core values of a reformed international community." (Robert Jackson, pp.64-67)

[**Author's Note**: The Blair doctrine became controversial because it was based on "sharing our values" which were viewed as Western values based on the expression of "natural law and natural rights" that are the foundation for freedom and democracy which are not necessarily the values of other nations. Its intent was to tie international security to humanitarianism and democracy in foreign countries. Most non-western nations disagree – it looks like imperialism and colonialism to them – which make it point of major contention today.]

In a later chapter, Stewart Patrick describes "U.S. foreign policy initiatives to construct an *open world* – a multilateral order conducive to the survival and spread of the international rule of law, collective security, commercial liberty, self-determination, and the free-flow of ideas." (p.165) This action emerged from the U.S. triumph in the Cold War and various *multilateral frame works such as the U.N., NATO Alliance, and other multilateral agreements*. The impact was that the U.S. set a course to address the problems of the world unilaterally, if needed, and refused to be bound by international norms and commitments. The complaint in many circles, the UN and nations, is that the U.S. "jeopardizes the legitimacy of its claims to world leadership and the prospects for the open world it has sought." U.S. policymakers are cautioned that "no state is 'bound to lead' unless others choose to follow…more self-restraint, timely consultation, mutual accommodation, and coalition building" should be exercised by the U.S. so as to conform to formerly agreed international standards for statecraft. (pp.164-165)

To better understand current U.S. foreign policy requires understanding the founding principles of the nation and its cultural foundation. Patrick says that: "*Americans embrace the Enlightenment proposition,* developed in the democratic political philosophy of John Locke and the laissez-faire economic theory of Adam Smith, *that the pursuit of individual self-interest maximizes the collective good.* The elements of this founding creed, enunciated in the Declaration of Independence and the U.S. Constitution, include attachments to representative government, the rule of law, freedom of speech and religion, private property, and commercial liberty. This faith in liberal principles is so wholly taken for granted that it has become synonymous with the American way of life." (p.169)

Patrick continues by commenting that: "Whereas other countries have intermittently supported democracy, human rights, and free enterprise, in no other country are universal political and economic values so constitutive of the nation's identity…The ultimate objective, in Anton DePorte's wonderful phrase, is to 'Lockeanize a hitherto Hobbesian world." (p.170)

[**Author's Note**: The <u>learnership philosophy and architecture</u> recognizes the apparent inconsistencies in U.S. foreign policy and diplomacy described in this section. While doing so, learnership advocates proactive Societal Systems Development (SSD) in which not only citizens of the U.S., but all people receive an opportunity to learn, develop, and participate in experiencing the *universal objectives of self-development, high performance, the common good, and human enlightenment.* Additionally, the six pairs of universal ideals: *Truth – Honesty, Beauty – Goodness, Freedom – Democracy, Justice – Equality, Love – Happiness, and Responsibility – Trust* should be available to all people, everywhere, all the time.]

<u>International Leadership</u>. In his book: *Birth of a New World* (1993), Harlan Cleveland presents an upbeat way of thinking about the spread of knowledge and the possible impact this will have as nations continue to learn and rethink their purposes, goals, strategies and international relationships. He states: "This book is for anyone who is concerned with the state of our world and wants to help shape a positive future: those in government and international affairs; current and future public administrators and corporate executives; people in private enterprise and nonprofit agencies; and anyone who, by voting, loving, and planning ahead, wants to help mold the new world now being born." (p.xvii)

Cleveland presents twelve examples from his own experience in which international successes were achieved: (1) weather forecasting, (2) eradication of infectious diseases, (3) international civil aviation, (4) allocation of the frequency spectrum, (5) globalization of information flows, (6) agricultural research for development, (7) UN peace-keeping and peace-making, (8) cooperation in outer space, (9) the Law of the Sea, (10) the High Commissioner for Refugees (UNHCR), (11) the ozone treaty, and (12) the Antarctic Treaty. His view is that there is much the nations and societies of the world can do that needs to be done – even when major disagreements and wars still dot the landscape. The challenge, he says is to ask: "Why does international cooperation work – when does it? He provides ten common threads that run through his dozen success stories – ten reasons why what works, *works.* Taken together, they are priceless ingredients for success in international cooperation:

1. There is a consensus on outcomes. *People who disagree on almost everything else can agree* that smallpox is a threat to all, more accurate weather forecasts would be useful, enclosed seas should be cleaned up, civil aircraft should not collide, and somebody should help refugees.

2. No one loses. Each of the dozen successes turned out…to be a win-win game.

3. Sovereignty is pooled. Whenever a nation cannot act effectively without combining its resources, imagination, and technology with those other nations; cooperation does not mean "giving up" independence of action but pooling it, that is, *using their sovereign rights together to avoid losing them separately.*

4. Cooperation is stimulated by a "cocktail of fear and hope." Fear alone produces irrational, sometimes aggressive, behavior. Hope alone produces good-hearted but unrealistic advocacy. *Reality-based fear and hope, combined, seem to provide the motivation to cooperate.*

5. Individuals make things happen. In the early stages of each of the success stories, a crucial role was played by *a few key individuals who acted as international people* in leading, insisting, inspiring, sharing knowledge, and generating a climate of trust that brushed past distrust still prevailing in other domains.

6. Modern information technologies are of the essence. Needs for complex data processing and rapid, reliable communication seem to be common to the success stories in international cooperation.

7. Non-governments play a key role. The recent story of international cooperation is replete with the contributions of scientific academies, research institutes, women's groups, international companies, and "experts" who don't feel the need to act as instructed representatives for their governments.

8. Flexible, decentralized systems work best. The more complicated the task the more diverse the players, the more necessary it is to spread the work around so that many kinds of people are improvising on an agreed sense of direction.

9. Educated local talent is essential. Especially here developing countries have major roles to play, cooperation works best when they use their own talent to do their part.

10. The United States is a key player. American initiative, research, resources, and *entrepreneurial bias* have been important factors. (pp.51-54)

Cleveland recognizes that on the international plane the issue that always begs for attention is: Are there occasions when a nation's internal affairs become an international concern? And if that occurs: What and how should be the position and response by those outside the nation's borders? Cleveland argues that: "The United Nations Charter, along with every first-year textbook on international law, frowns on international intervention 'in matters which are essentially within the domestic jurisdiction of any state.' The obsolescence of this tattered doctrine is obvious, rapid, and welcome. The real-world map is a jumble of deep mutual inter-penetrations that more and more blur what used to be the political geography of the globe." (p.120)

Cleveland notes that there are two questions used as a litmus test to tell whether one nation's actions inside another nation were all right: (1) Do the outsiders have an international mandate for their actions? (2) Were the outsiders invited to intervene? On the former, he points out that from an American perspective we had the mandate in Korea and Kuwait and had a successful outcome. In Vietnam and Iraq we did not, and did/will not succeed. For the latter question outsiders are often "invited-in" by military action making this a useless ethical guide. He states that recent memory provides some useful fragments for tomorrow's use in determining the appropriateness and extent of permissible intervention:

1. Once you have a valid mandate to push an invader back across his own frontier, it's okay to invade the invader too. Example: General Schwartzkopf in Kuwait-Iraq and General MacArthur's Inchon landing in North Korea.

2. It is alright to use force to deprive a rogue government of dangerous exotic weapons. Example: Israel's bombing of an Iraqi power plant.

3. The intervention of a peacekeeping force mandated by the UN Security Council.

4. Genocide and other gross violations of human rights justify international intervention.

5. When a country's central authority loses control, it's okay for outsiders *acting together* to help cobble together a workable government.

6. Intervention is justified to suppress terrorists, especially when they are sponsored by national governments.

7. Rescuing hostages by force is usually acceptable.

8. Drug traffickers and other criminals may be chased by international police teams that don't have to pay any more attention to national frontiers than do the criminals.

9. Refugees and their repatriation or resettlement elsewhere are an international responsibility.

10. Coping with catastrophe, whether occasioned by natural forces (hurricanes) or human error (Chernoble), is clearly an international obligation regardless of the national state in which people may need emergency help.

[**Author's Note**: From a learnership viewpoint, the goal should always be to focus on humanity's needs and find the common ground that needs to be fertilized and turned into productive use. Also, when action is needed that crosses national borders or counters another society's activities that directly contravene international standards, intervention is a legitimate act to maintain the common good.]

Colliding Worlds. In *The Battle for Peace* (2006), authors General Tony Zinni (with Tony Koltz) shares a military leader's experience and perspective on the differences between stable and developing nations whose *institutions* and *environment* are strong, and those nations and societies in which political, economic, and social relationships have collapsed into pervasive instability with the attendant decline in safety, health, employment, and human welfare. He compares the world's stable, orderly, progressive, prosperous, and law-abiding societies (e.g., the U.S. and most others that exist on every continent) with the chaotic, destitute, impoverished, uneducated, and crime infested (e.g., Somalia, Collapse of Yugoslavia, Kurdish society, Afghanistan) countries that barely exist at the subsistence level. In the latter, huge instabilities have led to a chain of events in which unreliable institutions and unsustainable environments have defeated society's ability to cope. What happens, he says, is that people react to this disintegration in different ways: (1) some take advantage of the lack of controls and become predators, (2) some hunker down and try just to survive in ever-threatening circumstances, (3) some migrate to safer places with better opportunities, and (4) some lash out in anger to those they perceive are responsible for their plight.

Zinni comments: "When a society blessed with *strong institutions* faces security challenges, economic challenges, social challenges, or environmental challenges, its institutions will hold up under stresses and pressures. They will adapt to the changes; they may bend; but they will put together programs that will take on the challenges and overcome them...*The institution that probably best indicates a society that's stable, or that's moving toward stability, is a viable, growing, and reasonably prosperous middle class*...while a middle class that's withering and fading into the lower class – as the oligarchs and elites grow more powerful and wealthy – is in clear sign of instability." (pp.106-107) Also, regarding the importance of a supportive environment, he says: "The second component of stability – or of instability – is a viable environment or its absence. I'm talking about environment not only in the totality of nature, but also the narrower sense of the specific conditions in which people live, the wherewithal needed to provide for the population – economic well-being, health, food, security, education. The environment is a society's essential capital; its substance of what makes a society viable." (p.107)

The point of Zinni's message is that the first world of successful nations and societies have to deal with the issues and conditions of the second and third worlds. These problem societies are no longer isolated and are on the world's stage demanding attention, fully expecting assistance, and threatening retaliation against those other's they perceive are responsible for their plight. War will exist between those claiming to stand for peace – and the previously secure and prosperous societies will have to develop strategies and actions, albeit extremely costly, to ameliorate the situations that occur. Part of the strategy that Zinni recommends is that "America must be good." He says: "We offer societies in danger of failing a two-hundred-year tested model for security, peace, prosperity, governance, and hope. We can apply every dimension of our power to the task of building order, security, and peace virtually anywhere we choose – though not everywhere at once." (p.222)

[**Author's Note**: It is often debated whether the U.S. is in the nation-building business. The answer is probably that we cannot avoid that responsibility that comes from having such enormous success – the only question is to what degree, at what pace, and what are the priorities we have chosen. Learnership as a philosophy has a role at the societal level of social system development because "learning and leading as a way-of-being" is how benchmarks are identified, strategies developed, and progressive action is taken.]

A New Foreign Policy. Barack Obama's book entitled *Audacity of Hope* (2006) was a review of his domestic and foreign policy experiences and perspectives. It contains a list of thoughtful recommendations for the future that are designed to guide how this nation's interests, and our societal expectations and standards, could be better articulated in conversations with other nations and societies. This was an effort to both reestablish a principled approach to U.S. self-management and for earning the respect and trust from others in the international arena. Obama said: "I'd suggest a few things that the American people should be able to agree on, starting points for a new consensus." (p.303) Two foundational principles he lists are:

1. "To begin with, we should understand that *any return to isolationism – or a foreign policy approach that denies the occasional need to deploy U.S. troops – will not work...*Globalization makes our economy, our health, and our security all captive to events on the other side of the world...Like it or not, if we want to make America more secure, we are going to have to make the world more secure." (pp.303-304)

2. The security environment we face today is fundamentally different from the one that existed fifty, twenty-five, or even ten years ago...In that world, America's greatest threats came from expansionist states like Nazi Germany and Soviet Russia, which could deploy large armies and powerful arsenals to invade territories, restrict our access to critical resources, and dictate the terms of world trade. That world no longer exists. "*The growing threat, then, comes primarily from those parts of the world on the margins of the global economy where the international 'rules of the road' have not taken hold.*" (pp.304-305)

Obama then asked: "...if the fastest growing threats are transnational – terrorist networks intent on repelling or disrupting the forces of globalization, potential pandemic disease like avian flu, or catastrophic changes in the earth's climate – *then how should our national security adapt*? He suggested:

1. "*Defense spending and the force structure of our military should reflect the new reality.* There will be times again when we must play the role of the world's reluctant sheriff.

2. *We should have the right to take unilateral military action* to eliminate an imminent threat to our security – so long as an imminent threat is understood to be a nation, group, or individual that is actively preparing to strike U.S. targets (or allies with which the United States has mutual defense agreements), and has the or will have the means to do so in the immediate future.

3. Once we get beyond matters of self-defense, though, I'm convinced that *it will be almost always in our strategic interest to act multilaterally rather than unilaterally when we use force around the world.* When the world's sole superpower willingly restrains its power and abides by internationally agreed-upon standards of conduct, it sends a message that these are rules worth following, and robs terrorists and dictators of the argument that these rules are simply tools of American imperialism."

4. Our challenge, then, is to make sure that U.S. policies move the international system in the direction of greater equity, justice, and prosperity – that the rules we promote serve both our interests and the interests of a struggling world." (pp.303-316)

[**Author's Note 1**: For Societal Systems Development (SSD) to continue to make progress in America our sense of common purpose, articulation of generally accepted values, and demonstrated leadership in humanitarian causes must be transparent to all those we assist and to those who witness our contributions and efforts. The likes of Jimmy Carter, Bill Gates and other philanthropists working along with other nations and non-governmental organizations illustrates this nation living consistently with its own values, and in a manner that engenders respect and trust – two commodities lost by U.S. leaders over the last decade. Learnership supports the learning and leadership that is so critical to educate, motivate and develop nations and societies, worldwide.]

[**Author's Note 2**: As a further testament to the ability of human society to reason and write in a manner that articulates what all decent people and nations must stand for in terms of both individual and government responsibility, the *United Nations Universal Declaration of Human Rights* speaks clearly to everyone. The introductory statements that: (1) "Whereas recognition of the inherent dignity and of the equal and inalienable rights of all members of the human family is the foundation of freedom, justice and peace in the world." and (2) "Whereas disregard and contempt for human rights have resulted in barbarous acts which have outraged the conscience of mankind, and the advent of a world in which human beings shall enjoy freedom of speech and belief and freedom from fear and want has been proclaimed as the highest aspiration of the common people," illustrate that there can be little doubt that the authors had in mind a Way of (human) Being that transcends the ineptitude and frailties demonstrated daily by the world's leaders and the unenlightened multitude. We here, however, can read this declaration and appreciate the power of its sentiment.]

6. Ecological Knowledge Sphere. The ecological knowledge sphere concerns the relationships between organisms, their environments and the goal of sustainable habitats. Emphasis is on the life processes and characteristic phenomena of living organisms. Focus is on bio-system management, energy production, population and demographics, and the availability of food and health services.

The Global Commons. In his book entitled *The Global Commons* (1990), Harlan Cleveland reports on the Aspen Institute's 1989 symposium on that subject. Identified are the four enormous environments that are treated in international law as parts of the Global Commons: the oceans, outer space, weather and climate, and Antarctica. These areas belong to the commons because they are essentially indivisible, no nation can claim ownership of them, issues concerning them are "sharing transactions" rather than "exchange transactions," and widespread cooperation is necessary for their use and protection. The concern for these areas is based on the view that there are limits to growth requiring the protection of those areas not yet overused or despoiled. Cleveland opines that: "The governance of the Global Commons…is to social science what "global change" is to the natural sciences…its not hard to be exhilarated by the tasks of institution-building that lie just ahead." (p.16)

Cleveland emphasizes the complexity and importance of the commons when he refers to them as a super system, and a "bundle of relations" in which human behavior, policies, and institutions determine the health of the planet and of its life support systems (p.29). His work, and that of his symposium colleagues, is clearly focused on avoiding the "tragedy of the commons" scenario so often seen in lesser social and economic arenas.

[**Author's Note**: This perspective is useful in terms of the LISA model in that it defines the largest part of the commons to which this section is dedicated. The condition of the *environmental commons* is gaining more and more attention as the "carrying capacity" of planet earth becomes a greater issue in international relations. The issue is not only global, however; every community has a subset of related issues having to do with air pollution, water quality, waste disposal, etc. Whenever a people share a locality, they need to concern themselves with the physical and ecological environmental systems of which they are a part.]

Building a Sustainable Society. In *State of the World* (1999), David Roodman writes the chapter on Building a Sustainable Society in which he ties together many of the themes and issues raised earlier in the book by other authors. His introduction sums up the challenge before all global societies and nations when he asks: "*What sort of world are we headed toward?*" He answers: "So far, the world order emerging is one almost nobody wants. Human numbers are growing, forests are shrinking, species are dying, farmland is eroding, freshwater supplies are dwindling, fisheries are collapsing, rivers are constricting, greenhouse gasses are accumulating, soot is contaminating the air, and lead is contaminating our blood." (p.170) He asks: *"What, then, will it take to construct a sustainable, modern society?"* And he answers: "*Governments* will need to aggressively demarcate and defend environmental limits, working domestically and cooperating internationally…*Businesses* will need to anticipate the transition and position themselves to exploit the huge investment opportunities created. *Nonprofit organizations* ranging from international environmental groups to neighborhood churches – collectively called "civil society" – will need to press both governments and businesses forward. And undergirding all their efforts will be *educated citizens* operating in their capacities as voters, consumers, charitable donors, and owners of land and resources." (p.170) Roodman organizes his observations and recommendation for the journey forward as follows: (paraphrased from Chapter Ten)

1. Getting the Signals Right. Governments will need to apply most of the pressure that will move modern society onto a sustainable path, but the magnitude and complexity involved requires planning and business innovation to achieve. What governments can do is to stop subsidizing environmental harm and to start taxing it. It violates common sense to tax heavily the activities societies generally want while taxing lightly the activities they do not want.

2. Reinventing Regulation. There is considerable room for improving regulations, but efforts to date have mostly created a patchwork of laws that worsen the situation. What is needed is to make regulations work more like taxes, in the sense of zeroing in on results rather than prescribing solutions.

3. Global Challenges, Global Cooperation. To date, governments have ratified more than 215 international treaties on everything from acid rain to desertification. Most are regional in scope. And, governments have signed numerous action plans and communiqués that lack legal status. However, most of the treaties and agreements have been inadequate to the problem at hand, either in design or in implementation and enforcement.

4. An Eco-Industrial Revolution. The proper role of business in creating a sustainable society would necessarily be subtle. On the one hand, *businesses would be the objects of change* as they are encouraged to innovate. On the other

hand, *business could be the agents of change* as they bring the results of their efforts to a waiting marketplace. Consumers want information and entertainment, and businesses can become a leader in providing sustainable processes, products, and services that meet societies higher expectations.

5. <u>Civil Society for a Sustainable Society</u>. A sustainable society almost certainly must be founded on a strong civil society, which is defined as the realm in which people may work as individuals or in groups to shape their world on a non-profit basis. Civil society includes voters, consumers, churches and mosques, political parties, unions, and a dizzying variety of other nongovernmental groups.

6. <u>The Power of an Educated Citizenry</u>. Teaching students about the environment merely extends the understanding of citizenship to encompass their responsibilities as citizens of planet earth. Doing it, however, requires major changes in how students are taught. Disciplines are mostly severed from one another even though it is the relationship among them that is key for solving our environmental predicament. H.G. Wells foreshadowed much of the twentieth century when he wrote that 'human history becomes more and more a race between education and catastrophe.' Our knowledge of the natural world has raced far ahead of our wisdom in using it.

[**Author's Note**: Once again, learnership as a philosophy and architecture for meta-cognitive reasoning and integrated social development reaches out and embraces an arena of universal importance. Societal *ecological* issues are inextricably woven into the *political, economic, social, technological*, and *geographical* issues and opportunities vying for attention in the other universal knowledge spheres.]

Factors Impacting American Development

At the highest (Meta) level of social and societal development the issues, problems and opportunities for consideration by leaders and countries are so extensive that diplomacy must be used to resolve differences of perspective and opinion. The world now appears to be flat and the planet smaller, and every person and group are much closer in proximity than we might want them to be. This closeness might just encourage some of us to extend our influence over others for either collegial or nefarious purposes.

Figure 13-3 is provided for readers' reflection and discussion. Three potential scenarios are proposed in which the United States acts to alter its economic, social and/or political policies to achieve better advantage in the world marketplace. Also, there are eighteen content or context setting factors that may come into play as the U.S. attempts to proceed with any of the three scenarios.

Scenario A -- U.S. debt reduction through currency adjustments and tariffs (raise prices of imports and lower prices of exports). Which of the eighteen factors are likely to be in play (encouraged) from within the U.S.? Which are likely to arise (be an issue) for other nations?

Scenario B -- U.S. reestablishes its leadership in energy development and innovation (makes investments in alternative energy sources and the reduction in fossil fuel consumption). Which of the eighteen factors are likely to be in play (encouraged) from within the U.S.? Which are likely to arise (be an issue) from other nations?

Scenario C -- U.S. significantly reduces national debt and reestablishes progressive tax system (reduction in social expenditures and restrictions on financial industry opportunities). Which of the eighteen factors are likely to be in play (encouraged) from within the U.S.? Which are likely to arise (be an issue) from other nations?

It should be clear here that in each scenario the breadth and interdependence of the factors potentially involved makes it difficult to definitively assert who and how the U.S. and other nations might benefit or be harmed over the longer term. Many are experiencing the same influences. National leadership and international diplomacy may be locked in perpetual battle with human rights and national expectations. Normally, economists would encourage all nations to assess their situation from a "comparative advantage" perspective – one in which each recognizes the give and take necessary when collaborating and competing with other nations. However, the situational complexity often defies easy social or political accommodation.

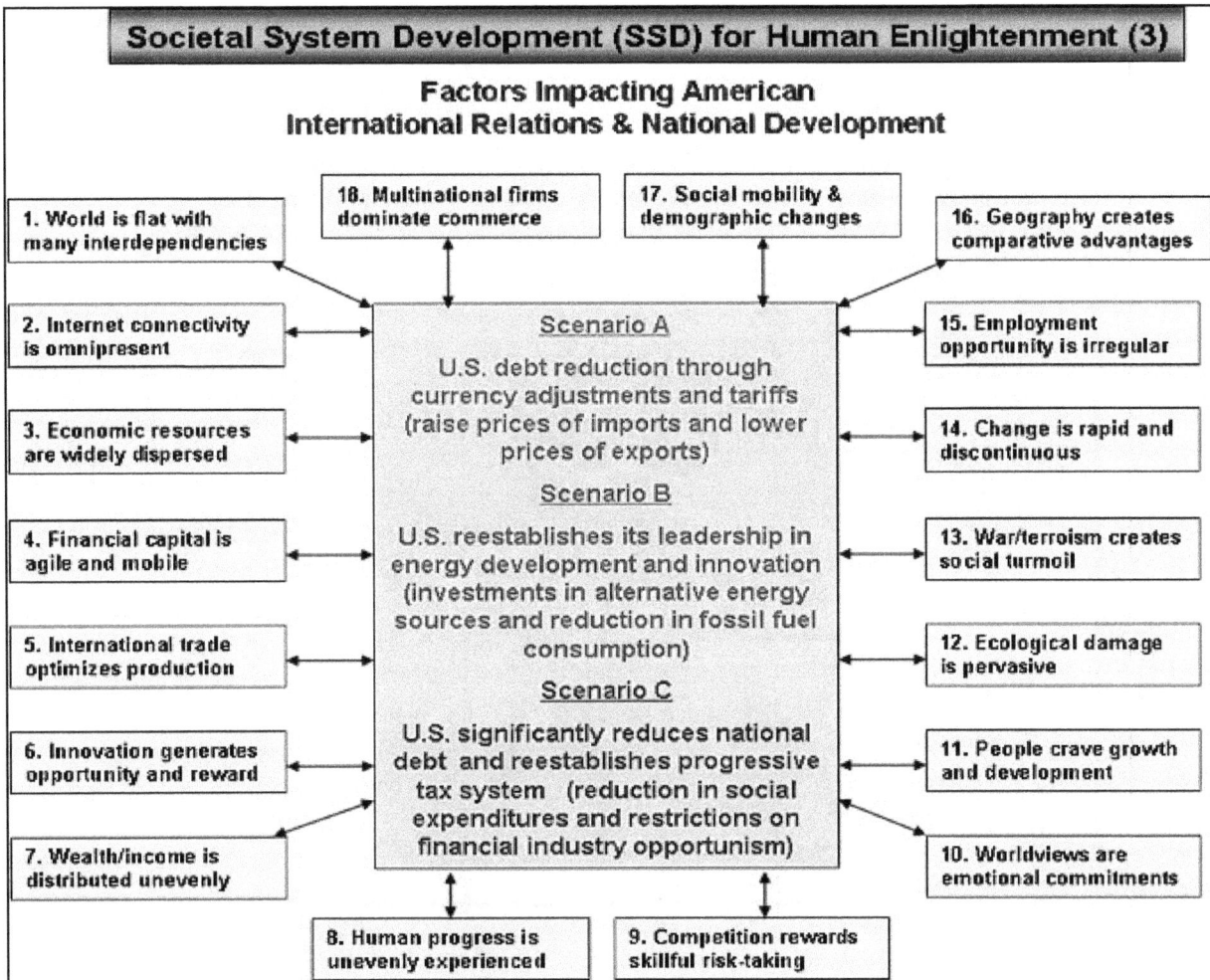

Figure 13-3

[**Author's Note:** Using Figure 13-3 for reference, a facilitator can form small groups to discuss the factors of major concern for Scenarios A, B and C. Each group can summarize and report the factors and outcomes of their respective conversations.]

Societal Discussion for Socio-Economic Management

Large broad-based societal issues are particularly challenging when citizens and leaders attempt to achieve consensus on future changes for healthier and more productive social progress. Figure 13-3 illustrates a nation facing a series of business, social and economic trends that appear in the past to be working at counter purposes in terms of overall societal growth and development. It does appear, however, that some changes have been proposed and implemented recently for the present that, hopefully, will establish societal improvement for the future. The problem is real life experience is that individuals and groups have difficulty in agreeing on societal factors such as goals and objectives, rewards and recognition, ideals and values and the wide variation of influential subjects in the Figure.

Societies and social groups have always been in both conflict and cooperation with others in their areas of perceived interest and authority. One way to understand this situation is to engage educated and experienced academics and leaders on ways to understand the underlying links and trends that are observable from a meta-level vantage point.

Societal Systems Development (SSD) for Human Enlightenment (4)

- How individuals and groups think needs to be explicated in order to see the context within which decisions are made, plans are constructed, and actions are implemented.

- Linear voice communication fails to convey the complete and rich variety of factors and assumptions that are involved – especially if recurring cycles of information sharing, parallel streams of intention, and trustful dialogue are absent.

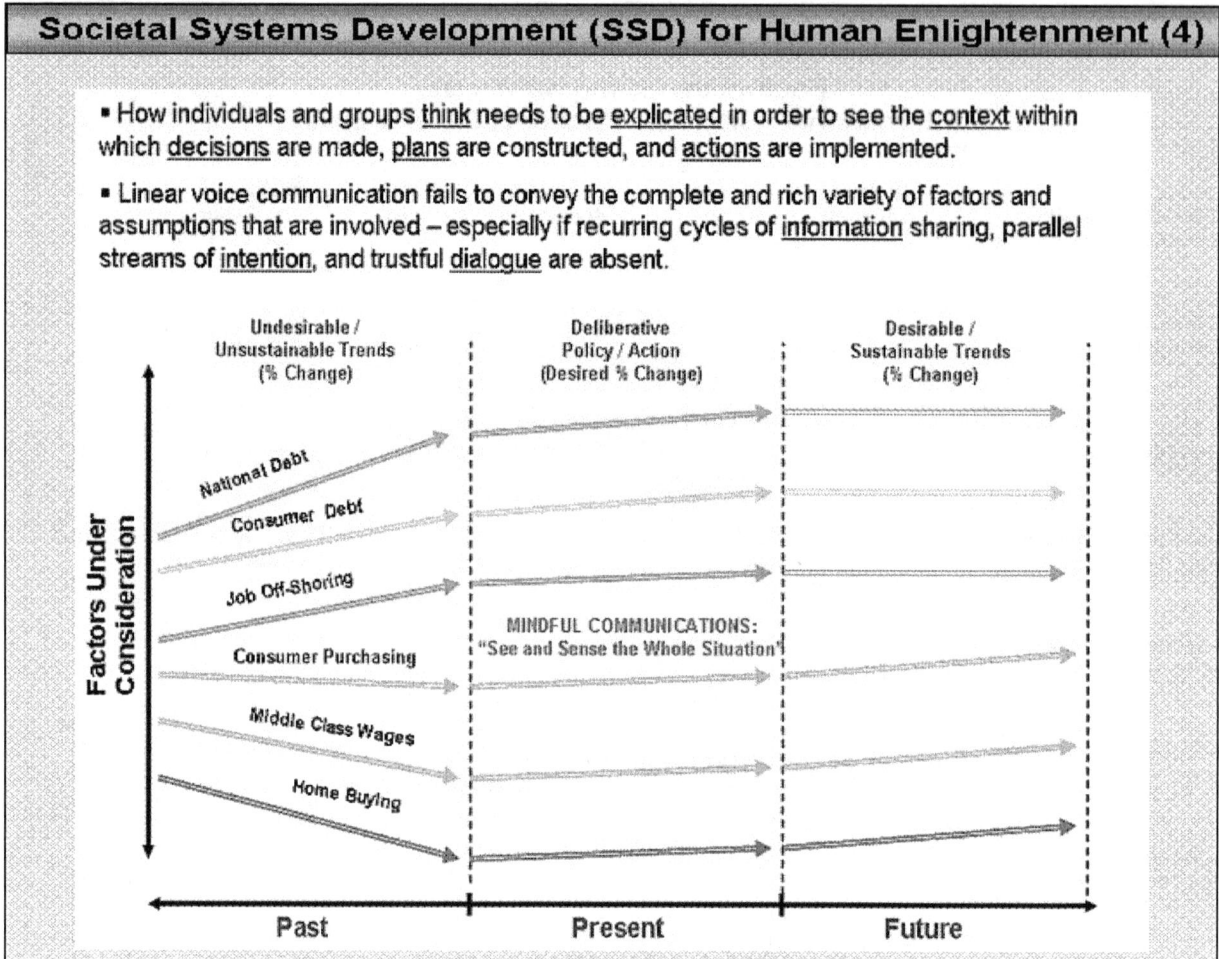

Figure 13-4

SSD is social synthesis at the meta-cognitive level, and consists of fully integrated reasoning and development across all four social system of systems domains that responds to influences from the six American learnership universal knowledge spheres (social, political, economic, technological, geographical and ecological). SSD strives to capture the spirit of John Sullivan's *To Come to Life More Fully* (1990), and suggests milestones for our timeless journey towards holistic personhood. The meta-level goal selected for the societal level is *human enlightenment*, and the key role to be played is *statesmanship*. Learning, knowing, and leading inform and activate SSD.

Theories of (Almost) Everything

A human being is part of the whole called by us universe, a part limited in time and space. He experiences himself, his thoughts and feelings as something separated from the rest, a kind of optical delusion of his consciousness. This delusion is a kind of prison for us, restricting us to our personal desires and to affection for a few persons nearest to us. Our task must be to free ourselves from this prison by widening our circle of compassion to embrace all living creatures and the whole of nature in its beauty. — Albert Einstein

Comprehensive Perspectives and Challenges. The contents of this chapter have addressed social systems at the highest level of interdependency – the *social system known as society*. From this viewing point:

1. Society represents the context within which lower level social systems e.g., the personal, organizational, and community levels become holistically integrated and through which they receive guidance

2. Society, itself, is the recipient and of all the turmoil, growth, and achievement accomplished at those lower levels.

Having constructed an initial treatise on how we might simultaneously contemplate the "Whole" and "Parts" of ourselves and our surroundings – and to construct a <u>Learnership Integrated Systems Architecture</u> (LISA) for education and development of those desiring a map for their life's journey, this chapter now introduces a select group of intellectual thinkers, leaders, and authors who have explored the "how does this all come together" territory from their own diverse viewing points.

The introduction to, and abstracts on, the books below are provided to further introduce you, the reader, to yet another level of systems thinking and comprehensive reasoning. Only a tantalizing amount of information has been extracted and provided so as to whet your appetite for more developmental reading. As the author of this book on learnership, I was pleased to discover that the concepts and perspectives I have presented strongly agree, and overlap with, the reasoning of the authors whose writings you are about to consider. What this learnership book does – that no others in this genre are known to do for their readers – is provide a holistic and integrated "theory to practice" methodology for reasoning and social development that readers can use to take practical action. Readers have been introduced to specific, actionable explanations and behavior that lead to real-life accomplishments and desired results. Finally, as you read ahead, be prepared to be mentally and emotionally stretched once again as you read the synopses below and should you choose to acquire copies of these books and enjoy their bounty.

Presence. Peter Senge along with other authors C. Otto Scharmer, Joseph Jaworski, and Betty Sue Flowers, wrote *Presence: An Exploration of Profound Change in People, Organizations, and Society* (2005) as a result of their collaborative exploration into the development of a new theory about learning and transformational change. "Their concept of *presence* is one borrowed form the natural world in which the whole is entirely present in any of its parts – to the worlds of business, education, government, and leadership. Drawing on the wisdom and experience of 150 scientists, social leaders, and entrepreneurs; *presence* is both revolutionary and hopeful in its message. It enables us to see, sense, and realize new possibilities in ourselves, in our institutions and organizations, and in society itself." (excerpt from book jacket)

At the core of the human challenge to change, to grow, and to learn, and to evolve is the limitation that: "As long as our thinking is governed by habit – notably by industrial, "machine age' concepts such as control, predictability, standardization, and 'faster is better' – we will continue to re-create institutions as they have been, despite their disharmony with the larger world, and the need of all living systems to evolve." (p.9) The major comparison the authors' make is to describe the difference between *reactive learning* and *deeper learning*. They say that all learning integrates thinking and doing; and in *reactive learning* thinking is governed by established mental models and doing is governed by established habit of action. Whereas, in *deeper learning* there is an increasing awareness of the larger whole – both as it is evolving – and actions that increasingly become part of creating alternative futures." (pp.10-11)

Presencing, according to the authors, occurs when people are able to take an inward-bound journey to a deeper place within themselves where they can become fully aware of the present moment, where deep listening can occur, where new information can get past pre-conceptions and historical preference, and where new choices and commitments can begin to emerge and become actionable. As a way of communicating their concept, the authors propose the concept of the "U" in which there are three stages. Starting at the upper left of the "U" a stage of "*Sensing*" begins in which the individual participates in intense "observation" to become one-with-the-world. Sliding down to the bottom of the "U" a stage of "*Presencing*" ensues in which the person reaches a heightened level of clarity and inner-knowing which is critical to begin a true change in thinking and feeling. No decisions have been made, however, new possibilities are allowed to be considered. Moving up the right side of the "U," the person now reaches the third stage of "*Realizing*" in which acting swiftly within the context of natural feelings and comfort, is possible.

Through additional conceptualization, the authors expand the basic "U" to recognize what they term the Seven Capacities of the "U" Movement. A separate set of activities are positioned around the periphery of the "U" starting at the upper left with *Suspending*, and then moving around the bottom of the "U" through *Redirecting, Letting Go, Letting Come, Crystallizing, Prototyping*; ending finally with *Institutionalizing* that coincides with *Realizing*. The key to satisfactory movement through the "U" is the willingness and ability of individuals to take the time to experience the value of each stage in the learning and transformation process.

One of the conclusions the authors experienced came in terms of international ecological concerns. They noted that: "The environmental movement is mostly focused on how we can be 'less bad,' how we can take or destroy less. But what if humans, as a species, actually have a purpose?

What if we have something distinctive to contribute – something to *give* rather than just *take*? Its one thing for a village or even a nation to take more than it leaves. But we humans in toto are now taking at an unprecedented rate globally…that will require us to think differently." (p.238)

Consilience: The Unity of Knowledge (1998). Author Edward O. Wilson begins his expansive treatise with the "great branches of learning" and the Enlightenment. He notes that "the Enlightenment thinkers got it right with the assumptions they made of *a lawful material world, the intrinsic unity of knowledge, and the potential of indefinite human progress*. He says the greatest enterprise of the mind has always been and always will be the attempted linkage of the sciences and humanities. The ongoing fragmentation of knowledge and resulting chaos in philosophy are not reflections of the real world but artifacts of scholarship. His view is that "consilience" is the key to unification and credits William Whewell as being the first to speak of consilience, literally a "jumping together" of knowledge by the linking of facts and fact-based theory across disciplines to create a common groundwork of explanation. Wilson credits Whewell who said: "The Consilience of Inductions takes place when an induction from one class of facts, coincides with an Induction obtained from another different class. This Consilience is a test of truth of the Theory in which it occurs." (p.8) For Wilson, the propensity of scholars and academics to narrowly constrain and distinguish their areas of research and expertise contributes to the difficulty in understanding the real world connections people experience and have to make sensible.

From this beginning, Wilson takes his readers through the Natural Sciences, the Construction and Functioning of the Human Mind, an explanation of Genes and Culture, the Fitness of Human Nature, the Social Sciences, the Arts and Their Interpretations, and Ethics and Religion – all using his unique intellect and skill in explicating their cross-influencing properties which when blended inductively create an understandable "consilience" toward a unity of knowledge. Along his journey, Wilson traces the rise and fall of religions as necessary stages to, but insufficient guides for understanding the universe; explains the many advancements in understanding evolution, DNA, genes, and their impact on developing cultures; describes the ecological and symbiotic relationships among all living things; and makes clear that the human brain is the most complex and sophisticated living organism of all time – and that it has not yet finished its work of fully understanding its own content and context – which it eventually will do.

As a way of summary and conclusion of his book, Wilson asks: "To What End?" He answers: "*The central idea of the consilience world view is that all tangible phenomena, from the birth of stars to the working of social institutions, are based on material processes that are ultimately reducible, however long and tortuous the sequences, to the laws of physics*. In support of this idea is the conclusion of biologists that humanity is kin to all other life forms by common descent. We share essentially the same DNA genetic code, which is transcribed into RNA and translated into proteins with the same amino acids. Our anatomy places us among the Old World monkeys and apes. The fossil record shows our immediate ancestor to be either *Homo ergaster* or *Homo erectus*. It suggests that the point of our origin was Africa about two hundred thousand years ago. Our heredity human nature, which evolved during hundreds of millennia before and afterward, still profoundly affects the evolution of culture." (pp.266-267)

He continues by saying that *the new century will find much greater emphasis on holistic thinking across distinctive domains of knowledge*, and that formerly unrecognized cause and effect relationships will continue to become understood leading to new kinds of synthesis. He explains that: "No compelling reason has ever been offered why the same strategy should not work to unite the natural sciences with social science and humanities. The difference between the two domains is the magnitude of the problem, not the principles needed for its solution." (p.267)

Lastly, Wilson comments: "Thanks to science and technology, access to factual knowledge of all kinds is rising exponentially while dropping in unit cost. It is destined to become global and democratic. Soon it will be available everywhere on television and computer screens. What then? The answer is clear: synthesis. We are drowning in information, while starving in wisdom. *The world henceforth will be run by synthesizers, people able to put together the right information, think critically about it, and make important choices wisely.*" (p.269)

A Theory of Everything (2000). Ken Wilber's book begins with his fascination with the concept of a "Kosmos." He says: "The Greeks have a beautiful word, *Kosmos*, which means the patterned Whole of all existence, including the physical, emotional, mental, and spiritual realms. Ultimate reality is not merely understanding the "cosmos," or the physical dimension, but the "Kosmos," or the physical and emotional and mental and spiritual dimensions all together. Not just matter, lifeless and insentient, but *the living Totality of matter, body, mind, soul, and spirit.*" (p.xi) Wilber's Theory of Everything (T.O.E.) strives to create an "integral vision" of how the seemingly disparate fields of knowledge and experience may be shown to be balanced, comprehensive, and inclusive – from science all the way through to morals. Wilber provides a summary of the work of Clare Graves in identifying the evolving "levels or waves of human existence," – and the further enhancements of that theory by Don Beck and Christopher Cowan who together created the concept of *Spiral Dynamics* (reference this book's Chapter Three for more explanation of this subject).

Spiral dynamics recognizes human development as proceeding through eight general stages, which are also called "memes" (basic stages of development that can be expressed in any activity). Individuals, groups, and cultures can be shown through analysis to favor one or more of the eight styles and/or descriptive patterns of thinking and behavior. An organizing scheme that illustrates the levels of development and assigned colors can be summarized as follows: (1)

survival stage – beige, (2) kin-spirits – purple, (3) power-gods – red, (4) truth-force – blue, (5) strive-drive – orange, (6) human-bond – green, (7) flex-flow – yellow, and (8) whole-view – turquoise. Wilber explains that Levels 1 through 6 are where most people and cultures are distributed today as a result of their past evolution and development; all still exist, but some advanced individuals and groups have achieved the *human-bond – green stage*. Their difficulty is continuing to grow through that stage to the second tier of human growth – yellow, and then turquoise. A summary of the desirable but hard to achieve yellow and turquoise levels of total growth and fulfillment includes: (1) *Flex-flow – Yellow*: Integration. Flexibility, spontaneity, and functionality have the highest priority. Differences and pluralities can be integrated into interdependent, natural flows. Knowledge and competency should supersede power, status, or group sensitivity. And, (2) *Whole-system – Turquoise*: Holistic. Universal holistic system, holons/waves of integrative energies; unites feeling with knowledge; multiple levels interwoven into one conscious system. A "grand unification is possible" such as a Theory of Everything (T.O.E.).

From this baseline, Wilber proposes the need for an "integral psychology" in understanding human development, and presents "A Full Spectrum (Interdependent) Approach" that depicts Four Quadrants of Human development/evolution. His four quadrant model refers to the most important dimensions of the "Kosmos," namely, the interior and the exterior of the individual and the collective. The four stages begin with (1) *Self and Consciousness* – the eight transpersonal waves of spiral dynamics – beige through turquoise, then (2) *Brain and Organism* – eight stages of physiological construction and development, (3) *Social System and Environment* – eight stages of social relationships from survival clans through holistic mesh-works, and finally, (4) *Culture and Worldview* – eight levels of social perspective from archaic through holonic. The concept recognizes that any combination across the four levels of human experience and preferences is possible, but that approaching stage/level eight in all four quadrants simultaneously would be akin to human optimization.

Wilber's intellectual journey proceeds further with observations and creative thinking on the topics of (1) Science and Religion, (2) the Real World, and (3) Maps of the Kosmos before drawing his work to a (temporary, I think) conclusion. Wilber comments at the end of his writing that: "In this Theory of Everything, I have one major rule: *Everybody* is right. More specifically, everybody – even me – has some important pieces of truth, and all of these pieces need to be honored, cherished, and included in a more gracious, spacious, and compassionate embrace, and genuine T.O.E." (p.140)

A History of Everything (2003). Bill Bryson's book is a compilation of subject area tome's that together provide an overarching view of the past, present, and the likely future of life (and death) on earth. He dedicated three years of his recent adult life traveling, interviewing, reading, researching, and writing the fundamental questions and most probable answers to as many fields of learning and education he could master. His book is a tour de force of the most eminent theories and intellectual compilations of how the universe, the earth, and biological life have come to be what they are.

The parts of his book include intriguing titles like:
1. Lost in the Cosmos
2. The Size of the Earth
3. A New Age Dawns
4. Dangerous Planet
5. Life Itself
6. The Road to Us

Along the way, his readers learn the latest thinking on subjects like:

1. How to build a universe,
2. How things are measured and their sizes
3. Movement within the earth – earthquakes and volcanoes
4. Details of the Big Bang
5. The rise of life
6. The richness of being
7. The stuff of life
8. The mysterious biped.

And, throughout his stories are interpersonal vignettes, introductions to past and present notable personalities, and a growing appreciation for this moment in time when modern life exists – albeit so short given the catastrophic events that may occur at any moment. Here are some facts and observations that most everyone would find interesting – assuming they are "systems thinkers:"

1. We have a universe. It is a place of the most wondrous and gratifying possibility, and beautiful, too. And it was all done in about the time it takes to make a sandwich…This all happened about 13.7 billion years ago. (p.10) And, the edge of the universe is 90 billion trillion miles away! (p.13)

2. The current best estimate for earth's weight is 5.9725 trillion metric tons…and the use of current technology has simply confirmed what Isaac Newton surmised about 110 years ago. (p.62)

3. Marine fossils can be found on top of mountain tops – not because the seas were once that high – but because the mountain chains had been pushed up from under the seas millions of years before. (p.64)

4. Einstein was a bright but not outstanding student. Before his brilliance was discovered he could not get a job as a university lecturer or even as a high school teacher – he was a Swiss patent office clerk. Experts now say: As the creation of a single mind, his Theory of Relativity is undoubtedly the high intellectual achievement of humanity." (p.123)

5. Recent evidence suggests that not only are the galaxies of the universe racing away from us, but they are doing so at a rate that is accelerating. This is counter to all expectations. It appears that the universe may not only be filled with dark matter, but with dark energy. Scientists sometimes call it vacuum energy or, more exotically, quintessence. (p.171)

6. Today we know that Earth's surface is made up of eight to twelve (tectonic) plates and twenty of so smaller ones, and they all move in different directions at different speeds. Europe and North America are parting at about the speed a finger nail grows – roughly two yards in a human lifetime. (p.182)

7. Suppose that there was a button you could push and you could light up all the Earth-crossing asteroids larger than ten meters, there would be over 100 million of these objects in the sky. Two or three pass close to the earth every week, but we usually would not know about them (a) until after they pass by because we are not tracking them, or (b) until they strike the earth's atmosphere because of the heat and pressure waves that are about to kill us and large portions of the planet. (pp.194-203)

8. Under the western United States there is a huge cauldron of magma, a colossal volcanic hot spot, which erupts, on the average, every 600,000 years. It has already been 630,000 years since the last eruption which buried eastern Nebraska in over ten feet of ash. The source of this horrific event has been Yellowstone National Park in Idaho. The power of the next explosive event could be thousands of times bigger than the explosion of Mt. St. Helens in Washington State.

9. 97 percent of all water on earth is in the seas, the greater part of it in the Pacific, which covers the planet and is bigger than all the landmasses put together. Of the 3 percent of the Earth's water that is fresh, most exist as ice sheets. The tiniest amount – 0.036 percent – is found in lakes, rivers, and reservoirs. (p.273)

10. At some point in an unimaginably distant past some little bag of chemicals fidgeted to life. It absorbed some nutrients, gently pulsed, had a brief existence…cleaved itself and produced an heir. It was the moment of creation for us all. Biologists sometimes call it the "Big Birth." All life is one, whether plants which came first – or after they produced oxygen – animals which came later. (p.294)

11. Every human body consist of 10 quadrillion cells, but about 100 quadrillion bacterial cells. We could not survive without them. There are few environments in which bacteria aren't prepared to live. They are finding now that when they push probes into ocean vents so hot that the probes actually melt, the bacteria are even there. (p.305)

12. A virus is a strange and unlovely entity – a piece of nucleic acid, smaller than and simpler than bacteria, about 5000 in number, and afflict us with many hundreds of diseases. Viruses prosper by hijacking the genetic material of a living cell and using it to produce more virus. (p.316)

13. It isn't easy to become a fossil. The fate of nearly all living organisms – over 99.9 percent of them – is to compost down to nothingness. When your spark is gone, every molecule you own will be nibbled off you or sluiced away to be put in some other system. (p.321)

14. Life wants to be; life doesn't always want to be much; life from time to time goes extinct; but life starts up again and goes on – in ways that are decidedly amazing. (p.349)

15. When Charles Darwin began his studies he was believer in creation. Darwin didn't use the phrase "survival of the fittest" in any of his work…nor did he employ the word *evolution* in print until the sixth edition of Origin of the Species, preferring instead "descent with modification."

16. Darwin and Alfred Wallace (a young naturalist) had developed independently, and then somewhat collaboratively, parallel theories that together explained what would become the origin of the species. They laid the groundwork for all life sciences. (pp.386-393)

17 Every human genome is different, but we are 99.9 percent the same. Chromosomes, attached to the genome DNA, constitute the complete set of instructions to make and maintain each of us. There are about six feet of DNA squeezed into almost every cell – each with 3.2 billion letters of coding.

18. DNA is not alive, but it uses RiboNucleic Acid (RNA) to send messages to proteins which direct all the work of the human body e.g., creating traits and bodily processes. Over 90 percent of human genes are also found in mice. Humans have 35,000 to 40,000 genes – about the same number as found in grass. All life is one. (pp.412-415)

19. Before fifty million years ago, Earth had no regular ice ages, but when we did have them they tended to be colossal. A massive freezing occurred about 2.2 billion years ago, followed by a billion years or so of warmth. The belief is that we were saved by volcanoes which pushed through the buried surface, pumping tons of heat and gasses that melted the snows and re-formed the atmosphere. (pp.428-429)

20. *Homo erectus*, the species that existed about 1.8 million years ago to possibly as recently as twenty thousand or so years ago is the dividing line between everything before – apelike creatures – and everything humanlike that came after. It was the first to hunt, the first to use fire, the first to fashion complex tools, the first to leave evidence at campsites, and the first to look over the weak and frail. (p.449)

21. Sometime over a hundred thousand years ago, a smarter, lither species of creature – the ancestors of every one of us alive today – arose on the African plains and began radiating outward. These new *homo sapiens* displaced their duller, less adept predecessors. (p.457)

22. We have been chosen, by fate or Providence or whatever you wish to call it. As far as we can tell, we are the best there is. We may be all there is. It's an unnerving thought that we may be the universe's supreme achievement and its worst nightmare simultaneously. (p.477)

Five Minds for the Future (2006). Author Howard Gardner, well known for developing the concept of "multiple intelligences" introduced earlier in this book, says in this his latest book "I concern myself here with the kinds of minds that people will need if they – if we – are to thrive in the world in the eras to come…I specify the operations of the minds that we will need…also the ones we should develop." (p.1) His book jacket (by Red Letter Design) captures the essence of the author's reasoning and will serve as a basis herein for further discussion: What is said is: "We live in a time of vast changes that include accelerating globalization, mounting quantities of education, the growing hegemony of science and technology, and the clash of civilizations. Those changes call for new ways of learning and thinking in school, business and the professions. In *Five Minds for the Future*, noted psychologist Howard Gardner defines the cognitive abilities that will command a premium in the years ahead:

1. The Disciplinary Mind. Mastery of major schools of thought (including science, mathematics, and history) and of least one professional craft

2. The Synthesizing Mind. Ability to integrate ideas from different disciplines or sphere into a coherent whole and to communicate that integration to others

3. The Creating Mind. Capacity to uncover and clarify new problems, questions, and phenomena

4. The Respectful Mind. Awareness of and appreciation for differences among human beings

5. The Ethical Mind. Fulfillment of one's responsibilities as a worker and a citizen

Armed with these well-honed capacities, a person will be equipped to deal with what is expected in the future – as well as what cannot be anticipated. Without these "minds," individuals will be at the mercy of forces that can't understand – overwhelmed by information, unable to succeed in the workplace, and incapable of making judicious decisions about personal and professional matters.

Renowned worldwide for his theory of multiple intelligences, Gardner takes that thinking to the next level in his book. Concise and engaging, *Fives Minds for the Future* will inspired lifelong learning in any reader and provide valuable insights for those charged with training and development organizational leaders – today and tomorrow."

[**Author's Note**: Learnership: Learning and Leading as a Way-of-Being, written before knowing of Gardner's thinking on this subject, appears to have a remarkable potential as a catalyst in pursuit of Gardner's stated objectives. This judgment is made based on the following factors:

1. The *Learnership Integrated Systems Architecture* (LISA) is a (right brain activity) systems model that illustrates the intricacies among *five essential human development competencies* and the *four fundamental social systems* within which everyone should strive for development – while the LISA is also described in writing (left brain activity) to ensure a holistic experience for readers

2. The *book content* is deliberately chosen to represent numerous fields of academic study and fields of experience e.g., engineering, business, public administration, education, philosophy, biology, physics, and personal health are just a few

3. The *book context* is presented in which universal goals, ideals, and spheres of knowledge are defined and used as both a foundation for lifelong learning and a guidebook for individual, organizational, and community development

4. The book is designed and provides discussion questions and a personal journal for *reference and reflection* by readers striving to learning and change not only to be entertained

5. The book is rich with theoretical and practical insights from noted experts across many diverse domains of expertise; and finally

6. The book is *Not the Answer* as so many books are inclined to be, but instead, is specifically designed to be a beginning stimulant for a *Holistic Societal Dialogue* to be hosted *by American Learnership Forum*. In summary, detailed review will indicate that all five of the author's "minds" are significantly designed into the learnership philosophy, architecture, and practices.]

Implications for Integral Learning and Knowledge Management

We now arrive at the *social systems domain* where the result of our knowledge building, with the assistance of the five learnership Interdisciplinary reasoning competencies, may be reviewed. The major determination for **SSD** is whether the knowledge recently created is "relevant" to the inquiry, study, problem or issue being considered. Quite often a paradox occurs at this juncture in which the conclusion reached appears to be inconsistent, conflicting or incompatible with what the individuals involved anticipated or desired. When analyzed, questions arise as to weather the Systems Thinking, Pattern Recognition or Situational Learning competencies have been utilized in an open, factual, unbiased, timely and convincing manner. That is, is the knowledge really correct and integral when considering that there are obvious limitations in people's minds and personal preferences – and their cultures, education, and beliefs are sometimes entirely in conflict. Effective and valued knowledge will need to be judged by the *SSD Personal, Organization, and Community* domains of thinking and behavior as interpreted by skilled and experienced leaders.

Conclusion

> Humanity is now learning the process of evolution and becoming consciously responsible
> for it. Through the maturation of consciousness and technology we are now co-evolutionary
> It is vital that we use that new power with love and wisdom. — Barbara Marx Hubbard

Capacity for Self-Transcendence. In his July 4, 1994 speech in acceptance of the Philadelphia Freedom Medal, Vaclav Havel spoke of "The New Measure of Man." He said that the modern age has ended and that we are now in a post-modern transitional period in which an amalgamation of cultures is taking place. It is a time when "everything is possible but nothing is certain;" a time when we have "globalized only the surface of our lives, but our inner self continues to have a life of its own." He says that "...individual cultures, increasingly lumped together by contemporary civilization, are realizing with new urgency their own inner autonomy." This leads to increasing tension and conflict as value differences strive to remain unaffected by pressures for accommodation and conformity.

According to Havel, what is needed is the "creation of a new model of co-existence among the various cultures, peoples, races, and religious spheres within a single interconnected civilization." He says that the basis for this new model begins with the fundamental ideas of modern democracy, and then reaches for something deeper – a set of generally held values – that link all men together. At the most basic level, he suggests that mankind must recognize its universal condition: it is anchored both to the earth and to the cosmos, and is part of a larger whole that must be revered. Acceptance of this state-of-being, he believes, "endows us with the capacity for self-transcendence." And, when motivated toward self-transcendence, mankind will be able to determine a reliable path for peaceful co-existence in a multicultural world.

[**Author's Note**: In terms of the learnership philosophy and architecture, the common good (Chapter Twelve) is offered as the higher level-of-(human) being wherein a community's individuals, organizations, institutions, and cultures can attain an optimized existence that respects and balances the rights and responsibilities of all concerned. If we enhance that vision with this chapter's aspiration for human enlightenment, understanding, and advancement among all people and societies, we can appreciate the altruistic and "other-regarding" aspects of the human condition expressed by history's writers in the philosophical, spiritual, and humanistic traditions. Our challenge in doing this is to transcend uninformed viewpoints and self-serving modalities for greater alignment within a universal order still in design.]

Application of Learnership Reasoning Competencies. A fundamental goal of learnership is to enable most readers of the book to gain a fuller understanding of how their personal lives and careers are progressing in terms of the larger social systems of which they are a part. This book provides a beginning baseline for this assessment by presenting a philosophical viewpoint, an architectural framework, selected initial content, and a methodology for immersing the reader horizontally into numerous knowledge disciplines, while vertically immersing that same reader into greater subject matter depth in topics they never knew they wanted to know more about. The long-term plan is for those individuals who desire to rapidly develop their skills in this arena – and to begin to train and consult with others – to become accomplished learnership practitioners. A little theory can go a long way once we start to appreciate the benefits of becoming holistic thinkers, lifelong learners, and adaptive leaders.

This section is presented at the end of each chapter on social system development (personal, organizational, community, and societal). A little effort is now required from readers desiring to exercise their evolving understanding of learnership. Your task: using Table 13-3 below and a separate piece of paper, write down some examples of how the five learnership competencies influence, drive, support, or otherwise have a powerful effect on the societal social system discussed in this chapter. Save your work for later reference and potential use in your American Learnership. for Life, Work Wealth and Legacy Fulfillment

Reasoning Competency	Societal Social System
Systems Thinking	Impact on the larger society?
Pattern Recognition	Impact on the larger society?
Situational Learning	Impact on the larger society?
Knowledge Management	Impact on the larger society?
Adaptive Leadership	Impact on the larger society?

Table 13-3

[**Author's Note**: Are the knowledge and skills you have acquired and using so far in your life sufficient for you to achieve your current goals, a meaningful life and a memorable legacy?]

Personal Reflection. This topic appears at the send of each chapter and is meant to serve two purposes: (1) be a reader's guide to main points and "takeaways," and (2) to encourage everyone to take a moment to engage their mental cognition and intuition on what the chapter means to them – especially at this time in their lives. Questions for chapter reflection follow immediately below; and for those readers inclined to maintain a self-assessment, your thoughts may be recorded in your American Learnership for Life, Work, Wealth, Health and Legacy Success at Appendix B.

Questions for Discussion:

1. How is the conceptual goal of *human enlightenment* achieved in the learnership architecture?

2. Explain the differences between attempting to resolve *convergent and divergent problems* arise in the public sector.

3. What does it mean to say that a government has an implied *social contract* with its people?

4. Why has there been a call for greater *interdisciplinary education* from some sources in the U.S.?

5. Can you list two to three major learning points from this chapter that you want to keep in mind to improve your ability to manage your life and career?

6. Can you identify two to three topics, models, or perspectives in this chapter you would like to learn more about?

7. Should you be making an entry into your *American Learnership for Life, Work and Legacy Success* at Appendix B?

Questions on the Meaning of Your Life

How have these "Surrogate" Goals worked for you so far? Now that you have completed Chapters One through Thirteen your learning and future objectives should have become more clearly defined. Please write them down as the answers to Chapter Two (Discovering the Meaning of Your Life) and later use in this handbook.

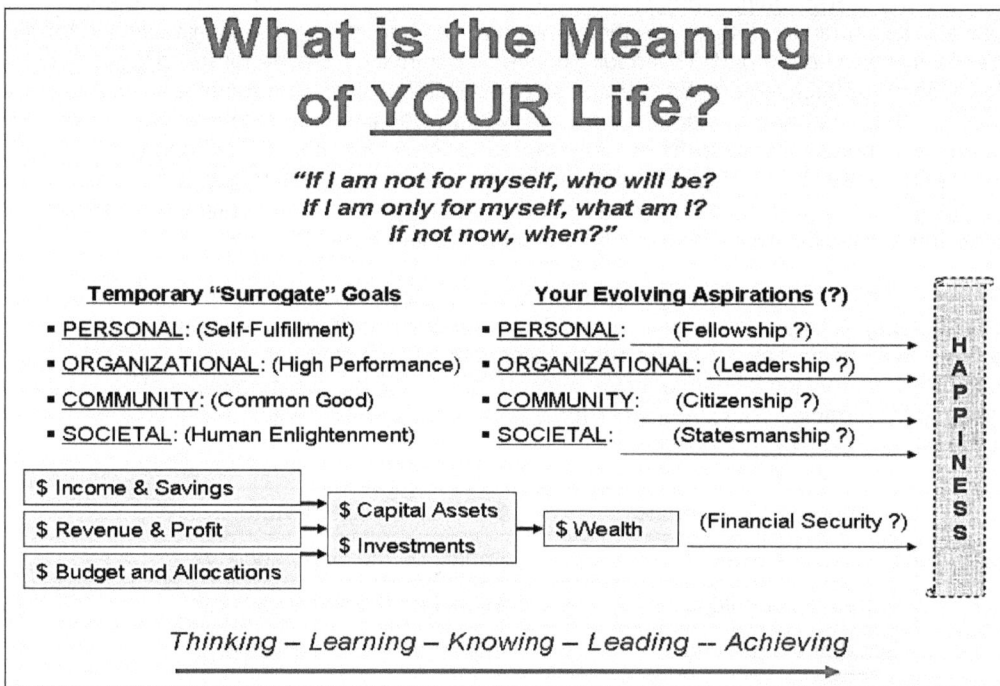

What is the Meaning of YOUR Life?

"If I am not for myself, who will be?
If I am only for myself, what am I?
If not now, when?"

Temporary "Surrogate" Goals	Your Evolving Aspirations (?)
• PERSONAL: (Self-Fulfillment)	• PERSONAL: (Fellowship ?)
• ORGANIZATIONAL: (High Performance)	• ORGANIZATIONAL: (Leadership ?)
• COMMUNITY: (Common Good)	• COMMUNITY: (Citizenship ?)
• SOCIETAL: (Human Enlightenment)	• SOCIETAL: (Statesmanship ?)

$ Income & Savings
$ Revenue & Profit → $ Capital Assets / $ Investments → $ Wealth (Financial Security ?)
$ Budget and Allocations

HAPPINESS

Thinking – Learning – Knowing – Leading -- Achieving

Figure 13-4

Insights, Commitments and Skills

If you plan to participate in the American Learnership for Life, Work, Wealth, Health and Legacy Success e-book developmental experience, it is suggested you record your Insights, commitments and skills to be developed here in this chapter, and again in Appendix B:

My learning in terms of new insights, changing priorities, new commitments or skills I want to acquire:

1. Insights (Example): Remind myself that ...

2. Commitments (Example): Continue to ask myself ...

3. Skills (Example): Apply my knowledge and skills to ...

Second Interlude

American Learnership: Reader Reflection and Development
A summary of what you have <u>accomplished</u> and the <u>options</u> available to you as you extract value
from this American Learnership Life Management, Authentic Living, and Legacy Success learning experience.

<u>Author's Note</u>: All readers and course participants should engage in the webinars and conversations included in this Mindset Handbook for full development. It is also advisable that new readers and course participants familiarize themselves with this instruction, and how to achieve the written Legacy Success e-books described in Appendix B and C. Lastly, those <u>already at age 50</u> may seek a shortened approach to their needs by choosing <u>My Senior Lifelong Learning and Memorable Legacy (Letter) option</u> at Chapter 15 and Appendix E. Contact <u>rgarrity@alforum.org</u> for assistance.

Accomplished by Participants Starting at Chapter One:

1. <u>Preliminary Insights and Aspirations</u> meant to serve as ice-breakers for your cognitive and emotional journey.

2. <u>Section I:</u> the *American Learnership* framework for organizing the Handbook (*Learnership Process, Personal Meaning, Project Management, Personal and Professional Branding*).

3. <u>Section II:</u> the five *Reasoning Competencies* that empower everyone to further develop their knowledge, skills and abilities – *System Thinking, Pattern Recognition, Situational Learning, Knowledge Management, Adaptive Leadership* and the *First Interlude.*

4. <u>Section III:</u> the four domains of Social Systems Development: *personal, organization, community* and *society* within the context of six spheres of knowledge: *social, political, economic, technological, ecological* and *geographical.*

5. <u>Appendix B and C Options.</u> Your notes, after studying chapters one to thirteen, enable your participation in both <u>learnership practitioner</u> e-book exercises at Appendices B and C.

<u>Appendix B.</u> [My] <u>Integral Life, Work, Wealth, Health and Legacy Success</u>. Your use of this personal learning and performance improvement product is described at the end of each chapter and is located for use at <u>Appendix B</u>. The appendix contains two items. The <u>first</u> item is an example completed by Dr. Garrity. The <u>second</u> item is a partially blank format for your e-book use. A <u>Certificate of Achievement</u> is awarded this item.

<u>Appendix C.</u> [My] <u>Authentic Personal and Professional Brand.</u> This Authentic Branding Methodology was developed by Dr. Hubert Rampersad and approved for use in this Mindset Handbook. This product is described back in <u>chapter four</u> and is located for use at <u>Appendix C</u>. This appendix contains two items. The <u>first</u> item is a personal example completed by Dr. Garrity. The <u>second</u> item is a partially blank form for your personal e-book use. A <u>Certificate of Achievement</u> is awarded for completing this item. (<u>Note</u>: For those interested in becoming a Certified Authentic Professional Brand Coach, Dr. Garrity will coordinate a meeting for you with Dr. Rampersad who created the product)

Option for Ages 50+: If you are age 50+ and are <u>just starting this program at Chapters fourteen and fifteen</u>, you may want to **start your learning plan** by first reviewing <u>Mid-Life/Career Transition and Renewal</u> (14) and <u>Senior Rejuvenation, Authentic Living and Legacy Success</u> (15) before making your choice between e-books at Appendix B or C. <u>As an Alternative</u>, you may choose to by-pass writing the e-books and only concentrate on writing your <u>Senior Life Learning and Memorable Legacy (Letter)</u> as described here (below) and in Chapter Fifteen and Appendix E.

<u>Appendix E.</u> [My] <u>Senior Life Learning and Memorable Legacy (Letter)</u>. The development of this product requires selected use of topics presented in this Handbook. This choice will result in your completion of what is sometimes referred to as an "ethical will" or "living legacy" to be shared with your family and friends. (<u>Note</u>: This option is explained in Chapter Fifteen and Appendix E can be combined with the e-book options offered in Appendix A or B if guided study of the earlier chapters is conducted. For assistance <u>rgarrity@alforum.org</u>.

Reminder for All: Read the <u>Epilogue: Summation and Review of Selected Major Topics</u>. to gain an understanding on how this Mindset Handbook achieves integration among selected topics.

Section IV

American Learnership Encore: Mid-Life Opportunities and Experiences

[**Author's Note 1:** If you opened this Handbook first to this section you have two choices based on your personal objectives. Read chapters fourteen and fifteen, and then decide how you choose to proceed.]

Choice 1 (Under age 50): Commit to studying chapters one through fifteen and the Epilogue: Summarization and Review of Selected Major Topics. Join many others who are dedicated to significantly improving their life, work and legacy by reading and attending seminars and webinars dedicated to your comprehensive lifelong learning and performance. This will encourage you to participate in one of two practical e-book exercises: (a) [My] Integral Life, Work, Wealth, Health and Legacy Success or (b) [My] Authentic Personal and Professional Branding.

Choice 2 (Age 50+): Commit to studying (a) Chapters One through Four, (b) chapters fourteen and fifteen, and (c) the Epilogue: Summarization and Review of Selected Major Topics. This choice focuses primarily on your Mid-Life/Career Transition and Renewal (Chapter 14) and on Senior Rejuvenation, Authentic Living, and Legacy Success (Chapter 15). It also encourages you to choose from the Appendix either the (a) [My] Integral Life, Work, Wealth, Health and Legacy Success or (b) [My] Authentic Personal and Professional Branding e-book projects for additional development.

Additional Option for Ages 50+: There is an additional option for those just starting this learning program and who may not want to do the e-book work offered above. If you are age 50+ and are just starting this program at Chapters Fourteen and Fifteen, you may want to **start your learning plan** by first reviewing Mid-Life/Career Transition and Renewal (14) and Senior Rejuvenation, Authentic Living and Legacy Success (15) before making your choice between e-books at Appendix B or C. As an Alternative, you may choose to by-pass writing the e-books and only concentrate at this time on writing [My] Senior Life Learning and Memorable Legacy (Letter) as described here and Chapter Fifteen.

Appendix E. [My] Senior Life Learning and Memorable Legacy (Letter). The development of this product requires selected use of topics previously presented in this Handbook. This choice will result in your completion of what is sometimes referred to as an "ethical will" or "living legacy" to be shared with your family and friends. (Note: This option is explained in Chapter Fifteen and can also be combined with the e-book options offered in Appendix A or B if guided study of the earlier chapters is conducted. For assistance with options contact Dr. Garrity, rgarrity@alforum.org.

Reminder for All: Read the Epilogue: Summation and Review of Selected Major Topics to gain an understanding on how this Mindset Handbook achieves integration among selected topics.

Since beginning this Handbook other very relevant references have been discovered with pertinent insights and practical skills. Highlights from these sources are advocated in Chapters 14 and 15, and their use requires obtaining a reference copy of the books (e.g. Amazon.com) by our readers and course members:

1. *The Encore Career Handbook: How to make a Living and a Difference in the Second Half of Life*, 2013, Marci Alboher, Workman Publishing Co. New York, NY.

2. *Live Smart after 50: The Experts' Guide to Life Planning for Uncertain Times,* 2012, Life Planning Network, Boston MA.

3. *Working with Older Adults: A Professional's Guide to Contemporary Issues of Aging*, 2015 Society of Certified Senior Advisors, Denver, CO.

4. *Legacies of the Heart: Living a Life that Matters, Meg Newhouse, 2016, EBook Bakery Books.*
All these senior life references contain recommendations and initiatives that motivated, mid-life/career people should consider for tackling personal renewal, senior rejuvenation and a memorable legacy.

Chapter Fourteen

Mid-Life/Career Transition and Renewal

For self-renewing men and women the development of their own potentialities and the process of self-discovery never end…Exploration of the full range of our own potentialities is not something that we can safely leave to the chances of life. It is something to be pursued systematically, or at least avidly, to the end of our days.
— *John Gardner*

Major Chapter Topics

Chapter Fourteen

Mid-Life/Career Transition and Renewal

This stage of cognitive and emotional awareness, and even discomfort, generally begins in the forty-five to sixty age range, but can vary significantly depending on an individual's particular life circumstances. It is often a period of disruptive feelings, cognitive dilemmas, and forced reflection on matters having to do with one's life purpose, progress, happiness, experiences and increasing age. Challenges include moving from independency to interdependency and from intimacy to generativity.

American Learnership Mental Model

The American Learnership Forum (ALF) is a non-profit education, coaching, consulting and fundraising community; and the developer of the products and services used to demonstrate that significant learning toward *personal self-fulfilment*, *organization high performance*, and the *community common good* pursued in a holistic manner can contribute to *societal human enlightenment*. Figure 14-1 encourages the concept that a person with a comprehensive perspective on the social system-of-systems of which we a part enables us to experience and enjoy the world more fully.

Figure 14-1

Figure 14-2 presents a dynamic illustration on how almost anyone can expect to experience adult development (think, learn, know, lead, achieve) over a successful lifetime. The major point being advocated is the extent to which the social systems-of-systems growth curve becomes integral over the years is a precursor to the rate and degree of achievement we can expect to attain. Typically there will be time periods when transitions are more difficult than the norm for each person or group, however, learning, support and innovation will usually be found by resilient people so that progress toward successful lives are realized. Even better, there may be a time when a "surge period" occurs wherein the person or group acquires the *knowledge, skill and abilities* to strike out on an even faster rate and degree of achievement due an encounter with a persuasive leader or the combination of fortuitous events the shine a light on new paths for greater accomplishment.

[**Author's Note**: With these two concepts in mind, the following pages describe how the learnership process, philosophy, architecture and practitioner characteristics build a solid foundation for further understanding and engagement with the subject of personal mid-life/career renewal.]

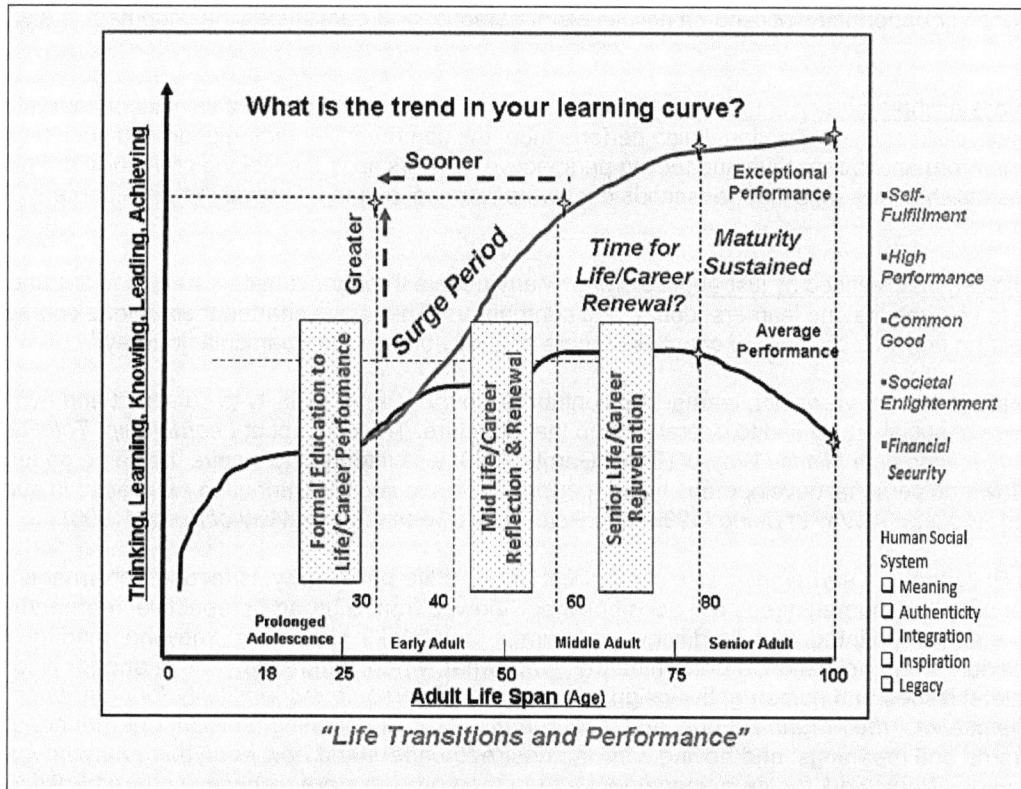

Figure 14-2

Learnership Development Process. Our description of learnership early in Chapter One proposed that it consisted of philosophical perspectives, architectural structures, and practical behaviors that together establish a distinctive human preference for action that we said was a recognizable "way-of-being." A short review of these aspects of learnership will serve to focus our attention and assist in summarizing what has been presented and learned in this book. (Reference Figure 14-3)

Learning is a complex human activity with the object of knowledge creation and use in virtually all human affairs. And, learners are people with an ability to learn although the development of this ability and willingness to use it varies widely across the general population. It follows, then, that there should be a term to describe people who are exceptional and influential learners, the breadth of their capabilities, and the extent of their influence on others. Learnership is the suggested term, and it is derived from: (1) *learner* – one who seeks to learn or to gain knowledge through experience or study, and (2) *–ship (suffix)* – to show or possess a quality, state, or condition. Additionally, learnership captures the essence and skill of leader*ship* in which people are skillful in influencing others. Some distinctive features of learnership are:

1. Learnership is an *activity* in the service of knowledge, its creation, and its application. Highly developed skill in learnership virtually assures highly developed and comprehensive use of knowledge across multiple interdisciplinary social systems. In today's terminology it could be said that learnership makes the concept of "Total Knowledge Management" (TKM) a distinct possibility.

2. Learnership is about *learning*, and about being a *learner*. More importantly, it's about the journey that begins when we *learn to become a skilled and purposeful learner* and make a lifelong commitment to create and realize our individual potential.

3. Learnership is about *knowing* and how lifelong learning leads to the acquisition and storage of information and knowledge that may be employed in a multifaceted manner to become an "intelligent and competent person." The more knowledge we can acquire, store, access, and apply in a timely and rational manner the more efficient and effective we become in all aspects of our lives.

4. Learnership is about *leading*, and about influencing action. Learning leads to knowledge but knowledge without action denies the learner and others the growth and development they may value. The ability of leaders to create a

sense of urgency or opportunity focused on new levels of personal or organizational development is a significant attribute.

5. Learnership is a whole-person competence. The objective of learnership is to be a significant catalyst in the pursuit of personal self-fulfillment, organizational high performance, the community common good and societal human enlightenment. From an introspective and feeling perspective learnership is the lifelong crafting of our potential *to become*; to establish a presence that transcends our own existence, and to influence the development of future generations.

6. Learnership can be practiced by just about anyone. Many people throughout history have had the understanding and courage to become lifelong learners, doers, and contributors. They have charted their unique course, realized their own purpose, and enriched the lives of countless others as they pursued their particular journeys.

From a knowledge system viewpoint, learnership contributes to the learner's ability to construct and evolve his or her own knowledge of social reality and to operate within that structure. The concept of *Learnership: Total Learning, Knowing, and Leading as a Mindful Way-of Being* (Garrity 2009) was intended to inspire the same generative perspective towards personal development, higher performance and social contribution expressed in such seminal works as Carl Rodgers' *A Way of Being* (1980) and Peter Vaill's *Learning as a Way of Being* (1996).

Learnership Philosophy. *Learnership*, as a component of one's life philosophy, is focused on what is worth knowing and doing, and on how human needs are accomplished. Viewed from a broad perspective, learnership practitioners maintain an integrative worldview that frames their thinking, learning, knowing, leading, and goal-seeking behavior. Their inclination to determine the: who, what, when, where, why, how, and for whom on a wide range of societal issues and human activity signifies a *sense of personal responsibility for contributing to the welfare of themselves, their organizations, and their communities*. Maintaining a broad, open-minded perspective on life's patterns and meanings; and having a strong desire to understand *how everything may be integrated into a compelling mental framework* for life management and human progress are distinctive characteristics of the learnership practitioner's philosophy of life.

On the philosophical level, learnership may be understood and appreciated as enthusiasm to participate in life and contribute to human progress by engaging in a broad set of mutually supportive and symbiotic practices that enrich peoples' knowledge and understanding. *Learning to learn, and to use what is learned for the betterment of humankind is an essential characteristic of the learnership philosophy.* Specific emphasis is placed on:

1. Purpose and Meaning – A commitment to engage with others in answering life's basic questions:

    a. What do I stand for? (*A sense of purpose*)
    b. How do I fit in with what has come before? (*A sense of history*)
    c. How am I related to other people/events/objectives? (*A sense of order*)
    d. What can I hope for as I take action? (*A sense of outcome*)

2. Societal Development – A willingness to embark on humanity's journey toward an understanding of life's mysteries, definition of human purpose, and equalization of societal opportunities.

3. Higher-Level-of-Being – A desire to motivate oneself and others to pursue a unique purpose, confront personal challenges, develop enlightened perspective, and experience mindful accomplishment.

4. Goal Achievement – A synthesis of skills in lifelong learning and knowledge management that leads toward the accomplishment of the universal human goals of self-fulfillment, high performance, the common good, and human enlightenment.

5. Responsibility and Motivation – A focus on the what, why, and how of lifelong learning and knowledge management so individuals may (1) take responsibility for their own learning and development, and (2) be motivated to achieve extraordinary results by first discovering their unique skills and purpose.

6. Role Performance – A capacity to improve human performance by applying the skills of kinship, fellowship, leadership, followership, stewardship, citizenship, statesmanship, and philanthropy.

7. Use of Dialogue – An appreciation for interpersonal dialogue anchored in open inquiry, rapid learning, interpersonal understanding, reasoned decision-making, and constructive action that achieves consensual results.

8. <u>Knowledge Management</u> – A willingness to participate in knowledge development focused on issues and challenges in the political, economic, social, technological, ecological, and geological spheres of societal knowledge and endeavor.

9. <u>Adult Life Cycle</u> – A developmental perspective on one's own lifetime that recognizes that individuals, organizations, and communities pass through phases of development, each with its own objectives, responsibilities, and rewards.

10. <u>Self-Renewal</u> – An understanding of life's uncertainty, complexity, and temporality – and the value of transformative learning for occasional reinvigoration of one's life and career.

11. <u>Learning-to-Learn</u> – A willingness to learn and apply contemporary skills and methods designed to increase the quality and speed of one's learning.

12. <u>Secular Reasoning</u> – A commitment to participate in the "public" sphere using fact-based objectivity and authentic subjectivity as opposed to supernatural appeals and narrowly prescribed dogma which can stress individual differences and limit collaboration.

13. <u>Future Orientation</u> – A desire to explore and discover new knowledge and innovations that can enhance the lives and careers of current and future individuals and societies.

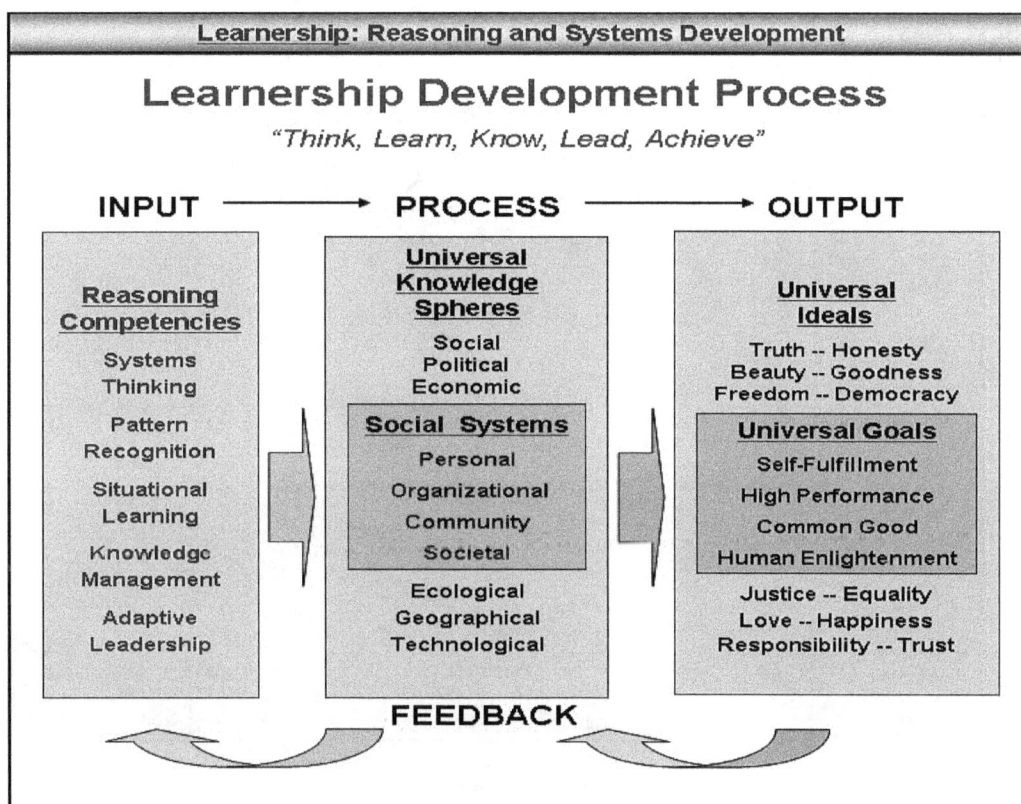

Learnership: Reasoning and Systems Development

Learnership Development Process

"Think, Learn, Know, Lead, Achieve"

INPUT ⟶ PROCESS ⟶ OUTPUT

Reasoning Competencies	**Universal Knowledge Spheres**	**Universal Ideals**
Systems Thinking	Social Political Economic	Truth -- Honesty Beauty -- Goodness Freedom -- Democracy
Pattern Recognition	**Social Systems** Personal	**Universal Goals** Self-Fulfillment
Situational Learning	Organizational Community	High Performance Common Good
Knowledge Management	Societal	Human Enlightenment
Adaptive Leadership	Ecological Geographical Technological	Justice -- Equality Love -- Happiness Responsibility -- Trust

FEEDBACK

Figure 14-3

<u>Learnership Architecture.</u> An architecture is established to provide a generally accepted, overarching description of significant relationships and dependencies among physical or intellectual objects that are components in building or maintaining specific capabilities and/or entities. The learnership architecture organizes the intellectual and experiential topics, functions, and behaviors necessary to understand and implement the learnership philosophy. The theoretical construct through which this occurs has *two major propositions*:

1. That *systems thinking, pattern recognition, situational learning, knowledge management and adaptive leadership* are foundational reasoning competencies that serve as building blocks for managing what is worth thinking, learning,

knowing, leading, and pursuing to select and achieve a holistic set of life goals: self-fulfillment, high performance, common good, and human enlightenment.

2. That to understand and accomplish these life goals, an architecture consisting of the five stated competencies and four interdependent social systems requires our thoughtful reflection. These four social systems consist of our *personal social system*, our *organizational social system*, our *community social system*, and the *societal social system* among nations and geopolitical networks.

The learnership development process initially described in chapter one of this book was systematically developed in chapters two through nine to become the *Learnership Integrated Systems Architecture* (LISA) depicted in the Interlude Section. The conceptual development and visual illustration of the LISA is the core theme of this text. In it (Figure 14-4), the reader can see all five learnership competencies and four social systems for integrated development interacting in dynamic complexity. The LISA is a learnership practitioner tool for remembering critical elements and dependencies when gathering, organizing, analyzing, using, and sharing information and knowledge during problem-solving and decision-making activities.

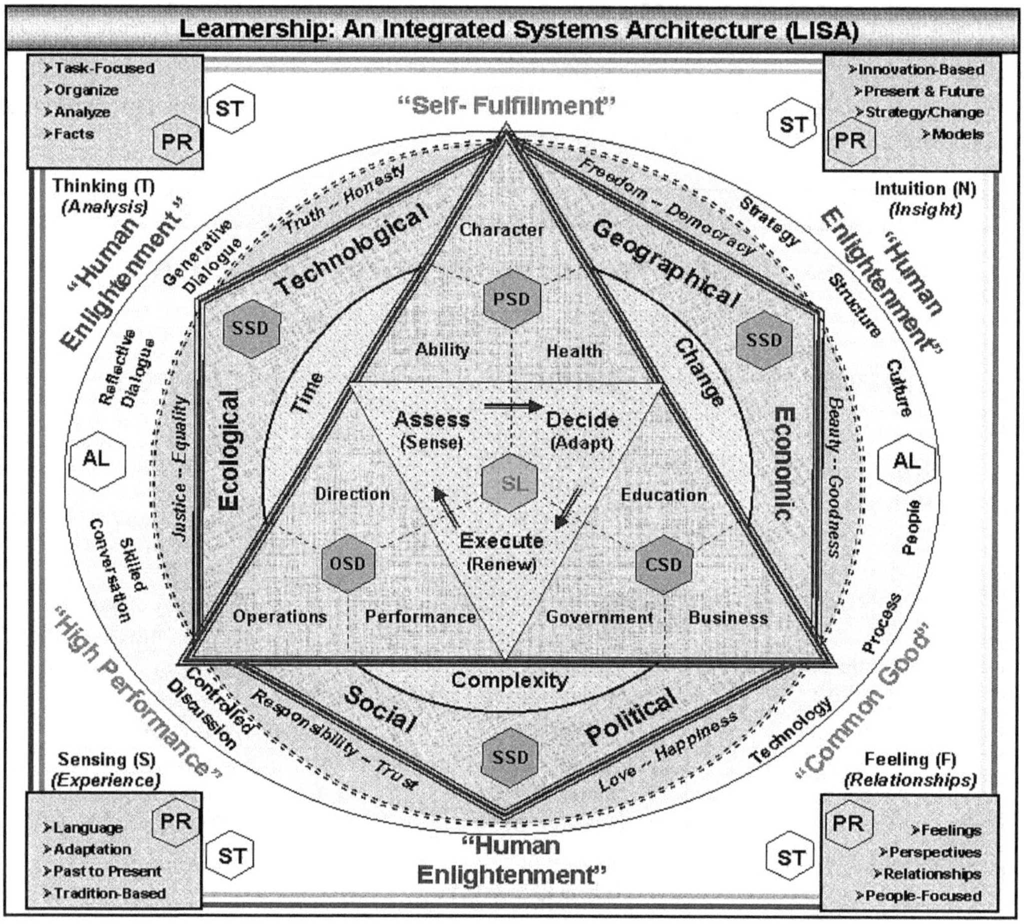

Figure 14-4

Learnership Practitioner. Learnership practitioner is the term used in this book to give special distinction to a special class of artful learners – those who immerse themselves in a lifelong quest for relevant learning, meaningful knowledge, and personal achievement. These people systematically increase their understanding of life's opportunities and challenges; develop their skills through questioning and learning; and produce products and services of value to others and themselves. These practitioners develop strong reasoning competencies, actively engage in social systems development, and strive to achieve synthesis in achieving their ultimate goals. The practitioner development process shown in Figures 14-5 and 14-6 serve as a pathway for individuals pursuing *learning, knowing and leading as a Mindful Way-of Being*, and the capabilities they develop and apply are listed below:

Learnership: Practitioner Characteristics (1 of 2)

1. **A desire to understand and appreciate** the fundamental theories in their fields of interest and education.

2. **A capacity for good cognitive and reflective skills.** But unlike their more academic counterparts, those skills are valued to the degree they align with their need to turn knowledge into action in a timely manner.

3. **A capacity for "learning-to-learn."** They get psychological rewards from the process of learning, and do it all their lives.

4. **A desire to operate as "free agent learners,"** and to be distinguished from many others that they are not bound by the limitations of the traditional educational curricula taught in formal school and classroom settings.

5. **A capacity for curiosity concerning the world around** them that enables them to achieve important career and life objectives through all phases of their adult lives.

6. **An enthusiasm to fully absorb their experiences** and to learn from them. They also become influential through their ability to put their knowledge into action.

7. **A willingness to embark on humanity's journey** toward mindful growth and an understanding of life's mysteries and human purpose.

8. **A desire to motivate themselves and others** to discover life's opportunities, pursue a unique purpose, confront personal challenges, develop enlightened perspective, and attain a higher level of being.

9. **An appreciation for interpersonal dialogue** based on open inquiry, rapid learning, interpersonal understanding, and reasoned decision making.

10. **A capacity to improve human relations** by exemplifying the principles of leadership, followership, stewardship, citizenship, fellowship, and statesmanship.

11. **An enthusiasm to participate in issue resolution** in the political, economic, social, technological, geographical, and ecological domains of societal knowledge and endeavor.

12. **A developmental perspective** on how individuals, organizations and communities progress through their respective phases of development – each with its own objectives, challenges and rewards.

13. **A systems perspective on societal learning and development** that balances the human need for both stability and change to achieve higher levels of societal development and performance.

Figure 14-5

Learnership: Practitioner Characteristics (2 of 2)

14. **A focus on personal learning and knowledge management** as key capabilities in the development of social systems: personal, organizational, community, and society.

15. **A personal commitment to learning reasoning competencies** that improve systems thinking, pattern recognition, situational learning, knowledge management, and adaptive leadership.

16. **An expectation that personal development depends primarily on being responsible** and responsive to the ever-changing political, economic and social forces occurring locally or on a global scale.

17. **A desire to replace differentiation with integration** as a lifelong practice – and the ultimate foundation for a mindful journey through life.

18. **A commitment to use knowledge, science, and practical experience** to challenge over-reliance on mysticism, superstition, and supernatural intervention.

19. **An advocate of the means between the extremes** – weighing personal rights with social responsibilities in order to negotiate adequate, inclusive outcomes.

20. **An appreciation for balancing inquiry and advocacy** in all one attempts to accomplish. No one knows all that could be known in life to reduce potential risk and to guarantee success.

21. **A capacity to perform multiple roles** such as consultant, coach, facilitator, student, mentor, thought leader, and project manager as situations require.

22. **Are people who systematically increase their understanding** of life's opportunities and challenges; develop their skills through questioning and learning; and produce products and services of value to themselves and others.

23. **Have historically been contributors to societal development** due to their "innovation and problem-solving" proclivities. They are people who have eclectic learning interests and acquire the skills and technologies that enable their achievements.

24. **Are "knowledge managers" in their own right** in that they continually identify, acquire, organize, use and share new found knowledge within their respective social systems.

25. **A willingness to apply the Learnership Integrated Systems Architecture** (LISA) model at all levels of personal and social systems development.

Figure 14-6

Learnership Mindful Way of Being. *Learnership practitioners* are people who systematically increase their understanding of life's opportunities and challenges; develop their skills through questioning and learning; and produce products and services of value to themselves and others. They are knowledge managers in that they continually identify, acquire, organize, use and share new found knowledge within their respective social systems. They learn and lead within their personal domains, they develop and apply knowledge practices and tools in their organizational roles, and they contribute as informed problem-solvers within their local communities. Using learnership, they seek to optimize the integration of their personal *self-fulfillment*, organizational *high performance*, community *common good*, and societal *human enlightenment*. They may even experience what Csikszentmihalyi (*Flow*, 1990), Senge et al (*Presence*, 2007), and Langer (*Mindfulness*, (1989) have eloquently described in their well-regarded writings. This is the learnership practitioner's vibrant and rewarding *mindful way-of-being* wherein learned people with significant understanding of interdisciplinary concepts, analytical frameworks and tools, and skilled in reasoning and decision making processes can solve problems and lead civilized societal development.

Social Systems Development

Integrated Pathways for Adult Development. This chapter reuses the Personal Systems Development Life Cycle Model introduced in Chapter Ten which is now shown as Figure 14-7. Once again, the *horizontal axis* represents a notional distribution of the adult life span, and the *vertical axis* displays selected dimensions of cognitive and emotional reasoning that may be used to discuss practical elements of human development. Particular emphasis is on the *Mid-Life/Career Transition* marker that often serves the individual as a re-awakening, a warning, and/or an opportunity to *make things right* while there is time to do so. The transition from the *Early* to *Middle Adult* stage is our main interest in this chapter.

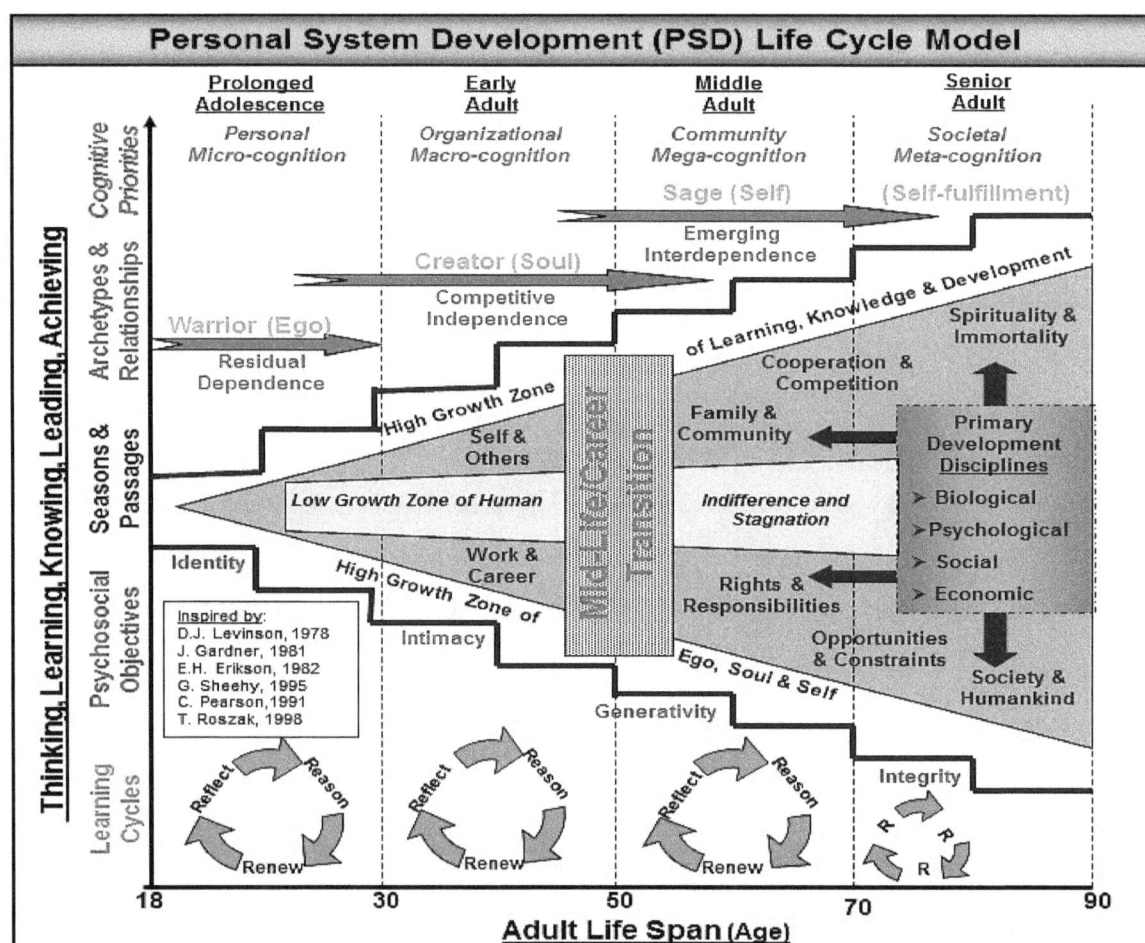

Figure 14-7

[**Author's Note**: A review of the dimensions of reasoning and development illustrated in Figure 14-7 is a useful prelude to the detailed perspectives and observations provided further-on in this chapter. The five sets of developmental activities and one special learning experience and challenge (Mid-Life/Career Transition), are summarized below: Using Figure 14-7 for reference, readers are invited to reflect on their own development and positioning in the figure in terms of the following topics. Where are you along your path of growth and development?]

1. Cognitive Priorities – The *Learnership Integrated Systems Architecture* (LISA) envisions four levels of social systems development, each one requiring its own level of personal cognitive activity in which we come to understand our unique purpose and our relationship with others in society. We realize both the breadth and depth of our interrelationships as we sequentially shift our mental energies from (1) *personal micro- cognition* when it is "all about us" as we pass through prolonged adolescence; (2) through *organizational macro-cognition* when we take on the responsibility of family and career, (3) through *community mega-cognition* as we invest additional time to help manage and guide the future of our local communities (city, county, state); and lastly (4) to *societal meta-cognition* when we have lived the majority of our lives and begin to take measure of our larger world (our nation, the world's nations) and our place in it – our search for a *sense of wholeness and completion.*

2. Learning Cycles – The vertical scale identifies five major categories of activities that generally unfold in an overlapping, but systematic manner. As each of these activities moves through the sequential time periods, other opportunities for lifelong learning and development are presented, but of course are optional. The *reflect-reason-renew cycle* inserted in each age period is a reminder that there are distinct cognitive and emotional insights available to each of us as we continue to grow and develop.

3. Psychological Objectives – As we move through our stages of adult development, we experience psycho-social changes. In the *prolonged adolescence* period our *identity* and personal *ego* are foremost in our attention. Who are we; what is our purpose; and how will our needs be satisfied are the questions that need to be answered. When we move to the *early adult* period our concerns expand to include getting in touch with ourselves (*soul*) and others (*intimacy*) at a deeper level. In *middle adult life* we evolve again as we attempt to gain a full understanding of what we really have become (*self*) and how we can begin to share with posterity (*generativity*) the best of our knowledge and insight. Lastly, if we are healthy and lucky, we transition into the *senior adult* level of psychological *integrity* when our interests, knowledge and accomplishments converge into mindfulness and *self-fulfillment.*

4. Archetypes and Relationships – Four distinctive periods of growth are recognizable across the human life cycle in terms of representative archetypes, psychological drivers and levels of dependence. The first three symbiotic relationships are: Warrior (*Ego*) – *Dependence*; Creator (*Soul*) – *Independence*; and Sage (*Self*) – *Interdependence*. In the last stage, personal *Self-fulfillment* is the culmination of a life well-lived. The learnership philosophy and architecture requires that self-fulfillment to be optimally achieved, that is, be supported by high performance, the common good, and human enlightenment achieved in the other social systems domains.

5. Seasons and Passages – Running horizontally through the middle of the model is a conceptual vision of how each of us could hopefully become self-fulfilled. This vision is the space between the *High Growth Zone of Human Knowledge and Development and the High Growth Zone of Ego, Soul and Self.* Our ever-expanding acquisition of learning, knowledge and skills permits us to master the challenges in each time period, refine and maintain our focus, and experience a well-lived and successful life. It is important, however, to acknowledge the reality that given the unequal allocation of knowledge and resources among most social groups, a significant portion of each population will enter what is termed the *Low Growth Zone of Human Indifference and Stagnation.* Once in this zone, an immense effort is required to re-emerge and get back onto the road of development for successful living.

[**Author's Note**: The mid-life/career challenge is to use the months, even years in this period, to invest in significant reflection, learning, and planning for renewed focus and energy. Additional education, new experiences, and conversations with a wider range of colleagues and contacts are helpful techniques to identify opportunities for development and greater purpose. New visions, goals, and strategies are all possible when this time period is used effectively.]

Learnership for Self-Renewal. A major audience for this book from its early conception has been those individuals

1. In the throes of their *mid-life/career transition*

2. Who are managing the *generative stage* of their adult life cycle

3. Who are focused on planning their senior adult *self-fulfillment* activities. The learnership philosophy, architecture, and practices offer a holistic and integrated approach for practicing *self-renewal* in a systematic, meaningful manner. John Gardner has written extensively on this subject (*Self-Fulfillment: The Individual and the Innovative Society* (1981) and some of his insights are summarized here for consideration – particularly by those actively transitioning to another stage of their lives:

1. <u>Self-Development</u> – "For self-renewing men and women the development of their own potentialities and the process of self-discovery never end…Exploration of the full range of our own potentialities is not something that we can safely leave to the chances of life. It is something to be pursued systematically, or at least avidly, to the end of our days." (pp.10-11)

2. <u>Self-Knowledge</u> – Human beings have always employed an enormous variety of clever devices for running away from themselves, the modern world is particularly rich in such stratagems." (p.12)

3. <u>Courage to Fail</u> – "We pay a heavy price for our fear of failure…If you want to keep on learning, you must keep on risking failure – all your life. It's as simple as that." (p.14)

4. <u>Love</u> – "The joy and suffering of those we love are part of our own experience. We feel their triumphs and defeats, their hopes and fears, their anger and pity, and our lives are richer for it." (p.15)

5. <u>Motivation</u> – "All of us cannot spend all our time pursuing our deepest convictions. But all of us…should be doing something about which we care deeply. If we are to escape the prison of the self, it must be something not essentially egocentric in nature." (p.16)

6. <u>Innovation</u> – "Today even the most potent innovators are unlikely to be effective unless their work coincides with a crisis, or a series of crises, that put people in a mood to accept innovation." (p.29)

7. <u>Individuality and its Limits</u> – "The moral for all of us is clear. We have a duty to nourish those qualities within ourselves that make us free and morally responsible beings. And we have an equally compelling duty to honor values beyond the self." (p.93)

8. <u>Moral Decay and Renewal</u> – "In a pluralistic society consensus must necessarily be sought at what one might call a *middle level of values*. Obviously it cannot deal with the surface trivialities on manners and daily customs; neither can it sound the depths. It can deal with fairly fundamental values governing man's behavior and with concepts such as *freedom* and *justice*. But those values float over still-deeper reaches of philosophic and religious beliefs…that gain their strength from man's deepest nature…to force consensus would be intolerable…*so a pluralistic society wisely seeks to establish its consensus in the middle depths*." (p.118)

[**Author's Note 1**: An appropriate reminder at this juncture is that the learnership philosophy is anchored to a set of *Universal Goals and Ideals* that virtually all educated and reasonable people, organizations, communities, and societies would likely support and attempt to attain. The four *Goals* are: *self-fulfillment, high performance, the common good,* and *human enlightenment*. The six pairs of *Ideals* thought to be sufficient for inspiring morality in a pluralistic society are: *Truth-Honesty, Freedom-Democracy, Beauty-Goodness, Love-Happiness, Responsibility-Trust,* and *Justice-Equality*.]

[**Author's Note 2**: Gardner's observation on "moral decay and renewal," above, is particularly insightful in that it recognizes that an extremely valuable aspect of a pluralistic democratic society is that a wide range of deeply held beliefs can be expressed and compete for attention in the public sphere. However, when those with strong beliefs or self-serving purposes attempt to seize or manipulate some aspect of American public policy or governance to favor their views – thereby disadvantaging other groups and beliefs in the process – they should be perceived as being out-of-bounds. The excessively wealthy, powerful, and/or charismatic people among us are still entitled to the one vote per person rule of democracy. The middle ground, where the vast majority of American citizens can participate in social, economic, and political affairs without threats and intimidation from self-absorbed individuals and groups, must be protected. Attempting to exclude or dominate others, whether those others are in the minority or majority status violates the American vision of freedom and justice.]

<u>Dealing with Loss</u>. Judith Viorst, author of *Necessary Losses: The Loves, Illusions, Dependencies and Impossible Expectations that all of Us have to Give Up in Order to Grow* (1986) has much to say on life transitions and the predictable changes in most everyone's sense of self as they proceed through their respective life cycles. Viorst quotes research psychologist Daniel Levinson on the process of separation and loss people experience as they move through various life phases and transitions: "The task of a developmental transition is to terminate a time in one's life; to accept the losses the termination entails; to review and evaluate the past; to decide which aspects of the past to keep and which to reject; and to consider one's wishes and possibilities for the future. One is suspended between the past and the future, and struggling to overcome the gaps that separate them. Much from the past must be given up – separated from, cut out of one's life, rejected in anger, renounced in sadness or grief. And there is much that can be used as a basis for the future. Changes must be attempted in both self and world." (p.266)

Viorst proceeds with her own story with the comment that: "…at about forty, those bridging years which take us from early to middle adulthood, Levinson calls this time the Mid-Life Transition. For most of us it's a crisis – a mid-life crisis. I have had one of my own…life begins at forty, we're told; we're getting better, not older; if Sophia Loren is what middle age is, it ain't bad. But before we can come to some positive view of the others side of the mountain, we need to acknowledge that middle age is sad, because – not all at once, but bit by bit and day by day – we lose and leave and let go of our young self." (p.267)

Viorst, the prolific writer of numerous books of poetry and prose and a contributing editor to Redbook magazine, continues with a series of insightful observations that illuminate the subject of this chapter. A synopsis of her factual, but sometimes humorous comments is presented here, in sequence, to capture the chaos of mid-life crisis:

1. The mid-life decline of youthful good looks is far more wounding for women than for men, for men can be wrinkled and balding and in other ways battered by time and still be viewed as sexually attractive.

2. Being physically attractive counts much more in a women's life than in a man's…identified as it is for women, with youthfulness, does not stand up well to age…a woman may fear aging because age will steal her power – her sexual power to attract a man.

3. And we may start to feel that this is a time of always letting go, of one thing after another after another: Our waistlines, Our vigor, Our sense of adventure, Our 20/20 vision, Our trust in justice.

4. We feel shaken. We feel scared. We do not feel safe. The center's not holding, and things are falling apart.

5. We want a second opinion that says; 'Don't you worry, you are going to live forever.'

6. We find in every ache and bodily change and diminished capacity intimations of our own mortality.

7. In mid-life we discover that we are destined to become our parents' parent. Few of us have factored that into our life's *plan.*

8. As past realities start to collapse, we challenge the self-definitions that have sustained us, finding that everything seems up for grabs, questioning who we are and what it is we are trying to be, and whether, in this life of ours, the only life we have, our achievements and our goals hold any value.

9. Faced with the losses that mid-life has already brought, or is soon to bring, faced with a sense of finiteness and mortality, few of us will renounce our youth with anticipation of gain. And many of us will fight it all the way.

10. The *change-resisters* defy the realities of time by holding on to their power and to their non-negotiable ways of doing things. The *youth seekers* do not want to stand pat; they want to go back in time. They liked what they had and want to have it again. The *psychosomatic sufferers* trade off psychic distress for physical ills, including heart attacks and perhaps even cancer. The *self-improvers* distract themselves by filling up their time; they are running too fast to notice what they have lost." (pp.268-272)

So, what can we do to manage our way through our mid-life transition or crisis? Can we get back into control of our mind and emotions? Can we reflect on our early life learning and renew ourselves for the later life that follows? And, what is it that we need to know or do differently, anyway? For what purpose? Viorst gives us a clue: "Integration – the unifying of seemingly opposite tendencies – is seen as the grand achievement of mid-life. But of course it's a process we've met with previously. It began with our childhood struggle to heal the split between good and bad mother, to heal the split between devil and angel me, to balance our wish for attachment with our wish to be separate and free. The struggle – now on a higher level – continues. And so we strive to integrate:

1. Our feminine self with our masculine self

2. Our creative self with the self that knows inner and outer destructiveness

3. Our separate self that must die alone with a self that craves connection and immortality

4. A wiser, more seasoned middle-aged self with the youthful zest of the self we are leaving behind. Our season is autumn; our springtime and summer are done." (p.282)

[**Author's Note**: And, now for the good news! The average 50 year old today can expect to live for 30 more years – half will live longer and experience more vitality, more enjoyment, and more learning and accomplishment than ever before in the history of humankind. Notwithstanding Viorst's well documented depiction of loss and diminution expertly written in the 1980s, we are now a new people; much healthier, still striving to find meaning, still in control of our ultimate destiny, and much more involved in leading and mentoring others to become all they can be.]

Insight into Mid-Life/Career Transition and Renewal

We shall renew neither ourselves, nor our society, nor our troubled world unless
we share a vision of something worth saving. — John Gardner

Mid-Life/Career Opportunities. This stage of cognitive and emotional awareness, and even discomfort, generally occurs in the 45-55 age range, but can vary significantly depending on an individual's particular life circumstances. It is often a period of disruptive feelings, cognitive dilemmas, and forced reflection on matters having to do with one's life purpose, progress, happiness, experiences, and increasing age. Challenges include moving from independency to interdependency and from intimacy to generativity. Greater emphasis is required on learning and preparing for later life and ensuring a *second life* identity and adulthood commensurate with the knowledge and experience already gained. Throwing off old stereotypes, letting go of outgrown priorities, and developing real clarity about one's own capabilities, purpose, and impact on posterity are the usual areas for concern and purposeful renewal.

The Future of Humanity. In *Crucial Questions about the Future* (1991), futurist Allen Tough poses several questions for our consideration regarding the future of humanity – questions such as: What is most important of all? Why do we act in ways that hurt our future? How can we achieve a satisfactory future? How can each person contribute? Discussing these questions and their potential solutions is fertile ground for everyone's meta-cognitive social development. The balance between what we can and should do for ourselves, and for others, becomes more obvious when conversations on topics such as these are organized, facilitated, and action is taken. Tough stimulates conversation by stating his views on what needs to be done to achieve an exceptional future in terms of five top priorities, future-relevant knowledge, and individual learning and change.

Five Top Priorities:

1. *Increase humanity's knowledge of world problems and social change* much faster than the problems themselves increase. A three-fold increase in future-relevant research, inquiry, disciplined thinking, knowledge, synthesis, and wisdom would probably be a highly beneficial expenditure, not a waste of money.

2. *Disseminate this knowledge* to political leaders, other key decision-makers, and the general public of all ages through education, books, mass media, and fresh approaches.

3. *Improve governance*, including planning, policies, governmental structure, and public administration. We need to sharply reduce the influence of unduly narrow and short-term pressures on all aspects of governance.

4. *Avoid the worst catastrophes* of all. In particular; world wars, population growth, deterioration of the planet, and the resulting misery and poverty

5. *Foster positive directions and improvement*. Not only avoid catastrophes, but devote effort and innovation toward improving various aspects of civilization.

Future-Relevant Knowledge:

1. We need more thoughtful *understanding of any traditional or false beliefs* that threaten our future, to decide why so much human behavior undermines a flourishing future for human civilization, and determine the most urgent and appropriate actions that we need to take.

2. We need *vigorous thinking and research* about the arrangements and institutions that are likely to produce individual and group behavior that is in the long-term interests of human civilization.

3. We need to determine how to get human *society to take its own future seriously* and to act accordingly.

4. There is a great need for *deep thoughtfulness*, from wrestling with the most important question of all, for seeing the big picture, and for acquiring wisdom and a broad perspective.

Individual Learning and Change:

1. *Never in history have so many people known so little* about the matters most important to their occupational, social, personal, and political future. This ignorance is a powder keg.

2. Once enough people *care about the future of human civilization*, choosing and implementing the necessary priorities and policies will be easier than at present.

3. Adult educators, college and university instructors, teachers, writers, artists, composers, public speakers, book publishers, and the mass media will all play a crucial role in *fostering the necessary learning and changes* in the people of every nation.

[**Author's Note**: These questions draw upon the thinking, learning, knowing, leading, and achieving learnership competencies presented in Chapters Five through Nine of this Handbook. Fundamentally, Tough is calling for the development and application of mature, adult reasoning by societal leaders. Nothing less than the future of human civilization is at stake.]

Timeless Pursuit of Purpose, Legacy and Spirituality. In their new book: *Live Smart after 50: The Expert's Guide to Life Planning for Uncertain Times* (2013) the Life Planning Network authors present a chapter entitled "Living in 3D: Enrich Your Life with Purpose, Legacy and Spirituality. They suggest that when people pass their respective mid-lives they become increasingly motivated by *meaning and authenticity* and by *experiencing significance rather than success.* Questions such as: What do I want to contribute to make the world a little better? And, what legacies will we leave for succeeding generations? Also on the spiritual level, they are often concerned with their connection to a larger purpose, spirit, knowledge, nature or God. Questions that need to be asked and answered are:

1. "What is my *Purpose*? – Ask yourself: What is my purpose? Why am I here? What is my life about? What do I really want to do with my time, money and talents?

2. What *Legacy* should I leave? – Ask yourself: What does the world need that calls forth my natural talents? What values, wisdom and life lessons do I want to pass on? What specific, tangible things do I want to leave behind?

3. What is my *Spiritual* nature? – Ask yourself: Who am I and why am I here? What will bring meaning into my life. Is there something wiser and bigger than myself that I can count on for guidance and support?

The authors make their emphasis on personal spiritual growth by summarizing the relationship between having a purpose that can lead towards the achievement of *wholeness*. They say: "If we live authentically and on purpose, we will inevitably leave legacies of the heart and become attentive to and guide by the larger mystery of life."

[**Author's Note**: This reference was discovered near the end of writing this Handbook, and is a comprehensive listing of practical learning and action that can empower people over 50 to continue to learn and grow. Other topics of discussion will be used from this LPN book during the training activities being planned for workgroup development, and group members should acquire their own copy for class participation.]

Longevity, Identity, and Moral Character. In *The Fountain of Youth: Cultural, Scientific, and Ethical Perspectives on a Biomedical Goal* (2004) editors Stephen Post and Robert Binstock present the research and perspective of numerous experts on extending youth and long life. A useful presentation is that made by Christine Overall in "Longevity, Identity, and Moral Character: A Feminist Approach." Overall says: "My point is that greater longevity, as a widespread social phenomenon, requires the development of new moral system. The reason is that as the human life span increases, different stages of life are being and will continue to be redefined…increasing longevity creates opportunities for new ways of living. For example (paraphrased):

1. What schooling and education mean will be redefined. *Lifelong learning* in the form of formal and informal schooling will permit people to continue to acquire skills, information, and understanding as need and interest dictate.

2. What marriage, partnership, friendship, sexuality, and gender mean will be redefined. There will be opportunities for more relationships at various points during the longer life.

3. What it means to be father, mother, parent, grandparent, and family will be redefined. Increasing technological control over conception, contraception, gestation, and birth make it possible to manage the timing and nature of reproductive behavior.

4. What it means to work, have a job or career, and retire will need to be redefined engage in several careers over a lifetime – and to choose the time and type of one's retirement."
All this will lead to the adoption of new roles and new identities as our life stages are reinterpreted. And, with new and redefined life stages, human beings will have the prospect of taking up new values and responsibilities." (pp.291-293)
"Morals and virtues will change with an increased focus on 'How should I live?' and 'What kind of person should I be?' and less on the more authoritarian notion of chastity and sexual purity...the focus of virtue ethics is on the individual agent and his or her character rather than in acts or rules. Character is the composite of the psychological qualities, both mental and moral, that make one a distinct person." (p.293)

Christine Overall presents *feminist virtue ethics* as a major contributor to the future social order in that it allows for the possibility that appropriate and genuine virtues may be defined in relation to the specific communities in which they are needed and valued...Since feminist ethics emphasizes the importance of personal and social contexts both in shaping moral challenges and in providing data for responding to them, it requires us to be aware of contexts of aging and of increasing longevity...Some virtues, like honesty and truthfulness may be important for a lifetime, while others, such as receptiveness and or assertiveness, may be more useful at some stages than at others. She states that "Ethicists ought not to make moral evaluations or construct moral theory in a vacuum. Morality and moral systems cannot be analyzed and assessed without attention to the social context in which moral values are transmitted and moral decisions are made. Ethicists must take into account the effects and implications of cultural categories such as gender, race, class, sexual orientation, ability, and age, and their attendant belief systems and stereotypes." (pp.295-296)

Christine Overall summarizes her thesis by saying that: "A longer life provides a greater chance for human flourishing, for learning virtues, and for living a good life. The person who seeks to foster in herself the appropriate virtues and who is successful to at least some degree is the person who will best be able to adapt to a changing environment, who will be more likely to transform herself, and will be able to flourish within the context of a longer life." (p.300)

[**Author's Note 1**: Much scientific activity today revolves around pro-longevity, countermanding the effects of senescence (aging), and helping people have choice in defining their own immortality. While we cannot be certain regarding the concept of life after death, we can absolutely begin to manage how posterity remembers us and our time on this planet. Perhaps taking time to assess and reflect on our state of mid-life/career development, we can plan and activate a second life stage of growth that is fully rewarding while we live, and is uniquely respected after we pass from this level of existence.]

[**Author's Note 2**: The next two perspectives look more closely into the needs and motivation of people as they move into the mid-life/career stage of their lives and begin to become concerned about how well their lives are really turning out. Questions such as: (1) Is this where I thought I would be, and still want to be? And, (2) Am I fulfilling the vision and goals I once held for myself? are often asked. Their answers may not be satisfactory. Their time for self-assessment and reflection might now be at hand and "second life/career" planning may need to begin.]

1. Answering Your Call – John Schuster, author of *Answering Your Call: A Guide for Living Your Deepest Purpose* (2003), is an executive coach, trainer, and speaker with a lifetime of learning and experience devoted to helping people achieve their best and become fulfilled. In his book he explains how successful people negotiate their lives and careers in the pursuit of their "calling," and why that pursuit, conducted in a mindful manner, yields meaningful long-term results. For purposes of this learnership discussion, six topics have been created within which a few of Schuster's developmental recommendations are summarized and presented for reflection:

2. Recognize Your Calling – A *call* is an influential awareness, part intellectual and part emotional, that motivates us to go beyond the surface level of an issue or topic in order to accomplish something of lasting purpose. A call may be heard as an inner voice, visually recognized as a mental picture, or a learning experience that commands our attention and stimulates us to action. Open-minded, lifelong learners experience many more calls due to their diversity of experience, accumulated knowledge, and interpersonal contacts. Calls are particularly notable as influencing factors affecting peoples' mid-life career transitions and personal crises. Schuster says: "Calls command that you attach yourself to something infinite and lasting so you can escape the life you thought you deserved and replace it with the life you were meant for." (p.14)

3. Outlast Your Saboteurs – Saboteurs are those occasional people you meet and need to work with whose self-importance and need for authority and control cause them to overlook, dismiss, ridicule or steal your ideas, contributions, and value. Saboteurs have narrow visions of others, withhold support and encouragement, and see the world as a small place dominated by competitive practices. The antidote is to acknowledge your situation; network and connect with open-minded and collaborative colleagues; develop greater tolerance by understanding the others' limitations and stop exposing your weaknesses to them; build courage and endurance as you pull away from their influence; and commit to benefiting others with your newfound insight concerning saboteurs. (pp.61-70)

4. Hear Your Evocateurs – Evocateurs evoke out of other people and their circumstances the skills, gifts, and potential they did not know they had. They understand the innate human longing to be more than we are, and help motivate us in ways that build direction and confidence. Evocateurs see more than others see in us and share their insights as "teachable moments" from which we can draw knowledge and energy. They work on the level of personal "identity" in that they coach us to understand our purpose and abilities so we can grow into an identity of our choosing. (pp.76-84)

5. Become a Provocateur – Provocateurs recognize unfairness, injustice, or other situations that restrain human growth and development, and they speak out in ways to draw attention to these matters. Sometimes they provoke others into action, sometimes they lead the action as provocateurs themselves, but always they work within the larger social system to create significant change for the betterment of humankind. To be successful requires a commitment to long-run, sometimes subtle activism because important change is often incremental. A compelling future vision, a sense of humor, a willingness for controversy, and a strong circle of likeminded friends helps maintain the energy and commitment for long-term change. (pp.97-102)

6. Constrain Your Ego – Our personality is the outer shell for our "egos" and "selves." *Self* may be understood as our higher will or essence striving for authenticity and meaning – the transcendent part of our connection to others and the universe. The *ego* is the operative part of our self in action, it is what we show to others as we create roles for ourselves and go about making life work for us. Schuster says: "Even the best-inclined egos pose challenges and can taint even our most noble thoughts with their own concerns." We must be alert for our ego's tendency toward dominance, and work to temper its potentially negative impact. (pp.112-114)

7. Pursue Your Purpose – "Answering a series of calls over our lifetimes will sanctify our lives and exalt our existence. A life is to be lived, a job is to be worked, a role is to be fulfilled. But a calling is something to become worthy of, to make a commitment to, to go on an extended journey for. A calling is like the bugle sound at a great coronation – the Notes ring out above the crowd and draw our attention to the highest of intentions and human possibilities." (pp.138-139)

Everyone can expect a "call" to occur a number of times in our lives. If we are alert to our own emerging capabilities within the context of our life and career interests and experiences we will have opportunity and choice. Being open to change and prepared for action are keys to our success.

Reclaiming the Fire. In *Reclaiming the Fire: How Successful People Overcome Burnout* (2001), author Steven Berglas uses his knowledge and experience as a clinical psychologist to dissect the causes and implications of high performer burnout. His data indicates that a large percentage of successful boomer generation people are not truly happy with their lives and actually experience ennui and depression that stems from their failure to self-actualize amid all their trappings of success. The causes of this problem include:

1. Being ambitious, but not for intrinsic reasons.

2. The inability to turn success into a significant life-altering occasion.

3. The stress of having to prove oneself over and over again.

The failure to establish a personal sense of purpose and meaning within the larger scope of life Berglas' solution focuses on coaching clients through a personal transformation that:

1. Reduces the perceived risk of failure.

2. Creates conditions to rebuild success and self-esteem.

3. Expands areas of interest and potential involvement.

4. Reframes opportunities for contribution and service.

Of particular value is Berglas' understanding of the built-in narcissism that underpins the drive and success of many accomplished people. He Notes that self-made people generate feelings of confidence in others because they are independent, but the degree to which these very people have dysfunctional attitudes and behaviors that belie their success – and lead to their own discomfort – is not usually recognized.

Berglas suggests that as these successful but troubled people move through life they become ripe for self-assessment that can open the doors to personal growth, renewal, and future opportunities. For those in the 45-55 age range who may be moving through their mid-life/career transition period, their learning might be that they can and should develop and embrace the *generative stage* of development toward which they are moving.

Berglas attributes the concept of generativity and its importance in human development to Erik Erickson who said: "Evolution has made man a teaching as well as a learning animal, for dependency and maturity are reciprocal: mature man needs to be needed, and maturity is guided by the nature of that which must be cared for. Generativity, then, is primarily the concern for establishing and guiding the next generation." (p.169) "People, who aim to achieve generativity utilize their wisdom and mental excellence in ways that allow them to realize their dreams – while enabling successive generations to also realize theirs. "The essence…to building a living legacy is the *attitude realignment* that is step one in the process of reclaiming the fire: divesting the worship for success and with it the squalid cash interpretation put on the word. In its place substitute 'relationships,' which have come to be called connectivity…connectivity is the result of taking responsibility for the intellectual and emotional development of others." (p183)

Clearly, this theme of moving away from ego-driven independence toward an enlarged self-identity that values social engagement and interdependence is insightful coaching for those who have been unusually successful in their past.

Mid-Career Perspectives

The Second Act of Your Life. Many of us were already embroiled in our mid-life/career issues before we realized that a crossroad had been reached without our even knowing it. Being invested in schooling, building a career, and raising a family had become so time-consuming we did not realize that our 40s had arrived and while much had gone well, not everything was to our liking. Without having stopped to take inventory of where we were going we were continuing to rush forward toward undefined personal and organizational objectives. When our situation change dramatically because of a career and/or life loss or redirection we were thrown into a situation of stress and uncertainty from which extricating ourselves was a major challenge.

In their book *Second Acts: Creating the Life You Really Want, Building the Career You Truly Desire* (2003) authors Stephen Pollan and Mark Levine comment that many people live two lives in one lifetime, and that being prepared for that eventuality makes that more likely to happen. What they recommend to get things started is much like the Boy Scout motto: "Be Prepared." In Chapter Three they say to "Develop the Second Act Mindset." That is, lay the building blocks that will enable the mid-life/careerist to understand what may be of significant value or interest to them and to recognize emerging opportunities when they begin to take form. Their nine building blocks are stated and interpreted here as follows:

1. Reach out for help…and give it back in return – Research your interests and explore the goals and opportunities you want to pursue with others when the right time comes. Don't be afraid to discuss your interest with others and to seek their input.

2. Embrace conflicting needs…don't settle – Use periods of stability and reliable income to prepare for your opportunity that might just be around the corner. Don't over extend, reserve some time and income which will be needed.

3. Cast lots of irons in the fire – Constantly explore, learn, and try new approaches; collaborate with new people with different experiences.

4. Go through open doors – Seek to engage others doing things similar to what you would like to do. Learn all you can from them, partner when possible, and do whatever make sense to continue moving forward.

5 Don't be ashamed of your shortcomings…be candid – Do a self-assessment of your current state of preparation, your strengths and weaknesses, and actions necessary to fill any gaps.

6. Practice bifocal vision – Maintain expertise in your current career while simultaneously building knowledge and skills for your next position.

7. Just row…leave the steering to God – Favorable events cannot always be planned, but they may emerge differently than anticipated so be ready to grab them when they emerge – whatever their basis, setting, or cause.

8. Embrace your incomparability – Everyone is one of a kind and not "average." Average is a mathematical concept not an actual place or capability. Seize on your special talents not on what everyone has in common.

9. The Keystone – have hope in the future – Be a hopeful realist. Avoid self-defeating pessimism by grabbing occasional opportunities as they come by.

The authors suggest that without this preparation a period of confusion and even chaos may ensue reducing the person's focus, efficiency, and increasing their level of unhealthful stress.

New Careers, New Workplace. In *JobShift: How to Prosper in a Workplace Without Jobs* (1994) author William Bridges explains that the past vision of U.S. jobs that entailed Monday to Friday, nine to five, twelve months a year, with promotions and then pensions beginning at age sixty-five are going, going, and will mostly be gone. Newly designed work methods and increased business focus on control of labor costs have enabled greater American competitiveness based on the economies from labor. Updated with today's competitive global marketplace, explosion of technological innovation, and benefits from internet-enhanced virtual operations; the jobs of old are an endangered species. Bridges warns that "*All* the jobs in today's economy are temporary – for two reasons:

a. The job is a social artifact on the wane along with the (past social and economic) conditions that created it

b. That work arrangements themselves are temporary in the sense they are created to meet the productivity needs in an immediate but changing situation." (p.55)

He comments that: "In the future your job security will depend on your developing three characteristics as a worker and as a person: *employability* (your momentary abilities and attitudes*), vendor-mindedness* (your being hired to accomplish a specific task), *and resiliency* (your ability to bend but not break and to deal with uncertainty).

Given how the cards have become stacked against being able to use the same knowledge and skills learned and applied for a lifetime of dedicated work with one firm or industry, Bridges encourages most people to prepare for inevitable changes while we still have the time and temporary financial stability to do so. He summarizes his guidance (p.60) as:

1. Learn to see every potential work situation, inside an organization as well as outside it, as a market. (Some day you may be marketing yourself.)

2. Survey your desires, abilities, temperament, and assets (DATA) and recycle them into a different and more viable "product." (Someday your services may be someone else's product.)

3. Build a business plan for your own personal enterprise, refine it as you move forward, and begin to see yourself as being in business for yourself. (Some day you may actually do this.)

4. Learn about the psychological impacts of life in this new world of work – and make a plan to handle them. (Don't be surprised by the emotional challenge.)

Concerning the last item (psychological impacts) Bridges reminds his readers of the research work done by Elizabeth Kubler-Ross on the process of mourning/grieving observed in a large number of people undergoing significant loss. The stages of denial, anger, bargaining, despair, and acceptance are usually witnessed – and people being traumatized by forced career change are known to experience many of these stages of adjustment. Using the Kubler-Ross framework, Bridges recommends a process that people in need of making such a transition adopt a procedure (p.195) along the following, overlapping lines:

1. An ending, during which one disengages from and breaks the old identity with "the way things were.

2. A neutral zone, when one is in between two ways of doing and being, having lost the old and not yet having found a way to live with the new.

3. A new beginning, after which one again feels at home and productive in "the way things are" with a new identity based on new conditions.

In his conclusion, Bridges offers a discerning perspective: "Life is a teacher. Periodically it destroys how things have been and forces us to say good-bye to how we have done things and define ourselves. The external details of the change may be unique and confusing, but the real transitional task is always the same: to let go of some reality or strategy or personal identity that characterized the previous leg of our journey. The question life asks is always, 'What is it time for you to say good-bye to?" (p.220)

[**Author's Note**: Everyone's the project manager of his or her own life and career. Periodically we need to plan, execute, and evaluate; and to re-plan, re-execute, and re-evaluate. These recurring, situational learning cycles must be accomplished in a timely, accurate, and informative manner if we are to optimize our personal, organizational, community, and societal capabilities and accomplishments. It is particularly important that today's workers prepare for a lifetime of work activity given the downsizing and outsourcing practices of American industry, the disappearance of traditional retirement programs, and the looming bankruptcy of social security and Medicare.]

Time Out for an Unreal Career. According to Ernie Zelinski author of *Real Success without a Real Job* (2006), a person does not have a "real job" if he or she works for him or herself, and loves the activity (work?) they choose (have?) to do. This change in how income earning activity is both perceived and conducted makes a big difference in how much we value our work-life. Many people not only change jobs they decide to work for themselves, and an AARP Policy Institute report says that the self-employed in the U.S. constitute over 10 percent of workers but account for 66 percent of the millionaires. A high percentage of individuals who go into business for themselves have the knowledge and commitment to overcome obstacles and to succeed in providing the products and services others find essential to their needs. Zelinski offers the following "advantages and disadvantages of working for oneself.

Advantages:

1. Flexibility to set your own work hours
2. Opportunity to use special skills and talents.
3. Opportunity to be innovative and creative.
4. No boss to tell you what to do.
5. Convenience and cost-saving of not having to commute every day.
6. Greater earning potential and a more direct connection between effort and reward.
7. Tax benefits.
8. Variety offered by working on a number of different projects and the mobility of working anywhere.

Disadvantages:

1. Capital usually needed to start a business
2. Uncertain income makes it hard to plan financially
3. Lack of paid-for-benefits such as health insurance, sick leave, and a retirement plan
4. Uncertain work hours
5. Pressure of having sole responsibility for your livelihood
6. Possibility of business failure and loss of capital
7. Perceptions of family and friends who think negatively that you don't have a real job
8. Having to chase clients to get paid" (pp.52-53)

The author continues with the comment: "…if you are a baby boomer quickly approaching retirement, you may be concerned whether you are saving enough for retirement. The good news is that many people may be overestimating how much money they need once they leave the workforce. Several research studies show that people generally spend a lot less as they age…With a retirement pension, you can retire early from your present boring job and find another job that is more interesting even if it does not pay as much. (p.75) This observation is valuable for anyone concerned that they would like to change career direction, but are not certain they can afford to do so. If you have been systematically preparing for an opportunity to make a strategic change, serious thought should given to whether the right time for a new direction is at hand. Zelinski reports that: "Clearly, for those stuck in a rut, early retirement from their present career is a way to replace it with one filled with joy and meaning. For retirees who are financially stable, starting a business is another option. Boredom is a key reason why retirees start a business." (p.76)

On the motivational front, Zelinski suggests that: "Do your best and the best of things will come your way…Doing your best should be a lifelong journey. The measure of your success is not how well you have done relative to anyone else in society. Instead, the measure of your success should be how well you have used your creativity and ability to achieve worthy goals, regardless of how humble those goals are. Doing your best means rising above the mediocrity so prevalent in society today. (pp.219-221)

Your Right Livelihood. In her *Discovering Your Right Livelihood* (1987), author Marsha Sinetar explains that many people are dutifully at work seeking to "pay their bills" without really understanding what they could be doing that is more in line with their unique purpose, knowledge, skills, and temperament. She argues for everyone to discover a way of earning a living that uses their talent and permits a degree of Maslow's "self-actualization" to be realized. According to Sinetar, "Right Livelihood is an idea about work which is linked to the natural order of things. It is doing our best at what we do best. The rewards that follow are inevitable and manifold…The original concept of Right Livelihood apparently comes from the teachings of Buddha, who described it as work consciously chosen, done with full awareness and care, and leading to enlightenment." (p.10) She continues to say that: "Right Livelihood, in both its ancient and contemporary sense, embodies self-expression, commitment, mindfulness, and conscious choice – it is a way of being. Work is:

1. Conscious Choice – The very best way to relate to our work is to choose it ourselves.

2. A Way of Being – Conducting our lives so as to experience the fullest life

3. Self-Expression – A natural vehicle for expressing our attitudes, feelings, and perceptions for meaningful productivity.

4. Commitment – The willingness to work hard on behalf of something we feel is meaningful.

5. Mindfulness – Deep involvement in the work itself and in the way in which each task is performed" (pp.11-17)

Sinetar cautions her readers to be aware that *resistance* is always lurking wherever people begin to think about making significant change in their lives or careers. To her, resistance is the subtle inner mechanism that urges us to back away from life's difficulties and demands. It intensifies the difficulties of problems, task, and routines. It undermines enthusiasm, energy, and our finest intentions. (p.82) "She contrasts the difference between those who succeed and those who continually get in their own way:

1. Successful People – Those who experience more of what they desire in life seem to be people who do not back away from problems, growth or difficult tasks…if we observe the behaviors of those people we think are successful (e.g., healthy, creative, materially and professionally fulfilled), we see that they do things willingly that others only talk about doing, but avoid…Discipline becomes a powerful tool for getting what they really want out of life.

2. Unsuccessful People – Such is not the case for the unsuccessful or the unfulfilled. Their habit patterns help them avoid challenges, demands, and the use of their talents. They prefer comfort over challenge, safety over growth, invisibility over visibility…They avoid confrontation and risk at all costs. Thus, professionally and personally, they back away from what would help them become more useful to themselves and others." (p.83)

[**Author's Note**: This author appreciates that people are different in knowledge, skills, and temperament and that these differences make certain occupations and endeavors better for some than for others. Extroverts are likely to pursue different interests and experiences than introverts, the left brain dominant tend to think and act somewhat differently than the right brain dominant, and intuition has more usefulness for many then sensing. Still, her emphasis on individuals having the courage, perseverance, and motivation to seek careers well suited to their talents and to be assertive in pursuit of high performance is commendable.]

Your Mid-Career Rewiring. Authors Jeri Sedler and Rick Miners book entitled *Don't Retire, Rewire!* (2003) provides a unique point of view on the mid-career transition. From their experience in the executive search and transition coaching they discovered that many people dislike the term "retiring." Instead, they found that "rewiring" was more suitable in that it expressed the attitude of today's generation of middle career workers who desire to be redirected toward other life pursuits rather than to retire. The positive aspect of becoming a *rewiree* is that numerous alternatives to traditional retirement are openly explored, selected, and pursued with vigor by people seeing themselves as much too young and energetic to be retirees. According to the authors, "retiring is a going *from* and rewiring is a going *to.*" (p.xiii) Sedler and Miners survey of the reasons people fail to find retirement satisfactory include:

1. Retired for the wrong reasons.
2. Didn't realize the emotional side of retiring.
3. Didn't know myself as well as I thought I did.
4. Didn't have a plan.
5. Expected retirement to evolve on it's own.
6. Thought rest, leisure, and recreation would be enough.
7. Didn't stay connected with society.
8. Expected my partner to be my social life.
9. Didn't know what I was leaving behind.

10. Was overcome by boredom. (p.19)

In order counter the negative effects of a failed retirement, the authors work with their clients to develop new mindset that lead toward successful rewiring. Their top 10 ingredients are:

1. A positive attitude.
2. Good health.
3. An awareness of the financial picture.
4. An open mind.
5. A desire to stay connected.
6. Self-knowledge.
7. Meaningful interests or a desire to discover them.
8. Intellectual curiosity.
9. A willingness to explore.
10. Flexibility.

When working with their clients, Sedler and Miners help identify the major "drivers" that motivate them to action. Some examples include the need for accomplishment, creativity, fulfillment, identity, lifelong learning, recognition, self-esteem, and visibility. These drivers, among many others, are the basis for making choices among different types of activities, organizations, relationships and commitments on which the clients will spend their time and energy. Given that each of us has only limited time in life to learn, develop, achieve and contribute, learning to prioritize our efforts is most valuable.

Once Sedler and Miners have gotten their clients to accept that:

1. Their rewiring helps going to a new mental place and capability
2. Their prioritized drivers become the foundation for moving forward
3. They help to choose the activities that support those drivers
4. They help to create a vision for the new person and career that is evolving
5. They help to prepare an action plan to ensure real progress is made toward the *new way of working and being.*

Your Professional Presence. No matter how much knowledge or experience we have as individuals or as team members, the social nature of our work and relationships makes it essential that we adhere reasonably well to the code of dress and manners generally accepted in our organizations and communities. Notwithstanding the current trends in American society toward more casual dress and informal conversation, the majority of people holding the reigns of power and influence expect to work with people whose dress, attitude, and conversational style appeal to the sensibilities of co-workers and customers. In all but a few business environments a tendency toward what might be termed "conservative" or "respectful" presentation of oneself is desired.

An unclean or disheveled appearance, exposed tattoos or body piercing, loud or annoying speech, or improper decorum or manners communicates to others that we might not be the "right fit" for teamwork or customer contact. While some might argue that "personal rights" in terms of these and other factors are at stake, there is little to be gained by going to an extreme to win a point with others who can affect our employability or opportunity to do the career we truly seek to pursue. Common sense indicates that a degree of care be employed when operating in our public arenas.

It is not our purpose in this text to delve into the details of individuals' professional presence or executive image other than to provide a couple of excellent sources for readers to get specific information and to make their own personal adjustments as they deem to be appropriate. Two books that are filled with contemporary information are: *5 Steps to Professional Presence* (2001) by Susan Bixler and Lisa Scherrer Dugan, and *Your Executive Image* (2000) by Victoria Seitz. For those transitioning in their mid-life/career phase of development it is especially useful to note that while "age is just a number" as many say, we still live in a society that likes to celebrate the healthy, vibrant, and cheerful attributes of people. Developing and/or maintaining these characteristics in our social activities help us in building friendships and collegial relationships with those both younger and older than ourselves.

Wealth Generation and Financial Security in Retirement

[**Author's Note 1:** This topic is part of an ongoing conversation that began in Chapter 2 and continued through Chapter Twelve. It is suggested that material be reviewed by Mid-Life and Senior readers of this chapter before proceeding further. The best way is to proceed directly to this Handbook's Epilogue, Item C, "Wealth Generation and

Financial Security." *Chapter Fourteen's content is only available here in its own chapter, and includes additional items of concern and action applicable to Chapter Fifteen.*]

[**Author's Note 2:** Because one of the best sources for consumer guidance on personal wealth and financial guidance is from Suze Orman's work and products, our readers are requested to go to Amazon.com and purchase her latest book entitled: *The Money Class* (2011) available as new and for resale, and follow her on the web (www.suzeorman.com). The discussion on Mid-Life Transition and Senior Rejuvenation in this Handbook will be accomplished assuming each participant has their own copy of Suze's textbook.]

Figure 10-4 that is located in both Chapter Ten and the Epilogue, is included below (14-8) for quick reference. Its significance is that it illustrates a number of financial topics that adults will need to consider and prioritize as they continue their journey from their 20s to their 80s. It features income derived from employment, savings, investments and social services – and then proposes that income be moved to other investments and products suitable for retirement planning and sustainment. There are a variety of strategies a person can devise on their journey depending on their rate of money and asset accumulation, and the economic variations the nation at large experiences.

Suze's Retirement Planning Suggestions

1. Getting Going in Your 20s and 30s: *[How many of us really tried to do this? How did that work out?]*
    a. Use time as an asset – Start saving early for great long term results
    b. Use your employer's savings and investment plans.
    c. Use 401(k)s, IRAs and Roth IRAs
    d. Stock investing and dollar cost averaging

2. Fine-tuning in Your 40s and 50s: *[Some of us are here now. Are we ready to finally start?]*
    a. Your mortgage – when and how to pay it off
    b. The "work until age 67" work plan
    c. Delay Social Security benefit payments
    d. Estimate retirement income
    e. Best investments outside your 401(k)
    f. Plan for healthcare, Medicare and Long-Term Care
    g. Choose only fee-based financial planners (no commissions)

3. Living in Retirement: *[Now we need to get serious. What have we done (will do) to succeed?]*
    a. Focus on affordability; your needs over your wants
    b. Protect your retirement savings from others' expectations
    c. Choose only dividend paying stocks and EFTs from low cost brokers
    d. Avoid long-term bonds and bond funds
    e. Go slow on selecting annuities (can be complex and deceptive)
    f. Eliminate mortgages when choosing to stay in same home
    g. Include donations and giving back to the community

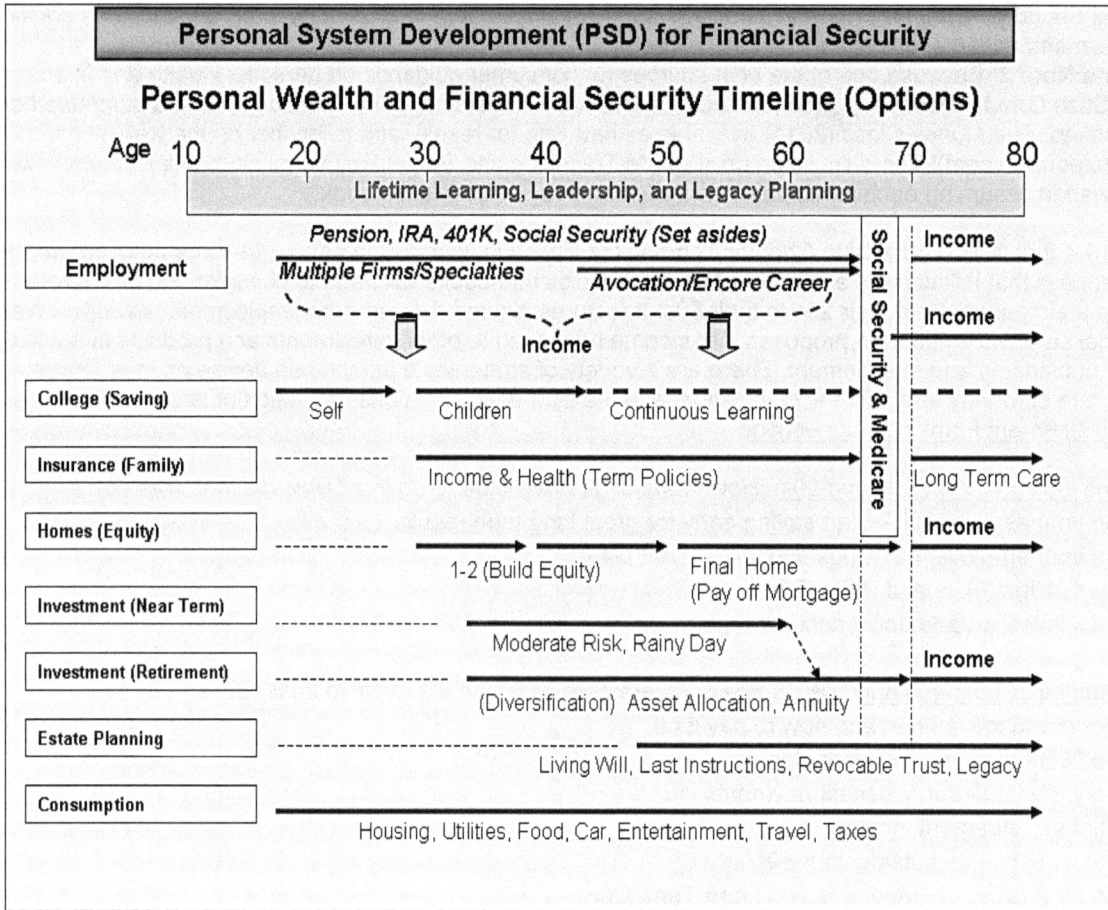

Figure 14-8

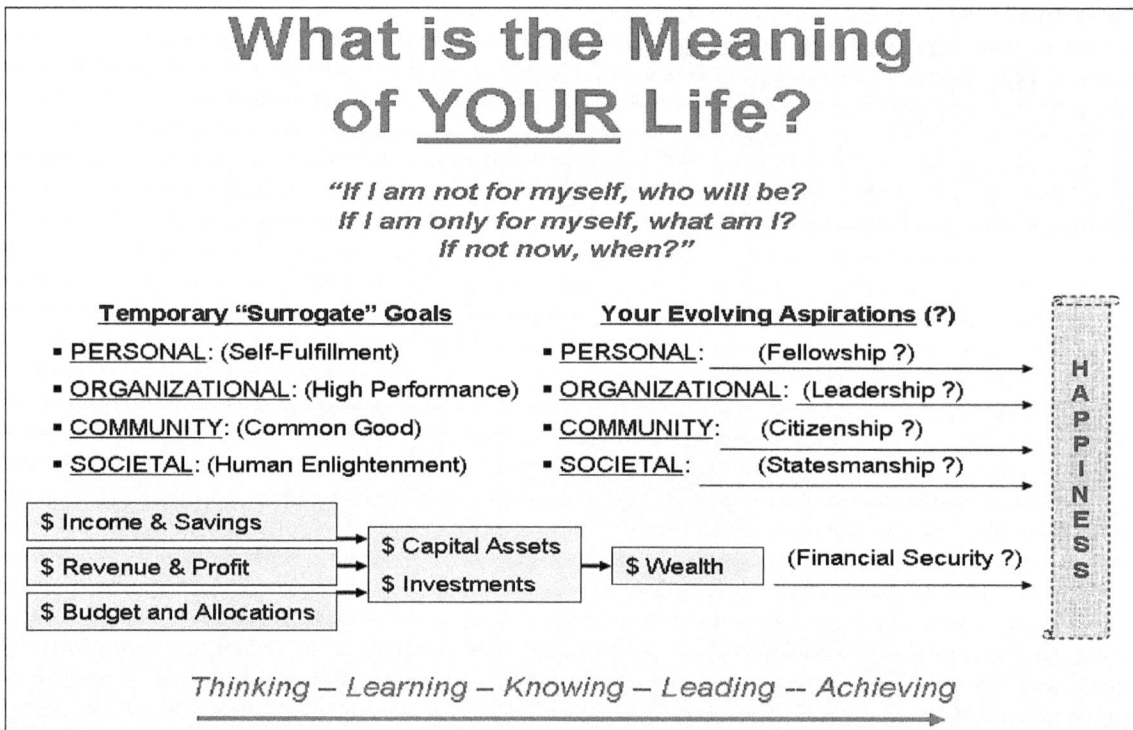

Figure 14-9

Summarization, Integration and Motivation (50+)

This is the last Handbook update on discovering the meaning of your life. The surrogate goals and evolving aspirations (Figure 14-9) should now become more definitive after completing the major chapters in this Handbook. Your goals and follow-on commitments should be clarified by now for final use in the e-book products and legacy letters that will become a significant part of you living and after death legacies.

Meaning, Happiness and Mindfulness

It has been said that human consciousness makes us aware of our mortality, and that the inevitability of our death often creates an imperative for us to produce something of worth that represents our societal mark and timeless immortality. This view suggests we have a fundamental desire to create a sense of order in the lives we live, to live up to the social standards we accept, and to establish our self-esteem as a counterbalance to our mortal anxiety. By leaving a positive mark on society it may be said we led a good life – and our lives were meaningful.

A meaningful life can also be thought of as our pursuit of satisfaction which occurs from establishing a reinforcing linkage between two interdependent desires: (1) a global way to understand and feel our inclusion, purpose, usefulness, value and self-worth, and (2) to cognitively and emotionally believe that life itself is meaningful. Within the field of positive psychology it has been proposed that one's sense of living a meaningful life results in fewer negative emotions and a lower sense of personal risk in life matters.

Having a meaningful life both in the present, and with the expectation of a continuation into the longer term, is a significant aspect of achieving a happiness -- a mental or emotional state of well-being defined by positive or pleasant emotions ranging from contentment or joy. The degree of happiness that each person can practically attain varies across individual differences and circumstances. Poet John Chiardi's essay on "Is Everybody Happy" (Example Essays.com) proclaims that "the long and trying road that runs toward what you want to become is also the road to happiness." Apparently, the road to happiness should be understood as the combination of the pursuit of material things (Western world emphasis on "having") and the pursuit of a spirituality (Eastern world emphasis on "being"). Chiardi opines that a mixture of both is required to fill a human need and that "having" and "being" are always partial stops on the road toward "becoming."

A contribution of this Handbook for reader development and life management is the explanation and graphical representation provided on how *meaning* and *happiness* intersect (Figure 14-9). The construction of the intersection among our personal, organizational, community and societal lives offers a taxonomy and methodology for reflection and integration of the basic domains of human activity. The breadth and depth of topics and issues requiring consideration for human understanding are explained as elements of *mindfulness*.

Living a Life that Matters

Sometimes we might wonder whether we are living an existence that matters, or are we fooling ourselves and others of our intent or meaning in life. Are we simply reacting to the dictates of our primitive brain or are we pursuing a higher purpose such as a in a religious belief or the advancement of humanity. Meg Newhouse, author of *Legacies of the Heart*, suggests we learn to "live from the heart" which is an authentic way of being that does not allow us to do intentional harm to others. She comments we "live a good, enlightened life, and that there are excellent books, audios, and self-help programs that can help us do so."

For her suggestion to happen we would assume we have learned and developed the life-affirming feelings and emotions that contribute to societal progress. Also, we would likely have established a level of cognition where we understood the essence our being and how we could demonstrate that quality in our relationships in the pursuit of our personal life vision and mission. She makes a wise observation that this cognition and emotional capability evolves through life learning and experience and that "our purpose manifests differently in the second half of life where we attempt to become more significant people and make a difference.

The author notes that a large part of our development relies in our conscious, or even unconscious acceptance of others' influence (legacies) on who we evolve to become. If we recognize these legacies we have a *choice* to continue, stop, change or pass them on to others while we still live – or share them as recommendations to others after death. *Choice* occupies the time between our "Sense and Respond" or "Assess and Act" activity when problem-solving or opportunity- finding is pursued. Of note, Meg comments that her choice for the second half of life has been for "Positive Aging."

Regarding the subject of living a life that matters and being intentional about our legacies elicits attention toward the topic of the inevitable fact of our personal immortality. While this is not the most pleasant aspect for most people, it does cause reflection on which parts of ourselves we choose to emphasize. If the inheritances we have learned and adopted have been uplifting and aspirational of our loving and generous selves, it is likely we would be motivated to share that information with others we deem as important during our lives. The author believes "the heart trusts that if its motives are as pure as possible the ultimate impact will be positive."

1. The author provides six keys to learn and create a living legacy [edited], pages 184-5:

2. Live your legacy consciously now.

3. Live, as best you can, from the heart.

4. Consider your legacy inheritance, especially those pieces that strongly affect who you are. Strengthen your ability to choose whether and how you want to pass them on.

5. Be thoughtful about the legacies you left and those you still want to give, whether through your essence, words, actions, public legacies or personal artifacts.

6. Seek company and support for the legacy journey.

7. Enjoy the ride. Just because your journey is important does not give it leave to become a grim taskmaster.

Implications for Integral Learning and Social Systems Development

We now arrive at the *social systems domain* where the result of our knowledge building, with the assistance of the five learnership Interdisciplinary reasoning competencies, may be reviewed. The major determination for Mid-Life/Career Transition and Renewal is whether the knowledge recently created is "relevant" to the inquiry, study, problem or issue being considered. *Quite often a paradox occurs* at this juncture in which the conclusion reached appears to be inconsistent, conflicting or incompatible with what the individuals involved anticipated or desired. When analyzed, questions arise as to whether the Systems Thinking, Pattern Recognition or Situational Learning competencies have been utilized in an open, factual, unbiased, timely and convincing manner. That is, is the knowledge really correct and integral when considering that there are obvious limitations in people's minds and personal preferences – and their cultures, education, and beliefs are sometimes in conflict? Effective and valued knowledge will need to be judged by thinking and behavior as interpreted by skilled and experienced leaders of the *Mid-Life Transition* domains.

Conclusion
Every act of creation is first an act of destruction — Picasso

Self-Assessment and Renewal. A major focus of this book is on the interests and needs of mid-life and career adults. For readers in that demographic group this chapter has hopefully served as a opportunity for reflection, learning, and renewed commitment to make the second half of your life even better than the first. If you are a part of the baby boom generation, you never were going to be satisfied with the status quo. Now with some living under your belt you may have the mindset to really make a difference for yourself and others. If so, you are invited to participate in the American Learnership Forum.com. The primary requirement is for individuals to read this book, answer the questions at the end of each chapter, and join our web-based organization. From then on, you will have the opportunity to be an active participant in many of the learning and development projects being developed to include publishing your own e-books.

[**Author's Note**: Are the knowledge and skills you have acquired and using so far in your life sufficient for you to achieve your current goals, a meaningful life and a memorable legacy?]

Personal Reflection. This topic appears at the end of each chapter and is meant to serve two purposes: (1) be a reader's guide to main points and "takeaways," and (2) to encourage everyone to take a moment to engage their mental cognition and intuition on what the chapter means to them – especially at this time in their lives. Questions for chapter reflection follow immediately below; and for those readers inclined to maintain a self-assessment, your thoughts may be recorded in [My] Integral Life, Work, Wealth, Health and Legacy Success located at Appendix B.

Questions for Discussion:

1. How prepared are you to renew yourself and seek a more *meaningful life* and/or a more *rewarding career*? What are the major speed bumps holding you back?

2. Which of the authors and subjects introduced in this chapter spoke to you most forcefully? Do you now know how to take some steps forward? What are they?

3. Have you received your "calling" yet? If so, what do you now need to do to let go of some things and embrace some others so that you can begin making progress? If not, are you open to doing research and data gathering so as to prepare for your calling when it comes?

4. Are you financially secure enough to take some risk and redirect your life energy and career goals? If not, are there actions you can take to increase income or reduce expenses to eventually put yourself in a state of preparedness? Is there someone you can work with to achieve your objective?

5. Can you list two to three major learning points from this chapter that you want to keep in mind to improve your ability to manage your life and career transition?

6. Should you be making an entry into your *American Learnership for Life, Work, Wealth, Health and Legacy Success* at Appendix B?

Insights, Commitments and Skills

If you plan to participate in the *American Learnership for Life, Work, Wealth, Health and Legacy Success* self-development e-book experience, it is suggested you record your Insights, commitments and skills to be developed here in this chapter, and again in Appendix B:

My learning in terms of new insights, changing priorities, new commitments or skills I want to acquire:

1. Insights (Example): Remind myself that …

2. Commitments (Example): Continue to ask myself …

3. Skills (Example): Apply my knowledge and skills to …

Chapter Fifteen

Senior Rejuvenation, Authentic Living and Legacy Success

If you would not be forgotten, as soon as you are dead and rotten,
Either write things worth reading, or do things worth the writing.
Benjamin Franklin (Poor Richard's Almanac)

Major Chapter Topics

Senior Rejuvenation, Authentic Living and Legacy Success

The title of this Handbook: *Your Integral Life Matters: Create a Life and Legacy Management Mindset for Personal, Organizational, Community and Societal Success in the American Tradition* was chosen to inspire, motivate and stretch its readers beyond the normal boundaries that often limit human growth and development. Our realization is that life is often shorter than we think it should be, that it encourages us to value the time we have available, and that it appeals to us to think, learn, know, lead and achieve while we still can do so. If we also take action to ensure our story continues as a constructive influence beyond our demise; then we have optimized our lifetime value and contribution.

Some writers have said that the boomers will complete America's transformation into a gerontocracy as they take control of the nation's social and economic power. From this demographically and politically dominant position, they will have the potential to realize their full intellectual, social, and political influence, not as baby boomers but as elders." (Ken Dychtwald in *Age Power).* Notwithstanding Dychtwald's argument, here in 2016 it is arguable as to which generation has become the most dominant. The millennials receive the most product advertising, but the seniors control the most income and wealth. And that wealth has been obtained through knowledge, skills, and experience acquired over five or more decades. Many of those seniors are over sixty five years of age, and fully one-half of them will live past the age of eighty. As a group they are healthier than ever, involved in mental and physical rejuvenation, and are spending more of their available time considering the form and contents of their lives and future legacies. For many this is the time they have been waiting for most of their lives and they want these later years to be the most influential on posterity as they can achieve.

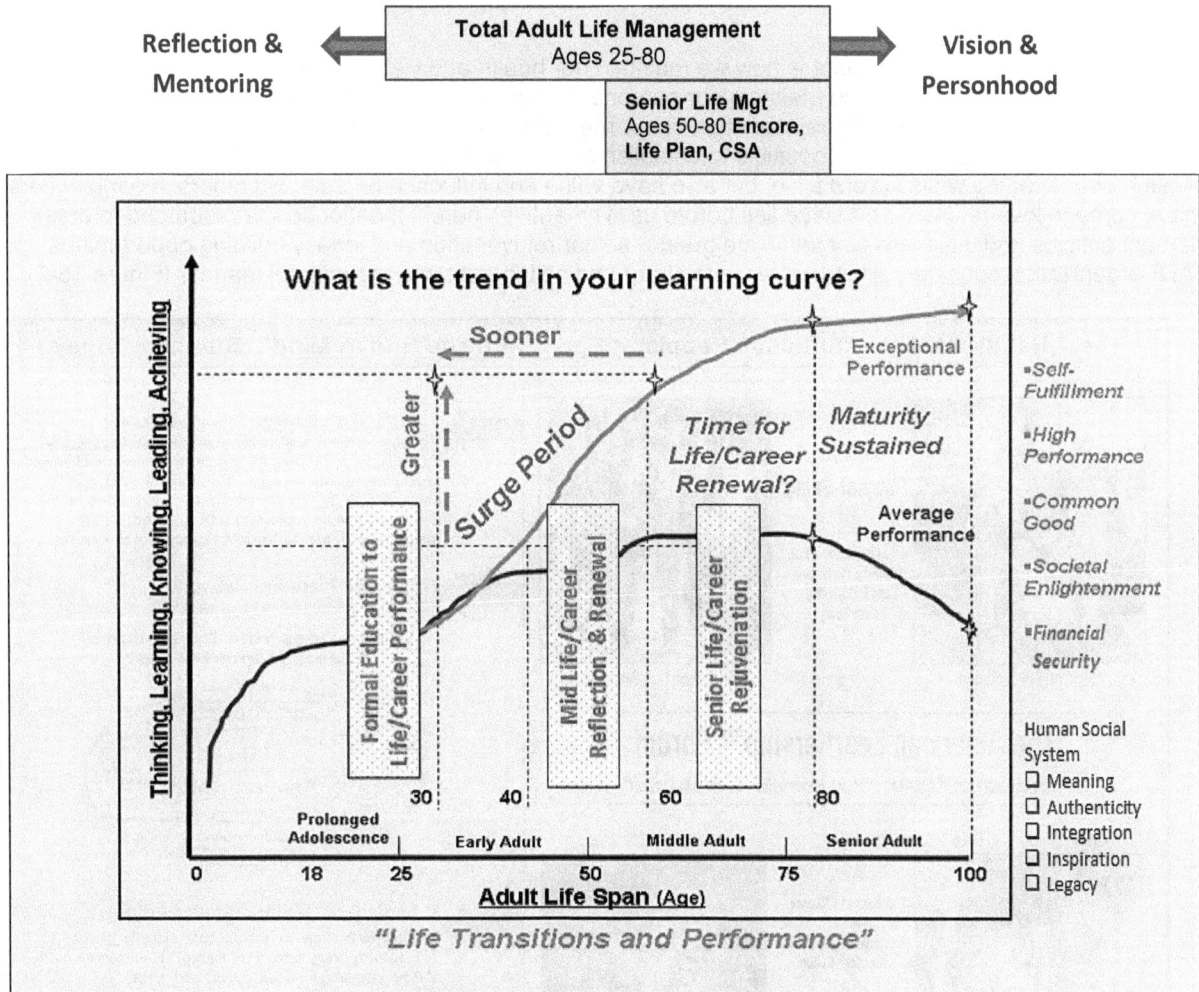

Figure 15-1

Lifelong Learning and Development

Lifelong learning and development is illustrated (Figure 15-1) as a notional lifetime of human growth and development in which people live their lives (emphasis on adults ages 25-80 on the X axis) and achieve knowledge, skills, abilities and achievement on the Y axis). Major points of transition are identified and representative graphs of development are shown wherein: **Blue** = average life trajectory and **Green** = highly developed achievement. The Green track is favored and attained through lifelong, attentive, and motivated, adaptive, learning – and is available to most people who adopt the American learnership principles and practices advocated in this Handbook.

A notable relationship is illustrated at the top of the graphic where ALF Total Adult Life Management focuses on adult development between ages 25 and 80 and begins to integrate (around age 50) with the Encore, Life Planning Network, and Society of Certified Senior Advisors positive aging senior programs already in operation and expansion. A useful way to understand the potential human value that can result is to view Learnership Life Management as a multi-disciplinary, whole brain, social meta-model that *creates a foundation for integral thinking, learning, knowing, leading, achieving many years before mid-life/career transition and senior renewal become an imperative for continued senior life success and contribution.*

Once the intersection of Learnership Life Management and the three Senior Life Management programs illustrated become mutually supportive, numerous concepts and projects are likely to become practical, resourced and implemented. This alliance is a purposeful objective of the "Your Integral Life Matters Handbook and Master Class." The opportunities within and among the contributing organizations can become even more extraordinary as age savvy and motivated seniors achieve additional purpose, learning, skills and motivation by contributing their talent to families, friends and communities.

Senior Connections

The topic for consideration at this point is how we maintain our health and viability while moving through this last phase of adult development. Is it possible to maintain our personal status quo, and also identify a new purpose, establish goals to achieve, and experience the rejuvenation of our mental and emotional processes so that more intense "life fulfillment" can be attained? And, is it possible to establish a series of ongoing life activities that not only have motivation and meaning while we are alive, but also have value and influence on selected others in earlier years that we have come to love respect. This issue lies before us. The entities herein mentioned are resourced to create and implement policies and initiatives that stimulate greater senior rejuvenation and legacy building opportunities – while the ALF organization considers additional ways to share and collaborate in a meaningful manner (Figure 15-2).

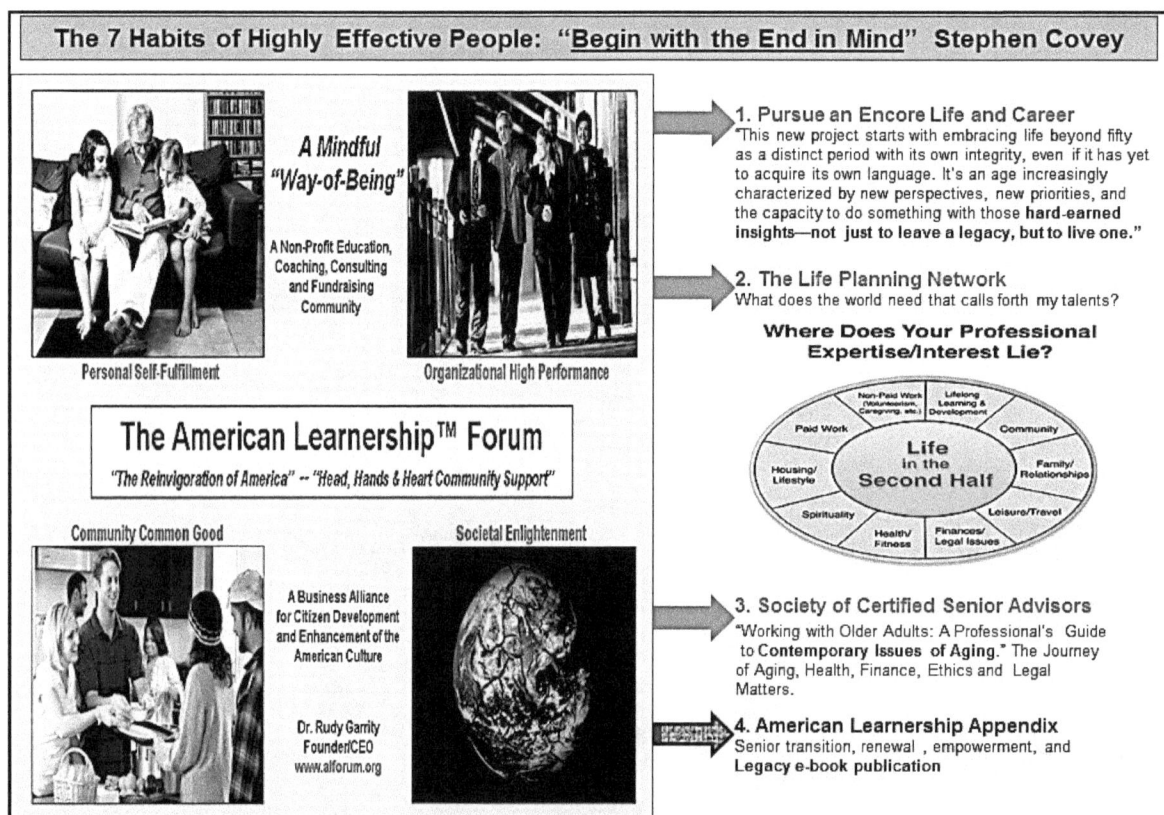

Figure 15-2

1. Pursue an Encore Life and Career. In the *Encore Career Handbook (2013)* introduction, Mark Freedman, founder and CEO of Encore.org suggests that a new life is open to current mid-life adults: "You've heard it all before. A gray wave of boomers is careening toward the second half of life, hitting retirement age, morphing suddenly into senior citizens, and bringing with them a new era of cross-generational conflict and economic despair." (Figure 15-2)

"Don't' believe it. Those of us at midlife and beyond are far from the scrap heap. We are poised to invent an entirely new stage of life - the encore years - between the end of midlife and anything resembling old-fashioned retirement."

"Society brands us as the young-old or the working retired. Maybe they should just call our predicament the oxymoronic years. On the one hand, we're implored to hang on to our former youth - sixty as the new forty it's said. On the other, "senior discounts" are dispensed indiscriminately at fifty or sixty. I'm all for saving a buck but the broader choice seems to be cling to the past or risk being sent off to some premature pasture."

"But sixty is not the new forty any more than it is the old seventy or eighty. It's the new sixty. And for that matter, fifty is the new fifty. Indeed, the whole post – midlife period is simply new territory and those of us flooding into this phase constitute a phenomenon unique to the twenty-first century…with close to 10,000 women and men a day crossing the midlife divide, it's high time to accelerate the social invention of the 'encore years.' This new project starts with embracing life beyond fifty as a distinct period with its own integrity, even if it has yet to acquire its own language. It's an age increasingly characterized by new perspectives, new priorities, and the capacity to do something with those hard-earned insights - not just to leave a legacy, but to live one."

"It also means recognizing that for most of us this period is a new stage of work, every bit as much as a new stage of life (who wants to play thirty years of golf – and who can afford it?). Indeed, a movement is afoot to fashion this next chapter into something we can genuinely look forward to. Millions are trading in the old dream of the freedom *from* work for a new one animated by what might be called the freedom *to* work. They are embracing encore careers, forging a new hybrid between the spirit of service and the practicality of continued income, looking for productive engagement that is not only meaningful but also means something beyond themselves."

"Some argue that this simply amounts to making virtue out of necessity. True enough, but what's wrong with virtue, or for that matter facing reality squarely with ingenuity? That goes for the nation too. We simply cannot afford to write off the most experienced segment of the population, consigning them to spend half their adult lives in a state of enforced leisure at a time that group is set to double in size – and at a juncture when the challenges facing the country in areas like education, health, and the environment are themselves spiralling."

"The encore career movement holds the potential to turn all this around, to create richer lives and a better society. And to do so on a grand scale. It promises the biggest potential human capital windfall since millions of women broke through to new productive roles in the 1960s and 1970s."

Marci Alboher is the author of the *Encore Career Handbook* (2013). Useful mid-life/career insights from reviewing a few of her chapter introductions are:

Understand the new world. "In the past one hundred years, the average life span in the United States has expanded from forty-seven to seventy-eight years. By any account, longer lives should be a cause for celebration. But all this extra time can also create anxiety. What do we do with these additional years?"

Learn what is out there. "You may know exactly what you want to do with this stage of your life. Or you may have no idea at all. It's possible that this is the first time in your life that you're asking what it is that you *want* to do. Not what you *can* do, Not what you *should* do. Not what *someone else* wants or expects you to do."

Perform self-assessment. "Money is a lot like sex. Everyone wants to know what everyone else is doing, but few people want to share what's happening in their own lives…there are a few things I can say with certainty. First, one of the biggest challenges of an encore transition – perhaps even bigger that the emotional side of things – is figuring out how to manage the financial side. Second, although people at every level of income find ways to move into an encore career, people who manage well financially have one critical thing in common: They have a good handle on what kind of lifestyle they want and how much money they need to support it."

Get comfortable with uncertainty. "For most people, transitions are intensely unsettling. So it's important to get comfortable with feelings of uncertainty – and to develop techniques to get you through any rough patches…you will no doubt hit a time when you are neither fully invested in what you have been doing, nor fully involved in what will be a new kind of work. When you're in that in-between nowhere space, expect to feel uneasy or even anxious."

Ask others for assistance. "People aren't just resources for ideas or sounding boards, they are also links to other communities, organizations and opportunities. Connecting yourself to new webs of ideas, people and organizations is fundamental not just for moving into a new stage of work but also for ensuing that you're effective in your new role when you get there. Expanding your circle also helps you find support along the way from like-minded folks who understand what you're going through and from those who can help you get there.

For those not comfortable with networking for various reasons, think of networking as a way to increase your capacity to give, not as a way to get others to do you a favor."

Update your skills. "It has been estimated that over 90 million people now participate in what is called adult or enrichment learning, and that adult learning is as much about job training as about expanding horizons. The latest research from Encore.org shows that 31 million people ages forty-four to seventy had increased by 20 percent over the last decade. When you're looking to retool in mid-life, some education or a new credential can help level the playing field and give you a better shot at a new job." Obtaining a new skill set, or even acquiring some advanced education may fill your learning gap.

Go Do Things." So maybe you're not sure of what encore direction to take, so you haven't taken action yet. Maybe you could "experiment" checking out what friends are doing or what volunteering opportunities might serve to get you started. Pro bono sharing of your skills and joining in some charitable activities might enhance relationship building and information gathering that could assist in making future contacts."

A CURRENT GRAY WAVE PROGRAM:
The Life Planning Network

In *Live Smart after 50: The Expert's Guide to Life Planning for Uncertain Times* (2013) the Life Planning Network authors suggest Living in 3D: Enrich Your Life with Purpose, Legacy and Spirituality – when people pass their respective mid-lives they become increasingly **motivated by meaning and authenticity and by experiencing significance rather than success**. They say: What do I want to contribute to make the world a little better? What **legacies** will we leave for succeeding generations?

What is my Purpose? Why am I here? What is my life about? What do I really want to do with my time, money and talents?

What Legacy should I leave? What does the world need that calls forth my talents? What values, wisdom and life lessons do I want to pass on? What tangible things do I want to leave behind?

What is my Spiritual nature? Who am I and why am I here? What will bring meaning into my life. Is there something wiser and bigger than myself that I can count on for guidance and support?

The authors recognize the achievement of *wholeness*. "**If we live *authentically* and on purpose, we will leave *legacies* of the heart and become attentive to and guide by the larger mystery of life.**"

Where Does Your Professional Expertise/Interest Lie?

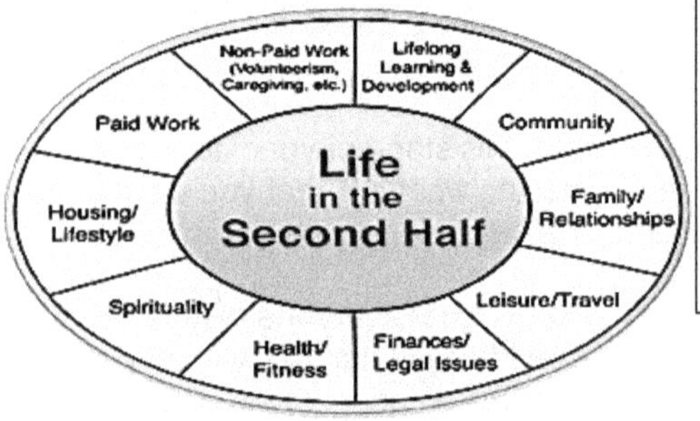

The *LPN Mission* is to create and communicate knowledge and resources that support professionals in their work to enhance people's later lives and thus benefit society.

Our vision is the intentional and holistic preparation for the complexities and possibilities of later life and becomes a common practice available to all.

Figure 15-3

2. Join the Life Planning Network. This network of professionals represents a wide range of interests and skillsets that seek to collaboratively develop age 50+ seniors' knowledge and skills so they may to maintain and attain better lives and careers as they move forward through their senior years. Their focus is on answering questions such as: What is my Purpose? What Legacy should I leave? And, What is my Spiritual Nature? (Figure 15-3)

Members of the LPN are also committed to assisting seniors in finding opportunities for continuous learning, volunteering, building communities, maintaining healthy lifestyles, and earning additional income to meet their retirement needs. Their organizational vision is the intentional and holistic preparation of the complexities of later life and becomes a common practice available to all.

This ALF Handbook educational and consulting program offers resources and support to the Life Planning Network based on a long history of change management and enterprise transformation conducted in both private and public sector organizations. We support the commitment to live authentically and on purpose, so that we can leave legacies of our hearts guided by the larger mysteries of life we are still learning to understand.

3. Employ Certified Senior Advisors Assistance. Emphasis by these professionally skilled service providers is on providing contemporary aging advice, coordination with health transitions as people grow steadily older, assistance with quality of life choices, counsel on financial and estate planning, access to federal and state programs, and establishment of essential ethics in communication and treatment. It may be that at the latest stages of our lives that availability of the most experienced and compassionate experts and specialists is critical. (Figure 15-4) Formal certification as a CSA is recommended for those with applicable knowledge and skill.

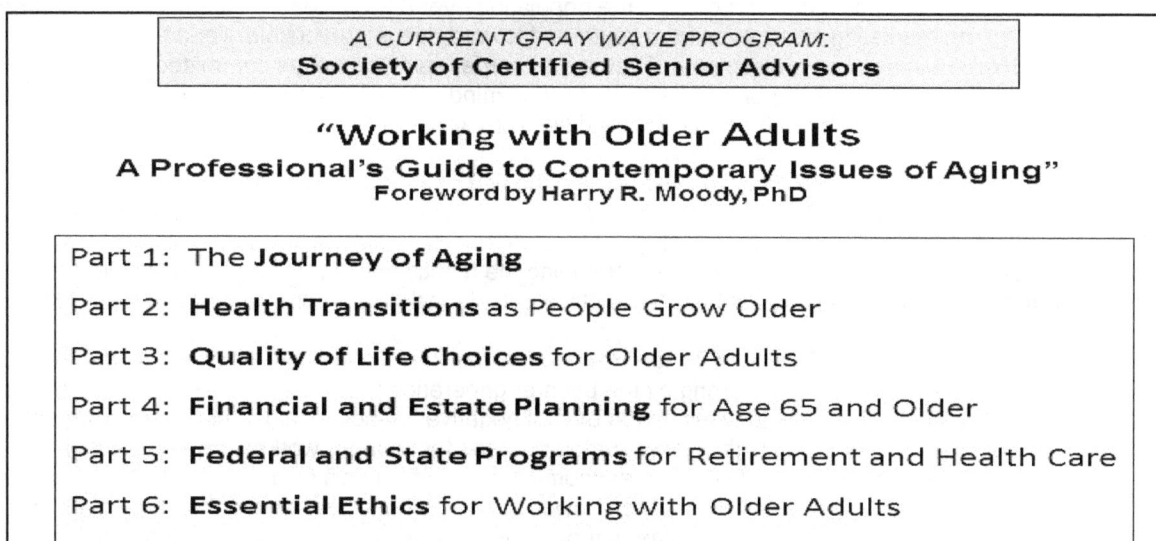

A CURRENT GRAY WAVE PROGRAM:
Society of Certified Senior Advisors

"Working with Older Adults
A Professional's Guide to Contemporary Issues of Aging"
Foreword by Harry R. Moody, PhD

Part 1: The **Journey of Aging**

Part 2: **Health Transitions** as People Grow Older

Part 3: **Quality of Life Choices** for Older Adults

Part 4: **Financial and Estate Planning** for Age 65 and Older

Part 5: **Federal and State Programs** for Retirement and Health Care

Part 6: **Essential Ethics** for Working with Older Adults

Figure 15-4

[Author's Note: The three organizations displayed above have a commitment to the future development of seniors beginning at the age of 50 all the way through their 80s. The significance is that their national prominence and comprehensive programs and practices are available to people at all stages of social interests, physical needs, educational levels, and mobility skills. The leaders involved are talented leaders with coaching capability.]

Senior Rejuvenation

The topics presented below (*Longevity Revolution; Age of Power; 50+ Reinventing America*) may enhance your motivation to take personal action.

1. The Longevity Revolution. In *America the Wise* (1998), Theodore Roszak describes the coming of a "new people" in American society. He says: "We are the first generation of the senior dominance. The beneficiaries of a *revolution in life-extending medicine and public health*, we enter the second half of our lives possessed of more political influence, greater wealth, and more vitality than any older generation before us. The values we choose to live by cannot help but be a commanding influence in shaping the century to come." (p.1) Some examples of near-term changes that will begin to have major impact on U.S. political, economic, and social affairs include:

a. Discovering a New People – More people are living longer and their extended participation in societal affairs will shape the course of history. The largest-growing sector of our population as of the early twenty-first century comprises those over eighty-five. Death, if one survives its first call, is a great awakener of our conscious and a call to serious reflection and radical reappraisal. The fifty million Americans now living on entitlements are the largest component of the welfare state. They will soon be joined by another eighty million Americans as the baby boomers age into retirement. (pp.9-11)

b. Concern about Entitlement Affordability – Increasing economic concern is being expressed from a number of public and private sector organizations that so large a percentage of retired people will become a drain on the U.S. economy. Some have suggested that senior entitlements are unsustainable, undeserved, unprincipled, and unfair – and that a "fiscal breakdown" is in the making. Additionally, some say the baby boom generation is uniquely identified for its "unseemly" and "ruinously dysfunctional" way of life. (p.27)

c. Rise of the Non-Profit Third Sector – The *Third Sector* is the sum total of all volunteer work outside the marketplace, either by individuals or through non-profit organizations. The third sector holds communities together in such fields of education, day care, health care, legal advocacy, sheltering and feeding the homeless, and drug rehabilitation. Women have traditionally been the main caregivers due to their greater longevity and social service skills, but more men are coming into the field. The third sector is becoming the main focus of work for retired seniors, the money spent by that sector is greater than the GNP of all but seven nations, and there are already more people in that sector than in
construction or transport or textiles. (p.99)

d. Maturity and the Media – The national media outlets for radio and TV services focus primarily on the 18-49 age group while seeming to forget that in the 21st century the population over 65 will steadily increase and outnumber the population under 25. The marketing trend away from youth and toward age is irreversible – and the older generation is more skeptical and less trusting of advertisements. They are a "harder sell" and not as committed to technological products. "Context" will become more important in entertainment, mindless adolescent behavior will be less tolerated, and sex will not be as large a draw for selling products and services. (pp.125-126)

e. Generativity and Mentoring – Erik Erickson was among the first psychologists to see aging as "a stage of growth of the healthy personality" and coined the word *generativity* to refer to the eldering project of our later years: "the interest in establishing and guiding the next generation," as he defined it. Daniel Levinson has sought to broaden generativity to mean *mentoring*: "It is a complex role, combining the function of teacher, sponsor, guide, exemplar, and counselor… mentoring is a social task that at best takes place outside the parent-child relationship." (pp.168-169)

2. The Age of Power. Author Ken Dychtwald, 50+*Age Power: How the 21st Century will be Ruled by the New Old* (1999) takes another view of the impact occurring by the boomer generation moving into their senior years -- and it is not too complementary. Most of his book focuses on the overall negative impact of such a high percentage of elders on the American economy: huge deficits, higher taxes, unfair burdens for younger workers, the heavy lobbying hand of seniors' organizations (e.g., the AARP), and negative economic trends. Still, in his concluding chapter: He does offer some coaching to that generation (he is one of them) on how they can do better as seniors than they did in the earlier stages of their development. Quoting pp.235-236, the author comments: "By now it will be obvious that America is becoming a "gerontocracy," and that four outcomes are certain:

a. More of us will live longer than in the previous generation.

b. The epicenter of economic and political power will shift from the young to the old.

c. We will need to change our current mind-set about how to spend the extra years of our life.

d. How we decide to behave as elders will, in all likelihood, become the most important challenge we will face in our lives."

Dychtwald continues: "In the decades ahead, the boomers will complete America's transformation into a gerontocracy as they take control of the nation's social and economic power. From this demographically and politically dominant position, they will have the potential to realize their full intellectual, social, and political influence, not as baby boomers but as elders. In youth, boomers were self-indulgent in their priorities. In their late teens and twenties, many shared an idealistic commitment to society. During the past several decades of career building and childrearing, many of their early ideals have been submerged.

As boomers shed the skin of youth, however, they could be migrating into the *most powerful years of their lives*. If they can step outside their generational tendency toward self-centeredness and wield this power with wisdom and generativity, they could rise to their greatest height and make a remarkable success of history's first multi-ethnic, multi-racial, and multi-generational melting pot. Or if, like silver-haired velociraptors, they use their size and influence to bully younger generations and gobble up all the available resources, they will find themselves in a Jurassic Park of their own making.

If this generation evolves to a deepened appreciation of the effect it has on others and can learn to exemplify a new kind of wise, mature leadership, when the boomers' time on earth is over, perhaps they will be remembered not just as the *largest* generation in history, but the *finest*."

3. Reinventing America. Authors Bill Novelli and Boe Workman (*50+ Igniting a Revolution to Reinvent America*, 2006) provide a much more upbeat look at the nation as its boomers move into the senior citizen ranks. They acknowledge the alarmist tone of much of the discussion surrounding the aging U.S. population, but propose strategies for alleviating some of the difficulties. First, they say it is a fact that:

a. "Boomers have not prepared adequately for their long futures.

b. Companies are rapidly shifting financial risks and responsibilities to workers and retirees without adequate preparation and safeguards.

c. Government programs are not working as well as they should, and many need to be modernized, better financed, and more engaging to the public.

d. We have a health-care system that is designed to pay bills but doesn't promote health and wellness.

e. We have a growing older population that by and large is vital and active and possesses great intellectual wealth.

But we have not structured a social model to optimize their continued involvement." (p.12) On the positive side, however, the authors recognize trends and opportunities designed to enable seniors to live better and contribute more to their communities. Some opportunities to:

a. Transform Health Care – Increase efficiencies, cut costs, decrease chronic disease, provide access to more people, and increase the availability and use of technology.

b. Conduct charitable volunteering – Continuing education, care-giving to family and others, better financial preparation, and phased retirement.

c. Revolutionize the Workplace – Adaptability to the changing workplace and technology, recognizing the advantages of stable, reliable, and part-time older workers.

d. Build Livable Communities – Modification of homes for better access and use of physical aids, provision of transportation services, and construction of senior communities and recreation facilities.

e. Change the Marketplace – Greater attention by marketers to the services and products required by seniors, and greater assistance fighting consumer fraud and financial scams.

f. Advocate for a Cause – Participation in public health and safety groups, social and political activism, and mentoring and coaching younger adults and children.

g. Opportunity to Leave a Legacy – Completing one's own life work, contributing to the betterment of others, and sharing experiences and wisdom accumulated over a lifetime."

This last item is particularly important for the next part of this chapter: What can you do to establish a life legacy that adequately represents your own personhood over the years of your life? Are you preparing to remind family and friends of the value of their presence and affection during your life, and to identify ways you can still share your best knowledge and experience with them that you never got a opportunity to do so? This may be the very time to take action on these matters. There is still time as long as the sun still shines (Figure 15-1).

Authentic Living

1. Living with Passion and Purpose. In their book *Life-Launch: A Passionate Guide to the Rest of Your Life* (1995) authors Frederic Hudson and Pamela McLean present a map designed to "…help you locate your deep energy and passion for the destinations you now want to pursue. Yesterday's passions may not serve tomorrow's goals, so ask yourself 'what motivates me the most at this time of my life to be the best I can be?' That's the fuel for your next Life-Launch." They say that: "After examining hundreds of biographies of twentieth century successful adults, we found that the persons we examined measured their lives with six different basic values or passions – often in combination with

one another." (pp.66-71) These are:

a. Personal Power: Know Thyself – (*Claiming Yourself*) Self-esteem, confidence, identity, inner motivation, a positive sense of self, clear ego boundaries, self-love, courage.

b. Achievement: Reach Your Goals – (*Proving Yourself*) Reaching goals, conducting projects, working, winning, playing in organized sports, having ambition, getting results and recognition and income, being purposive, doing.

c. Intimacy: Love and Be Loved – (*Sharing Yourself*) Loving, bonding, caring, being intimate, making relationships work, touching, feeling, close, nesting, coupling, parenting, and being a friend.

d. Play and Creativity: Follow Your Intuition – (*Expressing Yourself*) Being imaginative, intuitive, playful, spontaneous, original, expressive, humorous, artistic, celebrative, creative, funny, curious, childlike, and non-purposive.

e. Search for Meaning: Spiritual Integrity – (*Integrating Yourself*) Finding wholeness, unity, integrity, peace, an inner connection to all things, spirituality, trust in the flow of life, inner wisdom, and sense of transcendence, bliss.

f. Compassion and Contribution: Leave a Legacy – (*Giving Yourself*) Improving, helping, feeding, reforming, leaving the world a better place, bequeathing, being generative, serving, social and environmental caring, institution-building, volunteerism.

[**Author's Note**: Throughout this book we have been developing and applying the *Learnership Integrated Systems Architecture (LISA)* as a framework for aspiration and inspiration toward living a life with passion and purpose. Authors Hudson and McLean have just captured the essence of this objective with their six values and passions.]

2. <u>Burnish Your Authentic Brand</u>. For many people the Mid-life/career Transition and Senior Rejuvenation phase can be a time of deep reflection, extensive learning and greater life satisfaction. This typically requires a degree of introspection and circumspection that stimulates better focus of our time on future opportunities and a personal determination to project more of our "real" selves to others. This drive for clarity and authenticity can lead to greater comfort in working with others without pretention and ego-involvement. It can enhance our satisfaction with interpersonal relationships within our own developing personhood.

In his book on *Authentic Personal Branding* (2009) Dr. Rampersad describes the importance of formulating and implementing our own Personal Ambition which specifically includes personal vision, mission and key roles to be played through life. He says: "Your Personal Ambition and Personal Brand allow you to formulate your dream, key roles, purpose in life, uniqueness and values honestly and make these available to you. Once completed, your Personal Ambition will impact your personal well-being and success at work and the rest of your life." It is during our senior years that we become especially interested in what we have achieved and how we are seen by others – basically, we want clarity of mind on our self-worth and personal well-being. Chapter two in this handbook is dedicated to authentic personal branding, and Appendix C provides an illustration on how readers can prepare their own e-book on the subject.

3. <u>Elders by the Fireside</u>. Here is your invitation to the fireside. If we were to describe our lives using the metaphor of fire, we would recognize that there comes the time when the flames have settled into a comfortable glow. The fire is steady, burning warmly, and in no danger of going out anytime soon. There is plenty of fuel to add to it, but no rush to do so. A bank of coals lies at the base of the fire, white hot and powerful. The fire has been well tended and is now ready to give back great heat and light for some time to come.

This book is for people who are moving into and through the stage of life characterized by that fire. It is for people who are ready to stroke the wisdom gained in the first half of their lives to burn with a brighter sense of purpose in the second half...we believe that the second half of life offers us unique opportunities for growing whole, not old. When we claim our place at the fire – by recalling our stories, re-finding our place, renewing our calling, and reclaiming our purpose – we are ultimately embrace the deepest expression of who we really are."

With that invitation, authors Richard Leiter and David Shapiro of *Claiming Your Place at the Fire: Living the Second Half of Your Life (2004)* proceed to tell us that as proper elders of today we should now be keeping our fire alive within ourselves. We do that by recalling our lives by asking the fire-starter question (Who am I?), followed by (Where do I Belong?), and then (What do I Care about?) and finally (What is My Legacy?). They say that these four *flames* in the fire represent *vital aging questions* for which are each responsible. (pp.2-4).

They observe that James Hillman in his book *The Force of Character* talks about the finish of our lives in a way that distinguishes "finish" from "end." Finishing our lives, says Hillman, is better understood as *burnishing our character* to a high gloss. He makes the natural connections between finishing our lives and leaving the legacy we leave. Both require us to develop the most authentic expression of who we are to claim our place at the fire. (p. 20).

Leiter and Shapiro continue on to say we elders need to embrace that stage of our lives where we reflect and reconstruct that which we have experienced and learned into thoughtful and interest stories that secure our place closest to the flames themselves. Others will sit and listen if we have good stories to tell – and these need to address four elements of the good life: Our place, the people, the work itself, and the purpose we sought in at the time are all foundational elements of sharing a story that is both memorable and informative.

[**Author's Note**: This book is an essential read for anyone coming into their senior years. Buy it and add it to your collection as a keepsake for your heirs.]

Legacy Success Products

The majority of people with successful lives and careers have achieved some appreciation and recognition for their productive activities and social contributions. The difficulty is that beyond their family members, friends and selective colleagues, few others are aware that just beyond their reach there may be unique and unexpressed knowledge and insight that could have been willingly shared had the opportunity been available. This situation is especially impactful for aging seniors whose associates are passing-on, thereby reducing the opportunities to exchange intellectual and emotional knowledge and hard-won experience. The resulting sense of increasing isolation concurrent with decreasing self-worth can surely be damaging to the one who is aging – and to others who failed to connect when time could still have been scheduled.

The design of this ALF Mindset Handbook and subsequent training initiatives has been focused on this quandary. Would it be possible to motivate people to be lifelong proactive learners seeking to optimize and integrate their intellectual and emotional capabilities all through their adult life stages and transitions? Could their evolving visions, missions, experience and learning carry them successfully through mid-life and into old age with a sense of continued accomplishment and compatibility with their changing environment? Could we all "live our legacy" and "leave our legacy" so our accumulated personhood could be an evolutionary moment in time?

A major objective has been to enable we seniors a "late in life voice" while we are still able to learn and share our perspectives with colleagues. These later in life conversations and reflections will often contain material and insights that have ongoing value to others when communicated as part of our own legacy documentation. The ALF approach has been to establish a proactive methodology for continued thinking, learning, knowing, leading and achieving that rapidly builds our capability for personal and societal system development. And, to be of lasting utility our learning and journeys should be recorded and shared after our death with those we love and value.

Legacy Products. There are two books and one Legacy Letter outlined in the Appendix that readers of this Handbook are invited to write for their own life education, integration and professional success. Each is a powerful testimony on the perspectives and experience we gleaned from proactive and successful living. For many of us, this might be the first and last time to define and illuminate the purpose of our authentic, complex, and meaningful lives. Completing this task would be the documentation of our individual life project and the summation of our unique personhood.

1. Personal e-Book Publishing (Continued at Appendix B): *American Learnership for "[My] Life, Work, Wealth, Health and Legacy Success"*

2. Personal e-Book Publishing (Continued at Appendix C): *American Learnership for "[My] Authentic Personal and Professional Branding"*

3. *[My] Senior Life Learning and Memorable Legacy* (Letter) (Continued in this chapter and Appendix E.)

Writing Procedure This feature is addressed by providing planned formats as illustrated in this chapter Appendices B, C and E. The specific steps to follow are:

1. Read these chapters and the Epilogue. Then contact Dr. Garrity at rgarrity@alforum.org. for assistance, options and associated costs, and further instructions for tasks 2, 3, or 4 below.

Chapter One: Introduction to American Learnership
Chapter Two: Discovering the Meaning of Your Life

Complete Your Unique Life Project

1. Read the acknowledgement statement that follows (next page), Chapter One of Dr Garrity's book in Appendix B

2. Prepare your writing plan following the Dr. Garrity's e-book example in either Appendices B or C (see below).

3. Begin preparation of [My] *Senior Lifelong Learning and Memorable Legacy* in accordance this chapter and Appendix E instructions.

4. Submit your product(s) for review by Dr. Garrity and for planned publication.

An American Perspective on Personal, Corporate, Community and Societal Branding

The American experiment in democratic governance deserves a mixed review in terms of its efficiency and effectiveness. A majority of Americans benefit from the security, wealth, and technological capability offered to those who through education, social connectivity, or birthright have the opportunity to participate, produce, and consume valued goods and services. However, in terms of serving the interests of *ALL Americans* more fully, the nation is failing to live up to its Constitutional guarantee of life, liberty, and the pursuit of happiness for all. There is little doubt that American society, in terms of its social and financial responsibilities, should be able to produce and distribute its bounty more equitably and in greater alignment with its founding principles. For a sizeable minority in the population these opportunities may not exist; or are missed due to their lack of preparation; or social barriers are perceived to be too difficult for them to overcome.

While the increasing pace of life, complexity of issues, and unpredictability of events threaten to consume many in whirlpools of societal turbulence, the systems that have been designed for support often fail to respond adequately. Chaos and rigidity co-exist to the detriment of social alignment and cohesion. Using the Federal government as an example, pluralistic gridlock that even James Madison might find difficult to accept has slowed policy and budget deliberations to a crawl. Americans seem to be losing their ability to recognize and act on issues of mutual concern. Unless a crisis is imminent, little action is taken, and even then that which is done may be ill-advised.

A critique of the growth and development of modern American society in terms of the core civic and ethical values envisioned in the American founding would hardly be complementary. The extent of our impressive economic and technological accomplishments coupled with seemingly intractable political, social, ecological, and international predicaments could have been difficult to anticipate and prevent, but surely we might have done much better than we have. The question of whether American society can proactively learn to manage its future for positive results, or simply act as inept caretakers of a diminishing heritage, may be worth considering. It appears that we, as citizens, are not sufficiently engaged in the most important conversations required to fully understand, expertly negotiate and firmly secure enlightened national progress here at home.

On the international scene, we may ask ourselves: "Where are the future U.S. leaders with outstanding minds and ethical personal character who can influence and establish America's national vision, mission and policies that are constitutionally authentic and internationally welcomed? Concurrently, we could ask ourselves to reflect on our seemingly self-imposed commitment to be the leader of the "free world." Are we willing to "walk our talk" by confronting the ignorant traditions, rampant greed, and inhumane behavior of billions of people distributed throughout planet earth? To what degree is human progress on an international scale the responsibility of American?" Is human progress limited to only a minority our nation's and the world's people? What share of the planet's human burden falls is the responsibility of the United States? Can we even articulate these multi-dimensional questions in an informed manner?

The topic of "authentic personal branding" has become very important in today's world of global competition, increasing pressure and constant communication. We all need to learn and improve ourselves continuously and be able to communicate our unique personal brand with passion in order to be successful in life. It will not only make us better people but also enable us to live happier and more productive lives.

My colleague, Dr. Hubert Rampersad, continually reinforces this in his books. I have built my own authentic personal brand successfully based on his authentic personal branding methodology, and I am happy to present this to you to encourage you to take the time to reflect, learn and make a similar investment in yourself.

For me, Dr. Rampersad's coaching has been instrumental in pursuing my career work as CEO of the American Learnership Forum which emphasizes lifelong learning, knowing and leading for a mindful way-of-being. We all have only one life in which to learn, achieve and contribute to our families, businesses, communities and society. Taking time to construct and document our personal visions, missions, goals, plans and accomplishments takes only a small time investment to advance our personhood and obtain appropriate rewards. I am privileged to act as a role model based on my authentic personal brand. I hope that this book will inspire you to build your personal brand as well and to attract success in your life and career.

I would like to thank Dr. Hubert Rampersad who inspired and stimulated me to develop and share my authentic personal brand with you, and who provided me the methodology to do so. And, I especially would like to recommend his most recent books for your learning and development: Authentic Governance: *Aligning Personal Governance with Corporate Governance* (2014), and *Authentic Personal Branding for Coaches and Executives* (2014). I hope that this book will assist you on your journey towards happiness and enduring success

Dr. Rudolph Garrity, Chairman, The American Learnership Forum, Inc. Potomac Dr. NE, # 602, Leesburg, VA 20176

Table – 1 (Acknowledgement)

Appendix B

Personal eBook Publishing: My Integral Life, Work, Wealth, Health and Legacy Success

ITEM I: Completed Example – Dr. Rudy Garrity's Personal Assessment
ITEM II: Blank Form – For others to complete.

ITEM I: Personal Example (Dr. Garrity)
[**Author's Note**: Readers planning on conducting a self-assessment for purposes of personal renewal or development are encouraged to record their end-of-chapter notes in <u>Part B</u> of this Journal—after reading each chapter in the book. When all chapters have been completed, readers should review and summarize their notes and complete the <u>Part A</u> **Overall Summary** topics, below.

Part A. Overall Summary (Author's Note: Complete **Part B** individual Chapter Summaries below first in preparation to complete **Part A** afterward)

1. **Personal Reflections** Cross reference with <u>Rudy's Authentic Personal Brand Balanced Scorecard (**Internal**)</u> when your own Part II (Chapter Four) Authentic Personal and Professional Balanced Scorecard is completed.

---

a. What *new insights* have I developed on my self, my life, and my career?

Everyone is entitled to dream and pursue their own life that is hopefully, worth living. For me, learning has provided the way forward, and *lifelong learning has granted significant rewards* for my life and career.

b. Is it time for me to become more holistic and integrated in my thinking, and to pursue my *higher purpose*? What is that higher purpose?

I have accumulated education and experience, but there is so much more to learn and do. Now is the time to consolidate and integrate important, but sometimes disparate concepts for further consideration. It has been enormously satisfying for me to envision the relationship among *self-fulfilment*, *high performance* and the *common good* as they intersect for *human enlightenment* and a *mindful way-of-being*.

c. What do I really want to accomplish in my life, and to leave something for *posterity, a legacy*?

The Enlightenment Period of European history was a profound time when intellectual prowess finally emerged from suppression by self-imposed mythmakers and religionists. Thankfully, American founders such as Benjamin Franklin, Thomas Jefferson and Thomas Paine to recognize just a few, had the wisdom to provide the leadership and craft the documentation to launch America into the forefront of scientific discovery and human development that continues to this day. *Our generation has added intellectual and emotional intelligence* to the bus destined for posterity; we must ensure this intelligence exceeds its cost of transportation.

Table – 2 (Sample)

<u>Appendix C</u>

Personal eBook Publishing: My Authentic Personal and Professional Brand

[**Author's Note**: This part is adapted from the work of Dr. Hubert Rampersad and includes excerpts from his book *Authentic Personal Branding (2009)* and *Rudolph Garrity's Personal Brand* (2014).

ITEM I: Completed Example – Dr. Rudy Garrity's Authentic Brand
ITEM II: Blank Form – For others to complete.

ITEM I: Completed Example – Dr. Garrity

Contents

Preface: Importance of an Authentic Personal and Professional Brand
Chapter 1: My Authentic Personal and Professional Branding
Chapter 2: My Authentic Personal Ambition
Chapter 3: My Authentic Personal Brand
Chapter 4: My Authentic Personal Balanced Scorecard
Chapter 5: My Authentic Personal Brand Implementation and Cultivation
Chapter 6: My Authentic Personal Brand Alignment with Myself and Corporation

Preface: Importance of an Authentic Personal and Professional Branding

Customers must recognize that you stand for something.
– Howard Schultz, Chairman of Starbucks

The underlying assumption of personal-branding philosophy is that each of us has unique gifts and a distinct purpose and dream in life. By connecting these gifts, purpose and dream, we open ourselves up to greater happiness and success in life (Frost, 2003). This fits very well to my holistic and authentic personal branding model, which will be discussed in the following sections. This new blueprint will help me to unlock my potential and build a trusted image of myself that I want to project in everything I do. It must therefore be in harmony with my true values, beliefs, dreams, and genius. When my brand is combined with powerful tools, it will deliver peak performance and create a stable basis for trustworthiness, credibility, and personal charisma.

This inside-out approach is durable and differs from traditional methods, and is based on a passion for developing human potential. This new approach places more emphasis on understanding myself and the needs of others, meeting those needs while staying true to my values, improving myself continuously, and realizing growth in life based on this personal branding journey. It focuses on the human side of branding, and includes my reputation, character and personality. If am well branded according to this approach, I will find it easier to convince others and I will attract the people and opportunities that are a perfect fit for me.

The authentic personal branding process starts with determining who I am at my core authentic self. Rather than inventing a brand that I would like to be perceived as and to sell myself to others, this one is based on my life philosophy, dreams, vision, mission, values, key roles, identity, self-knowledge, self-awareness, self-responsibility, positive attributes, and self-management. With an authentic personal brand, my strongest characteristics, attributes, and values can separate me from the crowd. Without this, I look just like everyone else. If I am not branded in an authentic, honest, and holistic way, if I don't deliver according to my brand promise, and if I focus mainly on selling, packaging, outward

Table – 3 (Sample)

Senior Lifelong Learning and Memorable Legacy

LIFE DOMAINS	LIFE STAGES ⟶			
	ADOLESCENCE (Childhood)	**EARLY ADULT** 25-45	**MID-LIFE ADULT** 45-60	**SENIOR ADULT** 60-80
PHILOSOPHY (Worldview/Ideals)				
REASONING (Competencies)				
PERSONAL (Family)				
ORGANIZATION (Career/Work)				
COMMUNITY (Society)				
	ADOLESCENCE (Childhood)	**EARLY ADULT** 25-45	**MID-LIFE ADULT** 45-60	**SENIOR ADULT** 60-80
PEOPLE (I Knew)				
EVENTS (I Experienced)				
SUCCESS (I Experienced)				
SADNESS (I Experienced)				

Appendix Table E-1

Conclusion

An important responsibility is recognized in this chapter. If you have successfully mastered your mid-life/work transition with assistance from information shared here and in the previous chapter (Chapter Fourteen) of this Handbook, how can you continue to achieve satisfactory life closure in your later adult years? Can you establish a meaningful legacy as an informative and caring gift to those who follow later? What are the subjects, activities, and artifacts in need of your near term attention so that you can efficiently transition your worldly knowledge, property and affairs to others, and give others advice on organizing their personal life/career accomplishments in a manner that enhances their own family, business and community common good.

Figure 15-5

Epilogue

Summarization and Review of Selected Major Topics

A	Implications of Integral Learning And Knowledge Management
B	American Learnership Practitioner Characteristics
C	Wealth Generation and Financial Security
D	Life Transitions and Architecture for Integrated Living and Development

Figure 1

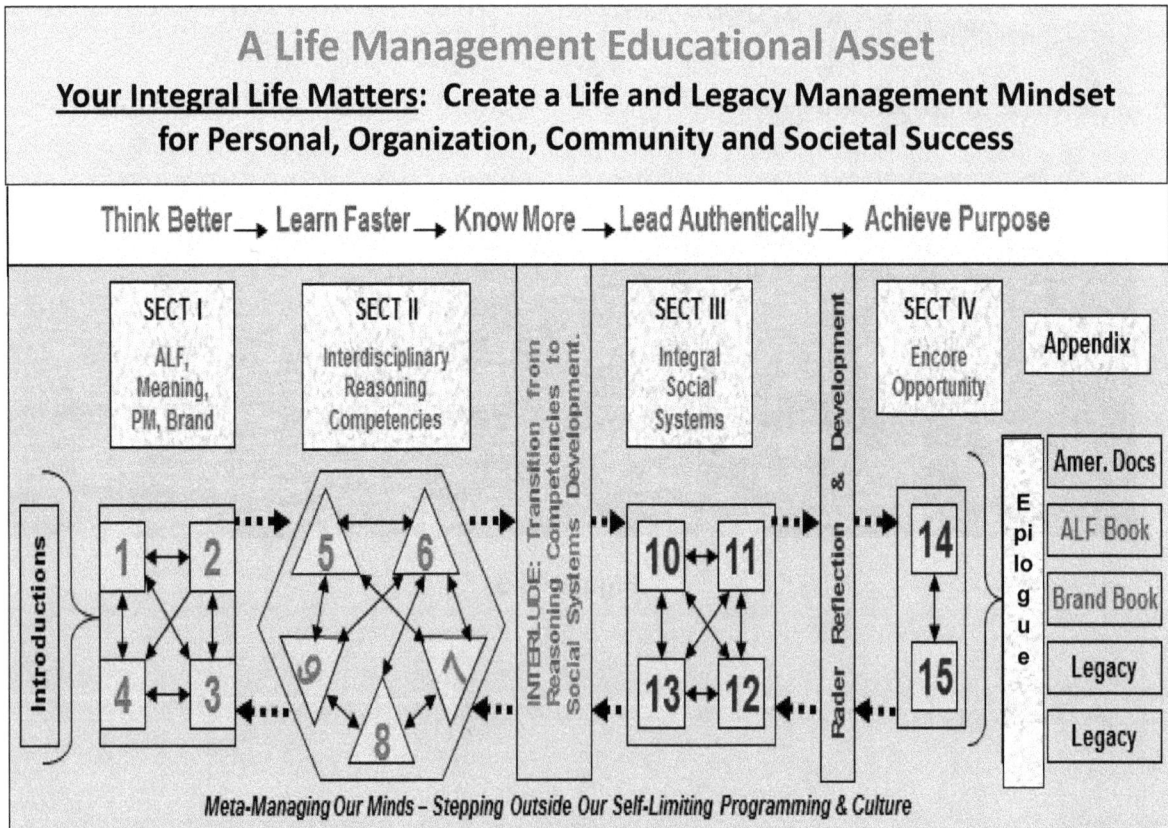

Figure 2

A. Implications of Integral Learning and Knowledge Management

Foreword: The American Experiment in Life, Liberty and the Pursuit of Happiness

The American experiment in democratic governance deserves a mixed review in terms of its efficiency and effectiveness. A majority of Americans benefit from the security, wealth, and technological capability offered to those who through education, social connectivity, or birthright have the opportunity to participate, produce, and consume valued goods and services. However, in terms of serving the interests of *ALL Americans* more fully, the nation is failing to live up to its Constitutional guarantee of life, liberty, and the pursuit of happiness for all.

There is little doubt that American society, in terms of its social and financial responsibilities, should be able to produce and distribute its bounty more equitably and in greater alignment with its founding principles. For a sizeable minority in the population these opportunities may not exist; or are missed due to their lack of preparation; or social barriers are perceived to be too difficult for them to overcome.

Preface: Preliminary Insights and Aspirations

Many of us go through our lives completing tasks and meeting responsibilities without thinking too much about where we are going and how we are going to get there. Only occasionally when a person or an event breaks our pattern of concentration do we take the time to reflect on what we have been doing and to determine whether it is meaningful to us or to anyone else, that we continue along the same path. When we do find time to mull over our direction, extent of commitments, and rate of progress, the thoughts that often emerge are:

1. When will I discover my true calling, and begin to live a more integrated and meaningful life?
2. How can I become more knowledgeable and competent in a rapidly changing and stressful world?
3. How can I manage my way through these mid-life/career disappointments, and have a second chance to succeed?
4. How can I make my life a memorable event, and become an example for those who follow in the future?

These questions, and others with similar heart-felt overtones, are clues to lives that lack the cognitive and emotional development that people in advanced societies have come to expect. How can we make the appropriate personal changes? How can we even think about what has happened and what is needed to be done? These are daunting challenges. These concerns and challenges mark the cornerstone of this work.

The research for this book has been an investigation into Americans' lives, careers, legacies and societal best practices; and a framework for integrating the resulting theories, perspectives, and practices so they may be understood, embraced, and applied for personal, organizational, and community improvement.

SECTION I. American Learnership: Lifelong Learning & Professional Performance Branding

Chapter One: Introduction to American Learnership

Learnership is a component of one's life philosophy on what is worth knowing and doing and on how human needs can be accomplished. Viewed from a broad perspective, *learnership practitioners* maintain a distinctive worldview that frames their thinking, learning, knowing, leading, and behavior. Their inclination to determine the: who, what, when, where, why, how, and for whom on a wide range of societal issues and human activity signifies a sense of personal responsibility for contributing to the welfare of themselves, their organizations, and their communities.

Implications for Integral Learning and Knowledge Management. *The comprehensive American Learnership Process Model and the Learnership Integrated Systems Architecture (LISA) in this chapter provide an all-inclusive framework suitable for both the book's primary subject of Integral learning and Knowledge Management (ILKM) and the companion subject of Total Knowledge Management (TKM). Both topics are based on the premise that "total learning, total knowing, and total leading" are a natural triad of activities in a lifetime of human development and achievement. More specifically, Situational Learning and Knowledge Management will be shown to be interdependent competencies supporting Adaptive Leadership in achieving Social System Progress.*

The ILKM (TKM) concept is anchored here in chapter one and is further developed in subsequent chapters through adaptive leadership (chapter nine). After that, it is applied in the four social system domains of personal, organization, community and societal development (chapters ten to thirteen). Along the way, Learning and Knowledge Management will be observed to be evermore interdisciplinary in educational scope and integral for social systems enrichment.

Chapter Two: Discovering the Meaning of Your Life

In the <u>pursuit of what we term our personal "*meaning"*</u> it is essential that we understand that while "meaning" is often thought to be something dynamic that we explicitly demonstrate outside ourselves, in fact, "meaning" always begins inside ourselves as our fundamental worldview of appropriate beliefs, values, motives and preferred actions before we reveal them to others.

Implications for Integral Learning and Knowledge Management. *This handbook uses a social system-of-systems perspective for understanding the thinking and behavior of human beings. Doing this recognizes the artifacts and relationships among the four principal social domains of personal (family), organization (business), local community and society (largest) that includes them all. Each of these domains creates a psycho-social set of accepted understandings or culture that defines them each as both individual entities and intergroup collaborators. The goals, boundaries, plans, resources and activities of all are based on the human needs, wants, and desires of all members. The thinking, learning and knowledge capabilities established within these groups are both interdisciplinary and integral. Knowing this truism encourages all of us to improve our reasoning and decision-making to obtain more meaningful outcomes.*

Chapter Three: Being the Project Manager of Your Life

<u>Project management is the selection and systematic application of knowledge, skills, tools and technologies to achieve a planned objective.</u> Project management requires the sequential implementation of five work process phases: initiation, planning, executing, controlling and closing. The project manager is responsible for the overall integration and completion of all activities leading to project success, and everyone can be the project manager of their own life.

The project management methodology may be extended and used at the executive level in an enterprise by integrating the Balanced Scorecard assessment capability. This capability is useful at the strategic or meta level of performance review because it emphasizes *internal* enterprise performance in workforce learning and development and the efficiency of organizational processes. Concurrently, *external* performance in marketing, sales, and customer satisfaction can be reviewed, as well as the status of earnings in revenue and profit may be determined.

Lastly, personal financial planning tools and organizational consulting strategies are highlighted to ensure adequate awareness is given to the fundamental personal wealth-building and business profit creating needs essential in the American socio-economic system.

Implications for Integral Learning and Knowledge Management. *This chapter illustrates that Personal Life Project Management is a methodology that encompasses both the qualitative and quantitative aspects of human aspirations and financial security. It also cautions that a reasonable person would recognize that a thoughtful, balanced and holistic approach in setting goals and taking action is advisable. Because the quality and quantity of our learning – developed over a lifetime of experience – evolves, major changes can occur as new knowledge replaces that which no longer serves our needs and interests. And, as the new learning and knowledge becomes influential our goals will require modification within our already integral mindsets and beliefs.*

Chapter Four: Crafting Your Authentic Personal and Professional Brand

The technological revolution has changed the structure of careers today. It used to be that you went to work for one or two companies in your entire career. Today we will all have as many as four to eight jobs or careers in our lifetime.

<u>Personal Branding is essential to personal and career development.</u> It is an effective career tool because it helps define who you are; what you stand for; what makes you unique, special, and different; how you are great; and why you should be sought out as a colleague.

Implications for Integral Learning and Knowledge Management. *The willingness and ability of people, organizations and communities to represent themselves as being authentic is based on the level of credibility they have accumulated in past and present encounters. To do so, they must have earned a reputation of being informed, open, honest and flexible in dealing with others in their family, business, community and marketplace. And, these characteristics are based, in part, on their intellectual, emotional and knowledgeable manner in conducting their relationships. Those who are multi-disciplinary and cross-trained in modern work practices and contemporary human* *relations are more valued and trusted by others. One's brand can be planned and improved by systematic reflection on who they are and how they want to be known.*

SECTION II. American Learnership: Interdisciplinary Reasoning Competencies

Chapter Five: Reasoning Competency # 1: Systems Thinking

A systems perspective on social matters that illustrates the interdependency and mutual support among the personal, organizational, and community subsystems within which we learn, develop, and strive for success.

The <u>systems thinking competency helps us develop a broader, more integrated outlook</u>, and to expand the contextual environment of our thoughts and decisions. The use of systems thinking inspires us to be integrative thinkers and discover opportunities to synthesize our learning for better understanding. *Systems Thinking (ST) and Pattern Recognition (PR) combine to assure more effective Situational Learning (SL).*

Implications for Integral Learning and Knowledge Management. *Working in a complex world and a competitive marketplace tends to cause leaders and employees alike to reduce the scope of their thinking and attention in an attempt to become more efficient in accomplishing their lives and employment responsibilities. Better, cheaper, faster can sometimes seem like an oxymoron; especially when "time is of the essence" or "the customer is on the phone." If we really learned from our not-so-positive experiences, why are we doing things over again so often? Part of the reason is that projects, problems, and workflow issues are being handled with minimal attention to the larger context, longer timeframe, or increasing risks associated with the status quo. Failure to take the time to observe, reflect, and consider all influential factors is the basis for attempting to solve the wrong problems and wasting time and resources on ill-conceived solutions. Effective knowledge management requires decision-making and problem-solving based on timely, accurate, and relevant information. Leaving out that which is relevant due to an unwillingness to pursue a larger, systems thinking approach is not wise personally or organizationally.*

Systems thinking is an essential part of knowledge management, and is particularly important in that the six Universal Knowledge Spheres described in this chapter are essential elements in the construction of the Learnership Integrated Systems Architecture (LISA); and by extension, are contributing elements in building an Integral Learning and Knowledge Management (ILKM) capability.

Chapter Six: Reasoning Competency # 2: Pattern Recognition

By definition, a pattern can be an archetype, a model, an ideal worthy of imitation, a representative sample of some thing, or a composite of traits and features characteristic of individuals. All biological life forms maintain and exhibit patterns of activity; and, the social development of humankind is inextricably anchored to our thought processes as revealed in our behavior. The cultural expectations, documented methodologies, and established practices that form our human experience and interpersonal and organizational relationships are the artifacts of inherited tendencies and learned values, beliefs, and experiences previously programmed into our computer-like minds.

The <u>Pattern Recognition Competency focuses on our ability to recognize those preprogrammed aspects and preferences of ourselves and others</u>, and on the need for us to better manage our reasoning based on the why and how we think, learn, know, lead, and pursue certain objectives in all our societal endeavors. *Pattern Recognition (PR) combines with Systems Thinking (ST) to ensure more effective Situational Learning (SL).*

Implications for Integral Knowledge Management. *The inability to skillfully recognize similarities and differences among workgroup members and/or between various types of work assignments and methods directly affects the quality of team relationships and performance. In every day life the factors that make us think and act somewhat differently from others are far more numerous than those that tend to make us similar. Differences in age, culture, gender, education, career fields, work assignments, social circles, experience, expectations, and other mental programming make organizational, community, and personal relationships very difficult when it comes to establishing the alignment and cohesion required for high performance.*

Effective leadership and management are necessary as well as a willingness among those involved to increase their sensitivity and awareness of the situation and be open to the information and clues that help to understand the roles, objectives, styles, and objectives always in play, but not always clearly expressed. Effective knowledge management depends on understanding what is needed by whom and when; clarity and accuracy matter as well an efficient communication and coordination. Knowledge and skill in pattern recognition enables the accuracy and speed of information sharing, task learning, and issue resolution.

Chapter Seven: Reasoning Competency # 3: Situational Learning

A major life responsibility is dealing with the wide variety of situations we encounter on a daily basis. Some situations are routine and need little attention while at the other end of a continuum they may be significantly life and/or career threatening. What is important to understand is that every situation we encounter requires some amount of information gathering and analysis followed by decision making and action. And, <u>every situation is a potential learning opportunity.</u>

The situational learning competency is a significant element in human capital development and in becoming a *learnership practitioner* which makes it a foundational anchor in the practice of learnership. *Situational Learning (SL) benefits from the support provided by Systems Thinking (ST) and Pattern Recognition (PR) – and, it is an essential foundation for the practice of Knowledge Management (KM).*

Implications for Integral Learning and Knowledge Management. *Unless there is efficient, effective learning, knowledge management will always be operating with too much decision-making risk. The reason is that "relevant" knowledge will often be inaccurate or arrive too late thereby causing decisions to be made under excessive uncertainty and risk. Performance will be less than optimal and individuals and organizations will under-perform their objectives. Assertive learners cycling rapidly through numerous learning cycles are part of the remedy. So too, is an organization skilled in authentic dialogue and trusted collaboration wherein the parties involved know each other's needs, are committed to each other's success, and use critical thinking effectively without engaging in unnecessary game-playing or politics. Skills in Systems Thinking and Pattern Recognition support Situational Learning, which in turn, enables effective Knowledge Management.*

Chapter Eight: Reasoning Competency # 4: Knowledge Management

Human development can only proceed as far as our combined knowledge will allow. Whether we view ourselves as individuals, organizations or communities, we are both empowered and constrained by our current knowledge, and our willingness and ability to acquire additional knowledge. Contemporary studies and writings indicate that knowledge may be systematically created, managed and used to enhance human development and to produce the products and services we need and desire.

The <u>knowledge management competency is the core element in becoming a</u> *learnership practitioner.* It is the knowledge repository for situational learning artifacts, and in turn, it is the storehouse for the tacit and explicit knowledge used by adaptive leaders in advancing personal and social initiatives. *Knowledge Management (KM) is enabled by Situational Learning (SL) which itself is supported by Systems Thinking (ST) and Pattern Recognition (PR).*

Implications for Integral Learning and Knowledge Management. *The concept of ILKM was introduced in Chapter One, has been developing through intermediary chapters, and has culminated here in Chapter Eight with a full, but high level explanation. All of the reasoning competencies and knowledge management capabilities described and discussed are now available for leader use to in integral social systems development section that follows.*

Notwithstanding the fact that knowledge management has been primarily discussed as an organizational capability in most management literature; all the issues, practices, challenges, and techniques discussed herein apply as well to personal and community social system development. Knowledge management is essentially a "personal" choice on how an individual chooses to learn and develop in the major social domains of his or her life.

Knowledge always needed to be managed and those who acquired knowledge and applied it well were generally better rewarded and more successful. This is now true more than ever, and the future belongs to those who step up to the challenges of lifelong learning and knowledge management. Learning organizations applying knowledge management practices and techniques are the wave of the future whether they are the bricks and mortar operations of today or the virtual, networked organizations of tomorrow. And, the learnership practitioners are individuals skilled in the use of IKM principles, practices, and technologies.

Chapter Nine: Reasoning Competency # 5: Adaptive Leadership

No amount of knowledge has practical value until it is applied to human needs or concerns. Someone needs to articulate what is known, show relevancy to the situation or challenge at hand, and propose a course of action that can create a meaningful result. It is the work of learning leaders to craft visions and futures that inspire others to accept change and become participants in the journey forward.

The adaptive leadership competency is another foundational anchor in the learnership discipline because it moves knowledge into action. Theory is turned into practice, and practice leads to meaningful accomplishment for individuals and social organizations. *Adaptive Leadership (AL) applies Knowledge Management (KM) which has been enabled by Situational Learning (SL) which is supported by Systems Thinking (ST) and Pattern Recognition (PR).*

Implications for Integral Learning and Knowledge Management. *Adaptive Leadership principles, practices, and technologies are of little use in an organization that does not take implementation action. Concurrent with the design and change of work processes and procedures and the addition of IT technology and tools; leadership is essential to communicate the business case for change, arrange for training and mentoring, and to advise everyone in the enterprise of the improvements and what they mean to both internal units and external customers and constituencies. Adaptive leadership is the critical skill at this juncture because more than likely the changes being implemented will be based on greater distribution of organizational functions and people, and might even require an increased virtuosity in the performance of tasks. Organizational changes require experienced, competent management by those well suited to stressful and oftentimes conflicted situations.*

The wide range of practices and technologies available for today's leaders means change is continuous and adaptability to new circumstances is a regular requirement for those in leadership positions. The learnership social system domains addressed in chapters ten through fourteen will all need a strong infusion of ILKM (TKM) to achieve their growth potential and universal goals (Self-Fulfillment, High Performance, the Common Good, Human Enlightenment).

First Interlude: Transition from Reasoning Competencies to Social Systems Development

An interlude is included at this point to convey the consolidation of proactive concepts and reasoning skills already established as a precursor to their application to the four major social system of systems domains: personal, organizational, community and societal.

The primary documents include the Learnership Integrated Systems Architecture (LISA), the Learnership Architecture & Collaboration Instrument (LACI), the Learnership Systems Building Blocks (LSBB), and the list of Twenty-Five Learnership Practitioner Characteristics.

SECTION III. American Learnership: Integral Social Systems Development

Chapter Ten: Personal (Micro) Systems Development (PSD)

PSD is social synthesis at the micro-cognitive level, and is the starting point for managing the quality of our individual lives. Priority at this level is focused on continuous improvement of our *health, character* and *ability.* The universal goal selected for individuals is *self-fulfillment*, and the key role to be played is that of *fellowship.* Learning, knowing, and leading inform and activate PSD.

Implications for Integral Learning and Knowledge Management. *We now arrive at the social systems domain where the result of our knowledge building, with the assistance of the five learnership interdisciplinary reasoning competencies, may be reviewed. The major determination for **PSD** is whether the knowledge recently created is "relevant" to the inquiry, study, problem or issue being considered. Quite often a paradox occurs at this juncture in which the conclusion reached appears to be inconsistent, conflicting or incompatible with what the individuals involved anticipated or desired. When analyzed, questions arise as to whether the Systems Thinking, Pattern Recognition or Situational Learning competencies have been utilized in an open, factual, unbiased, timely and convincing manner. That is, is the knowledge really correct and integral when considering the obvious limitations in people's minds and personal preferences – and their cultures, education, and beliefs are sometimes entirely in conflict. Effective and valued knowledge will need to be judged by the PSD Health, Character, and Ability domains of thinking and behavior as interpreted by skilled and experienced leaders.*

Chapter Eleven: Organizational (Macro) Systems Development (OSD)

OSD is social synthesis at the macro-cognitive level, and uses recognized benchmarks for achieving highly efficient and effective organizational performance. The organizational elements selected for intense management focus are the organization's *direction, operations* and *performance.* The universal goal selected for organizations is *high performance*, and the key role to be played is *leadership.* Learning, knowing, and leading inform and activate OSD.

Implications for Integral Learning and Knowledge Management. We now arrive at the social systems domain where the result of our knowledge building, with the assistance of the five learnership interdisciplinary reasoning competencies, may be reviewed. The major determination for **OSD** is whether the knowledge recently created is "relevant" to the inquiry, study, problem or issue being considered. Quite often a paradox occurs at this juncture in which the conclusion reached appears to be inconsistent, conflicting or incompatible with what the individuals involved anticipated or desired. When analyzed, questions arise as to whether the Systems Thinking, Pattern Recognition or Situational Learning competencies have been utilized in an open, factual, unbiased, timely and convincing manner. That is, is the knowledge really correct and integral when considering the obvious limitations in people's minds and personal preferences – and their cultures, education, and beliefs are sometimes entirely in conflict. Effective and valued knowledge will need to be judged by the OSD Direction, Operations and Performance domains of thinking and behavior as interpreted by skilled and experienced leaders.

Chapter Twelve: Community (Mega) Systems Development (CSD)

CSD is social synthesis at the mega-cognitive level, and uses community selected benchmarks for achieving highly efficient and effective town, city, county or state performance. The community elements selected for intense management focus are the community's *business*, *education* and *government* contributors. The universal goal selected for communities is the common good, and the key role to be played is *citizenship*. Learning, knowing, and leading inform and activate CSD.

Implications for Integral Learning and Knowledge Management. We now arrive at the social systems domain where the result of our knowledge building, with the assistance of the five learnership interdisciplinary reasoning competencies, may be reviewed. The major determination for **CSD** is whether the knowledge recently created is "relevant" to the inquiry, study, problem or issue being considered. Quite often a paradox occurs at this juncture in which the conclusion reached appears to be inconsistent, conflicting or incompatible with what the individuals involved anticipated or desired. When analyzed, questions arise as to weather the Systems Thinking, Pattern Recognition or Situational Learning competencies have been utilized in an open, factual, unbiased, timely and convincing manner. That is, is the knowledge really correct and integral when considering the obvious limitations in people's minds and personal preferences – and their cultures, education, and beliefs are sometimes entirely in conflict. Effective and valued knowledge will need to be judged by the CSD Business, Education, and Government domains of thinking and behavior as interpreted by skilled and experienced leaders.

Chapter Thirteen: Societal (Meta) Systems Development

SSD is social synthesis at the meta-cognitive level, and consists of fully integrated reasoning and development across all four social system of systems domains that responds to influences from the six American learnership universal knowledge spheres (social, political, economic, technological, geographical and ecological). SSD strives to capture the spirit of John Sullivan's *To Come to Life More Fully* (1990), and suggests milestones for our timeless journey towards holistic personhood. The meta-level goal selected for the societal level is *human enlightenment*, and the key role to be played is *statesmanship*. Learning, knowing, and leading inform and activate SSD.

Implications for Integral Learning and Knowledge Management. We now arrive at the social systems domain where the result of our knowledge building, with the assistance of the five learnership Interdisciplinary reasoning competencies, may be reviewed. The major determination for **SSD** is whether the knowledge recently created is "relevant" to the inquiry, study, problem or issue being considered. Quite often a paradox occurs at this juncture in which the conclusion reached appears to be inconsistent, conflicting or incompatible with what the individuals involved anticipated or desired. When analyzed, questions arise as to whether the Systems Thinking, Pattern Recognition or Situational Learning competencies have been utilized in an open, factual, unbiased, timely and convincing manner. That is, is the knowledge really correct and integral when considering that there are obvious limitations in people's minds and personal preferences – and their cultures, education, and beliefs are sometimes entirely in conflict. Effective and valued knowledge will need to be judged by the SSD Personal, Organization, and Community domains of thinking and behavior as interpreted by skilled and experienced leaders.

SECTION IV. American Learnership Encore: Mid-Life Opportunities and Experiences

Chapter Fourteen: Mid-Life/Career Transition and Renewal

This stage of cognitive and emotional awareness, and even discomfort, generally begins in the forty-five to fifty-five age range, but can vary significantly depending on an individual's particular life circumstances. It is often a period of disruptive feelings, cognitive dilemmas, and forced reflection on matters having to do with one's life purpose, progress, happiness, experiences and increasing age. Challenges include moving from independency to interdependency and from intimacy to generativity.

Implications for Integral Learning and Knowledge Management. *We now arrive at the social systems domain where the result of our knowledge building, with the assistance of the five learnership Interdisciplinary reasoning competencies, may be reviewed. The major determination for Mid-Life/Career Transition and Renewal is whether the knowledge recently created is "relevant" to the inquiry, study, problem or issue being considered. Quite often a paradox occurs at this juncture in which the conclusion reached appears to be inconsistent, conflicting or incompatible with what the individuals involved anticipated or desired. When analyzed, questions arise as to whether the Systems Thinking, Pattern Recognition or Situational Learning competencies have been utilized in an open, factual, unbiased, timely and convincing manner. That is, is the knowledge really correct and integral when considering that there are obvious limitations in people's minds and personal preferences – and their cultures, education, and beliefs are sometimes entirely in conflict. Effective and valued knowledge will need to be judged by thinking and behavior as interpreted by skilled and experienced leaders of the Mid-Life Transition Personal, Organization, and Community domains.*

Chapter Fifteen: Senior Rejuvenation, Authentic Living and Legacy Success

"In the decades ahead, the boomers will complete America's transformation into a gerontocracy as they take control of the nation's social and economic power. From this demographically and politically dominant position, they will have the potential to realize their full intellectual, social, and political influence, not as baby boomers but as elders." (Ken Dychtwald in *Age Power: How the 21st Century will be Ruled by the New Old*, 1999)

Notwithstanding Dychtwald's argument, here in 2015 it is arguable as to which generation has become the most dominant. The millennials receive the most product advertising, but the seniors control the most income and wealth. And that wealth has been obtained through knowledge, skills, and experience acquired over five or more decades. Many of those seniors are over sixty five years of age, and fully one-half of them will live past the age of eighty. As a group they are healthier than ever, involved in mental and physical rejuvenation, and are spending more of their available time considering the form and contents of their lives and future legacies. For many this is the time they have been waiting for most of their lives and they want these later years to be the most influential on posterity as they can achieve.

Implications for Integral Learning and Knowledge Management. *Conceptually, mentally healthy adults of this age can possibly be the most holistically informed and knowledge sharing benefactors of the younger generations that follow. This group has the benefit of a lifetime of continuous learning, working and leading through hundreds, if not thousands, of both positive and negative experiences that demanded attention, adjustment and change. The new and better have continually chased the old and weaker out of the main arena. And yet, much of what humanity has needed has survived the on-slot of products and services so that these seniors are not necessarily irrelevant or nonproductive. In fact, considering their breadth of knowledge and experience, they may have the best advice for confronting complex issues due to their interdependent and integral wisdom.*

END

B. American Learnership Practitioner Characteristics (25)

If there is a new social contract implicit between employers and employees today it should be this:
You give me your labor and I will guarantee that as long as you work here,
I will give you every opportunity – through either career advancement or training to become more
employable and more versatile. — Thomas Friedman

"Learnership practitioner" is the term used in this Handbook to give distinction to a special class of artful learners – those who immerse themselves in a lifelong quest for relevant learning, meaningful knowledge, and personal achievement. These are people who, over time, continuously learn and develop the capability to understand and integrate the myriad of influences and experiences to which life exposes them. They display a personal "presence" which others often interpret as being rational, balanced and competent. Additional attributes often characteristic of learnership practitioners is they have or are:

1. Are people who systematically increase their understanding of life's opportunities and challenges; develop their skills through "questioning and learning;" and produce products and services of value to themselves and others.

2. Have historically been contributors to societal development due to their "innovation and problem-solving proclivities." They are people who have eclectic learning interests and acquire the skills and technologies that enable their achievements.

3. Are also "knowledge managers" in their own right in that they continually identify, acquire, organize, use and share new found knowledge within their respective social systems. They learn and lead within their personal social system, develop and apply knowledge practices and tools in their organizational roles, and contribute as informed problem solvers within their local communities.

4. Understand and appreciate the fundamental theories in their fields of interest and education. However, they are "primarily committed to the practical application" of what they need to learn and know in order to pursue their goals and achieve their priorities. In particular, these highly interdependent personalities appear to have a high degree of resilience and resourcefulness in acquiring new knowledge and in their ability to learn from practical experience. These people have good cognitive and reflective skills, but unlike their more academic counterparts, those skills are valued to the degree they align with their need to turn "knowledge into action" in a timely manner.

5. Have "learned-to-learn," they get psychological rewards from the process of learning, and they do it all their lives. They may be distinguished from the majority of others who are bound by the excessive differentiation and lack of integration of the traditional educational curricula that fail to connect theory to practice, and have little motivational impact when taught in formal classroom settings.

6. Operate as "free agent learners" and may be distinguished from many others in that they are not bound by the limitations of the traditional educational curricula taught in formal school and classroom settings. Instead, they are, and have been imbued with the "adult learning," "learn-as-needed," "just-in-time-training," and "virtual knowledge worker" practices encouraged by the rapidly changing social, economic, and technological work practices of the last two decades.

7. Pursue "cycles of rapid learning" across formal and informal boundaries and social and electronic networks. Instant messaging, internet scanning, and blog participation are viewed as sources of potentially useful information, while smart phones and laptops are essential tools for communications, learning, and knowledge-building.

8. Possess a "curiosity concerning the world around them" that enables history, learnership practitioners have been "people with distinguished lives and careers." They are here today working among us in large numbers, and will be valued for their unique contributions by generations yet to come.

9. Relish the opportunity to "fully absorb their experiences and to learn from them." They also become influential through their ability to put their knowledge into action.

10. A willingness to embark on humanity's journey toward mindful growth and an understanding of life's mysteries and human purpose.

11. A desire to motivate oneself and others to discover life's opportunities, pursue a unique purpose, confront personal challenges, develop enlightened perspective, and attain a higher level-of-being.

12. An appreciation for interpersonal dialogue based on open inquiry, rapid learning, interpersonal understanding, and reasoned decision making.

13. A capacity to improve human relations by exemplifying the principles of leadership, followership, stewardship, citizenship, fellowship, and statesmanship.

14. A willingness to participate in issue resolution in the political, economic, social, technological, territorial, and ecological domains of societal knowledge and endeavour.

15. A developmental perspective on how individuals, organizations and communities progress through their respective phases of development – each with its own objectives, challenges and rewards.

16. A systems perspective on societal learning and development that balances the human need for both stability and change to achieve higher levels of societal development and performance.

17. A focus on personal learning and knowledge management as key capabilities in the development of social systems: personal, organizational, community, and societal.

18. A desire to replace differentiation with integration as a lifelong perspective – and the ultimate foundation for a mindful journey through life.

19. A commitment to use knowledge, science, and practical experience to overcome excessive reliance on mysticism, superstition, and supernatural intervention when operating in the public spheres where everyone needs to feel comfortable and secure.

20. An advocate of the means between the extremes – weighing personal rights with social responsibilities in order to negotiate adequate, inclusive outcomes.

21. An appreciation for balancing inquiry and advocacy in all one attempts to accomplish. No one knows all that could be known to reduce potential risk and to guarantee success.

22. A capacity to perform multiple roles such as consultant, coach, facilitator, student, mentor, thought leader, and project manager as situations require.

23. A willingness to apply the Learnership Integrated Systems Architecture (LISA) model at all levels of personal and social systems development.

Thomas Friedman, in his recent book *The World is Flat* (2005) suggested a few new thoughts that integrate into the learnership practitioner description. When explaining what will be required for those individuals worldwide to remain vital and competitive during the rapid changes in the immediate future, Friedman emphasizes: (a) learning-to-learn, (b) pattern recognition and problem solving, (c) striving to become untouchable, and (d) becoming a "*versalist.*"

Learning-to-learn is a fundamental anchor in learnership philosophy and practice. It is the capacity to recognize individual, organizational and societal patterns of thinking and action. Problem solving and decision-making are essentially learnership reasoning practices. Striving to become an "untouchable" in the new world economy requires that we keep ourselves well educated and skilled in order to remain marketable in the international marketplace.

Lastly, more careerists will stay competitive to strike a balance between being a specialist and a generalist – both of which have their place in the economy. We who become "*versalists,*" however, will progress through our careers by continually adding new specialties to our respective repertoires thereby allowing us multiple opportunities for gainful employment. Two additional learnership practitioner capabilities should now be added to the list:

24. A personal commitment to learning reasoning competencies that improve systems thinking, pattern recognition, situational learning, knowledge management, and adaptive leadership.

25. An expectation that personal development depends primarily on being responsible and responsive to the ever-changing political, economic, and social forces occurring locally or on a global scale.

C. Wealth Generation and Financial Security

[Reference Chapters 2, 3, 4, 10, 11, 12, and 14]

Chapter 2. Discovering the Meaning of Your Life

While the previous topic emphasized human "qualitative aspirations" it is essential that financial or "quantitative aspirations" be given equal consideration. This chapter is the first of many following chapters that consider the importance in everyone's life of earning money and acquiring wealth. For some, this is the overarching purpose to which they are committed and the one that assists them in measuring and quantifying the ultimate value of their lives. However, significant research on the lives of the most successful and wealthy people does not show that having significant wealth negates the desire for success – and the happiest people are most often people of ordinary financial means.

How we think about financial security, acquired wealth, and their importance in achieving prosperity is significant in much of our personal and work lives. Our conscious and unconscious attitudes which were learned from early experiences with family, community and culture establish how we deal with others and make choices when acquiring and managing money. If we have thought about our purpose, success and happiness in terms of our personal, organizational and community relationships we are likely to maintain a balanced perspective in which money and the ownership of property and assets are mutually desirable but with due respect for the interests of others in the larger social system.

In the *Psychology of Wealth* (2012), author Charles Richards PhD advises people to review their principles and values to assure that their personal beliefs and behaviors demonstrate the positive side of wealth instead of the negative side of wealth:

1. The Negative Side of Wealth is illustrated when fear, insecurity, anxiety and stress make us appear to be miserly, arrogant, self-serving, restrictive and judgmental towards others.

2. The Positive Side of Wealth is depicted when higher human purpose is on display in the form of generosity, proficiency, creativity, and discerning or considerate behavior.

According to Dr. Richards the psychology of wealth is, in fact, a psychology of self-esteem and self-respect. And, it is a mistake to pursue wealth believing that first acquiring wealth leads to those important psychological objectives. Each of us should invest in ourselves by pursuing meaningful objectives, assuming self-responsibility and maintaining integrity similar to those illustrated in this Mindset Handbook. Dr. Richards advises that personal development leads to high self-esteem versus low self-esteem:

1. Having high self-esteem includes: being open to other points of view, learning from mistakes, accepting others' differences gracefully, and living in the present.

2. Having low self-esteem includes: being hypersensitive to criticism, blaming others for your circumstances, fearing change and avoiding taking risks, and having difficulty in making decisions.

Dr. Richards advises that "The psychology of wealth is a simple and pragmatic call to nurture the qualities and attitudes within ourselves that will create a prosperous life," and that "We expect the best of ourselves, and we recognize that the golden path to true prosperity, to a life of happiness and fulfillment, begins by showing up and putting one foot in front of the other." (pp. 224-5)

[**Author's Note:** This topic on Wealth Generation leading to adequate Financial Security begins in this chapter and is developed in greater detail, as appropriate, in Personal Project Management (Chapter 3) Authentic Branding (Chapter 4), Personal Development (Chapter 10), Organization Development (Chapter 11) and Community Development (Chapter 12). In each chapter, the theme of *earning financial security from productive activity* serves to remind the reader that lifelong learning, knowing, leading, and achieving is a multi-functional responsibility in human progress.

Chapter 3. Being the Project Manager of Your Life

Wealth and Financial Security Using an Integrated Balance Scorecard
The graphic at Figure 3-6 represents the American Learnership interpretation of the Kaplan and Norton model as

a <u>Learnership Integrated Balanced Scorecard</u>. It begins with business *high performance* (HP) domain in the center, personal *self-fulfillment* (SF) domain on the left, and the community *common good* (CG) domain on the right. Simultaneously, it interlinks the balanced scorecard financial, customer, internal processes and knowledge and learning assessment factors to communicate a social system-of-systems framework. The result is an ambitious conceptualization of how future project managers, business leaders and social system architects can reflect and   collaborate on interdisciplinary societal improvement and development in terms of the *planned and achieved financial management outcomes* for participants in all societal domains.

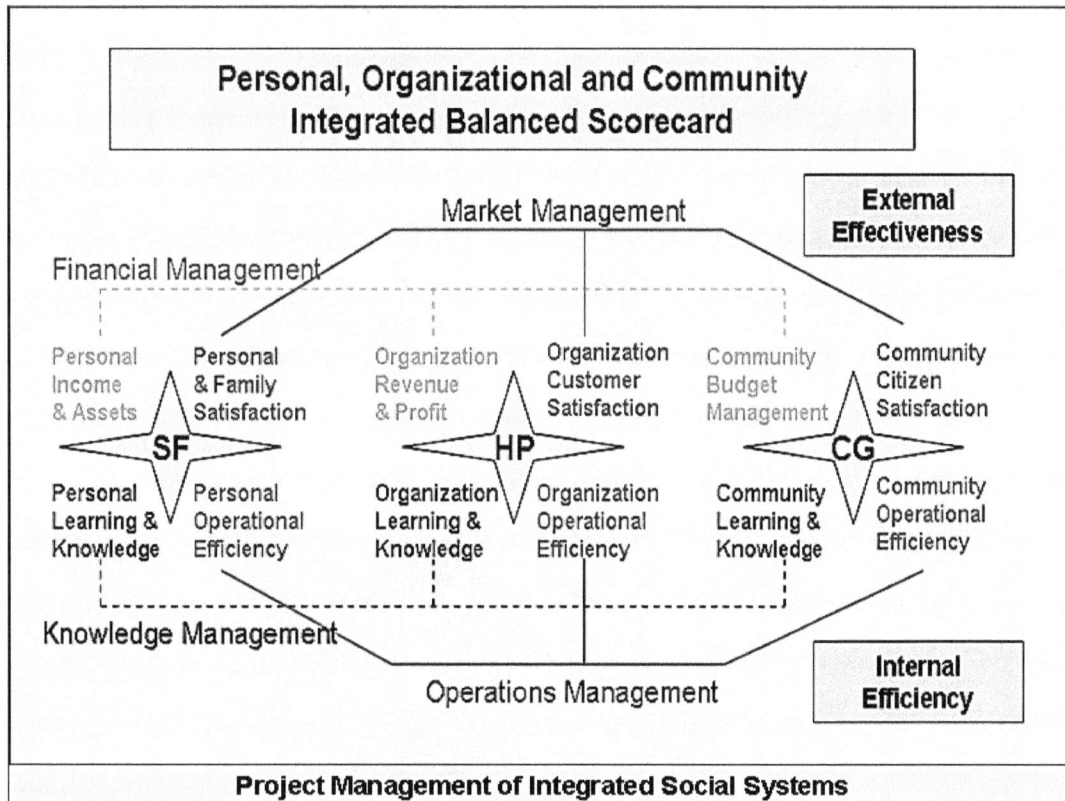

Figure 3-6

The efficiency and effectiveness of all domains can be best determined by reviewing systems performance in a counter-clockwise manner starting with the <u>Knowledge Management</u> domain, proceeding through the <u>Operations Management</u> and the <u>Market Management</u> domains, and ending at the <u>Financial Management</u> results domain:

a. <u>Personal Self-Fulfillment</u> – From this viewpoint, an assessment that reviews an individual's personal level of learning and knowledge development, followed by how that development enables personal (family) operational efficiency, followed by the effectiveness in achieving personal (family) satisfaction, results in the near and longer-term accumulation of personal (family) income and capital assets. This process may be termed **personal (family) wealth and financial security** which is the result continuous review and learning in the other quadrants and is discussed in detail later in Chapter Ten.

b. <u>Organization High Performance</u> – From this viewpoint, an assessment that reviews an organization's level of learning and knowledge development, followed by how that development enables organizational operational efficiency, followed by the effectiveness in achieving organization market satisfaction, results in the near and longer-term accumulation of organization income and capital assets. This process may be termed **organization (business) wealth and financial security** which is the result continuous review and learning in the other quadrants and is discussed in detail later in Chapter Eleven.

c. <u>Community Common Good</u> – From this viewpoint, an assessment that reviews a community's level of learning and knowledge development, followed by how that development enables community operational efficiency, followed by the effectiveness in achieving community citizen satisfaction, results in the near and longer-term accumulation of community income and capital assets. This process may be termed **community wealth and financial security** which is the result continuous review and learning in the other quadrants and is discussed in detail later in Chapter

Twelve.

[**Author's Note:** Figure 3-7 has been modified to illustrate the wealth and financial security aspect of assessing the Meaning of our Lives as we continue through this Handbook.]

Chapter 4. Crafting Your Personal and Professional Brand

Wealth and Financial Security

By the time individuals begin thinking about establishing their Personal Brand they have generally begun reflecting on who they are and what they hope to accomplish in their lives. For some, they may already been stimulated by thoughts of the level of income they are earning, whether it is satisfactory at the present time in their lives, and if they want to equal or exceed that of those they see as competitors in achieving progress and respect. Once again, significant meaning in life may be attained by focusing primarily on the societal qualitative factors (personal, organizational, community, social) with or without excessive concern for financial factors. And, yet without a modest effort in this area they cannot assume sufficient income and wealth accumulation that will support them achieving all that they may hope to achieve.

The advantage of participating in the authentic personal and professional branding initiative in this handbook is that its process blends the personal branding and the corporate (organization) branding initiatives to form a synthesis of ambition, branding, and balanced scorecard commitments toward integrated personal success and financial security (Figure 4-5). The required planning, documentation and execution of the project ensures a disciplined assessment of measurable progress. Setting wealth and financial security goals should be reviewed and action taken regularly.

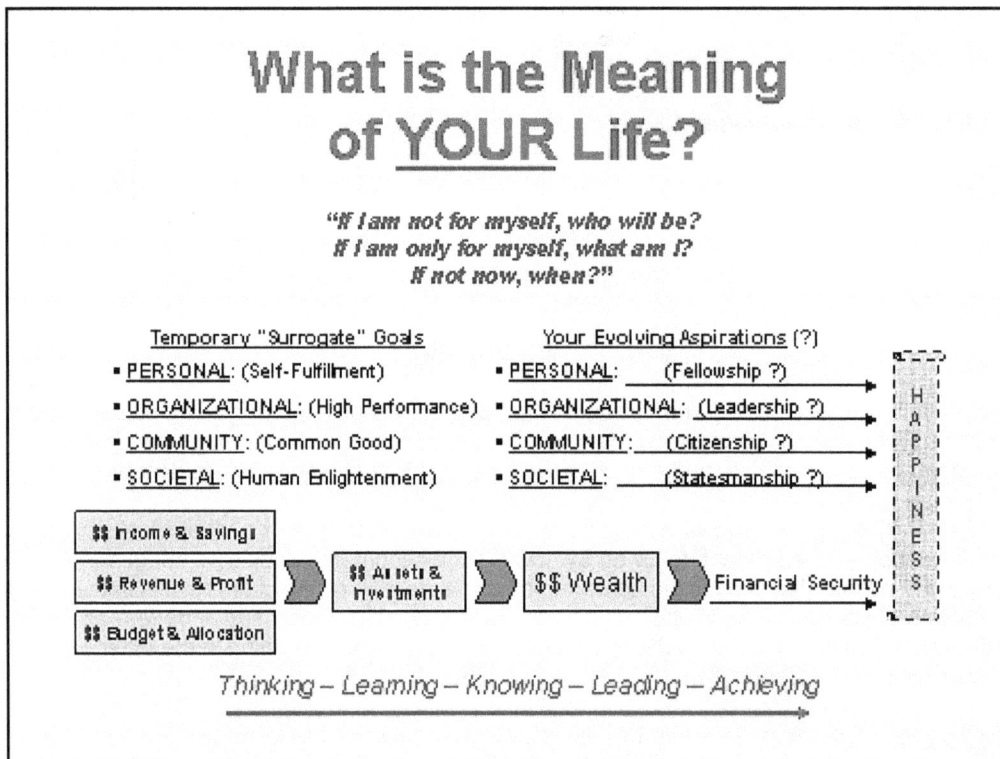

Figure 4-5

Chapter 10. Personal (Family) Development

Personal Wealth and Financial Security (Observations and Recommendations)

As explained starting back in Chapter Two, our Personal (Family) System Development can be evaluated on how well we make progress on achieving our meta-level life goals – specifically, how well we contribute toward self-fulfilment, high performance, the common good and human enlightenment. However, all of these qualitative socio-economic measures are enabled by the productivity of our knowledge and skills in growing personal wealth and attaining financial security. Figure 10-4 is a comparative illustration of the major income and expenditure categories during a typical adult lifetime. Points for consideration are:

1. **Employment** – A lifetime of career work and development that provides the income necessary for expenditures. Primary approaches to save for future needs are pensions, IRAs, 401(k)s, and payroll taxes. Part time work is often considered to accumulate sufficient income even through the retirement years.

2. **College (Savings)** – Lifelong learning is essential for successful career growth and retirement. It is recommended that we save and pay for part of our own education. And then, if children are a responsibility, begin a 529 savings or other investment account for their education.

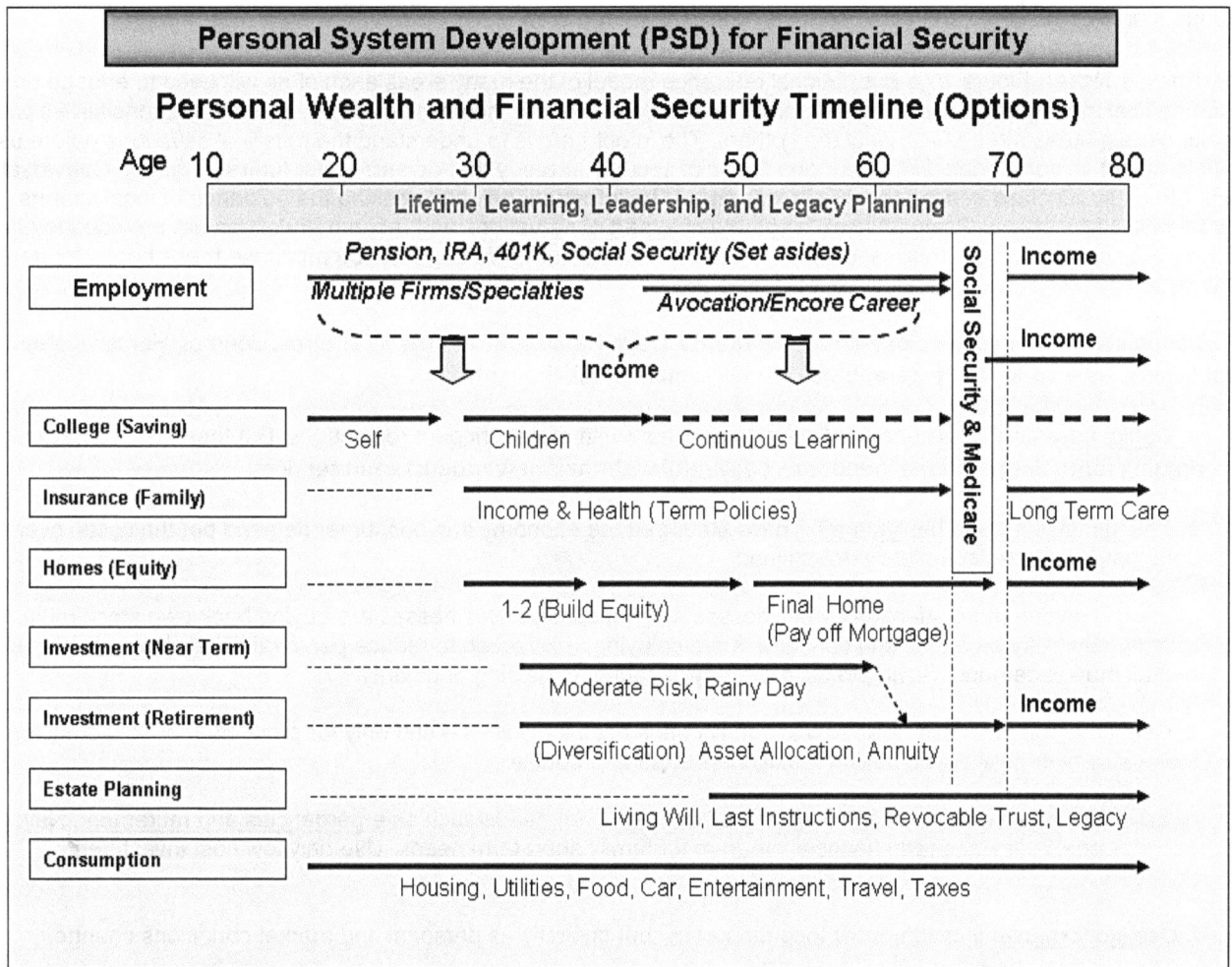

Figure 10-4

3. **Insurance (Family)** – Insurance is needed primarily for family health and financial security upon our own death, and should be term life only. Long term insurance is recommended for our retirement period when other income and assets are insufficient to pay for group residential expenses. Medicare is federal government health insurance assistance starting at age sixty-five after federal Social Security is being received.

4. **Homes (Equity)** – Saving early and purchasing a starter home with equity growth potential can start an advantageous series of sell and buy transactions ending in the ultimate purchase of a final home that can be paid off by the owner's retirement.

5. **Investment (Near Term)** – Either saving or near term investments (5-8 years) may be a good way to acquire the money needed for a large purchase such as a house down payment. If funds are available when getting close to retirement, that surplus can be transferred to increase the value of the retirement account.

6. **Investment (Retirement)** – In today's financial environment when so many are underfunded for their retirement years it advisable that retirement investments are begun much earlier in life than was previously recommended. Starting by age 30 – and concurrently with near term investments – would not be too soon.

7. **Estate Planning** – While having a written will is advisable as soon as one has assets that need to be distributed after death, one should not wait past their mid-life period (age 45-50) to prepare a more detailed expression of the their wishes once they have a family situation wherein accumulated money, physical assets and other personal matters must assuredly be addressed. Professional estate planning is recommended to ensure legal and administrative processing is achieved.

8. **Consumption** – The amount of income allocated for all the above items still needs to be allotted in a manner that all weekly and monthly expenses can be comfortably accommodated. In reality, for most people their early life/family budgets are not sufficient and some serious trade-offs are required.

[Author's Note: Figure 10-4 is a notional reference model of the many areas each of us will need to engage during our financial management lives. The combination and degree of our incomes, interests, age and responsibilities will make certain areas more of a priority than others. The intent here is to understand the personal situations before us and to select an appropriate life wealth and financial security strategy that optimizes our future progress. Conversation with others in our class and personal networks should be informational, and seeking the guidance of local experts is certainly a smart option. Going forward, a sample of expert observations and recommendations are provided to enrich our discussions in terms of this Handbook's informational structure. We suggest you purchase these books for detailed advice.]

1. A Guide to the New Rules of Personal Finance, Dave Kansas, 2011, The Wall Street Journal, Harper-Collins Publishers, New York, NY. To paraphrase a small sample of his thoughts:

a. Banks have been chastened and have to deal now with more stringent regulations. But they are aggressively arguing for their operational freedom – be careful with their new products and services.

b. The stimulus bill and healthcare bill have stabilized the economy and consumer demand but the costs, over time, have not been completely determined.

c. Thrift is getting more attention by businesses and consumers. Businesses are buying back own stock rather than offering new risky products, and consumers are delaying satisfaction to reduce personal risks which diminishes overall market demand. Saving to build a "rainy day fund" is gaining popularity.

d. Consumer loans should be limited to family *needs* not simply *likes* – and only for products that hold or increase their value over time. Avoid buying rapidly depreciating products.

e. Save and invest much earlier than in the past for long run needs such as emergencies and retirement. Never sacrifice one's own long term financial program for family short term needs. Use only low cost investment providers.

f. Use stock market investment for long run needs, but diversify as personal and market conditions change.

g. Delay taking Social Security payments past age 62 up to 70 to maximize retirement funding. Sign up for Medicare at age 65 or Medicaid when the conditions apply.

h. Consider annuities which include initial investments and guaranteed lifetime payouts during retirement. However,
deal only with the highest rated organizations due to the complexity of these instruments and the many unscrupulous sales practices in this arena.

2. *The Money Class,* Suze Orman, 2011, Spiegel and Grau, Random House Publishing Group, New York, NY. To paraphrase a small sample of her thoughts:

a. We need to move beyond materialism to actual happiness in life. Put your finger on what is authentic to you.

b. Having lasting security requires standing in your own truth. Recognize, embrace and trust what is real for you and use that to understand the choices you make and the real needs you have.

c. Create your own balance sheet. Review your income and expenses. Get your FICO score. Balance your short term and long term needs and choose to live below your means.

d. Recognize the power of cash. Spend what you have today not what you hope to have in the future. Plan to have an eight month reserve for income emergencies. Get extra years out of cars, houses and appliances.

e. Use term insurance, not whole life insurance. Take advantage of all employer savings and investment benefits.

f. Do not invest in bonds or bond funds as they are only occasionally advantageous during periods of low and stable interest rates. It is far more likely that market rates (managed by the Federal Reserve Board) will soon be encouraged to rise for the benefit of businesses, thereby driving down the base value of long term bonds.

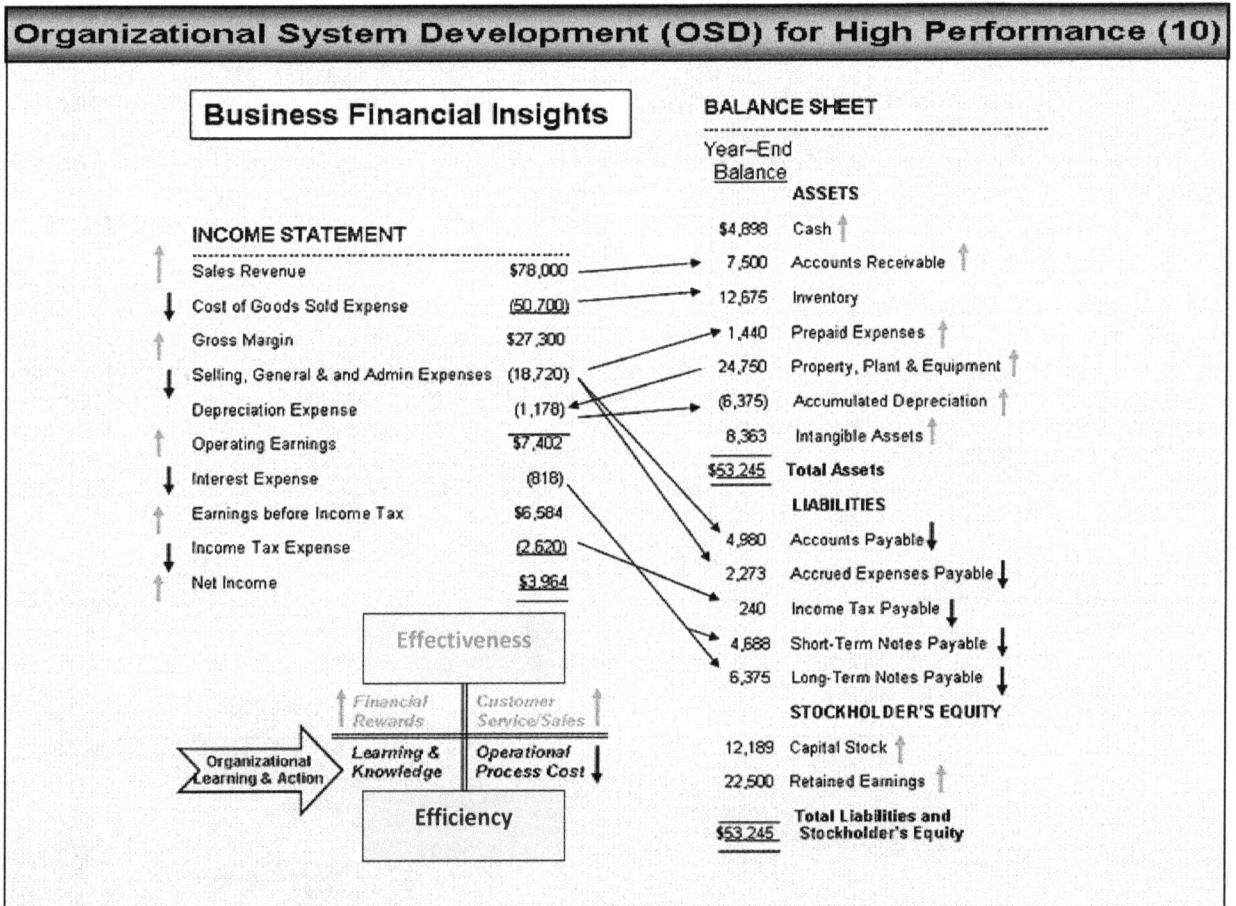

Figure 10-5

g. Always use Roth IRAs, federal loans not private loans for college loans. Do not co-sign loans, sacrifice retirement savings for others, and plan to create experiences for grandchildren rather than leave large cash inheritances.

h. Use estate planning in addition to a will to protect and allocate resources that remain after death. Consider the benefits of a "revocable living trust."

A reminder at this junction provided by Suze Orman is: that in terms of one's career, the American Dream in the past of steady employment opportunity is being replaced by a new American Dream in which there will be increasing competition for fewer good full time jobs. And, in this new Dream, only the rapidly developing person in the right location at the right time will experience an observable ladder for steady socio-economic progress throughout their lifetime.

Chapter 11. Organization (Business) Development

Organization (Business) Financials for Growth, Wealth and Financial Security
Organization leaders, chief financial officers and enterprise consultants have a common interest in assuring the firm's financial status is growing so as to achieve its stated mission. Their daily decision making activities must stay focused on improvements as illustrated in the balanced scorecard model inserted at the bottom of Figure 11 – 10. That model shows that improvement in workforce learning and knowledge can stimulate operational efficiency. Additionally, emphasis on business efficiency should always be directed toward supporting greater customer service effectiveness resulting in the achievement of desired financial results.

Chapter 12. Community (Societal) Development

Community Wealth and Financial Security

Individuals and the organizations for which they work and support are inevitably members of local communities in which they and their families participate in shopping, recreation, school events, public associations, and the use of government services and school activities. Commercial and industrial businesses, government and non-government associations, schools for children ages 5 to 18 as well as those for whom colleges and private academies provide training for adult life interact in a myriad of communications and transactions that build both a sense of community and culture.

Using a balanced scorecard perspective (Chapters two to four) it can be illustrated that community wealth and financial security may be positively influenced (1) by the level of human knowledge and skill developed over time, (2) that stays within in the community and adds to public and private efficiency, and (3) is applied to effectively meet the needs and satisfaction of the community's citizens. When these factors and associated community values are present, well-intentioned leaders are able to collaborate to determine their community's priorities and desires, establish conservative and reasonable budgets, and gain consensus on an administrative process to collect operational income and to allocate and appropriate funding within budget guidelines – mostly through taxes and revenue from individuals, businesses and various levels of government administration.

Figure 12-6 illustrates approved budget limits for FY 2016 of one state county. It shows residents the result of numerous meetings and debates among community members prior to the beginning of the FY. Every member of the community who contributed their respective knowledge and skills to complete the deliberations and final budget – and those who will contribute their payment – are worthy of recognition for their commitment to finding the *Community Common Good.*

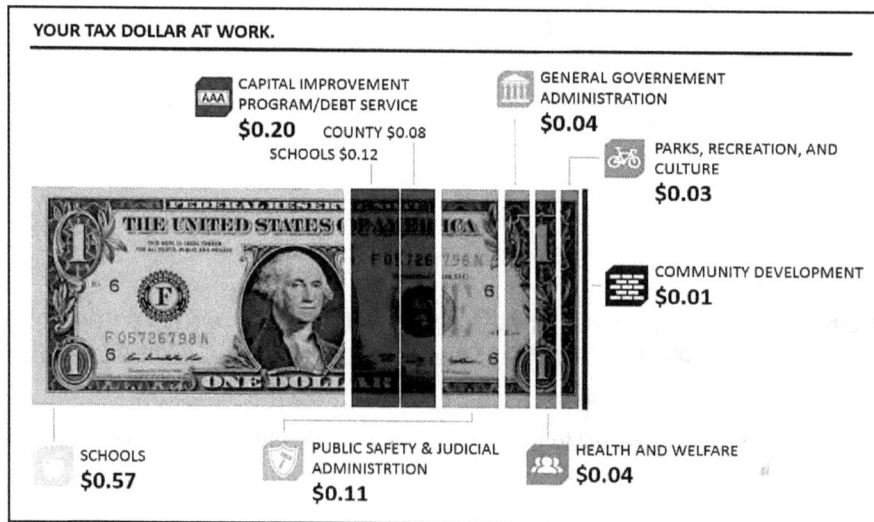

Figure 12-5

The chart above shows how each dollar of real property tax revenue is allocated between the General Government and the Schools in FY 2016. The School system receives 69 cents of every tax dollar, with 57 cents going toward operating expenses and 12 cents toward capital improvements and debt service. The County receives 31 cents of every local tax dollar, 8 cents of which is devoted to capital improvements and debt service while the remaining 23 cents covers annual operating costs. The chart shows the distribution of the 23 cents in County operating costs across the five functional areas of County government. Operating expenses for the Public Safety and Judicial Administration function will require 11 cents. of every tax dollar in FY 2016.

Chapter 14. Mid-Life/Career Transition and Renewal

Suze's Retirement Planning Suggestions
1. Getting Going in Your 20s and 30s: *[How many of us really tried to do this? How did that work out?]*
   a. Use time as an asset – Start saving early for great long term results
   b. Use your employer's savings and investment plans.
   c. Use 401(k)s, IRAs and Roth IRAs
   d. Stock investing and dollar cost averaging

2. Fine-tuning in Your 40s and 50s: *[Some of us are here now. Are we ready to finally start?]*
   a. Your mortgage – when and how to pay it off
   b. The "work until age 67" work plan
   c. Delay Social Security benefit payments
   d. Estimate retirement income
   e. Best investments outside your 401(k)
   f. Plan for healthcare, Medicare and Long-Term Care
   g. Choose only fee-based financial planners (no commissions)

3. Living in Retirement: *[Now we need to get serious. What have we done (will do) to succeed?]*
   a. Focus on affordability; your needs over your wants
   b. Protect your retirement savings from others' expectations
   c. Choose only dividend paying stocks and EFTs from low cost brokers
   d. Avoid long-term bonds and bond funds
   e. Go slow on selecting annuities (can be complex and deceptive)
   f. Eliminate mortgages when choosing to stay in same home
   g. Include donations and giving back to the community

D. Life Transitions and Architecture (LISA) for Integrated Living and Development

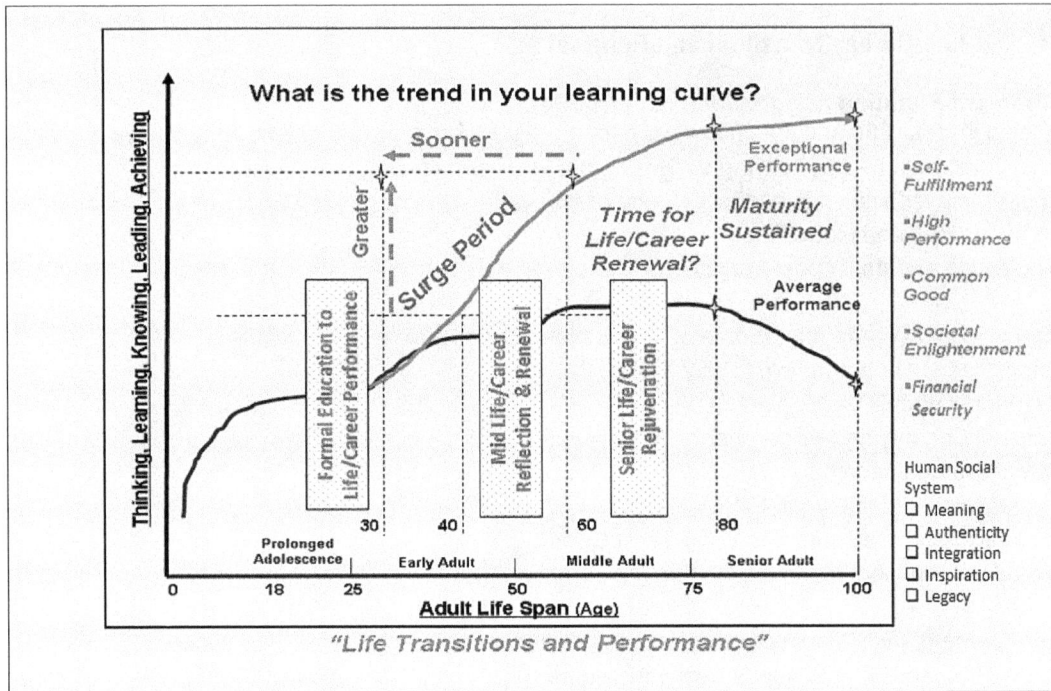

Figure 1

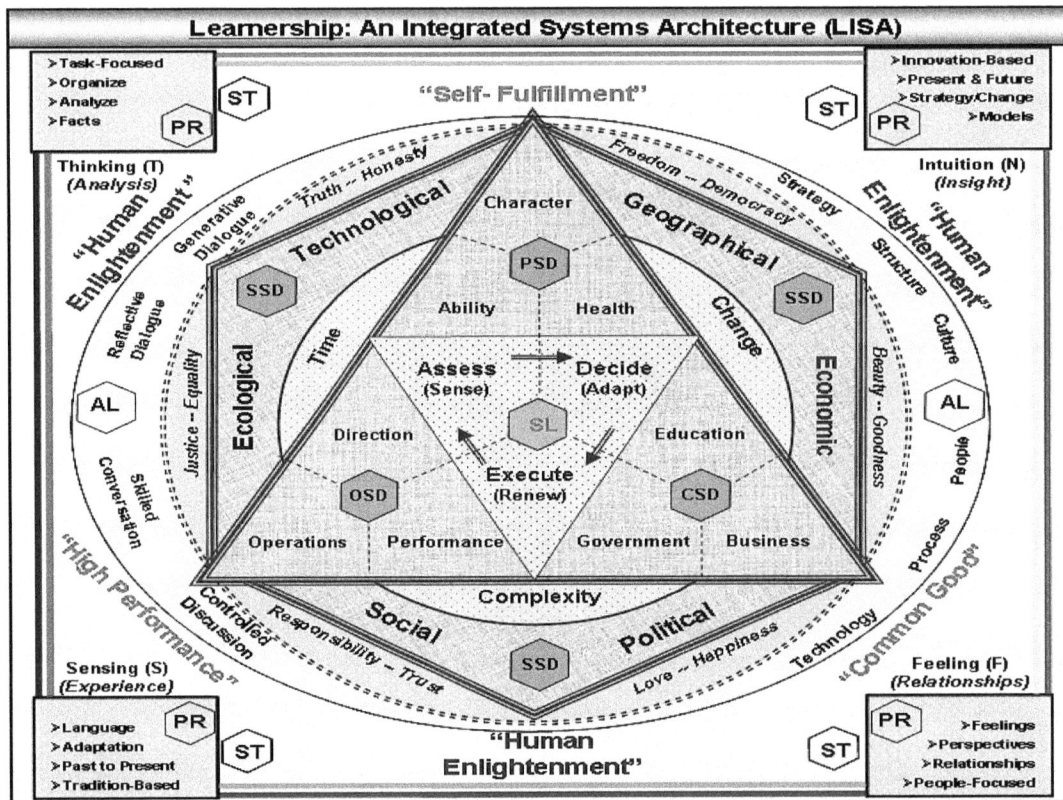

Figure 2

Appendix

Appendix A	**American Founding Documents:** p.420 U.S. Declaration of Independence U.S. Bill of Rights U.N. Declaration of Human Rights
Appendix B	** **Personal eBook Publishing:** p.426 My Integral Life, Work, Wealth, Health, and Legacy Success
Appendix C	** **Personal eBook Publishing:** p.446 My Authentic Personal and Professional Brand
Appendix D	**Encore Example:** p.494 The Author's Encore Journey
Appendix E	**Complete Your Unique Life Project** p.496 Your Legacy Package ** My Mid-Life/Career Transition and Personal Renew ** My Senior Lifelong Learning and Memorable Legacy (Letter) Your Legal, Administrative and Financial Affairs
Appendix F	Your Legal, Administrative and Financial Affairs p.501
Appendix G	**American Learnership Organization and Author** p.503 Organization: AL Solutions and AL Forum Author: Rudolph B. Garrity, Dr. Public Administration

[**Author's Note:** Readers and participants in ALF programs and courses are reminded that while improved learning and performance are expected by everyone who contributes to the huge volume of concepts and materials that make this educational experience worthwhile; action is required to gain the benefits suggested by the many contributing experts whose insight and knowledge have been included in this ALF Mindset and Handbook]

ALF Website: http://www.alforum.org/read-handbook.html
(Includes: Handbook, Website, Curriculum, Videos, Chapter PDFs, Exercise)

Mastermind for Project Leaders: American Family Life Management and Professional Performance
(Description Location: Handbook Preface; Website Master Class Tab)

Age 25-50 Projects:

My Integral Life, Work, Wealth, Health and Legacy Success ** (Personal Fulfillment) & (Optional: e-book)

My Authentic Personal and Professional Brand ** (Enterprise High Performance) & (Optional: e-book)

Age 50-75 Projects:

My Mid-Life/Career Transition and Personal Renewal ** (Encore Life Planning) & (Optional: e-book)

My Senior Lifelong Learning and Memorable Legacy ** (Optional: Family Letter)

Appendix A

The United States Declaration of Independence
The Declaration of Independence: A Transcription [Original Text]
IN CONGRESS, July 4, 1776

The unanimous Declaration of the thirteen united States of America,

When in the Course of human events, it becomes necessary for one people to dissolve the political bands which have connected them with another, and to assume among the powers of the earth, the separate and equal station to which the Laws of Nature and of Nature's God entitle them, a decent respect to the opinions of mankind requires that they should declare the causes which impel them to the separation.

We hold these truths to be self-evident, that all men are created equal, that they are endowed by their Creator with certain unalienable Rights, that among these are Life, Liberty and the pursuit of Happiness. –That to secure these rights, Governments are instituted among Men, deriving their just powers from the consent of the governed, –That whenever any Form of Government becomes destructive of these ends, it is the Right of the People to alter or to abolish it, and to institute new Government, laying its foundation on such principles and organizing its powers in such form, as to them shall seem most likely to effect their Safety and Happiness. Prudence, indeed, will dictate that Governments long established should not be changed for light and transient causes; and accordingly all experience hath shewn, that mankind are more disposed to suffer, while evils are sufferable, than to right themselves by abolishing the forms to which they are accustomed. But when a long train of abuses and usurpations, pursuing invariably the same Object evinces a design to reduce them under absolute Despotism, it is their right, it is their duty, to throw off such Government, and to provide new Guards for their future security. –Such has been the patient sufferance of these Colonies; and such is now the necessity which constrains them to alter their former Systems of Government. The history of the present King of Great Britain is a history of repeated injuries and usurpations, all having in direct object the establishment of an abso lute Tyranny over these States. To prove this, let Facts be submitted to a candid world.

–– He has refused his Assent to Laws, the most wholesome and necessary for the public good.

–– He has forbidden his Governors to pass Laws of immediate and pressing importance, unless suspended in their operation till his Assent should be obtained; and when so suspended, he has utterly neglected to attend to them.

––– He has refused to pass other Laws for the accommodation of large districts of people, unless those people would relinquish the right of Representation in the Legislature, a right inestimable to them and formidable to tyrants only.

–– He has called together legislative bodies at places unusual, uncomfortable, and distant from the depository of their public Records, for the sole purpose of fatiguing them into compliance with his measures.

–– He has dissolved Representative Houses repeatedly, for opposing with manly firmness his invasions on the rights of the people.

–– He has refused for a long time, after such dissolutions, to cause others to be elected; whereby the Legislative powers, incapable of Annihilation, have returned to the People at large for their exercise; the State remaining in the mean time exposed to all the dangers of invasion from without, and convulsions within.

–– He has endeavoured to prevent the population of these States; for that purpose obstructing the Laws for Naturalization of Foreigners; refusing to pass others to encourage their migrations hither, and raising the conditions of new Appropriations of Lands.

–– He has obstructed the Administration of Justice, by refusing his Assent to Laws for establishing Judiciary powers.

–– He has made Judges dependent on his Will alone, for the tenure of their offices, and the amount and payment of their salaries.

–– He has erected a multitude of New Offices, and sent hither swarms of Officers to harrass our people, and eat out their substance.

–– He has kept among us, in times of peace, Standing Armies without the Consent of our legislatures.

–– He has affected to render the Military independent of and superior to the Civil power.

–– He has combined with others to subject us to a jurisdiction foreign to our constitution, and unacknowledged by our laws; giving his Assent to their Acts of pretended Legislation:

For Quartering large bodies of armed troops among us: For protecting them, by a mock Trial, from punishment for any Murders

which they should commit on the Inhabitants of these States:

For cutting off our Trade with all parts of the world: For imposing Taxes on us without our Consent:

For depriving us in many cases, of the benefits of Trial by Jury: For transporting us beyond Seas to be tried for pretended offences:

For abolishing the free System of English Laws in a neighbouring Province, establishing therein an Arbitrary

government, and enlarging its Boundaries so as to render it at once an example and fit instrument for introducing the

same absolute rule into these Colonies:

For taking away our Charters, abolishing our most valuable Laws, and altering fundamentally the Forms of our Governments:

For suspending our own Legislatures, and declaring themselves invested with power to legislate for us in all cases whatsoever.

-- He has abdicated Government here, by declaring us out of his Protection and waging War against us.

-- He has plundered our seas, ravaged our Coasts, burnt our towns, and destroyed the lives of our people.

-- He is at this time transporting large Armies of foreign Mercenaries to compleat the works of death, desolation and tyranny, already begun with circumstances of Cruelty & perfidy scarcely paralleled in the most barbarous ages, and totally unworthy the Head of a civilized nation.

-- He has constrained our fellow Citizens taken Captive on the high Seas to bear Arms against their Country, to become the executioners of their friends and Brethren, or to fall themselves by their Hands.

-- He has excited domestic insurrections amongst us, and has endeavoured to bring on the inhabitants of our frontiers, the merciless Indian Savages, whose known rule of warfare, is an undistinguished destruction of all ages, sexes and conditions.

In every stage of these Oppressions We have Petitioned for Redress in the most humble terms: Our repeated Petitions have been answered only by repeated injury. A Prince whose character is thus marked by every act which may define a Tyrant, is unfit to be the ruler of a free people.

Nor have We been wanting in attentions to our Brittish brethren. We have warned them from time to time of attempts by their legislature to extend an unwarrantable jurisdiction over us. We have reminded them of the circumstances of our emigration and settlement here. We have appealed to their native justice and magnanimity, and we have conjured them by the ties of our common kindred to disavow these usurpations, which, would inevitably interrupt our connections and correspondence. They too have
been deaf to the voice of justice and of consanguinity. We must, therefore, acquiesce in the necessity, which denounces our Separation, and hold them, as we hold the rest of mankind, Enemies in War, in Peace Friends.

We, therefore, the Representatives of the united States of America, in General Congress, Assembled, appealing to the Supreme Judge of the world for the rectitude of our intentions, do, in the Name, and by Authority of the good People of these Colonies, solemnly publish and declare, That these United Colonies are, and of Right ought to be Free and Independent States; that they are Absolved from all Allegiance to the British Crown, and that all political connection between them and the State of Great Britain, is and ought to be totally dissolved; and that as Free and Independent States, they have full Power to levy War, conclude Peace, contract Alliances, establish Commerce, and to do all other Acts and Things which Independent States may of right do. And for the support of this Declaration, with a firm reliance on the protection of divine Providence, we mutually pledge to each other our Lives, our Fortunes and our sacred Honor.

END

The United States Bill of Rights to the Constitution

The Bill of Rights: A Transcription [Original Text]

The Preamble to:The Bill of Rights:
The **Congress of the United States** begun and held at the City of New-York
on Wednesday the fourth of March one thousand seven hundred and eighty nine.

THE Conventions of a number of the States, having at the time of their adopting the Constitution, expressed a desire, in order to prevent misconstruction or abuse of its powers, that further declaratory and restrictive clauses should be added: And as extending the ground of public confidence in the Government, will best ensure the beneficent ends of its institution.

RESOLVED by the Senate and House of Representatives of the United States of America, in Congress assembled, two thirds of both Houses concurring, that the following Articles be proposed to the Legislatures of the several States, as amendments to the Constitution of the United States, all, or any of which Articles, when ratified by three fourths of the said Legislatures, to be valid to all intents and purposes, as part of the said Constitution; viz.

ARTICLES in addition to, and Amendment to the Constitution of the United States of America proposed by Congress, and ratified by the Legislatures of the several States, pursuant to the fifth Article of the original Constitution.

Note: The following text is a transcription of the first ten amendments to the Constitution in their original form. These amendments were ratified December 15, and from what is known as the "Bill of Rights" and from what is known as the "Bill of Rights."

Amendment I
Congress shall make no law respecting an establishment of religion, or prohibiting the free exercise thereof; or abridging the freedom of speech, or of the press; or the right of the people peaceably to assemble, and to petition the Government for a redress of grievances.

Amendment II
A well-regulated Militia, being necessary to the security of a free State, the right of the people to keep and bear Arms, shall not be infringed.

Amendment III
No Soldier shall, in time of peace be quartered in any house, without the consent of the Owner, nor in time of war, but in a manner to be prescribed by law.

Amendment IV
The right of the people to be secure in their persons, houses, papers, and effects, against unreasonable searches and seizures, shall not be violated, and no Warrants shall issue, but upon probable cause, supported by Oath or affirmation, and particularly describing the place to be searched, and the persons or things to be seized.

Amendment V
No person shall be held to answer for a capital, or otherwise infamous crime, unless on a presentment or indictment of a Grand Jury, except in cases arising in the land or naval forces, or in the Militia, when in actual service in time of War or public danger; nor shall any person be subject for the same offence to be twice put in jeopardy of life or limb; nor shall be compelled in any criminal case to be a witness against himself, nor be deprived of life, liberty, or property, without due process of law; nor shall private property be taken for public use, without just compensation.

Amendment VI
In all criminal prosecutions, the accused shall enjoy the right to a speedy and public trial, by an impartial jury of the State and district wherein the crime shall have been committed, which district shall have been previously ascertained by law, and to be informed of the nature and cause of the accusation; to be confronted with the witnesses against him; to have compulsory process for obtaining witnesses in his favor, and to have the Assistance of Counsel for his defence.

Amendment VII
In Suits at common law, where the value in controversy shall exceed twenty dollars, the right of trial by jury shall be preserved, and no fact tried by a jury, shall be otherwise re-examined in any Court of the United States, than according to the rules of the common law.

Amendment VIII
Excessive bail shall not be required, nor excessive fines imposed, nor cruel and unusual punishments inflicted.

Amendment IX
The enumeration in the Constitution, of certain rights, shall not be construed to deny or disparage others retained by the people.

Amendment X
The powers not delegated to the United States by the Constitution, nor prohibited by it to the States, are reserved to the States respectively, or to the people. **END**

Universal Declaration of Human Rights [Original Text]

Preamble

Whereas recognition of the inherent dignity and of the equal and inalienable rights of all members of the human family is the foundation of freedom, justice and peace in the world,

Whereas disregard and contempt for human rights have resulted in barbarous acts which have outraged the conscience of mankind, and the advent of a world in which human beings shall enjoy freedom of speech and belief and freedom from fear and want has been proclaimed as the highest aspiration of the common people,

Whereas it is essential, if man is not to be compelled to have recourse, as a last resort, to rebellion against tyranny and oppression, that human rights should be protected by the rule of law,

Whereas it is essential to promote the development of friendly relations between nations,

Whereas the peoples of the United Nations have in the Charter reaffirmed their faith in fundamental human rights, in the dignity and worth of the human person and in the equal rights of men and women and have determined to promote social progress and better standards of life in larger freedom,

Whereas Member States have pledged themselves to achieve, in cooperation with the United Nations, the promotion of universal respect for and observance of human rights and fundamental freedoms,

Whereas a common understanding of these rights and freedoms is of the greatest importance for the full realization of this pledge,

Now, therefore,
The General Assembly,

Proclaims this Universal Declaration of Human Rights as a common standard of achievement for all peoples and all nations, to the end that every individual and every organ of society, keeping this Declaration constantly in mind, shall strive by teaching and education to promote respect for these rights and freedoms and by progressive measures, national and international, to secure their universal and effective recognition and observance, both among the peoples of Member States themselves and among the peoples of territories under their jurisdiction.

Article I
All human beings are born free and equal in dignity and rights. They are endowed with reason and conscience and should act towards one another in a spirit of brotherhood.

Article 2
Everyone is entitled to all the rights and freedoms set forth in this Declaration, without distinction of any kind, such as race, colour, sex, language, religion, political or other opinion, national or social origin, property, birth or other status. Furthermore, no distinction shall be made on the basis of the political, jurisdictional or international status of the country or territory to which a person belongs, whether it be independent, trust, non-self-governing or under any other limitation of sovereignty.

Article 3
Everyone has the right to life, liberty and security of person.

Article 4
No one shall be held in slavery or servitude; slavery and the slave trade shall be prohibited in all their forms.

Article 5
No one shall be subjected to torture or to cruel, inhuman or degrading treatment or punishment.

Article 6
Everyone has the right to recognition everywhere as a person before the law.

Article 7
All are equal before the law and are entitled without any discrimination to equal protection of the law. All are entitled to equal protection against any discrimination in violation of this Declaration and against any incitement to such discrimination.

Article 8
Everyone has the right to an effective remedy by the competent national tribunals for acts violating the fundamental rights granted him by the constitution or by law.

Article 9
No one shall be subjected to arbitrary arrest, detention or exile.

Article 10
Everyone is entitled in full equality to a fair and public hearing by an independent and impartial tribunal, in the determination of his rights and obligations and of any criminal charge against him.

Article 11
1. Everyone charged with a penal offence has the right to be presumed innocent until proved guilty according to law in a public trial at which he has had all the guarantees necessary for his defence.
2. No one shall be held guilty of any penal offence on account of any act or omission which did not constitute a penal offence, under national or international law, at the time when it was committed. Nor shall a heavier penalty be imposed than the one that was applicable at the time the penal offence was committed.

Article 12
No one shall be subjected to arbitrary interference with his privacy, family, home or correspondence, nor to attacks upon his honour and reputation. Everyone has the right to the protection of the law against such interference or attacks.

Article 13
1. Everyone has the right to freedom of movement and residence within the borders of each State.
2. Everyone has the right to leave any country, including his own, and to return to his country.

Article 14
1. Everyone has the right to seek and to enjoy in other countries asylum from persecution.
2. This right may not be invoked in the case of prosecutions genuinely arising from non-political crimes or from acts contrary to the purposes and principles of the United Nations.

Article 15
1. Everyone has the right to a nationality.
2. No one shall be arbitrarily deprived of his nationality nor denied the right to change his nationality.

Article 16
1. Men and women of full age, without any limitation due to race, nationality or religion, have the right to marry and to found a family. They are entitled to equal rights as to marriage, during marriage and at its dissolution.
2. Marriage shall be entered into only with the free and full consent of the intending spouses.
3. The family is the natural and fundamental group unit of society and is entitled to protection by society and the State.

Article 17
1. Everyone has the right to own property alone as well as in association with others.
2. No one shall be arbitrarily deprived of his property.

Article 18
Everyone has the right to freedom of thought, conscience and religion; this right includes freedom to change his religion or belief, and freedom, either alone or in community with others and in public or private, to manifest his religion or belief in teaching, practice, worship and observance.

Article 19
Everyone has the right to freedom of opinion and expression; this right includes freedom to hold opinions without interference and to seek, receive and impart information and ideas through any media and regardless of frontiers.

Article 20
1. Everyone has the right to freedom of peaceful assembly and association.
2. No one may be compelled to belong to an association.

Article 21
1. Everyone has the right to take part in the government of his country, directly or through freely chosen representatives.
2. Everyone has the right to equal access to public service in his country.
3. The will of the people shall be the basis of the authority of government; this will shall be expressed in periodic and genuine elections which shall be by universal and equal suffrage and shall be held by secret vote or by equivalent free voting procedures.

Article 22
Everyone, as a member of society, has the right to social security and is entitled to realization, through national effort and international co-operation and in accordance with the organization and resources of each State, of the economic, social and cultural rights indispensable for his dignity and the free development of his personality.

Article 23
1. Everyone has the right to work, to free choice of employment, to just and favourable conditions of work and to protection against unemployment.
2. Everyone, without any discrimination, has the right to equal pay for equal work.

3. Everyone who works has the right to just and favourable remuneration ensuring for himself and his family an existence worthy of human dignity, and supplemented, if necessary, by other means of social protection.
4. Everyone has the right to form and to join trade unions for the protection of his interests.

Article 24
Everyone has the right to rest and leisure, including reasonable limitation of working hours and periodic holidays with pay.

Article 25
1. Everyone has the right to a standard of living adequate for the health and well-being of himself and of his family, including food, clothing, housing and medical care and necessary social services, and the right to security in the event of unemployment, sickness, disability, widowhood, old age or other lack of livelihood in circumstances beyond his control.
2. Motherhood and childhood are entitled to special care and assistance. All children, whether born in or out of wedlock, shall enjoy the same social protection.

Article 26
1. Everyone has the right to education. Education shall be free, at least in the elementary and fundamental stages. Elementary education shall be compulsory. Technical and professional education shall be made generally available and higher education shall be equally accessible to all on the basis of merit.
2. Education shall be directed to the full development of the human personality and to the strengthening of respect for human rights and fundamental freedoms. It shall promote understanding, tolerance and friendship among all nations, racial or religious groups, and shall further the activities of the United Nations for the maintenance of peace.
3. Parents have a prior right to choose the kind of education that shall be given to their children.

Article 27
1. Everyone has the right freely to participate in the cultural life of the community, to enjoy the arts and to share in scientific advancement and its benefits.
2. Everyone has the right to the protection of the moral and material interests resulting from any scientific, literary or artistic production of which he is the author.

Article 28
Everyone is entitled to a social and international order in which the rights and freedoms set forth in this Declaration can be fully realized.

Article 29
1. Everyone has duties to the community in which alone the free and full development of his personality is possible.
2. In the exercise of his rights and freedoms, everyone shall be subject only to such limitations as are determined by law solely for the purpose of securing due recognition and respect for the rights and freedoms of others and of meeting the just requirements of morality, public order and the general welfare in a democratic society.
3. These rights and freedoms may in no case be exercised contrary to the purposes and principles of the United Nations.

Article 30
Nothing in this Declaration may be interpreted as implying for any State, group or person any right to engage in any activity or to perform any act aimed at the destruction of any of the rights and freedoms set forth herein.

END

Appendix B

Personal eBook Publishing: My Integral Life, Work, Wealth, Health and Legacy Success

ITEM I: Completed Example – Dr. Rudy Garrity's Personal Assessment
ITEM II: Blank Form – For others to complete.

ITEM I: Personal Example (Dr. Garrity)
[**Author's Note**: Readers planning on conducting a self-assessment for purposes of personal renewal or development are encouraged to record their end-of-chapter notes in **Part B** of this Journal—after reading each chapter in the book. When all chapters have been completed, readers should review and summarize their notes and complete the **Part A Overall Summary** topics, below.

Part A. Overall Summary (**Author's Note**: Complete **Part B** individual Chapter Summaries below first in preparation to complete **Part A** afterward)

1. Personal Reflections Cross reference with Rudy's Authentic Personal Brand Balanced Scorecard (**Internal**) if and when your own Part II (Chapter Four) Authentic Personal and Professional Balanced Scorecard is completed.

---

a. What *new insights* have I developed on my self, my life, and my career?

Everyone is entitled to dream and pursue their own life that is hopefully, worth living. For me, learning has provided the way forward, and *lifelong learning has granted significant rewards* for my life and career.

b. Is it time for me to become more holistic and integrated in my thinking, and to pursue my *higher purpose*? What is that higher purpose?

I have accumulated education and experience, but there is so much more to learn and do. Now is the time to consolidate and integrate important, but sometimes disparate concepts for further consideration. It has been enormously satisfying for me to envision the relationship among *self-fulfilment*, *high performance* and the *common good* as they intersect for *human enlightenment* and a *mindful way-of-being*.

c. What do I really want to accomplish in my life, and to leave something for *posterity, a legacy*?

The Enlightenment Period of European history was a profound time when intellectual prowess finally emerged from suppression by self-imposed mythmakers and religionists. Thankfully, American founders such as Benjamin Franklin, Thomas Jefferson and Thomas Paine to recognize just a few, had the wisdom to provide the leadership and craft the documentation to launch America into the forefront of scientific discovery and human development that continues to this day. *Our generation has added intellectual and emotional intelligence* to the bus destined for posterity; we must ensure this intelligence exceeds its cost of transportation.

---

2. **Human Relations** Cross reference with <u>Rudy's Authentic Personal Brand Balanced Scorecard (**External**)</u> if and when your own Part II (Chapter Four) Authentic Personal and Professional Balanced Scorecard is completed.

---

a. Are there *dependencies* on others I need to reduce to free myself to move forward? With whom are they?

Our minds are full with past images, experiences and situations that demand recall at many inopportune times. That pre-programming requires review to determine its relevance now and in future situations. All of us are best served when we commit to think and learn in the present without inviting disempowering memories from the past. I need to *moderate the lingering emotions and debilitating thoughts* that sometimes cloud my judgment; judgment that always requires accurate information and critical thinking – *often from family members.*

b. Are there *connections* with others I need to make to expand my vision and learning? With whom are they?

Successful lives and careers are most often achieved through a combination of an individual's knowledge and motivation and the person's relationships and willingness to take advantage of social factors that occasionally work in their favor. I should extend my network to include, and engage, *organizational leaders* and *academic thought leaders.*

c. Is it time for me to moderate my independence, and become more *interdependent*? What specifically can I do and with whom?

Dependence and independence define an individual's relationship with other individuals and organizations from their youth up through their adult mid-life/career experiences. However, normal adult development requires intellectual and emotional development after mid-life toward a *greater sense of mutuality and generativity*. The interactions among family members, friends and colleagues, community leaders and the public evolve towards a feeling of statesmanship wherein rights and rewards, responsibilities and accountability are viewed *negotiable for the common good.* Being in this stage of life myself, I am obliged to increase my *engagement with others at the intersection of business, education, government, and non-profit community activities.*

3. Learning and Commitment Cross reference with <u>Rudy's Authentic Personal Brand Balanced Scorecard</u> (**Knowledge and Learning**) if and when your own Part II (Chapter Four) Authentic Personal and Professional Balanced Scorecard is completed.

---

a. What specific elements of the _learnership_ philosophy most appeal to me? Describe.

Learning is a lifelong responsibility with major influence on the quality and progressive growth of human life. Only through learning and leadership within a participative democracy can the nation's and world's populations _obtain the information and skills to build lives worth living_. The learnership philosophy conforms to the social system-of-systems within which people need to live. And, the complexity and pace of life _requires rapid knowledge building_ to create and enjoy the intellectual and physical products and services available in developing economies.

b. Which of the five _learnership_ reasoning competencies and four _domains of social systems development_ are most useful for my personal development? Why?

Situational learning is the reasoning competency that uses the benefits from _systems thinking_ and _pattern recognition_ to encourage informed, critical thinking. And, critical thinking is essential for _knowledge management_ and _adaptive leadership_ to obtain practical results. American society and culture is grounded in the U.S. Constitution and Bill of Rights, and history will tell if that structure proves to be the ultimate arrangement for human learning, knowing, leading and being for the next millennia.

c. Do I see myself becoming a _learnership_ practitioner and adopting the corresponding characteristics and skills?

Learnership practitioners have a proclivity toward holistic and rapid learning for knowledge building and management. These skills develop as people recognize the interdependencies among social domains and the responsibilities and opportunities that result from proactive socio-economic decision-making. Learnership practitioners have always existed, and they may be termed academics, entrepreneurs, statesmen, craftsmen, philanthropists, anthropologists and even poets – anyone with a broad-based curiosity and a desire to understand life in its greatest complexity. They want to understand what is, as well as envision what could be, in this dynamic and evolving world.

4. Next Steps: Planning for an Improved Life, Career and Legacy

> **a. *Who are the people* I need to talk with to help clarify my future path and provide support?**
>
> Assistance from family, friends, colleagues, co-workers, community and spiritual leaders
>
> **b. *What resources* do I need to identify and acquire to outline an actionable plan?**
>
> A comprehensive methodology administered through an experienced life and career coach.
>
> **c. *What timeframe* is both reasonable and motivational to assure my progress?**
>
> Forty five to sixty days of part-time reflection, interviews, learning, discussion and preparing an Integrated Learning and Knowledge Report suitable as an addendum to Rudy's American Learnership Personal Brand.

5. Vision for Myself

> **a. Describe the "new me" three year and five years in the future.**
>
> In three years I will have practiced all the developmental efforts listed for myself in this Learnership Journal. Additionally, in five years I will have successfully *transferred my new knowledge and experience* to hundreds of individuals and organizations.
>
> **b. What will I have given up in my renewal effort? What will be added or enhanced?**
>
> Along the way I will have *unlearned certain attitudes and behaviors that have limited my life and career development and progress.* I will have achieved the authenticity and skills associated with being a Learnership practitioner.
>
> **c. How will I measure my success?**
>
> Progress and success will be anecdotally viewed by me and others and in personal and business relationships.

6. Mission for Myself

a. Describe what I have become and achieved three year and five years in the future.

In three years my ALF business will be judged as a successful not-for-profit organization. In five years I will have *transferred ownership to another enterprise* for further growth and development during and after my retirement.

b. What will I have given up in my renewal effort? What will be added or enhanced?

Nothing will need to be given up to achieve renewal. However, the depth and breadth of my *written papers and projects will be recognized as major contributions* to the understanding of lifelong learning for the betterment of human performance and happiness.

c. How will I measure my success?

Progress and success will be through community recognition and published books and articles.

7. Major Roles for Myself

a. Describe changes in my current and new roles three and five years into the future.

In three years my primary role as an advocator of lifelong learning for personal, organizational and community development and progress will begin to *transition into that of a personal coach and mentor to societal seniors* striving to record their life and career legacies. Within five years, that work will be completed and I will be retired having finished my own lifetime professional learning – hopefully *being just a father to and grandfather to my children.*

b. What will I have given up in my renewal effort? What will be added or enhanced?

I will have given up trying to demonstrate personal and professional success in favor of *giving and experiencing love* as my time will be exceedingly short.

c. How will I measure my success?

My family's appreciation of my life and work..

Part B. Chapter Summaries (**Author's Note**: Complete this section first, then proceed back to the **Part A Overall Summary,** above)

Chapter One: **Introduction to American Learnership**: [**Author's Note**: This Chapter One Summary has been completed in advance and is suggested for **All** participants]

Learnership is a component of one's life philosophy on what is worth knowing and doing and on how human needs are accomplished. Viewed from a broad perspective, learnership practitioners maintain a distinctive worldview that frames their thinking, learning, knowing, leading, and behavior. Their inclination to determine the: who, what, when, where, why, how, and for whom on a wide range of societal issues and human activity signifies a sense of personal responsibility for contributing to the welfare of themselves, their organizations, and their communities.

My learning in terms of new insights, changing priorities, new commitments or skills I want to acquire:

1. Insight: Learnership is a conjunction of _Learning_ and _Leadership_ that translates into "_lifelong learning for a mindful way of being._" And, learnership is presented as both a philosophy for life and career management, and as the architecture for a structured approach for thinking, learning, knowing, leading and action. In practice, learnership is a comprehensive and integrated social process that encompasses the concepts of _human capital and total knowledge management_.

2. Insight: The components in the learnership architecture include: _five reasoning competencies_ that enable the progressive improvement of _four social system domains_ that are interoperable with six societal responsibilities represented as _universal knowledge spheres_. The goals of each domain are meaningful cultural outcomes within a set of values and behaviors presented as _universal ideals._

3. Commitment: I will continue to pursue multidisciplinary thinking, learning and reasoning to enhance my personal and career accomplishments.

4. Skill: Adopt and implement the _learnership personal benefits from learning and development_ in Figure 1-3.

5: Skill: Adopt and implement the _learnership practitioner development process_ in Figure 1-6.

Chapter Two: **Discovering the Meaning of Your Life**

In the pursuit of discovering what we term our "_meaning_" it is essential that we understand that while "meaning" is often thought to be something dynamic we objectively demonstrate outside ourselves, in fact, "meaning" always begins inside ourselves as our worldview of appropriate beliefs, values, motives and preferred actions before we reveal them to others.

My learning in terms of new insights, changing priorities, new commitments or skills I want to acquire:

1. Insight: Remind myself that clarifying my personal meaning will assist me in making better choices that influence my unique sense of self, vision, mission and personhood.

2. Commitment: Continue to ask myself: What aspirations are still unfulfilled, and how can I continue to pursue them?

3. Skill: Apply my knowledge and skills to maximize my own performance, accomplishments and happiness.

Chapter Three: **Being the Project Manager of Your Life**

Project management is the selection and systematic application of knowledge, skills, tools and technologies to achieve a planned objective. Project management requires the sequential implementation of five work process phases: initiation, planning, executing, controlling and closing. The project manager is responsible for the overall integration and completion of all activities leading to project success, and everyone can be the project manager of their own life.

My learning in terms of new insights, changing priorities, new commitments or skills I want to acquire:

1. Insight: Project management is the selection and systematic application of knowledge, skills, tools and technologies to achieve a planned objective. And, project management requires the sequential implementation of five work process phases: initiation, planning, executing, controlling and closing

2. Commitment: Apply the project management discipline as a preeminent skill set for converting social and organizational theories and concepts into my personal and organizational capabilities and practices.

3. Skill: I will develop the ability to cross-link learnership social system domains using the Balanced Scorecard concept.

Chapter Four: Crafting Your Authentic Personal and Professional Brand

The technological revolution has changed the structure of careers today. It used to be that you went to work for one or two companies in your entire career. Today we will all have as many as four to eight jobs or careers in our lifetime.

Personal Branding is essential to personal and career development. It is an effective career tool because it helps define who you are; what you stand for; what makes you unique, special, and different; how you are great; and why you should be sought out as a colleague.

My learning in terms of new insights, changing priorities, new commitments or skills I want to acquire:

1. Insight: The authentic personal branding process starts with determining who I am at my core authentic self. Rather than inventing a brand that I would like to be perceived as and to sell myself to others, this one is based on my life philosophy, dreams, vision, mission, values, key roles, identity, self-knowledge, self-awareness, self-responsibility, positive attributes, and self-management.

2. Commitment: I understand that my "personal brand" involves defining and formulating an authentic, distinctive, and memorable personal brand promise to others I know and meet. As such, I should use it as the focal point of my thinking and behavior which must be in harmony with my "personal ambition."

3. Skill: I will apply Authentic Personal Branding to my own life and career, and go forward by sharing that knowledge and skill with others.

Chapter Five: Reasoning Competency # 1: Systems Thinking

A system perspective on social matters that illustrates the interdependency and mutual support among the personal, organizational, and community subsystems within which we learn, develop, and strive for success.

The system thinking competency helps us develop a broader, more integrated outlook, and to expand the contextual environment of our thoughts and decisions. The use of system thinking inspires us to be integrative thinkers and discover opportunities to synthesize our learning for better understanding. *Systems Thinking (ST) and Pattern Recognition (PR) combine to assure more effective Situational Learning (SL).*

My learning in terms of new insights, changing priorities, new commitments or skills I want to acquire:

1. Insight: Systems thinking requires a willingness and ability to consider the topic or situation under observation in terms of both obvious *content* but also the influencing *context. I must empower myself* to reach out and understand the larger complexity that surrounds important issues.

2. Commitment: Human life is conducted in a social system of systems, and our brains are aware of the interdependent forces that are integrated across those intersections: personal/family, organizational/business and community/society. *I need to remind myself* to work in a balanced way across those intersections.

3. Insight: It is human nature to continuously fragment learning and knowledge into smaller and narrower disciplines so as to understand the parts of the whole more completely. However, *I must remind myself* that understanding and acting on piece parts causes us to forget the larger whole of a subject – thereby, reducing our ready access to larger meanings and forces.

4. Commitment: A useful strategy for me to become a better systems thinker is to practice *stepping outside myself"* mentally to a new viewing point where my biases and preferences are temporarily on hold to allow for critical thinking.

5: <u>Commitment</u>: Understand the dynamic relationships and forces illustrated in Figure 2-3.

6. <u>Skill</u>: Practice systems thinking on a daily basis by pausing to expand discussions and decision-making by *expanding the range of content and contextual factors* that influence the quality of my problem-solving.

Chapter Six: Reasoning Competency # 2: Pattern Recognition

By definition, a pattern can be an archetype, a model, an ideal worthy of imitation, a representative sample of some thing, or a composite of traits or features characteristic of individuals. All biological life forms maintain and exhibit patterns of activity; and, the social development of humankind is inextricably anchored to our thought processes as revealed in our behavior. The cultural expectations, documented methodologies, and established practices that form our human experience and interpersonal and organizational relationships are the artifacts of inherited tendencies and learned values, beliefs, and experiences previously programmed into our computer-like minds by ourselves and others.

The <u>pattern recognition competency focuses on our ability to recognize those preprogrammed aspects of ourselves and others</u>, and on the need for us to better manage our reasoning based on the why and how we think, learn, know, lead, and pursue certain objectives in all our societal endeavors. *Pattern Recognition (PR) combines with Systems Thinking (ST) to ensure more effective Situational Learning (SL).*

<u>My learning in terms of new insights, changing priorities, new commitments or skills I want to acquire:</u>

1. <u>Insight</u>: Life is full of patterns necessary for thinking, reasoning, behavior and taking action. Through nature and nurture we have been, and are continuously becoming, programmed in terms of our beliefs, values, preferences and biases. I need *conscious awareness of this reality*, and then manage my development carefully.

2. <u>Insight</u>: The brain is the pattern maker and repository for all personal and social cognition and physical and emotional development. It is my responsibility to manage the *evolution of my mental models* for growth, behavior, achievement and success.

3. <u>Commitment</u>: The universal goals and ideals presented in the Learnership Architecture are foundational beliefs in the American culture. It is my responsibility to *inculcate these beliefs in my life's work* and be authentic when dealing with others.

4. <u>Commitment</u>: Given the wide variety of human programming, learning styles and preferences; I should strive to first observe and *understand these similarities and differences* before coming to conclusions and taking action.

5. <u>Commitment</u>: The nine *general principles of high achievers* illustrate attitudes, skills and activities I need to make part of my personal and professional way of being.

6. <u>Skill</u>: Investigate the psychological methodologies on which the Myers-Briggs, Hermann Brain Dominance, and Spiral Dynamics personality profiles have been developed.

Chapter Seven: Reasoning Competency # 3: Situational Learning

A major life activity is dealing with the wide variety of situations we encounter on a daily basis. Some situations are routine and need little attention while at the other end of the continuum they may be significantly life and/or career threatening. What is important to understand is that every situation we encounter requires some amount of information gathering and analysis followed by decision making and action. And, <u>every situation is a potential learning opportunity.</u>

The <u>situational learning competency is a significant element in human capital development and in becoming a learnership practitioner</u> which makes it a foundational anchor in the practice of learnership. *Situational Learning (SL) benefits from the support provided by Systems Thinking (ST) and Pattern Recognition (PR) – and, it is an essential foundation for the practice of Knowledge Management (KM).*

<u>My learning in terms of new insights, changing priorities, new commitments or skills I want to acquire:</u>

1. <u>Commitment</u>: The concept of *double-loop learning* is an essential skill in becoming a proactive lifelong learner. *I need to enhance my willingness and ability* to not only work my way through an experience, but to also observe that

experience from a distance as it happens for the purpose of learning how well the process itself influenced the outcome.

2. Insight: What distinguishes a good situational learner is the patience and ability for critical thinking; which almost by definition requires the *knowledge of known reasoning errors* that can diminish my capacity to reason.

3. Insight: No two situations are exactly the same. Information availability and interpersonal dynamics are always at play as are other influential factors. Hence some *uncertainty and complexity* must be considered in my discussions and deliberations.

4. Insight: Every day is different from every day before. This requires a willingness and ability to incorporate mental learning cycles (assess – decide – execute) and (sense – adapt – respond) into my conscious activity.

5. Commitment: Information overload is pervasive and cannot be stopped. However, I can and will *prepare myself with a mental model and selective use of information* to build valid knowledge and make thoughtful decisions.

6. Skill: Adapt and apply the Facilitating Group Dialogue technique illustrated in Figure 7-2.

Chapter Eight: Reasoning Competency # 4: Knowledge Management

Human development can only proceed as far as our combined knowledge will allow. Whether we view ourselves as individuals, organizations or communities, we are both empowered and constrained by our current knowledge, and our willingness and ability to acquire additional knowledge. Contemporary studies and writings indicate that knowledge may be systematically created, managed and used to enhance human development and to produce the products and services we need and desire.

The knowledge management competency is the core element in becoming a learnership practitioner. It is the knowledge repository for situational learning artifacts, and in turn, it is the storehouse for the tacit and explicit knowledge used by adaptive leaders in advancing personal and social initiatives. *Knowledge Management (KM) is enabled by Situational Learning (SL) which itself is supported by Systems Thinking (ST) and Pattern Recognition (PR).*

My learning in terms of new insights, changing priorities, new commitments or skills I want to acquire:

1. Insight: Selective use of data and information is essential for the recipient to build and enhance what they consider to be knowledge. However, each individual's knowledge base is slightly different than that of others due to different prior knowledge and experience. *Not all knowledge is created equal.*

2. Insight: Some knowledge is created through *explicit exchanges between people*, and other knowledge may be obtained indirectly through *tacit exchanges between people* working and socializing together. Sharing that knowledge with others either explicitly or tacitly empowers learning, knowing, leading, and achieving for myself, organizations and communities.

3. Insight: Knowledge building and management results in the *creation of intellectual capital* which may be categorized as human, structural or customer capital. It is the accumulation of intellectual capital by myself, organizations and communities that define the growth and success of societies.

4. Commitment: Becoming a lifelong learner and proactive knowledge builder and manager inspires rapid social and economic progress. I need to make a daily *commitment to inquire, collect, create and apply new knowledge* to achieve my goals and life mission.

5. Commitment: Learn to recognize, understand and *apply knowledge management technologies and practices* within the social system-of-systems I experience on a daily basis.

6. Skill: Learn and implement elements of the *Knowledge Management Competency: Process, Practices and Technologies (Figure 5-2, page 181)* in my own personal and organizational knowledge-sharing activities.

Chapter Nine: Reasoning Competency # 5: Adaptive Leadership

No amount of knowledge has practical value until it is applied to human needs or concerns. Someone needs to articulate what is known, show relevancy to the situation or challenge at hand, and propose a course of action that can create a meaningful result. It is the work of leaders to craft visions and futures that inspire others to accept change and become participants in their journey forward.

The adaptive leadership competency is another foundational anchor in the learnership discipline because it moves knowledge into action. Theory is turned into practice, and practice leads to meaningful accomplishment for individuals and social organizations. *Adaptive Leadership (AL) applies Knowledge Management (KM) which has been enabled by Situational Learning (SL) which is supported by Systems Thinking (ST) and Pattern Recognition (PR).*

My learning in terms of new insights, changing priorities, new commitments or skills I want to acquire:

1. Insight: Understand the relationship among the learnership five reasoning competencies: *systems thinking* and *pattern recognition* together set the stage for improved *situational learning* – which, in turn, provides the data and information essential for accurate *knowledge building and management*. Only when these first three reasoning competencies are selectively and regularly employed can *adaptive leadership* be embraced by me for effective decision-making and action.

2. Insight: Uncertainty, complexity, competing demands and rapid speed all collude to make providing leadership a daunting challenge – often with time constraints and significant risk to individual and organizations.

3. Commitment: Learn to recognize the differences and appropriate use of *Sense and Respond* versus the *Make and Sell* business strategies. I need to understand when one is more effective than the other.

4. Commitment: Understand that the systematic *action learning* process, that includes *double-loop learning*, is a formidable methodology for optimizing group and team collaboration and decision-making.

5: Skill: Adapt and apply the *Social Systems Change and Development* technique in Figure 9-1.

6: Skill: Adapt and apply the *Leader Attributes, Roles and Dialogue* technique in Figure 9-2.

First Interlude: Transition from Reasoning Competencies to Social Systems Development

An interlude is included at this point to convey the consolidation of proactive concepts and reasoning skills already established precursors for their application to the four major social system of systems domains: personal, organizational, community and societal.

The primary documents include the Learnership Integrated Systems Architecture (LISA), the Learnership Architecture & Collaboration Instrument (LACI), the Learnership Systems Building Blocks (LSBB), and the list of Twenty-Five Learnership Practitioner Characteristics.

My learning in terms of new insights, changing priorities, new commitments or skills I want to acquire:

1. Commitment: Learn to understand and use the Learnership Integrated Systems Architecture (LISA) (Figure 1) as my personal mental model for organizing and applying critical thinking and problem solving.

2. Commitment: Learn to analyze and contribute to dialogue and decision-making using the Learnership Architecture and Collaboration Instrument (LACI) (Figure 6) when participating in teamwork and problem solving.

Chapter Ten: Personal (Micro) Systems Development

PSD is social synthesis at the micro-cognitive level, and is the starting point for managing the quality of our individual lives. Priority at this level is focused on continuous improvement of our *health, character* and *ability*. The universal goal selected for individuals is *self-fulfillment*, and the key role to be played is that of *fellowship*. Learning, knowing, and leading inform and activate PSD.

My learning in terms of new insights, changing priorities, new commitments or skills I want to acquire:

1. Insight: Understand the *personal systems development model* wherein subsystems *personal health, personal ability and personal character* are mutually reinforcing for me to achieve *self-fulfillment*.

2. Insight: Continuous *self-development* is based on my ability to acquire *self-knowledge* and willingness to pursue *self- renewal*.

3. Commitment: To learn and pursue the variety of behaviors that, together, define *"self-fulfillment"* – especially *letting my true self emerge*, being free from cognitive constraints imposed by others.

4. Commitment: Learn to appreciate *sane self-talk rather than crazy self-talk (Ellis and Harper)* as I continue to develop and evolve to be rational, enjoy having choices, avoid perfectionism, attempt to be objective, and strive for continuous improvement.

5. Skill: Continue to *develop as a learnership practitioner* by opening my mind to new avenues for investigation and integration into my own unique perspective of the human social system of systems.

6: Skill: Continue to *develop a professional presence* which requires building strong interpersonal relationships based on excellent communication skills and genuine good manners and productive business skills.

7. Skill: Pursue *physical and emotional health* as the foundation for a long life filled with learning, professional achievement and societal contribution.

Chapter Eleven: Organization (Macro) Systems Development

OSD is social synthesis at the macro-cognitive level, and uses recognized benchmarks for achieving highly efficient and effective organizational performance. The organizational elements selected for intense management focus are the organization's *direction*, *operations* and *performance*. The universal goal selected for organizations is *high performance*, and the key role to be played is *leadership*. Learning, knowing, and leading inform and activate OSD.

My learning in terms of new insights, changing priorities, new commitments or skills I want to acquire:

1. Insight: Understand the *organizational systems development model* wherein subsystems *organization direction*, *organization operations*, and *organization performance* are mutually reinforcing for organizations to achieve *high performance*.

2. Insight: Continuous *high performance* is based on my ability to achieve organization external goals in terms of customer and client satisfaction and desired revenue and profit objectives.

3. Insight: Recognize that managing and consulting with leaders at the executive level of an organization requires my *holistic perspective and a commitment to integrated* planning, organizing, sales management and production efficiency.

4. Commitment: Reflect on the elements required to *build an intelligent organization*. According to authors Gifford and Elizabeth Pinchot there needs to be a balance between (1) individual rights – widespread truth and rights, freedom of enterprise and liberated teams; and (2) organizational responsibilities – equality and diversity, voluntary learning networks and democratic self-rule. An overarching condition I recognize as limited corporate governance.

5. Commitment: Understand the benefits of using a *comprehensive model for change and transformation* innovations when leading, coaching or consulting near the top of a large and complex enterprise. An example is the National Baldrige Award Model offered through the National Institute of Science and Technology (NIST) which I will continue to apply.

6. Skill: Expand my opportunities to deliver coaching and consulting services focused on *workforce development and transformation*.

8. Skill: Incorporate the *attributes of self-initiated followership* into my professional writing and coaching and consulting projects

9. Skill: I will conduct *transformational decision-making* (Figure 8-6) by ensuring that collecting information and making choices includes conducting systematic analysis, avoiding psychological traps, and considering appropriate policy trade-offs.

Chapter Twelve: Community (Mega) Systems Development

CSD is social synthesis at the mega-cognitive level, and uses community selected benchmarks for achieving highly efficient and effective town, city, county or state performance. The community elements selected for intense management focus are the community's *business, education* and *government* contributions. The universal goal selected for communities is the *common good*, and the key role to be played is *citizenship*. Learning, knowing, and leading inform and activate CSD.

My learning in terms of new insights, changing priorities, new commitments or skills I want to acquire:

1. Insight: Understand the *community systems development model* wherein subsystems *community government, community business,* and *community education* are mutually reinforcing for communities to achieve the *common good*.

2. Insight: Achieving the *common good depends on a spirit of citizenship* which acts as a catalyst for collaboration among the individuals and organizations with a vested interest in living and working in close proximity with one another.

3. Insight: The importance of effective *community social dialogue* is a foundational tenet of community learnership. There are ten principles in this chapter that illustrate how dialogue differs from discussion, debate, and argumentation.

4. Commitment: Remember the book title: *All Organizations are Public (Barry Bozeman)* in which he argues that all organizations are based upon economic authority or political authority or some combination of the two – which are established by the society in which they reside. This concept is particularly appropriate for understanding the unique function of not-for-profit entities and public-private partnerships.

5. Commitment: Author John Gardner states that "apathy and lower motivation are the most widely noted characteristics of a civilization in decline." My commitment is for action to counter that trend.

6. Skill: As a person who has made public service a long time part of his career, it is incumbent that I maintain and support people and initiatives that require public leaders to be ethical and experienced in the roles they assume and the decisions they make.

7. Skill: As an educator my concern is for the development of the next generation of citizens and leaders. I will make it my mission to act on John Dewey's observation that "in a democracy, society accomplishes its objectives when schools place emphasis on development of individuals with the community."

Chapter Thirteen: Societal (Meta) Systems Development

SSD is social synthesis at the meta-cognitive level, and consists of fully integrated reasoning and development across all four levels of social synthesis. SSD strives to capture the spirit of John Sullivan's *To Come to Life More Fully* (1990), and suggests milestones for our timeless journey towards holistic personhood. The universal goal selected for the societal level is *human enlightenment*, and the key role to be played is *statesmanship*. Learning, knowing, and leading inform and activate SSD.

My learning in terms of new insights, changing priorities, new commitments or skills I want to acquire:

1. Insight: Aspiration for human enlightenment is inspired by the unique relationship between the *American founding and the legacy of the European Enlightenment* during the period of 1650 to 1800. It is through the work of luminaries such as Jefferson, Franklin, and Paine that the emerging progressive and socially participative ideas that the founding American documents got their energy and intellectual influence.

2. Insight: *Societal systems development for human enlightenment* represents the highest order of system-of-systems social integration. It is where people, organizations and communities optimize their use of *learnership reasoning competencies* and *learnership practitioner practices* through fellowship, leadership, citizenship and statesmanship to advance human evolution and development for posterity.

3. Insight: "The most exciting way to cope with life challenges requires that we cherish the courage to become, the capacity to reason, and the ability to care for other human beings." (Paul Kurtz)

4. Commitment: Understanding the impact of the *learnership universal knowledge spheres* on the everyday lives and careers of individuals, organizations, communities and the society at large is an essential component of systems thinking, critical thinking and societal decision-making. Any issue that requires thinking and action across socio-

economic or political boundaries is sure to have impact on, or be impacted by, one or more of the social, political, economic, ecological, technological or geographic spheres of information and knowledge.

5. Skill: The book *Consilience: The Unity of Knowledge* by Edward O. Wilson argues that there is currently a "jumping together of knowledge" between the fields of science and the humanities over the long years of their seemingly fractured evolution. I believe that this convergence is an opportune time for integrating data, information and knowledge across the social system-of-systems in which we all live and hopefully prosper. I must continue to articulate the union of these domains.

6. Skill: The *Universal Declaration of Human Rights* (United Nations) illustrates how the world's peoples should cast aside ignorant and destructive human thinking and behavior in order to make progress possible for humanity. Little international and individual state progress can be seen on this fifty year old visionary initiative. I will take this as a one person challenge to make a difference in this matter.

Chapter Fourteen: Mid-Life Transition and Renewal

This stage of cognitive and emotional awareness, and even discomfort, generally begins in the 45-55 age range, but can vary significantly depending on an individual's particular life circumstances. It is often a period of disruptive feelings, cognitive dilemmas, and forced reflection on matters having to do with one's life purpose, progress, happiness, experiences and increasing age.

My learning in terms of new insights, changing priorities, new commitments or skills I want to acquire:

1. Commitment: I am committed to further research and obtaining additional content for the Integrated Pathways for Adult Development model presented in Chapter Fourteen at Figure 14-7.

2. Commitment: I am committed to the twenty-five Learnership Practitioner behavior modifications summarized in this chapter.

3. Insight: I recognize that the term "*generativity*" applies to my mode of work and living here in the later stage of my life.

4. Insight: I have learned to agree with Marsha Sinetar when she encourages us that discovering our right livelihood leads to moving up the Maslow scale of human actualization to our highest level of personal achievement.

5. Skill: I will continue to learn to understand, adapt and take action to enhance my "*personal presence*" in life, work and legacy as I use the time I have left to take action..

Chapter Fifteen: Senior Rejuvenation, Authentic Living, and Legacy Success.

This stage of personal accomplishment is dedicated to completing a person's lifetime of learning and development in preparation for the explanation and documentation of thoughts, feelings and transformational insights that may be useful for others to know. It is the place for prioritization of topics and removal of issues required to achieve self-fulfillment.

My learning in terms of new insights, changing priorities, new commitments or skills I want to acquire:

1. Commitment. Commit to building an exceptional 50+ lifestyle and career.

2. Commitment. Commit to establishing a memorable legacy.

3. Insight. Achieving cognitive and emotional integration is an admirable life objective.

4. Insight. Becoming an "elder by the fireside" is a worthy senior life accomplishment.

[Author's Note: After completing the above task, you are reminded to return back to <u>Part A</u> where you will create <u>seven summary level statements</u> that mobilize your activities over the next three to five years.]

Appendix B (Continued)

Guest eBook Publishing: My Integral Life, Work, Wealth, Health and Legacy Success

ITEM I: Completed Example
ITEM II: Blank Form – For others to complete

ITEM II Blank Form – For others to complete

Part A. Overall Summary (**Author's Note**: Complete **Part B** individual Chapter Summaries (below) first in preparation to complete this **Part A** summary afterward)

1. Personal Reflections (Cross reference with your Authentic Personal Brand Balanced Scorecard (**Internal**) if and when your own Part II (Chapter Four) Authentic Personal and Professional Balanced Scorecard is completed.

2. Human Relations [Cross reference with your Authentic Personal Brand Balanced Scorecard (**External**) if and when your own Part II (Chapter Four) Authentic Personal and Professional Balanced Scorecard is completed.

3. Learning and Commitment [Cross reference with Rudy's Authentic Personal Brand Balanced Scorecard (**Knowledge and Learning**) if and when your own Part II (Chapter Four) Authentic Personal and Professional Balanced Scorecard is completed.

4. Next Steps: Planning for an Improved Life, Career and Legacy

5. Vision for Myself

6. Mission for Myself

7. Major Roles for Myself

Part B. Chapter Summaries (**Author's Note**: Complete this section first, then proceed back to the **Part A, Overall Summary,** above)

Chapter One: **Introduction to American Learnership: [Author's Note**: This Chapter One Summary has been completed in advance and is suggested for **All** participants]

Learnership is a component of one's life philosophy on what is worth knowing and doing and on how human needs are accomplished. Viewed from a broad perspective, learnership practitioners maintain a distinctive worldview that frames their thinking, learning, knowing, leading, and behavior. Their inclination to determine the: who, what, when, where, why, how, and for whom on a wide range of societal issues and human activity signifies a sense of personal responsibility for contributing to the welfare of themselves, their organizations, and their communities.

My learning in terms of new insights, changing priorities, new commitments or skills I want to acquire:

1. Insight: Learnership is a conjunction of _Learning_ and _Leadership_ that translates into "*lifelong learning for a mindful way of being.*" And, learnership is presented as both a philosophy for life and career management, and as the architecture for a structured approach for thinking, learning, knowing, leading and action. In practice, learnership is a comprehensive and integrated social process that encompasses the concepts of *human capital and total knowledge management.*

2. Insight: The components in the learnership architecture include: *five reasoning competencies* that enable the progressive improvement of *four social system domains* that are interoperable with six societal responsibilities represented as *universal knowledge spheres.* The goals of each domain are meaningful cultural outcomes within a set of values and behaviors presented as *universal ideals.*

3. <u>Commitment</u>: I will continue to pursue multidisciplinary thinking, learning and reasoning to enhance my personal and career accomplishments.

4. <u>Skill</u>: Adopt and implement the *learnership personal benefits from learning and development* in Figure 1-3.

5: <u>Skill</u>: Adopt and implement the *learnership practitioner development process* in Figure 1-5.

Chapter Two: Discovering the Meaning of Your Life

In the pursuit of discovering what we term our "*meaning*" it is essential that we understand that while "meaning" is often thought to be something dynamic we objectively demonstrate outside ourselves, in fact, "meaning" always begins inside ourselves as our worldview of appropriate beliefs, values, motives and preferred actions before we reveal them to others.

<u>My learning in terms of new insights, changing priorities, new commitments or skills I want to acquire:</u>

1. <u>Insight</u>:

2. <u>Commitment</u>:

3. <u>Skill</u>:

Chapter Three: Being the Project Manager of Your Life

Project management is the selection and systematic application of knowledge, skills, tools and technologies to achieve a planned objective. Project management requires the sequential implementation of five work process phases: initiation, planning, executing, controlling and closing.

The project manager is responsible for the overall integration and completion of all activities leading to project success, and everyone can be the project manager of their own life.

<u>My learning in terms of new insights, changing priorities, new commitments or skills I want to acquire:</u>

1. <u>Insight</u>:

2. <u>Commitment</u>:

3. <u>Skill</u>:

Chapter Four: Crafting Your Authentic Personal and Professional Brand

The technological revolution has changed the structure of careers today. It used to be that you went to work for one or two companies in your entire career. Today we will all have as many as four to eight jobs or careers in our lifetime.

Personal Branding is essential to personal and career development. It is an effective career tool because it helps define who you are; what you stand for; what makes you unique, special, and different; how you are great; and why you should be sought out as a colleague.

<u>My learning in terms of new insights, changing priorities, new commitments or skills I want to acquire:</u>

1. <u>Insight</u>:

2. <u>Commitment</u>:

3. <u>Skill</u>:.

Chapter Five: Reasoning Competency # 1: Systems Thinking

A system perspective on social matters that illustrates the interdependency and mutual support among the personal, organizational, and community subsystems within which we learn, develop, and strive for success.

The system thinking competency helps us develop a broader, more integrated outlook, and to expand the contextual environment of our thoughts and decisions. The use of system thinking inspires us to be integrative thinkers and discover opportunities to synthesize our learning for better understanding. *Systems Thinking (ST) and Pattern Recognition (PR) combine to assure more effective Situational Learning (SL).*

My learning in terms of new insights, changing priorities, new commitments or skills I want to acquire:

1. Insight:

2. Commitment:

3. Insight:

Chapter Six: Reasoning Competency # 2: Pattern Recognition

By definition, a pattern can be an archetype, a model, an ideal worthy of imitation, a representative sample of some thing, or a composite of traits or features characteristic of individuals. All biological life forms maintain and exhibit patterns of activity; and, the social development of humankind is inextricably anchored to our thought processes as revealed in our behavior. The cultural expectations, documented methodologies, and established practices that form our human experience and interpersonal and organizational relationships are the artifacts of inherited tendencies and learned values, beliefs, and experiences previously programmed into our computer-like minds.

The pattern recognition competency focuses on our ability to recognize those preprogrammed aspects of ourselves and others, and on the need for us to better manage our reasoning based on the why and how we think, learn, know, lead, and pursue certain objectives in all our societal endeavors. *Pattern Recognition (PR) combines with Systems Thinking (ST) to ensure more effective Situational Learning (SL).*

My learning in terms of new insights, changing priorities, new commitments or skills I want to acquire:

1. Insight:

2. Commitment:

3. Skill:

Chapter Seven: Reasoning Competency # 3: Situational Learning

A major life activity is dealing with the wide variety of situations we encounter on a daily basis. Some situations are routine and need little attention while at the other end of the continuum they may be significantly life and/or career threatening. What is important to understand is that every situation we encounter requires some amount of information gathering and analysis followed by decision making and action. And, every situation is a potential learning opportunity.

The situational learning competency is a significant element in human capital development and in becoming a learnership practitioner which makes it a foundational anchor in the practice of learnership. *Situational Learning (SL) benefits from the support provided by Systems Thinking (ST) and Pattern Recognition (PR) – and, it is an essential foundation for the practice of Knowledge Management (KM).*

My learning in terms of new insights, changing priorities, new commitments or skills I want to acquire:

1. Commitment:

2. Insight:

3. Skill:

Chapter Eight: Reasoning Competency # 4: Knowledge Management

Human development can only proceed as far as our combined knowledge will allow. Whether we view ourselves as individuals, organizations or communities, we are both empowered and constrained by our current knowledge, and our willingness and ability to acquire additional knowledge. Contemporary studies and writings indicate that knowledge may be systematically created, managed and used to enhance human development and to produce the products and services we need and desire.

The knowledge management competency is the core element in becoming a learnership practitioner. It is the knowledge repository for situational learning artifacts, and in turn, it is the storehouse for the tacit and explicit knowledge used by adaptive leaders in advancing personal and social initiatives. *Knowledge Management (KM) is enabled by Situational Learning (SL) which itself is supported by Systems Thinking (ST) and Pattern Recognition (PR).*

My learning in terms of new insights, changing priorities, new commitments or skills I want to acquire:

1. Commitment:

2. Insight

3. Skill:

Chapter Nine: Reasoning Competency # 5: Adaptive Leadership

No amount of knowledge has practical value until it is applied to human needs or concerns. Someone needs to articulate what is known, show relevancy to the situation or challenge at hand, and propose a course of action that can create a meaningful result. It is the work of leaders to craft visions and futures that inspire others to accept change and become participants in the journey forward.

The adaptive leadership competency is another foundational anchor in the learnership discipline because it moves knowledge into action. Theory is turned into practice, and practice leads to meaningful accomplishment for individuals and social organizations. *Adaptive Leadership (AL) applies Knowledge Management (KM) which has been enabled by Situational Learning (SL) which is supported by Systems Thinking (ST) and Pattern Recognition (PR).*

My learning in terms of new insights, changing priorities, new commitments or skills I want to acquire:

1. Commitment:

2. Insight:

6: Skill:

First Interlude: Transitioning from Reasoning Competencies to Social Systems Development

An interlude is included at this point to convey the consolidation of proactive concepts and reasoning skills already established as a precursor to their application to the four major social system of systems domains: personal, organizational, community and societal.

The primary documents include the Learnership Integrated Systems Architecture (LISA), the Learnership Architecture & Collaboration Instrument (LACI), the Learnership Systems Building Blocks (LSBB), and the list of Twenty-Five Learnership Practitioner Characteristics.

My learning in terms of new insights, changing priorities, new commitments or skills I want to acquire:

1. Commitment:

2. Insight:

3. Skill:

Chapter Ten: Personal (Micro) Systems Development

PSD is social synthesis at the micro-cognitive level, and is the starting point for managing the quality of our individual lives. Priority at this level is focused on continuous improvement of our *health*, *character* and *ability*. The universal goal selected for individuals is *self-fulfillment*, and the key role to be played is that of *fellowship*. Learning, knowing, and leading inform and activate PSD.

My learning in terms of new insights, changing priorities, new commitments or skills I want to acquire:

1. Commitment:

2. Insight:

5. Skill:

Chapter Eleven: Organization (Macro) Systems Development

OSD is social synthesis at the macro-cognitive level, and uses recognized benchmarks for achieving highly efficient and effective organizational performance. The organizational elements selected for intense management focus are the organization's *direction*, *operations* and *performance*. The universal goal selected for organizations is *high performance*, and the key role to be played is *leadership*. Learning, knowing, and leading inform and activate OSD.

My learning in terms of new insights, changing priorities, new commitments or skills I want to acquire:

1. Commitment:

2. Insight:

3. Skill:

Chapter Twelve: Community (Mega) Systems Development

CSD is social synthesis at the mega-cognitive level, and uses community selected benchmarks for achieving highly efficient and effective town, city, county or state performance. The community elements selected for intense management focus are the community's *business*, *education* and *government* contributions. The universal goal selected for communities is the common good, and the key role to be played is *citizenship*. Learning, knowing, and leading inform and activate CSD.

My learning in terms of new insights, changing priorities, new commitments or skills I want to acquire:

1. Commitment:

2. Insight

3. Skill:

Chapter Thirteen: Societal (Meta) Systems Development

SSD is social synthesis at the meta-cognitive level, and consists of fully integrated reasoning and development across all four levels of social synthesis. SSD strives to capture the spirit of John Sullivan's *To Come to Life More Fully* (1990), and suggests milestones for our timeless journey towards holistic personhood. The universal goal selected for the societal level is *human enlightenment*, and the key role to be played is *statesmanship*. Learning, knowing, and leading inform and activate SSD.

My learning in terms of new insights, changing priorities, new commitments or skills I want to acquire:

1. Commitment:

2. Insight:

3. Skill:

Chapter Fourteen: Mid-Life Transition and Renewal

This stage of cognitive and emotional awareness, and even discomfort, generally begins in the 45-55 age range, but can vary significantly depending on an individual's particular life circumstances. It is often a period of disruptive feelings, cognitive dilemmas, and forced reflection on matters having to do with one's life purpose, progress, happiness, experiences and increasing age. Challenges include moving from independency to interdependency and from intimacy to generativity.

My learning in terms of new insights, changing priorities, new commitments or skills I want to acquire:

1. Commitment:

2. Insight:

3. Skill:

Chapter Fifteen: Senior Rejuvenation, Authentic Living, and Legacy Success.

This stage of personal accomplishment is dedicated to completing a person's lifetime of learning and development in preparation for the explanation and documentation of thoughts, feelings and transformational insights that may be useful for others to know. It is the place for prioritization of topics and removal of issues required to achieve self-fulfillment.

My learning in terms of new insights, changing priorities, new commitments or skills I want to acquire:

1. Commitment:

2. Insight:

3. Skill:

[Author's Note: After completing the above task, you are reminded to return back to Part A where you will create seven summary level statements that mobilize your activities over the next three to five years.]

Appendix C

Personal eBook Publishing: My Authentic Personal and Professional Brand

[**Author's Note**: This part is adapted from the work of Dr. Hubert Rampersad and includes excerpts from his book *Authentic Personal Branding (2009)* and *Rudolph Garrity's Personal Brand* (2014).

ITEM I: Completed Example – Dr. Rudy Garrity's Authentic Brand
ITEM II: Blank Form – For others to complete.

ITEM I: Completed Example – Dr. Garrity

Contents

Preface: Importance of an Authentic Personal and Professional Branding

Customers must recognize that you stand for something.
– Howard Schultz, Chairman of Starbucks

The underlying assumption of personal-branding philosophy is that each of us has unique gifts and a distinct purpose and dream in life. By connecting these gifts, purpose and dream, we open ourselves up to greater happiness and success in life (Frost, 2003). This fits very well to my holistic and authentic personal branding model, which will be discussed in the following sections. This new blueprint will help me to unlock my potential and build a trusted image of myself that I want to project in everything I do. It must therefore be in harmony with my true values, beliefs, dreams, and genius. When my brand is combined with powerful tools, it will deliver peak performance and create a stable basis for trustworthiness, credibility, and personal charisma.

This inside-out approach is durable and differs from traditional methods, and is based on a passion for developing human potential. This new approach places more emphasis on understanding myself and the needs of others, meeting those needs while staying true to my values, improving myself continuously, and realizing growth in life based on this personal branding journey. It focuses on the human side of branding, and includes my reputation, character and personality. If am well branded according to this approach, I will find it easier to convince others and I will attract the people and opportunities that are a perfect fit for me.

The authentic personal branding process starts with determining who I am at my core authentic self. Rather than inventing a brand that I would like to be perceived as and to sell myself to others, this one is based on my life philosophy, dreams, vision, mission, values, key roles, identity, self-knowledge, self-awareness, self-responsibility, positive attributes, and self-management. With an authentic personal brand, my strongest characteristics, attributes, and values can separate me from the crowd. Without this, I look just like everyone else. If I am not branded in an authentic, honest, and holistic way, if I don't deliver according to my brand promise, and if I focus mainly on selling, packaging, outward appearances, promoting myself, and becoming famous, I will be perceived as not being authentic.

LEARNING OBJECTIVES
After reading this authentic branding methodology and applying its concepts, I am learning to:
--Build, implement, and cultivate an authentic, distinctive, inspiring, compelling, enduring personal brand.
--Create positive perceptions and emotions in the mind of my prospects (that I am different, special, unique, and authentic) based on my personal brand.
--Build a truly lasting and trusted relationship with my clients, make an emotional connection with them, and managing their expectations and perception effectively.
--Manage and influence how others perceive me and think of me.

> --Use my brand to communicate my unique service that provides a sense of value for my target audience, which is in line with my dreams, purpose in life, values, passion, competencies, uniqueness, genius, specialization, characteristics, and things that I love doing.
> --Position myself strongly in relation to my competitors, built a strong reputation, and develop an effective image of myself that I want to project in everything I do.
> --Communicate what I stand for in a unique way that is different from others in my field and that gets inside people's minds.
> --Provide value to others continuously, create visibility, build trust, and reinforce integrity, honesty, trustworthiness, credibility, transparency, and personal charisma.
> --Build a trusted image of myself, which is based on my true values, beliefs, dream, and genius.
> Make a difference in relationships throughout my life, fire my passion, and be happy and attract success.

Remember what Albert Einstein said: *Try not to become a person of success but a person of value.*

Chapter 1: My Authentic Personal and Professional Branding

Having a strong personal brand seems to be a very important asset in today's online, virtual, and individual age. It is becoming increasingly essential and is the key to personal success. Everyone has a personal brand but most people are not aware of this and do not manage this strategically, consistently, and effectively. I should take control of my brand and the message it sends and affects how others perceive me. This will help me to actively grow and distinguish myself as an exceptional professional.

My personal brand should be authentic, which means that it always should reflect my true character, and should be built on my dreams, life purpose, values, uniqueness, genius, passion, specialization, characteristics, and things what I love doing. If I am branded in this organic, authentic and holistic way my personal brand will be strong, distinctive, meaningful, inspiring, and memorable. I will also create a life that is fulfilling, automatically attract the people and opportunities that are a perfect fit for me, and increase my ability to deliver peak performances.

Branding isn't just for corporations anymore. There is a new trend called "*Personal Branding*". The reason for this is (Jane Tabachnick, 2007):

1. The technological revolution has changed the structure of careers today. It used to be that we went to work for one or two companies in our entire career. Today we will all have as many as four to eight jobs or careers in our lifetime. Personal Branding is essential to career development and an effective career tool because it helps define who we are, what we stand for, what makes us unique, special, and different, how we are great, and why we should be sought out.

2. The change in the way we communicate. The internet has elevated each of us to the position of publisher. Email, newsgroups, bulletin boards, blogs, and online network and discussion groups afford all of us the opportunity to learn, network and get exposure for our businesses and ourselves. People want to do business with people they know or people they feel they can trust, with whom they feel some sort of connection, and with whom they relate. If we are a familiar, friendly, and consistent presence and brand online, people will have the sense that they know us and be more receptive to doing business with us. So Personal Branding is also essential to business development.

According to Randall Hansen (2007) *" Branding can be defined as a promise... a promise of the value of the product... a promise that the product is better than all the competing products... a promise that must be delivered to be successful"*. Being good and accomplished in our field is not enough. It's time to give serious effort to discovering our genius, passion, and our authentic dream, imagining and developing ourselves as powerful, consistent, and memorable people with our own specific brand, as we do related work we love. We can shape the market's perception of our Personal Brand by defining our unique strengths, values, and personality, sharing it with others in an exciting, persuasive manner, and cultivating our brand continuously. It's something that we can develop and manage, which is essential for future employability and success in life. Everyone has a chance and should take the responsibility to learn, improve, build their skills and be a strong brand.

Everyone has a personal brand but most people are not aware of this and do not manage this strategically and effectively. I should take control of my brand, the message it sends and its affect on how others perceive me. This will help me to actively grow and distinguish myself as an exceptional professional. Having a strong personal brand has benefits. It:

1. Stimulates meaningful perceptions about the values and qualities that I stand for

2. Tells others: who I am, what I do, what makes me different, how I create value for them, and what they can expect when they deal with me, and influences how others perceive me

3. Creates expectations in the mind of others of what they will get when they work with me

4. Creates an identity around me which makes it easier for people to remember who I am.

5. Gets my prospects to see me as the only solution to their problem.

6. Puts me above the competition and makes me unique and better than my competitors in the marketplace

An Authentic Branding Model:

A great brand taps into emotions....Emotions drive most, if not all, of our decisions. A brand reaches out with a powerful connecting experience. It's an emotional connecting point that transcends the product....A great brand is a story that's never completely told. A brand is a metaphorical story that's evolving all the time..... Stories create the emotional context people need to locate themselves in a larger experience. -- Scott Bedbury

This chapter emphasizes the organic, holistic and authentic branding model, which provides an excellent framework and roadmap to develop, implement, and cultivate an authentic personal and corporate brand in a sustainable way.

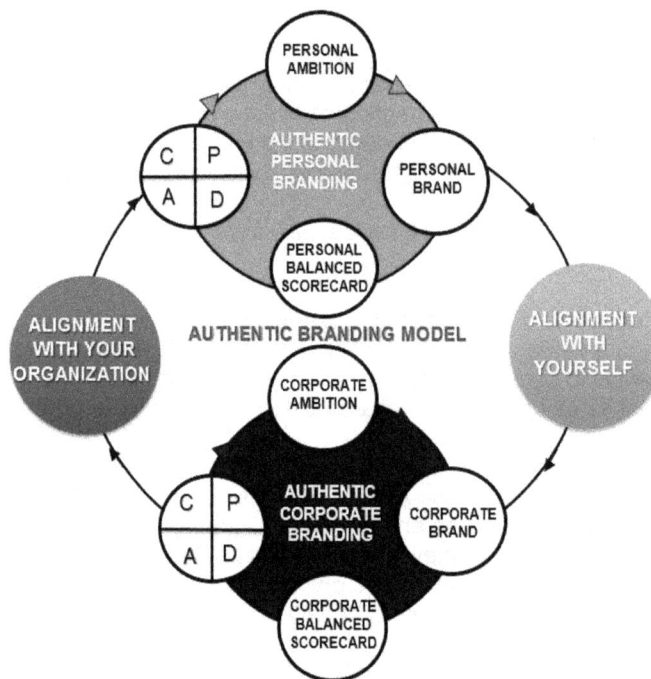

Figure 1-1: Authentic Branding Model

The authentic branding model consists of four phases which are the building blocks of sustainable personal leadership branding (Rampersad, 2009, 2014):

1. Authentic Personal Branding:

a. <u>Personal Ambition</u>; this phase involves a soul-searching process based on thought, introspection, and self-reflection supported through use of a "breathing and silence exercise." Questions which I can ask myself are: Who am I, What do I stand for?, What makes me happy?, What do I live for?, Why do I want to lead? What's the purpose of my leadership? The result of this phase is the formulation of my personal mission, vision and key roles. On the basis of insights acquired through this process, I can develop self-awareness and self-regulation, which are the foundation of trustworthiness, integrity, and openness to learn. (See chapter 2)

b. <u>Personal Brand</u>; this phase involves defining and formulating an authentic, distinctive, and memorable personal brand promise, and using it as the focal point of my behavior and actions. This must be in harmony with my personal ambition. (See chapter 3)

c. <u>Personal Balanced Scorecard</u> (PBSC); personal ambition has no value unless I take action to make it a reality. Therefore the emphasis in this stage is developing an integrated and well-balanced action plan based on my personal ambition to realize your life objectives. It's about translating my personal ambition into action. Personal branding without continuous improvement of yourself based on your PBSC is merely cosmetic and will not lead to my sustainable growth. My PBSC entails my personal critical success factors that are related to my personal ambition and my corresponding objectives, performance measures, targets and improvement actions (Rampersad, 2006). It is divided into the four perspectives: internal, external, knowledge & learning, and financial perspectives. (See chapter 4)

d. <u>Implementation and Cultivation of My Personal Brand</u>; personal ambition and personal balanced scorecard have no value unless I implement them to make them a reality. Therefore the next step is to implement, maintain, and cultivate my ambition, personal brand and PBSC to manage myself effectively. This focuses on my private life and business life. To guide me in this process I have used a unique learning cycle called the Plan-Deploy-Act-Challenge cycle (PDAC cycle), which should be followed continuously (Rampersad, 2003, 2006, 2009). To live in accordance with my personal ambition and related PBSC through its implementation using the PDAC cycle, results in a journey towards self-awareness, flow and happiness. (See chapter 5)

2. Alignment with Yourself:

Aligning your personal ambition with my behavior and my way of acting is needed to develop personal integrity. I need to commit myself to live and act according to my personal ambition and to keep promises that I make to myself. Personal branding built on a person's true character is sustainable and strong. I should reflect my true self and must adhere to a moral and behavioral code set down by my personal ambition. This means that who I really am, what I care about, and my passions should come out in my personal ambition, and I should act and behave accordingly (I should be myself) to build trust.

These first two stages in the authentic branding model focus on personal leadership development by cultivating my inner compass.

3. Authentic Corporate Branding:

a. <u>Corporate Ambition</u>; this phase involves defining and formulating the shared corporate ambition. It entails the soul, core intention and the guiding principles of the organization and encompasses the corporate mission, vision, and core values.

b. <u>Corporate Brand</u>; this phase involves defining and formulating an authentic, distinctive, and memorable corporate brand promise, and using it as the focal point of the organization's behavior and actions. This must be in harmony with the shared corporate ambition.

c. <u>Corporate Balanced Scorecard</u> (CBSC); the emphasis in this stage is developing an integrated and well-balanced action plan based on the corporate ambition to realize the corporate objectives. It offers a means to maintain balance between financial and nonfinancial measures and to connect strategic and operational standards. The CBSC entails the related corporate critical success factors, objectives, performance measures, targets and improvement actions, divided into four perspectives: financial, external, internal, and knowledge & learning. The CBSC is needed to improve the business processes continuously based on the corporate ambition in order to add value to customers and satisfy them.

d. <u>Implementation and Cultivation of the Corporate Brand</u>; the next step is to implement, maintain, and cultivate the corporate ambition, the corporate brand and CBSC in order to govern my organization effectively, to deliver peak performance, and to create competitive advantage. To guide you in this process I have introduced the Plan-Deploy-Act-Cultivate cycle (PDAC cycle), which should be followed continuously. To operate in accordance with the corporate ambition, corporate brand and related CBSC, through its implementation using the PDAC cycle, results in a journey towards sustainable business success.

4. Alignment with My Corporation:

An Integrated Breathing and Silence Exercise

(Rampersad, 2009, 2014)

Step 1: Breathing Exercise

1. Look for a quiet spot with fresh air and make sure that you will not be disrupted.
2. Sit in a comfortable chair with an upright back, and your shoulders and neck relaxed.
3. Gently rest your hands on your knees, with your palms upward and close your eyes.
4. Breath deeply through your nose according to the following rhythm: inhale deeply during a count to four (your stomach fills like a balloon), hold your breath during four counts, and exhale fully and slowly during a count of six (your stomach flattens again) and stop for two counts. Focus on the rhythm of breathing in and out.
5. Focus your attention entirely on your breathing during this process and observe how your life energy flows through your body. During the breathing you will become more relaxed. Concentrate on the feeling of relaxation in your whole body (face, shoulders, hands, feet, etc.).
6. Repeat this process during 10-15 minutes.

Step 2: Silence Exercise

After finishing the breathing exercise, remain in your sitting position with your back straight, relax your arms, keep your eyes closed and breathe normally through your nose.

1. Focus entirely on your thoughts; do not concentrate on anything else. If thoughts do enter, do not force them out but simply let them pass like clouds making way for the beautiful blue sky.
2. Allow your thoughts to come and go, including the thoughts related to the Personal Brand questions.
3. Be open to all images that come up in your mind. Imagine that you are in a garden and that a wise man approaches you who, after introducing himself, asks you some of the Personal Brand questions mentioned below. Listen carefully to the answers of your inner voice and write these down immediately after this exercise.
4. Listen carefully to the answers of your inner voice and write these down immediately after this exercise.

Open your eyes slowly after 10-15 minutes and write the answers of your inner voice in your personal ambition statement and your personal brand diary. The purpose of this diary is to be able to use this information to update your personal ambition and personal brand and keep record of your experiences and progress in each session.

Table 1-1

The emphasis in this final stage is aligning personal ambition with corporate ambition and creating uniformity of personal and organizational values. It's about aligning personal branding with corporate branding and getting the optimal fit and balance between these two activities in order to enhance labor productivity, to create a climate of trust, and to stimulate engagement, commitment, integrity, and passion in the organization. This is needed because staff members don't work with devotion or expend energy on something they do not believe in or agree with. If there is a match between their interests and those of the organization, or if their values and the organization's values align, they will be engaged and will work with greater commitment and dedication towards realizing the corporate objectives. The effective combination of all these four phases creates a stable basis for a high-performance and ethical organization. As we can see from Table 1-1, the authentic branding model gives us insight into both the way authentic branding can be developed effectively and the coherence between its different aspects.

[**Author's Note**: The Breathing and Silence Exercise below is known to be helpful for deep contemplation and relaxation when preparing to complete some of the tasks included in Authentic Personal Branding.]

Chapter 2. My Authentic Personal Ambition

"The future belongs to those who believe in the beauty of their dreams"
-- Eleanor Roosevelt

Before anyone can clearly define and describe an Authentic Personal Brand, they need to start with the dream or vision of the person behind the brand. They need to define their purpose in life, values, roles in life, the meaning of your life, and what you want with their life. They should give serious effort to discovering their genius and authentic dream, imagining and developing themselves as a powerful, consistent, and memorable Personal Brand.

[**Author's Note**: Following Dr. Rampersad's method, I will present below my own up-to-date Authentic Personal Branding results starting with Personal Ambition (vision, mission, key roles) which focuses on my defined purpose in life, values, roles in life, the meaning of my life, and what I want to accomplish with my life.

The first stage in the authentic personal branding journey is primarily concerned with defining and formulating my Personal Ambition in an exciting and persuasive manner and make it visible (see Figure 2.1). My Personal Ambition entails my dream (vision), my identity (mission) and my key roles in life. My dream is related to a *higher calling* and to my *uniqueness*. I am aware of this higher calling, a so-called *inner assignment*. I am aware of this higher calling and have the commitment to follow it in order to be successful and have more meaning in life.

My own dream can be thought of as a synonym for my Personal vision. While personal "mission" is aimed at my *being* (an articulation of what I'm all about*), personal "vision" is focused on who and what I are *becoming*. My personal vision motivates me, my personal mission inspires me, and my personal key roles guide my relationships with others. My values are included in all these three elements. Personal Ambition, here, is defined as personal vision, mission, and key roles, which are divided into four unique perspectives for deeper personal assessment: *internal, external, knowledge & learning, and financial.*

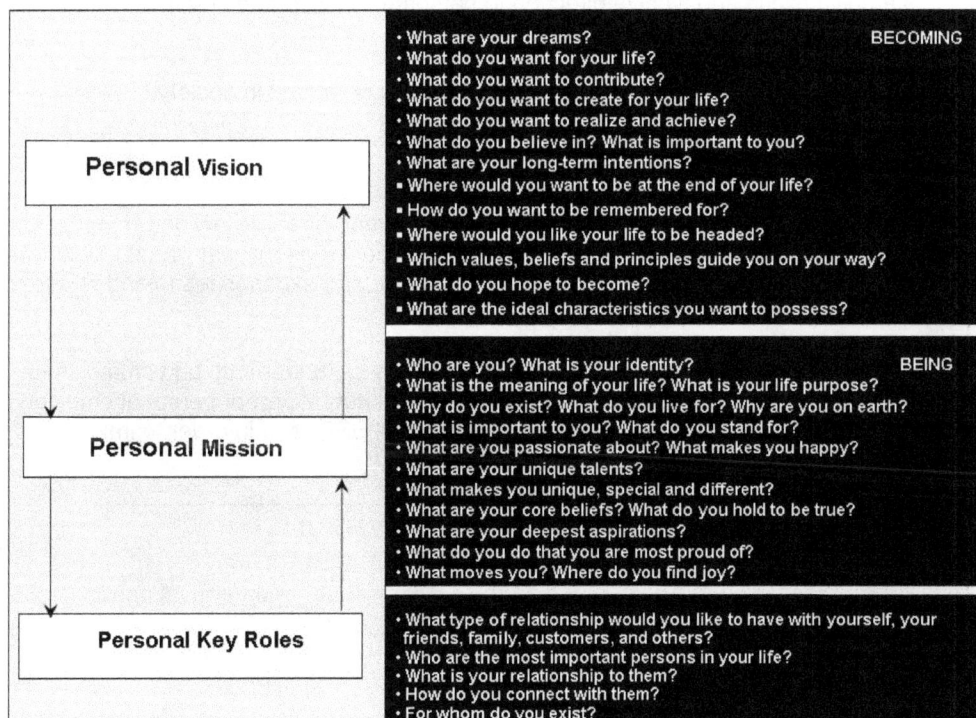

Figure 2-1: Personal Ambition Stage

The four perspectives that follow should be in balance and are of essential importance for my self-development, personal well-being, and marketing success of my brand. These are:

1. **Internal**: my physical health and mental state. How can I control these in order to create value for myself and others?

2. **External**: my relations with my customers, spouse, children, friends, manager, colleagues, and others. How do they see me?

3. **Knowledge and learning**: my skills and learning ability. How do I learn, and how can I remain successful in the future?

4. **Financial**: financial stability. To what degree am I able to fulfil my financial needs?

[**Author's Note**: The formulation of everyone's Personal Ambition is most effective when it complies with the following criteria.]

1. Your personal vision motivates you, your personal mission inspires you, and your key roles guide your relationships.

2. Your personal vision is about _becoming_ and your personal mission about _being_.

3. The four perspectives: financial, external, internal, and knowledge and learning are a part of it.

4. The emphasis is on unselfishness and authenticity.

5. Your values should explicitly be included in your personal vision, mission, and key roles.

6. Is specific to each person and includes ethical starting points, with an emphasis on your dream, uniqueness, genius, skills, principles, and values

7. Personal mission is short, clear, simple, and formulated in the present tense; it is concrete and may be used as a guideline.

8. Personal vision is ambitious and should give direction to personal initiative and creativity, and combines personal power and energy.

9. Personal mission indicates how a person wants to distinguish him or herself in society.

My Personal Vision:

My personal vision statement is a description of the way in which I want to realize my dream in the long term. It indicates where I am going, which values, beliefs and principles guide me on my way, what I want to achieve, what I want for my life, what my long-term intentions are, what talents, skills and experiences I need to add value to others, and where I want to be at the end of my life.

My values and the four basic perspectives: internal, external, knowledge & learning, and financial are clearly recognizable in my ambition statement. These perspectives are an integral part of personal ambition in order to be able to completely formulate my Personal Ambition and my Personal BSC, and in order to improve continuously based on my Personal BSC (to live a balanced life).

Rudy's Personal Vision

To become a happy and respected family man and an exceptional leader of an educational organization that provides innovative training, coaching and consulting to individuals, organizations, and communities. I want to realize this in the following way:

--Enjoy _health and economic security_ to secure family relationships
--Acquire _fame_ and financial security to enjoy life and _contribute_ to the community common good
--Be _generous_ and _compassionate_ to inspire others and _earn their respect_
--_Influence learning_ organizations to build human capital and produce innovative services
--Model the best practices in personal management and professional performance for greater _achievement_
--Experience enjoyment in my work by being full of initiative, accepting challenges continuously, and to seek opportunities for _learning_

My Personal Mission:

My personal mission is about being and giving meaning to my life. It encompasses my philosophy of life and my overall objectives, indicating who I am, the reason for my existence, why I am here on earth, what I stands for, what makes me unique, special and different, what is decisive for my success, what are my unique talents, what are my overall life objectives, and what is my life purpose. I reflected on these questions and answered them honestly:

1. What moves me?

2. Where do I find joy?

3. What words would others use to describe me?

4. What can others depend on me for?

5. Am I seen as someone who is reliable? Or, am I seen as someone who is self-serving?

6. Do I stand out among my competitors and colleagues? I know I need to identify what makes me unique, and then stick with it, not lose sight of it, and maintain my focus.

To get an accurate picture about his mission, I also considered how I am introduced to others, and what my friends, family and colleagues might say about me when I am not around. I wondered how others might perceive my values and what others would gladly pay me to do? This took a good bit of my thinking and self-knowledge. I also reflected on how to distinguish myself from others and figure out what it takes to create a distinctive role for myself in society.

My Personal Ambition is formulated as a high level statement to reflect on the whole of my life and everything my life has yet to achieve as I go forward. Everyone is invited to take a look at my short and supporting Personal Mission statement below. I think there is some differentiation from others.

Rudy's Personal Mission

Want to be a personal success and a valued contributor to *organizational high performance* and *American societal* development. I want to fulfil my vision in the following way:

Internal: As I progress through my senior years, it is important that I adhere to good nutrition, maintain a healthy weight, and participate in regular exercise. This routine will help me remain mentally alert, avoid excessive physical diminishment, and maintain long-term loving relationships with my family, friends and colleagues.

External: I am obliged to stay engaged with others in a friendly, collegial manner so that strong and trusted relationships continue to support my longevity. Additionally, I need to enjoy my later stages of life where mentoring and sharing with others may prove to be life affirming activities.

Knowledge & Learning: I remind myself that my lifelong pursuit of learning for knowledge building and innovative action is essential for me to obtain closure on what I have come to understand is my vision and mission. There remains only a short time for me to integrate and holistically explain what I have come to know as indispensable for experiencing a mindful way-of-being.

Financial: I know that I now have the benefit of modest and continuing income. However, as I choose to work to achieve my vision and mission, I must seek considerable additional income that will sustain not only my wife and me, but will leave a respectable legacy so my children and grandchildren have the opportunity to experience their own significant personal growth and professional development

---

My Key Roles:

In order to continue building a strong Personal Ambition I need to identify and add the key roles and relationships I plan to have with people who truly matter to me. These relationships are related to the essential roles in my life I wish to fulfill. The Key Roles indicate what type of trustworthy relationships I would like to have with my life companion, children, friends, customers, employer, co-workers, and others. This relationship evolves and grows; the deeper the relationship, the better the mutual understanding.

Of course, the most intimate relationship I have is with me. This is covered in my authentic personal vision and mission, which is based on self-awareness – and extended to others as my Key Roles. I made a list of these that I am fulfilling in life with my family, friends and important others; and selected my key roles in this list, which illustrates my personal vision and mission in action.

Rudy's Key Roles

In order to achieve my vision and mission, the following key roles have top priority:

Spouse: To be happy together with my wife; give and receive love and companionship.

Father: To love and help my children and grandchildren seek and find their respective paths to mindful ways-of-being.

Sibling: To continue a kind and loving relationship with my sister throughout our senior years.

Educator: Become a lifelong learner who exemplifies constant intellectual and emotional development as I pass through many stages of life. And, be an exemplar of personal reflection to discover hidden talents for utilization and weaknesses for modification.

Leader: Become an authentic manager and leader who are thoughtful, fair, and motivational towards those subject to my influence. And, be a person who demonstrates remarkable self-management and professional capabilities in the presence of others.

Friend and Colleague: Become an honest and trustworthy supporter that provides encouragement and assistance during trying times. And, be known as a mentor who guides others toward choices and opportunities they desire.

My Personal Ambition (vision, mission, and key roles) are now ready to set the stage for developing my Personal Brand and then my Personal Balanced Scorecard.

Chapter 3. My Authentic Personal Brand

A product is something made in a factory; a brand is something that is bought by the customer. A product can be copied by a competitor; a brand is unique. A product can be quickly outdated; a successful brand is timeless.
-- Stephen King, WPP Group

The second stage in the Personal Branding journey is primarily concerned with defining and formulating a sustainable, strong, authentic, consistent, and memorable Personal Brand identity, which is in harmony with my Personal Ambition.

Personal SWOT	• What are my strengths and weaknesses? What are my most important shortcomings? What are the external opportunities and threats in my chosen domain? • Evaluating myself and defining my personal life style
Personal Brand Objectives	• Which results do I want to achieve with my Personal Brand? • What do I want to be known for?
Specialization, Service, Dominant Attribute	• What is my specialty? What do I do? • What is my service? What is my work style? • What makes me unique, special and different? • What is my single most dominant characteristic?
Domain	• In what arena do I want to achieve my brand objectives? • What is my target market? • Who are my customers? • Who are my main competitors?
Personal Brand Statement	• Concise, meaningful, and inspiring brand promise, based on my Personal Ambition and my dominant attribute, that states what I am committed to being for others.
Personal Brand Story	• The essence of what I want to say about my unique talents, personality and your leading attribute to produce an emotional reaction • Is my Elevator Pitch
Personal Logo & Slogan	• Name, slogan, and icon that represent my Personal Brand and that tell something useful about what I do, for whom I do it, and what the related benefit is.

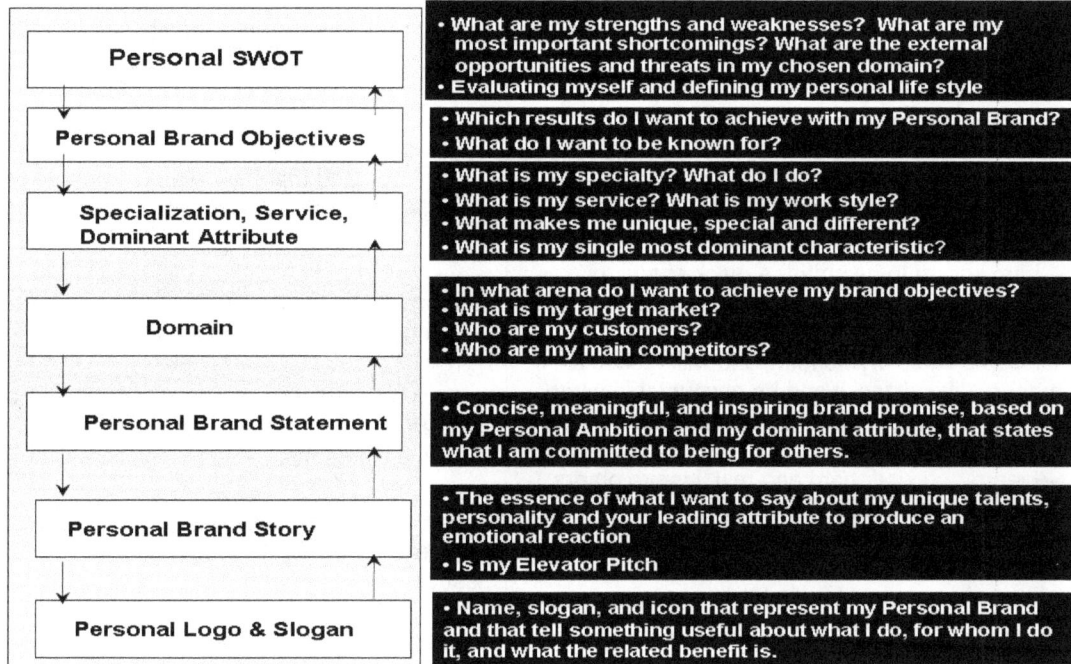

Figure 2-2: Personal Brand Stage

First of all, I performed a personal SWOT analysis and evaluated myself honestly calling to mind the results of the previous breathing and silence exercise. The result of this analysis and evaluation is the definition of my personal life style. This relates to my Personal Brand objectives, what results I want to achieve with my Personal Brand. These are related to the four perspectives: internal, external, knowledge & learning, and financial.

I determined my specialization, concentrating on a single core talent, what my main specific services are, what my key characteristics are, what my single leading and most powerful attribute is, who my audience (domain) is, and what their greatest needs are. My Personal Brand Statement entails the total of my Personal Ambition, brand objectives, specialty, service, dominant attribute, and domain. My Unique Value Proposition (UVP) is part of this.

The next step was to define my Personal Brand Story (Elevator Pitch), which is the essence of what I want to say about my Personal Brand in order to produce a positive emotional reaction. Finally, I designed my Personal Logo and Slogan which is a single graphical symbol that represents my Personal Brand.

My Personal SWOT Analysis:

My personal SWOT analysis forms the basis of my brand and personal objectives, by examining my strengths and weaknesses in the internal environment and opportunities and threats in the external environment. This self-assessment also helped me to identify areas where I may need to improve. I examined my own situation, by asking myself some of the following questions -- and answering them honestly:

1. What are my strengths and weaknesses?
2. How can I capitalize on my strengths and overcome my weaknesses?
3. What are the external opportunities and threats in my chosen field and domain?
4. What would my colleagues or my customers say is my greatest and clearest strength?
5. What would they say is my greatest weakness?
6. What are some of the strengths that have contributed to my success up to the present?
7. How might these create problems for me in the future?
8. Which problems would I like to solve first?

Also, I asked myself this question—what is the most important challenge I face regarding my work and career? Factors that may be related to these questions were, for example, talent, ability, intelligence, goal-orientation, perseverance, self-control, health, integrity, creativity, tolerance, enthusiasm, the home and work environments, responsibility, job prestige, status, power, freedom, and having more free time. Take a look at my SWOT in Table 3.1. I have included some improvement actions in my Personal BSC based on this, so that I can turn my weaknesses into strengths.

	POSITIVE ASPECTS	NEGATIVE ASPECTS	
INTERNAL ENVIRONMENT	**My Strengths (S)** Internal positive aspects that are under control and upon which I will capitalize in my Personal BSC: -- I am known to be smart, a quick study, a reliable subordinate, and a forthright colleague. -- People value my honesty and willingness to pursue difficult tasks and be accountable when tough decisions have to be made. -- I learn and work hard and fast, inspire others to be open-minded, and to reach inside themselves for holistic insight. -- I have a life agenda which I aspire to complete over the next few years.	**My Weaknesses (W)** Internal negative aspects that are under my control, and that I will plan to improve (my objectives and related improvement actions in my Personal BSC) -- I am known to show irritation and impatience when time and money are being wasted. -- I am sometimes outspoken or cause others' embarrassment when witnessing illegal, unkind or abusive situations. -- My work/life balance easily gets skewed due to my heightened sense of responsibility for external issues. -- While I am compassionate, I do express little sympathy for those without the responsibility and courage to lift themselves out of oppressive circumstances.	**ASPECTS THAT ARE NOT COMPLETELY UNDER MY CONTROL**
EXTERNAL ENVIRONMENT	**Opportunities (O) in My Field and Domain:** Positive external conditions that I do not completely control, but of which I plan to take advantage (my objectives and related improvement actions in my Personal BSC) -- I have the education and social awareness to create opportunities for myself under competitive socio-economic conditions. -- There are community needs and paid employment positions for which I am competitive -- My decision to establish a business that offers products and services is making progress, and I will gain greater recognition and publicity as I continue to brand myself and my business. -- It is likely that I will receive training and speaking chances at local universities, and that my writing and publishing efforts will yield encouraging results.	**Threats (T) in my Field and Domain:** Negative external conditions that I do not completely control, but the effect of which I will be able to lessen (my objectives and related improvement actions in my Personal BSC) -- My friends and clients network have not adequately been developed, and my business capacity to perform must be expanded to accommodate work with more than just a couple of clients concurrently. -- The competition for my type of services in my locality is very strong, and differentiation of my skills, while unique, is a challenge. -- Being that I am already of retirement age makes continuous employment difficult when much younger workers with lower financial expectations may appear to be better investments to potential employers to be better investments.	**ASPECTS THAT NOT COMPLETELY UNDER MY CONTROL**

Table 3.1: Personal SWOT

My Evaluation of My Life Style

On the basis of the list I made of all my strengths and weaknesses and opportunities and threats, I evaluated myself honestly and defined my personal life style, which is in harmony with my personal ambition and life story. While evaluating myself, I reflected on the following questions:

1. How do I relate to others?

2. What are my most important values?

3. What are my strongest areas? Do they add value to my domain?

4. What is the strongest personality characteristic I project to others?

5. For what ability, talent or skill am I best known?

6. What is the value that others associate with me most?

7. What moral principle or value do I associate with myself?

8. What do others say about me?

9. How do others, who have never met me, describe me?

10. How am I perceived?

Take a look at my personal life style below. It includes aspects of my <u>Personal Ambition</u>. It entails my perspective regarding life -- which personalizes my brand and reflects my values. I spend time thinking about my life, by performing the breathing exercises regularly. Consequently my <u>Personal Brand</u> reflects distinctiveness, relevancy, and consistency.

Rudy's Personal Life Style

A passionate and compassionate lifelong learner and versalist; who leads a life and career where honesty, reliability, hard work, holistic thinking, and open-mindedness inspire others.

My Personal Brand Objectives:

After I analyzed my strengths, weaknesses, and related threats and opportunities, I performed the breathing and silence exercise, evaluated myself, and defined my personal style; and used that information to define my <u>Personal Brand</u> objectives. For this, I reflected on the following questions:

Rudy's Personal Brand Objectives
I am a partially retired senior executive that enjoys the results of my evolving education and continued accomplishments. I am physically and mentally rejuvenated as I continue to explore new experiences and work related engagements.
I make new friends easily and enjoy interludes with noted people from various industries and locations. I gain satisfaction from occasional opportunities for training, coaching, mentoring, consulting, and charitable fundraising
I am a practitioner of lifelong learning in that I read voraciously, attend stimulating meetings and conferences, and I engage others on substantive life matters through writing or discussion.
I value the use of my time and strive to achieve and maintain a satisfactory work/life balance. When I work and provide value I expect to be paid. When I spend time with my wife, family and friends I anticipate meaningful relations and affection. When I assist in my local community I anticipate positive outcomes for others.

1. What do I want my Personal Brand to accomplish? Is this: Increased business? Recognition? Satisfaction?

2. What do I want to be known for in my profession and domain?

3. What emotions would I like my brand to produce in others? What do I want others to think about me?

My Personal Brand objectives should be realistic and related to the four perspectives: internal, external, knowledge & learning, and financial. Take a look at my Personal Brand objectives.

My Specialization:

After I defined my Personal Brand objectives, I determined my specialization and expertise. I know my unique gift is meta-cognition – which is a specialization in the brain's ability to conduct knowledge "integration." In this authentic Personal Branding concept focused on Personal Ambition, my Personal Brand is built around my dream, values, key roles, and purpose in life.

I have identified and bounded the scope of what I do, which is in line with my strengths. I specialize in patterns of relationships and integration. This is my niche that I love, that I am passionate about, and which is related to my Personal Ambition:

Rudy's Specialization

I have been a specialist in many fields of study and occupations over a 45 year career. This has helped me become what is known as a "versalist" in contemporary language. My specialty now is enquiry into the human ability for integration, synthesis, meta-cognition and holistic aspects of human system learning, knowledge, leadership and performance.

My Service:

After I defined my specialization, I determined my service and tailored this to my target market (domain). I reflected on the following questions:

1. What do I do?

2. What are my primary services?

3. What is my related work style?

4. How do I want prospects in my target market to view my service?

Rudy's Service

I serve myself and others by writing non-fiction descriptions of human learning, knowledge, motivation and performance. These left-brain based writings are supplemented by emergent right-brain graphics and visuals that depict substantive interdependencies that are often subtle or overlooked by others. I assist people, organizations, and communities to attain a mindful way-of-being.

I also defined what makes me unique, special and different. I reflected on the following questions:

1. What are my key characteristics that are very clear to anyone and which add value to others?

2. What unique parts of my personal life style and my work style make an impact on others when I am on top of my performance?

3. What are the top five characteristics that reflect my brand?

4. What is the single leading and most powerful attribute of my Personal Ambition?

5. What are my unique and natural talents?

6. What separates me from the masses?

7. What are my personal core competencies?

8. How do I want prospects and key influencers to think about me and describe me to others?

9. How am I introduced to others? How do my friends describe me to others?

10. What makes me distinctive, related to my most prized personal value?

11. What is the strongest personality characteristic I project to others?

12. What do others say about me when I am not around?

13. How do others react when they first meet me?

Rudy's Top Five Key Characteristics

Passionate, Compassionate, Holistic, Mindful, Lifelong Learning

---

My Dominant Attribute:

These characteristics are the foundation of his brand. My single most dominant characteristic, called dominant attribute, is being a lifelong learning practitioner. I have chosen this characteristic because this is who I am, what makes me distinctive, what correlates to my most prized value, and what appeals to and is valued by my target market. I have the courage to consistently display this with everyone. I am therefore including this attribute in my Personal Brand statement and my brand story. This is what makes my brand unique.

Rudy's Dominant Attribute
Lifelong Learning Practitioner

I hope that *lifelong learning practitioner* is the first idea that enters others' minds when they hear or read about me at this stage of my life. This is also what my target market needs and what can creates value for others.

My Domain:

Once I defined my dominant attribute, the next step was to choose and define my audience (which should be in harmony with my Personal Ambition, brand objectives, specialty, service, and dominant attribute); and to know his audience and their greatest needs. In this inside-out approach, I reflected on the following questions:

1. In what arena do I want to achieve my Personal Brand objectives?

2. What is my target market? Does it have the potential to make money? Do I enjoy working in this target market?

3. Who are my customers?

4. What are their greatest needs? What do they want? What do they value? What do they expect? What are they worried about?

5. What do they expect from me?

6. What are the values of my domain?

7. Who will find me and my unique strengths valuable in the marketplace?

8. What original knowledge or skills do I bring to my clients, industry or company?

Take a look at my domain; the greatest needs of my customers and my key competitors as I now see them.

Rudy's Domain

The American social system-of-systems: Individual learners, organizations, and communities creating aspirations, seeking learning and knowledge, and performing coherently within the nation's founding documents and cultural agreements.

My Customers:

I am focusing on people and companies that are willing to learn and improve consciously. I don't have much time and energy to waste trying to help people and companies who are not committed to change and learning.

My Personal Brand must be relevant to my domain, which means that I must understand and care about what's important to my customers. For corporate customers, employee engagement, a happy and passionate workforce, personal effectiveness & growth, high labor productivity, and awareness for integrity are very important to them.

Rudy's Customers Greatest Needs

Societal alignment and cohesion: Individual self-fulfillment, organizational high performance, and the community common good.

My Key Competitors:

I fill this need with my products/services and brand, and I am convinced that my key competitors don't have sufficient concepts and tools to fill this need in a durable, holistic, and humanized way.

Rudy's Key Competitors

Major coaching organizations and management consulting behemoths that dominate their markets by providing similar, but less effective products and services.

My Personal Brand Statement:

My Personal Brand identity or Personal Brand Promise is a statement that I use _internally_ to focus my efforts on what my Personal Brand must deliver _externally_ in order to satisfy the needs of others. It states what I am committed to "being" for others, and the impact a relationship with me will have on them.

With my Personal Brand statement I wanted to create a particular impression in the mind of others to whom I am important, and to make an emotional connection with them. It includes my Unique Value Proposition (UVP), which entails a core element what makes me more unique, more valuable, and more visible in the market. A powerful Unique Value Proposition makes marketing and selling my services much easier.

The formulation of my Personal Brand promise is most effective when it complies with the following criteria:
1. Should be based on my Personal Ambition, personal SWOT, brand objectives, domain, specialty, service, and dominant attribute.

2. Must be formulated positively, in a distinctive, relevant, consistent, concise, meaningful, exciting, inspiring, active, action-oriented, compelling, memorable, ambitious, and persuasive manner.

3. The emphasis is on authenticity, integrity, consistency, relevancy, and distinctiveness.

4. Should state how I will make a difference in relationships throughout my life.

5. Should include a strong slogan to position me and how to distinguish myself in society

6. Should reflect how I provide value to others

7. Should be unique to me, relevant to the market place, reflect who I really am, and to be used by people at work, family, and friends (to all my relationships in your life).

8. Should differentiate me and direct the way I think and behave.

My authentic Personal Brand Statement below summarizes me. I have formulated this for myself to be used as guidance for my Personal Brand "story" and to keep me moving in the right direction. This makes my Personal Brand more personal and continuously creates a personal touch and bond with my target audience. It provides me energy that helps me consistently build distinctive relationships with important people in my life. It also helps me to understand myself better.

Rudy's Personal Brand Statement

Linking Lifelong Learning to Human Potential – I employ my passion for systems thinking and learning to illuminate the path others may take to an intellectually and emotionally satisfying mindful way-of-being. I craft social system frameworks that elevate people's desire to benefit from experiencing, concurrently: individual *self-fulfillment*, organizational *high performance*, the community *common good* and societal *human enlightenment*.

I am using my brand statement to communicate my unique service that provides a sense of value for my target audience. It is in line with my dreams, life purpose, values, creativity, passion, competencies, specialization, characteristics, and things what I love doing. This statement should evoke strong emotions (warmth, confidence, respect) in my target market -- which is exactly how I want to be perceived by my colleagues and clients.

My Personal Brand statement reflects who I really am, what I do well, what I love to do, for whom I am doing it, and what I care about. It's a commitment that I make to important people in my life, including my customers, and about what I am willing to do on their behalf. It's clearly defined so that my target audience quickly grasps what I stand for.

I have included my Personal Brand statement on my website, in my books, articles, resume and brochures. I uses it as a compass for marketing and sales of my brand, keeping me focused, guiding me in the right direction, and defining and communicating my Personal Brand story effectively.

My Personal Logo and Slogan

A Personal Logo is a single graphical symbol that represents and packages my Personal Brand. It tells something useful about what I do, for whom I do it, and what the benefit happens to be. A Personal Logo consists of: a name, a slogan and an icon. A Personal Logo & Slogan makes my Personal Brand visible.

Take a look at my Personal Logo & Slogan below. My brand name and slogan are based on my first book: *American Learnership: Total Learning, Knowing, and Leading as a Mindful Way-of-Being.* My slogan "Linking Lifelong Learning to Human Potential" implies a future vision to my domain, and my icon is strongly related to my personal life style and my Personal Ambition. These entail the essence of my market positioning, and uses America's colors (red, white blue) to convey dedication to my country.

My Brand Name: The American Learnership Forum

My Slogan: Linking Lifelong Learning to Human Potential

My Icon:

My Logo:

Linking Lifelong Learning to Human Potential

A nice Personal Brand without an execution plan in order to make is a reality, will not lead to sustainable development of my potential and marketing success. My plan and Personal Balance Scorecard, are discussed in detail in the next chapter.

4. My Authentic Personal Balanced Scorecard

> *Life is like riding a bicycle. To keep your balance you must keep moving.*
> -- Albert Einstein

I recognized that once my Personal Ambition and Personal Brand were developed, the next step was to translate these into my Personal Balanced Scorecard (a personal branding strategy and an execution plan) in order to make my brand a reality. My Personal Ambition and Personal Brand are related to my heart (emotions) and the right half of my brain. My Personal BSC, however, is related to the left half of my brain. With the left half of my brain having mainly an analytical, logical and quantitative function, the right half of my brain has an intuitive, spiritual, emotional, and holistic function. One of the results of applying this holistic and authentic Personal Branding model, along with the tools introduced here, is the balance of the left and right side of my brain and the balance of my heart and head.

My Critical Success Factors:

My Personal Critical Success Factors (CSFs) are derived from my Personal Ambition and Personal Brand. They are related to the four perspectives, *internal, external, knowledge and learning, and financial*. A Personal Ambition and Personal Brand without these four perspectives results in an incomplete Personal BSC. The personal CSFs form the bridge between the Personal Ambition and Personal Brand (long term) -- and on the other side the personal objectives, performance measures, targets, and improvement actions (short term). This link is made by identifying my personal core competencies, uniqueness, genius, dominant attribute, values in my Personal Ambition and Personal Brand and translating these into concrete personal objectives. (See figure 4.1)

My Personal Objectives:

My Personal Ambition and Personal Brand are tied to my personal objectives. These objectives should be realistic and are based on my Personal Ambition/Brand statement and the results of the self assessment executed with the help of my personal SWOT analysis. The central questions here are:

1. Which measurable short-term personal results do I want to achieve?
2. Which problems would I like to handle better?
3. What are my five-year career goals and life objectives?

My objectives describe a result that I want to achieve in order to realize my Personal Ambition, and successfully launch my Personal Brand. My ambition is aimed at my personal objectives both in the short-term and the future. My personal objectives give me ambition and brand direction. The personal Critical Success Factors form the bridge between these. My personal objectives are derived from my personal Critical Success Factors and from my SWOT analysis (See figure 4.1: Personal Brand Stage Factors and Actions).

Personal Critical Success Factors	• Which factors in my Personal Ambition and Personal Brand, related to the four BSC perspectives, are decisive for my success?
Personal Objectives	• What short-term results do I want to achieve? • Which problems would I like to handle better?
Personal Performance Measures	• How can I measure my personal results? • What makes my Personal Ambition, Personal Brand objectives and personal life objectives measurable?
Personal Targets	• Which values do I have to obtain? • What are my targets?
Personal Improvement Actions	- How do I want to achieve the results? Which improvement actions do I need to achieve this? - How to make my personality appropriate for my target market. What talents, skills and experience do I need to add value to others? How will I communicate my Personal Brand?

Figure 4.1: Personal Branding Factors and Actions

My Personal Performance Measures:

Performance Measures are standards to measure the progress of my Personal and Brand objectives. With these measures, I can assess my functioning in relation to my personal Critical Success Factors and objectives. Without performance measures and targets, it is difficult to coach/manage myself with feedback from others. Performance measures urge me to action if they are related to my Personal and Brand objectives, giving me certain direction. (See figure 4.1)

My Personal Targets:

My personal target is a quantitative objective of a personal performance measures. On the basis of my performance targets I can get clear feedback about the progress of my improvement actions; which is needed to refine my Personal Brand and to better manage myself. My personal targets indicate values that I want to achieve, and depend on my level of ambition. They should be:

Specific -- they must be specifically formulated so that they can also influence behavior.

Measurable -- they must be formulated in such a way that they can measure the objective.

Achievable -- they must be realistic, realizable, feasible and acceptable.

Result--oriented -- they must be related to concrete results.

Time--specific -- they must be time-constrained. (See figure 4.1)

My Personal Improvement Actions:
My personal improvement actions are personal strategies used to realize my Personal Ambition and Personal Brand. They are utilized to develop my skills, improve my behavior, master myself, and improve my performance. I used two ways to define my personal improvement actions:

1. By selecting Critical Success Factors in my Personal Ambition and Brand statement, and translating these into personal objectives, performance measures, targets, and related improvement actions

2. By performing my personal SWOT analysis and transforming my strengths, weaknesses and related opportunities and threats into personal improvement actions. (See figure 4.1)

My Authentic Personal Balanced Scorecard:

Table 4.1 shows my Personal BSC, which is related to my Personal Ambition, my SWOT, my Personal Brand Statement, and is related to my Personal Critical Success Factors. It shows how I monitor the progress of my Personal Brand and my related personal objectives and improvement actions.

Some important questions in this evaluation process are:

1. Do I make more money?
2. Do I get more referrals?
3. Are opinions about my work stronger?
4. Do more people know who I am, what I do, and what I stand for (brand awareness)?
5. Am I being considered for more work?

By continuously checking the data I am receiving from my own observations, I am keeping my brand relevant, focused, and emotionally connected with my target market.

Table 4.1: Rudy's Personal Balanced Scorecard

		Internal		
Personal Critical Success Factors	**Personal Objectives**	**Personal Performance Measures**	**Personal Targets**	**Personal Improvement Actions**
1. Maintain good health	1. Adhere to a good health practices	1. Twice a year physical check-up and dental exam	1. Lose 20 lbs	1. Increase regular physical activity (weekly)
2. Provide love and support to family	2. Take action to show appreciation, love and respect	2a. Make time to listen to family members interests and needs	2a. Communicate daily about interpersonal matters	2a. Eat out weekly with my wife, and call/talk with my children at least once a week.
		2b. Provide assistance and helpful guidance	2b. Seek to determine issues in need of concern	2b. Check in with sister two times per week to discuss matters of health and finance
3. Make Progress on my life/work agenda	3. Become efficient in using my resources	3. Make a schedule for achieving essential tasks	3a. Write and publish my Authentic Personal Brand book	3a. Submit book for publishing by Jan. 2014
			3b. Modify and re-publish American Learnership textbook	3b. Submit book for publishing by Feb. 2014
4. Conquer impatience with others' failings	4. Become less sensitive to others' behavior	4. Practice understanding and forgiveness	4. Identify people and situations that lead to my stress	4. Take a pause every day to think quietly and breath deeply
5. Achieve happiness	5. A mindful way-of-being	5. Gain exposure to new countries and cultures	5. Increase travel outside the U.S.	5. Take two extended business trips or vacations in 2014

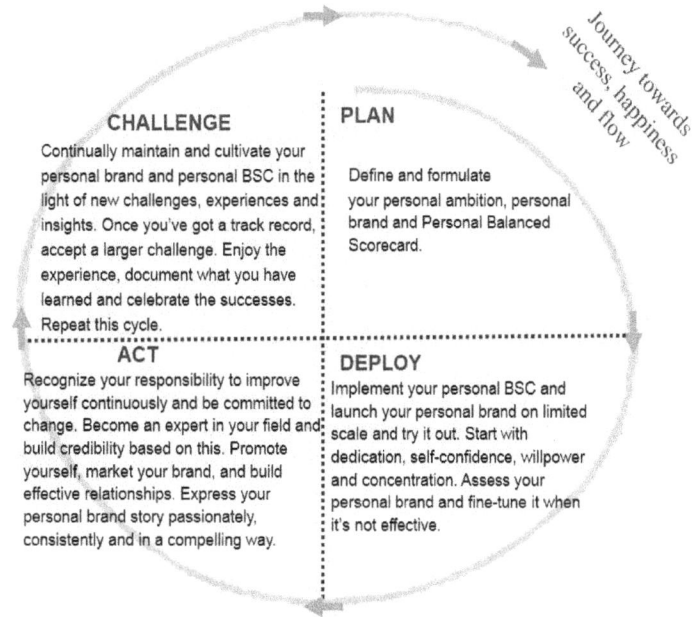

Figure 5.1 Plan-Deploy-Act-Challenge Cycle

ACT

I have become an expert in my field and building credibility based on this effort. I am promoting myself and my personal code of ethics, marketing my brand, building effective relationships, networking with fellow professionals, and expressing my Authentic Personal Brand relentlessly, passionately, constantly, consistently, and in a compelling way to everyone I meet.

I find venues for my voice, express myself, and communicate my brand story in most everything I say and do. I keep my Personal Brand statement in mind when carrying out activities and dealing with others. I develop my talent and skills to achieve my Personal and Brand objectives.

I recognize my responsibility to improve myself continuously and be committed to change. I know that it is my ethical duty and moral responsibility to change – not only for my own good but also for my loved ones, my work, my organization, my country, and for the world of which I am a part.

I am building a solid reputation within my industry and doing work I love that is consistent with my passion, Personal Ambition and Personal Brand.

I am creating a representative and professional personal website that is specifically designed to deliver my brand message and showcase my key accomplishments, skills, education, successes, and summary of my career. My website also includes his articles, speeches, awards, and testimonials.

I have designed a great looking logo for my business card, building a network of contacts that know my brand value and am able to communicate it, and keep my network strong.

I also remember what Ralph Waldo Emerson said; "*Our greatest glory is in never failing, but in rising up every time we fail*".

CHALLENGE

I am cultivating and maintaining my brand continuously in the light of new challenges, experience, and insights. I monitor, refine, fine tune, and cultivate this as I am going along, figuring out which parts work and which don't, in order to create brand loyalty. I am constantly checking and monitoring my target market and making adjustments as necessary. I am constantly updating my brand to reflect the new challenges I accept and the lessons I learn in order to keep people interested and committed in my life and work.

Chapter 6. My Authentic Personal Brand Alignment with Myself and Corporation

In the 21st Century great companies will figure out how to tap into people's hearts—their passion and their desires to make a difference through their work. Those companies that link these passions to the generation of innovative ideas will have the capacity to sustain their growth for decades.
-- Bill George, former Chairman of Medtronic Inc.

Increasingly, successful organizations are beginning to recognize that good brand relationships with their employees are as important as good brand relationships with their customers; employees should be happy first in order to make the customers happy. Corporate brand loyalty starts with employee's happiness; with the linkage between employee's ambition/brand and employer's ambition/brand. Both must be put side by side to check if there are similarities or not. Both don't have to match exactly but should align in key places, such as in Personal Ambition and Personal Brand.

The final stage in the Authentic Branding Model entails aligning and synchronizing my Personal Ambition and Personal Brand with my Corporation's Ambition and Brand; (see figure 6.1). Also, the development of a Corporate Balanced Scorecard should be added to the mix because greater leadership alignment and workforce cohesion occur when these relationships exist.

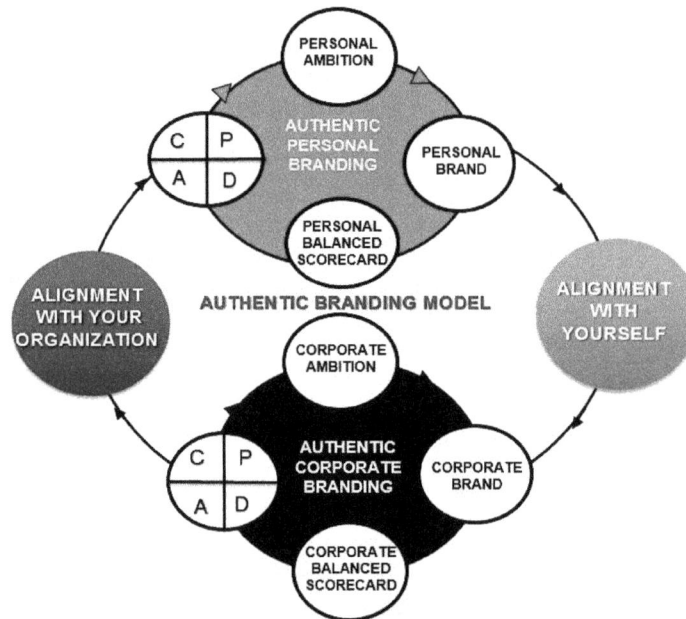

Figure 6.1 <u>Alignment Stage</u> in the Authentic Governance Model

I find that it is essential to strive for the optimal fit and balance in order to enhance my productivity and to stimulate engagement, commitment, and passion in the organization. This alignment process has to do with reaching a higher degree of compatibility between personal and organizational objectives and accomplishing mutual value.

Research has shown that when an individual has some input regarding the shared ambition that affects his or her work, the person will be more supportive, motivated, and receptive towards organizational change. I know that I am often willing to work together towards the goals of the organization with dedication when there is a match between myself and their personal ambition and the corporate ambition. All people have different personal values and principles that must be understood and linked to the corporation's values.

This alignment process is about matching my personal ambition/brand with the corporate ambition/brand. It has to do with reaching a higher degree of compatibility between my personal objectives and those of my corporate organization. The larger the intersection area between these two parties, the greater the degree of integral operations and the achievement of higher performance. (See figure 6.2)

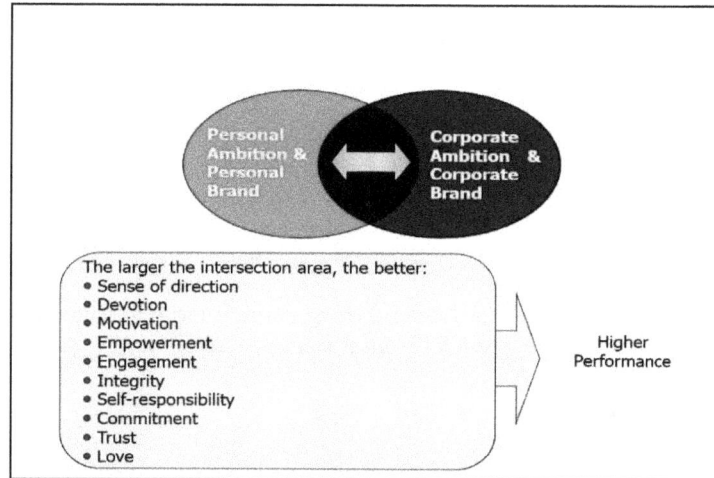

Figure 6.2: Matching the Personal Ambition/Brand with the Corporate Ambition/Brand

How to Align with my Organization:

Dr. Rampersad has been encouraging managers and employees to establish their personal ambitions brands, so that they become energized to share that information. I too, recommend introducing an _Ambition Meeting_ within organizations between the line-manager or superior and his/her employees. The Ambition Meeting is a periodical, informal, voluntary and confidential meeting of a maximum duration of one hour between line-manager and his/her employees -- with the employee's personal ambition/brand/BSC and the corporate ambition/brand/BSC as topics for friendly discussion. For consideration:

1. Why informal? _Because they will learn more from informal than from formal meetings._ It is recommended that the meeting is held structurally at least once every two months, preferably more often. The outcome of these informal meetings should be highly confidential and should be kept out of the personnel file and not be used against the employee. The line-manager or supervisor plays a crucial role in worker well-being and engagement. He/she should act as a trusted person, coach, and role model in this process.

2. Why as a trusted person? _Because if there is distrust and fear, there will be no sharing and learning._ To be able to talk about the employee's personal ambition/brand/BSC, one needs a confidential, informal and friendly atmosphere, an atmosphere of trust and open communication. This is essential as human values will be discussed. Experience has shown that this intimate atmosphere can be reached if the manager formulates his/her own personal ambition/brand/BSC beforehand and shares it with his/her employee.

The implementation of the employee's personal ambition/brand/BSC comes up for discussion, and may include selected private matters that have an impact on job performance that can be discussed confidentially. During the alignment process, the manager should act as a trusted and informal coach and provide social support to the employees by being a good listener, providing help, and being someone on which the employee can rely.

I selected the following ambition questions as the basis for having an ambition meeting with my future employees and colleagues (Rampersad, 2009):

1. Does your personal ambition/brand correspond with the corporate ambition/brand?

2. Does your personal ambition/brand match the corporation's ambition/brand? Where do they align and where do they contradict each other? Do they conflict? Are there compatibilities? Are there linkages?

3. Is there a win-win situation between your own interests and the ones of your organization?

4. What makes you feel good at work?

5. Are you proud of working for the organization?

6. Whose life is improved because of your work?

7. Which skills do you need to be a pillar of the organization and thus realize the organization ambition/brand? What do you want to gain through this?

8. Are your developmental expectations in tune with those of the organization?

9. Do your job requirements match your capabilities and needs?

10. What motivates you? What de-motivates you? What makes you happy or sad? What do you enjoy the most?

11. What contribution are you trying to make to the realization of our corporate ambition/brand? Which job do you aspire? What are your wishes? What do you strive for? What are your concerns?

12. Have you considered a job change?

Conclusion

As Authentic Personal and Corporate Branding comes to closure, you the reader, have the opportunity to decide if you have achieved your life and work objectives by recording your *own what, why, how* and *for whom* you live and work. If you have completed this project in order to become a <u>Certified Personal Brand Coach</u> you will need to discuss how that might be accomplished by talking with Dr. Garrity: <u>rgarrity@alforum.org</u> or Dr. Rampersad: <u>h.rampersad@tps-international.com</u>.

(See Blank Form Below)

Appendix C (Continued)

Guest eBook Publishing: My Authentic Personal and Professional Brand

[**Author's Note**: This part is adapted from the work of Dr. Hubert Rampersad and includes excerpts from his book *Authentic Personal Branding (2009)* and *Rudolph Garrity's Personal Brand* (2014).

ITEM II: Blank Form – For others to complete.

Contents

Preface: Importance of an Authentic Personal and Professional Brand
Chapter 1: My Authentic Personal and Professional Branding
Chapter 2: My Authentic Personal Ambition
Chapter 3. My Authentic Personal Brand
Chapter 4: My Authentic Personal Balanced Scorecard
Chapter 5: My Authentic Personal Brand Implementation and Cultivation
Chapter 6: My Authentic Personal Brand Alignment with Myself and Corporation

Preface: Importance of an Authentic Personal and Professional Branding

Customers must recognize that you stand for something.
– Howard Schultz, Chairman of Starbucks

The underlying assumption of personal-branding philosophy is that each of us has unique gifts and a distinct purpose and dream in life. By connecting these gifts, purpose and dream, we open ourselves up to greater happiness and success in life (Frost, 2003). This fits very well to my holistic and authentic personal branding model, which will be discussed in the following sections. This new blueprint will help me to unlock my potential and build a trusted image of myself that I want to project in everything I do. It must therefore be in harmony with my true values, beliefs, dreams, and genius. When my brand is combined with powerful tools, it will deliver peak performance and create a stable basis for trustworthiness, credibility, and personal charisma.

This inside-out approach is durable and differs from traditional methods, and is based on a passion for developing human potential. This new approach places more emphasis on understanding myself and the needs of others, meeting those needs while staying true to my values, improving myself continuously, and realizing growth in life based on this personal branding journey. It focuses on the human side of branding, and includes my reputation, character and personality. If am well branded according to this approach, I will find it easier to convince others and I will attract the people and opportunities that are a perfect fit for me.

The authentic personal branding process starts with determining who I am at my core authentic self. Rather than inventing a brand that I would like to be perceived as and to sell myself to others, this one is based on my life philosophy, dreams, vision, mission, values, key roles, identity, self-knowledge, self-awareness, self-responsibility, positive attributes, and self-management. With an authentic personal brand, my strongest characteristics, attributes, and values can separate me from the crowd. Without this, I look just like everyone else. If I am not branded in an authentic, honest, and holistic way, if I don't deliver according to my brand promise, and if I focus mainly on selling, packaging, outward appearances, promoting myself, and becoming famous, I will be perceived as not being authentic.

LEARNING OBJECTIVES
After reading this authentic branding methodology and applying its concepts, I am learning to:
- Build, implement, and cultivate an authentic, distinctive, inspiring, compelling, enduring personal brand.
- Create positive perceptions and emotions in the mind of my prospects (that I am different, special, unique, and authentic) based on my personal brand.
- Build a truly lasting and trusted relationship with my clients, make an emotional connection with them, and managing their expectations and perception effectively.
- Manage and influence how others perceive me and think of me.
- Stimulate meaningful perceptions about the values and qualities I stand for.
- Use my brand to communicate my unique service that provides a sense of value for my target audience, which is in line with my dreams, purpose in life, values, passion, competencies, uniqueness, genius, specialization, characteristics, and things that I love doing.

- Position myself strongly in relation to my competitors, built a strong reputation, and develop an effective image of myself that I want to project in everything I do.
- Communicate what I stand for in a unique way that is different from others in my field and that gets inside people's minds.
- Provide value to others continuously, create visibility, build trust, and reinforce integrity, honesty, trustworthiness, credibility, transparency, and personal charisma.
- Build a trusted image of myself, which is based on my true values, beliefs, dream, and genius.
- Make a difference in relationships throughout my life, fire my passion, and be happy and attract success.

Remember what Albert Einstein said: *Try not to become a person of success but a person of value.*

Chapter 1: My Authentic Personal and Professional Branding

Having a strong personal brand seems to be a very important asset in today's online, virtual, and individual age. It is becoming increasingly essential and is the key to personal success. Everyone has a personal brand but most people are not aware of this and do not manage this strategically, consistently, and effectively. I should take control of my brand and the message it sends and affects how others perceive me. This will help me to actively grow and distinguish myself as an exceptional professional.

My personal brand should be authentic, which means that it always should reflect my true character, and should be built on my dreams, life purpose, values, uniqueness, genius, passion, specialization, characteristics, and things what I love doing. If I am branded in this organic, authentic and holistic way my personal brand will be strong, distinctive, meaningful, inspiring, and memorable. I will also create a life that is fulfilling, automatically attract the people and opportunities that are a perfect fit for me, and increase my ability to deliver peak performances.

Branding isn't just for corporations anymore. There is a new trend called "*Personal Branding*". The reason for this is (Jane Tabachnick, 2007):

1. The technological revolution has changed the structure of careers today. It used to be that we went to work for one or two companies in our entire career. Today we will all have as many as four to eight jobs or careers in our lifetime. Personal Branding is essential to career development and an effective career tool because it helps define who we are, what we stand for, what makes us unique, special, and different, how we are great, and why we should be sought out.

2. The change in the way we communicate. The internet has elevated each of us to the position of publisher. Email, newsgroups, bulletin boards, blogs, and online network and discussion groups afford all of us the opportunity to learn, network and get exposure for our businesses and ourselves. People want to do business with people they know or people they feel they can trust, with whom they feel some sort of connection, and with whom they relate. If we are a familiar, friendly, and consistent presence and brand online, people will have the sense that they know us and be more receptive to doing business with us. So Personal Branding is also essential to business development.

According to Randall Hansen (2007) "*Branding can be defined as a promise… a promise of the value of the product… a promise that the product is better than all the competing products… a promise that must be delivered to be successful*". Being good and accomplished in our field is not enough. It's time to give serious effort to discovering our genius, passion, and our authentic dream, imagining and developing ourselves as powerful, consistent, and memorable people with our own specific brand, as we do related work we love. We can shape the market's perception of our Personal Brand by defining our unique strengths, values, and personality, sharing it with others in an exciting, persuasive manner, and cultivating our brand continuously. It's something that we can develop and manage, which is essential for future employability and success in life. Everyone has a chance and should take the responsibility to learn, improve, build their skills and be a strong brand.

Everyone has a personal brand but most people are not aware of this and do not manage this strategically and effectively. I should take control of my brand, the message it sends and its affect on how others perceive me. This will help me to actively grow and distinguish myself as an exceptional professional. Having a strong personal brand has benefits. It:

1. Stimulates meaningful perceptions about the values and qualities that I stand for

2. Tells others: who I am, what I do, what makes me different, how I create value for them, and what they can expect when they deal with me, and influences how others perceive me

3. Creates expectations in the mind of others of what they will get when they work with me

4. Creates an identity around me which makes it easier for people to remember who I am.

5. Gets my prospects to see me as the only solution to their problem.

6. Puts me above the competition and makes me unique and better than my competitors in the marketplace

An Authentic Branding Model:

A great brand taps into emotions….Emotions drive most, if not all, of our decisions. A brand reaches out with a powerful connecting experience. It's an emotional connecting point that transcends the product….A great brand is a story that's never completely told. A brand is a metaphorical story that's evolving all the time…..Stories creates the emotional context people need to locate themselves in a larger experience. -- Scott Bedbury

This chapter emphasizes the organic, holistic and authentic branding model, which provides an excellent framework and roadmap to develop, implement, and cultivate an authentic personal and corporate brand in a sustainable way.

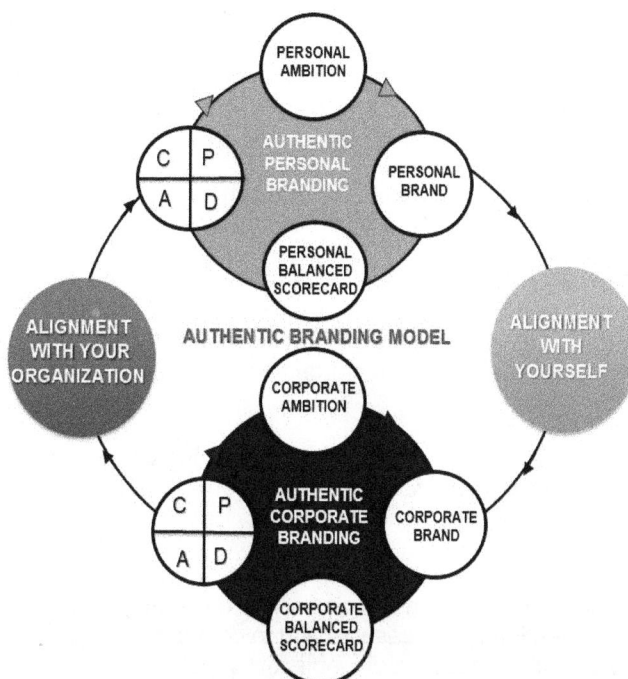

Figure 1-1: Authentic Branding Model

The authentic branding model consists of four phases which are the building blocks of sustainable personal leadership branding (Rampersad, 2009, 2014):

1. Authentic Personal Branding:

a. Personal Ambition; this phase involves a soul-searching process based on thought, introspection, and self-reflection supported through use of a "breathing and silence exercise." Questions which I can ask myself are: Who am I, What do I stand for?, What makes me happy?, What do I live for?, Why do I want to lead? What's the purpose of my leadership? The result of this phase is the formulation of my personal mission, vision and key roles. On the basis of insights acquired through this process, I can develop self-awareness and self-regulation, which are the foundation of trustworthiness, integrity, and openness to learn. (See chapter 2)

b. Personal Brand; this phase involves defining and formulating an authentic, distinctive, and memorable personal brand promise, and using it as the focal point of my behavior and actions. This must be in harmony with my personal ambition. (See chapter 3)

c. Personal Balanced Scorecard (PBSC); personal ambition has no value unless I take action to make it a reality. Therefore the emphasis in this stage is developing an integrated and well-balanced action plan based on my personal ambition to realize your life objectives. It's about translating my personal ambition into action. Personal branding without continuous improvement of yourself based on your PBSC is merely cosmetic and will not lead to my sustainable growth. My PBSC entails my personal critical success factors that are related to my personal ambition and my corresponding objectives, performance measures, targets and improvement actions (Rampersad, 2006). It is divided into the four perspectives: internal, external, knowledge & learning, and financial perspectives. (See chapter 4)

d. <u>Implementation and Cultivation of My Personal Brand</u>; personal ambition and personal balanced scorecard have no value unless I implement them to make them a reality. Therefore the next step is to implement, maintain, and cultivate my ambition, personal brand and PBSC to manage myself effectively. This focuses on my private life and business life. To guide me in this process I have used a unique learning cycle called the Plan-Deploy-Act-Challenge cycle (PDAC cycle), which should be followed continuously (Rampersad, 2003, 2006, 2009). To live in accordance with my personal ambition and related PBSC through its implementation using the PDAC cycle, results in a journey towards self-awareness, flow and happiness. (See chapter 5)

2. Alignment with Yourself:

Aligning your personal ambition with my behavior and my way of acting is needed to develop personal integrity. I need to commit myself to live and act according to my personal ambition and to keep promises that I make to myself. Personal branding built on a person's true character is sustainable and strong. I should reflect my true self and must adhere to a moral and behavioral code set down by my personal ambition. This means that who I really am, what I care about, and my passions should come out in my personal ambition, and I should act and behave accordingly (I should be myself) to build trust.

These first two stages in the authentic branding model focus on personal leadership development by cultivating my inner compass.

3. Authentic Corporate Branding:

a. <u>Corporate Ambition</u>; this phase involves defining and formulating the shared corporate ambition. It entails the soul, core intention and the guiding principles of the organization and encompasses the corporate mission, vision, and core values.

b. <u>Corporate Brand</u>; this phase involves defining and formulating an authentic, distinctive, and memorable corporate brand promise, and using it as the focal point of the organization's behavior and actions. This must be in harmony with the shared corporate ambition.

c. <u>Corporate Balanced Scorecard</u> (CBSC); the emphasis in this stage is developing an integrated and well-balanced action plan based on the corporate ambition to realize the corporate objectives. It offers a means to maintain balance between financial and nonfinancial measures and to connect strategic and operational standards. The CBSC entails the related corporate critical success factors, objectives, performance measures, targets and improvement actions, divided into four perspectives: financial, external, internal, and knowledge & learning. The CBSC is needed to improve the business processes continuously based on the corporate ambition in order to add value to customers and satisfy them.

d. <u>Implementation and Cultivation of the Corporate Brand</u>; the next step is to implement, maintain, and cultivate the corporate ambition, the corporate brand and CBSC in order to govern my organization effectively, to deliver peak performance, and to create competitive advantage. To guide you in this process I have introduced the Plan-Deploy-Act-Cultivate cycle (PDAC cycle), which should be followed continuously. To operate in accordance with the corporate ambition, corporate brand and related CBSC, through its implementation using the PDAC cycle, results in a journey towards sustainable business success.

4. Alignment with My Corporation:

The emphasis in this final stage is aligning personal ambition with corporate ambition and creating uniformity of personal and organizational values. It's about aligning personal branding with corporate branding and getting the optimal fit and balance between these two activities in order to enhance labor productivity, to create a climate of trust, and to stimulate engagement, commitment, integrity, and passion in the organization. This is needed because staff members don't work with devotion or expend energy on something they do not believe in or agree with. If there is a match between their interests and those of the organization, or if their values and the organization's values align, they will be engaged and will work with greater commitment and dedication towards realizing the corporate objectives. The effective combination of all these four phases creates a stable basis for a high-performance and ethical organization.

As we can see from Table 1-1, the authentic branding model gives us insight into both the way authentic branding can be developed effectively and the coherence between its different aspects.

[**Author's Note**: The Breathing and Silence Exercise below is known to be helpful for deep contemplation and relaxation when preparing to complete some of the tasks included in Authentic Personal Branding.]

An Integrated Breathing and Silence Exercise

(Rampersad, 2009, 2014)

Step 1: Breathing Exercise

1. Look for a quiet spot with fresh air and make sure that you will not be disrupted.
2. Sit in a comfortable chair with an upright back, and your shoulders and neck relaxed.
3. Gently rest your hands on your knees, with your palms upward and close your eyes.
4. Breath deeply through your nose according to the following rhythm: inhale deeply during a count to four (your stomach fills like a balloon), hold your breath during four counts, and exhale fully and slowly during a count of six (your stomach flattens again) and stop for two counts. Focus on the rhythm of breathing in and out.
5. Focus your attention entirely on your breathing during this process and observe how your life energy flows through your body. During the breathing you will become more relaxed. Concentrate on the feeling of relaxation
   in your whole body (face, shoulders, hands, feet, etc.).
6. Repeat this process during 10-15 minutes.

Step 2: Silence Exercise

After finishing the breathing exercise, remain in your sitting position with your back straight, relax your arms, keep your eyes closed and breathe normally through your nose.

1. Focus entirely on your thoughts; do not concentrate on anything else. If thoughts do enter, do not force them out but simply let them pass like clouds making way for the beautiful blue sky.
2. Allow your thoughts to come and go, including the thoughts related to the Personal Brand questions.
3. Be open to all images that come up in your mind. Imagine that you are in a garden and that a wise man approaches you who, after introducing himself, asks you some of the Personal Brand questions mentioned below.
4. Listen carefully to the answers of your inner voice and write these down immediately after this exercise.

Open your eyes slowly after 10-15 minutes and write the answers of your inner voice in your personal ambition statement and your personal brand diary. The purpose of this diary is to be able to use this information to update your personal ambition and personal brand and keep record of your experiences and progress in each session.

Table 1-1

Chapter 2. My Authentic Personal Ambition

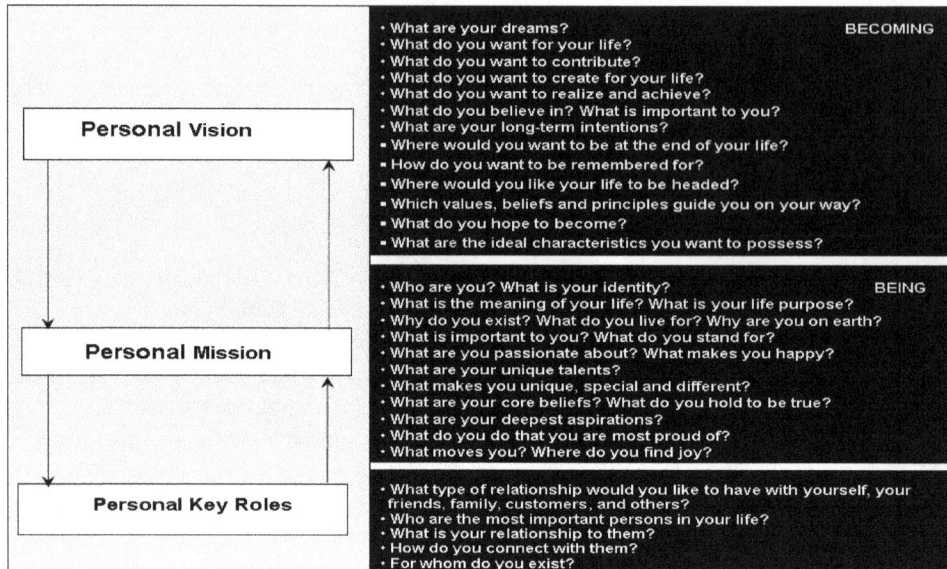

Figure 2-1: Personal Ambition Stage

The four perspectives that follow should be in balance and are of essential importance for my self-development, personal well-being, and marketing success of my brand. These are:

1. Internal: my physical health and mental state. How can I control these in order to create value for myself and others?

2. External: my relations with my customers, spouse, children, friends, manager, colleagues, and others. How do they see me?

3. Knowledge and learning: my skills and learning ability. How do I learn, and how can I remain successful in the future?

4. Financial: financial stability. To what degree am I able to fulfil my financial needs?

[**Author's Note**: The formulation of everyone's Personal Ambition is most effective when it complies with the following criteria.]

1. Your personal vision motivates you, your personal mission inspires you, and your key roles guide your relationships.

2. Your personal vision is about _becoming_ and your personal mission about _being_.

3. The four perspectives: financial, external, internal, and knowledge and learning are a part of it.

4. The emphasis is on unselfishness and authenticity.

5. Your values should explicitly be included in your personal vision, mission, and key roles.

6. Is specific to each person and includes ethical starting points, with an emphasis on your dream, uniqueness, genius, skills, principles, and values.

7. Personal mission is short, clear, simple, and formulated in the present tense; it is concrete and may be used as a guideline.

8. Personal vision is ambitious and should give direction to personal initiative and creativity, and combines personal power and energy.

9. Personal mission indicates how a person wants to distinguish him or herself in society.

My Personal Vision:

Personal Vision

My Personal Mission:

Personal Mission

My Key Roles:

Key Roles

My <u>Personal Ambition</u> (vision, mission, and key roles) are now ready to set the stage for developing my <u>Personal Brand</u> and then my <u>Personal Balanced Scorecard</u>.

Chapter 3. My Authentic Personal Brand

A product is something made in a factory; a brand is something that is bought by the customer. A product can be copied by a competitor; a brand is unique. A product can be quickly outdated; a successful brand is timeless.
-- Stephen King, WPP Group

The second stage in the Personal Branding journey is primarily concerned with defining and formulating a sustainable, strong, authentic, consistent, and memorable <u>Personal Brand</u> identity, which is in harmony with my <u>Personal Ambition</u>.

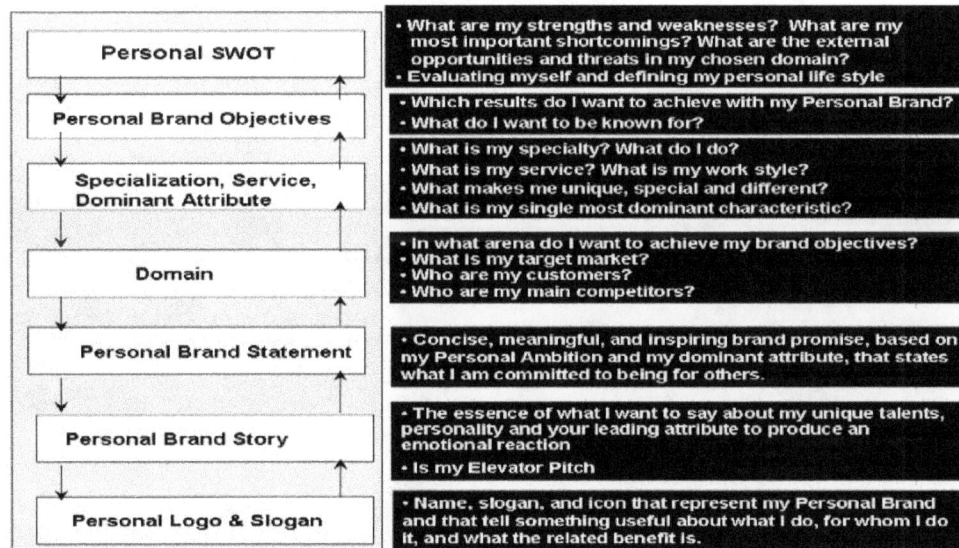

Personal SWOT	• What are my strengths and weaknesses? What are my most important shortcomings? What are the external opportunities and threats in my chosen domain? • Evaluating myself and defining my personal life style
Personal Brand Objectives	• Which results do I want to achieve with my Personal Brand? • What do I want to be known for?
Specialization, Service, Dominant Attribute	• What is my specialty? What do I do? • What is my service? What is my work style? • What makes me unique, special and different? • What is my single most dominant characteristic?
Domain	• In what arena do I want to achieve my brand objectives? • What is my target market? • Who are my customers? • Who are my main competitors?
Personal Brand Statement	• Concise, meaningful, and inspiring brand promise, based on my Personal Ambition and my dominant attribute, that states what I am committed to being for others.
Personal Brand Story	• The essence of what I want to say about my unique talents, personality and your leading attribute to produce an emotional reaction • Is my Elevator Pitch
Personal Logo & Slogan	• Name, slogan, and icon that represent my Personal Brand and that tell something useful about what I do, for whom I do it, and what the related benefit is.

Figure 3.1: Personal Brand Stage

First of all, I performed a personal SWOT analysis and evaluated myself honestly calling to mind the results of the previous breathing and silence exercise. The result of this analysis and evaluation is the definition of my personal life style. This relates to my Personal Brand objectives, what results I want to achieve with my Personal Brand. These are related to the four perspectives: <u>internal</u>, <u>external</u>, <u>knowledge & learning</u>, and <u>financial</u>.

I determined my specialization, concentrating on a single core talent, what my main specific services are, what my key characteristics are, what my single leading and most powerful attribute is, who my audience (domain) is, and what their greatest needs are. My Personal Brand Statement entails the total of my Personal Ambition, brand objectives, specialty, service, dominant attribute, and domain. My <u>Unique Value Proposition</u> (UVP) is part of this.

The next step was to define my Personal Brand Story (Elevator Pitch), which is the essence of what I want to say about my Personal Brand in order to produce a positive emotional reaction. Finally, I designed my Personal Logo and Slogan which is a single graphical symbol that represents my Personal Brand.

My Personal SWOT Analysis:

My personal SWOT analysis forms the basis of my brand and personal objectives, by examining my strengths and weaknesses in the internal environment and opportunities and threats in the external environment. This self-assessment also helped me to identify areas where I may need to improve. I examined my own situation, by asking myself some of the following questions -- and answering them honestly:

1. What are my strengths and weaknesses?

2. How can I capitalize on my strengths and overcome my weaknesses?

3. What are the external opportunities and threats in my chosen field and domain?

4. What would my colleagues or my customers say is my greatest and clearest strength?

5. What would they say is my greatest weakness?

6. What are some of the strengths that have contributed to my success up to the present?

7. How might these create problems for me in the future?

8. Which problems would I like to solve first?

Also, I asked myself this question—what is the most important challenge I face regarding my work and career? Factors that may be related to these questions were, for example, talent, ability, intelligence, goal-orientation, perseverance, self-control, health, integrity, creativity, tolerance, enthusiasm, the home and work environments, responsibility, job prestige, status, power, freedom, and having more free time.

Take a look at my SWOT in Table 3.1. I have included some improvement actions in my Personal BSC based on this, so that I can turn my weaknesses into strengths.

	POSITIVE ASPECTS	NEGATIVE ASPECTS	
INTERNAL ENVIRONMENT	**My Strengths (S)**	**My Weaknesses (W)**	**ASPECTS THAT ARE UNDER MY CONTROL**
EXTERNAL ENVIRONMENT	**Opportunities (O) in My Field and Domain:**	**Threats (T) in my Field and Domain:**	**ASPECTS THAT ARE NOT COMPLETELY UNDER MY CONTROL**

Table 3.1: Personal SWOT

My Evaluation of My Life Style

On the basis of the list I made of all my strengths and weaknesses and opportunities and threats, I evaluated myself honestly and defined my personal life style, which is in harmony with my personal ambition and life story. While evaluating myself, I reflected on the following questions:

1. How do I relate to others?

2. What are my most important values?

3. What are my strongest areas? Do they add value to my domain?

4. What is the strongest personality characteristic I project to others?

5. For what ability, talent or skill am I best known?

6. What is the value that others associate with me most?

7. What moral principle or value do I associate with myself?

8. What do others say about me?

9. How do others, who have never met me, describe me?

10. How am I perceived?

Take a look at my personal life style below. It includes aspects of my Personal Ambition. It entails my perspective regarding life -- which personalizes my brand and reflects my values. I spend time thinking about my life, by performing the breathing and silence exercises regularly. Consequently my Personal Brand reflects distinctiveness, relevancy, and consistency.

Personal Life Style

My Personal Brand Objectives:
After I analyzed my strengths, weaknesses, and related threats and opportunities, I performed the breathing and silence exercise, evaluated myself, and defined my personal style; and used that information to define my Personal Brand objectives. For this, I reflected on the following questions:

1. What do I want my Personal Brand to accomplish? Is this: Increased business? Recognition? Satisfaction?

2. What do I want to be known for in my profession and domain?

3. What emotions would I like my brand to produce in others? What do I want others to think about me?

My Personal Brand objectives should be realistic and related to the four perspectives: internal, external, knowledge & learning, and financial. Take a look at my Personal Brand objectives that follow:

Personal Brand Objectives

My Specialization:

After I defined my Personal Brand objectives, I determined my specialization and expertise. I know my unique gift is meta-cognition – which is a specialization in the brain's ability to conduct knowledge "integration." In this authentic Personal Branding concept focused on Personal Ambition, my Personal Brand is built around my dream, values, key roles, and purpose in life.

I have identified and bounded the scope of what I do, which is in line with my strengths. I specialize in patterns of relationships and integration. This is my niche that I love, that I am passionate about, and which is related to my Personal Ambition:

Specialization

My Service:

After I defined my specialization, I determined my service and tailored this to my target market (domain). I reflected on the following questions:

1. What do I do?

2. What are my primary services?

3. What is my related work style?

4. How do I want prospects in my target market to view my service?

Service

I also defined what makes me unique, special and different. I reflected on the following questions:

1. What are my key characteristics that are very clear to anyone and which add value to others?

2. What unique parts of my personal life style and my work style make an impact on others when I am on top of my performance?

3. What are the top five characteristics that reflect my brand?

4. What is the single leading and most powerful attribute of my Personal Ambition?

5. What are my unique and natural talents?

6. What separates me from the masses?

7. What are my personal core competencies?

8. How do I want prospects and key influencers to think about me and describe me to others?

9. How am I introduced to others? How do my friends describe me to others?

10. What makes me distinctive, related to my most prized personal value?

11. What is the strongest personality characteristic I project to others?

12. What do others say about me when I am not around?

13. How do others react when they first meet me?

Top Five Key Characteristics

My Dominant Attribute:

These characteristics are the foundation of his brand. My single most dominant characteristic, called dominant attribute, is being a lifelong learning practitioner. I have chosen this characteristic because this is who I am, what makes me distinctive, what correlates to my most prized value, and what appeals to and is valued by my target market. I have the courage to consistently display this with everyone. I am therefore including this attribute in my Personal Brand statement and my brand story. This is what makes my brand unique.

Dominant Attribute

I hope that *lifelong learning practitioner* is the first idea that enters others' minds when they hear or read about me at this stage of my life. This is also what my target market needs and what can creates value for others.

My Domain:

Once I defined my dominant attribute, the next step was to choose and define my audience (which should be in harmony with my Personal Ambition, brand objectives, specialty, service, and dominant attribute); and to know his audience and their greatest needs. In this inside-out approach, I reflected on the following questions:

1. In what arena do I want to achieve my Personal Brand objectives?

2. What is my target market? Does it have the potential to make money? Do I enjoy working in this target market?

3. Who are my customers?

4. What are their greatest needs? What do they want? What do they value? What do they expect? What are they worried about?
5. What do they expect from me?

6. What are the values of my domain?

7. Who will find me and my unique strengths valuable in the marketplace?

8. What original knowledge or skills do I bring to my clients, industry or company?

Take a look at my domain; the greatest needs of my customers and my key competitors as I now see them.

Domain

My Customers:

I am focusing on people and companies that are willing to learn and improve consciously. I don't have much time and energy to waste trying to help people and companies who are not committed to change and learning.

My Personal Brand must be relevant to my domain, which means that I must understand and care about what's important to my customers. For corporate customers, employee engagement, a happy and passionate workforce, personal effectiveness & growth, high labor productivity, and awareness for integrity are very important to them.

Customers Greatest Needs

My Key Competitors:

I fill this need with my products/services and brand, and I am convinced that my key competitors don't have sufficient concepts and tools to fill this need in a durable, holistic, and humanized way.

Key Competitors

My Personal Brand Statement:

My Personal Brand identity or Personal Brand Promise is a statement that I use _internally_ to focus my efforts on what my Personal Brand must deliver _externally_ in order to satisfy the needs of others. It states what I am committed to "being" for others, and the impact a relationship with me will have on them.

With my Personal Brand statement I wanted to create a particular impression in the mind of others to whom I am important, and to make an emotional connection with them. It includes my Unique Value Proposition (UVP), which entails a core element what makes me more unique, more valuable, and more visible in the market. A powerful Unique Value Proposition makes marketing and selling my services much easier.

The formulation of my Personal Brand promise is most effective when it complies with the following criteria:

1. Should be based on my Personal Ambition, personal SWOT, brand objectives, domain, specialty, service, and dominant attribute.

2. Must be formulated positively, in a distinctive, relevant, consistent, concise, meaningful, exciting, inspiring, active, action-oriented, compelling, memorable, ambitious, and persuasive manner.

3. The emphasis is on authenticity, integrity, consistency, relevancy, and distinctiveness.

4. Should state how I will make a difference in relationships throughout my life.

5. Should include a strong slogan to position me and how to distinguish myself in society

6. Should reflect how I provide value to others

7. Should be unique to me, relevant to the market place, reflect who I really am, and to be used by people at work, family, and friends (to all my relationships in your life).

8. Should differentiate me and direct the way I think and behave.

My authentic Personal Brand Statement below summarizes me. I have formulated this for myself to be used as guidance for my Personal Brand "story" and to keep me moving in the right direction. This makes my Personal Brand more personal and continuously creates a personal touch and bond with my target audience. It provides me energy that helps me consistently build distinctive relationships with important people in my life. It also helps me to understand myself much better.

Personal Brand Statement

I am using my brand statement to communicate my unique service that provides a sense of value for my target audience. It is in line with my dreams, life purpose, values, creativity, passion, competencies, specialization, characteristics, and things what I love doing. This statement should evoke strong emotions (warmth, confidence, respect) in my target market -- which is exactly how I want to be perceived by my colleagues and clients.

My Personal Brand statement reflects who I really am, what I do well, what I love to do, for whom I am doing it, and what I care about. It's a commitment that I make to important people in my life, including my customers, and about what I am willing to do on their behalf. It's clearly defined so that my target audience quickly grasps what I stand for.

I have included my Personal Brand statement on my website, in my books, articles, resume and brochures. I uses it as a compass for marketing and sales of my brand, keeping me focused, guiding me in the right direction, and defining and communicating my Personal Brand story effectively.

My Personal Logo and Slogan

A Personal Logo is a single graphical symbol that represents and packages my Personal Brand. It tells something useful about what I do, for whom I do it, and what the benefit happens to be. A Personal Logo consists of: a name, a slogan and an icon. A Personal Logo & Slogan makes my Personal Brand visible.

Take a look at my Personal Logo & Slogan below.

My Brand Name:
My Slogan:
My Icon:
My Logo:

A nice Personal Brand without an execution plan in order to make is a reality, will not lead to sustainable development of my potential and marketing success. My plan and Personal Balance Scorecard, are discussed in detail in the next chapter.

4. My Authentic Personal Balanced Scorecard

My Critical Success Factors:

My Personal Critical Success Factors (CSFs) are derived from my Personal Ambition and Personal Brand. They are related to the four perspectives, _internal, external, knowledge and learning, and financial_. A Personal Ambition and Personal Brand without these four perspectives results in an incomplete Personal BSC. The personal CSFs form the bridge between the Personal Ambition and Personal Brand (long term) -- and on the other side the personal objectives, performance measures, targets, and improvement actions (short term). This link is made by identifying my personal core competencies, uniqueness, genius, dominant attribute, values in my Personal Ambition and Personal Brand and translating these into concrete personal objectives. (See figure 4.1)

My Personal Objectives:

My Personal Ambition and Personal Brand are tied to my personal objectives. These objectives should be realistic and are based on my Personal Ambition/Brand statement and the results of the self-assessment executed with the help of my personal SWOT analysis. The central questions here are:

1. Which measurable short-term personal results do I want to achieve?
2. Which problems would I like to handle better?
3. What are my five-year career goals and life objectives?

My objectives describe a result that I want to achieve in order to realize my Personal Ambition, and successfully launch my Personal Brand. My ambition is aimed at my personal objectives both in the short-term and the future. My personal objectives give me ambition and brand direction. The personal Critical Success Factors form the bridge between these. My personal objectives are derived from my personal Critical Success Factors and from my SWOT analysis (See figure4.1 1: Personal Brand Stage Factors and Actions).

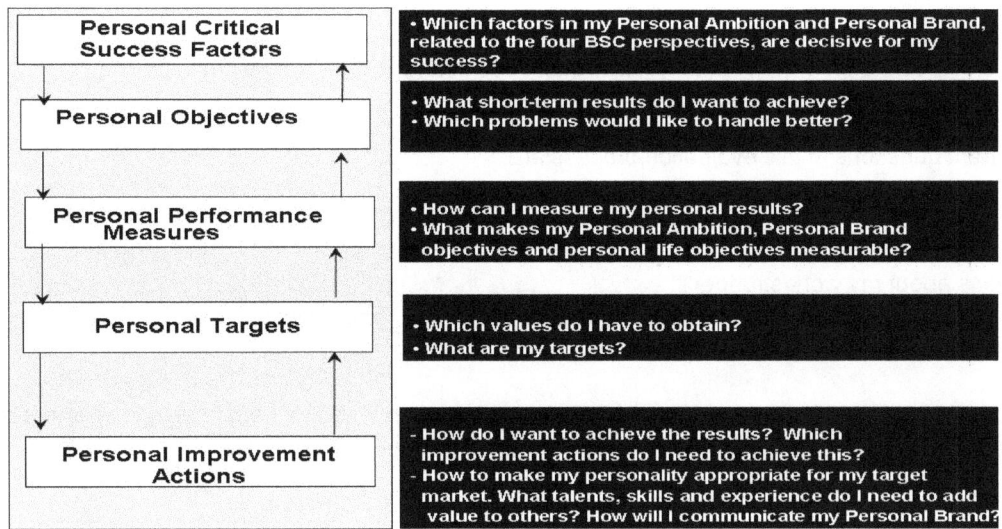

Figure 4.1: Personal Branding Factors and Actions

My Personal Performance Measures:

Performance Measures are standards to measure the progress of my Personal and Brand objectives. With these measures, I can assess my functioning in relation to my personal Critical Success Factors and objectives. Without performance measures and targets, it is difficult to coach/manage myself with feedback from others. Performance measures urge me to action if they are related to my Person al and Brand objectives, giving me certain direction. (See figure 4.1)

My Personal Targets:

My personal target is a quantitative objective of a personal performance measures. On the basis of my performance targets I can get clear feedback about the progress of my improvement actions; which is needed to refine my Personal Brand and to better manage myself. My personal targets indicate values that I want to achieve, and depend on my level of ambition. They should be:

Specific -- they must be specifically formulated so that they can also influence behavior.

Measurable -- they must be formulated in such a way that they can measure the objective.

Achievable -- they must be realistic, realizable, feasible and acceptable.

Result-oriented -- they must be related to concrete results.

Time-specific -- they must be time-constrained. (See figure 4.1)

My Personal Improvement Actions:

My personal improvement actions are personal strategies used to realize my Personal Ambition and Personal Brand. They are utilized to develop my skills, improve my behavior, master myself, and improve my performance. I used two ways to define my personal improvement actions:

1. By selecting Critical Success Factors in my Personal Ambition and Brand statement, and translating these into personal objectives, performance measures, targets, and related improvement actions

2. By performing my personal SWOT analysis and transforming my strengths, weaknesses and related opportunities and threats into personal improvement actions. (See figure 4.1)

My Authentic Personal Balanced Scorecard:

Table 4.1 shows my Personal BSC, which is related to my Personal Ambition, my SWOT, my Personal Brand Statement, and is related to my Personal Critical Success Factors. It shows how I monitor the progress of my Personal Brand and my related personal objectives and improvement actions.

Some important questions in this evaluation process are:

1. Do I make more money?
2. Do I get more referrals?
3. Are opinions about my work stronger?
4. Do more people know who I am, what I do, and what I stand for (brand awareness)?
5. Am I being considered for more work?

By continuously checking the data I am receiving from my own observations, I am keeping my brand relevant, focused, and emotionally connected with my target market.

Table 4.1: Personal Balanced Scorecard

Internal				
Personal Critical Success Factors	Personal Objectives	Personal Performance Measures	Personal Targets	Personal Improvement Actions
External				
Personal Critical Success Factors	Personal Objectives	Personal Performance Measures	Personal Targets	Personal Improvement Actions
Knowledge & Learning				
Personal Critical Success Factors	Personal Objectives	Personal Performance Measures	Personal Targets	Personal Improvement Actions
Financial				
Personal Critical Success Factors	Personal Objectives	Personal Performance Measures	Personal Targets	Personal Improvement Actions

My Strategic Map:

The position of my objectives, within the four perspectives, and their mutual relationships are made visible in Figure 4.2. In this cause-effect diagram, my personal objectives are interrelated and affect one another. My final objective – like that of a majority of people, is to be _happy_. All my goals result in this final overall objective. On the basis of this diagram, I can improve myself continuously based on the feedback I get from others. It is also a handy tool in communicating my brand and PBSC to trusted persons.

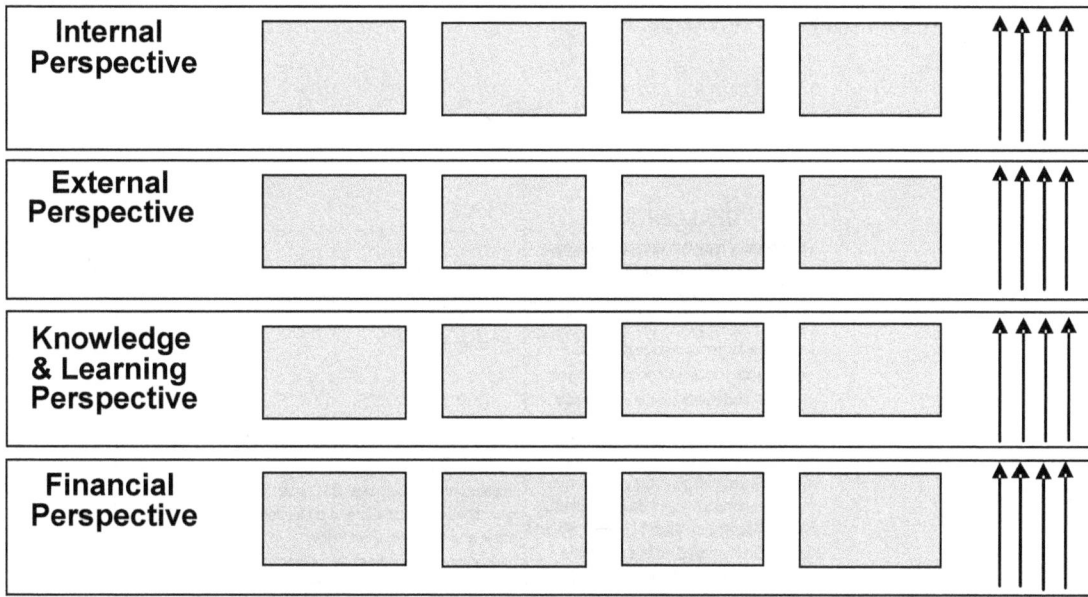

Figure 4.2: Cause and Effect Diagram

Chapter 5. My Authentic Personal Brand Implementation and Cultivation

My Personal Brand will be of no use to me if I don't implement and cultivate my Personal Ambition, Personal Brand and Personal BSC (brand strategy) effectively. This entails the final stage in the Personal Branding journey. To guide me with this, Dr. Rampersad provided the Plan-Deploy-Act-Challenge (PDAC Cycle) which I am following continuously.

In the following sections, each of the phases in the Plan, Deploy, Act, and Challenge cycle (see Figure 5.1) are discussed as tasks that I need to accomplish in an iterative, lifelong learning manner.

PLAN

First of all, I recognize my responsibility to define, formulate, and update my authentic Personal Ambition, Personal Brand, and related Personal Balanced Scorecard. I should review my core competencies, my dominant attribute, my service, my competitors, and my target audience. I should occasionally update my Ambition, Brand and my PBSC in a scheduled manner.

DEPLOY

In this stage of the PDAC cycle I launched myAuthentic Personal Brand on a limited scale and tried it out with trusted persons who can give me honest feedback; get the word out through a variety of media channels; publish articles that showcase my expertise, seek out conferences and meetings where I can give speeches and presentations. When I respond to my Authentic Personal Brand with passion, courage, purpose and faith in myself, I live up to my brand promise.

I first implemented my Personal BSC on a limited scale, keeping in mind the priorities that I had identified. I started with a simple objective and related improvement action with dedication, self-confidence, willpower and concentration. I constantly monitoring and evaluating the progress of my brand. In doing this I reflect on the following questions of this stage:

1. Are opinions about my work stronger?
2. Do more people know who I am, what I do, and what I stand for?
3. Am I being considered for more work?

By constantly monitoring and evaluating my personal objectives and actions I will keep my brand relevant, focused, and remain emotionally connected with my target market.

Figure 5.1 Plan-Deploy-Act-Challenge Cycle

ACT

I have become an expert in my field and building credibility based on this effort. I am promoting myself and my personal code of ethics, marketing my brand, building effective relationships, networking with fellow professionals, and expressing my Authentic Personal Brand relentlessly, passionately, constantly, consistently, and in a compelling way to people..

I find venues for my voice, express myself, and communicate my brand story in most everything I say and do. I keep my Personal Brand statement in mind when carrying out activities and dealing with others. I develop my talent and skills to achieve my Personal and Brand objectives.

I recognize my responsibility to improve myself continuously and be committed to change. I know that it is my ethical duty and moral responsibility to change – not only for my own good but also for my loved ones, my work, my organization, my country, and for the world of which I am a part.

I am building a solid reputation within my industry and doing work I love that is consistent with my passion, Personal Ambition and Personal Brand.

I am creating a representative and professional personal website that is specifically designed to deliver my brand message and showcase my key accomplishments, skills, education, successes, and summary of my career. My website also includes his articles, speeches, awards, and testimonials.

I have designed a great looking logo for my business card, building a network of contacts that know my brand value and am able to communicate it, and keep my network strong.

I also remember Ralph Waldo Emerson said; "*Our greatest glory is not in never failing, but in rising up every time we fail*".

CHALLENGE

I am cultivating and maintaining my brand continuously in the light of new challenges, experience, and insights. I monitor, refine, fine tune, and cultivate this as I am going along, figuring out which parts work and which don't, in order to create brand loyalty. I am constantly checking and monitoring my target market and making adjustments as necessary. I am constantly updating my brand to reflect the new challenges I accept and the lessons I learn in order to keep people interested and committed in my life and work.

Chapter 6. My Authentic Personal Brand Alignment with Myself and Corporation

Increasingly, successful organizations are beginning to recognize that good brand relationships with their employees are as important as good brand relationships with their customers; employees should be happy first in order to make the customers happy. Corporate brand loyalty starts with employee's happiness; with the linkage between employee's ambition/brand and employer's ambition/brand. Both must be put side by side to check if there are similarities or not. Both don't have to match exactly but should align in key places, such as in Personal Ambition and Personal Brand.

The final stage in the Authentic Branding Model entails aligning and synchronizing my Personal Ambition and Personal Brand with my Corporation's Ambition and Brand; (see figure 6.1). Also, the development of a Corporate Balanced Scorecard should be added to the mix because greater leadership alignment and workforce cohesion occur when these
relationships exist.

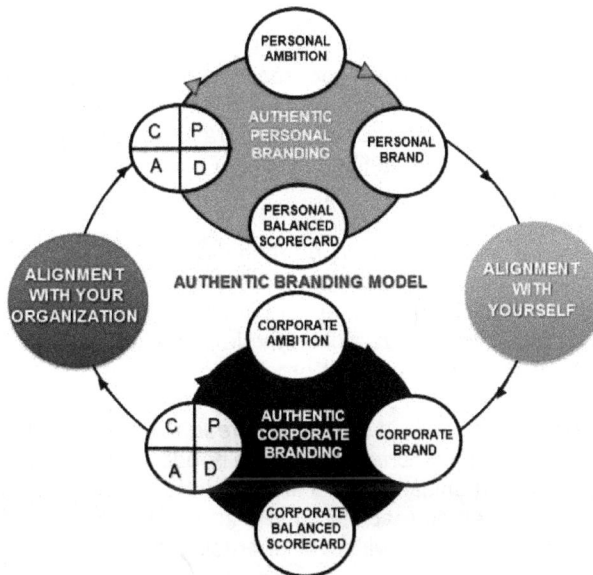

Figure 6.1 <u>Alignment Stage</u> in the Authentic Governance Model

I find that it is essential to strive for the optimal fit and balance in order to enhance my productivity and to stimulate engagement, commitment, and passion in the organization. This alignment process has to do with reaching a higher degree of compatibility between personal and organizational objectives and accomplishing mutual value.

Research has shown that when an individual has some input regarding the shared ambition that affects his or her work, the person will be more supportive, motivated, and receptive towards organizational change. I know that I am often willing to work together towards the goals of the organization with dedication when there is a match between myself and their personal ambition and the corporate ambition. All people have different personal values and principles that must be understood and linked to the corporation's values.

This alignment process is about matching my personal ambition/brand with the corporate ambition/brand. It has to do with reaching a higher degree of compatibility between my personal objectives and those of my corporate organization. The larger the intersection area between these two parties, the greater the degree of integral operations and the achievement of higher performance. (See figure 6.2)

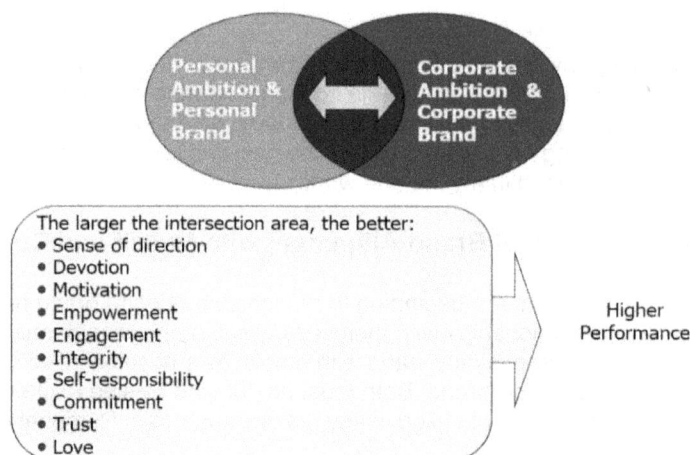

Figure 6.2: Matching the Personal Ambition/Brand with the Corporate Ambition/Brand

How to Align with my Organization:

Dr. Rampersad has been encouraging managers and employees to establish their personal ambitions brands, so that they become energized to share that information. I too, recommend introducing an *Ambition Meeting* within organizations between the line-manager or superior and his/her employees. The Ambition Meeting is a periodical, informal, voluntary and confidential meeting of a maximum duration of one hour between line-manager and his/her employees -- with the employee's personal ambition/brand/BSC and the corporate ambition/brand/BSC as topics for friendly discussion. For consideration:

1. Why informal? *Because they will learn more from informal than from formal meetings.* It is recommended that the meeting is held structurally at least once every two months, preferably more often. The outcome of these informal meetings should be highly confidential and should be kept out of the personnel file and not be used against the employee. The line-manager or supervisor plays a crucial role in worker well-being and engagement. He/she should act as a trusted person, coach, and role model in this process.

2. Why as a trusted person? *Because if there is distrust and fear, there will be no sharing and learning.* To be able to talk about the employee's personal ambition/brand/BSC, one needs a confidential, informal and friendly atmosphere, an atmosphere of trust and open communication. This is essential as human values will be discussed. Experience has shown that this intimate atmosphere can be reached if the manager formulates his/her own personal ambition/brand/BSC beforehand and shares it with his/her employee.

The implementation of the employee's personal ambition/brand/BSC comes up for discussion, and may include selected private matters that have an impact on job performance that can be discussed confidentially. During the alignment process, the manager should act as a trusted and informal coach and provide social support to the employees by being a good listener, providing help, and being someone on which the employee can rely.

I selected the following questions as the basis for having an ambition meeting with my future employees and colleagues:

1. Does your personal ambition/brand correspond with the corporate ambition/brand?

2. Does your personal ambition/brand match the corporation's ambition/brand? Where do they align and where do they contradict each other? Do they conflict? Are there compatibilities? Are there linkages?

3. Is there a win-win situation between your own interests and the ones of your organization?

4. What makes you feel good at work?

5. Are you proud of working for the organization?

6. Whose life is improved because of your work?

7. Which skills do you need to be a pillar of the organization and thus realize the organization ambition/brand? What do you want to gain through this?

8. Are your developmental expectations in tune with those of the organization?

9. Do your job requirements match your capabilities and needs?

10. What motivates you? What de-motivates you? What makes you happy or sad? What do you enjoy the most?

11. What contribution are you trying to make to the realization of our corporate ambition/brand? Which job do you aspire? What are your wishes? What do you strive for? What are your concerns?

12. Have you considered a job change?

Conclusion

As Authentic Personal and Corporate Branding comes to closure, you the reader, have the opportunity to decide if you have achieved your life and work objectives by recording your *own what, why, how* and *for whom* you live and work. If you have completed this project in order to become a <u>Certified Personal Brand Coach</u> you will need to discuss how that might be accomplished by talking with Dr. Garrity: <u>rgarrity@alforum.org</u> or Dr. Rampersad: <u>h.rampersad@tps-international.com</u>.

Appendix D

Encore Example: The Author's Encore Journey

Prior to 1994 (The Adolescence to Early Adult Transition)

For three years my adult life was similar to that of a large number of Americans. First, I left adolescence with minimal parental support, few employable skills, minimal post high school education, and with no money or place to live. The U.S. Army was the only welcoming employer offering training and employment for those in my status. They were willing to provide six months of training as a Crypto-Security Equipment Technician in exchange for three years of military service. A place to live and a skill with private sector possibilities motivated me into action. What a great deal!

Within eight additional years I completed my military service, worked with a major information technology corporation for a year as a field engineer, decided to start a federal government career using my accumulated private and public sector (military and civilian) capabilities. Concurrently, I became a married man raising the first of two children, and was enjoying independent, but low budget apartment living. My wife and I were following the traditional American family story experienced by others. During this period, the need for a college education became quite clear as I learned that many other people were pursuing career advancement and promotion by learning the skills, knowledge and abilities required for greater job performance and remuneration. By this time I had established in my mind the view that there was a symbiotic relationship between pursuing continuously higher education (social, economic and technological) and obtaining the benefits of work and career success.

For the next twenty years my personal and family life continued to expand and develop across multiple fields of education, locations, specialties, responsibilities, cultures – and all family members appeared to benefit from the growth, education, experiences and new opportunities that they experienced. I acquired extensive formal education (four degrees through PhD) through continuous part-time training, I attended numerous technical and organizational courses and certifications, I held leadership positions in technical project management, training division management, enterprise development and change management, financial and logistics management, and I served as adjunct faculty at various universities. On the home front, my wife established her own interests and career opportunities, my children received college degrees and started their own lives – and after twenty-two years of marriage my wife and I decided to divorce and pursue our individual interests. I was now fifty years of age after thirty years of work, and I was contemplating an unplanned future. And yet, I recognized that new opportunities often come with the acceptance of change.

[Author's Note 1: The result at this time was an unexpected, but welcomed life/career change.]

In 1994 (The Mid-Life/Career Transition Begins)

By 1994 I had been in the University of Southern California part time doctorate program for five years. I experienced a major awakening at the time of acceptance into the program. New students were required to conduct a self-reflective examination of our personal and work lives so we could **better understand who we had become and where we thought we were going as our lives progressed**. The result of our effort was used to assess and plan our respective futures in a way that assured a doctorate in public administration made sense for each of us. The psychological and sociological methods we used elicited new information that most of us had not known or expected. Did we really understand our life purpose, and how could we ensure the life each of us had left was going to be productive and meaningful in the PA field?

After my studies were completed the challenge of choosing a dissertation topic that mattered equally to the school faculty and to me became challenge for consideration. Again, what did I really care enough about to do all the work involved – and to meet the school's graduation requirement? The USC list of typically narrow topics was not acceptable to me because I had developed an interest in understanding "how the integration of human life knowledge and work experience could be modeled and used for human progress in today's world." I thought that defining a system-of-systems model for approaching one's adult life management would be worth my time. At first the faculty said no to the topic, but then relented if I could reframe the project to meet their graduation requirements. I was required to do additional research and submit a new proposal to align my work with the school's needs. To do so I performed six months of research to eventually submit a proposal acceptable to the faculty.

Our collaboration finally resulted in the dissertation topic: ***The Construction and Evaluation of a Quality Learning Systems Model for Societal Dialogue and Development*** which combined sufficient topics and elements to be acceptable. In part, the description said: *Society is experiencing a strong undercurrent of dysfunctional tension which constrains the quality of its long term development. It is in need of an integrated strategy and comprehensive model for* *finding solutions to its systematic issues, and for capitalizing on its capabilities and opportunities. This study is an inquiry into what type and form of common ground, overarching concept, or pervasive belief might be learned to enhance the administration of society's activities. The clients for this work are the leaders of American public and private sector organizations.* At my graduation, the leader of my committee commented: **"You now have you life's work ahead of you."** Indeed I did! Can a differentiated life/career be better understood when viewed as an interdependent social system from 50,000 feet above the ground? Shouldn't someone set out to study the issue, and then become an advocate of a comprehensive and integrated life journey?

[Author's Note 2: An education/work life change had occurred once again.]

Concurrent with my improved education status, a work assignment designed to implement a Total Quality Management (TQM) agency transformation was assigned to me incorporating the use of my recent doctorate education. The wide scope of the program encouraged significant use of my formal education and experience. However, within three years the agency executive leadership team decided enough had been done (not even close) and the program was closed. My expectations for success were not realized.

Shortly thereafter, other disruptive changes in my federal career track became a regular occurrence as the agency went through external influences on its purpose and functions. About the same time, I reached my own thirty year service point and became eligible for early retirement. Due to the fact my agency planned on making staff cutbacks, was willing to encourage selective retirements using financial incentives, and I had achieved the highest grade level likely for my own career development; I retired and went immediately to work for a federal government support contractor. This change of venue encouraged me to re-think what I wanted to do at this 50+ age of life and how I might deliberately fashion a new life and career became a matter of focus.

[Author's Note 3: Another work/career change had occurred.] The concept of pursuing a purposeful "Encore Life and Career" slowly occurred to me."

In 2001 (Mid-Life/Career Transition in Progress)

From 2001 through 2007 I crafted a proactive series of products and services to realign my accumulated knowledge and experience to synchronize with emerging professional services opportunities. Accomplishments included: establishing a small not-for-profit educational services business that conducted pro bono community services as well as working as an enterprise change subcontractor to various federal government contractors. I also became an adjunct professorial lecturer and researcher in knowledge management and organizational learning at a local university, and began authoring books in the interdisciplinary field of life/work management.

In 2007 (Senior Adult Transition and Rejuvenation)

Late in 2007 at age sixty-six I finished my last federal government contractor support project and desired to concentrate on my educational research and authoring initiatives. It had been about twelve years since I accepted the USC doctoral challenge to go off and prove my thesis that was eventually approved for graduation. Since then I have written two print books and eight e-books advancing much of what I have learned mostly later in life. Now in 2016 my ultimate print book (this book) will soon be published: *Your Integral Life Matters: A Life Management Handbook for American Learning, Leading and Legacy Success.* The approach used has been to demonstrate an educational innovation wherein holistic, interdisciplinary learning and action supports greater comprehension of issue factors and grounded knowledge.

END

Appendix E

Complete Your Unique Life Project

Whatever you can do in advance of your death to ease the burden on your estate executor and heirs will be heartily welcomed by them. If you have witnessed the numerous times (like your author has) wherein those who remained had to labor furiously to locate, organize, and share the documents and property; pay the immediate bills; relocate children; and work with the legal and interpersonal matters a death in the family requires – all the while mourning your loss and assisting those nearly incapacitated – you would be ashamed at your thoughtlessness. We must do better by others, especially when the memories of us linger for many years.

[**Author's Note**: *It is anticipated that some elders would enjoy this time in their lives collecting, reflecting and writing their own Living Legacy Package. However, for many this very important life accomplishment could not be thoroughly accomplished without the assistance of a family member or close friend – in addition to obtaining occasional financial or estate planning specialist to ensure written material is properly communicated.*

For this reason, your Handbook author (Dr. Garrity) proposes to coach an elder (you) and one of their family members preparing and completing some of the tasks below (paragraphs a and b). Task c. will require the elder to select their own expert to assist. Before proceeding you should contact Dr. Garrity (www.rgarrity@alforum.org) to discuss the time and cost required to schedule and complete tasks a. and/or b.]

A. Your Legacy Package

In addition to writing your final and detailed Last Will and Testament of your wishes, the people impacted, and the things that should be accomplished, you need to identify a location(s) for your legacy items. Provide a list of what can be found there, and make the list readily available (Open Only After my Death) for a few people you trust to see the list and to take the actions you desire. Then attend to the following matters:

1. Assemble, organize and store other small property not in current use such as jewelry, books, electronics, clothing, tools, pictures, videos, recordings, games, loaned equipment and athletic equipment that may be given promptly by your executor (in accordance with your Last Will and Testament) to the proper recipients. And, a contemporary guide for organized disconnection from the world we all have embraced is *Your Guide to Leaving Your Internet Legacy* by Monna Elithorpe, Biz Lady Journal Publishing, 2013. Make sure your identification and passwords are listed and available for someone to close your online activity.

2. One or both of the e-books you completed as described in Chapter 15 and the Appendix B/C are very unique additions to your legacy package. They speak for you in terms of your learning, intellect, feelings, insights and capabilities – some of which others may never have known or suspected. They allow you to bring closure to your fully developed personhood. You are entitled to be heard both during and after your life is lived. It does not matter much if these books were actually done years ago to meet your needs, as you can prepare an addendum for subsequent years, title them and place them into your Legacy Package.

B. My Mid-Life/Career Transition and Personal Renewal (Encore)

This senior level writing project is appropriate for those program participants aged 50 to 60 years who are inclined to focus on creating an encore (second) life career or avocation based in large part on their earlier career education and experience. In this case, the instructions provided in either Appendix B or C above would apply equally as well here. Appendix B should be followed if a significant increase in life learning is the priority for the new avocation, or the guidance in Appendix C would apply better if the additional of Personal Branding is required to focus and plan a new, but related avocation.

C. My Senior Lifelong Learning and Memorable Legacy (Letter)

Your Senior Lifelong Learning and Memorable Legacy (Letter) to family, friends, colleagues and others. There are many ways to construct a personal *Legacy Letter* that enables you to express yourself to others more fully, or to convey additional insights and feelings that you may have overlooked while you are alive. Some include preparing an actual letter, a video, a journal, a memoir, a poem, a history, a picture album, a song – and other creative ways to stay connected and relevant to selected people long after your death. Even better, we recommend that you include additional information to turn this letter into a "legacy of the heart" or "living legacy" as proposed by Meg Newhouse in Chapter 15. Doing so will infuse your letter with the major ideals, values and goals you have adopted during life. Subsequently, you can build continuity by demonstrating your desire to share these thoughts with your descendants after your death.

The detail for systematic reflection, selection, organization and presentation designed by this author follows the foundational concepts and graphics used herein to create, write and present a few of the American Learnership perspectives presented throughout this Handbook. This approach reflects on the thoughts and concepts stressed throughout the Handbook, and focuses us on the foundational concepts upon which the Handbook is based: Figures 14-1, 14-2, 14-3 and 14-9 (snapshots below). The Senior Lifelong Learning and Memorable Legacy worksheet (Appendix Table E-1) enables us to accumulate and record our legacy notes according to the Life Domains (9) and Life Stages (4) in which they occurred. A five-stage procedure is facilitated for collecting information by the program participant, and followed by the completion of their Legacy Letter.

Figure 14-1

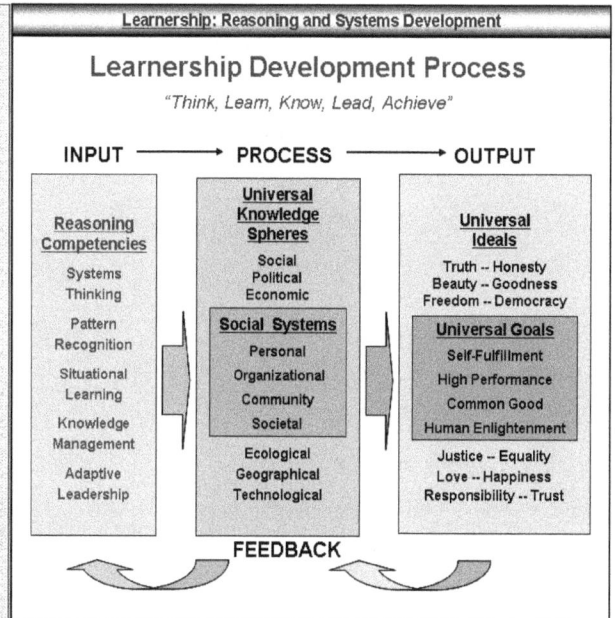

Figure 14-2

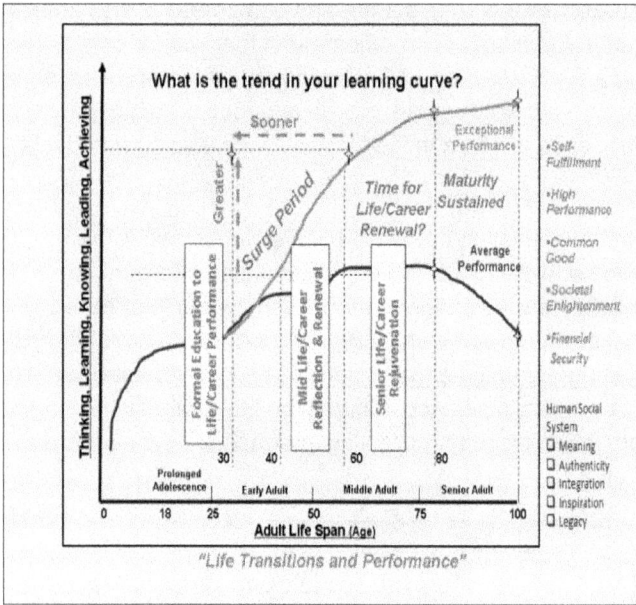

Figure 14-3

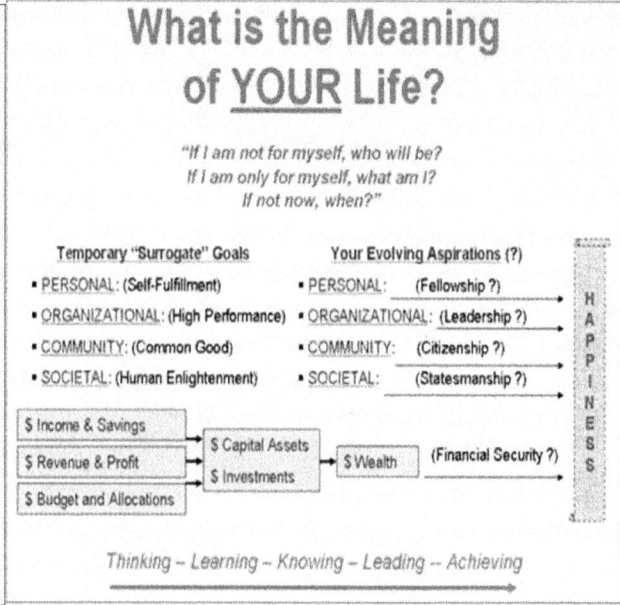

Figure 14-9

Senior Lifelong Learning and Memorable Legacy (Letter)

LIFE DOMAINS	LIFE STAGES			
	ADOLESCENCE (Childhood)	EARLY ADULT 25-45	MID-LIFE ADULT 45-60	SENIOR ADULT 60-80
PHILOSOPHY (Worldview/Ideals)				
REASONING (Competencies)				
PERSONAL (Family)				
ORGANIZATION (Career/Work)				
COMMUNITY (Society)				
	ADOLESCENCE (Childhood)	EARLY ADULT 25-45	MID-LIFE ADULT 45-60	SENIOR ADULT 60-80
PEOPLE (I Knew)				
EVENTS (I Experienced)				
SUCCESS (I Experienced)				
SADNESS (I Experienced)				

Appendix Table E-1

The concepts and graphics presented in this Mindset Handbook have been selected to stimulate our personal reflection on the principles and practices that can assist us in experiencing an "Integral Life that Matters," The lifetime development of our abilities (thinking, learning, knowing, leading, achieving) have been organized for review into the nine domains of Appendix Table E-1. Discovering, recognizing and having success in accommodating the social expectations identified here are known to enhance our long-term personal presence, skill development and interpersonal competence. The program author or a designated coach will facilitate this procedure. Contact Dr. Rudy Garrity at http://www.alforum.org.

Five Stage Procedure:

1. Prepare for author-led learning conversations. Make blank copies of the Appendix Table E-1, and prepare to record short notes that come to mind during facilitated discussion. Keep in mind that some notes will lend themselves to be listed as "insight about yourself" or as a "living legacy," Other notes will be structured as cognitive or emotionally based comments to others to understand or take action based on your advice.

2. For each of the top five domains (Philosophy, Reasoning, Personal, Organization and Community), reflect on the *What, Why and When* the item became very important in your life experience. Expect that you will eventually winnow the number down to only the most impactful 5-6 items for each domain. (Two groups: *Insight about Yourself*, and *Comments to Others*)

3. For each of the lower four domains (specific People, Events, Success and Sadness), plan to identify and record any related thoughts or situations that come to mind while participating in #2 above. These notes will serve as temporary place-holders until item #2 is completed.

4. Using copies of Appendix E-1 once again, conduct a facilitated review of the lower four domains. Be sure to address each of the four domains and four life cycle stages – in an iterative manner – until a representative list of items have been identified and explained at a summary level suitable for sharing. (Two groups: *Insight about Yourself,* and *Comment to Others*)

5. Consolidate and create a story. Separate *Insight about Yourself* from *Comments to Others*. Write your personal narratives in a paragraph format (either by domain or by life stage) using the information collected Ensure your communication tone and language choice is careful and considerate. Statements of love and encouragement confirm a wish for other's growth and happiness – a unique gift among human beings.

References for Reflection and Discussion:

Program Orientation: Life Learning Educational Asset (Introduction, C. Ambitions: Preliminary Insights and Aspirations)

Handbook Highlights

    Section I – Chapters 1-4 (Figures 1-5, 2-2, 4-2, Table 3-1)

    Section II – Chapters 5-9 (Figures 5-2, 6-1, 7-3, 7-4, 8-1, 9-1)

    First Interlude (I-1 through I-8)

    Section III – Chapters 10-13 (Figures 10-2, 11-2, 12-2, 13-2)

    Second Interlude; Epilogue A-B; Appendix A-C

    Section IV – Chapters 14-15 (Figures 14-1 through 14-9 and 15-1 through 15-4)

F. Your Legal, Administrative and Financial Affairs

This topic places emphasis on the broad range of strategies, products and services that should gain increasing attention as we progress from our early adult, through mid-life adult, to senior adult lives. And, a general piece of advice that applies to a large number of people is that "the earlier you begin to take a more holistic view of your life's direction, and balance spending and investments with (hopefully) steadily increasing income; the better off you will be during periods of unexpected financial impact and when unemployment and retirement are on the horizon."

Consideration of this responsibility has begun early in this Handbook in Chapters 2, 3, 4,10,11,12 and 14, and has been summarized for easy review in Epilogue Section C: Wealth Generation and Financial Security. It is suggested that you take the time now to review that section to enable its use going forward. Certain perspectives should be given extra attention, for example:

1. Author Charles Richard's advice to distinguish between the positive and negative sides of wealth, and the nature of high and low self-esteem

2. The inclusion of financial security along with other non-monetary aspects of discerning the "meaning" of life

3. The Personal Wealth and Financial Security Timeline, and discussion centered on Figure 10-4

4. The observations and suggestions offered by Dave Kansas and Suze Orman in their respective books and seminars.

With this information as a baseline, and recognizing the wide variation in people's circumstances: incomes, wealth, health, needs and interests as the population moves through mid-life into retirement, the selected approach here is to advocate administrative and financial considerations most often under discussion. Most of the topics and tools will need to be considered for use with help from expert advisers. Everyone's objective needs to determine a course of action that help them as individuals to balance the relevant benefits and life risks while moving toward the closure of their respective lives.

With the assumption that your "*legacy package*" (above) is underway, here are some important administrative and financial responsibilities that require special deliberation and action. Assistance from a certified professional accountant and/or an estate planning attorney is strongly recommended.

[**Author's Note:** The material that follows provides guidance and forms to accomplish the preparation of essential documents needed to plan and complete one's meaningful life journey and end of life tasks. After a short summary of the key documents, the reader is referred, enthusiastically, to the best estate planning reference your author has found for his own life management and end of life purposes: The Suze Orman series of books, videos, products and website at: http://www.suzeorman.com/index.php/books-kits/collections-and-kits/must-have-documents/. One comment in case it is not addressed to your satisfaction by Suze, is that we need to be sure there is adequate cash available to our selected executor (that is outside any trust or probate proceeding) that may be used for immediate needs such as funeral, mortgage and/or utility payments. Too many people find themselves not prepared to finance these expenses even temporarily for the decreased.]

Following Suze's comprehensive coverage address these responsibilities in your own life, here is what you need to consider and act upon:

1. **Will and Last Testament** – A **will** or **testament** is a legal document through which a person discloses his or her wishes as to how their property is to be distributed at death, and names one or more persons to manage the until its final distribution.

2. **Revocable Living Trust** – A trust document is established by you, the grantor, the person setting up the trust and placing assets into it. The assets in the trust are managed for your benefit during your lifetime, however life insurance and retirement accounts may not be included in a trust. You should name yourself as the trustee who manages the trust and another responsible person to assume management responsibility after you death and distributes the assets

according to your beneficiaries. The major advantage of a trust is to keep your property out of complication of estate probate, and the trust may revoked if you choose to do so.

3. **Financial Power of Attorney** – A document that lets you name someone to make your financial decisions for you. This document takes effect at a stated time, applies when and if you become mentally unable to handle your affairs, and can be deleted by you when no longer needed. The specific types of decisions for which the document applies may be explicitly listed.

4. **Durable Power of Attorney for Healthcare** – A document that lets you name someone to make decisions on how to proceed when certain of your life management situations cannot be made by yourself. The law recognizes your choice and reduces the likelihood that attending medical professionals will be held responsible when making important decisions that may impact your life and death. The specific types of conditions when this document is essential is when you may have a terminal condition or when you might experience permanent unconsciousness.

5. **Protection Portfolio** – A state of the art case that provides protection for valuable documents, assets, and personal Information. The portfolio includes a water-resistant case. Integrated organize, must have documents, DNA lifeline. Insurance evaluator, protection library, and a grab & go wallet.

[**Author's Note**: Additional guides for selecting and preparing these mostly written products are: *Writing About Your Life* by William Zinsser, Marlowe and Company, New York, 2004; and *Writing Life Stories* by Bill Roorbach, Writer's Digest Books, Cincinnati, Ohio, 2008. Particularly important, recognize that the e-books described in this Handbook (#2 above) employ a systems framework for chronological thinking and learning that can help you integrate your story – and can be your intellectual and emotional baseline for reflection and expression of the interpersonal topics you choose to include.]

END

Appendix G

American Learnership™ Organization and Author

American Learnership Solutions and Forum

Individuals and organizations can achieve their goals and improve their performance with the help of the innovative educational programs and consulting services of American Learnership™ Solutions (ALS) and American Learnership Forum (ALF) in Leesburg, Virginia. These two organizations offer educational, coaching, consulting, enterprise and charitable support services based in large part on the education, experience, research, writings, courses and videos created and presented by Dr. Rudy Garrity.

1. As a community services enterprise, ALS/ALF provides a comprehensive and interdisciplinary social systems perspective on American life and career in which products and services – informed by American Constitutional declarations and cultural traditions – are shared among individuals, organizations, and communities seeking continual societal progress.

2. ALS is the business home base and is responsible for the interdisciplinary reasoning and integral social systems architecture that distinguishes American Learnership in the educational, coaching and consulting marketplace. Its foundational concepts are depicted in its trademark "Learnership" architecture and "University of the Mind" metaphor.

3. The ALF is a not-for-profit subsidiary of ALS and operates a Center for American Life Management and Professional Branding that creates, organizes, produces and delivers American Learnership products and services through communities of public service (e.g. schools, charities) that contribute to social problem-solving.

4. The ALF subsidiary welcomes skilled writers, coaches, educators, consultants, leaders, artists and other informed people working to build human capital and American socio-economic progress. We celebrate America's traditions and responsibilities at this time in world history, and we solicit your insights, accomplishments, and artistry for reflection, dialogue, and notable publication.

American Learnership Author, Dr. Rudolph B. Garrity

Rudolph (Rudy) Garrity has been a public and private sector product and service specialist, manager, executive, educator, coach, consultant and project manager in a wide variety of technical fields, educational roles and human capital activities in U.S. Defense and Intelligence organizations. His formal education (BS, MBA, MPA, DPA) and over 45 years of progressive leadership responsibilities has enabled him to transition into and lead nonprofit initiatives in his semi-retirement status. Professional distinctions include:

- Trademark Owner: "*American Learnership*"
- Certified Life and Career Success Coach
- Professional Life/Work Transitions Coach
- Chief Learning Officer and Senior Life Advisor
- Member, Continental Who's Who Registry
- Certified Master Authentic Personal Branding Coach
- Professional Enterprise Consultant/Project Manager
- Director Community Outreach: "Mentor America Program"
- Member, Worldwide Who's Who and Global Network
- University Lecturer: Learning and Knowledge Management
- Founder/Chairman: American Learnership Solutions/Forum, Inc.
- Book Author: *Your Integral Life Matters: Create a Life and Legacy Management Mindset for Personal, Organizational, Community and Societal Success in the American Tradition*
- Book Author: *"Total Learning, Knowing and Leading for a Mindful Way-of-Being"*

Bibliography

A Treasure Trove of Knowledge References for
Your Integral Life Matters

[**Author's Note:** A major effort has been conducted to include every reference beyond a few words (some from multiple references) that are included in this work. Some references were documented right at the point of use to ensure readers followed my suggestion that the book/item be purchased or acquired soon after a new subject was introduced. A sincere apology if offered to anyone who has not received credit for their work, and changes to subsequent issues of this book will be made after the author has received a request to do so – rgarrity@alforum.org.]

Adler, Mortimer J. (1981). Six great ideas. New York: Colliers Books.

_____ (1985). Ten philosophical mistakes. New York: Macmillan Publishing Company.

_____ (1988). The Paideia proposal: An American manifesto. New York: Collier Books.

Albrecht, Karl (1988). At America's service. New York: Warner Books.

Argyris, Chris (1982). Reasoning, learning, and action. San Francisco: Jossey-Bass Publishers.

Ausubel, D. P. (1967). A cognitive structure theory of school learning. In L. Siegel (ed.), Instruction: some contemporary viewpoints. San Francisco: Chandler.

Beck, Don Edward & Christopher C. Cowan (2006). Spiral dynamics: Mastering values, leadership and change. Malden MA: Blackwell Publishing.

Bennet, William (1993). Book of virtues. New York: Simon & Schuster.

Bennett, Alex & David Bennett (2004). Organizational survival in the new world. Burlington, MA: Elsevier.

Berger, Peter L., & Luckmann, Thomas (1967). The social construction of reality. New York: Anchor Books.

Berglas, Steven (2001). Reclaiming the fire. New York: Random House.

Bixler, Susan & Dugan, Lisa Scherrer (2001). 5 Steps to professional presence. Avon, MA. Adams Media Corporation.

Block, Peter (1993). Stewardship: Choosing service over self-interest. San Francisco: Berrett-Koehler Publishers.

Bok, Derek (1990). Universities and the future of America. Durham, NC: Duke University Press.

Boorstin, Daniel J. (1998).   The seekers: The story of man's continuing quest to understand his world. New York: Random House.

Bornstein, David (2005). How to change the world. India: Penguin Books.

Brodie, Richard (1996) Virus of the mind" New science of the meme. Seattle: Integral Press.

Bozeman, Barry (1987). All organizations are public. San Francisco: Jossey-Bass Publishers.

Bridges, William (1994). Jobshift: how to prosper in a workplace without jobs. Reading, MA: Addison-Wesley Publishing.

Brookfield, Stephen D. (1986). Understanding and facilitating adult learning. San Francisco: Jossey-Bass Publishers.

_____ (1987). Developing critical thinkers. San Francisco: Jossey-Bass Publishers.

Brooking, Annie. (1999). Corporate memory: Strategies for knowledge management. London: International Thomson Business .

Browne, M. Neil and Stuart Keeley (2001). Asking the right questions: A guide to critical thinking. Upper Saddle River, NJ: Prentice-Hall.

Bryson, Bill (2003). A short history of nearly everything. New York: Broadway Books.

Bryson, John M., & Crosby, Barbara C. (1992). Leadership for the common good. San Francisco: Jossey-Bass.

Butler, Gillian & Tony Hope (1995). Managing your mind: The mental fitness guide. New York: Oxford University Press.

Callahan, David. (2006) Moral center: How we can reclaim our country from die-hard extremists, rogue corporations, Hollywood hacks and pretend patriots. Orlando, FL: Harcourt.

Campbell, Joseph (1949). The hero with a thousand faces. New York: MJF Books.

Carnevale, Anthoney P., Gainer, Leila J., & Meltzer, Ann S. (1990). Workplace basics: The essential skills employers want. San Francisco: Jossey- Bass.

Cavanaugh, Gerald (1984). American business. Upper Saddle River, NJ: Prentice-Hall

Claxton, Guy (1999). Wise-up: The challenge of lifelong learning. New York: Bloomsbury.

Cleveland, Harlan (1990). The global commons. Lanham, MD: University Press of America.

_____ (1993). Birth of a new world: An open moment for international leadership. San Francisco: Jossey-Bass.

Cohen, Don & Laurence Prusak (2001). In good company: How social capital makes organizations work. Boston: Harvard Business School Press.

Collins, Jim (2001). Good to great: Why some companies make the leap and others don't. New York: HarperCollins.

Conklin, Jeff (2005). Dialogue mapping: Building shared understanding of wicked problems. London: John Wiley & Sons Ltd.

Cooper, Robert K. & Ayman Sawat (1997). Executive EQ: Emotional intelligence in leadership and organizations. New York: The Berkley Publishing Group.

Cooper, Terry L. (1982). The responsible administrator. Port Washington, NY: Kennikat Press.

Covey, Stephen R. (1989). The seven habits of highly effective people. New York: Simon and Schuster.

_____ (1991). Principle-centered leadership. New York: Summit Books.

_____ (2004). The 8th Habit. New York: Free Press.

Csikszentmihalyi, Mihali (1990). Flow: The psychology of optimal experience. New York: Harper and Row, Publishers.

_____ (1993). The evolving self. New York: HarperCollins.

Cummings, Thomas G. & Edgar F. Huse (1989). Organization development and change. New York: West Publishing Company.

Daly, Herman E. & John B. Cobb, Jr. (1989) For the common good: Redirecting the economy toward community, the environment, and a sustainable future. Boston: Beacon Press

Davenport, Thomas H. (2005). Thinking for a living. Boston: Harvard Business School Press.

Davenport, Thomas H. & John C. Beck (2001) The attention economy: Understanding the new currency of business. Boston: Harvard Business School Press.

Davenport, Thomas H. & Lawrence Prusak (1998) Working knowledge. Boston: Harvard Business School Press.

Davidow, William H. & Michael S. Malone (1992). The virtual corporation: Structuring and revitalizing the corporation for the 21st century. New York: Harper-Collins.

Davidson, Mark (1983). Uncommon sense. Los Angeles: J. P. Tarcher.

Dewey, John (1915). The school and society. Chicago: Centennial Publications of the University of Chicago Press.

Despres, Charles & Daniele Chauvel (2000). Knowledge horizons: The present and the promise of knowledge management. Woburn, MA: Butterworth-Heinemann.

Dobbs, Lou (2006). War on the middle class. New York: Penguin Group.

Dotlich, David L. & Peter C. Cairo (1999). Action coaching: How to leverage individual performance for company success. San Francisco: Jossey-Bass.

Drucker, Peter F. (1992). Managing for the future: The 1990s and beyond. New York: Truman Talley Books/Dutton.

Dychtwald, Ken (1999). Age power: how the 21st century will be ruled by the new old. New York: Penguin Putnam.

Eldridge, Natalie et al (2013). Live smart after 50!. Boston, Life Planning Network.

Ellis, Albert & Robert A. Harper (1961). A new guide to rational living. Englewood Cliffs, NJ: Prentice-Hall.

Erikson, Erik H. (1963). Childhood and society. New York: W.W. Norton and Company.

Erikson, Erik H. (1982). The life cycle completed. New York: W.W. Norton and Company.

Etzioni, Amitai (1991). A responsive society. San Francisco: Jossey-Bass.

Finch, Charles E. (1927). Guideposts to citizenship. New York: American Book Company.

Fiske, Marjorie & David A. Chiriboga (1990). Change and continuity in adult life. San Fancisco: Jossey-Bass.

Follett, Mary Parker (1924). Creative experience. New York: Longmans, Green and Company.

Frame, J. Davidson (1999). Building project management competence. San Francisco: Jossey-Bass.

Frankl, Viktor E. (1959). Man's search for meaning. Boston: Beacon Press.

Friedman, Thomas L. (2005). The world is flat: A brief history of the twenty-first century. New York: Farrar, Strauss and Giroux.

Frost, S. E., Jr. (1962). Basic teachings of the great philosophers. New York: Doubleday.

Fuller, Graham E. (1991) The democracy trap: Perils of the post-cold war world. New York: The Penguin Group.

Fuller, Robert (2001). Spiritual but not religious. New York: Oxford University Press.

Gans, Herbert (1999). Popular culture and high culture. New York: Basic Books.

Gardner, Howard (1983). Frames of mind: The theory of multiple intelligences. New York: Basic Books.

Gardner, John (1963). Self-renewal: The individual and the innovative society. New York: W. W. Norton and Company.

 (1981). Self-development: The individual and the innovative society. New York: W. W. Norton and Company.

_____ (2006). Five minds for the future. Boston, MA: Harvard Business School Press.

Garrity, Rudolph B. (1995). The construction and evaluation of a quality learning systems model for societal

dialogue and development. Ann Arbor MI: UMI Dissertation Services.

_____ 2007). American Learnership: Total learning, knowing and leading as a mindful way of being. Leesburg, Virginia: ALF Press

Garvin, David A. (2000) Learning in action: A guide to putting the learning organization to work. Boston: Harvard Business School Press.

Gates, Bill (1999). Business at the speed of light. New York: Warner Books.

Gawthrop, Louis C. (1984). Public sector management, systems, and ethics. Bloomington, IL: Indiana University Press.

Gazzaniga, Michael S. (1985). The social brain: Discovering the networks of the mind. New York: Basic Books.

_____ (2005). The ethical brain: The science of our moral dilemmas. New York: Harper Perennial.

Gellermann, William, Frankel, Mark S., & Ladenson, Robert F. (1990). Values and ethics in organization and human systems development. San Francisco: Jossey-Bass.

George, Stephen (1992). The baldrige quality system: the do-it-yourself way to transform your business. New York: Wiley & Sons.

Gergen, Kenneth J. (1991). <u>The saturated self: Dilemmas of identity in contemporary life.</u> New York: Basic Books.

Gilley, Jerry & Amy Coffern (1994). <u>Internal consulting for HRD professionals</u>. New York: Irwin Publishers.

Gilbert, Dennis (2002) <u>The American class structure in an age of growing inequality</u>. Belmont, CA: Wadsworth Publishing.

Gilbert, G. Ronald & Ardel E. Nelson (1991). <u>Beyond participative management: Toward total employee empowerment for quality</u>. New York: Quorum Books.

Giamatti, Bartlett A. (1981). <u>The university on the public interest</u>. New York: Atheneum.

Glenn, Jerome C., Theodore J. Gordon, & Elizabeth Florescu (2008). 2008 State of the Future. Washington D.C.: The Millennium Project

Goffman, Erving (1974). <u>Frame analysis: An essay on the organization of experience</u>. Boston: Northeastern University Press.

Goldberg, Elkhonon (2005) <u>The wisdom paradox: How your mind can grow stronger as your brain grows older</u>. New York: Penguin Group.

Goldthwait, John T. 1996). <u>Values: What they are & how we know them</u>. New York: Prometheus Books.

Goleman, Daniel (1995). <u>Emotional intelligence</u>. New York: Bantam Books.

_____ (1998). <u>Working with emotional intelligence</u>. New York: Bantam Books.

Gore, Al (2006). <u>An inconvenient truth: The planetary emergency of global warming and what we can do about it</u>. New York: Rodale.

_____ (2007). <u>The assault on reason</u>. New York: The Penguin Press.

Grenier, Ray & George Metes (1995) <u>Going virtual: Moving your organization into the 21st century</u>. Upper Saddle River, NJ: Prentice Hall.

Griessman, B. Eugene (1987). <u>The achievement factors.</u> New York: Dodd, Mead & Company.

Haeckel, Stephan H. (1999) <u>Adaptive enterprise: Creating sense and respond organizations</u>. Boston: Harvard Business School Press.

Halal, William E. (1986). <u>The new capitalism.</u> New York: John Wiley and Sons.

Hamel, Gary & C.K. Prahalad (1994). <u>Competing for the future</u>. Boston: Harvard Business School Press.

Hammer, Michael & James Champy. (1993). <u>Reengineering the corporation: A manifesto for business revolution</u>. New York: Harper-Collins.

Hammond, John, Ralph Lee and Howard Raiffa (1999). <u>Smart choices: A practical guide to making better decisions</u>.

Handy, Charles (1989). <u>The age of unreason.</u> Boston: Harvard Business School Press.

Hart, Leslie A. (1983). <u>Human brain and human learning.</u> Oak Creek, AZ: Books for Educators.

Heibroner, Robert L. (1975). <u>An inquiry into the human prospect.</u> New York: W. W. Norton and Company.

Herrmann, Ned (1996). <u>The whole brain business book</u>. New York: McGraw-Hill.

Hersey, Paul, & Blanchard, Kenneth H. (1979). <u>Management of organization behavior</u> (3rd ed.). Englewood Cliffs, NJ: Prentice-Hall.

Hubbard, Barbara Marx. (1993). Conscious evolution: Examining humanity's next step. The Futurist, Volume 27, No.5, September-October, 1993.

Hudson, Frederic M. (1999) <u>The adult years: Mastering the art of self-renewal</u>. San Francisco: Jossey-Bass.

Hudson, Frederic M. & Pamela D. McLean (1995). Life launch: A passionate guide to the rest of your life. Santa Barbara: The Hudson Institute Press.

Hughes, Robert (1993). Culture of compliant: The fraying of America. New York: Oxford University Press.

Hyman, Mark & Mark Liponis (2003). Ultra-prevention: The 6 week plan that will make you healthy for life. New York: Simon and Schuster.

Iacocca, Lee (2007). Where have all the leaders gone? New York: Simon and Schuster..

Issacs William N. (Autumn, 1993). Taking flight: dialogue, collective thinking, and organizational learning. Organizational Dynamics,

Issacs, William (1999). Dialogue and the art of thinking together. New York: Random House.

Janis, Irving L. (1989). Crucial decisions: leadership in policymaking and crises management. New York: The Free Press.

Johansen, Robert and Rob Swigart (1994). Upsizing the individual in the downsized organization. New York: Addision-Wesley Publishing Company.

Kanter, Rosabeth Moss (2001). Evolve: Succeeding in the digital culture of tomorrow. Boston: Harvard Business School Press.

Kaplan, Robert (1996). The balanced scorecard: Translating strategy into action.

Kepner, Charles H. & Benjamin B. (1981). The new rational manager. Princeton, NJ: Princeton Research Press.

Kilmann, Ralph H., Saxton, Mary J., & Roy Serpa and Associates (1985). Gaining control of the corporate culture. San Francisco: Jossey-Bass.

Kline, Peter, & Saunders, Bernard (1993). Ten steps to a learning organization. Arlington, VA: Great Ocean Publishers.

Kohlberg, Lawrence (1981). The philosophy of moral development. San Francisco: Harper and Row.

Kolb, David A. (1974). Building a learning community. Washington, DC: National Training and Development Press.

_____ (1983). Experiential learning: Experience as the source of learning and development. Upper Saddle River, NJ: Prentice-Hall.

Kotter, John P. (1996) Leading change. Boston: Harvard Business School Press.

Kramnick, Issac & R. Laurance Moore (1996). The godless constitution. New York: W&W Norton and Company.

Langer, Ellen J. (1989). Mindfulness. New York: Addison-Wesley Publishing Company.

Lawler, Edward E. (1986). High involvement management. San Francisco: Jossey-Bass.

Lengnick-Hall, Mark L. & Cynthia A. Lengnick-Hall (2003). Human resource management in the knowledge economy. San Francisco: Berrett-Koehler Publishers.

Levinson, Daniel J. (1978). The seasons of a man's life. New York: Ballantine Books.

Lindblom, Charles E., & Cohen, David K. (1979). Usable knowledge: social science and social problem solving. New Haven, CT: Yale University Press.

Marquardt, Michael J. (1999) Action learning in action: transforming problems and people for world-class organizational learning. Palo Alto, CA: Davies-Black Publishing.

Martin, James (1996). Cybercorp: The new business revolution. New York: AMACOM.

Maslow, Abraham H. (1968). Toward a psychology of being. New York: D. Van Norstrand Company.

_____ (1970). Motivation and personality (2nd ed.). New York: Harper and Row.

_____ (1971). <u>The farther reaches of human nature.</u> New York: Penguin Books.

Maxwell, John C. (2003) <u>Thinking for a change: 11 ways highly successful people approach life and work</u>. New York: Time Warner Books.

McCall, Morgan W., Jr., Lombardo, Michael M., & Morrison, Ann M. (1988). <u>The lessons of experience: How successful executives develop on the job.</u> Lexington, MA: Lexington Books.

McClelland, David C. (1975). <u>Power: The inner experience.</u> New York: Irvington Publishers.

McCain, John & Mark Salter (2005)<u> Character is destiny: Inspiring stories every young person should know and every adult should remember</u>. New York: Random House

McGee, James & Laurence Prusak (1993). <u>Managing information strategically.</u> New York: John Wiley & Sons, Inc.

Mead, George Herbert (1934) edited by Charles W. Morris (1967) <u>Mind, self , & society: From the standpoint of a social behaviorist.</u> Chicago: University of Chicago Press.

Meister, (1994). <u>Corporate quality universities, Lessons in building a world class workforce.</u> New York: Irwin Professional Publishing.

Merriam, Sharan B. & Caffarella, Rosemary S. (1991). <u>Learning in adulthood: A comprehensive guide.</u> San Francisco: Jossey-Bass Inc., Publishers.

Myers, Isabel Briggs with Peter B. Myers (1980). <u>Gifts differing.</u> Palo Alto, CA: Consulting Psychologists Press, Inc.

Nagel, Stuart S. (1989). <u>Higher goals for America: Doing better than the best.</u> Lanham, MD: University Press of America.

Newhouse, Meg (2016), <u>Legacies of the heart: living a life that matters</u>. Bakery Books.

Novelli, Bill (2006). <u>50+ Igniting a revolution to reinvent America</u>. New York: St. Martin's Press.

Obama, Barack (2006) The audacity of hope: <u>Thoughts on reclaiming the American dream</u>. New York: Crown.

Osborne, David, & Ted Gaebler (1992). <u>Reinventing government: How the entrepreneurial spirit is transforming the public sector.</u> New York: Addison-Wesley Publishing Company.

Pascale, Ricahrd T., Mark Millemann, Linda Gioja (2000) <u>Surfing the edge of chaos</u>. New York: Three Rivers Press.

Patterson, Kerry, Joseph Grenny, Ron McMillan, & Al Switzler (2002) <u>Crucial conversation tools for talking when stakes are high.</u> New York: McGraw-Hill

Pearson. Carol S. (1991) <u>Awakening the heroes within: Twelve archetypes to help us find ourselves and transform our world.</u> New York: HarperCollins.

Peck, Scott (1978). <u>The road less traveled: A new psychology of love, transitional values and spiritual growth</u>. New York: Simon and Schuster.

Peterson, Brooks ((2004). <u>Cultural Intelligence: A guide for working with people from other cultures</u>. Boston: Nicholas Brealey Publishing.

Piaget, Jean (1966). <u>Psychology of intelligence</u>. Totowa, NJ : Littlefield, Adams.

Pinchot, Gifford, & Pinchot, Elizabeth (1993). <u>The end of bureaucracy and the rise of the intelligent organization.</u> San Francisco: Berrett-Koehler.

Pinchot, Gifford & Ron Pellman (1999). <u>Intrapreneuring in action: a handbook for business innovation</u>. San Francisco: Berrett-Koehler Publishers.

Pollan, Stephen M. & Mark Levine (2003). <u>Second Acts: creating the life you really want, Building the career you truly desire.</u> New York: HarperCollins.

Post, Stephen G. & Robert H. Binstock (2004) editors. <u>The fountain of youth</u>. New York: The Oxford Press.

Prusak, Lawrence (1997). Knowledge in organizations. Boston: Butterworth-Heinemann.

Quinn, Robert E. (1988). Beyond rational management: Mastering the paradoxes and competing demands of high performance. San Francisco: Jossey-Bass.

Rampersad, Hubert (2014). Rudolph Garrity's Authentic Personal Brand. Miami: Authentic Personal Brand Coach Certification.

Rappaport, Herbert (1990). Marking time: what our attitudes toward time reveal about our personalities and conflicts. New York: Simon and Schuster.

Ridley, Matt (1996) The origins of virtue: Human instincts and the evolution of cooperation. New York: Penguin Books.

_____ (1999). Genome: The autobiography of a species in 23 chapters. New York: Harpers-Collins Publishers.

_____ (2003). Nature via nurture. New York: HarperCollins.

Rodgers, Carl R. (1980). A way of being. Boston: Houghton Mifflin Company.

Rohr, John A. (1986). To run a constitution: The legitimacy of the administrative state. Lawrence, KS: University of Kansas Press.

_____ (1989). Ethics for bureaucrats. New York: Marcel Dekker.

Roizen, Michael F. & Mehmet C. Oz (2006) You, the smart patient: An insider's handbook for getting the best treatment. New York: Free Press.

_____ (2006). You, on a diet: The owner's manual for waist management. New York: Simon and Schuster.

Roszak, Theodore (1998). America the wise: The longevity revolution and the true wealth of nations. New York: Houghton Mifflin Company.

Rothwell, William J. (2002). The workplace learner: How to align training initiatives with individual learning competencies. New York: AMACOM.

Rousseau, Jean-Jacques. Translation by Maurice Cranston (1968). The social contract. New York: Penguin Books.

Ruchlis, Hy (1990). Clear thinking. Buffalo, NY: Prometheus Books.

Rummler, Geary A. & Alan P. Brache (1994) Improving performance: How to manage the white space on the organization chart. San Francisco: Jossey-Bass.

Savage, Charles (1996). 5th generation management. Newton, MA: Butterworth-Heinemann

Sayers, Dorothy (1954). Introductory papers on Dante, in A guide for the perplexed. See Schumacher (1977)

Schein, Edgar H. (1993, Autuum). On dialogue, culture, and organizational learning. Organizational dynamics.

Schmidt, Warren H., & Finnigan, Jerome P. (1992). The race without a finish line: America's quest for total quality. San Francisco: Jossey-Bass.

Schon, Donald A. (1979). Beyond the stable state. New York: W. W. Norton & Company.

_____ (1983). The reflective practitioner. New York: Basic Books.

Schott, Richard L. (1986). The psychological development of adults: implications for public policy. Public Administration Review, 657-667.

Schumacher, E. F. (1977). A guide for the perplexed. New York: Harper and Row.

Schuster, John P. (2003). Answering your call: A guide for living your deepest purpose. San Francisco: Berrett-Koehler.

Sedlar, Jeri & Rick Miners (2003). Don't retire, rewire. New York: Penguin Group.

Seitz, Victoria A. (2000). Your executive image. Avon, MA.: Adams Media Corporation.

Selye, Hans (1976). The stress of Life. New York: McGraw Hill Book Company.

Senge, Peter et al (1990). The fifth discipline: The art and practice of the learning organization. New York: Doubleday Currency.

_____ (2005). Presence: An exploration of profound change in people, organizations, and society. New York: Random House.

Sheehy, Gail (1998). Understanding men's passages: Discovering the new map of men's lives. New York: Random House.

_____ (1995). New passages: Mapping your life across time. New York: Random House.

Sims, Henry P., Jr., & Dennis A. Gioia and Associates (1986). The thinking organization: Dynamics of organizational social cognition. San Francisco: Jossey-Bass.

Sinetar, Marsha (1987). Discover your right livelihood. New York: Random House.

Singer, Peter (1979). Practical ethics. Cambridge, England: Cambridge University Press.

Skinner, B. F. (1971). Beyond freedom and dignity. New York: Knopf.

Smith, David E. (2000). Knowledge, groupware and the internet. Woburn, MA: Butterworth-Heinemann.

Smith, Robert M. (1982). Learning how to learn: Applied theory for adults. Buckingham, England: Open University Press.

Stankosky, Michael editor (2005). Creating the discipline of knowledge management. Burlington, MA: Elsevier.

Stewart, Thomas A. (2001). The wealth of knowledge: Intellectual capital and the twenty-first century organization. New York: Currency Books.

_____ (1997). Intellectual capital: The new wealth of organizations. New York: Bantam Doubleday Dell Publishing Group.

Stoner, James A. F. (1982). Management. Englewood Cliffs, NJ: Prentice-Hall.

Sullivan, John Greenfelder (1990). To come to life more fully. Columbia Maryland: Traditional Acupuncture Institute.

Sveiby, Karl Erik. (1997) The new organizational wealth: Managing & measuring knowledge-based assets. San Francisco: Berrett-Koehler Publishers.

Tapscott, Don. (1996). Digital economy: Promise and peril in the age of networked intelligence. New York: McGraw-Hill.

Theobald, Robert (1987). The rapids of change: Social entrepreneurship in turbulent times. Indianapolis, IN: Knowledge Systems.

Thompson, William & Joseph Hickey (2005). Society in focus: An introduction to sociology. Boston: Allyn and Bacon.

Tough, Allen (1991). Crucial questions about the future. New York: University Press of America.

Vaill, Peter B. (1996). Learning as a way of being. San Francisco: Jossey-Bass.

Van Ness, Peter (1996). Spirituality and the secular quest. New York: Crossroad Publishing Company.

Wade, Nicholas (2001) Book of the Brain. New York: New York Times.

Walter, Susan, & Pat Choate (1984). Thinking strategically: A primer for public leaders. Washington DC: The Council of State Planning Agencies.

Waldo, Dwight (1988). The enterprise of public administration. Novato, CA: Chandler and Sharp Publishers.

Watson, Gregory H. (1993). Strategic benchmarking: How to rate your company's performance against the world's best. New York: John Wiley & Sons.

Weisbord, Marvin R. (1992). Discovering common ground. San Francisco: Berrett-Koehler Publishers.

Wheelis, Allen (1958). The quest for identity. New York: W&W Norton & Company.

Wiig, Karl (2004). <u>People-centered knowledge management</u>. Burlington, MA: Elsevier.

Wilber, Ken (2000). <u>A theory of everything: An integral vision for business, politics, science, and spirituality</u>. Boston: Shambhala Publications.

Wilkins, Alan L. (1989). <u>Developing Corporate Character</u>. San Francisco: Jossey-Bass.

Wilson, Edward O. (1998). <u>Consilience: The unity of knowledge</u>. New York: Knopf.

Wolfe, Alan (2001) <u>Moral freedom: The search for virtue in a world of change</u>. New York: W.W. Norton and Company.

Yankelovich, Daniel (1990). <u>Coming to public judgment: Making democracy work in a complex world.</u> New York: Syracuse University Press.

Zelinski, Ernie J. (2007). <u>Real success without a real job</u>. Berkeley: Ten Speed Press.

Zinni, Tony & Tony Koltz (2006). <u>The battle for peace: A frontline vision of America's power and purpose</u>. New York: Palgrave Macmillan.

Zurcher, Louis A., Jr. (1977). <u>The mutable self: A self-concept for social change.</u> Beverly Hills: Sage Publications.

[Reader Notes]

[Reader Notes]

www.ingramcontent.com/pod-product-compliance
Lightning Source LLC
Chambersburg PA
CBHW062024210326
41519CB00060B/6973